The Lion Christian Quotation Collection

Hannah Ward and Jennifer Wild are freelance writers and editors. Formerly members of Anglican Franciscan communities, their publications include *The Lion Christian Meditation Collection* (Lion, 2002) and *Conversations: Meeting Our Forebears in Faith* (SPCK, 1997).

THE LION CHRISTIAN QUOTATION *Collection*

Over 5,000 quotations, past and present

Compiled by Hannah Ward and Jennifer Wild

A LION BOOK

Published by
Lion Publishing plc
Mayfield House, 256 Banbury Road,
Oxford OX2 7DH, England
www.lion-publishing.co.uk
ISBN 0 7459 5096 5

First hardback edition 1997
First paperback edition 2002
10 9 8 7 6 5 4 3 2 1 0

A catalogue record for this book is available from the British Library

Typeset in Berkeley Oldstyle
Printed and bound in Finland

CONTENTS

PREFACE

It has been an exciting, if sometimes daunting, task to gather and arrange the material for this collection of Christian quotations, and now that the house is up and complete, the main purpose of this Preface is to ensure that you, the reader and user of this book, know how to find your way around, so that you can make yourself at home in it.

You will see that the entries are arranged chronologically, beginning with Clement of Rome, who just scrapes into the first century. Among other things, the invention of movable type in the fifteenth century means that the last few centuries are far more fully represented than all that went before them. It is often difficult to date writers of the first ten centuries accurately, so you will notice much less precise figures here in many cases.

Even when dates are known, we had to decide which century to place people in. Generally speaking, it is the century in which they lived most of their lives, or at least most of their writing lives. But, for instance, some early martyrs, whose stories were recorded by their contemporaries (they are not all near-fictitious legends!) are placed in the century in which they died, since it is precisely their dying in witness to their faith in Jesus Christ that has given them a place in our collection. Hence Perpetua and Felicitas are included in the third century, because they died in 203 (or thereabouts); whereas later on, Julian of Norwich, who was aged about seventy in 1413, is included in the fourteenth century because her revelations, on which our knowledge of her depend, happened in or about 1373. Nearer our own time, Florence Nightingale, who died at the age of ninety in 1910, is included in the nineteenth century, because that is the century in which she became well known and completed her public work.

When we arrived at our own century, now nearly over, the choice was even more difficult because there was so much material, not yet thinned out by the passing of time. We have tried to help by dividing the entries between those who died before 1950, and those who have died since, or who are still alive—so that there are two alphabetical lists for the twentieth century.

Of course, we cannot hope to give a 'God's eye' view of Christian thought. Apart from ordinary human limitations—our own as compilers, the uneven distribution of surviving material to choose from—an enormously high proportion of available material from the earlier centuries is written by monks and a good deal of the rest by clergy of one kind or another, and only for the present day does one not have to search hard to find a decent proportion of contributions from women. Innumerable Christians have lived and died without leaving any written evidence of their lives, let alone their thoughts.

What we have included has necessarily been available in English, but we have tried to ensure that the scope is wider than that often covered by English-speaking and commonly translated writers. In particular, we have looked for writing by Christians from all parts of the world, especially from the uprush of theological activity in Third World countries and cultures. And because women have not been well represented in writing surviving from earlier periods, we have collected quotations from present-day women (as well as men) from as many parts of the world as possible—and there is an increasing amount to choose from.

The number of quotations given from each person is not an indication of the importance we assign to that person as a Christian thinker. A Thomas Aquinas, a Martin Luther or Karl Barth can only be glimpsed through a series of short quotations, whereas some seventeenth- or eighteenth-century preachers and essayists seem to produce an endless stream of quotable pithy sayings. Nor have we set out to define people as Christian—or not. We believe that all those we have included would define themselves as Christian, and we have not stood in judgment. On the other hand, we have not set out to reveal 'Christian thinkers, warts and all'. Though a great variety of views and beliefs are expressed in this collection, it does not pretend to reveal all the terrible things Christians have at times said to and about each other, or about those of other faiths or none, or men about women, and so on. We hope, all the same, that an honest picture of the writers chosen is given, and that there is plenty for everyone both to agree and to disagree with.

In terms of language we have not intentionally tampered with the words actually used. Some translations of ancient or medieval writers are now in inclusive language. We have used what we found, so there is considerable variety, but on the whole we have preferred versions that leave people speaking how they might actually have spoken in their own language, in their own time.

To find your way round: if you look at the Index of Sources, you will see that each name is followed by two figures. The first figure after each person's name is their century. C.S. Lewis (1898–1963), for instance, has the figure 20.352 after his name. In the main body of the book he is listed alphabetically in the second half of the twentieth century, and is the 352nd entry in the twentieth century overall. Under his name there are twenty-three quotations, and each of these is numbered. If you look in the Index of Themes under 'motherhood', you will find, among the other entries, 20.352.2, which refers to the second entry under Lewis' name. If you vaguely remembered a remark about parental loss in terms of Atlantis, you would be able to trace this same saying back to C.S. Lewis via the Index of Key Words, where 'Atlantis' is followed by the same three figures. So the three figures correspond to the century, name, and number of the particular quotation. Armed with this knowledge, you can easily use the Index of Themes or the Index of Key Words to find what different Christians across the centuries have had to say on any given theme.

Finally: this collection represents the thoughts of a few of the many Christians of whom we have a record over the past 2,000 years. Think how many more there have been who could not write, who were not highly enough regarded for their words to be recorded, who did not have a great deal to say. And in our own articulate and talkative age, if we only take note of what was written yesterday or last week, and rather look down on anything else as 'old hat' or (worse!) 'archaic', how much poorer will be our approach to the words and writers of the Hebrew and Christian Testaments that form the Bible? Here is a sample, only, of that great 'cloud of witnesses'. We are the richer for their lives—indeed, without them we would have lost all knowledge of the gospel of Jesus Christ. They may seem strange, awkward, difficult or funny, but they are our fellow human beings, who have found their place in what Jesus called the 'many rooms in my Father's house'.

PART 1

First to Fifteenth Centuries

Let us hang upon the lips of all the faithful,
for the Spirit of God is upon every one of them.

Paulinus of Nola
(d.431)

First Century

1.1
Clement of Rome (d.c.95)
Bishop of Rome

1 O God, make us children of quietness, and heirs of peace.

2 Christ is with those of humble mind, not with those who exalt themselves over his flock.

3 Through him we see as in a mirror the spotless and excellent face of God.

4 It is through faith that Almighty God has justified all that have been from the beginning of time.

5 Have we not one God and one Christ and one Spirit of grace shed upon us?

6 Let us run towards the goal which from the beginning has been handed down to us, the goal which is peace; and let us fix our gaze on the Father and Creator of the whole universe, and cling to his splendid and superlative gifts of peace.

7 Let us think of the host of angels, how they stand by and serve his will.

8 Where can any of us escape from his mighty hand? What world will receive anyone who deserts from his service?

9 Out of love our Lord took us to himself; because he loved us and it was God's will, our Lord Jesus Christ gave his life blood for us—he gave his body for our body, his soul for our soul.

10 We must look on all things of this world as none of ours, and not desire them. This world and that to come are enemies. We cannot therefore be friends to both, but must resolve which to forsake and which to enjoy.

Second Century

2.1
Abercius (?2c.)
Bishop of Hieropolis in Phrygia (in modern Turkey)

1 My name is Abercius. I am a disciple of the holy shepherd who feeds his flocks on the mountains and in the plains. His eyes are large and everything comes within the range of his vision...

2 Faith was my guide everywhere and everywhere set food before me: a fish from the spring, very big and sound, caught by a holy virgin. This she would give her friends to eat at all times. And to drink, there was an excellent wine she had and served with bread.

2.2
Acts of Peter and Andrew (?2c.)
Early Christian writings

1 Peter got up and girded his cloak and undergarment, and said to Andrew, 'It is not right for us to rest and be idle, especially when the old man has left his work and is working for us.' Then Peter took hold of the plough and sowed the wheat, and Andrew was behind the oxen. He took the plough out of Peter's hand and sowed the wheat, saying, 'O seed cast into the ground in the field of the righteous, let the young men of the city therefore come forth, for the apostles of Christ are coming, pardoning the sins of those who believe, and healing every disease.'

2.3
Aristides of Athens (early or mid 2c.)
Christian Apologist (defender of Christian belief against paganism)

1 As for the Christians, they trace their line from the Lord Jesus Christ. He is confessed to be the Son of the most high God, who came down from heaven, by the Holy Ghost, for the salvation of mankind, and was born of a pure virgin... and took flesh, and in a daughter of man there dwelt the Son of God.

2 If there is a man among them who is poor and in need, and they have not an abundance of what is needed, they fast for two or three days so that they may supply the needy with their necessary food.

3 For Christ's sake they are ready to lay down their lives: they keep his commandments faithfully, and live righteous and holy lives, as the Lord commanded them; and they give him thanks every morning and every hour of the day, for food and drink and every blessing.

4 I have no doubt that the world stands because of the prayer of Christians.

2.4
Athenagoras (2nd half 2c.)

Christian Apologist (see under Aristides)

1 In our case [as Christians] we are hated for our name.

2 The Holy Spirit himself, which also operates in the prophets, we assert to be an effluence of God, flowing from him and returning back again like a beam of the sun.

2.5
Barnabas (?early 2c.)

Probably a Christian of Alexandria in Egypt

1 The doctrines of the Lord are three: the hope of life is the beginning and the end of our faith; righteousness is the beginning and end of Judgement; and glad and joyful love is the evidence of the works of righteousness.

2 What does 'milk and honey' mean? A child is first fed on milk, and afterwards on honey. In the same way after we have been given life by believing in the word of promise, we shall go on to live and possess the world.

3 This then is the Way of Light: if anyone wants to journey to the place appointed for him, he must work zealously at it. And this is the knowledge that has been given us so that we can walk in this Way. You shall love your maker, and fear the one who formed you, and you shall give glory to the one who ransomed you from death.

2.6
Blandina (d.177)

Slave girl martyred in Lyons in 177

1 I am a Christian; we do nothing to be ashamed of.

2.7
Carpus, Papylus and Agathonike

Martyred at Pergamum (in modern Turkey)

1 Blessing to you, Lord Jesus Christ, Son of God: you have thought me fit to share this fate with you, sinner though I am. (Carpus)

2 Lord Jesus Christ, receive my soul. (Papylus)

3 Lord, Lord, Lord, come to my help; I turn to you for refuge. (Agathonike)

2.8
Didache

Title of a short book on Christian behaviour and church practice

1 Baptize thus: Having first recited all these things, baptize 'in the name of the Father, and of the son, and of the Holy Spirit', in running water. If you have no running water, baptize in other water; if you cannot baptize in cold water, use warm. If you have neither, pour water on the head thrice.

2 Give thanks in this manner. First, over the cup: 'We give thanks to thee, our Father, for the holy vine of thy son David, which thou hast made known to us through Jesus thy Son: thine be the glory for ever.'

3 Then over the broken bread: 'We give thanks to thee, our Father, for the life and knowledge which thou didst make known to us through Jesus thy Son: thine be the glory for ever.'

4 As this broken bread was scattered upon the mountains and was gathered together and became one, so let thy Church be gathered together from the ends of the earth into thy kingdom.

5 Let grace come, and let this world pass away.

6 Allow the prophets to give thanks as much as they will.

7 The false and the genuine prophet will be known by their ways. If a prophet teaches the truth but does not practise what he teaches, he is a false prophet.

2.9
Diognetus, Epistle to
Anonymous letter to otherwise unknown recipient

1 Christians are not distinguished from the rest of mankind by country or language or customs.

2 Christians live in countries of their own, but as sojourners. They share all things as citizens; they suffer all things as foreigners.

3 We may say that Christians are in the world what the soul is to the body.

4 How will you love him who so loved you first? Why, in loving him you will be an imitator of his kindness. And do not marvel that a human being can imitate God. By the will of God he can.

2.10
Dionysius of Corinth (c.170)
Bishop of Corinth

1 In these ways you [Roman Christians] also, by your admonition have united the planting that Peter and Paul did, in the case of Romans and Corinthians. For indeed both planted in Corinth here, and likewise taught us; and likewise they taught together in Italy also, and were martyred on the same occasion.

2.11
Hermas, Shepherd of
Author of The Shepherd *and one of the earliest church writers (Apostolic Fathers)*

1 Remove every evil desire and clothe yourself with good and holy desire. For if you are clothed with good desire, you will hate evil desire and bridle it as you please.

2 The devil cannot lord it over those who serve God with their whole heart and who put their hope in him. The devil can wrestle with them, but cannot overcome them.

3 Fear the Lord and you will do everything well.

4 Hold fast to simplicity of heart and innocence. Yes, be as babes who do not know the wickedness that destroys grown people's lives.

5 Those who are rich in this world cannot be made useful for the Lord unless their riches have been cut out of them.

2.12
Ignatius of Antioch (d.107)
Bishop of Antioch in Syria, martyred in Rome

1 There is only one physician, a physician who is at once fleshly and spiritual, generate and ingenerate, God in man, true life in death, born of Mary and of God, first passible then impassible, Jesus Christ our Lord.

2 For when you meet frequently the forces of Satan are annulled and his destructive power is cancelled in the concord of your faith.

3 The virginity of Mary and her child-bearing was hidden from the prince of this world; so likewise was the death of the Lord—three mysteries that are to be proclaimed with a shout, which were effected in the quiet of God.

4 Meet together in common—every single one of you—in grace, in one faith and one Jesus Christ.

5 I am God's wheat, and I am being ground by the teeth of the beasts so that I may appear as pure bread.

6 My birth pangs are at hand. Bear with me, my brothers. Do not hinder me from living: do not wish for my death... Allow me to receive the pure light; when I arrive there I shall be a real man. Permit me to be an imitator of the passion of my God.

7 My love has been crucified and there is not in me any sensuous fire, but living water springing up in me, and saying within me, 'Come to the Father'.

8 I desire the bread of God, which is the flesh of Christ who was of the seed of David; and for drink I desire his blood, which is love incorruptible.

2.13
Irenaeus (130-202)

Bishop of Lyons, possibly from Smyrna (in modern Turkey), theologian

1 For where the church is there is the Spirit of God, and where the Spirit of God is, there is the church and all grace.

2 Breaking one bread, which is the medicine of immortality, the antidote against death which gives eternal life in Jesus Christ.

3 The glory of God is man fully alive; and the life of man consists in beholding God.

4 This is the Creator: in respect of his love, our Father; in respect of his power, our Lord; in respect of his wisdom, our Maker and Designer.

5 In the beginning God fashioned Adam, not because he had need of human beings, but so that he might have beings on whom to bestow his benefits.

6 God made man lord of the earth, but he was small, being but a child. He had to grow and reach full maturity.

7 As through a conquered man our race went down to death, so through a conqueror we ascend to life.

8 Our Lord Jesus Christ, the word of God, of his boundless love, became what we are that he might make us what he himself is.

9 Thus there is one God the Father, and one Christ Jesus our Lord who came in fulfilment of God's comprehensive design and consummates all things in himself.

10 God the Word restored in himself humankind, his ancient handiwork, that he might do to death sin, strip death of its power and give life to humankind.

11 Through the Spirit humankind ascends to the Son, through the Son to the Father.

12 As dry flour cannot be united into a lump of dough, or a loaf, but needs water, so we who are many cannot be made one in Christ Jesus without the water that comes from heaven.

13 He takes to himself our good endeavours so that he may repay us with his good things.

14 The Lord has taught us that no one can know God unless he is taught by God.

15 To bring man into existence, to make a creature living and rational, made of bones, muscle, veins and all the other human parts, which as yet did not exist—this was a harder task and more incredible than to restore this creature to life once it had dissolved into earth.

16 Just as through a tree we became God's debtors, so through a tree we receive the cancellation of our debts.

17 Just as the bread, which is made from the earth, when God is invoked is no longer common bread but the Eucharist, both earthly and heavenly, so our bodies, after we have received the Eucharist, are no longer corruptible, since they hold the hope of the resurrection.

18 It was the ground God cursed, not Adam.

19 God pitied man and tried to prevent him from continuing in sin forever and in evil without end or remedy, so he ended man's wickedness by bringing in death and thus making an end of sin, so that by dying man should begin to live to God.

20 Just as the sun, God's creature, is one and the same the whole world over, so also the church's preaching shines everywhere, giving light to all who want to come to a knowledge of truth.

2.14
Justin Martyr (c.100-c.165)
Christian Apologist (see under Aristides)

1 Thus we are called atheists. And we admit that in respect of such supposed gods we *are* atheists; but not in regard to the most true God, the Father of righteousness.

2 We are not atheists, for we worship the Creator of the universe with the word of prayer and thanksgiving.

3 The master who taught us this worship, and who was born to this end, was crucified under Pontius Pilate in the reign of Tiberius Caesar.

4 At the end of the prayers we embrace each other with a kiss.

5 For all that we receive we bless the maker of all things through his Son Jesus Christ and the Holy Spirit.

6 The Father of all has no name given him since he is unbegotten. For a being who has a name given him has someone older than him to give him that name. 'Father' and 'God', 'Creator', 'Lord', 'Master', are not names but titles derived from his benefits and works.

7 Consider whether the business of the world could be carried on without the figure of the cross. The sea cannot be crossed unless this sign of victory, the mast, stands upright. Without it there would be no ploughing, nor could diggers or mechanics do their work without their cross-shaped tools. Humans are distinguished from other animals by their upright posture and the way they can extend their arms. The very nose through which we breathe is set at right angles to the brow, fulfilling the prophet's words, 'Our Lord Christ is the breath before our face'.

8 We hope to suffer torment for our Lord Jesus Christ and so to be saved.

9 Christ is the firstborn of God, and he is the Word of whom all mankind have a share, and those who lived according to reason are Christians even though they are counted among the atheists. For example, among the Greeks, Socrates and Heraclitus; among the non-Greeks, Abraham, Ananias, Azarias and Misael, Elias and many others.

10 We hold this gathering on Sunday, since this is the first day on which God, by making a transformation of darkness and chaos, made the universe, and on the same day Jesus Christ our Saviour rose from the dead.

2.15
Melito of Sardis (d.c.190)
Bishop of Sardis, devotional writer

1 What is this new creation?
The judge is judged and is silent;
The invisible is seen on the cross
and is not ashamed;
The infinite is contained
and does not complain;
The impassible suffers
and does not seek vengeance,
The immortal dies and says nothing,
The King of heaven is buried
and endures it.
What is this strange mystery?

2 He was led forth like a lamb; he was slaughtered like a sheep. He ransomed Israel from the land of Egypt; he freed us from our slavery to the devil as he had freed Israel from the hand of Pharaoh. He sealed our souls with his own Spirit and the members of our body with his own blood.

3 It is he who endured every kind of suffering in all those who foreshadowed him. In Abel he was slain, in Isaac bound, in Jacob exiled, in Joseph sold, in Moses exposed to die. He was sacrificed in the passover lamb, persecuted in David, dishonoured in the prophets.

2.16
Polycarp (69-155)
Bishop of Smyrna (in modern Turkey), martyred

1 God the Father of our Lord Jesus Christ increase us in faith and truth and gentleness, and grant us part and lot among his saints.

2 Leave me as I am, the one who gives me strength to endure the fire will also give me strength to stay quite still on the pyre, even without the precaution of your nails.

3 For eighty and six years have I been his [Christ's] servant, and he has done me no wrong, and how can I blaspheme my King who saved me?

2.17
Protevangelium of St James (?2c.)

An apocryphal account of the birth of Jesus

1 An order came from Augustus for the enrolment of all the inhabitants of Bethlehem in Judaea. Joseph said: 'I will enrol my sons, but what shall I do with this girl? How shall I put her down? As my wife? I am ashamed to do that. As my daughter? But all the children of Israel know that she is not my daughter. The day of the Lord will bring it about as the Lord wills.'

2.18
Quadratus (early 2c.)

Christian Apologist (see under Aristides)

1 But the works of our Saviour were always present (for they were genuine): namely, those who were healed, those who were raised from the dead; they were not only seen in the act of being healed or raised, but also continued to be present; and not only when the Saviour was on earth, but after his departure as well, they lived for a considerable time, to such an extent that some of them have survived even to our own day.

2.19
Mother of Symphorian (d. in 2c.)

Mother of a martyr

1 My son, my son Symphorian, remember the living God and be of good cheer. Raise your heart to heaven, and think of the one who reigns there. Do not be afraid of death which leads to certain life.

2.20
Thecla (c.150-200)

Early Christian virgin, reputedly a convert and co-worker of St Paul

1 [Seeing a ditch full of water she said:] Now it is time to wash myself. [And she threw herself in, saying:] In the name of Jesus Christ I am baptized on my last day.

2 I am indeed a servant of the loving God; and as to what there is about me, I have believed in the Son of God, in whom he is well pleased... For he alone is the end of salvation, and the basis of immortal life; for he is a refuge to the tempest-tossed, a solace to the afflicted, a shelter to the despairing; and once for all, whoever shall not believe on him, shall not live for ever.

2.21
Theophilus of Antioch (d.180)

Bishop of Antioch and Apologist (see under Aristides)

1 Hear further, O man, of the work of resurrection going on in you, even though you were unaware of it. For perhaps you have sometimes fallen sick, and lost flesh, and strength, and beauty; but when you once more received mercy and healing from God, you regained flesh and appearance and also recovered your strength.

2 God set man in paradise, giving him the opportunity to advance, so that by growing and becoming mature, and by sharing in the divine life, he might thus ascend to heaven. For man was created in an intermediate state, neither entirely mortal nor wholly immortal, but capable of becoming either.

Third Century

3.1
Clement of Alexandria (c.150-c.215)
Theologian, probably born in Athens

1 All our life is a celebration for us; we are convinced, in fact, that God is always everywhere. We sing while we work, we sing hymns while we sail, we pray while we carry out all life's other occupations.

2 Elijah offers an excellent example of frugality: he sat down under the juniper tree and the angel brought him food. The Lord sent that sort of meal as the best sort for him. It seems, then, that we should travel light on our road towards truth.

3 The faithful person lives constantly with God; he is always serious and joyful: serious because he remembers God, joyful because he dreams of all the good things that God has given to humankind.

4 If you do not hope, you will not find out what is beyond your hopes.

5 Christ has turned all our sunsets into dawn.

6 As the sun illumines not only the heaven and the whole world, shining on both land and sea; but also sends his rays through windows and small chinks into the furthest recesses of a house; so the Word, poured out everywhere, beholds the smallest actions of human life.

7 The Father does not exist without the Son, for 'Father' immediately implies 'Father of a Son'; and the Son is the true teacher about the Father.

8 O wonderful mystery! The Father of all things is one; the Word of all things is one; the Holy Spirit is one and the same everywhere.

9 Being baptized, we are enlightened; being enlightened, we are adopted as children; being adopted, we are made perfect; being made complete, we are made immortal.

3.2
Cyprian (?200-258)
Bishop of Carthage (in North Africa) and martyr

1 He cannot have God for his father who has not the church for his mother. If anyone could escape outside of Noah's ark, then they can also escape outside the doors of the church.

2 When I had drunk the Spirit from heaven, and the second birth had restored me so as to make a new man of me, then at once in an amazing way my doubts began to be resolved, doors that had been closed to me opened, dark places became light, and what before had seemed difficult now seemed easy to me.

3 We should not mourn for our brethren who have been freed from the world by the divine summons, since we know that they are not lost, but only sent on ahead.

4 There can be salvation for none outside the church.

5 This sacrament of unity, this bond of peace inseparable and indivisible, is indicated when in the Gospel the robe of the Lord Jesus Christ was not divided at all or rent, but they cast lots for the raiment of Christ, to see who should put on Christ for clothing.

6 He who rends and divides the church of Christ cannot possess the clothing of Christ.

7 All our power for good is derived from God.

3.3
Felicitas (d.203)
North African martyr

1 [Awaiting martyrdom, she gave birth to her child prematurely, and while in labour was taunted by the prison guards with the words: 'If you are complaining now, what will you do when you are thrown to the beasts?' She replied:] Now it is I who suffer, but there another will suffer in me, since I am now suffering for him.

3.4
Genesius of Rome (d.c.205)
Early martyr, possibly an actor

1 There is no King but him whom I have seen; he it is that I worship and adore. Were I to be killed a thousand times for my allegiance to him, I should still go on as I have begun, I should still be his man. Christ is on my lips, Christ is in my heart; no torments can take him from me.

3.5
Gregory Thaumaturgus (?213-?270)
Early missionary in what is now Turkey. His nickname means 'wonderworker'

1 Origen taught us, inspiring us as much by his humbleness as by his assurance, that our minds have a natural desire to know the truth of God and the causes of things, in just the same way as our eyes have a natural desire for light and our bodies for food.

3.6
Hippolytus (c.160-235)
Roman theologian and martyr

1 Joy to all creatures, honour, feasting, delight.
Dark death is destroyed
and life is restored everywhere.
The gates of heaven are open.
God has shown himself man,
man has gone up to him a God.
The gates of hell God has shattered,
the bars of Adam's prison broken.
The people of the world below
have risen from the dead,
bringing good news;
what was promised was fulfilled.
From the earth has come singing
and dancing.

2 This is God's passover.
Heaven's God, showing no meanness,
Has joined himself to us in the Spirit.

3 Eternal God, to whom the hidden is as clearly known as the visible: before you your people bow their heads, to you they submit their hard hearts and unruly bodies. Send down blessing from your glorious dwelling on these men and women, lend them a ready ear and answer their prayers. Set them up firmly with your strong hand and protect them against all evil passions. Preserve their bodies and souls, increase their faith and fear and increase ours, through your only Son.

3.7
Lactantius (?240-?320)
Christian Apologist (see under Aristides)

1 Modesty in human beings is praised because it is not a matter of nature, but of will.

3.8
Lucian and Marcian (d.c.250)
Martyrs in Bithynia (in modern Turkey)

1 We offer you our poor praises, Lord Jesus, because you have defended us—poor undeserving creatures though we are—from the errors of paganism, and in your mercy have brought us to these supreme sufferings, which it is a privilege to undergo for the glory of your name; and you have given us a share in the glory of your saints.

3.9
Origen (c.185-c.254)
Alexandrian biblical scholar, theologian and spiritual writer

1 We know that in saying 'everything is possible to God', 'everything' is understood as not extending to the impossible and the inconceivable. We also assert that shameful things are impossible to God, for if they were it would mean that God is able to cease to be God.

2 It may well be that human sins afflict with grief even God himself.

3 Let us enter the contest to win perfectly not only outward martyrdom, but also the martyrdom that is in secret, so that we too may utter the apostolic cry 'For this is our boast, the martyrdom of our conscience that we have believed in the world with holiness and godly sincerity'.

4 We must suppose that the presence of the angels who watch over us and minister to God comes together with someone who prays, so that the angels may be united with him in what he asks in prayer.

5 The power of choosing between good and evil is within the reach of all.

6 Stronger than all the evils in the soul is the Word, and the healing power that dwells in him.

7 Let us have clean hearts ready inside us for the Lord Jesus, so that he will be glad to come in, gratefully accepting the hospitality of those worlds, our hearts; he whose glory and power will endure throughout the ages.

8 When Plato says that it is 'difficult to see the maker and Father of the universe', we Christians agree with him. And yet he can be seen; for it is written, 'Blessed are the pure in heart, for they shall see God'. Moreover, he who is the image of the invisible God has said, 'He who has seen me has seen the Father.'

9 If we consult the scriptures about the stock into which we have to be grafted, and the kind of tree it is, we find this text concerning wisdom: She is a tree of life to those who hope in her and put their trust in her, as in their Lord. This tree of life into which we have to be grafted is Christ who is the power and the wisdom of God—Christ who by his death, that unprecedented gift of divine love, became for us a tree of life.

3.10
Pectorius of Autun (early 3c.)
Writer of an inscription found at Autun, France

1 Fish-born, divine children of a heavenly father,
drink with heartfelt reverence God's waters,
the source of immortality to mortals.
Eat as a hungry man eats
of the Fish you hold in your hands.

3.11
Perpetua (d.203)
North African martyr

1 My father was the only one of my family who could find no reason to rejoice at my suffering. I tried to comfort him, telling him 'What happens at this tribunal will be what God wants, for our power comes not from us but from God.'

3.12
Tertullian (?150-?212)
North African Church Father

1 They converse as those would who know that God hears.

2 It is certainly no part of religion to compel religion.

3 However often we are mown down by you, we increase in numbers; it is Christian blood that is the seed.

4 If the Tiber reaches the walls, if the Nile does not rise, if the sky does not move or if the earth does, if there is a famine or a plague, the cry is 'To the lions with the Christians!'.

5 O evidence of a soul naturally Christian!

6 It is certain because it is impossible.

7 God is invisible, though he is seen; incomprehensible, though manifested by grace; inconceivable, though conceived by human senses.

8 The world was made up of all kinds of good things, and gives sufficient indication of the great good in store for the one for whom all this was provided.

9 We define the soul as born of the breath of God.

10 No angel ever descended for the purpose of being crucified, of experiencing death, of being raised from the dead.

11 The name of the feast explains the reason for it; it is called by the Greek name for love [agape].

12 Faith keeps watch for that day, and daily fears that for which she daily hopes.

Fourth Century

4.1
Agape (d.304)

One of several martyrs at Salonike (northern Greece)

1 I believe in the living God, and refuse to destroy my conscience.

4.2
Ambrose (340-397)

Bishop of Milan and Church Father

1 When we speak about wisdom, we are speaking of Christ. When we speak about virtue, we are speaking of Christ. When we speak about justice, we are speaking of Christ. When we speak about peace, we are speaking of Christ. When we speak about truth and life and redemption, we are speaking of Christ.

2 To renounce riches is the beginning and sustaining of virtues.

3 Riches are the beginning of all vices, because they make us capable of carrying out even our most vicious desires.

4 Born of the Virgin, he came forth from the womb as the light of the whole world to shine on all. His light is received by those who long for the splendour of perpetual light that can never be destroyed by darkness. The sun we know every day is followed by the darkness of night, but the sun of righteousness never sets, because wisdom cannot give way to evil.

5 You were rubbed with oil like an athlete, Christ's athlete, as though in preparation for an earthly wrestling match, and you agreed to take on your opponent.

6 For all in common [the church] prays, for all in common she works, in the temptations of all she is tried.

7 When I go to Rome, I fast on Saturday; when I am at Milan I do not: so, you too, whatever church you happen to go to, follow its custom, if you want to avoid giving scandal.

8 The will of God is the measure of things.

9 What is impossible to God? Not that which is difficult to his power, but that which is contrary to his nature.

10 Let us have reason for beginning, and let our end be within due limits. For a speech that is wearisome only stirs up anger.

11 She [St Agnes] was still too young for punishment, but already ripe for victory, too young for battle, yet ready to win the crown. Her tender age was a disadvantage, but she won the trial of virtue.

12 He would never come and knock at our door unless he wanted to come in, and if he does not always come in, that is our fault.

13 If you want my estate, you may have it;
if you want my body, I willingly give it up.
If you want to put me in irons or kill me,
I am content. I will not flee to the people
for protection, or cling to the altar. Rather, I
choose to be sacrificed for the sake of the altar.

14 As often as the Lord's blood is shed, it is poured out for the forgiveness of sins; so I ought to receive it always, that my sins may always be forgiven.

15 The church's foundation is unshakeable and firm against the assaults of the raging sea. Although the elements of the world crash against it and batter it, the church offers the safest harbour of salvation for all in distress.

16 Let no word pass your lips in vain, no meaningless word be uttered.

17 To give new natures to things is no less wonderful than to change their nature.

18 Do not limit the benefit of fasting merely to abstinence from food, for a true fast means refraining from evil. Loose every unjust bond, put away your resentment against your neighbour, forgive him his offences. Do not let your fasting lead to wrangling and strife. You do not eat meat, but you devour your brother; you abstain from wine, but not from insults. So all the labour of your fast is useless.

4.3
Ammonas the Hermit (c.288-350)
Egyptian ascetic

1 It is indeed essential for a man to take up the struggle against his thoughts, if the veils of thought that cover his intellect are to be removed, so that he can turn his gaze freely to God, and not follow wherever his wandering thoughts want to lead him.

4.4
Antony of Egypt (c.251-c.356)
Egyptian ascetic

1 My life is with my brother.

2 Do not trust in your own righteousness; do not grieve about a sin that is past and gone; and keep your tongue and your belly under control.

3 Whatever you find in your heart to do in following God, that do, and remain within yourself in him.

4 I tell you truly, beloved, that our carelessness and our weakness and our turning aside from the way are a loss not to us alone, but a weariness to the angels and to all the saints in Jesus Christ. Our weakness gives grief to them all, just as our salvation gives joy and refreshment to them all.

5 As long as we have peace with this world, we are at war with God and his angels and all the saints.

6 He who knows himself, knows everyone. He who can love himself, loves everyone.

7 The mind is not perfectly at prayer until the one praying does not think of himself or know he is praying.

8 There are some people who at first are hardhearted and persist in sin; somehow the good God in his mercy sends them the chastisement of affliction, so that they grow weary of their ways and come to their senses, and are converted. They draw near to God and come to knowledge and repent wholeheartedly, and attain to the true way of life.

9 I pray that since we are all made of the same substance, which has a beginning but no end, we may love one another with a single love. For all who know themselves know that they are of one immortal substance.

10 The demons know that the devil fell from heaven through pride, so they attack first those who are advanced in the way, by trying to set them against each other through pride and boastfulness. They know that this way they can cut us off from God.

11 By his word of power God gathered us out of all lands, from one end of the earth to the other, raised up our minds, forgave our sins, and taught us that we are members one of another.

12 There is no need for us to go abroad to attain the kingdom of heaven, nor to cross the sea in search of virtue: as the Lord has already told us, the kingdom of God is within you.

13 Distribute my garment as follows: let bishop Athanasius have the one sheepskin I sleep on, which he gave me new, and which has grown old with me; let bishop Serapion have the other sheepskin. As for my hairshirt, keep it for yourselves.

14 Demons are always cowardly.

15 Envious of us Christians, the demons meddle in everything in their efforts to stop us getting to heaven: they do not want us to make it to the place from which they fell.

16 Wherever you are on earth, so long as you remain on earth, 'the Lord is near, do not be anxious about anything'.

4.5
Aphrahat (mid 4c.)
Monk, a Syriac Church Father

1 Let us come now to the prayer of silence, that Samuel's mother, Hannah, prayed: how it was pleasing before God...

2 And I will show you, my beloved, how God was in each one of our righteous ancestors who prayed. When Moses prayed on the

mountain he was alone, and God was with him, and it was certainly not the case that he was not heard because he was alone. No, Moses' prayer was very much heard, and it appeased the wrath of God.

3 As I urged you above, the moment you start praying, raise your heart upwards, and lower your eyes downwards; enter inside your inner person and pray in secret to your Father who is in heaven.

4 If you are willing to forgive, then Gabriel who offers up prayers will receive your offering and raise it up; but if you do not forgive, then he will say to you: 'I will not bring your unclean offering before the sacred throne'. Instead, you will go there to give an account to your Creditor, taking your offering with you, while Gabriel will leave your offering and go off.

5 Now it says in the prophet: 'This is my rest; give it to the tired' [Isaiah 28.12]. Therefore effect this 'rest', and you will have no need to say 'forgive me'. Give rest to the weary, visit the sick, make provision for the poor; this is indeed prayer, as I shall explain to you. All the time that someone effects the 'rest' of God, that is prayer.

6 Watch out, my beloved, lest, when some opportunity of 'giving rest' to the will of God meets you, you say 'the time for prayer is at hand. I will pray and then act'. And while you are seeking to complete your prayer, that opportunity for 'giving rest' will escape from you.

7 I have written to you, my beloved, to the effect that a person should do the will of God, and that constitutes prayer. That is how prayer seems to me to excel. Nevertheless, just because I have said this to you, do not neglect prayer; rather, be all the more eager for prayer, and do not weary in it.

8 At a time when you are in trouble, offer up petition, and when you are well supplied with good things, you should give thanks to the Giver, and when your mind rejoices, offer up praise.

4.6
Apollos
Monk in Egypt

1 [To a brother who was discouraged by evil thoughts] Do not be surprised, my child, and do not lose hope. I too, old and grey as I am, am still much troubled by these thoughts. Do not be discouraged by this burning desire, which is healed not so much by human effort as by God's compassion.

2 O Lord, who puts us to the test for our own benefit, let [me] be given the brother's battle, so that in old age he may learn through experience what he has not been taught over these many years: how to feel sympathy with those who are under attack by the demons.

4.7
Arius (d.336)
Probably born in Libya, condemned for his views about the divinity of Jesus Christ

1 If the Father begot the Son, the One who was begotten has a beginning of existence; and from this it is evident that there was when the Son was not.

2 As for us, what do we say, and believe, and what have we taught, and what do we teach? That the Son is not unbegotten, nor in any way part of the unbegotten; nor from some lower essence; but that by his own [the Father's] will and counsel he has subsisted before time, and before ages as God full [of grace and truth], only-begotten, unchangeable.

3 The Son had a beginning, but God is without beginning.

4 We believe in one God, the Father Almighty; and in the Lord Jesus Christ his only begotten Son, who was begotten of him before all ages, God the Word through whom all things were made...

4.8
Athanasius (?296-373)
Bishop of Alexandria, Church Father

1 He built himself a temple, a body, that is, in the Virgin, and so made himself an instrument in which to dwell.

2 He became what we are that he might make us what he is.

3 For the Word was not degraded by receiving a body; rather, he deified what he put on.

4 The Word of God was not made for us; rather we were made for him.

5 Everything in the world is sold for what it is worth, and people trade objects for their equivalent. But the promise of eternal life is purchased for next to nothing.

6 Anthony begged the vision that appeared to him, 'Where were you? Why didn't you appear right from the start, to put an end to my distress?' And a voice said to him, 'I was here, Anthony, but I waited to watch your struggle. Now, because you persevered and did not give in, I will be your helper for ever, and will make you famous everywhere.'

7 I think the Psalms are like a mirror, in which one can see oneself and the movements of one's own heart.

8 God would not be true to himself if man did not die once God had pronounced sentence against him. On the other hand it would not be fitting that rational beings who have shared in God's Word should perish and return to non-existence.

4.9
Basil (330-379)
Bishop of Caesarea in Cappadocia (in modern Turkey), Church Father

1 Despise the flesh, for it passes away; be solicitous for your soul, for it will never die.

2 It is right to submit to a higher authority when a commandment of God would not be violated.

3 Truly unexpected news make both ears tingle.

4 Christians should offer their brethren simple and unpretentious hospitality.

5 The indwelling of God is this—to hold God always in memory, his shrine established within us.

6 This is the definition of vice: the wrong use, in violation of the Lord's command, of what has been given us by God for a good purpose.

7 God chooses those who are pleasing to him. He put a shepherd at the head of his people, and of the goat-herd Amos he made a prophet.

8 Good family, athletic prowess, a handsome face, tall stature, the esteem of others, control over others—none of these are important to us or fit matter for our prayers; we do not pay court to those who can boast of them. Our ideals are far higher than that.

9 Prudence must precede all our actions since, if prudence is lacking, there is nothing, however good it may seem, that is not turned into evil.

10 Self-renunciation means to loosen the chains of this earthly life which comes to an end, and to set ourselves free from worldly business, and so make ourselves more fit to enter on the path that leads to God. We free our spirit to win and use those things that are far more valuable and precious than gold or precious stones.

11 What is the mark of a Christian? Faith working by love. What is the mark of faith? Unhesitating conviction of the truth of the inspired words, unshaken by any argument either based on the plea of physical necessity or masquerading in the guise of piety. What is the mark of a believer? To hold fast by such conviction in the strength of what Scripture says and to dare neither to set it at nought nor to add to it.

12 What is the mark of him who is born of the Spirit? That he should be, according to the measure given him, that very thing of which he

was born, as it is written: 'That which is born of the flesh is flesh, and that which is born of the Spirit is spirit.'

13 What is the mark of a Christian? To love one another, even as Christ also loved us. What is the mark of a Christian? To see the Lord always before him. What is the mark of the Christian? To watch each night and day and in perfectly pleasing God to be ready, knowing that the Lord will come at an hour that he does not expect.

4.10
Bessarion (?late 4c.)
Desert ascetic

1 The monk ought to be as the cherubim and the seraphim: all eye.

4.11
Boniface of Tarsus (d.306)
Martyr

1 Lord, Lord almighty, Father of our Lord Jesus Christ, I am your servant; come to my help. Send me your angel; take my soul and give it peace. That will stop the foul dragon with his reek of blood from blocking my way; no malice of his will then obstruct my soul, none of his stratagems will deceive me.

4.12
Book of Steps
Late fourth-century Syrian writing

1 That body and heart in which our Lord dwells—also because the Spirit resides there—is in truth a temple and an altar, seeing that our Lord resides there.

2 Now the person who shepherds the flock of Christ cannot go off and work with a plough or labour on the visible land; he will be gathering in, shepherding, and pacifying the sheep entrusted to him. He shall stand with unabashed face on that final day before him who bade him 'Shepherd my flock, my ewes and my lambs'.

3 Let it be a law for ourselves, then, that we should run after perfection. Once we have heard the word of truth and of mercy, let us be 'the good soil' for it, and let it put forth in us rootlets, striking root in our souls, and sprouting so as to 'give fruit, thirty-fold, sixty-fold and a hundred-fold'.

4.13
Crispina (d.304)
Martyred for her defence of the Christian faith

1 My God who is and who abides for ever ordered me to be born; it was he who gave me salvation through the saving waters of baptism: he is at my side, helping me, strengthening his handmaid in all things so that she will not commit sacrilege.

4.14
Cronius (c.285-c.386)
Desert father

1 If Moses had not led his sheep to Mt Sinai, he would not have seen the fire in the bush... Truly it is written: 'Looking unto Jesus, the pioneer and perfector of our faith, who for the joy which was set before him, endured the cross.' David also said: 'I will not give sleep to mine eyes, nor slumber to my eyelids, until I find a place for the Lord.'

4.15
Cyril of Jerusalem (c.315-386)
Bishop and teacher

1 If anyone does not receive baptism, they have no salvation; except only that martyrs, even without water, receive the kingdom.

2 Temptation is like a river that is difficult to cross. Those who are not overwhelmed by temptation are good swimmers; they cross the river without sinking. But those who cannot swim are submerged when they enter the water.

3 Christ did not pass through the Virgin as through a channel, but truly took flesh and was truly fed with milk from her. He truly ate as we eat and drank as we drink. For if the incarnation was a figment then so was our salvation.

4 Why did Christ refer to the grace of the Spirit under the name of water? Because through water all plants and animals live. The rain comes down from heaven, and though it comes in one form, its effects have various forms: yes, indeed, one spring watered all of paradise, and the same rain falls on the whole world, yet it turns white in the lily, red in the rose, and purple in the violet.

5 You are standing before God in the presence of the hosts of angels. The Holy Spirit is about to set his seal on each of your souls. You are about to be drawn into the service of the great king.

6 The Lord's body became a bait for death, so that the dragon, hoping to swallow him up, would be forced to disgorge with him everyone else he had swallowed.

7 What a strange and inconceivable thing it is! We did not really die, we were not really buried; we were not crucified and raised again; our imitation of Christ was but in a figure, while our salvation is truth. Christ actually was crucified and buried, and truly rose again; and all these things have been transmitted to us, that we might by imitation participate in his sufferings, and so gain salvation in truth.

4.16
Cyrillona

Poet and hymn-writer, probably from Mesopotamia (in modern Iraq)

1 Your hand upholds the universe,
your love gives rest to the world.

4.17
Desert fathers and mothers (anonymous sayings)

Monks and nuns of the Egyptian desert

1 Just as we carry our own shadow everywhere with us, so we ought to have tears and compunction with us wherever we are.

2 The children of Israel entered the promised land after forty years. When you reach that land, you will no longer fear the battle. God, indeed, wills that you should be worried, so that you may ceaselessly desire to enter into that land.

3 A poor man, sleeping with a single mat half under, half on top, was heard saying: I thank you, Lord: How many rich people are in prison wearing irons at present; how many more have their feet fastened to wood, not being able so much as to satisfy their bodily needs—whereas I am like a king with my legs stretched out.

4 If a bodily illness comes to you, do not be disturbed. For truly, if your Master wants you to be sick in body, who are you to resist? Will he not himself care for you in all things? Can you live without him? Live without bitterness, then, and beg him to supply you with what is necessary. This is what his will is, that you should remain in patience, eating the charity which is brought you.

5 What condemns us is not that thoughts enter into us but that we use them badly; indeed, through our thoughts we can be shipwrecked, and through our thoughts we can be crowned.

6 Look, I am going to play the part of God and seat myself on the throne of judgment. What do you want me to do for you, then? If you say, 'Have mercy on me', God says to you, 'If you want me to have mercy on you, do you also have mercy on your brother; if you want me to forgive you, do you also forgive your neighbour.' Can there be injustice in God? Certainly not, but it depends on us whether we wish to be saved.

7 The prophets wrote books, then came our Fathers who put them into practice. Those who came after them learnt them by heart. Then came the present generation, who have written them out and put them into their window seats without using them.

8 Do not agree with every word. Be slow to believe, quick to speak the truth.

9 If the soul has the word but not the work, it is like a tree with leaves but no fruit. But just as a tree full of fruit also has beautiful foliage,

so words are appropriate in the soul whose activity is good.

10 Do not do anything you hate to another. You do not like it when someone slanders you? Then do not slander anyone. You do not like it if someone denounces you falsely? Then do not denounce anybody. You do not like it if someone despises you, injures you, or steals something from you? Then do nothing of this sort to another. He who can keep this saying has what he needs for salvation.

11 He who loses gold or silver can find more to replace it, but he who loses time cannot find more.

12 The reason why we do not make progress is because we do not know our own measure, and we do not persevere in the work we undertake, and we want to acquire virtue without labour.

13 I would rather have a defeat with humility than a victory with pride.

4.18
Dioscorus (late 4c.)

Desert father

1 If we wear our heavenly robe, we shall not be found naked, but if we are found not wearing this garment, what shall we do, brothers? We, even we also, shall hear the voice that says, 'Cast them into outer darkness; there men will weep and gnash their teeth.'

4.19
Egeria (late 4c.)

Pilgrim and diarist

1 It was always our custom that when we had reached the place we wanted to go, first we said a prayer, then a selection from Scripture was read, then an appropriate psalm was sung, and we again said a prayer. We always maintained this custom, God willing, whenever we arrived at the place we desired to visit.

4.20
Ephraem the Syrian (c.306-373)

Syriac Church Father, poet

1 If the womb holds back the child, then both mother and child will die; may my mouth, Lord, not hold back my faith with the result that the one perish and the other be quenched, the two of them perishing, each because of the other.

2 Fish are both conceived and born in the sea; if they dive deep, they escape those who would catch them. In luminous silence within the mind let prayer recollect itself, so as not to stray.

3 Truth and Love are wings that cannot be separated, for Truth cannot fly without Love, nor can Love soar aloft without Truth; their yoke is one of amity.

4 Blessed is the person who has consented to become the close friend of faith and of prayer: he lives in singlemindedness and makes prayer and faith stop by with him.

5 Sunrise marks the hour for toil to begin, but in our souls, Lord, prepare a dwelling for the day that will never end.

6 You are the guest who filled the jars
with good wine,
Fill my mouth with your praise.

7 In the bread we eat the power that
cannot be eaten,
In the wine we drink the fire that
cannot be drunk.

8 O Lord and Master of my life, take from me the spirit of laziness, faint-heartedness, lust for power and idle talk. Give, rather, the spirit of chastity, humility, patience and love to your servant. Yes, my Lord and King, grant that I may see my own errors and not judge my brothers and sisters, for you are blessed from all ages to all ages.

4.21
Epiphanius (c.315-403)
Desert father

1 Since I took the habit [became a monk] I have not allowed anyone to go to sleep with a complaint against me and I have not gone to rest with a complaint against anyone.

4.22
Epitaph from Cairo
A prayer for the dead

1 God of spirits and of all flesh,
you have conquered death,
trampled Hades underfoot
and given life to the world.
Give rest to the soul of my father, Sinethe...
in the bosom of Abraham, of Isaac
and of Jacob,
a place of light and refreshment,
where no sorrow is, or pain, or sighing.

4.23
Euplus (d.c.304)
A deacon, martyred in Sicily

1 Thank you, Christ, for this. Take care of me, because it is for you that I am suffering. Lord, protect your servants: stay with them to the end, and then they will be able to glorify your name for all eternity.

4.24
Eusebius of Caesarea (c.260-c.330)
The 'Father of Church History'

1 The race of the Hebrews is not new, but is honoured among all men for its antiquity and is itself well known to all.

2 [At the victory of Constantine] there was taken away from men all fear of those who had formerly oppressed them; they celebrated brilliant festivals; all things were filled with light, and men formerly downcast looked at each other with smiling faces and beaming eyes; with dancing and hymns in city and country alike they gave honour first of all to God the universal King... and then to the godly Emperor.

4.25
Eusebius of Vercelli (c.283-371)
Born in Sardinia, Bishop of Vercelli in northern Italy

1 Like a farmer tending a sound tree, untouched by axe or fire because of its fruit, I want not only to serve you good people in the body, but also to give my life for your well-being.

4.26
Evagrius of Pontus (c.305-400)
Spiritual writer, born in Pontus (in modern Turkey)

1 It is better to begin from one's feeble state and end up strong, to progress from small things to big, than to set your heart from the very first on the perfect way of life, only to have to abandon it later.

2 It is the same with people who travel: if they tire themselves out on the very first day by rushing along, they will end up wasting many days as a result of sickness. But if they start out walking at a gentle pace until they have got accustomed to walking, in the end they will not get tired, even though they walk great distances.

3 Allow the Spirit of God to dwell within you; then in his love he will come and make a habitation with you; he will reside in you and live in you.

4 A sinner who begins to show concern over his soul and who becomes penitent is like a kitchen utensil which is full of filth and blackened; yet once washed and scrubbed it glistens.

5 A single word said with an attentive mind is better than a thousand when the mind is far away.

6 Blessed are you if you have to struggle hard in prayer. Say your words, offer up your complaint, seek out your Judge.

7 Set off on the path of prayer with confidence, then swiftly and speedily will you reach the place of peace, which is your stronghold against the place of fear.

8 If you pray truly, you will feel within yourself a great assurance; and the angels will be your companions.

9 Strive never to pray against anyone.

10 God cannot be grasped by the mind. If God could, he would not be God.

11 Do not think you have acquired virtue, unless you have struggled for it to the point of shedding your blood.

4.27
Gregory of Nazianzus (c.330-c.390)
Church Father from Cappadocia (in modern Turkey)

1 My mind is, if I must write the truth, to keep clear of every conference of bishops, for of conference never saw I good come, or a remedy so much as an increase of evils. For there is strife and ambition, and these have the upper hand of reason.

2 To do no wrong is really superhuman, and belongs to God alone.

3 The Creator Word... formed man as a second universe, great in his littleness.

4 Christ is born: glorify him. Christ comes from heaven: go out to meet him. Christ descends to earth: let us be raised on high.

5 The whole of human life is but a single day, to those who labour with love.

4.28
Gregory of Nyssa (c.335-c.394)
Church Father from Cappodocia (in modern Turkey)

1 The creature is like a mighty trumpet that speaks to us of God.

2 His descent to our lowliness is the supreme expression of his power.

3 He who gives you the day will also give you the things necessary for the day.

4 Cling only to what is necessary.

5 This truly is the vision of God: never to be satisfied in the desire to see him. But one must always, by looking at what he can see, rekindle his desire to see more.

6 The one who keeps his eyes on the head and origin of the whole universe has them on the perfection of virtue, on truth, on justice, on immortality, and on everything else that is good, because Christ is goodness itself.

7 Just as those at sea, who have been carried away from the direction of the harbour they are making for, regain the right course by the clear sign of some beacon or mountain peak, so the Scripture guides those adrift on the sea of life back to the harbour of God's will.

8 Truly barren is secular education which is always in labour and never brings anything to birth.

4.29
Hilarion (c.291-371)
Born in Gaza, became a hermit

1 An wanton horse and an unchaste body should have their provender cut down.

4.30
Hilary of Poitiers (d.c.367)
Bishop of Poitiers (in France), theologian

1 His abasement is our glory. What he is, while appearing in the flesh, that we in turn have become: restored to God.

2 Faith ought in silence to fulfil the commandments, worshipping the Father, reverencing with him the Son, abounding in the Holy Spirit. The error of others compels us to err in daring to embody in human terms truths which ought to be hidden in the silent veneration of the heart.

3 Christ dwells in us; and when Christ thus dwells, God dwells. And the Spirit of Christ dwells; and it is not another Spirit than the Spirit of God who dwells. But if Christ is understood to be in us through the Holy Spirit, we must recognize this as both the Spirit of God and the Spirit of Christ.

4 It was not necessary for him through whom man was made to become man, but it was necessary for us that God should be made flesh and dwell with us, that is to say, dwell within all flesh by assuming one fleshly body.

4.31
Irenaeus of Sirmium (d.c.304)
Bishop of Sirmium (in Hungary), martyred

1 Thanks be to you, Lord Jesus Christ: in all my trials and sufferings you have given me the strength to stand firm; in your mercy you have granted me a share of eternal glory.

4.32
Isaac of the Cells (late 4c.)
Desert father

1 Our fathers... wore old garments woven from palm fronds and mended all over; now you are foppishly dressed. Go away from here; leave this place.

4.33
Isidore of Pelusia
Desert father

1 To live without speaking is better than to speak without living. For the former who does rightly does good even by his silence, but the latter does no good even when he speaks. When words and life correspond to one another they are together the whole of philosophy.

4.34
Isidore the Priest (?4c.)
Desert father

1 Now is the time to labour for the Lord, for salvation is found in the day of affliction: for it is written, 'By your endurance you will gain your lives'.

4.35
John Chrysostom (?347-407)
From Antioch in Syria (in modern Turkey), later Archbishop of Constantinople (Istanbul), preacher and Church Father

1 God has made for us two kinds of eyes: those of flesh and those of faith. When you come to the sacred initiation, the eyes of the flesh see water; the eyes of faith behold the Spirit. Those eyes see the body being baptized; these eyes see the old existence being buried.

2 People will not attend to what we say, they will look carefully at what we do; and they will say to us 'First obey your own words and then you can exhort others.'

3 However just your words, you spoil everything when you speak them with anger.

4 Read the prophetic books without seeing Christ in them, and how flat and insipid they are! See Christ there, and what you read is fragrant.

5 You are a poor soldier of Christ if you think you can overcome without fighting, and suppose you can have the crown without the conflict.

6 By the cross we know the gravity of sin and the greatness of God's love towards us.

7 The world is meant to be like a household in which all the servants receive equal allowances, for all men are equal, since they are brothers.

8 God waits for the chances we give him to show his great generosity.

9 The magi worshipped this body even when it lay in a manger. Those heathen foreigners left home and country and went on a long journey, and came and worshipped him with fear and great trembling. We are citizens of heaven; let us imitate these foreigners.

10 Attention to little things is a great thing.

11 Patience is the queen of the virtues.

12 You can set up an altar to God in your mind by means of prayer. And so it is fitting to pray at your trade, on a journey, standing at a counter or sitting at your handicraft.

13 Every sermon should be an agony of soul, a passion to beget Christ in the souls of men.

14 God draws, but he draws the willing.

15 He [the devil] does not dare to look at you directly because he sees the light blazing from your head and blinding his eyes.

16 What does light give me compared with what your love gives? The light is useful to me in my present life, but your love weaves for me a crown in the future.

17 You yourself both offer and are offered, you yourself both receive and are distributed, O Christ our God.

18 Every day bring God sacrifices and be the priest in this reasonable service, offering your body and the virtue of your soul.

19 Do you want to honour Christ's body? Then do not despise him when you see him naked, and do not honour him here in church by wearing silk, while you neglect him outside the church where he is cold and naked.

20 A woman is led by her natural love for her child to feed it from her overflowing breast; and in the same way Christ always feeds with his own blood those whom he has brought to new birth.

21 There are many mothers who after the pains of childbirth give their children to strangers to nurse. But Christ could not bear his children to be fed by others. He feeds us himself with his own blood.

22 How could twelve uneducated men, who lived on lakes and rivers and deserts, conceive of such a great enterprise? Their preaching was clearly divinely inspired.

23 I consider that the one who knows how to form the mind of the young is truly greater than all painters, sculptors and others like that.

24 If you want to rise, avoid luxury, for luxury lowers and degrades.

25 I am afraid that no one has ever not been pleased at being praised.

26 There is only one thing to be feared, and that is sin. Everything else is beside the point.

27 The highest point of philosophy is to be both wise and simple; this is the angelic life.

28 The monks have no sadness. They wage war on the devil as though they were performing a dance.

4.36
John the Dwarf (c.339)
Desert father

1 [In response to the jealous accusation that 'his vessel is full of poison'] That is very true, abba; and you have said that when you only see the outside, but if you were able to see the inside as well, what would you say then?

2 Do your work in peace.

4.37
Joseph of Panephysis
Desert father

1 If you want to find rest here below, and hereafter, in all circumstances say, Who am I? and do not judge anybody.

4.38
Liturgical fragments
From documents dating back to very early Christian times

1 Great is the mystery, O Lord,
of your resurrection.

What you are receiving
is the body of Christ,
what you are drinking,
the source of immortality.

2 Today we have gained possession
of the burning coal in whose shadow
the cherubim sing.
Today we have heard
a voice say, sweet and strong:
This body burns the thorns of sin.
This body gives light to the souls
of all believers.

3 This is the Pasch:
holy the feast we celebrate today.
The Pasch opens to us the gates of paradise.

4 We give you the fruit of our lips
and we say to you:
Glory to you for your baptism.
Glory to you for your cross.
Glory to you for your burial.
Glory to you for rising
and raising us with you.

4.39
Macarius of Alexandria (c.296-c.393)
Desert father

1 Correct and judge justly those who are subject to you, but judge no one else. For truly it is written: 'Is it not those inside the church whom you are to judge? God judges those outside.'

4.40
Macarius the elder (of Egypt) (c.300-c.390)
Desert father

1 There is no need to talk a lot in prayer, but stretch out your hands often and say, 'Lord, as you want and as you know, have mercy on me.' But if there is war in your soul, add, 'Help me.' And because he knows what we need, he shows us his mercy.

2 Receive poverty, want, sickness and all miseries joyfully from the hand of God, and with equal joy receive consolation, refreshment and every kind of abundance. If you always have this same joy in the will of God you will deaden the goad of your passions.

4.41
Macrina (327-379)
Older sister and great influence on Basil of Caesarea and Gregory of Nyssa, and founder of a community of women in her native Pontus (in modern Turkey)

1 O Lord, you have freed us from the fear of death. You have made the end of this life into the beginning of true life. One day you will take back again what you have given, transfiguring our mortal remains with the grace of immortality. Lord, you have saved us from the curse and from sin, having become both for our sake.

2 That which is 'made in the image' of the Deity necessarily possesses a likeness to its prototype in every respect.

4.42
Methodius of Olympus (d.c.311)
Bishop in Lycia (in modern Turkey), religious writer

1 Decay is destroyed; disease,
with its pain and its tears, has gone.
Death is no more, folly has fled
and grief, that gnaws the mind,
is dead. A sudden shaft of joy
from Christ our God,
and now this mortal world is shining.

4.43
Monica (c.331-387)
African Christian mother of Augustine of Hippo

1 Son, for my part, I have no further delight in anything in this life. What I do here any longer, and to what end I am here, I do not know, now that my hopes in this world are accomplished. The one thing for which I desired to linger for a while in this life—that I might see you a Catholic Christian before I died—my God has done for me.

2 Nothing is far, to God; and I have no need to be afraid that at the end of the world he will not know where the place is, when the time comes to raise me up.

4.44
Moses
Desert father

1 [To a monk] Go and sit in your cell, and your cell will teach you everything.

2 If a man's deeds are not in harmony with his prayer, he labours in vain.

4.45
Nicholas of Myra (early 4c.)
Bishop in Lycia (in modern Turkey), subject of many legends

1 This office [of bishop] demands a different sort of conduct, so that one may live no longer for oneself but for others.

4.46
Gospel of Nicodemus (?4c.)
An apocryphal account of the life, death and resurrection of Jesus

1 While Hades so debated with Satan, the King of glory held out his right hand, and took hold of our father Adam and raised him. He turned to the rest and said: 'All of you come with me, as many as have died through the touch of his hand on the tree; for behold, I raise you all up through the tree of the cross.'

4.47
Nilus
Desert father

1 Everything you do in revenge against a brother who has harmed you will come back to your mind at the time of prayer.

4.48
Or (d.c.390)
Desert father

1 Do not speak in your heart against your brother like this: 'I am a man of more sober and austere life than he is,' but put yourself in subjection to the grace of Christ, in the spirit of poverty and genuine charity, or you will be overcome by the spirit of vain-glory and lose all you have gained... let your salvation be founded in the Lord.

4.49
Pachomius (290-346)
Egyptian founder of Christian monastic life in its communal form

1 Strive, my brothers, to attain that to which you have been called. Meditate on the Psalms, and the lessons from the rest of the Bible, especially from the Gospel. And I myself find rest in serving God and you according to God's commandment.

4.50
Pambo (c.303-373)
Desert father

1 From the time that I came into this solitude and built my cell and dwelt in it, I cannot remember eating any food that I have not earned with my own hands, nor speaking any word that I have been sorry for until now. And so I go to the Lord, as one who has not yet begun to serve God.

4.51
Paphnoutios
Desert father

1 During the whole lifetime of the old men, I used to go and see them twice a month... I told them each of my thoughts and they never answered me anything but this: 'Wherever you go, do not judge yourself and you will be at peace.'

4.52
Paul the Great
Desert father

1 Keep close to Jesus.

4.53
Paula (347-404)
Roman Christian, settled in Bethlehem near Jerome, founding convents of nuns and of monks

1 My prayer is that I may die a beggar, not leaving a penny to my daughter and indebted to strangers for my winding sheet... If I beg, I will find many to give to me; but if this beggar does not obtain help from me when by borrowing I can give it to him, he will die; and if he dies, of whom will his soul be required?

4.54
Poemen the Shepherd
Desert father

1 As the breath which comes out of our nostrils, so do we need humility and the fear of God.

4.55
Sarah
Desert mother

1 If I prayed God that all men should approve of my conduct, I should find myself a penitent at the door of each one, but I rather pray that my heart may be pure towards all.

4.56
Serapion
Bishop of Thmuis on the Nile delta, religious writer

1 We beg you, make us really alive. Give us the spirit of light, that we may know you, the supremely true...

4.57
Severus of Thrace (Heraclea) (d.c.304)
Martyr in Thrace (northern Greece)

1 To all who are tossed by the waves, you are the calm of the harbour; you are the hope of the hopeful.

4.58
Silvanus
Desert father

1 Mary needs Martha. It is really thanks to Martha that Mary is praised.

4.59
Simeon bar Sabba'e (d.c.339-344)
Bishop of Seleucia in Persia, martyred

1 Give me this crown, Lord; you know how I long for it, for I have loved you with all my heart and all my being. When I see you I shall be filled with joy and you will give me rest.

4.60
Sisoes
Desert father

1 It is no great thing to be with God in your thoughts, but it is a great thing to see yourself as inferior to all creatures. It is this, coupled with hard work, that leads to humility.

4.61
Theodora
Desert mother

1 Let us strive to enter by the narrow gate. Just as the trees, if they have not stood before the winter's storms cannot bear fruit, so it is with us: this present age is a storm and it is only through many trials and temptations that we can obtain an inheritance in the kingdom of heaven.

4.62
Theodore of Eleutheropolis
Desert father

1 If you are temperate, do not judge the fornicator, for you would then transgress the law just as much. And he who said, 'Do not commit fornication', also said, 'Do not judge'.

4.63
Theodore of Enaton
Desert father

1 When I was young, I lived in the desert. One day I went to the bakery to make two loaves, and there I found a brother also wanting to make bread, but there was no one to help him. So I put mine on one side, to lend him a hand. When the work was done, another brother came, and again I lent him a hand in cooking his food. Then a third came, and I did the same; and similarly one after the other, I baked for each of those who came. I made six batches. Later I made my own two loaves, since no one else came.

4.64
Theodore of Heraclea (d.c.306)
Martyr from Pontus (on the Black Sea)

1 I know not your gods. Jesus Christ, the only Son of God, is my God. Beat, tear or burn me, and if my words offend you, cut out my tongue; every part of my body is ready when God calls for it as a sacrifice.

4.65
Theodore of Pherme
Desert father

1 There is no other virtue than that of not being scornful.

4.66
Theophilus of Alexandria (d.412)
Bishop of Alexandria

1 Abandoned to outer darkness and condemned to everlasting fire, the careless soul will be punished through the ages without end. Where then is the vanity of the world? Where is vain glory? Where is carnal life? Where is enjoyment? Where is imagination? Where is ease?

Fifth Century

5.1
Agathon
Desert father

1 Whatever good work a man undertakes, if he perseveres in it, he will attain rest, but prayer is hard work and warfare to one's last breath.

5.2
Alonius
Desert father

1 If a man does not say in his heart, in the world there is only myself and God, he will not gain peace.

5.3
Anoub
Desert father

1 We are seven brethren. If you wish us to live together, let us be like this statue, which is not moved whether one beats it or whether one flatters it.

5.4
Apollo
Desert father

1 When you see your brother, you see the Lord your God.

5.5
Apostolic Constitutions
A collection of worship material

1 You are knowledge that never had a beginning, eternal sight, hearing that did not need to be given birth, wisdom that required no teaching.

5.6
Arsenius (c.360-440)
Desert father

1 Be solitary, be silent, and be at peace.

5.7
Asterius of Amasia (d.c.410)
Bishop of Amasia in Pontus (on the Black Sea)

1 O night more light than day,
more bright than the sun,
O night more white than snow,
more brilliant than many torches,
O night of more delight than is paradise.

5.8
Augustine of Hippo (354-430)
Born in North Africa (modern Tunisia), bishop, Church Father

1 I did not yet love, and yet I loved to love... I was looking for someone to love, because I loved being a lover.

2 Christ came when all things were growing old. He made them new.

3 You have made us for yourself, and our heart is restless till it finds its rest in you.

4 I kept my heart from assenting to anything, being afraid to fall headlong; but by hanging in suspense, I met a worse death.

5 To err is human, to persist in error is devilish.

6 I inquired into the nature of evil and found no substance in it.

7 Faith is to believe what you do not yet see; the reward for this faith is to see what you believe.

8 Envy and hatred try to pierce our neighbour with a sword. But the blade cannot reach our neighbour unless it first passes though our own body.

9 Taking trouble over a funeral, giving dignified burial, having a grand funeral procession: all this is more to comfort the living than to be of use to the dead.

10 God is more truly imagined than expressed, and exists more truly than can be imagined.

11 I beg you to come into my heart, for by inspiring it to long for you, you make it ready to receive you.

12 Give what you command; and ask what you will.

13 Man still wishes to be happy even when he so lives as to make happiness impossible.

14 The whole point of this life is the healing of the heart's eye through which God is seen.

15 See how the unlearned start up and take heaven by storm while we with all our learning grovel upon the earth.

16 He who is filled with love is filled with God himself.

17 Two works of mercy set a man free: forgive and you will be forgiven, and give and you will receive.

18 It is the mystery of yourselves that is laid on the Lord's table; it is the mystery of yourselves that you receive. To that which you are, you answer 'Amen', and in answering you assent. For you hear the words 'the body of Christ', and you reply 'Amen'.

19 If you have received well, you are what you have received.

20 You have put salt in our mouths that we may thirst for you.

21 Understanding is the reward of faith. So do not seek to understand in order that you may believe, but believe, so that you may understand.

22 We make a ladder of our vices, if we trample those same vices under foot.

23 We do the works, but God works in us the doing of them.

24 Too late I came to love you, beauty so ancient and so new, too late I came to love you! And see! You were within me, and I was outside myself and searching for you there.

25 St John appears as the boundary between the two testaments. As representative of the past, he is born of elderly parents; as herald of the new age, he is declared to be a prophet while still in the womb of his mother. For while yet unborn he leapt in Elizabeth's womb at the arrival of the blessed Mary.

26 He humbled himself for us; let us glorify him.

27 He that saves you, the same saves your horse and your sheep; to come to the very least, your hen too.

28 If you plan to build a high house of virtues, you must first lay deep foundations of humility.

5.9
Balai (d.c.460)
Syrian poet and hymn-writer

1 God, who is all-powerful, could have made himself a house as easily as he brought the world into existence, with a wave of his hand. But he preferred to build man instead, and man in turn was to build for him. Blessed be the mercy that showed us such love.

5.10
John Cassian (360-435)
Monk, writer, traveller

1 Every art and every discipline has a particular objective, that is to say, a target and an end peculiarly its own. Someone keenly engaged in any one art calmly and freely endures every toil, danger, and loss.

2 The aim of our profession is the kingdom of God or the kingdom of heaven. But our point of reference, our objective, is a clean heart, without which it is impossible for anyone to reach our target.

3 Not to be jealous, not to be puffed up, not to act heedlessly, not to seek what does not belong to one, not to rejoice over some injustice, not to plan evil—what is this and its like if not the continuous offering to God of a heart that is perfect and truly pure, a heart kept free of all disturbance?

4 What we gain from fasting does not compensate for what we lose in anger.

5 All gifts have been given for reasons of temporal use and need and they will surely pass away at the end of the present dispensation. Love, however, will never be cut off. It works in us and for us, and not simply in this life.

6 When our gaze has wandered even a little from Christ let us immediately turn the eyes of our heart back to him and let our vision be directed to him as though along the straightest line.

7 What is more suitable and appropriate to true blessedness than an eternity of peace and joy?

8 Contemplation of God can be understood in more than one fashion. For God is not solely known by way of the astonished gaze at his ungraspable nature, something hidden thus far in the hope that comes with what has been promised us. He can also be sensed in the magnificence of his creation, in the spectacle of his justice, and in the help he extends each day to the running of the world. He can be sensed too when with well-purified minds we consider what he has achieved in each generation by means of his saints.

9 God can be sensed when we gaze with trembling hearts at that power of his which controls, guides, and rules everything, when we contemplate his immense knowledge and his knowing look which the secrets of the heart cannot evade.

10 It is discernment which in Scripture is described as the eye and the lamp of the body... The eye sees through all the thoughts and actions of a man, examining and illuminating everything which we must do. And if it is not sound... that is, if it is not fortified by good judgement and by well-founded knowledge, if it is deluded by error and by presumption, this makes for darkness in our entire body.

11 Discernment is the mother, the guardian, and the guide of all the virtues.

12 If sin and worldly preoccupation have not weighed the soul down, if dangerous passion has not sullied it, then, lifted up by the natural goodness of its purity, it will rise to the heights on the lightest breath of meditation and, leaving the lowly things, the things of earth, it will travel upward to the heavenly and the invisible.

13 The same kind of prayers cannot be uttered continuously by any one person. A lively person prays one way. A person brought down by the weight of gloom or despair prays another. One prays another way when the life of the spirit is flourishing, and another way when pushed down by the mass of temptation.

14 These, then, are the four rich sources of prayer. Out of contrition for sin is supplication born. Prayer comes of the fidelity to promises and the fulfilment of what we have undertaken for the sake of a pure conscience. Pleading comes forth from the warmth of our love. Thanksgiving is generated by the contemplation of God's goodness and greatness and faithfulness. And all this, as we know, often evokes the most fervent and fiery prayers.

15 'May your will be done on earth as it is in heaven.' No greater prayer can be offered than that the things of earth should be put on a level with the things of heaven.

16 'Give us this day our daily bread.' With 'daily' the evangelist shows that without this bread we cannot live a spiritual life for even a day.

17 We shall be forgiven proportionately with the forgiveness we display to those who, whatever their malice, have injured us.

18 Sometimes the soul lies low, hidden in the depths of silence. The stunning onset of sudden light takes all sound of voice away. All its senses are withdrawn into its own depths or else are let go and with unspeakable groanings it pours out its longings to God.

19 We must therefore not be hesitant and lacking in faith. We must persist in our prayers, and our persistence will quite certainly win us, as God has told us, everything we ask for. No doubt about this at all!

20 We pray in our room whenever we withdraw our hearts completely from the tumult and noise of our thoughts and our worries and when secretly and intimately we offer our prayers to the Lord.

21 We pray with the door shut when without opening our mouths and in perfect silence we offer our petitions to the One who pays no attention to words but who looks hard at our hearts.

22 To keep the thought of God always in your mind you must cling totally to this formula for piety: 'Come to my help, O God; Lord, hurry to my rescue'.

23 Three things keep a wandering mind in place—vigils, meditation, and prayer. Constant attention to them and a firm concentration upon them will give stability to the soul.

24 For wrath that is nursed in the heart, although it may not injure the bystanders, yet excludes the splendour of the radiance of the Holy Spirit, equally with wrath that is openly manifested.

5.11
Chromatius of Aquileia (d.c.407)

Italian bishop and scholar

1 Since he is the Sun of Justice, he fittingly calls his disciples the light of the world. The reason for this is that through them, as through shining rays, he has poured out the light of the knowledge of himself upon the entire world. For by manifesting the light of truth, they have dispelled the darkness of error from the hearts of men.

2 The Lord called his disciples the salt of the earth because they seasoned with heavenly wisdom the hearts of men that were rendered insipid by the devil.

5.12
Cyril of Alexandria (c.376-444)

Bishop, theologian

1 That anyone could doubt the right of the holy Virgin to be called the mother of God fills me with astonishment. Surely she must be the mother of God if our Lord Jesus Christ is God, and she gave birth to him!

2 The one who will come is the one who suffered death in human fashion, but rose again in a divine manner and went up to heaven... He will come, as I have said, revealed not in human lowliness but in the glory of supreme divinity.

3 He undertook to help the descendants of Abraham, fashioning a body for himself from a woman and sharing our flesh and blood, so that we could see in him not only God, but also, because of this union, a man like ourselves.

5.13
Diodochos of Photiki (c.400-486)
Bishop in northern Greece, spiritual writer

1 Evil does not exist by nature, nor is any man naturally evil, for God made nothing that was not good.

2 All men are made in God's image; but to be in his likeness is granted only to those who through great love have brought their own freedom into subjection to God.

5.14
Dionysius the Areopagite
(?end 5c. or beg. 6c.)
Mystical theologian

1 Let us quietly receive the beneficent rays of the truly good, the transcendently good Christ and let us be led by their light towards his divinely good deeds.

2 Does [Christ] not come lovingly to those who have turned away from him? Does he not contend with them, and beg them not to spurn his love? Does he not support his accusers and plead on their behalf? He even promises to be concerned for them and when they are far away from him they have only to turn back and there he is, hastening to meet them. He receives them with completely open arms and greets them with the kiss of peace.

3 Others, as they puzzle over the nature of Jesus, acquire an understanding of this divine work on our behalf and it is Jesus himself who is their instructor, teaching them directly about the kindly work he has undertaken out of love for man.

4 It is not possible to be gathered together towards the one and to partake of peaceful union with the One while divided among ourselves.

5 The most divine knowledge of God, that in which he is known through unknowing, according to the union that transcends the mind, happens when the mind, turning away from all things, including itself, is united with the dazzling rays, and there and then illuminated in the unsearchable depth of wisdom.

6 It is as if there were a great chain of light let down from the summit of the heavens and reaching down to the earth, and as we grasp it first with one hand, then another, we seem to be drawing it down, but really it remains there and it is we who are being raised up to the most exalted splendours of its shining rays.

7 For this is to see and to know truly, and to praise in a transcendent way him who is beyond being through the negation of all things, just as those who make statues with their own hands cut away everything which obscures the clear beholding of the hidden form, and thus make it manifest its hidden beauty solely by the process of cutting away.

8 Love for God is ecstatic, making us go out from ourselves: it does not allow the lover to belong any more to himself, but he belongs only to the Beloved.

9 God exists not in any single mode, but embraces and prepossesses all beings within himself, absolutely and without limit.

5.15
Doulas
Desert father

1 Detach yourself from the love of the multitude lest your enemy question your spirit and trouble your inner peace.

5.16
Epitaph
From Egypt

1 O God, give him rest with the devout
and the just
in the place where green things grow
and refreshment is and water,
the delightful garden
where pain and grief and sighing
are unknown.

5.17
Faustus of Riez (c.400-480)
British or Breton, monk and bishop in southern France

1 At the font the Holy Spirit gave all that is needed for innocence; at confirmation he gives an increase for grace, for in this world those who survive through the different stages of life must walk among dangers and invisible enemies.

5.18
Gelasios
Desert father

1 The eye of God always sees the works of a man and nothing escapes him and he knows those who do good.

5.19
Inscription
Discovered in an Egyptian sarcophagus

1 From all eternity he has pointed out
the true way of life:
Jesus, the Christ.
Jesus Christ, son of Mary.

5.20
Isaac of Antioch (fl.c.460)
Syriac monk and writer

1 Your mind dwells in the deep,
beyond our reach,
and your thoughts are a mystery
no man has explored.

5.21
Isaiah the Solitary (d.c.490)
Desert father in Egypt and Gaza

1 Without anger a man cannot attain purity: he has to feel angry with all that is sown in him by the enemy.

2 Keep hell's torments in mind; but know that your helper is at hand.

5.22
Jerome (331-420)
Church Father and Bible translator, born in southern France, educated in Rome, settled finally in Bethlehem

1 When you are preaching in church do not look to arouse applause, but lamentation; the tears of your hearers are your praise. A preacher's discourse should be based on his reading of Scripture. Don't be a declaimer or a gabbling ranter, but be skilled in God's mysteries and learned in his sacraments.

2 For those who love nothing is hard, and no task is difficult if your desire is great.

3 Affection has no price.

4 Avoid, as you would the plague, the clergyman who is also a man of business.

5 When the stomach is full it is easy to talk of fasting.

6 A friend is long sought, hardly found and with difficulty kept.

7 The friendship that can cease has never been real.

8 It is worse still to be ignorant of your ignorance.

9 Love is not to be purchased.

10 Do not let your deeds belie your words, lest when you speak in church someone may say to himself, 'Why do you not practise what you preach?'

11 Therefore, since we have now journeyed a great part of our life over rough waters, and

our ship has been pounded by gales, and holed on rocks, as soon as possible let us enter the haven of a country retreat.

12 When I was a young man, though I was protected by the rampart of the lonely desert, I could not endure against the promptings of sin and the ardent heat of my nature. I tried to crush them by frequent fasting, but my mind was always in a turmoil of imagination. To subdue it I put myself in the hands of one of the brethren who had been a Hebrew before his conversion, and asked him to teach me his language. Thus... I began to learn the alphabet again and practise harsh and guttural words... I thank the Lord that from a bitter seed of learning I am now plucking sweet fruits.

13 Nothing is more to be feared than too long a peace. You are deceived if you think that a Christian can live without persecution. The person who suffers the most persecution is the one who lives under none. A storm puts a man on his guard and obliges him to do all he can to avoid shipwreck.

14 The toil my writing cost me, the difficulties I underwent, how often I gave up in despair, and how I started again, both I who knew the burden, and those who lived with me can bear witness.

15 If you will send your little Paula, I promise that I myself will be both teacher and foster-father to her. I (old man that I am) will carry her on my shoulders and teach her as she stumbles to speak.

16 We marvel at the Creator, not only as the one who made heaven and earth, sun and ocean, elephants, camels, horses, oxen, leopards, bears and lions, but also as the one who made the small creatures: ants, gnats, flies, worms and the like—things whose shape we know better than their names. And as in all creation we revere his skill, so the one whose mind is given to Christ is earnest in small things as in great, knowing that an account must be given even for an idle word.

17 One ought to rise from a meal able to apply oneself to prayer and study.

18 The immoderate long fasts of many displease me, for I have learned by experience that the ass that is too much wearied by the road looks for rest at any cost. In a long journey, strength must be supported.

19 Everything that we read in the sacred books shines and glitters even in the outer shell; but the marrow is sweeter. He who wants to eat the kernel must first crack the shell.

20 It is a candid and ingenuous kind of confession that praises in others what is wanting in oneself.

5.23
John of Apamea (1st half 5c.)

Syriac monk and spiritual writer

1 Greet everyone, and you should be the first in greeting people, just as our Lord taught the apostles how, whenever they entered, they should be the first to make the greeting. You only need a word, and you will thereby gladden someone's mind.

2 Let everyone be important in your eyes, and do not despise those whose knowledge is less than yours.

3 Think about people in a way that will profit you, so that you sorrow for the lost, feel pain for those gone astray, suffer for those in pain, pray for sinners, and in the case of the good, entreat God to preserve them.

4 Do not impose on yourself a labour that is beyond your strength, otherwise you will enslave yourself to the need to please others.

5 Pay attention to the reading of the words of Scripture, in order to learn from them how to be with God.

6 Be both a servant, and free: a servant in that you are subject to God, but free in that you are not enslaved to anything—either to empty praise or to any of the passions.

7 Do not make hard and fast decisions over anything in the future, for you are a created being and your will is subject to changes.

8 Be attentive to the thoughts of the mind. If some evil thought passes through you, do not get upset, for it is not the transient thoughts of your mind that the knowledge of the Lord of all observes, rather, he looks at the depths of mind to see if you take pleasure in that evil thought which resides there.

9 Let the love of God be stronger than death in you.

10 Rebuke hatred rather by your deeds than by your words.

11 Honour peace more than anything else. But strive first of all to be at peace in yourself.

12 Be a proclaimer of the gospel at all times. You will become a proclaimer of the gospel when you lay upon yourself the gospel's way of life.

13 When evening comes, collect your thoughts and ponder over the entire course of the day.

14 It is folly that, when someone who is more important than us is angry with us, we sleep in fear and sorrow, whereas we go to sleep untroubled by any thought of regret for the fact that we have provoked God all day long in our ingratitude for all his goodness.

5.24
Leo I (d.461)
Pope

1 Accordingly, God, the Word of God, the Son of God... in order to deliver man from eternal death, became man; humbling himself in such a way as to assume our low estate without lessening his own majesty: he remained what he was, and put on what he was not, uniting the true 'form of a servant' to that form in which he was equal to the Father, and combined both natures in a league so close, that the lower was not consumed by receiving glory, and the higher was not lessened by assuming lowliness.

2 What was visible in Christ has now passed over into the sacraments of the church.

3 Thus there was born true God in the entire and perfect nature of true man, complete in what is properly his, complete in what is ours.

4 The Word does not withdraw from his equality with the Father's glory; the flesh does not desert our human nature.

5 Recognize your dignity, O Christian, and once made sharer in the divine nature, do not by your evil conduct return to the base servitude of the past. Keep in mind of whose head and body you are a member.

6 As the Lord Jesus was made our flesh by being born, so we too have been made his body by being born again.

7 Let the people of God acknowledge that they are a new creation in Christ Jesus, and with souls on the watch, understand by whom they have been assumed and whom they have assumed.

5.25
Lot
Desert father

1 Abba Lot came to Abba Joseph and said to him: 'Father, according to my strength I keep a moderate rule of prayer and fasting, quiet and meditation, and as far as I can I control my imagination; what more must I do?' And the old man rose and held his hands towards the sky so that his fingers became like flames of fire and he said: If you will, you shall become all flame.

5.26
Mark the Ascetic (?early 5c.)
Monk and spiritual writer

1 At the times when you remember God, increase your prayers, so that when you forget him, the Lord may remind you.

2 God and our conscience know our secrets. Let them correct them.

3 He who is humble in his thoughts and engaged in spiritual work, when he reads the holy Scriptures, will apply everything to himself and not to his neighbour.

4 Thieves do not readily attack a place where they see royal weapons prepared against them, and the one who has prayer grafted into his heart is not easily robbed by thieves of the mind.

5.27
Mary of Egypt (5c.)

By legend, a converted prostitute who became a hermit

1 When I think from what evils the Lord has freed me, I am nourished by incorruptible food, and I cover my shoulders with the hope of my salvation. I feed upon and cover myself with the Word of God, who contains all things.

5.28
Nestorius (d.c.451)

Archbishop of Constantinople, deposed on grounds of unorthodoxy

1 All greatness grows great by self-abasement, and not by exalting itself.

5.29
Niceta of Remesiana (c.335-414)

Italian bishop, possible author of the ancient hymn 'Te Deum' ('We praise you, God')

1 O God, we praise you,
as Lord we confess you.
Eternal Father, all the earth reveres you.

5.30
Nilus of Ancyra (d.c.430)

Greek monk and writer

1 If you do not love the blessed and truly divine words of Scripture, you are like the beasts that have neither sense nor reason. In our natural desire for life we eat and drink, we talk and listen; and in the same way with an insatiable thirst we should devote ourselves to reading the words of God.

5.31
Ninian (c.360-c.432)

Missionary to Scotland, of Cumbrian British family

1 The potter's vessels crumble in the heat
of the furnace,
And just men are spent by the weight
of their burdens;
I long for release, to behold Christ,
and be with him.

5.32
Patrick (c.389-c.461)

The 'Apostle of the Irish', of Romano-British family

1 I was like a stone lying deep in mud but he that is mighty lifted me up and placed me on top of the wall.

2 See now, I commend my soul to God for whom I am an ambassador because he chose me for this task, despite my obscurity, to be one of the least among his servants.

3 I was a free man in a good position, and I bargained away my noble status—and I am not ashamed of this or regretful about it—for the sake of others. In short, I am a slave of Christ in a remote country because of the unspeakable glory of eternal life which is in Christ Jesus our Lord.

4 I read the heading of the letter which said 'the cry of the Irish', and at that very moment I heard the voice of those who were by the Wood of Voclut near the Western Sea; and they cried with one voice, 'Holy boy, we are asking you to come and walk with us again.'

5 In a single day I have prayed as many as a hundred times, and in the night almost as often.

6 When by misfortune I came to Ireland, every day I used to look after sheep. I used to pray often during the day, and the love of God and the fear of him increased in me more and more; my faith began to grow and my spirit was stirred, so that in one day I would say as many as one hundred prayers. I used to rise at dawn for prayer, in snow, frost or rain, because of the glow of the Spirit in me.

7 I have been promoted beyond measure by the Lord, and I was not worthy or the kind of person to whom the Lord might grant this, as I know for certain that poverty and misfortune are more appropriate for me than riches and luxury.

8 On another night—I do not know, God knows, whether it was interior or external to me—someone was speaking in the most beautiful language, and I listened but could not understand, except that at the end he spoke these words: 'He who gave his life for you, he it is who speaks in you', and at that I awoke, full of joy.

5.33
Paulinus of Nola (d.431)
Italian bishop and poet

1 This temple has two porches,
as the Church has two testaments;
but the temple and the Church
are each blessed with one fount.
The old law gives strength to the new,
the new completes the old;
in the old was hope,
in the new is faith.
But old and new
are joined by the grace of Christ:
which is why a fountain
has been put in the place between.

2 Not only pagan literature, but the whole sensible appearance of things is the lotus flower; so men forget their own land, which is God, the country of all of us.

3 We have dared to attempt our work of perfection, relying not on our own deeds and strength but on the power and mercy of God. He is almighty, and can complete in us this work. He has deigned to lay the foundation and to put up the scaffolding, and he can construct the building according to his plan, and complete it right up to the roof.

4 The body derives its steadfastness from the mind's courage; the servant obeys in accordance with the disposition of the master.

5 I pray that we may be found worthy to be cursed, censured, and ground down, and even put to death in the name of Jesus Christ, so long as Christ himself is not put to death in us.

6 I bowed my neck, then, to the yoke of Christ, and now I see myself engaged in tasks that are greater than I deserve or can understand. I know that I have been admitted and accepted into the mysteries of the most high God, that I partake of heavenly life, and that I have been brought nearer to God so as to dwell in the very spirit, body and light of Christ. With my poor mind I can barely understand the holy burden I have taken on me. I know my weakness and I tremble at the gravity of my task.

7 Do you address as lords and greet with bowed head those whom you see to be enslaved to wood and stone? They worship gold and silver under the name of gods, and their religion is one beloved by greed's corruption.

8 Let us hang upon the lips of all the faithful, for the Spirit of God is upon every one of them.

5.34
Pelagius (early 5c.)
British(?) monk, critic of Augustine of Hippo, and strongly criticized by him

1 Perhaps you want to know what it means to be a Christian? A Christian is a man or woman in whom can be found these three attributes which all Christians should possess: knowledge, faith, obedience; knowledge by which we know God, faith by which we believe in him whom we know, obedience by which we render our allegiance and service to him in whom we believe.

5.35
Peter Chrysologus (c.406-c.450)
Italian bishop and preacher

1 Christ is born so that by his birth he might restore our nature. He became a child, was fed and grew so that he might bring in the one perfect age to remain forever as he created it.

He holds mankind up so that they may no longer fall. The creature he formed of earth he now makes heavenly.

2 As Christ was pleased to be comforted by an angel, so it was needful that the Virgin should be encouraged by an angel.

5.36
Proclus of Constantinople (d.c.447)
Archbishop, preacher and theologian

1 Glory of virgins, joy of mothers, support of the faithful, crown of the church, model of true faith, abode of devotion, dwelling place of the Holy Trinity.

5.37
Prudentius (348-410)
Spanish-born poet and hymn-writer

1 Let, let the weary body
Lie sunk in slumber deep.
The heart shall still remember
Christ in its very sleep.

Take him, earth, for cherishing,
To thy tender breast receive him.
Body of a man I bring thee,
Noble even in its ruin.

Once was this a spirit's dwelling,
By the breath of God created.
High the heart that here was beating,
Christ the prince of all its living.

Guard him well, the dead I give thee;
Not unmindful of his creature
Shall he ask it: he who made it
Symbol of his mystery.

5.38
Rabbula of Edessa (d.436)
Syriac theologian

1 You take the sinfulness from sinners, O Christ, and when we repent you make us welcome beside you.

5.39
Schenute (d.466)
Egyptian (Coptic) monk and writer

1 May I not be afraid or disturbed when the time comes for my soul to leave my body.

2 O God, sharpen my will. May it be like a sword and cut all sinful thoughts out of my mind.

5.40
Sedulius (?early 5c.)
Spanish or Gallic (French) poet and hymn-writer

1 'Glory' saints and angels sang:
heaven with their praises rang;
while shepherds saw with wondering eyes
the shepherd who had made the world.

5.41
Syncletica (5c.)
Desert mother

1 When we are driven by the spirits who are against us, we hold to the cross as our sail, and so we can set a safe course.

2 It is like those who wish to light a fire:
at first they are choked by the smoke and cry,
and by this means obtain what they seek;
so we also must kindle the fire in ourselves
through tears and hard work.

3 There is grief that is useful and grief that is destructive. The first kind consists in weeping over one's own faults and weeping over the weakness of one's neighbours, in order not to destroy one's purpose, and attach oneself to the perfect good. But there is also the grief that comes from the enemy, full of mockery, which some call accidie. This spirit must be cast out, mainly by prayer and psalmody.

5.42
Synesius (d.414)
Libyan scholar and poet

1 Send, O Christ, the Spirit, send
the Father to my soul;
steep my dry heart in this dew,
the best of all your gifts.

5.43
Theodoret (?393-?466)
Syrian bishop and theologian

1 Grace sometimes precedes the sacrament, sometimes follows it, and sometimes does not even follow it.

2 It was not the law which bestowed this gift [of reconciliation] but the Lord Christ, who paid your debt, and handed over his body to death.

5.44
Zeno
Desert father

1 If a man wants God to hear his prayer quickly, then before he prays for anything else, even his own soul, when he stands and stretches out his hands towards God, he must pray with all his heart for his enemies. Through this action God will hear everything that he asks.

Sixth Century

6.1
Anonymous, Irish *Life* of Columba

1 God counselled Abraham to leave his own country and go in pilgrimage into the land which God has shown him, that is, the 'Land of Promise'... Now the good counsel which God enjoined here on the father of the faithful is incumbent on all the faithful, that is, to leave their country and their land, their wealth and their worldly delight, for the sake of the Lord of the elements, and go in perfect pilgrimage in imitation of him.

6.2
Babai (?early 6c.)
Syriac spiritual writer

1 Use your discernment and choose the course which takes you farthest away from the deadening activities of the stifling world, and brings you close to God; direct your footsteps towards Bethlehem like the blessed Magi your fellow companions, until you reach the appointed place of that blessed star which shone from Jacob.

2 Let nothing ever urge you on except the love of God, for whose sake you should cause yourself to toil. Otherwise what is the use of wearing yourself out, spending your life to no advantage? You would be like the man who laid a plank of wood over a well's mouth and drew up water on one side and poured it out on the other.

3 Do not be zealous over externals, lest you become like someone who wears fine clothes, but who has nothing in his house.

4 If someone considers himself to something when he has nothing, then he is just a fool. He is like the man who chases after gazelles while riding on a donkey: he fatigues his body, but fails to catch the gazelles.

5 Make it your care to pray without ceasing, for prayer is light to the soul, and it acts as a guard to the body.

6 Human beings know what is behind them, but in front of them is infinity. And for those who seek the Lord, evening and morning is more than enough. Their road goes a long way, but it is close at hand as they travel along it.

6.3
Barsanuphius and John (early 6c.)
Syriac spiritual writers

1 We must know that the constant calling on the name of God is a medicine which cures not only all the passions but also all their effects. Just as a doctor applies a remedy or a poultice to the patient's wound, and they take effect even though the patient does not know how this happens, so the invocation of the name of God puts all passions to death, even though we do not know how this happens.

6.4
Benedict (480-543)
Italian monk, 'Father of Western Monasticism'

1 Let everything be done in moderation.

2 Let the weaker be helped so that they may not do their work in sadness.

3 There is an evil bitter zeal which cuts us off from God, and leads to hell, and there is also a good zeal which shields us from vice and leads to God and eternal life.

4 Before all things and above all things, care must be taken of the sick, so that they may be served in very deed as Christ himself... But let the sick on their part consider that they are being served for the honour of God, and not provoke their brethren who are serving them by their unreasonable demands.

5 Let the abbot aim to be loved rather than feared. He must not be worried or anxious, nor too exacting and harsh, nor jealous, or over-suspicious, for then he will never be at rest. He must temper everything so that the strong may not be held back and the weak not frightened off.

6 'Who is it that wants to live, and desires to see good days?' What can be more agreeable, my dear brothers, than the voice of the Lord inviting us! See! In his lovingkindness he shows us the way of life.

7 When anyone receives the name of abbot he should rule his followers with a twofold teaching: that is, he should be first with deeds rather than just words in all that is good and holy. To those who have understanding he may indeed expound the Lord's commands in words; but for the hard-hearted and the simple he must show forth the commandments of God in his own life.

6.5
Boethius (c.480-c.524)
Roman philosopher and statesman

1 In every down-turn of fortune the most unhappy aspect of being unfortunate is to have once been happy.

6.6
Brigid or Bride (d.c.523)
Irish nun, venerated patron of Ireland

1 I ask for the angels of heaven to be among us.
I ask for the abundance of peace.
I ask for full vessels of charity.
I ask for rich treasures of mercy.
I ask for cheerfulness to preside over all.
I ask for Jesus to be present.

6.7
Caesarius of Arles (470-543)
Gallic (French) bishop, preacher and teacher

1 Christ hungers now, my brethren; it is he who deigns to hunger and thirst in the persons of the poor. And what he will return in heaven tomorrow is what he receives here on earth today.

6.8
Cassiodorus (?490-?585)
Roman author and monk

1 He is invited to do great things who receives small things greatly.

6.9
Columba (?521-597)
Irish monk and missionary in Scotland

1 Be thou a bright flame before me,
Be thou a guiding star above me,
Be thou a smooth path below me,
Be thou a kindly shepherd behind me,
Today—tonight—and for ever.

2 Dear cell, what happy hours I have spent in you, with the wind whistling through the loose stones and the sea spray clinging to my hair!

6.10
Columbanus (540-615)
Irish monk and missionary in various parts of Europe

1 Those who love you do not know you; those who despise you understand you. You are not truthful, but deceitful: you make yourself out to be true, but you show yourself false.

2 Nothing is sweeter than a good conscience, nothing more secure than purity of soul; but no one can bestow these on himself, because they are properly the gift of another.

3 Let us concern ourselves with things divine, and as pilgrims ever sigh for and desire our homeland; for the end of the road is ever the object of travellers' hopes and desires, and thus, since we are travellers and pilgrims in the world, let us ever ponder on the end of the road, that is, of our life, for the end of our roadway is our home.

4 Yet of his being who shall be able to speak? Of how he is everywhere present and invisible, or of how he fills heaven and earth and every creature, according to that saying, Do I not fill heaven and earth? saith the Lord, and elsewhere, The Spirit of God, according to the prophet, has filled the round earth, and again, heaven is my throne, but earth is the footstool of my feet?

6.11
David (d.602)
Patron saint of Wales

1 My brethren, persevere in what you have learned from me and seen with me. On the third day of the week on the first of March I shall go the way of my fathers. Farewell in the Lord. I shall depart. Never shall we be seen on the earth again.

6.12
Dorotheus of Gaza (6c.)
Greek spiritual writer

1 The nearer we draw to God in our love for him, the more we are united together by love for our neighbour; and the greater our union with our neighbour, the greater is our union with God.

6.13
Fulgentius of Ruspe (468-533)
North African bishop and writer

1 We have not received the Spirit of God because we believe, but that we may believe.

2 Christ made love the stairway that would enable all Christians to climb up to heaven. So hold fast to love in all sincerity, give each other practical proof of it, and by your progress in it, make your ascent together.

6.14
Gregory the Great (540-604)
Pope, Church Father, administrator and teacher

1 The woman who stayed behind to seek Christ was the only one to see him. For persistence is essential to any good deed, as the voice of truth tells us: 'Whoever perseveres to the end will be saved'.

2 Who, dear brother, can possibly describe the great joy of believers when they have learned what the grace of Almighty God and your own labours have done for the Angles?

3 Obedience is the only virtue that plants the other virtues in the heart and preserves them after they have been planted.

4 In other sacrifices the flesh of another is put to death, but in obedience our own will is offered.

5 Every earthly possession is just a kind of garment, so that anyone who is about to have strife with the devil must cast aside these garments, so as not to be pulled down by them.

6 It is impossible to engage in spiritual conflict unless the appetite for food has first been subdued.

7 The virtue of innocence is regarded as foolishness by the wise of this world. Anything done out of innocence they doubtless consider stupid; and whatever is approved by truth, by the worldly wise will be called folly.

8 You should know that the word 'angel' denotes a function rather than a nature. Those holy spirits of heaven have always been spirits, but they can only be called angels when they deliver a message.

9 When we are linked by the power of prayer, we hold each other's hand, as it were, while we walk along a slippery path; and so by the generous bounty of charity it comes about that the harder each one leans on the other, the more firmly we are bonded together in brotherly love.

10 In order to attain the citadel of contemplation you must begin by exercising yourself in the field of labour.

11 Faith has no merit where human reason supplies the truth.

12 Now I am in this place tossed by such billows of this world that I am in no way able to steer into port the old and rotten ship over which, in the hidden dispensation of God, I have assumed the guidance.

13 The person who acquires any virtues without humility is like someone carrying powdered spices in the open air.

6.15
Philoxenus of Mabbug (d.523)
Syriac theologian and bishop

1 If then you are temples and shrines of God by reason of the Spirit of God dwelling within us, then no sin, whether it be by deed or by thought, can destroy the temple of God.

2 Thus it is that when we approach the Mysteries of our Saviour, we approach as needy sinners; for there is no need for medicine except in the case of an illness, or for healing except when someone is sick.

3 For he is our true baptism, and for this reason we remain always baptized, for the Holy Spirit is within us always, and no sin can strip us of our baptism—only the denial of God and consorting with demons can do this, for in such cases the Holy Spirit really does depart, for he does not consent to remain in a place where Satan dwells.

4 Anyone who prays should pray having his heart in touch with his mouth and his mind with his lips.

6.16
Samhthann (?6c.)
Celtic virgin

1 If God could not be found on this side of the sea we would indeed journey across. Since, however, God is near to all who call upon him, we are under no obligation to cross the sea. The kingdom of heaven can be reached from every land.

6.17
Simeon of Emesa (d.c.589)
A 'holy fool', hermit in the Sinai desert and in Syria

1 Love knows that among the poor, and especially among the blind, there are people who shine like the sun, cleansed by their endurance and by the ills they have suffered.

6.18
Varsanuphius the Great (early 6c.)
A hermit living near Gaza, spiritual guide

1 As for the rule of life you ask me to give you: you are following too many roundabout ways in order to delay entering through the narrow gate that leads to eternal life. See, Christ tells you briefly how to enter. Leave men's rules, and listen to what he says: 'He who endures to the end will be saved'. Do not ask me to give you orders, for I want you to be 'not under the law but under grace'.

6.19
Venantius Fortunatus (?530-609)
Italian by birth, Bishop of Poitiers (France)

1 Thus the work for our salvation
He ordained to be done;
To the traitor's art opposing
Art yet deeper than his own;
Thence the remedy procuring
Whence the fatal wound begun.

Fulfill'd is now what David told
In true prophetic song of old,
How God the heathen's King should be;
For God is reigning from the Tree.

Seventh Century

7.1
Abraham of Nathpar (c.600)
Syriac spiritual writer

1 Be eager in prayer, and vigilant, without wearying; and remove from yourself drowsiness and sleep. You should be watchful both by night and by day; do not be disheartened.

2 You should pray, therefore, in spirit, seeing that he is spirit.

3 For God is silence, and in silence is he sung and glorified by means of that psalmody and praise of which he is worthy.

4 If God is slow in answering your request, and you ask but do not promptly receive anything, do not be upset, for you are not wiser than God.

5 Thirst for Jesus, so that he may inebriate you with his love. Blind your eyes to all that is held in honour in the world, so that you may be held worthy to have the peace which comes from God reign in your heart.

6 Humility restrains the heart. Then, once someone has become humble, immediately God's mercy surrounds him and embraces him.

7 Prayer is supplication, or concern and yearning for something; or the wish to escape from present or future evils, or a desire for the promises, or some request by which a person is aided in drawing closer to God.

8 You should not wait till you are cleansed from wandering thoughts before you pray.

9 Wandering is good when the mind wanders on God during the entire extent of one's prayer.

7.2
Adamnan (c.624-704)
Abbot of Iona

1 He [Columba] was a man of most acute mind, and exceedingly shrewd. For thirty-four years he lived and fought upon the island. Not an hour passed that was not spent in prayer, or reading, or writing, or work of some sort. In unwearied vigils and fasting he toiled day and night under burdens so heavy that each one of them seemed beyond human strength. And in the midst of all this he was universally loved, his face always cheerful, his secret heart glad with the joy of the Holy Spirit of God.

7.3
Aidan (d.651)
Monk of Iona, Bishop of Lindisfarne, missionary to the English

1 It seems to me, brother, that you were too hard on those unlearned folk who came to listen to what you had to say. You were not like the Apostles, feeding them first with the milk of easier lessons, so that they could bit by bit grow strong enough to receive more advanced teaching and carry out God's higher commands.

7.4
Austrebertha (7c.)
Nun in northern Gaul (France)

1 O my dear mother, you have given me a heart so tender that creatures can never fill it. Let me, then, be the bride of Christ and of no other.

7.5
Caedmon (d.678)
The earliest English Christian poet

1 Let us sing how the eternal God, the author of all marvels, first created the heavens for the sons of men as a roof to cover them, and how their almighty protector gave them the earth for their dwelling place.

2 Light was first
through the Lord's word
named day;
beauteous bright creation.

3 The fiend with all his comrades
Fell then from heaven above
Through as long as three nights and three days
The angels from heaven into hell;
And them all the Lord transformed into devils
Because they his deed and word would not revere.

7.6
Colman the Irishman (7c.)
One of many Irish Colmans

1 Hear me, my son; little have I to say.
Let the world's pomp go by.
Swift it is as a wind, an idle dream,
Smoke in an empty sky.

Go to the land whose love gives thee no rest,
And may Almighty God,
Hope of our life, lord of the sounding sea,
Of winds and waters lord,

Give thee safe passage on the wrinkled sea,
Himself thy pilot stand,
Bring thee through mist and foam to thy desire
Again to Irish land.

Live, and be famed and happy: all the praise
Of honoured life to thee.
Yea, all this world can give thee of delight,
And then eternity.

7.7
Cuthbert of Lindisfarne (d.687)
Monk in Scotland, later monk and Bishop of Lindisfarne

1 What am I lying here for? God will certainly have heard the prayers of so many good men. Fetch me my coat and staff!

2 If I could live in a tiny dwelling on a rock in the ocean, surrounded by the waves of the sea and cut off from the sight and sound of everything else, I would still not be free of the cares of this passing world, or from the fear that somehow the love of money might still come and snatch me away.

7.8
Dadisho (2nd half 7c.)
Syriac spiritual writer

1 The entire way of life of stillness is interwoven with the following three virtues: with faith that comes from listening, and with hope and with love, out of which real faith is made known.

7.9´
Isaak the Syrian (of Nineveh) (7c.)
Syriac spiritual writer

1 When it is time for sleep and you approach your bed, say 'Bed, perhaps this night you will become my grave, I do not know.'

2 Speech is the organ of this present world. Silence is the mystery of the world to come.

3 The humble man approaches the beasts of prey, and as soon as they see him their wildness is tamed. They come up to him and follow him as their master, wagging their tails and licking his hands and feet. For they smell on him the smell that Adam had before the Fall, when the animals gathered before him in paradise and he gave them their names.

7.10
Isidore of Seville (c.560-636)
Spanish archbishop and scholar

1 The bishop points out what each [of the clergy] should do.

2 Custom is a kind of law; its origin is in usage, and this takes the place of law when law is lacking.

3 We spend the night before Easter in vigil because of the coming or our King and Lord, so that when the time of his resurrection comes, we may be found awake, and not sleeping.

4 The Lord's Day is called this, because on that day the joy of our Lord's resurrection is celebrated.

5 The whole science of the saints consists in finding out and following the will of God.

6 The pleasure that a man seeks in gratifying his own desires quickly turns to bitterness and leaves nothing behind it except regret that he has not discovered the secret of true blessedness and of the way of holiness.

7 Teaching that lacks grace may enter our ears but it never reaches the heart. When the grace of God really touches our inmost mind so as to bring understanding, then the word that reaches our ear can also sink deeply into the heart.

8 My dear son, when you receive a letter from a friend, you should not hesitate to embrace it as a friend. It is a great consolation for friends who are apart, that a letter can be embraced in the absence of its beloved writer.

7.11
John (?7c.)
Egyptian monk

1 What shall I do to be saved? For my intellect vacillates to and fro and strays after all the wrong things. [For the answer he was given, see under Philimon.]

7.12
John of Carpathos (?7c.)
Greek monk and spiritual guide

1 It is God's will that everything he has made should offer him glory.

2 Nothing so readily obliterates virtue as frivolous talk and making fun of things.

3 Just as the elephant fears the mouse, so the holy man is still afraid of sin, lest after preaching to others he himself 'should be cast away'.

4 There is a tiny fish called the remora, which is supposed to have the power to stop a large ship simply by attaching itself to the keel. In a similar manner, by God's permission a person advancing on the spiritual way is sometimes hindered by a small temptation.

5 When you follow the Lord with burning love, it may happen that on the road of life you strike your foot against the stone of some passion and fall unexpectedly into sin; or else, finding yourself in a muddy place, you may slip involuntarily and fall headlong. Each time you fall and in this way injure your body, you should get up again with the same eagerness as before, and continue to follow after your Lord until you reach him.

6 Peter was first given the keys, but then he was allowed to fall into the sin of denying Christ; and so his pride was humbled by his fall.

7 It is more serious to lose hope than to sin.

8 Let the fire of your prayer, ascending upwards as you meditate on the oracles of the Spirit, burn always on the altar of your soul.

9 Much toil and time is needed in prayer, so that one may reach a state of mind that is not liable to be disturbed by anything—the new heaven of the heart where Christ dwells, as St Paul says: 'Do you not yourselves know how Christ dwells in you?'

7.13
John Climacus (?570-649)

Greek monk and Abbot of Sinai, spiritual writer

1 I know a man who, when he saw a woman of striking beauty, praised the Creator for her. The sight of her lit within him the love of God.

2 Flog your enemies with the name of Jesus, for there is no weapon more powerful in heaven or on earth.

3 If God in his love for the human race had not given us tears, those being saved would be few indeed and hard to find.

4 Chastity is the longed for house of Christ and the earthly heaven of the heart.

5 How can I hate this body of mine when it is my nature to love it? How can I break away from it when I am bound to it for ever? How can I escape from it when it is going to rise with me?

6 In his ineffable providence God arranged that some received the blessed reward of their labours even before they had set to work, others while they were still working, and others again at the time of their death. Reader, ask yourself which of them was made more humble.

7 We should choose our director according to the nature of our passions. If your problem is lust, do not choose for your guide a wonder-worker who has a meal and a welcome for all comers. Choose rather an ascetic who will refuse any of the consolation of food. If you are arrogant, choose someone who is harsh and unyielding, not someone who is gentle and accommodating.

8 Obedience is the tomb of the will and the resurrection of humility.

9 Let us arm ourselves against our spiritual enemies with courage. They think twice about engaging with one who fights boldly.

10 An old man once admonished a proud brother who blindly said, 'Forgive me, father, but I am not proud.' 'My son,' said the wise old man, 'what better proof could you give of your pride that by denying it?'

11 Men can heal lust. Angels can heal malice. God alone can cure pride.

12 If you pass judgement on another you brazenly usurp God's prerogative; if you condemn another, you destroy your own soul.

13 The demons say one thing to get us into sin, and another to overwhelm us in despair.

14 Avarice is the worship of idols and the child of unbelief. The person who claims to possess both money and charity is a self-deluding fool.

15 If knowledge can cause most people to become arrogant, it may be that ignorance and lack of learning can make them humble. Yet every now and then you do find people who pride themselves on their ignorance.

7.14
Jonas
Author of life of Columbanus

1 [Columbanus] went up to the bear and told her not to hurt the hide, which was needed for the use of those who make sandals. The beast forgot her fierceness, and began to be tame and, contrary to her nature, caressed him. Submitting her neck to be patted, she left the carcass.

7.15
Martin I (d.c.656)
Pope

1 The Lord himself will take care of this lowly body of mine as befits his providence, whether this means unending suffering or some small consolation. Why am I anxious? 'The Lord is at hand.' But I hope that in his compassion he will bring me speedily to the end of the course he has laid out for me.

7.16
Martyrius Sahdona (1st half 7c.)
Syriac spiritual writer

1 Right at the beginning of our converse with God, as we stand before him, we should use those humble words of the blessed patriarch Abraham: 'See, I have begin to speak in the Lord's presence, I who am but dust and ashes!'

2 We stand laxly in his presence as though it were just a game, and we do not show any patience in our service even for a short period of time; instead, like people who have been set on fire, we dash in and out.

7.17
Maximus the Confessor (c.580-662)
Greek theologian and spiritual writer

1 Blessed is the man who can love all men equally.

2 There are three causes for inordinate love of money: desire for pleasure, ostentation, and lack of trust—and the last is more powerful than the other two.

3 Love is a holy state of the soul, disposing it to value knowledge of God above all created things.

4 Do not listen gleefully to gossip at your neighbour's expense or chatter to a person who likes finding fault.

5 We do not know God from his essence. We know him rather from the grandeur of his creation and from his providential care for all creatures.

6 If you are about to enter the realm of theology, do not seek to descry God's inmost nature, for neither the human intellect nor that of any other being under God can experience this; but try to discern, as far as possible, the qualities that appertain to his nature—qualities of eternity, infinity, indeterminateness, goodness, wisdom, and the power of creating, preserving and judging creatures, and so on.

7 The perfect peace of the holy angels lies in their love for God and their love for one another. This is also the case with all the saints from the beginning of time.

8 The Lord's commandments teach us to use neutral things intelligently.

9 Out of love for us the Word of God, born once for all in the flesh, wills continually to be born in a spiritual way in those who desire him. Becoming a little child, he fashions himself in them by their virtues and gives them as much knowledge of himself as he knows them to be capable of receiving... This is why the Word of God is always being manifested in the lives of those who share in him, yet remains for ever invisible to all in the transcendence of the mystery.

7.18
Philimon (?6 or 7c.)
Egyptian monk and spiritual guide

1 Keep watch in your heart; and with watchfulness say in your mind with awe and trembling: 'Lord Jesus Christ, have mercy upon me.'

2 When you are in church... think that you are standing in heaven, and that in the company of the holy angels you are meeting God and receiving him in your heart.

3 The radiance of the divine beauty is wholly inexpressible: words cannot describe it, nor the ear grasp it.

7.19
Sophronius (d.c.638)

Born in Damascus, monk in Egypt, Bishop of Jerusalem

1 Our lighted candles are a sign of the divine glory of the one who comes to dispel the dark shadows of evil and to make the whole universe radiant with the brightness of his eternal light. Our candles also show how bright our souls should be when we go to meet Christ.

7.20
Thalassios the Libyan

Libyan abbot and spiritual advisor

1 Perfume is not to be found in mud, nor the fragrance of love in the soul of a rancorous man.

2 There is a new wonder in heaven and on earth: God is on earth and man is in heaven.

3 The tongue of a back-biting soul is three-pronged: it injures the speaker, the listener, and sometimes the person being maligned.

4 If you share secretly in the joy of someone you envy, you will be freed from your jealousy; and you will also be freed from your jealousy if you keep silent about the person you envy.

5 Our actions disclose what goes on within us, just as its fruit makes known a tree otherwise unknown to us.

6 Jesus is the Christ, one of the Holy Trinity. You are destined to be his heir.

7 Free us from the tyranny [of the passions], so that we may worship thee alone, the eternal light, having risen from the dead and dancing with the angels in the blessed, eternal and indissoluble dance.

8 Paradoxically, the One moves from itself into the Three and yet remains One, while the Three return to the One and yet remain Three.

7.21
Wilfrid (634-709)

Northumbrian abbot, Bishop of York

1 Let us show how great our faith is by praying together with one accord that God may restore life to this lad's body and hear our prayers for him, just as he heard the prayers of St Paul.

2 If I am to be restored to my diocese, I shall follow and venerate your decision with all my might, as long as you issue a decree authorizing the removal of those who have usurped positions. But if, on the other hand, you think fit to appoint other bishops in my diocese, let them be the kind of men I can serve God alongside, in unity, peace and concord, so that we can all acknowledge the laws established by the church and be careful to guard the flock entrusted to us.

Eighth Century

8.1
Alcuin (735-804)
Born in York, advisor to Charlemagne, scholar

1 You should not listen to those who keep saying that the voice of the people is the voice of God, since a riotous crowd is always next door to madness.

2 Because we are a royal and priestly nation, we are anointed after the washing of baptism, that we may be bearers of the name of Christ [the 'anointed'].

8.2
Andrew of Crete (660-740)
Born in Damascus, hymn-writer

1 If you would understand that the cross is Christ's triumph, hear what he himself said: 'I, if I am lifted up, will draw all people to myself'. See now that the cross is Christ's glory and triumph.

2 The end draws near, my soul,
the end draws near;
Yet you do not care or make ready.
The time grows short, rise up;
the Judge is at the door.
The days of our life pass swiftly,
as a dream, as a flower.
Why do we trouble ourselves
over what is all in vain?

3 Like the thief I cry to thee,
'Remember me';
Like Peter I weep bitterly;
Like the publican I call out,
'Forgive me, Saviour';
Like the harlot I shed tears.
Accept my lamentation,
as once thou hast accepted
The entreaties of the woman of Canaan.
Have mercy on me, O God,
have mercy on me.

8.3
Anonymous, 'St Patrick's Breastplate' (?8c.)
Ancient Irish hymn, probably much later than Patrick

1 I gird myself today with the might of heaven:
The rays of the sun,
The beams of the moon,
The glory of fire,
The speed of wind,
The depth of the sea,
The stability of earth,
The hardness of rock.

8.4
Bede (?673-735)
English monk, Bible scholar and 'Father of English History'

1 He alone loves the Creator perfectly who manifests a pure love for his neighbour.

2 'Such, O King,' he said, 'in my view is the present life of humans on earth, in comparison with that time of which we have no certain knowledge. It is as if, when sitting feasting with your ealdormen and thegns in winter, one sparrow should appear and fly swiftly through the house, coming in by one door and immediately going out by another. In that time while it is inside the house it is untouched by the winter weather; yet this tiny patch of calm is left behind in a moment, and it returns from winter into winter again, and disappears from your sight. Human life seems rather like this; we simply do not know what precedes or follows it.

3 Learn quickly, for I know not how long I shall hold out, or whether my Maker will take me before long.

4 I have had a long life, and the merciful Judge has ordered it graciously. The time of my departure is at hand, and my soul longs to see Christ my King in his beauty.

5 All the ways of the world are as fickle and changeable as a freak storm at sea.

6 Therefore, with integrity of mind, firm faith, undaunted courage, thoroughgoing love, let us be ready for whatever God's will brings. Let us keep his commandments faithfully, and be innocent in our simplicity, peaceable in love, modest in humility, diligent in our service, merciful in assisting the poor, firm in standing for the truth and strict in our keeping of discipline.

7 O truly blessed mother church, adorned with the glorious blood of the victorious martyrs, clothed in unassailable praise by the white garment of virginity—your garments lack neither roses nor lilies!

8 Spurred on by his heavenly vision of the joys of everlasting happiness, Cuthbert was ready to undergo hunger and thirst in this life so as to enjoy the heavenly banquet in the next.

9 If it was a praiseworthy forwardness in the woman who, though diseased, touched our Lord's robe, why can the same concession not be granted to all women who have to bear nature's weakness?

8.5
Boniface (c.680-754)
English name Wynfrith, born in Devon, missionary to Germany

1 Pour into their untaught minds the preaching of both the Old and the New Testaments in the spirit of virtue and love and sobriety and with reasoning suited to their understanding.

2 The church is like a great ship pounded by the waves of life's various stresses. Our job is not to abandon ship, but to keep it on its course.

3 If indeed the English people, as is rumoured abroad and cast up against us in France and Italy, despise lawful marriage, a people that is unworthy and degenerate will come into being, and our nation will cease to be strong. We suffer because of the disgraceful conduct of our people.

4 I cannot give you a kiss, so I am sending, via the bearer of this letter, two little kegs of wine, asking you to make use of them, for love of me, for a couple of day's rejoicing with your friends.

8.6
Gregory II (d.731)
Pope and reformer

1 We have been greatly distressed to hear that certain peoples in Germany, east of the Rhine, are wandering in the shadow of death, still enslaved to the worship of idols. So we have resolved to send our brother Boniface into that country to bring to them eternal life.

2 The field of the Lord had been lying fallow, bristling with the thistles of unbelief. Now it has been ploughed by your teaching, and is bringing forth an abundant harvest of true faith.

8.7
Gregory III (d.741)
Pope

1 Absolutely reject all divination, fortune-telling, sacrifices to the dead, prophecies in groves or by fountains, amulets, incantations, sorcery (that is, evil spells), and all those sacrilegious practices that used to go on in your country.

8.8
Hesychios of Sinai
Greek abbot and spiritual writer

1 Let us learn humility from Christ, humiliation from David, and from Peter to shed tears over what has happened; but let us also learn to avoid the despair of Samson, Judas, and that wisest of men, Solomon.

2 When we are in trouble or despair or have lost hope, we should do what David did: pour out our hearts to God and tell him of our needs and troubles, just as they are.

8.9
John of Damascus (c.675-749)
Greek theologian, born in Damascus

1 God is a sea of infinite substance.

2 The day of resurrection,
earth tell it out abroad!
The Passover of gladness,
the Passover of God.
From death to life eternal,
from this world to the sky,
Our Christ has brought us over,
with hymns of victory.

3 Providence is the care God takes of all existing things.

4 God who knows everything, and provides for each one of us what will be profitable for us, has revealed what it was to our profit to know; but what we could not bear to know he has kept secret.

5 The thoughts that encompass all evil are eight in number: those of gluttony, unchastity, avarice, anger, dejection, listlessness, self-esteem and pride. It does not lie within our power to decide whether or not these eight thoughts are going to arise and disturb us. But to dwell on them or not to dwell on them, to excite the passions or not to excite them, does lie within our power.

6 I do not venerate matter but I venerate the Creator of matter, who for my sake has become material, who has been pleased to dwell in matter, and has through matter effected my salvation. I shall not cease to venerate matter, for it was through matter that my salvation came to pass. Do not insult matter, for it is not without honour; nothing is without honour that God has made.

8.10
John the Elder (of Dalyatha)
Syriac spiritual writer

1 Your door is open, Lord, and no one is entering. Your glory is revealed, but no one pays attention. Your light shines out in the pupils of our eyes, but we are not willing to see. Your right hand is extended, ready to give, but there is no one who takes from it!

2 Grant us, Lord, to cling to you, not in our outward beings but in our hidden selves, and may we follow you until we behold your face.

3 O Christ, the ocean of our forgiveness, allow me to wash off in you the dirt I am clothed in, so that I may become resplendent in the raiment of your holy light.

8.11
Joseph the Visionary (Abdisho)
Syriac spiritual writer

1 During the time of prayer the soul resembles a ship positioned in the middle of the sea. The mind is like the steersman in charge of the boat. The impulses convey the boat like the winds.

2 May our Lord Jesus Christ in his mercy make us all worthy of his glorious vision—here in pledge, but there in reality.

8.12
Leoba (700-779)
Born in Wessex, teacher and friend to many

1 May Christ our Creator and Redeemer grant that we shall meet again without shame on the day of judgement.

8.13
Zacharias (d.752)
Pope

1 You ask for advice as to whether it is permitted to flee from the persecution of the heathen or not. We give you this wholesome counsel: so long as it can be done, and you can find a suitable place, carry on your preaching, but if you cannot endure their assaults you have the Lord's authority to go into another city.

Ninth Century

9.1
Alfred (849-899)
Anglo-Saxon King of Wessex

1 If you have a fearful thought, do not share it with someone who is weak; whisper it to your saddle-bow, and ride on singing.

2 No wise man wants a soft life.

3 Power is never good, unless the one who has it is good.

9.2
Dhuoda (803-843)
Educated laywoman who wrote a book to guide her son

1 [To her son] Beseech God your Creator, cherish him, love him; if you do so, he will be a keeper, a leader, a companion, and a fatherland for you, the way, the truth, and the life, granting you generous prosperity in the world, and he will turn your enemies to peace.

2 If it should happen, my son, that you do something bad, or even if you perceive that your soul is afflicted, hasten as soon as you can to make amends in all things. Turn to him who sees everything.

9.3
Edmund the Martyr (841-870)
King of the East Angles, murdered by Danes

1 Why should others cause me to offend God, or to lose the charity which I owe and bear them? If any person were to cut off my arms or pluck out my eyes, they would be the dearer to me, and would seem the more to deserve my tenderness and compassion.

2 Countless multitudes are deceived into multiplying prayers. I would sooner say five words devoutly in my heart than five thousand words which my soul does not relish with affection and understanding.

9.4
Hrabanus Maurus (788-856)
German abbot and archbishop

1 Christ who first gave thee for a friend to me,
Christ keep thee well, where'er thou art,
for me.
Earth's self shall go and the swift wheel
of heaven
Perish and pass, before our love shall cease.

Do but remember me, as I do thee,
And God, who brought us on this earth
together,
Bring us together in his house of heaven.

2 Adam, the first man and the first prophet, made this prophecy with regard to Christ and the Church, for our Lord and Saviour left God his Father and the heavenly Jerusalem his mother, and came to earth for the sake of his body the Church, which he formed from his own side. For her sake the Word became flesh.

9.5
John Scotus Erigena (c.810-877)
Irish philosopher

1 Every visible or invisible creature is a theophany or manifestation of God.

2 Nothing can be said properly of God, because he transcends all understanding... he is known better by not knowing; ignorance concerning him is true wisdom. It is more in accord with truth and faith to deny anything of him than to affirm anything.

3 The human mind was not made for divine Scripture, for it would not have any need of Scripture if it did not sin; but for the sake of the human mind holy Scripture has been woven into the various creeds and doctrines so that it may guide our rational nature, which has fallen by sin from the contemplation of the truth, on its return to its original height of pure contemplation.

4 True authority does not oppose right reason, nor right reason true authority. For it is not to be doubted that both come from one source, namely, the divine wisdom.

5 The authority of Scripture must be followed in all things, for in it we have the truth as it were in its secret haunts.

6 God is properly called love because he is the cause of all love and is poured through all things and gathers all things into one and returns into himself in an unutterable way and brings to an end in himself the loves of every creature.

9.6
Sedulius Scotus (fl.848-858)
Irish scholar and poet

1 Last night did Christ the Sun rise from
the dark,
The mystic harvest of the fields of God,
And now the little wandering tribes of bees
Are brawling in the scarlet flowers abroad.
The winds are soft with birdsong;
all night long
Darkling the nightingale her descant told,
And now inside the church the happy folk
The Alleluia chant a hundredfold.
O father of thy folk, be thine by right
The Easter joy, the threshold of the light.

2 I read or write, I teach or wonder what
is truth,
I call upon my God by night and day.
I eat and freely drink, I make my rhymes,
And snoring sleep, or vigil keep and pray.
And very ware of all my shames I am;
O Mary, Christ, have mercy on your man.

9.7
Theodore the Studite (759-826)
Greek monk

1 Because man is made in the image and likeness of God, there is something divine about the act of painting an icon.

2 You were called and really are the most gracious of all joys, for from you was born Christ, the eternal joy and the vanquisher of our grief.

Tenth Century

10.1
African hymn

1 The cross is the way of the lost
the cross is the staff of the lame
the cross is the guide of the blind
the cross is the strength of the weak
the cross is the hope of the hopeless
the cross is the freedom of the slaves
the cross is the water of the seeds
the cross is the consolation of the
bonded labourers
the cross is the source of those who
seek water
the cross is the cloth of the naked.

10.2
Ethelwold (908-984)
Bishop of Winchester

1 There is no reason for the temples of God that lack senses to abound in riches, while the living temples of the Holy Spirit starve for hunger.

10.3
Hrotsvit of Gandersheim (935-1002)
German nun and writer

1 At least I do not pretend to have knowledge where I am ignorant. On the contrary, my best claim to indulgence is that I know how much I do not know.

2 So that my natural gifts might not be wasted through neglect, I have taken trouble, whenever I have been able to pick up some threads and scraps torn from the old garment of philosophy, to weave them into the fabric of my own book.

10.4
Nilus (c.910-1004)
Greek monk from Southern Italy

1 The spiritual combat in which we kill our passions in order to put on the new man is the most difficult of all the arts.

10.5
Odilo of Cluny (962-1949)
Benedictine monk, Abbot of Cluny (in France)

1 With God the Father from all eternity, before Abraham existed (more accurately, before anything existed) he had his eternal being; and yet he chose to be born in time from the stock of Abraham—Abraham who was told by God the Father: In your posterity all the peoples of the earth will be blessed.

10.6
Radbod of Utrecht (c.900)
Bishop of Utrecht

1 Hunger and thirst, O Christ, for sight of thee,
Thou sole provision for the unknown way.
Long hunger wasted the world wanderer,
With sight of thee may he be satisfied.

Eleventh Century

11.1
Anselm of Canterbury (1033-1109)
Italian-born monk, scholar and Archbishop of Canterbury

1 O Lord our God, grant us grace to desire you with our whole heart; that so desiring, we may seek, and seeking, find you; and so finding you, may love you; and loving you, may hate those sins from which you have redeemed us.

2 God is that than which nothing greater can be conceived.

3 How distant you are from my sight while I am present to your sight! You are wholly present everywhere and I do not see you.

4 God often works more by the illiterate seeking the things that are God's than by the learned seeking the things that are their own.

5 Lord my God, you have formed me and reformed me.

6 I was created to see God, and I have not yet accomplished that for which I was made.

7 I long to understand to some degree your truth, which my heart believes and loves. For I do not seek to understand in order that I may believe, but I believe in order that I may understand. For I believe this also, that if I did not believe, I would not understand.

8 If God is pleased so long as we do not deny his commandments, what enormous pleasure we must give him when we accept his will cheerfully, in sufferings that affect our own person.

9 Souls well-beloved of my soul, my eyes ardently long to behold you; my arms stretch out to embrace you; my lips sigh for your kisses; all the life that is left to me is eaten up with waiting for you. How could I forget those whom I have set as a seal upon my heart?

10 If wisdom delights you, 'the very wisdom of God will show herself to them'. If friendship, they shall love God more than themselves, and each other as themselves; and God will love them more than they love themselves, for they love him and themselves and each other through him, while he loves himself and through himself them.

11.2
Bruno (c.1030-1101)
Monk, founder of the Carthusian Order

1 I rejoice indeed, as is right, for the growth of the fruits of your virtues, but I lament and am ashamed that I lie inert and torpid in the filth of my sins.

11.3
Clement II (d.1047)
Pope

1 Let us consider, beloved, how the Lord is continually revealing to us the resurrection that is to be. He has constituted the Lord Jesus Christ as the first-fruits of this, by raising him from the dead.

11.4
Edward the Confessor (1004-1066)
Last Anglo-Saxon King of England before the Norman Conquest

1 Weep not, I shall not die; and as I leave the land of the dying I trust to see the blessings of the Lord in the land of the living.

11.5
Fulbert (c.960-1028)
Italian-born Bishop of Chartres

1 For Judah's Lion bursts his chains,
Crushing the serpent's head;
And cries aloud through death's domains
To wake the imprisoned dead.

11.6
Gregory VII (c.1020-1085)
(Hildebrand) reforming Pope

1 It is the custom of the Roman Church which I unworthily serve with the help of God, to tolerate some things, to turn a blind eye to some, following the spirit of discretion rather than the rigid letter of the law.

11.7
Herman of Reichenau (1013-1034)
Monk, scholar and writer

1 The whole of this present world and all that belongs to it—yes, this mortal life itself, has become cramped and tedious to me; and on the other hand, the world to come, the one that will not pass away, and eternal life have become so unutterably desirable and precious to me, that I regard all these passing things as light as thistledown. I am tired of this life.

11.8
Peter Damian (1007-1072)
Italian-born church reformer

1 Nobody can fight properly and boldly for the faith, if he clings to a fear of being stripped of earthly possessions.

2 If believers in Christ are one, wherever one member seems to be to the natural eye, there indeed is the whole body by the sacramental mystery. Whatever belongs to the whole in some way seems to fit in with any part.

3 Strengthen your patience with understanding, and look forward serenely to the joy that comes after sadness.

4 One can only praise God's way with people: he cuts them down before he heals them; he throws them down only to raise them to new life.

5 As your soul leaves your body, may the shining cohorts of angels hurry to greet you... and may our Lord Jesus appear to you with kindly and welcoming countenance, and give you a place among those who stand in his presence for evermore.

11.9
Simeon the New Theologian (949-1022)
Monk and mystic of the Eastern Church

1 The Holy Trinity, pervading all men from first to last, from head to foot, binds them all together.

2 O Light that none can name,
for it is altogether nameless,
O Light with many names,
for it is at work in all things,
O single glory and authority,
rule and kingdom,
O Light that is one in will and thought,
in counsel and strength,
Have mercy, take pity on me in my affliction.
O power of the divine Fire, O strange energy!

3 He was so bound [to his brethren] spiritually by a holy love in the Holy Spirit that he would have preferred not to enter the kingdom of heaven itself if it meant being separated from them.

4 The saints in each generation are joined to those who have gone before, and filled like them with light to become a golden chain in which each saint is a separate link, united to the next by faith, works and love. So in the one God they form a single chain which cannot quickly be broken.

5 I, who am but grass, partake of fire, and... am refreshed with dew.

6 Do not say, Men do not see the divine light,
Or else, It is impossible in these present times.
This is a thing never possible, my friends,
But on the contrary altogether possible
for those who so wish.

7 Do not try to be a mediator on behalf of others until you have yourself been filled with the Holy Spirit, until you have come to know and to win the friendship of the King of all with conscious awareness in your soul.

8 My blood has been mingled with your blood,
And I know that I have been united also to your Godhead.

9 Where shall I rest these limbs that have become your own?
In what works or actions shall I employ
These members that are terrible and divine?

10 [Of his spiritual father]

He was not ashamed
of the limbs of anyone,
Or to see others naked
and to be seen naked himself.
For he possessed the whole Christ
and was himself wholly Christ;
And always he regarded all his own limbs
and the limbs of everyone else,
Individually and together,
as being Christ himself.

11.10
Theophylact of Bulgaria (c.1050-1108)
Greek-born archbishop and writer

1 The Lord is a wrecker of evil in our hearts, but a renewer of the good; lust decays, prudence rises.

11.11
Vladimir (956-1015)
The 'Apostle of the Russians and Romanians'

1 O God, who hast created heaven and earth, look down, I beseech thee, on this thy new people, and grant them, O Lord, to know thee as true God, just as other Christian nations have come to know thee.

Twelfth Century

12.1
Peter Abelard (1079-1142)
French philosopher and scholar

1 I think that the purpose and cause of the incarnation was that God might illuminate the world by his wisdom and excite it to the love of himself.

2 O what their joy and their glory must be
Those endless sabbaths the blessed ones see!

3 The first key to wisdom is assiduous and frequent questioning. For by doubting we come in enquiry and by enquiry we arrive at the truth.

12.2
Adam of St Victor (d. between 1177 and 1192)
French monk and religious poet

1 Lo, these the winged chariots,
That bring Emmanuel nigh,
The golden staves, uplifting
God's very ark on high;
And these the fourfold river
Of paradise above,
Whence flow for all the nations
New mysteries of love.

12.3
Aelred of Rievaulx (1109-1167)
English monk and writer

1 No medicine is more valuable, none more efficacious, none better suited to the cure of all our temporal ills than a friend to whom we may turn for consolation in time of trouble—and with whom we may share our happiness in time of joy.

2 We can find no greater inspiration to love even our enemies as brothers and sisters—as we must if our love is to be perfect—than grateful remembrance of Christ's wonderful patience.

3 [Epiphany's] new star reiterates the heavenly message: Arise and be enlightened! A sign of the Lord's birth has appeared in the sky to invite us to detach ourselves from the love of earthly things and raise ourselves heavenward; and this sign consists of a star, so that we may understand that through Christ's birth we shall be flooded with new light.

12.4
Baldwin of Canterbury (d.1190)
English monk, Archbishop of Canterbury

1 Our first resurrection begins when we first show obedience to God, and is brought to completion by our perseverance in doing his will. Our second resurrection begins with our glorification and endures for all eternity. If we continue in obedience till the end of our lives, then we shall also abide in a glory that knows no end.

12.5
Thomas à Becket (1118-1170)
Chancellor of England, later Archbishop of Canterbury and murdered in the Cathedral

1 I have committed my cause to the great judge of all mankind, so I am not moved by threats, nor are your swords more ready to strike than is my soul for martyrdom.

12.6
Bernard of Chartres (d.c.1130)
French scholar

1 We are like dwarfs on the shoulders of giants: we can see more than they can, and things further off, not because we are keener-sighted or physically distinguished, but because we are being carried high, lifted up by their great size.

12.7
Bernard of Clairvaux (1091-1153)
French monk, founder of the Cistercian Order

1 All things are possible to one who believes.

2 When a man is content with the testimony of his own conscience, he does not care to shine with the light of another's praise.

3 Love is self-sufficient; it is pleasing to itself and on its own account. Love is its own payment, its own reward.

4 By his first work he gave me to myself; and by the next he gave himself to me. And when he gave me himself, he gave me back myself that I had lost.

5 First learn to love yourself, then you can love me.

6 Theirs is an endless road, a hopeless maze, who seek for goods before they seek for God.

7 Arouse yourself, gird your loins, put aside idleness, grasp the nettle and do some hard work.

8 He alone is God who can never be sought in vain—even when he cannot be found.

9 Whether in this life, or in death, or in the resurrection, the body is of great service to the soul that loves the Lord. First, it produces the fruits of penitence, second, it brings the gift of rest, and third, the final state of beatitude.

10 I will remind myself of all the labours Jesus undertook in preaching, his weariness in journeying, his temptations during his fast, his watchings in prayer, his tears of compassion. I will also remember his sorrows, and the insults, spit, blows, mocking, rebukes, the nails and all the rest of the sufferings that rained down on him.

11 If ever there should be a monastery without an awkward and ill-tempered member, it would be necessary to go and find one and pay him his weight in gold—so great is the profit that results from this trial, when it is used properly.

12 Poverty was not found in heaven. It abounded on earth, but human beings did not know its value. The Son of God treasured it, and came down from heaven to choose it for himself, and so make it precious to us.

13 The mortified man is able to suck honey from the rock and oil from the flinty stones.

14 If you notice something evil in yourself, correct it; if something good, take care of it; if something beautiful, cherish it; if something sound, preserve it; if something unhealthy, heal it. Do not weary of reading the commandments of the Lord, and you will be adequately instructed by them so as to know what to avoid and what to go after.

15 What else do those attached to this world think we are doing than just playing about, when we shun what they most like and go after what they flee from? We are like jesters and tumblers—heads down, feet in the air, they draw all eyes to themselves. The game we play is a joyful one, decent, serious and praiseworthy; it delights the gaze of those who are watching from heaven.

16 If you are wise you will show yourself rather as a reservoir than a canal. For a canal spreads abroad the water it receives, but a reservoir waits until it is filled before overflowing, and thus shares without loss to itself its superabundance of water.

12.8
Bernard of Cluny (fl.c.1130)

French monk and writer

1 Jerusalem the golden,
 with milk and honey blest,
Beneath thy contemplation sink heart
 and voice oppressed.

12.9
Elizabeth of Schönau (1129-1164)

German nun, visionary, writer

1 Arise, my soul, arise,
it is good to rejoice and join the
 angels' praises,
it is our health and strength
 to share in God's own feast.

2 Help me,
Lord my God.

By God's grace
I am what I am.

12.10
Gerald of Wales (c.1146-1220)
Welsh bishop and historian

1 If you take the trouble to look very closely [at the Book of Kells, a copy of the Gospels] and to penetrate with your eyes to the secrets of the artistry, you will notice such intricacies, so delicate, so subtle... so involved and bound together, so fresh still in their colourings, that you will not hesitate to declare that all those things must have been the work not of men but of angels.

12.11
Gratian (d.c.1179)
Italian monk, 'Father of Canon Law'

1 Paintings are the Bible of the laity.

12.12
Guigo II the Carthusian (d.c.1188)
Carthusian monk and writer

1 What is the use of spending one's time in continuous reading, turning the pages of the lives and sayings of holy men, unless we can extract nourishment from them by chewing and digesting this food so that its strength can pass into our inmost heart?

2 What use is it to anyone if he sees in his meditation what is to be done, unless the help of prayer and the grace of God enable him to achieve it?

3 If meditation is to be fruitful, it must be followed by devoted prayer, and the sweetness of contemplation may be called the effect of prayer.

12.13
Henry II (1133-1189)
King of England

1 Will no one rid me of this turbulent priest?

12.14
Hildebert (1056-1133)
Archbishop of Tours, poet and canonist (church lawyer)

1 O Holy Ghost, O faithful paraclete,
love of the Father and the Son...
you who alone
are worthily adored
with Father and with Son
to you in heart and word
be honour, worship, grace,
here and in every place,
world without end.

12.15
Hildegard of Bingen (1098-1179)
German nun, scholar, artist, visionary

1 This salvation of love did not spring from us, because we did not know, neither were we able to love God unto salvation, but because he the Creator and lord of all so loved the world, that he sent his Son for its salvation, the Prince and Saviour of the faithful, who washed and dried our wounds, and from him also came that most sweet medicine, from which all the good things of salvation flow.

2 As the flame in one fire has three powers, so the One God is in Three persons. In what manner? For in the flame abides splendid light, innate vigour and fiery heat, but it has splendid light that it may shine, innate vigour that it may flourish, and fiery heat that it may burn.

3 They of the first rank, who have as it were wings on their breasts, and bear before them faces like human faces, in which human countenances appear as if reflected in pure water: these are angels, expanding the desires of a profound intellect like wings, not that they do in fact have wings like birds, but that they perform the will of God speedily in their desires, as a man flies speedily to his thoughts.

4 All of creation God gives to humankind to use. If this privilege is misused, God's justice permits creation to punish humanity.

12.16
Hugh of Lincoln (1140-1200)
French-born monk, Bishop of Lincoln

1 Indeed I am sharper and more biting than pepper, and not infrequently when I preside over my Chapter I flare up over quite little matters. But they know that they have to endure the bishop whom they have been given, and so make a virtue of necessity and give way to me.

2 Tomorrow morning we will agree on some good course to take, under the guidance of the Lord, which he will know how to make redound to the greater glory of his name. For night brings its counsels, as we have often learned from experience.

3 Surely Almighty God should be greatly loved by women, since he did not disdain to be born of a woman. Hereby he conferred a wonderful honour and dignity on women, for although no man has been gifted with the right to be called the father of God, a woman has received this great distinction of being called the mother of God.

4 Three things are demanded of a Christian; if a man being judged lacks even one of these things, then the name of Christian will have no power to protect him... Love in the heart, truth on the lips and chastity in the body: these are what a man must have to be truly and in deed a Christian.

5 Now my doctors and my diseases may fight it out as they will, I shall have little care for either. I have given myself to God; I have received him, I will hold him and rest fast in him; it is good to abide fast in him, it is a blessed thing to hold him; he who receives him is safe and sound.

12.17
Hugh of St Victor (1096-1141)
German-born monk and writer

1 Learn everything you possibly can, and you will discover later that none of it was superfluous.

2 Brothers and sisters, it is now the season of the Lord's coming, and we must use the time to prepare ourselves by some spiritual devotion... We must strive to enter the house of our hearts, open the windows, and notice what is seemly and what unseemly in that house. We must brush away the cobwebs, sweep the floors, clear out the dust and dirt, strew the clean floors with freshly gathered rushes, fragrant herbs, and sweet-smelling flowers.

3 The difference between the love of God and the love of the world is this: the love of this world seems at the outset sweet, but has a bitter end; the love of God, by contrast, is bitter to begin with, but is full of sweetness in its end.

4 Maybe you are asking where this house of God is to be sought, and where it may be found. God's house is the whole world; God's house is the Catholic Church; God's house is also every faithful soul. But God inhabits the world in one way, the Church in another, and every faithful soul in yet a third. He is in the world as ruler of his kingdom; he is in the Church as head of the family in his own home; he is in the soul as the bridegroom in the wedding chamber.

5 God dwells in the human heart after two modes—namely, by knowledge and by love. Yet these two are one abiding, for the double reason that everyone who knows him loves him, and that nobody can love him without knowing him.

6 God has become everything to you, and God has made everything for you. He has made the dwelling, and is become your refuge. This one is all, and this all is one. It is the house of God, it is the city of the King, it is the body of Christ, it is the bride of the Lamb. It is the heaven, it is the sun, it is the moon, it is the morning star, the daybreak and the evening. It is the trumpet, it is the mountain, and the desert, and the promised land.

7 This is the tree of life indeed, the word of the Father, the wisdom of God in the highest, which in the hearts of the saints, as in an unseen paradise, is sown in fear, watered by grace, dies through grief, takes root by faith, buds by devotion, shoots up through compunction, grows by longing, is strengthened by charity, grows green by hope, puts out its leaves and spreads its branches through caution, flowers through discipline, bears fruit through virtue, ripens through patience, is harvested by death, and feeds by contemplation.

8 Here the gospel parable comes to my mind, in which the kingdom of heaven is likened to treasure hidden in a field. The kingdom of heaven is of course eternal life. But Christ is life eternal, Christ also is wisdom, and wisdom is the treasure. And this treasure was hidden in the field of the human heart when man was created in the image and likeness of his Maker.

9 You will build a house for the Lord your God *in and of yourself*. He will be the craftsman, your heart the site, your thoughts the materials. Do not take fright because of your own lack of skill; he who requires this of you is a skilful builder, and he chooses others to be builders too.

12.18
Isaac of Stella (c.1105-1178)
English-born monk and abbot in France

1 He became Son of man and made many men and women children of God, uniting them to himself by his love and power so that they became as one. In themselves they are many by reason of their human descent, but in him they are only one by divine rebirth.

12.19
Joachim of Fiore (c.1130-1201)
Italian monk and mystic

1 The true ascetic counts nothing his own but his harp.

12.20
Peter Lombard (?1100-1160)
Italian theologian

1 Eve was not taken from the feet of Adam to be his slave, nor from his head to be his lord, but from his side to be his partner.

12.21
Marie de France (fl.c.1150)
French poet

1 I am from France, my name's Marie
and it may hap that many a clerk
will claim as his what is my work
but such pronouncements I want not!
It's folly to become forgot.

12.22
Lawrence O'Toole (1128-1180)
Irish monk and archbishop

1 My will? What are you talking about? Thank God, I haven't a penny left in the world.

12.23
Peter of Celle (d.1182)
French monk

1 Notice his [Christ's] power in the abyss. He broke the iron bars. He cut off the heads of the dragon which was lying there. From its belly he extracted the riches which it had swallowed up. He filled his net with the fish of the patriarchs and prophets. With a strong hand and out-stretched arm he recovered the treasures hidden there from the beginning of the world.

2 Not inappropriately, Jesus' ways are called walkways rather than routes, because on this road there is no deviation, no giving rein to what is unlawful... It is difficult and narrow; there are few who find it.

3 [Jesus] gave his one body, but he acquired thousands upon thousands. He yielded up his one soul, but how many did he restore and take back to heaven? He was in the heart of the earth for three days, but he acquired eternity and length of days for his family.

4 After work a rest is welcome.

5 The mind has a more extensive and expansive leisure within the six surfaces of a room than it could gain outside by traversing the four parts of the world. In fact, the smaller the place the more extended the mind, for when the body is constrained the mind takes wing.

6 [A Frenchman writing to an Englishman] Your island is surrounded by water, and not unnaturally its inhabitants are affected by the nature of the element in which they live. Unsubstantial fantasies slide easily into their minds. They think their dreams to be visions, and their visions to be divine... It is different in France, which is not so wet and windy, and where the mountains are of stone and the earth is weighed down with iron.

12.24
Richard of St Victor (d.1173)
British-born mystic and theologian in France

1 It is plain that in a plurality of persons the nearer is their relationship, the closer is their union with one another, and the more intimate their unity, the greater is their joy. Who then would dare to contend or to take for granted that in the fullness of supreme felicity there is absent what is known to be a great source of joy...?

2 For charity to be true, it requires more than one person; for it to be perfected, it requires a Trinity of persons.

3 I do not know whether God can bestow upon a man anything greater than this grace, that by his work wayward men might be changed into better, and sons of the devil be changed into sons of God.

4 If you are in a hurry to reach higher things, you will go safely if truth goes ahead of you. Without truth your labour is in vain. Truth does not want to deceive, and so it cannot be deceived. If you do not want to go astray, follow Christ.

12.25
William of Malmesbury (1080-1143)
English monk and historian

1 In the sickness at the end of his life [Swithun] commanded that his body should be buried outside the church, where it would be trodden by the passers-by and made wet by the rain that falls from heaven.

12.26
William of St Thierry (1085-1148)
French religious philosopher

1 A man who has lost his sense of wonder is a man dead.

2 You alone are the Lord. By ruling us you save us and we are saved by you. Lord, you save your people and bless them, but what does it mean to be saved by you if not to receive the grace of loving you and being loved by you?

3 Seek not to explore the heights of the divine majesty, but to find salvation in the saving deeds of God our Saviour.

4 Hasten therefore to share in the Holy Spirit. He is with you when you call upon him; you can call upon him only because he is already present. When he comes in answer to your prayer, he comes with an abundance of blessings. He is the river whose streams give joy to the city of God.

Thirteenth Century

13.1
Agnellus of Pisa (c.1195-1236)
Italian leader of first Franciscans in England

1 [On examining the friars' increased expenses] Alas, I am in prison!

2 Come, sweetest Jesus!

13.2
Albert I (?1255-1308)
King of Germany

1 A man receives God in the soul as often as for love of God he abstains from a fault, be it only a word or an idle glance.

13.3
Albert the Great (1200-1280)
German-born theologian

1 God can be offered no greater gift than a good will; for the good will is the source of all good and the mother of all virtues; whoever begins to have that good will has gained all the help he needs for the good life.

13.4
Alfonso the Wise (1221-1284)
Spanish King of Leon and Castile

1 Had I been present at the creation, I would have given some useful hints for the better ordering of the universe.

13.5
Ancrene Riwle **(between 1190 and 1230)**
English book on the spiritual life

1 Reading is good prayer. Reading teaches how, and for what, we ought to pray; and afterwards prayer obtains it. In reading, when the heart feels delight, devotion is increased, and that is worth many prayers.

2 Confession must be our own: we must expose no one except ourselves, as far as possible.

13.6
Angela of Foligno (1248-1309)
Italian mystic

1 I saw in myself two sides and it was as if these had been separated by a furrow. On one side I saw fullness of love and every good, which was from God and not from me. On the other side I saw myself as arid and saw that nothing good originated in me. By this I discovered that it was not I who loved—even though I saw myself as total love—but that which loved in me came from God alone.

2 I praise you God my beloved; I have made your cross my bed. For a pillow or cushion, I have found poverty, and for other parts of the bed, suffering and contempt to rest on.

3 Holy Scripture is so sublime that there is no one in the world wise enough, not even anyone with learning and spirit, who would not find it totally beyond their capacity to understand Scripture fully; still, they babble something about it.

4 And pray in this fashion, namely, always reading the Book of Life, that is, the life of the God-man Jesus Christ, whose life consisted of poverty, pain, contempt, and true obedience.

5 Those persons who best know God are those who least presume to speak of him.

6 Inquire and meditate on all the ways of the passion and the cross. Even if you cannot do this from the heart, at least do it earnestly and carefully with your lips; because when a thing is often said, in the end it imparts warmth and fervour to the heart.

7 The world mocks at what I now say, namely that a man can weep for his neighbour's sins as though they were his own, or even more than for his own, for it seems contrary to nature, but the charity that leads to this action is not of this world.

8 There is no one either father or mother or son or any other person, who can embrace the person loved by them with a love as great as that with which God embraces the soul.

9 By nothing that we can think or say can God be exalted.

10 Christ appeared not as a philosopher or wordy doctor, or noisy disputer, or even as a wise and learned scribe, but he talked with people in complete simplicity, showing them the way of truth in the way he lived, his goodness and his miracles.

11 O marvellous, indescribable and joyful love, in you is all savour and sweetness and all delight, the contemplation of which exalts the soul above the world, making it able to stand alone in joy, peace and rest.

12 Exalted, drawn, and absorbed into the uncreated Light, I beheld that which cannot be related.

13.7
Anthony of Padua (1195-1231)
Portuguese-born Franciscan

1 Consider every day that you are then for the first time—as it were—beginning; and always act with the same fervour as on the first day you began.

2 Our thoughts ought by instinct to fly upwards from animals, men and natural objects to their Creator. If created things are so utterly lovely, how gloriously beautiful must he be who made them! The wisdom of the worker is revealed in his handiwork.

3 Happy the man whose words come from the Holy Spirit and not from himself!

4 See these little pieces of straw which the world tramples underfoot: they are the good qualities practised by your Saviour, and he himself has set you an example of meekness, humility, poverty, penitence, patience and self-discipline.

13.8
Roger Bacon (1214-1292)
English Franciscan philosopher

1 The wisdom of philosophy is completely revealed by God and given to philosophers; and it is he who illumines the souls of men in all wisdom.

13.9
Beatrice of Nazareth (c.1200-1268)
Flemish nun and writer

1 As the fish swims in the vastness of the oceans and rests in the deeps, and as the bird boldly soars in the heights and the vastness of the air, in the same way she feels her spirit roam free through the depths and the heights and the immensity of love.

2 The soul seeks God in his majesty; she follows him there and gazes upon him with heart and spirit. She knows him, she loves him, and she so burns with desire for him that she cannot pay heed to any saints or sinners, angels or creatures, except with that all-comprehending love of him by whom she loves all things.

13.10
Bonaventure (1221-1274)
Italian Franciscan theologian

1 The memory of Christ Jesus crucified was ever present in the depths of his [Francis'] heart like a bundle of myrrh.

2 If therefore a man would get up as high as he can, and there rest, and not go back at all, and the next day go up higher, and there set the foot of his heart, and after that ascend higher and higher, and thus do always, I say to you that such a one would profit more in one month than another, that goes back to take his rest, and returns from whence he first came, would do in forty years.

3 If this passing over is to be perfect, all intellectual operations must be given up, and the sharp point of our desire must be directed toward God and transformed in him. Such a motion as this is something mystical and very secret, and no one receives it except him who desires it, and no one desires it unless the fire of the Holy Spirit, whom Christ sent to earth, inflames him to the very marrow.

4 If you wish to know how such things come about, consult grace, not doctrine; desire, not understanding; prayerful groaning, not studious reading; the Spouse, not the teacher; God, not man; darkness, not clarity.

5 Consult not light, but the fire that completely inflames the mind and carries it over to God in transports of fervour and blazes of love. This fire is God, and his furnace is in Jerusalem. Christ starts the flame with the fiery heat of his intense suffering.

6 Let us die, then, and pass over into the darkness; let us silence every care, every craving, every dream; with Christ crucified, let us pass out of this world to the Father.

7 In beautiful things Francis saw Beauty itself, and through Beauty's traces imprinted on creation he followed his beloved everywhere, making everything a ladder by which he could climb up and embrace the One who is utterly desirable.

8 No matter how carefully our inner progress is ordered, nothing will come of it unless by God's help. And this is available to those who seek it from the heart, humbly and devoutly; which means, in this vale of tears, yearning for it in fervent prayer.

9 In all your deeds and words, you should look on Jesus as your model, whether you are keeping silence or speaking, whether you are alone or with others.

10 One Lent Francis whittled a little cup to occupy his spare moments. When he was reciting the office of Terce, it came into his mind and distracted him a little. Whereupon he burned the cup in the fire, saying, 'I will sacrifice this to the Lord, whose sacrifice it has impeded.'

11 When [Francis] stood up to present his homily, he went completely blank, and could not say anything at all. Humbly he said what had happened, and told himself to ask the help of the Holy Spirit—and at once he began to overflow with eloquence.

12 Food ought to be a refreshment for the body and not a burden.

13 Every creature is by its nature a kind of effigy and likeness of the eternal Wisdom, but this is particularly so of a creature which in the Scripture has been raised up by the spirit of prophecy to image spiritual things.

14 Since happiness in nothing but the enjoyment of the highest good, and since the highest good is above, then no one can be happy unless he rise above himself, not by a physical ascent, but by an ascent of the heart.

15 Heaven is not divided by the number of those who reign, nor diminished by being shared, nor disturbed by the multitude of those there, nor disordered by its various ranks, nor changed by motion, nor measured by time.

16 Every creature is a divine word because it proclaims God.

13.11
Clare of Assisi (c.1193-1253)

Friend of St Francis and founder of the Poor Clares

1 O blessed poverty, who bestows eternal riches on those who love and embrace her! O holy poverty, to those who possess and desire you God promises the kingdom of heaven and offers, indeed, eternal glory and blessed life! O God-centred poverty, whom the Lord Jesus Christ, who ruled and now rules heaven and earth, who spoke and things were made, condescended to embrace before all else!

2 What a great and laudable exchange: to leave the things of time for those of eternity, to choose the things of heaven for the goods of earth, to receive the hundredfold in place of one, and to possess a blessed and eternal life.

3 What you hold, may you always hold. What you do, may you always do and never abandon. But with swift pace, light step, and unswerving feet, so that even your steps stir up no dust, go forward securely, joyfully and swiftly on the path of prudent happiness.

4 Place your mind before the mirror of eternity! Place your soul in the brilliance of glory! Place your heart in the figure of the divine substance! And transform your whole being into the image of the Godhead itself through contemplation.

5 Cling to his sweet Mother who carried a son whom the heavens could not contain, and yet she carried him in the little enclosure of her holy womb, and held him on her virginal lap.

6 Our toil here is brief but its reward is eternal. Do not be disturbed by the clamour of the world, which passes like a shadow.

7 Our body is not made of iron. Our strength is not that of a stone. Live and hope in the Lord and let your service be according to reason. Season your whole-offering with the salt of prudence.

8 If a Lord so great and good, on coming to the Virgin's womb, chose to appear despised, needy and poor in this world, so that people who were themselves in utter poverty and want and in total need of heavenly nourishment might become rich in him by possessing the kingdom of heaven, then rejoice and be glad! Be filled with amazing happiness and spiritual joy! Contempt of the world has pleased you more than its honours, poverty more than earthly riches.

9 Love him totally who gave himself totally for your love.

10 The Lord be with you always, and be you with him always and in every place.

11 My Lord, I thank you for having created me.

13.12
Dominic (1170-1221)
Spanish-born founder of the Order of Preachers

1 I shall be more useful to you and more fruitful after my death than I was in my life.

2 I refuse to study dead skins [books] while men are dying of hunger.

3 The heretics are to be converted by an example of humility and other virtues far more readily than by any external display or verbal battles. So let us arm ourselves with devout prayers and set off showing signs of genuine humility and barefooted to combat Goliath.

4 Go, my son, and go confidently. I will hold you before God twice every day. Do not doubt, you will win many for God and bring forth much fruit.

5 A man who is ruler of his passions is master of the world.

13.13
John Duns Scotus (c.1266-1308)
Scottish Franciscan philosopher

1 Human nature has ineffable dignity.

2 The Creator is author of all arts that are truly arts.

3 The creation of things is executed by God not out of any necessity, whether of essence or of knowledge or of will, but out of a sheer freedom which is not moved—much less constrained—by anything external.

4 It is impossible that a nature should be perfectly happy and perfectly at peace unless it be wholly at peace and not only in part. Therefore the will cannot be at peace without the intellect, nor conversely, for each is a power of the one undivided nature. Consequently, beatitude consists in the perfection of both powers.

13.14
Edmund of Abingdon (?1175-1240)
English Archbishop of Canterbury

1 Into your hands, O Father and Lord, we commend our souls and bodies, our parents and homes, friends and servants, neighbours and kindred, our benefactors and brethren departed, all folk rightly believing, and all who need your pity and protection. Light us all with your holy grace, and suffer us never to be separated from you, O Lord in Trinity, God everlasting.

13.15
Elizabeth of Hungary (1207-1231)
Hungarian princess, devoted to the service of the poor

1 I gave to God what belonged to him, and God kept for us what was yours and mine.

2 Here before my eyes is my God and my King, the mild and merciful Jesus, crowned with sharp thorns; shall I, lowly creature that I am, remain before him crowned with pearls, gold and precious stones, and mock his crown with mine?

3 I have lost everything. O my beloved brother, O friend of my heart, O my good and devout husband, you are dead, and have left me in misery! How shall I live without you? Ah, poor lonely widow and miserable woman that I am, may he who does not forsake widows and orphans console me. O my God, console me! O my Jesus, strengthen me in my weakness!

4 As in heaven your will is promptly performed, so may it be done on earth by all creatures, particularly in me and by me.

13.16
Francis of Assisi (1182-1226)

Italian founder of the Franciscan Order

1 Praised be you, my Lord, with all your creatures, especially Sir Brother Sun, who is the day and through whom you give us light. And he is beautiful and radiant with great splendours and bears likeness of you, Most High One.

2 When I was in sin the sight of lepers nauseated me beyond measure; then God himself led me into their company, and I had a pity on them; what had previously nauseated me became a source of spiritual and physical consolation. After that I did not wait long before leaving the world.

3 Each one should confidently make known his needs to the other, so that he might find what he needs and minister to him. And each one should love and care for his brother in all those things in which God will give him grace, as a mother loves and cares for her son.

4 Blessed is the servant who esteems himself no more highly when he is praised and exalted by people than when he is considered worthless, foolish and to be despised; since what a man is before God, that he is and nothing more.

5 You damned spirits! You can only do what the hand of God allows you to do.

6 I consider you to be the servant of God and I love you more, the more you are attacked by temptations. Truly I tell you: no one should consider himself a perfect friend of God until he has passed through many temptations and tribulations.

7 Bring to the Lord, O you peoples of the gentiles, bring to the Lord glory and honour, bring to the Lord the glory due to his name. Bring your own bodies and bear his holy cross, and follow to the end his most holy precepts.

8 In the name of holy love which is God I implore all my brothers... to lay aside every obstacle, every care, every trouble, and to serve, love, adore and honour the Lord with all their might, with a pure heart and a whole mind which he seeks above all. Let us make a temple and a dwelling within us for the Lord God Almighty, Father, Son and Holy Spirit.

9 I am pleased for my brothers to study the Scriptures as long as they do not neglect application to prayer, after the example of Christ, of whom we read that he prayed more than he read.

10 Holy obedience puts to shame all natural and selfish desires. It mortifies our lower nature and makes it obey the spirit and our fellow men.

11 Most High, glorious God, enlighten the darkness of my heart and give me a right faith, a sure hope, a perfect charity, sense and knowledge, so that I may carry out your holy and true command.

12 It is no use walking anywhere to preach unless we preach as we walk.

13 St Paul tells us, 'The letter kills, but the spirit gives life'. A man has been killed by the letter when he wants to know quotations only so that people will think he is very learned.

14 My God and my all!

13.17
Gertrude the Great (1256-1302)
German mystic

1 On the Feast of the Annunciation I saw the heart of the Virgin Mother so bathed by the rivers of grace flowing out of the Blessed Trinity that I understood the privilege Mary has of being the most powerful after God the Father, the most wise after God the Son, and the most kindly after God the Holy Spirit.

13.18
Giles of Assisi (d.1262)
Italian companion of Francis

1 Blessed is he who does good to others and desires not that others should do him good.

2 The things that worldly men scorn and shun are honoured and valued by God and his saints; and those that worldly men embrace and prize are scorned and hated and shunned by God and his saints. Men hate everything that should be loved and love what should be hated.

3 Grace does not want to be praised, and vice does not want to be scorned. In other words, the man who has grace does not want to be praised and does not go looking for it, whereas the man who has vices does not want to be scorned or blamed—and this comes from pride.

13.19
Robert Grosseteste (c.1168-1253)
English scholar and bishop

1 [On Scripture's 'unchallengeable authority'] The time especially appropriate for laying foundation stones... is the morning hour when you lecture... therefore all your lectures especially at that time should be on the books of the New Testament or the Old.

13.20
Hadewijch of Brabant (early 13c.)
Belgian mystic

1 If you wish to possess finally all that is yours, give yourself entirely to God.

2 You should rely on love, and then you shall know what to love and what to hate.

3 People think they are led by the spirit, when mostly it is their own will that leads them.

4 To lose our way in [love] is to arrive,
To hunger for her is to feed and to taste.

5 Love's finest speech is without words.

6 We all wish to be God with God. But, God knows, there are few enough of us who want to live as men and women with his humanity or to bear his cross with him, and be crucified with him in order to pay for the sins of the whole world.

7 You should live on earth with the humanity of God when you experience suffering and troubles, while inwardly loving and rejoicing with the almighty and eternal Godhead in sweet abandonment.

8 Whoever loves, allow themselves willingly to be corrected, without seeking excuses, in order to be freer in love.

9 We wish to be godly in church but at home and elsewhere we wish to know about all those worldly things that help us or harm us.

10 [Love] made me like the hazel trees,
Which blossom early
in the season of darkness,
And bear fruit slowly.

11 Whatever gifts God bestowed upon us
There was no one who could
Understand true love
Until Mary, in her goodness,
And with deep humility,
Received the gift of Love.
She it was who tamed wild Love
And gave us a lamb for a lion;
Through her a light shone in the darkness
That had endured so long.

13.21
Hartmann von Aue (c.1170-1215)
German poet

1 He who helps in the saving of others, saves himself as well.

13.22
Hedwig of Silesia (c.1174-1243)
Bavarian noblewoman and philosopher

1 Do you not know that fasting can overcome concupiscence, lift up the soul, confirm it in the way of virtue and prepare a great reward for the Christian?

13.23
Humbert of Romans (c.1200-1277)
Dominican friar

1 There is nothing surprising in angels being called preachers, since their mission is for the sake of those who are to inherit salvation, just as preachers are sent out for the salvation of humankind.

2 Again, without preaching, which sows the word of God, the whole world would be barren and without fruit.

3 A preacher must apply himself very carefully to doing all that is in him to practise his job well and with grace. In this attempt, there are three things which are particularly helpful: the first is meticulous study, the second is to observe how other preachers tackle the job, and the third is prayer to God.

13.24
Jacopone da Todi (c.1230-1306)
Italian Franciscan

1 God does not dwell in a heart that's confined,
And a heart is only as big as the love it holds:
In the great heart of Poverty
God has room to dwell.

2 To live as myself and yet not I,
My being no longer my being,
This is a paradox
We cannot pretend to understand!

3 Poverty is having nothing, wanting nothing,
And possessing all things
in the spirit of freedom.

4 What death is to the body,
Sin is to the soul, but worse.

5 Should his wife and children
Put on weight, he is displeased—
The bread and wine in his house
He considers all his.

6 Wisdom lies in trusting no one;
He who is bitten by a snake
comes to fear the lizard.
Keep a wary eye on all sheep
you do not know,
And your conscience will not reproach you.

7 Were John the Baptist to return and denounce
The sin of the world, once more they'd
cut off his head.

13.25
Jordan of Saxony (d.1237)
Dominican friar

1 Good brother, do not fail to apply yourself to whatever inspires the most devotion in you. The most beneficial prayer will be the one which moves your heart in the most beneficial way.

2 May the supreme comforter, the Spirit of truth, possess your heart and comfort you and grant that we may be together in that heavenly Jerusalem for ever, by the gift of our Lord Jesus Christ, who is blessed above all else for ever.

3 After all, my dear, it is only a small thing that we write to each other; there is a fire of love in our hearts, in the Lord, and there you speak to me and I speak to you the whole time, in feelings of affection which no tongue could adequately express and which no letter could adequately contain.

4 Sometimes we get unduly elated when things go well, and at other times we are too dejected when they go badly... What we need is to establish our hearts firmly in God's strength, and struggle as best we can to place all our confidence and hope in him; in this

way we shall be like him, as far as is possibility, even in his unchanging rest and his stability.

5 So long as we are in this place of pilgrimage, so long as men's hearts are warped and prone to sin, lazy and weak in virtue, we need to be encouraged and stirred up, so that brother may be helped by brother, and the eagerness of heavenly love rekindle the flame in our spirit which our daily carelessness and lukewarmness tend to put out.

13.26
Robert Kilwardby (d.1279)
Dominican friar, Archbishop of Canterbury

1 It is profitless to fuss over human statutes and neglect the command of God which bids us love our neighbour as ourselves—on which St Augustine teaches that 'neighbour' must be taken to mean everybody.

13.27
Stephen Langton (d.1228)
English Archbishop of Canterbury

1 Come, thou Holy Spirit, come,
And from thy celestial home
Shed thy light and brilliancy...

13.28
Louis IX of France (1214-1270)
King of France

1 Take care not knowingly to do or say anything which, if everyone were to know of it, you could not own, and say, 'Yes, that is what I did, or what I said.'

2 Keep yourself, my son, from everything you know that displeases God, from every grave sin. You ought to let yourself be tortured by every kind of martyrdom rather than allow yourself to commit grave sin.

13.29
Margaret of Cortona (1247-1297)
Italian mystic

1 [Christ speaks:] Why do you ceaselessly ask to taste my pleasures and refuse the tribulations?

2 This morning my soul is greater than the world, since it possesses you, whom heaven and earth cannot contain.

3 The way of salvation is easy: it is enough to love.

4 [Christ speaks:] My daughter, I see more Pharisees among the Christians than I did around Pilate.

5 [Christ speaks:] I am concealing myself from you so that you may discover by yourself what you are without me.

6 Where now is the joy of your presence which I prize above everything?

7 I am his daughter. He said so. Oh the infinite gentleness of my God!

13.30
Mechtilde of Hackeborn (1241-1299)
German nun

1 Beyond all telling was your joy,
when your blest humanity was glorified
by the Father of divine glory
at your resurrection.
Then with divine power the Father
gave eternal glory
to all who have been chosen
to share the life of God.

13.31
Mechtilde of Magdeburg (c.1220-c.1280)
German nun

1 Fish cannot drown in the water,
Birds cannot sink in the air,
Gold cannot perish
In the refiner's fire.
This has God given to all creatures
To foster and seek their own nature.
How then can I withstand mine?

2 Think ye that fire must utterly slay my soul?
Nay! Love can both fiercely scorch
And tenderly love and console.

3 Lord, you are my lover,
My longing,
My flowing stream, my sun,
And I am your reflection.

4 [Lord], your glory pours into my soul like sunlight against gold.

5 God leads his chosen children
Along strange paths.
And it is a strange path,
And a holy path
God himself walked:
To suffer pain without sin or guilt.
But this gives delight to the soul
Who desires God.

6 It is a rare
And a high way
Which the soul follows,
Drawing the senses after,
Just as the person with sight leads the blind.

7 His soul is groundless in desire,
Burning in love,
Kind in his presence,
A mirror of the world,
Humble in his greatness,
True in his help,
Gathered in God.

8 If you love the justice of Jesus Christ more than you fear human judgment, then you will seek to do compassion.

9 The manifold delight I learn to take
in earthly things
can never drive me from my love.
For in the nobility of creatures,
in their beauty and in their usefulness,
I will love God—
and not myself!

13.32
William Peraldus (d. after 1261)
French Dominican preacher and writer

1 Prayer is a dove, the bird of the Holy Spirit, which brings the olive branch and wins peace for humankind.

13.33
Peter Martyr (1205-1252)
Italian Dominican friar

1 You have gone up into the mountain of sacrifice, while I still dwell in the valley of care, and have spent almost all my life for others. You take the wings of contemplation and soar above all this, but I am so stuck in the glue of concern for other people that I cannot fly.

13.34
Peter of Rheims (d. after 1247)
French Dominican friar

1 Anyone who is not burning will not be able to set anyone else on fire.

13.35
Raymond of Peñafort (1175-1275)
Spanish Dominican friar

1 Living, as I do, in the whirlwind of the court, I am hardly ever able to reach, or, to be quite honest, even to see from afar, the tranquillity of contemplation. I am so busy with Leah's morning shortsightedness and fruitfulness that in my present position I cannot reach the beauty of Rachel to which I have aspired, however feebly.

13.36
Richard of Chichester (1197-1253)
English bishop

1 Do you know what I mean? This is that of which St Philip said to our Lord: 'Show us the Father, and it is enough for us.' May the Lord give me that dish for my supper.

2 O most merciful Redeemer, Friend
and Brother,
May I know thee more clearly,
love thee more dearly,
follow thee more nearly,
day by day.

13.37
Thomas Aquinas (1225-1274)
Italian Dominican theologian

1 Although our view of the most sublime things is limited and weak, it is a great pleasure to be able to catch even a glimpse of them.

2 It is not that our body feels while our mind thinks, but we, as single human beings, both feel and think.

3 If you are looking for the way by which you should go, take Christ, for he is himself the way.

4 The proper effect of the Eucharist is the transformation of man into God.

5 No one can live without delight, and that is why a man deprived of spiritual joy goes over to fleshly pleasures.

6 Happiness is the natural life of man.

7 An angel can illumine the thought and mind of man by strengthening the power of vision, and by bringing within his reach some truth which the angel himself contemplates.

8 Charity is never a waste of time. Tonight I have given up my prayer in order to write to you.

9 If you are looking for an example of humility, look at the cross.

10 Every evil is based on some good, for it is present in a subject which is good and having some sort of nature. Evil cannot exist but in good, sheer evil is impossible.

11 Sheer joy is God's, and this demands companionship.

12 God of all goodness, grant us to desire ardently, to seek wisely, to know surely and to accomplish perfectly thy holy will, for the glory of thy name.

13 Reason in man is rather like God in the world.

14 The end of my labours is come. All that I have written appears to be as so much straw after the things that have been revealed to me.

15 O saving Victim, opening wide
The gate of heaven to man below,
Our foes press hard on every side,
Thine aid supply, thy strength bestow.

16 Three things are necessary for the salvation of man: to know what he ought to believe, to know what he ought to desire; and to know what he ought to do.

17 The divine nature is really and entirely identical with each of the three persons, all of whom can therefore be called one.

18 If all evil were prevented, the universe would lack much good: the lion would cease to live, if there were no slaughter of animals; and without persecuting tyrants, there would be no patient suffering of martyrs.

19 This food satisfies the hunger of the devout heart. Faith is the seasoning, devotion and love of the brethren the relish. The teeth of the body break this food, but only an unfaltering faith can savour it.

13.38
Thomas of Cantimpré (c.1201-c.1276)
Dominican friar

1 While they [monks] sit at home in their monasteries—and let us hope that it is with Mary—you go touring round with Paul [the Apostle], doing the job you have been given to do.

13.39
Thomas of Celano (c.1190-1260)
Franciscan, biographer of Francis

1 [Francis'] safest haven was prayer; not of a single moment or idle, but prayer of long devotion... walking, sitting, eating or drinking, he was always intent upon prayer.

2 St Francis ordered a plot to be set aside for the cultivation of flowers when the convent garden was made, in order that all who saw them might remember the Eternal Sweetness.

13.40
Thomas of Eccleston (mid 13c.)
English Franciscan friar

1 Once he [one of the first Franciscan novices in England] suffered such extreme cold that he thought he was about to die on the spot. As the brothers did not have the wherewithal to make him warm, their brotherly love taught them a remedy: they all gathered round him, and like a litter of piglets pressed close to him and so warmed him.

Fourteenth Century

14.1
Thomas Bradwardine (1290-1349)
English Archbishop of Canterbury

1 Grant, most gracious God, that we may love you always and everywhere, above all things, and for your sake, in this present life, and at length find you and forever hold you fast in the life to come.

14.2
Bridget of Sweden (1303-1373)
Wife, mother, foundress of the Brigittine Order

1 If we saw an angel clearly, we would die of pleasure.

2 Light has been made so that human beings, who share in the nature of both higher and lower beings, may be able to support themselves by working hard during the day, remembering the pleasure of the everlasting light they have lost. Night has been made so that they may rest their bodies with the intention of reaching that place where there is neither night nor toil, but rather eternal day and everlasting glory.

14.3
Nicolas Cabasilas (d.1371)
Greek mystical writer

1 The water of baptism destroys one life and reveals another: it drowns the old man and raises up the new. To be baptized is to be born according to Christ; it is to receive existence, to come into being out of nothing.

2 Under normal circumstances food is changed into the person who consumes it: fish, bread and the like become human flesh and blood. But in holy communion the exact opposite happens. The Bread of Life himself changes the person who eats, assimilating and transforming him into himself.

14.4
Catherine of Siena (1347-1380)
Italian mystic

1 You are the garment that covers every nakedness. You feed the hungry in your sweetness.

2 Then was seen God-and-Man, as might the clearness of the sun be seen. And he stood wounded, and received the blood [of the man being executed]; and in that blood a fire of holy desire, given and hidden in the soul by grace. He received it in the fire of his divine charity. When he received his blood and his desire, he also received his soul, which he put into the open treasure-house of his side, full of mercy; the primal Truth showing that by grace and mercy alone he received it, and not for any other work.

3 Build yourself a cell in your heart and retire there to pray.

4 'I can love you more than you can love yourself, and I watch over you a thousand times more carefully than you can watch over yourself.'

5 The martyrs wanted to die, not to flee from labour but to attain their purpose.

6 'The important thing is not to love me for your own sake, or yourself for your own sake, or your neighbour for your own sake, but to love me for myself, and yourself for myself, and your neighbour for myself. Divine love cannot bear to share with any earthly love.'

7 Eternal God, accept the offering of my life for the mystical body of your holy church.

8 Every light that comes from Holy Scripture comes from the light of grace. This is why foolish, proud and learned people are blind even in the light, because the light is clouded by their own pride and selfish love. They read the Scripture literally, not with understanding, and they have lost the light by which the Scripture was formed and proclaimed.

9 'O stupid people, don't you see that you are not the source of your own knowledge? It is my goodness, providing for your needs, that has given it to you.'

10 You are a fire that takes away the coldness, enlightens the mind with its light, and causes me to know your truth. And I know that you are beauty and truth itself, and wisdom itself.

11 Then the soul is in God and God in the soul, just as the fish is in the sea and the sea in the fish.

12 A soul cannot live without loving. It must have something to love, for it was created to love.

13 The more perfectly you abandon yourself and resign yourself to me, the more I will console you with my grace and make you feel my presence. But you will never reach this measure of perfection except by a firm, constant and absolute denial of self-will.

14.5
Geoffrey Chaucer (1340-1400)
English poet

1 Ful swetely herde he confessioun,
And plesaunt was his absolucion.

2 Therefore behoveth him a full long spoon
That shall eat with a fiend, thus heard I say.

3 Whoso will pray, he must fast and be clean,
And fat his soul and make his body lean.

4 Nature, the vicaire of the almyghty lorde.

5 Christ's lore, and his apostles twelve,
He taught, and first he followed it himself.

6 This noble example to his sheep he gave,
That first he wrought, and afterward he taught.

7 Truth is the highest thing that man may keep.

14.6
Clement VI (d.1352)
Pope

1 I will whatever you will,
I will because you will it,
I will just as you will,
I will for as long as you will.

14.7
Cloud of Unknowing
Book on the spiritual life

1 Charity means nothing else but to love God for himself above all creatures, and to love one's fellowmen for God's sake as one loves oneself.

2 The higher part of contemplation is wholly caught up in darkness and in this cloud of unknowing, with an outreaching of love and a blind groping for the naked being of God, himself and him alone.

3 For this reason this darkness which is between you and your God, I do not call a cloud of air, but a cloud of unknowing.

4 Reconcile yourself to wait in this darkness as long as is necessary, but still go on longing after him whom you love.

5 Whatever you possess, and however fruitful your activities, regard them all as worthless without the inward certainty and experience of Jesus' love.

6 For silence is not God, nor speaking; fasting is not God, nor eating; solitude is not God, nor company; nor any other pairs of opposites. He is hidden between them and cannot be found by anything your soul does, but only by the desire of your heart.

7 See what you lack and not what you have, for that is the quickest path to humility.

8 God wants us to pray, and will tell us how to begin where we are.

9 Surely pride is harboured within, wherever such mock humility is so plentifully displayed.

10 For as the cloud of unknowing lies above you, between you and your God, you must fashion a cloud of forgetting beneath you, between you and every creature.

11 Although we cannot have knowledge of God, we can love him: by love he may be touched and embraced, by thought, never.

12 Believe me when I say that the devil has his contemplatives as surely as the Lord has his.

13 In anticipation of this eternal glory, God will sometimes enflame the senses of his devoted friends with unspeakable delight and consolation even here in this life. And not just once or twice, but perhaps very often, as he judges to be best.

14 God in his great mercy decides what is best for each one.

15 The way to heaven is through desire. The one who longs to be there really is there in spirit. The path to heaven is measured by desire and not in miles.

16 And therefore, you are to strike the thick cloud of unknowing with the longing darts of love, and never to retreat, no matter what comes to pass.

17 In one little moment, short as it is, heaven may be lost.

18 Virtue is nothing else than an ordered and measured affection directed towards God for his sake alone.

14.8
Dante Alighieri (1265-1321)
Italian poet

1 O faithful conscience delicately pure,
How doth a little failing wound thee sore!

2 Consider your origin: you were not made to live like brutes, but to follow virtue and knowledge.

3 In his will is our peace.

4 The love that moves the sun and the other stars.

14.9
Dorothea of Montau (1347-1394)
German laywoman, mystic and (later) recluse

1 You are my hope,
my food,
my trust,
my comfort,
and all my desire.
Lord my God,
now make my soul grow
and open wide my heart!

14.10
Margaret Ebner (d.1351)
German nun and mystic

1 Jesus Christ,
guide us with your boundless compassion
and compel us with your perfect love
to love according to your will
in the truth...
that the truth may live in us
and we in the truth.

14.11
Meister Eckhart (?1260-1327)
Dominican mystic

1 One must not always think so much about what one should do, but rather what one must be. Our works do not ennoble us; but we must ennoble our works.

2 In silence man can most readily preserve his integrity.

3 Our Lord says to every living soul, 'I became man for you. If you do not become God for me, you do me wrong.'

4 God can no more do without us than we can do without him.

5 The eye with which I see God is the same as that with which God sees me.

6 The knower and the known are one. Simple people imagine that they should see God, as if he stood there and they here. This is not so. God and I, we are one in knowledge.

7 The more God is in things, the more he is outside them. The more he is within, the more without.

8 How can we ever be sold short, or cheated, we who for every service have long ago been overpaid?

9 If God were able to backslide from truth, I would fain cling to truth and let God go.

10 Nothing in all creation is so like God as stillness.

11 Human beings ought to communicate and share all the gifts they have received from God. If a person has something that he or she does not share that person is not good.

12 There is no such thing as 'my' bread. All bread is *ours* and is given to me, to others through me and to me through others.

13 Whatever God does, the first outburst is always compassion.

14 To rejoice at another person's joy is like being in heaven.

15 If anyone thinks he will obtain God in meditation and sweet thoughts and special devotions rather than by the fireside or in the byre, he is seeking to take God and wrap his head in a blanket and thrust him under the table.

16 He who seeks God in some external routine will find the routine and lose God.

17 The seed of God is in us.
Now the seed of a pear tree
grows into a pear tree;
and a hazel seed
grows into a hazel tree;
a seed of God
grows into God.

18 A flea, to the extent that it is in God, ranks above the highest angel in his own right.

19 Only the hand that erases can write the true thing.

14.12
Elizabeth of Portugal (1271-1336)
Queen and friend of the poor

1 I would rather die of hunger myself than deny aid to the poor in this season, and thus become guilty before God of their death.

14.13
Gregory Palamas (1296-1359)
Greek mystical theologian

1 There is an unknowing that is higher than all knowledge, a darkness that is supremely bright; and in this dazzling darkness divine things are given to the saints.

2 When we are engaged in manual labour and when we walk or sit down, when we eat or when we drink, we can always pray inwardly and practise prayer of the mind, true prayer, pleasing to God. Let us work with our body and pray with our soul.

3 [Christ] has made the flesh an inexhaustible source of sanctification.

4 The body is deified along with the soul.

14.14
Walter Hilton (d.1396)
English spiritual writer

1 I am nothing, I have nothing, I desire nothing but the love of Jesus in Jerusalem.

2 Although we may never attain it in this life, we should desire to recover some degree and likeness of that dignity [which we lost through Adam's sin], so that the soul may be re-formed by grace to a shadow of the image of the Trinity which it once had by nature, and which it will have fully in heaven.

3 Anyone who thinks himself a perfect follower of Christ's teaching and way of life—as some do, in that they preach and teach and are poor in worldly goods as Christ was—but who cannot follow Christ in having love and charity towards all, both good and bad, friends and foes, without pretence or flattery, contempt, anger, or spiteful criticism, is indeed deceiving himself.

4 Do your utmost to guard your heart, for out of it comes life.

5 Ask nothing of God, then, but this gift of divine Love, that is, the Holy Spirit.

14.15
John Huss (?1372-1415)
Bohemian reformer

1 O holy simplicity!

14.16
John of Alverna (1259-1322)
Italian Franciscan

1 Reawaken my soul by the grace of your love, since it is your commandment that we love you with all our heart and strength, and no one can fulfil that commandment without your help.

14.17
John of Ruysbroeck (1293-1381)
Flemish mystic

1 God in the depths of us receives God who comes to us; it is God contemplating God.

2 The inward stirring and touching of God makes us hungry and yearning; for the Spirit of God hurts our spirit; and the more he touches it, the greater our hunger and craving.

3 Christ is a sun of righteousness and also of mercy, who stands in the highest part of the firmament, on the right hand of the Father, and from there he shines into the depths of the humble heart; for Christ is always moved by helplessness whenever a person complains of it and lays it before him humbly.

4 The love of all spirits is measured; and for this reason their love perpetually begins afresh, so that God may be loved according to his command and to the spirits' own desires. This is why all the blessed spirits are perpetually gathered together to form a burning flame of love, so that they may perform this work, and so that God may be loved as his majesty deserves.

5 When we rise again with glorious bodies, in the power of the Lord, these bodies will be whiter and brighter than snow, more brilliant than the sun, clearer than crystal; and each one will have a special mark of honour and glory, according to the sufferings and torments they have endured and freely borne for the honour of God.

6 What we are, that we behold; and what we behold, that we are: for our thought, our life and our being are uplifted in simplicity, and made one with the Truth which is God.

7 All those who follow our Lord Jesus Christ hear the voice of the Father, for it is of them all that the Father says 'These are my chosen sons, in whom I am well pleased'.

8 When we are born anew of God's Spirit, then our will is free, for it is made to be one with the free will of God. There our spirit, through love, is raised and taken up into one Spirit, one will, one freedom in Christ.

9 The Holy Spirit works in us, and we together with him, perform all our good deeds. He cries in us with a loud voice and yet without words: *Love the love which loves you eternally*. His cry is an interior touching with our spirit. His voice is more terrifying than thunder. The lightnings that break from it open up heaven to us and show us the Light and eternal Truth. The heat of his touch and love is so great that it would burn us up. His touching of our spirit cries without ceasing, it keeps crying: *Repay your debt! Love the love which loves you eternally*.

10 One person works upon another person from outside inwards, but God alone comes to us from within outwards.

14.18
Julian of Norwich (?1342-c.1413)
English recluse

1 I saw our Blessed Lady—grounded in humility she was filled with grace and all virtues, and is thus higher than all other creatures.

2 He did not say, 'You shall not be tempted; you shall not be travailed; you shall not be afflicted.' But he said, 'You shall not be overcome.'

3 Every act of kindness and compassion done by any man for his fellow Christian is done by Christ working within him.

4 I saw three properties: the first is, that God made it. The second is, that God loveth it. The third is, that God keepeth it. But what beheld I therein? Verily the Maker, the Keeper, the Lover.

5 Our life is grounded in faith, with hope and love besides.

6 In his love he clothes us, enfolds and embraces us; that tender love completely surrounds us, never to leave us.

7 God is everything that is good, in my sight, and the goodness that everything has is his.

8 Peace and love are always alive in us, but we are not always alive to peace and love.

9 Rightfulness has two qualities: it is right and it is full. Such are all the works of God. They lack neither mercy nor grace, for they are altogether right, and nothing is lacking in them.

10 Pray inwardly, even if you do not enjoy it. It does good though you feel nothing, even though you think you are doing nothing.

11 When the soul gives up all for love, so that it can have him that is all, then it finds true rest.

12 It is true that sin is the cause of all this pain; but all shall be well, and all shall be well, and all manner of things shall be well.

13 God never deserts the soul, but abides there in bliss for ever.

14 Prayer oneth the soul to God.

15 Of all the pains that lead to salvation, this is the greatest, to see your love suffer. How could any pain be more to me than to see the one who is all my life, my bliss, my joy, suffer? Here I felt truly that I loved Christ so much more than myself that there was no pain I could suffer that could match the sorrow I had in seeing him in pain.

16 A mother may feed her child with her own milk, but our precious mother Jesus feeds us with himself, and does it with great courtesy and tenderness, in feeding us with the blessed sacrament that is the precious food of life.

14.19
William Langland (c.1330-1386)
English poet

1 Longsuffering is a sovereign virtue, and a swift vengeance. Who suffers more than God?

2 Adam, whilst he spake not, had paradise at will.

3 Chastity without charity lies chained in hell;
It is but an unlighted lamp.
Many chaplains are chaste,
but where is their charity?
There are no harder, hungrier men
than men of the church.

4 We should be low and lovelike and
lean each man to the other
And patient as pilgrims,
for pilgrims are we all.

5 Do not be ashamed to endure and to be needy, since he that made all the world chose to be needy.

6 My righteousness and right shall rule
In hell, and mercy over all mankind
before me
In heaven. I were an unkind king
If I did not help my kin.

14.20
Ludolf of Saxony (c.1300-1378)
Carthusian writer

1 If you want to draw fruit from the mysteries of Christ's life, you must offer yourself as present to whatever was said or done through our Lord Jesus Christ with the whole affective power of your mind, with loving care, with lingering delight; thus laying aside all other worries and cares... And though many of these are narrated as past events, you must meditate them all as though they were happening in the present moment.

14.21
Raymond Lull (c.1232-1316)
Spanish spiritual writer and missionary

1 Far above love is the Beloved; far beneath it is the lover; and Love, which lies between these two, makes the Beloved to descend to the lover and the Lover to rise toward the Beloved. And this ascending and descending is the being and the life to Love.

2 He who possesses patience possesses himself.

3 Truth walks by daylight, falsehood by night.

4 The shepherd who speaks ill of his flock speaks ill of himself.

5 The more you understand, the better you can believe.

6 The paths of love are both long and short. For love is clear, bright and pure, subtle yet simple, strong, diligent, brilliant, and abounding both in fresh thoughts and in old memories.

7 When you give, see that you give that which multiplies in giving.

14.22
Francesco Petrarch (1304-1374)
Italian poet

1 A good death does honour to a whole life.

2 To be able to say how much love, is to love but little.

14.23
Marguerite Porete (d.1310)
Spiritual writer, from Hainault (now part of France and Belgium)

1 No one is afraid to climb the heights, at least not if they have brave hearts and high courage. But the heart that is little from lack of love does not dare to undertake any great task, and does not venture to climb the heights.

14.24
Richard Rolle (1290-1349)
English hermit and spiritual writer

1 Let us make God the beginning and end of our love, for he is the fountain from which all good things flow and into him alone they flow back. Let him therefore be the beginning of our love.

2 We have a long way to go to heaven, and as many good deeds as we do, as many good prayers as we make, and as many good thoughts as we think in truth and hope and charity, by so many paces do we go heavenwards.

3 Some are deceived by too much abstinence from meat and drink and sleep. That is a temptation of the devil, to make them fall down in the middle of their work, so that they do not bring it to an end as they would have done if they had known reason and maintained discretion.

4 The name of Jesus is in my mind as a joyful song, in my ear a heavenly music, and in my mouth sweet honey.

14.25
Elisabeth Staeglin of Thöss
German mystic

1 Praise God!
I have been shown, as far as can be,
what God is and where God is...

I swim in the Godhead
like an eagle in air.

14.26
Henry Suso (c.1295-1365)
German mystic

1 In God, time and eternity are one and the same thing.

2 God has not called his servants to an ordinary, mediocre sort of life, but to the perfection of a sublime holiness: as he said to his disciples, 'Be perfect, as your heavenly Father is perfect.'

3 The cross possesses such power and strength that, whether they like it or not, it attracts and draws and carries away those who bear it.

4 Those who wish to live a spiritual life must not delude themselves that they can make progress in virtue unless they first apply themselves to gaining peace of mind and a good conscience. Christ loves to abide in pure and peaceful consciences, a fact that is quite understandable.

5 No mother could be quicker to snatch her child from a burning building that God is compelled to bring help to a penitent soul, even if the person has committed every imaginable sin a thousand times over.

6 I wish I could fight in your place, receiving in my own soul the attacks and wounds that you are enduring. But if I could do that, you would not then receive the palm of victory in heaven with the other soldiers of Christ.

7 Scrupulous people, forever tormented by doubts and anxiety, have hearts which are not well-prepared to receive Jesus Christ. Instead of that peace which religion is meant to give, these people make their lives miserable, and full of trouble and temptation. Scrupulous people distress themselves in many ways; in fact they believe no one, and no advice brings calm to their troubled spirits. They keep going back to their sins and doubts, and the more they brood over them, the more troubled they become.

8 They appear to be leading an austere life, but inwardly their passions still have full reign. They have fed and strengthened their own wills.

9 My beloved ones are surrounded by my love and are absorbed into the one thing: a love without images and without spoken words. They are gathered into me, the good from which they came forth.

14.27
Johann Tauler (1300-1361)
German Dominican mystic

1 God has all power in heaven and earth, but the power to do his work in man against man's will he has not got.

2 We should make ourselves poor, that we may altogether die, and in this dying be made alive again.

3 Therefore forsake everything for God, and then God will truly be given to you in everything.

4 We find more than a thousand testimonies in Scripture to the great usefulness of temptation; for it is a special sign of God's love for a person to be tempted and yet kept from falling.

14.28
Theognostus (?14c.)
Spiritual writer of the Eastern Church

1 When you realize that you have nothing and know nothing, then you will become rich in the Lord.

2 Be persuaded by me, all you who ardently and in all seriousness long for salvation: make haste, search persistently, ask ceaselessly, knock patiently, and continue until you reach your goal.

14.29
Theologia Germanica (late 14c.)
Anonymous mystical treatise

1 If you know yourself well, you are better and more praiseworthy before God, than if you did not know yourself, even though you understood the course of the heavens and all the planets and stars, the powers of all herbs, and the structure and dispositions of humankind, and also the nature of beasts and in such matters had all the skill of heaven and earth.

2 True peace and rest do not lie in outward things; if it were so, the Evil One would also have peace when things go according to his will.

3 What is paradise? All that is; for everything is good and pleasant, and so may fitly be called a paradise. It is said also that paradise is an outer court of heaven. In the same way this world is truly an outer court of the Eternal, or of eternity.

14.30
William of Occam (c.1300-1350)
English Franciscan philosopher

1 The knowledge of a simple [i.e. real] thing is never the sufficient cause for knowing another simple thing.

2 Nothing can be known naturally in itself, unless it is known intuitively. But God cannot be known by us intuitively from our natural powers.

14.31
John Wycliffe (?1330-1384)
English reformer

1 I believe that in the end truth will conquer.

2 This Bible is for the government of the people, by the people, and for the people.

3 There was good reason for the silence of the Holy Spirit as to how, when, in what form Christ ordained the apostles, the reason being to show the indifferency of all forms of words.

4 Our clerics neither evangelize like the apostles, nor go to war like the secular lords, nor toil like labourers.

5 The higher the hill, the stronger the wind: so the loftier the life, the stronger the enemy's temptations.

Fifteenth Century

15.1
Bernadine of Siena (1380-1444)
Italian Franciscan reformer

1 As flies are driven away by a great fire, so were the evil spirits driven away by her ardent love for God.

2 How would you like this wife of yours to be? 'I want her not to be greedy.' And you are always at your food! 'I'd like her to be active.' And you are a proper sluggard! 'I'd like her peaceful.' And you would burst into a rage at a straw if it crossed your feet! 'Obedient.' And you obey neither father nor mother nor anyone. You don't deserve her. 'I want a wife who is good and attractive and wise and well brought up.' My answer is that if you want her to be like this, then you must be the same.

3 When St Paul's voice was raised to preach the gospel to all nations, it was like a great clap of thunder up above. His preaching was a blazing fire, carrying all before it. It was the sun rising in full glory. Unbelief was consumed by it, wrong beliefs fled away, and the truth was made manifest like a great candle lighting the whole world with its bright flame.

4 By this action Christ our Master teaches us how in prayer we ought to use gestures by which the mind may be moved and uplifted, as we raise our eyes above, and join our hands, and bend our knees, using outward actions. Not that these outward signs make our prayer more effectual with God, for God is a searcher of hearts, and he is not moved by outward signs. But these actions are done, or ought to be done, so that you may know that body and soul are united in prayer.

15.2
Catherine of Genoa (1447-1510)
Italian mystic

1 I saw the body and the soul conversing together, arguing with one another. The soul was saying: God made me to love and to be

happy. So I would like to set out on a voyage of discovery to find out what it is that I am drawn to. Do come with me, of your own free will, for you too will share my joy. We will travel over the whole world together; if I find what pleases me, I will enjoy it. If you do the same, the one who finds more will be the truly happy one.

2 I do not believe it would be possible to find any joy that compares with that of a soul in purgatory, except for the joy of the blessed in paradise—a joy that goes on increasing day after day, as God more and more flows into the soul. And this he does abundantly in proportion as hindrances to his entrance are done away.

15.3
Vincent Ferrer (1350-1419)
Spanish Dominican preacher

1 Whoever proudly disputes and contradicts will always stand outside the door. Christ, the master of humility, reveals his truth only to the humble, and hides himself from the proud.

15.4
Frances of Rome (1384-1440)
Italian laywoman

1 It is most laudable in a married woman to be devout, but she must never forget that she is a housewife, and sometimes she must leave God at the altar to find him in her housekeeping.

15.5
Francis of Paola (c.1416-1507)
Italian Franciscan reformer

1 Pardon one another so that later on you will not remember the injury. The remembering of an injury is itself a wrong: it adds to our anger, feeds our sin and hates what is good. It is a rusty arrow and poison for the soul.

15.6
Lawrence Giustiniani (1381-1455)
Archbishop of Venice

1 God sets more store by our good will in all that we do than by the deeds themselves. Whether we devote ourselves to God in the work of contemplation, or whether we serve the needs of our neighbour in deeds of charity, we accomplish these things because the love of Christ urges us on.

15.7
Isabella of Spain (1451-1504)
Queen of Spain

1 In all human affairs there are things both certain and doubtful, and both are equally in the hands of God, who is accustomed to guide to a good end the causes that are just and are sought with diligence.

15.8
Joan of Arc (1412-1431)
French patriot, betrayed and executed

1 If I am not in God's grace, may God bring me there; if I am in it, may he keep me there.

2 I come, not in the strength of steel, but mailed in the panoply of righteousness, to offer my services to my king and country. I ask not the royal signet as a proof of my commission; my credentials are from heaven.

15.9
Margery Kempe (1373-c.1438)
English laywoman

1 [A clerical friend says to her:] 'Margery, you are welcome to me, for I have long been kept from you, and now our Lord has sent you here so that I may speak with you. Blessed may he be!' There was a dinner of great joy and gladness, much more spiritual than bodily, for it was given sauce and savour by stories from Holy Scriptures. And then he gave the said creature [i.e. Margery] a pair of knives, as a token that he would stand by her in God's cause, as he had done previously.

2 Our merciful Lord, speaking to her inwardly, reproached her for her fear, saying: 'Why are you in such dread? Why are you so afraid? I am as mighty here on the sea as on the land. Why do you mistrust me? All that I have promised you I will surely fulfil, and I will never deceive you.'

15.10
Nicholas of Cusa (1401-1464)
German philosopher

1 You, my God, are love who loves, and love who is lovable, and love who is the bond between these two.

2 You [Jesus Christ] are the Word of God humanified, and you are humanity deified.

3 We know about God what he is not, rather than what he is.

4 There is no way of comparing finite and infinite.

5 Led in learned ignorance to the mountain that is Christ... we come, as in a thinner cloud, to perceive him more clearly.

6 [God's face] is not seen unveiled until beyond all faces one enters into a certain secret and hidden silence where there is no knowledge or concept of a face... That very darkness reveals your face to be there, beyond all veils.

15.11
Nicholas of Flüe (1417-1487)
Swiss farmer, later recluse

1 O man, believe in God with all your might, for hope rests on faith, love on hope, and victory on love; the reward will follow victory, the crown of life the reward, and the crown is the essence of everything that is eternal.

15.12
Girolamo Savonarola (1452-1498)
Italian Dominican preacher and reformer

1 Nothing is more abhorrent to the tyrant than the service of Christ.

15.13
Nilus Sorsky (c.1433-1508)
Russian monk

1 Above all, pray for the gift of tears.

2 Listen to your heart.

3 As to the different kinds of food, we should take a little of everything, even sweets... We should never pick and choose, or push our food aside, but should thank God for everything.

4 It is useful for those whose faith is weak, or who are wavering, to abstain from certain foods especially the most palatable ones, because they have not enough faith in God's protection. As the Apostle says: 'The one who believes may eat everything, but the one who is weak should eat herbs'.

5 The fiend chooses for his most furious attacks the times when we feel most unable to pray.

15.14
Thomas à Kempis (c.1380-1471)
German spiritual writer

1 Give me grace ever to desire and to will what is most acceptable to thee and most pleasing in thy sight.

2 You will always have joy in the evening if you spend the day fruitfully.

3 Never be entirely idle; but either be reading, or writing, or praying, or meditating, or endeavouring something for the public good.

4 For a man to rejoice in adversity is not grievous to him who loves; for so to joy is to joy in the cross of Christ.

5 Suffer with Christ, and for Christ, if you desire to reign with Christ.

6 Have a good conscience and you will always have gladness.

7 Jesus now has many lovers of his heavenly kingdom, but few bearers of his cross.

8 If you bear your cross cheerfully, it will bear you.

9 What is required of you is faith and a sincere life, not loftiness of intellect or deep knowledge of the mysteries of God.

10 We are glad to want to make others perfect but we are not willing to correct our own fault.

11 How swiftly passes away the world's glory!

12 Man proposes but God disposes.

13 Humble yourself in everything.

14 Truly at the day of judgement we shall not be examined on what we have read, but what we have done; not how well we have spoken, but how religiously we have lived.

15 At least bear patiently, if you cannot bear joyfully.

16 We should have great peace if we did not busy ourselves with what others say and do.

17 A humble knowledge of yourself is a surer way to God than an extensive search after learning.

18 We feel and weigh soon enough what we suffer from others, but how much others suffer from us, of that we take no notice.

19 I would far rather feel compunction than know how to define it.

20 Sometimes we are filled with passion and we think it is zeal.

21 With God it is impossible that anything, however small, that is suffered for God's sake, should fail to meet with its reward.

PART 2

Sixteenth Century

If we recognize the Spirit of God as the unique fountain of truth, we shall never despise the truth wherever it may appear.

John Calvin
(1509-1564)

16.1
Arminius (Jakob Hermandszoon) (c.1560-1609)
Dutch Reformed Theologian

1 In his lapsed and sinful state, man is not capable, of and by himself, either to think or to will or to do that which is really good. But it is necessary for him to be regenerated and renewed in his intellect, affections or will and in all his powers, by God in Christ through the Holy Spirit, that he may be qualified rightly to understand, esteem, consider, will and perform whatever is truly good.

16.2
Thomas Becon (?1511-1567)
English Reformation theologian

1 For commonly, wheresoever God buildeth a church, the devil will build a chapel just by.

2 When the wine is in, the wit is out.

16.3
Thomas Bilney (d.1537)
English Protestant martyr

1 When I read that Christ Jesus came into the world to save sinners, it was as if day suddenly broke on a dark night.

16.4
Hermes Bolsec (d.1585)
French Carmelite monk

1 Faith depends not on election, but election on faith. God's grace is universal and some are not predestined to salvation more than others.

16.5
Katherine von Bora (1499-1552)
German nun, later wife to Martin Luther

1 Dear Lord, I thank thee for all the trials, through which thou didst lead me, and by which thou didst prepare me to behold thy Glory. Thou hast never forsaken nor forgotten me.

16.6
Francis Borgia (1510-1572)
Spanish Jesuit

1 Thou alone knowest best what is for my good. As I am not my own but altogether thine, so neither do I desire that my will be done, but thine, nor will I have any will but thine.

16.7
Charles Borromeo (1538-1584)
Archbishop of Milan, leader of the Counter-Reformation

1 If teaching and preaching is your job, then study diligently and apply yourself to whatever is necessary for doing the job well. Be sure that you first preach by the way you live. If you do not, people will notice that you say one thing, but live otherwise, and your words will bring only cynical laughter and a derisive shake of the head.

2 The best way not to find the bed too cold is to go to bed colder than the bed is.

3 He who desires to make any progress in the service of God must begin every day of his life with new ardour, must keep himself in the presence of God as much as possible, and must have no other view or end in all his actions but the divine honour.

16.8
John Bradford (1510-1555)
English Protestant martyr

1 [On seeing some criminals being taken to the gallows] But for the grace of God there goes John Bradford.

2 O Wisdom of the eternal Father, lighten my mind, that I may see only those things that please you and may be blinded to all other things. Grant that I may walk in your ways and that nothing else may be light and pleasant.

16.9
Alexander Briant (d.1581)
English Roman Catholic martyr

1 The first day that I was tortured upon the rack, before I came to the torture chamber, giving myself up to prayer, I was filled with a supernatural sweetness of spirit, and even while I was calling upon the Most Holy Name of Jesus and upon the Blessed Virgin Mary (for I was saying my rosary) my mind was cheerfully disposed, well comforted, and readily inclined and prepared to suffer and endure these torments.

16.10
Martin Bucer (1491-1551)
Alsace-born Reformation theologian

1 Flee formulae, bear with the weak. While all faith is placed in Christ, the thing is safe. It is not given for all to see the same thing at the same time.

2 [The five tasks of pastoral care are] to seek and to find all the lost; to bring back those that are scattered; to heal the wounded; to strengthen the sickly; to protect the healthy and to put them to pasture.

16.11
Christopher Buxton (d.1588)
English Roman Catholic martyr

1 I will not purchase corruptible life at so dear a rate; and indeed, if I had a hundred lives, I would willingly lay down all in defence of my faith.

16.12
Cajetan of Thiene (1480-1547)
Italian founder of the Theatine Order

1 I shall never cease to give all I can to those in need until I find myself reduced to such a state of poverty that there will scarcely remain to me five feet of earth for my grave or a penny for my funeral.

16.13
John Calvin (1509-1564)
French-born Reformation theologian

1 It is of the nature of man to feel pain, to be moved by it, to resist it nevertheless, and to accept consolations, but never to have no need of them.

2 I know not if I shall ever marry. If I did so, it would be in order to devote my time to the Lord, by being the more relieved from the worries of daily life.

3 They suspect everything we say. If I simply said it was daytime at high noon, they would begin to doubt it.

4 The entire sum of our wisdom, of that which deserves to be called true and certain wisdom, may be said to consist of two parts: namely, the knowledge of God and of ourselves.

5 What we think about [God] of ourselves is but foolishness and all we can say about him is without savour.

6 [God's] essence is so incomprehensible that his majesty is hidden, remote from all our senses.

7 The saints of the past have never known God otherwise that by looking to him in his Son, as in a mirror.

8 Because God does not speak to us every day from the heavens, and there are only the Scriptures alone, in which he has willed that his truth should be published and made known unto even the end, they can be fully certified to the faithful by no other warrant than this: that we hold it to be decreed and concluded that they came down from heaven, as though we heard God speaking from his own mouth.

9 In every part of the world, in heaven and earth, [God] has written and as it were engraven the glory of his power, goodness, wisdom and eternity.

10 For the little singing birds sang of God, the animals acclaimed him, the elements feared and the mountains resounded with him, the rivers and springs threw glances toward him, the grasses and the flowers smiled.

11 What is noblest and most to be valued in our souls is not only broken and wounded, but altogether corrupted, whatever of dignity it may reflect.

12 If we recognize the Spirit of God as the unique fountain of truth, we shall never despise the truth wherever it may appear, unless we wish to do dishonour to the Spirit of God; for the gifts of the Spirit cannot be disparaged without scorn and opprobrium to himself.

13 When it is a question of our justification, we have to put away all thinking about the Law and our works, to embrace the mercy of God alone, and to turn our eyes away from ourselves and upon Jesus Christ alone.

14 We ought not to dwell upon the vices of men, but rather contemplate in them the image of God, which by his excellence and dignity can and should move us to love them and forget all their vices which might turn us therefrom.

15 No one can enter into the glory of the heavenly kingdom unless he has been in this manner called and justified; seeing that without any exception the Lord promotes and manifests his election in this way in all the men he has elected.

16 Wherever we see the Word of God purely preached and heard, there a church of God exists, even if it swarms with many faults.

17 A sense of Deity is inscribed on every heart.

18 No one gives himself freely and willingly to God's service unless, having tasted his fatherly love, he is drawn to love and worship him in return.

19 My heart I give you, Lord, eagerly and entirely.

20 The real trouble-makers are those who prolong religious and social disorder by protecting it. Those reactionary conservatives who through their injustice and violence hold on to the lie, and who refuse to listen to the truth.

16.14
Edmund Campion (1540-1581)
English Jesuit, executed at Tyburn

1 Be it known unto you that we have made a league—all the Jesuits in the world—cheerfully to carry the cross that you shall lay upon us and never to despair your recovery while we have a man left to enjoy your Tyburn, or to be racked with your torments, or to be consumed with your prisons. The expense is reckoned, the enterprise is begun; it is of God—it cannot be withstood. So the Faith was planted, so it must be restored.

16.15
Peter Canisius (1521-1597)
Jesuit theologian

1 Let the world indulge its madness, for it cannot endure and passes like a shadow. It is growing old, and I think, is in its last decrepit stage. But we, buried deep in the wounds of Christ, why should we be dismayed?

2 At the mention of this name [Blessed Virgin Mary] the angels rejoice and the devils tremble; through this invocation sinners obtain grace and pardon.

16.16
Sebastien Castellio (1515-1563)
French Bible translator

1 To kill a man is not to defend a doctrine, but to kill a man.

16.17
John Colet (1467-1519)
English theologian and humanist scholar

1 Love God.
Thrust down pride.
Forgive gladly.

16.18
Vittoria Colonna (1490-1547)
Influential Italian Roman Catholic

1 When writhe the Saviour's shoulders on the tree
And droops the holy body from the weight
Is there then no key to fit the gate
That heaven should not open for to see?

16.19
Miles Coverdale (1488-1568)
English Bible translator

1 Whereas some men think translations make divisions in the faith, that is not so, for it was never better with the congregation of God than when every church almost had a sundry translation. Would to God it had never been left off after the time of St Augustine, then we should never have come into such blindness and ignorance, such errors and delusions.

16.20
Thomas Cranmer (1489-1556)
Archbishop of Canterbury and main compiler of the Book of Common Prayer

1 Therefore, every man that cometh to the reading of this holy book ought to bring with him first and foremost this fear of Almighty God, and then next a firm and stable purpose to reform his own self according thereunto.

2 [Matrimony] was ordained for the mutual society, help, and comfort, that the one ought to have of the other, both in prosperity and adversity.

3 In the Scriptures be the fat pastures of the soul; therein is no venomous meat, no unwholesome thing; they be the very dainty and pure feeding. He that is ignorant, shall find there what he should learn.

4 O Lord our God,
give us by your Holy Spirit
a willing heart and a ready hand
to use all your gifts to your praise and glory.

5 [At the stake] This was the hand that wrote it [his recantation], therefore it shall suffer first punishment.

16.21
Thomas Cromwell (?1485-1540)
Chief organizer of the dissolution of the monasteries in England

1 O Lord Jesu, who art the only health of all men living, and the everlasting life of those who die in thy faith: I give myself wholly unto thy will, being sure that the thing cannot perish which is committed unto thy mercy.

16.22
Edward Dering (?1540-1576)
English Puritan clergyman

1 The weight of sin is not in substance of matter, but in the majesty of God that is offended, and be the thing never so little, yet the breach of his commandment deserveth death.

2 Though a man had all the wisdom of the world and by his wit could compass upon earth what his heart could wish, yet if he fail in providing for true happiness all his wisdom is but madness.

16.23
Francis Drake (?1540-1596)
English admiral

1 There must be a beginning of any great matter, but the continuing unto the end until it be thoroughly finished yields the true glory.

16.24
Elizabeth I (1533-1603)
Queen of England

1 O Lord, thou hast set me on high. My flesh is frail and weak. If I therefore at any time forget thee, touch my heart, O Lord, that I may again remember thee. If I swell against thee, pluck me down in my own conceit.

2 The eyes of all things do look up and trust in thee; O Lord, thou givest them their meat in due season, thou dost open thy hand and fillest with thy blessing everything living.

3 [Speech to Members of Parliament] I am your anointed Queen. I will never be by

violence constrained to do anything. I thank God that I am endued with such qualities that if I were turned out of the Realm in my petticoat, I were able to live in any place in Christome.

4 Though God hath raised me high, yet this I count the glory of my crown that I have reigned with your loves.

5 I think that, at the worst, God has not ordained that England shall perish.

6 I would not open windows into men's souls.

7 'Twas God the word that spake it,
He took the bread and brake it;
And what the word did make it,
That I believe, and take it.

8 If thy heart fails thee, climb not at all.

9 [To the Countess of Nottingham] God may pardon you, but I never can.

10 [To the wife of the Archbishop of Canterbury, expressing her disapproval of married clergy] Madam I may not call you; mistress I am ashamed to call you; and so I know not what to call you; but howsoever, I thank you.

11 All my possessions for a moment of time.

16.25
Jerome Emiliani (1481-1537)

Venetian priest, worker for the poor, the sick, orphans and prostitutes

1 God wishes to test you like gold in the furnace. The dross is consumed by the fire, but the pure gold remains and its value increases.

16.26
Desiderius Erasmus (1467-1536)

Dutch humanist scholar

1 No gift is more precious than good advice.

2 I would to God that a ploughman would sing a text of the scripture at his plough and that the weaver would hum them to the tune of his shuttle.

3 These writings bring back to you the living image of that most holy mind, the very Christ himself speaking, healing, dying, rising, in fact so entirely present, that you would see less of him if you beheld him with your eyes.

4 If elephants can be trained to dance, lions to play, and leopards to hunt, surely preachers can be taught to preach.

5 Sever me from myself
that I may be grateful to you;
may I perish to myself
that I may be safe in you;
may I die to myself
that I may live in you;
may I wither to myself
that I may blossom in you;
may I be emptied of myself
that I may abound in you;
may I be nothing to myself
that I may be all to you.

6 The great part of Christianity is wholeheartedly to want to become a Christian.

7 [Of faith] Believe that you have it, and you have it.

8 By identifying the new learning with heresy we make orthodoxy synonymous with ignorance.

9 It is the chiefest point of happiness that a man is willing to be what he is.

10 No one respects a talent that is concealed.

11 Fruitless is the wisdom of him who has no knowledge of himself.

12 Let others wear the martyr's crown; I am not worthy of this honour.

16.27
John Fisher (1469-1535)

Bishop of Rochester, scholar and martyr

1 Our chiefest labour in prayer must be to inflame and set our hearts on fire, with this fervency of charity, and then as it were to spin out our prayer, so long until we have attained unto this end. But when through weariness of our frail body we find this heat and fervour in us to grow cold, then must we desist and pray no longer, but presently apply ourselves to some other works of virtue.

16.28
John Foxe (1516-1587)
Martyrologist

1 I have never made any statement that I knew to be untrue.

2 [Parishioners in Hadleigh, Suffolk] became exceedingly well learned in the Holy Scriptures, as well women as men, so that a man might have found among them many that had often read the whole Bible through, and that could have said a great sort of St Paul's epistles by heart, and very well and readily have given a godly learned sentence in any matter of controversy.

16.29
John Frith (c.1503-1533)
English Reformation scholar

1 The people should come together to hear God's word, receive the sacraments, and give God thanks. That done, they may return to their houses, and do their business as well as on any other day.

16.30
Aloysius Gonzaga (1568-1591)
Italian Jesuit

1 I confess that I am bewildered and lose myself at the thought of the divine goodness, a sea without shore and fathomless, a God who calls me to an eternal rest after such short and tiny labours—summons and calls me to heaven, to that supreme Good that I sought so negligently, and promises me the fruit of those tears that I sowed so sparingly.

2 I believe my days are few. I feel such an extraordinary desire to work and to serve God, I feel it so passionately, that I cannot believe God would have given it to me if he did not mean to take me away at once.

16.31
Richard Greenham (?1535-?1594)
English Puritan minister

1 The seat of faith is not in the brain, but in the heart, and the head is not the place to keep the promises of God, but the heart is the chest to lay them up in.

2 To a mind which misliketh this world, nothing can come so welcome as death, because it takes him out of the world.

3 Paradise is our native country, and we in this world be as exiles and strangers.

16.32
John Hamilton (1511-1571)
Archbishop of St Andrews and Benedictine monk

1 Meekness is love at school, at the school of Christ. It is the disciple learning to know, and fear, and distrust himself, and learning of him who is meek and lowly of heart, and so finding rest to his soul.

16.33
Richard Hooker (1554-1600)
English Anglican theologian

1 He that goeth about to persuade a multitude, that they are not so well governed as they ought to be, shall never want attentive and favourable hearers.

2 Of Law there can be no less acknowledged, than that her seat is the bosom of God, her voice the harmony of the world: all things in heaven and earth do her homage, the very least as feeling her care, and the greatest as not exempted from her power.

3 Alteration though it be from worse to better hath in it inconveniences, and those weighty.

4 I hold it for a most infallible rule in the exposition of scripture, that when a literal construction will stand, the furthest from the literal is commonly the worst.

5 The Church is in Christ as Eve was in Adam.

6 Sacraments are the powerful instruments of God to eternal life. For as our natural body consisteth in the union of the body with the soul, so our life supernatural is in the union of the soul with God.

7 With us one society is both Church and Commonwealth... which people are not part of them the Commonwealth, and part of them the Church of God, but the selfsame people whole and entire.

8 The power of the ministry of God translateth out of darkness into glory; it raiseth men from the earth, and bringeth God himself down from heaven.

16.34
John Hooper (d.1555)
English Protestant martyr and bishop

1 [Written the night before his execution as a heretic.]

Let nothing cause thy heart to fail;
Launch out thy boat, hoist up thy sail,
Put from the shore;
And be sure thou shalt attain
Unto the port that shall remain
For evermore.

2 [Upon being urged to recant, or be burned—since 'Life is sweet and death is bitter'] True, quite true! But eternal life is more sweet, and eternal death is more bitter.

16.35
Ignatius of Loyola (1491-1556)
Spanish founder of the Society of Jesus

1 I desire and choose poverty with Christ poor, rather than riches; insults with Christ loaded with them, rather than honours;
I desire to be accounted as worthless and a fool for Christ rather than to be esteemed as wise and prudent in this world. So Christ was treated before me.

2 Let him who is in consolation think how it will be with him in the desolation that will follow, laying up fresh strength for that time.

3 Obedience is a whole burnt-offering in which the entire man, without the slightest reserve, is offered in the fire of charity to his Creator and Lord by the hands of his ministers.

4 It is better to keep silence and to be, than to talk and not to be.

5 A bishop is most like God when he is silent.

6 We must take care lest, by exalting the merit of faith, without adding any distinction of explanation, we furnish people with a pretext for relaxing in the practice of good works.

7 We must adapt the Society [of Jesus] to the times, not the times to the Society.

8 Although it is true that no one can be saved unless he is predestined, and has faith and grace, we must be very careful how we speak and treat these subjects.

9 It is true that the voice of God, having once fully penetrated the heart, becomes strong as the tempest and loud as the thunder; but before reaching the heart it is as weak as a light breath which scarcely agitates the air. It shrinks from noise, and is silent amid agitation.

10 Teach us, good Lord, to serve thee
as thou deservest;
To give, and not to count the cost,
To fight, and not to heed the wounds,
To toil, and not to seek for rest,
To labour, and not to ask for any reward
Save that of knowing that we do thy will.

11 Let us work as if success depended upon ourselves alone; but with heartfelt conviction that we are doing nothing and God everything.

16.36
Bishop John Jewell (1522-1571)
Bishop of Salisbury

1 A bishop should die preaching.

2 In old time we had treen chalices and golden priests, but now we have treen priests and golden chalices.

16.37
John of Avila (1500-1569)
Spanish mystic

1 Those who imagine they can attain to holiness by any wisdom or strength of their own will find themselves after many labours, and struggles, and weary efforts, only the farther from possessing it, and this in proportion to their certainty that they of themselves have gained it.

2 I pray God may open your eyes and let you see what hidden treasures he bestows on us in the trials from which the world thinks only to flee.

3 One act of thanksgiving when things go wrong with us is worth a thousand thanks when things are agreeable to our inclination.

4 What our Creator and Redeemer puts into the heart and what moves it most to piety is the best.

16.38
John of the Cross (1542-1591)
Spanish Carmelite mystic

1 God passes through the thicket of the world, and wherever his glance falls he turns all things to beauty.

2 Never listen to accounts of the frailties of others and if anyone should complain to you of another, humbly ask him not to speak of him at all.

3 Live in the world as if God and your soul only were in it; that your heart may be captive to no earthly thing.

4 Keep your heart in peace; let nothing in this world disturb it: everything has an end.

5 There cannot be perfect transformation without perfect pureness.

6 Seek by reading, and you will find meditating; cry in prayer, and the door will be opened in contemplation.

7 An instant of pure love is more precious to God and the soul, and more profitable to the church, than all other good works together, though it may seem as if nothing were done.

8 Where there is no love, pour love in, and you will draw love out.

9 In the evening of our lives we shall be examined in love.

10 Love of God and love of created things are contrary the one to the other; two contraries cannot coexist in one and the same person.

11 The soul that is united with God is feared by the devil as though it were God himself.

12 Love unites the soul with God and the more love the soul has the more powerfully it enters into God and is centred on him.

13 All visions, revelations, heavenly feelings and whatever is greater than these, are not worth the least act of humility, being the fruits of that charity which neither values nor seeks itself, which thinketh well, not of self, but of others. Many souls, to whom visions have never come, are incomparably more advanced in the way of perfection than others to whom many have been given.

14 Contemplation is nothing else but a secret, peaceful, and loving infusion of God, which, if admitted, will set the soul on fire with the Spirit of love.

15 Ecstasy is naught but the going forth of a soul from itself and its being caught up in God, and this is what happens to the soul that is obedient, namely, that it goes forth from itself and from its own desires, and thus lightened, becomes immersed in God.

16 In sorrow and suffering, go straight to God with confidence, and you will be strengthened, enlightened and instructed.

17 The purest suffering hears and carries in its train the purest understanding.

18 One who does not seek the cross of Jesus isn't seeking the glory of Christ.

19 The soul of one who loves God always swims in joy, always keeps holiday, and is always in a mood for singing.

20 A dark night through which the soul passes in order to attain to the Divine light of the perfect union of the love of God.

21 That you may have pleasure in everything
Seek your own pleasure in nothing.
That you may know everything
Seek to know nothing.
That you may possess all things
Seek to possess nothing.
That you may be everything
Seek to be nothing.

22 My spirit has become dry because it forgets to feed on you.

23 Faith tells us of things we have never seen, and cannot come to know by our natural senses.

24 In order to arrive at that which thou knowest not,
Thou must go by a way that thou knowest not.
In order to arrive at that which thou possessest not
Thou must go by a way that thou possessest not.

25 I die because I do not die.

16.39
John of God (1495-1550)
Spanish founder of the Brothers Hospitallers

1 Just as water extinguishes a fire, so love wipes away sin.

16.40
John Knox (1505-1572)
Scottish Protestant and controversialist

1 The word of God is plain in itself; and if there appear any obscurity in one place, the Holy Ghost, which is never contrarious to himself, explains the same more clearly in other places.

2 In youth, in middle age, and now after many battles, I find nothing in me but corruption.

3 The Lord sanctify and bless you,
the Lord pour the riches of his grace
upon you,
that you may please him
and live together in holy love
to your lives' end.
So be it.

4 A man with God is always in the majority.

5 [Title of Pamphlet, 1558] The First Blast of the Trumpet Against the Monstrous Regiment of Women.

6 Live in Christ, live in Christ, and the flesh need not fear death.

7 The notes of the true Kirk, therefore, we believe, confess and avow to be: first, the true preaching of the Word of God, in which God has revealed himself to us, as the writings of the prophets and apostles declare; secondly, the right administration of the sacraments of Christ Jesus, with which must be associated the Word and promise of God to seal and confirm them in our hearts; and lastly, ecclesiastical discipline uprightly ministered, as God's Word prescribes, whereby vice is repressed and virtue nourished.

16.41
Stanislaus Kostka (c.1550-1568)
Young Polish Jesuit

1 I find a heaven in the midst of saucepans and brooms.

16.42
Hugh Latimer (1485-1555)
Bishop, preacher, Reformer, burnt at the stake

1 Who is the most diligent bishop and prelate in England? I will tell you. It is the devil. He is never out of his diocese. The devil is diligent at his plough.

2 [In a sermon before Edward VI] 'Take heed and beware of covetousness.'... 'Take heed and beware of covetousness.'... 'Take heed and beware of covetousness.'... What if I should say nothing else these three or four hours?

3 [In a sermon before Henry VIII] Latimer! Latimer! Latimer! Be careful what you say. Henry the king is here. [Pause.] Latimer! Latimer! Latimer! Be careful what you say. The King of kings is here.

4 The drop of rain maketh a hole in the stone, not by violence, but by oft falling.

5 We must first be made good
before we can do good;
we must first be made just
before our works can please God.

6 Wherever you see persecution, there is more than a probability that truth is on the persecuted side.

7 [Prior to being burnt for heresy] Be of good comfort Master Ridley, and play the man. We shall this day light such a candle by God's grace in England, as (I trust) shall never be put out.

16.43
Luis de Leon (c.1527-1591)
Augustinian canon and theologian

1 Christ is given so many names because of his limitless greatness and the treasury of his very rich perfections and with them the host of functions and other benefits which are born in him and spread over us. Just as they cannot be embraced by the soul's vision, so much less can a single word name them.

16.44
Leonardo da Vinci
Italian painter, sculptor, architect and engineer

1 Life well spent is long.

2 Iron rusts from disuse; stagnant water loses its purity and in cold weather becomes frozen; even so does inaction sap the vigour of the mind.

16.45
Martin Luther (1485-1546)
German monk and theologian, leader of the Protestant Reformation

1 I felt myself absolutely born again. The gates of Paradise had been flung open and I had entered. There and then the whole of scripture took on another look to me.

2 This epistle [Romans] is in truth the most important document in the New Testament, the gospel in its purest expression. Not only is it well worth a Christian's while to know it word for word by heart, but also to meditate on it day by day. It is the soul's daily bread, and can never be read too often, or too much.

3 We reach the conclusion that faith alone justifies us and fulfils the law; and this because faith brings us the spirit gained by the merits of Christ. The spirit, in turn, gives us the happiness and freedom at which the law aims; and this shows that good works really proceed from faith.

4 Faith, however, is something that God effects in us.

5 Flesh and spirit must not be understood as if flesh had only to do with moral impurity, and spirit only with the state of our hearts. Rather, flesh... means everything that is born from the flesh, i.e. the entire self, body and soul, including our reason and all our senses.

6 A man who is in the grip of fear or distress speaks of disaster in a quite different way from one who is filled with happiness; and a man who is filled with joy speaks and sings about happiness quite differently from one who is in the grip of fear.

7 I shall set down the following two propositions concerning the freedom and the bondage of the spirit: A Christian is a perfectly free lord of all, subject to none. A Christian is a perfectly dutiful servant of all, subject to all.

8 [The commandments] are intended to teach man to know himself, that through them he may recognize his inability to do good and may despair of his own ability.

9 Works, being inanimate things, cannot glorify God, although they can, if faith is present, be done to the glory of God.

10 Not only are we [Christians] the freest of kings, we are also priests forever, which is far

more excellent than being kings, for as priests we are worthy to appear before God to pray for others and to teach one another divine things.

11 There are a few who preach Christ and read about him that they may move men's affections to sympathy with Christ, to anger against the Jews, and such childish and effeminate nonsense. Rather ought Christ to be preached to the end that faith in him may be established that he may not only be Christ, but be Christ for you and me, and that what is said of him and is denoted in his name may be effectual in us.

12 Behold, from faith thus flow forth love and joy in the Lord, and from love a joyful, willing, and free mind that serves one's neighbour willingly and takes no account of gratitude or ingratitude, of praise or blame, of gain or loss.

13 There are very many who, when they hear of this freedom of faith, immediately turn it into an occasion for the flesh and think that now all things are allowed them.

14 As wealth is the test of poverty, business the test of faithfulness, honours the test of humility, feasts the test of temperance, pleasures the test of chastity, so ceremonies are the test of the righteousness of faith.

15 Do we work nothing for the attaining of this righteousness? I answer: Nothing at all. For the nature of this righteousness is, to do nothing, to hear nothing, to know nothing whatsoever of the low or of works, but to know and to believe this only, that Christ is gone to the Father and is not now seen; that he is seated in heaven at the right hand of his Father, not as a judge, but made for us by God wisdom, righteousness, holiness and redemption.

16 When we have thus taught faith in Christ, thẽn do we teach also good works. Because thou hast laid hold upon Christ by faith, through whom thou art made righteous, begin now to work well.

17 Because he [the Christian] feels all things within sweet and comfortable, therefore he does and suffers all things willingly. But when a man walks in his own righteousness, whatever he does is grievous and tedious to him, because he is doing it unwillingly.

18 This must be our ground and anchor-hold, that Christ is our only perfect righteousness.

19 These are fine, heart-warming words—that God wants to come down to us, God wants to come to us and we do not need to clamber up to him, he wants to be with us to the end of the world.

20 In this way, I take it, the word of Christ is reconciled with the passages which establish the sword, so that this is the meaning: no Christian shall wield or invoke the sword for himself and for his cause; but for another he can and ought to wield and invoke it, that wickedness may be hindered and godliness defended.

21 Probably one of our greatest needs is to abolish all mendicancy everywhere in Christendom. No one living among Christians ought to go begging. It would be an easy law to make, if only we dared, and were in earnest that every town should support its own poor.

22 Too many Christians envy the sinners their pleasures and the saint their joy, because they don't have either one.

23 The feast we call the Annunciation to Mary, when the angel came to her and brought her the message from God, may fitly be called the Feast of Christ's humanity, for then our deliverance began.

24 There will be little dogs, with golden hair, shining like precious stones.

25 The best thing you can do is to rap the devil on the nose at the very start. Act like that man who, whenever his wife began to nag and snap at him, drew out his flute from under his belt and played merrily until she was exhausted and let him alone.

26 Here stand I. I can do no other. God help me. Amen.

16.46
Mary Queen of Scots (1542-1589)
Queen of Scotland

1 In my end is my beginning.

2 O Lord my God, I have hoped in thee,
O dear Jesus, set me free.
Though hard the chains that fasten me,
And sore my lot, yet I long for thee.
I languish and groaning bend my knee,
Adoring, imploring, O set me free.

3 I fear John Knox's prayers more than any army of ten thousand men.

16.47
Mary Tudor (1516-1558)
Queen of England

1 When I am dead and opened, you shall find 'Calais' lying in my heart.

16.48
Philip Melanchthon (1497-1560)
Humanist scholar and Lutheran theologian

1 To know Christ is not to speculate about the mode of his incarnation, but to know his saving benefits.

2 To you, O Son of God, Lord Jesus Christ, as you pray to the eternal Father, we pray, make us one in him. Lighten our personal distress and that of our society. Receive us into the fellowship of those who believe. Turn our hearts, O Christ, to everlasting truth and healing harmony.

3 We do better to adore the mysteries of deity than to investigate them.

4 Unless you know why Christ put on flesh and was nailed to the cross, what good will it do you to know merely the history about him?

16.49
Angela Merici (1474-1540)
Born in Lombardy, founder of the Ursuline Order, the first great teaching order for women

1 In the fulfilment of your duties, let your intentions be so pure that you reject from your actions any other motive than the glory of God and the salvation of souls.

2 Our Saviour says that a good tree, that is, a good heart as well as a soul on fire with charity, can do nothing but good and holy works. This is why St Augustine could say 'Love, and do what you will'—that is, possess love and charity, and then do what you will. It is as though he said 'Charity cannot sin'.

3 Consider that the devil does not sleep, but seeks our ruin in a thousand ways.

4 In order to become an instrument in God's hands we must be of no account in our own eyes.

16.50
Paul Miki (1562-1597)
Japanese Jesuit martyr

1 My religion teaches me to pardon my enemies and all who have offended me.

16.51
Thomas More (1478-1535)
English statesman, author and martyr

1 These things, good Lord, that we pray for, give us Thy grace to labour for.

2 [Personal prayer for use whilst in the Tower] Give me, good Lord, a humble, lowly, quiet, peaceable, patient, charitable, kind, tender and pitiful mind; with all my works and all my words and all my thoughts to have a taste of the holy blessed spirit.

3 The devil... the proud spirit... cannot endure to be mocked.

4 The devil is ready to put out men's eyes that are content willing to wax blind.

5 Men desire authority for its own sake that they may bear a rule, command and control other men, and live uncommanded and uncontrolled themselves.

6 Comfort in tribulation can be secured only on the sure ground of faith holding as true the words of Scripture and the teaching of the Church.

7 For what is fame in itself but the blast of another man's mouth as soon passed as spoken?

8 It is a shorter thing, and sooner done, to write heresies, than to answer them.

9 When we feel us too bold, remember our own feebleness. When we feel us too faint, remember Christ's strength.

10 Occupy your minds with good thoughts, or the enemy will fill them with bad ones: unoccupied they cannot be.

11 A man may very well lose his head and yet come to no harm—yea, I say, to unspeakable good and everlasting happiness.

12 Is not this house [the Tower of London] as nigh heaven as my own?

13 What wholesome receipt this is. 'Remember,' saith this bill, 'thy last things, and thou shalt never sin in this world.' Here is first a short medicine containing only four herbs, common and well known, that is to wit, death, doom, pain, and joy.

14 [On the scaffold] See me safe up: for my coming down I can shift for myself.

15 [Last letter to daughter Margaret Roper] Farewell my dear child and pray for me, and I shall for you and all your friends that we may merrily meet in heaven.

16.52 Philip Neri (1515-1595)

Italian priest, founder of the Oratory

1 Christian joy is a gift of God flowing from a good conscience.

2 I will have no sadness in my house.

3 O Lord, put no trust in me; for I shall surely fail if Thou uphold me not.

4 Bear the cross and do not make the cross bear you.

5 The greatness of God must be tested by the desire we have of suffering for his sake.

6 As a rule, people who aim at a spiritual life begin with the sweet and afterwards pass on to the bitter.

7 Leave something for the angels.

8 Cast yourself into the arms of God and be very sure that if He wants anything of you, He will fit you for the work and give you strength.

9 Entire conformity and resignation to the divine will is truly a road on which we cannot go wrong, and it is the only road that leads us to taste and enjoy that peace which sensual and earthly men know nothing of.

10 A glad spirit attains to perfection more quickly than any other.

11 It is an old custom of the servants of God to have some little prayer ready and to be frequently darting them up to Heaven during the day, lifting their minds to God out of the mire of this world. He who adopts this plan will get great fruits with little pains.

16.53 John Northbrooke

English preacher

1 We must take heed that in the church nothing be sung without choice, but only those things which are contained in the holy scriptures, or which are by just reason gathered out of them, and do exactly agree with the word of God.

16.54
Mary Magdelene Dei Pazzi (1566-1607)
Italian Carmelite mystic

1 All for God and nothing for self.

2 Poverty should be the badge of religious; and as men of the world distinguish their property by stamping it with their names, so the works of religious should be known to be such by the mark of holy poverty.

3 Holy Spirit, Spirit of truth, you are the reward of the saints, the comforter of souls, light in the darkness, riches to the poor, treasure to lovers, food for the hungry, comfort to those who are wandering; to sum up, you are the one in whom all treasures are contained.

16.55
William Perkins (1558-1602)
English Puritan theologian

1 A man that does but begin to be converted is even at that instant the very child of God, though inwardly he be more carnal than spiritual... The first material beginnings of the conversion of a sinner, or the smallest measure of renewing grace, have the promises of this life and the life to come.

2 A constant and earnest desire to be reconciled to God, to believe and to repent, if it be in a touched heart is accepted by God as reconciliation, faith, repentance itself.

3 To see and feel in ourselves the lack of any grace pertaining to salvation, and to be grieved therefore, is the grace itself.

16.56
Peter of Alcantara (1499-1562)
Spanish Franciscan and spiritual writer

1 We should endeavour to unite meditation and contemplation, making the first a ladder for attaining to the second.

16.57
Catherine dei Ricci (1522-1590)
Italian-born Dominican mystic

1 The sooner you forgive him, the sooner he will recover from his illness. You are the person to restore him to health of soul and body. Speak to your son again. Do not refuse me, Father! If I am truly your daughter and you love me as much as you profess, you will grant me what I ask.

16.58
Nicholas Ridley (1500-1555)
Bishop of London, preacher, burnt at the stake

1 I confess that Christ's body is in the sacrament in this respect; because there is in it the Spirit of Christ, that is the power of the Word of God, which not only feedeth the soul but cleanseth it.

2 It was a great pity and a lamentable thing to have seen in many places the people so loathsomely and unreligiously to come to the Holy Communion and to the Common Prayer... in comparison of that blind zeal and indiscreet devotion which they had aforetime to those things whereof they understood never one whit.

3 I cannot burn. Good people, let me have more fire.

16.59
Rose of Lima (d.1586)
Peruvian saint, the first canonized saint of America

1 No one would complain about his cross or about troubles that may happen to him if he could come to know the scales on which they are weighed when they are distributed to men.

2 Our Lord and Saviour lifted up his voice and said with incomparable majesty: 'Let all men know that grace comes after tribulation. Let them know that without the burden of afflictions it is impossible to reach the height of grace. Let them know that the gifts of grace increase as the struggles increase.'

16.60
Philip Sidney (1554-1586)
English poet and soldier

1 Biting my truant pen, beating myself
for spite:
'Fool!' said my Muse to me, 'look in thy
heart and write.'

2 There have been many most excellent poets that have never versified, and now swarm many versifiers that need never answer to the name of poets.

3 They love indeed who quake to say they love.

4 Laughter almost ever cometh of things most disproportioned to our selves, and nature. Delight hath a joy in it either permanent or present. Laughter hath only a scornful tickling.

5 Comedy is an imitation of the common errors of our life.

6 Shallow brooks murmur most, deep silent slide away.

7 [Giving his water bottle to a wounded soldier after he himself had been wounded] Thy need is yet greater than mine.

8 Love my memory; cherish my friends; but above all, govern your will and affection by the will and word of your creator; in me beholding the end of this world, with all her vanities.

16.61
Menno Simons (1496-1561)
Anabaptist leader in Holland and north-west Germany, whose followers became known as Mennonites

1 We have not a single command in the Scriptures that infants are to be baptized, or that the apostles practised it, therefore we confess with good sense that infant baptism is nothing but human invention and notion.

2 We are not regenerated because we are baptized... but we are baptized because we are regenerated.

3 [The 'true and natural fruits of the new heavenly birth' are] humility, long-suffering, mercy, pure and chaste love, true faith, certain knowledge, sure hope, obedience to God, spiritual joy, inward peace and an unblameable life.

16.62
Robert Southwell (1561-1595)
English Roman Catholic poet and martyr

1 Times go by turns, and chances change
by course,
From foul to fair, from better hap to worse.

2 To rise by other's fall
I deem a losing gain;
All states with others' ruins built
To ruin run amain.

3 Much sorrow for the dead is either the child of self-love or rash judgement.

4 Christianity is a warfare, and Christians spiritual soldiers.

5 There are many among the martyrs of my age or younger, and as weak or weaker than I; but the Divine Grace that did not fail them will sustain me.

16.63
Edmund Spenser (c.1552-1599)
English poet

1 So let us love, dear love, like as we ought;
Love is the lesson which the Lord us taught.

16.64
Thomas Tallis (?1505-1585)
Organist and composer

1 To God who gives our daily bread
A thankful song we raise,
And pray that he who sends us food
May fill our hearts with praise.

16.65
Teresa of Avila (1515-1582)
Spanish Carmelite mystic

1 To wish to act like angels while we are still in this world is nothing but folly.

2 Contemplation is a gift of God which is not necessary for salvation nor for earning our eternal reward, nor will anyone require you to possess it.

3 There is no such thing as bad weather. All weather is good because it is God's.

4 Nothing is small if God accepts it.

5 Rapture, being drawn out of oneself by God, is an experience in which one learns that God is the stronger.

6 Die! Die as the silkworm does when it has fulfilled the office of its creation, and you will see God and be immersed in His Greatness, as the little silkworm is enveloped in its cocoon. Understand that when I say 'you will see God', I mean in the manner described, in which He manifests Himself in this kind of union.

7 God gives when he will, as he will and to whom he will.

8 God deliver us from sullen saints.

9 Settle yourself in solitude and you will come upon Him in yourself.

10 Don't imagine that if you had a great deal of time you would spend more of it in prayer. Get rid of that idea! Again and again God gives more in a moment than in a long period of time, for his actions are not measured by time at all.

11 We need no wings to go in search of Him, but have only to find a place where we can be alone—and look upon Him present within us.

12 Making my will one with the will of God, this is the union which I myself desire and should like to see in everyone, and not just a few of those raptures, however delightful, which go by the name of union.

13 Let nothing disturb you,
nothing frighten you;
All things are passing;
God never changes;
Patient endurance
Attains all things;
Whoever possesses God
Lacks nothing;
God alone suffices.

14 Know that even when you are in the kitchen, our Lord moves amidst the pots and pans.

15 Remember that there must be someone to cook the meals, and count yourselves happy in being able to serve like Martha.

16 Our Lord does not care so much for the importance of our works as for the love with which they are done.

17 It is not a matter of thinking a great deal but of loving a great deal, so do whatever arouses you most to love.

18 We are always in the presence of God, yet it seems to me that those who pray are in his presence in a very different sense.

19 The soul which gives itself to prayer—whether a lot or only a little—must absolutely not have limits set on it.

20 To reach something good it is very useful to have gone astray, and thus acquire experience.

21 Do not think of the faults of others but of what is good in them and faulty in yourself.

22 To give our Lord a good hospitality, Mary and Martha must combine.

23 Cursed be that loyalty which reaches so far as to go against the law of God.

24 Untilled ground, however rich, will bring forth thistles and thorns; so also the mind of man.

25 In all created things discern the Providence and wisdom of God, and in all things give Him thanks.

26 It is a great grace of God to practise self-examination; but too much is as bad as too little.

27 God is full of compassion, and never fails those who are afflicted and despised, if they trust in him alone.

16.66
Thomas of Villanova (1488-1555)
Spanish archbishop, healer and preacher

1 The bush seen by Moses, which burnt without being consumed, was a real symbol of Mary's heart.

16.67
William Tyndale (?1492-1536)
Father of the English Bible, scholar and translator

1 [In an argument with a scholar] If God spare my life, ere many years I will cause a boy who drives the plough to know more of the scriptures than you do.

2 Marriage was ordained for a remedy and to increase the world and for the man to help the woman and the woman the man, with all love and kindness.

3 Faith is, then, a lively and steadfast trust in the favour of God, wherewith we commit ourselves altogether unto God. And that trust is so surely grounded and sticks so fast in our hearts, that a man would not once doubt of it, although he should die a thousand times therefor.

4 [When copies of his translation of the New Testament were being bought and burnt] I am the gladder, for these two benefits shall come thereof: I shall get money of him [the Bishop of London] for these books to bring myself out of debt (and the whole world shall cry out upon the burning of God's word). And the overplus of the money that shall remain to me shall make me more studious to correct the said New Testament, and so newly to imprint the same once again.

5 [Request to have things brought to him in prison] A warmer cap, a candle, a piece of cloth to patch my leggings... But above all, I beseech and entreat your clemency to be urgent with the Procureur that he may kindly permit me to have my Hebrew Bible, Hebrew Grammar and Hebrew Dictionary, that I may spend time with that in study.

16.68
William Whittingham (?1524-1579)
Calvinist minister

1 [Calvin] dreams of reforming the whole world. One Lord, one faith, one baptism.

16.69
Thomas Woodhouse (d.1573)
English Roman Catholic martyr

1 Would God I might suffer ten times as much that thou might go free for the blow thou hast given me. I forgive thee, and pray to God to forgive thee even as I would be forgiven.

16.70
Francis Xavier (1505-1552)
Jesuit teacher and missionary in India

1 My God I love thee not because
I hope for heaven thereby,
Or because they that love thee not
Must burn eternally.

2 The Japanese are in all matters naturally curious, eager to learn as much as they possibly can; and so they never cease to ply us with one question or another, and to enquire further about our answers. Especially they seek most eagerly to hear what is new about religion.

3 Give me the children until they are seven and anyone may have them afterwards.

4 I remember not ever to have tasted such interior delights, and these consolations of the soul are so pure, so exquisite, and so constant, that they take from me all sense of my corporal suffering.

5 The better friends you are, the straighter you can talk, but while you are only on nodding terms, be slow to scold.

6 Be great in little things.

16.71
Anthony Zaccaria (1502-1539)
Priest, founder of the Barnabite Order

1 We should love and feel compassion for those who oppose us, rather than abhor and despise them, since they harm themselves and do us good, and adorn us with crowns of everlasting glory while they incite God's anger against themselves.

16.72
Huldreich (Ulrich) Zwingli (1484-1531)
Founder of Swiss Protestantism

1 Gold, silver, jewellery, and both silken and sumptuous clothing are either laid aside or sold and the proceeds distributed to the poor.

2 Our confidence in Christ does not make us lazy, negligent, or careless, but on the contrary it awakens us, urges us on, and makes us active in living righteous lives and doing good. There is no self-confidence to compare with this.

3 Man is nothing so much as a lump of muddy earth plunged into a very clear, pure brook.

4 He who is pious does not contend but teaches in love.

5 I believe that in the holy eucharist (that is, the supper of thanksgiving) the true body of Christ is present by the contemplation of faith. In other words, those who thank the Lord for the kindness conferred on us in his Son acknowledge that he assumed true flesh and in it truly suffered and truly washed away our sins by his own blood.

PART 3

Seventeenth Century

We are all strings in the concert of his joy;
the spirit from his mouth strikes the note
and the tune of our strings.

Jakob Boehme
(1575-1624)

17.1
Margaret Mary Alacoque (1647-1690)
French Visitandine, chief founder of devotion to the Sacred Heart

1 I need nothing but God, and to lose myself in the heart of Jesus.

17.2
William Alexander (?1567-1640)
Scottish politician and poet

1 Of all the tyrants that the world affords,
Our own affections are the fiercest lords.

2 The weaker sex, to piety more prone.

17.3
Lancelot Andrewes (1555-1626)
English Anglican bishop and Bible translator

1 Verily, here must the spirit rise to grace, or else neither the body nor it shall there rise to glory.

2 If by knowledge only, and reason, we could come to God, then none should come but they that are learned and have good wits... But God hath made his way 'via Regiam'—the King's Highway.

3 The nearer to church, the farther from God.

4 Open my eyes that I may see,
Incline my heart that I may desire,
Order my steps that I may follow
The way of your commandments.

5 Let this day, O Lord, add some knowledge or good deed to yesterday.

17.4
Johann Arndt (1555-1621)
German Lutheran pastor

1 By the lowliness and humility of our Lord Jesus Christ, we climb up as on a true ladder to heaven into the heart of God, our dear Father, and we rest in his love.

17.5
Francis Bacon (1561-1626)
English philosopher and essayist

1 It was a high speech of Seneca (after the manner of the Stoics) that 'the good things which belong to prosperity are to be wished, but the good things that belong to adversity are to be admired'.

2 Prosperity doth best discover vice, but adversity doth best discover virtue.

3 I had rather believe all the fables in the legends and the Talmud and the Al-coran, than that this universal frame is without a mind.

4 They that deny a God destroy man's nobility for certainly man is of kin to the beasts by his body; and if he be not of kin to God by his spirit, he is a base and ignoble creature.

5 If a man be gracious and courteous to strangers, it shews he is a citizen of the world, and that his heart is no island cut off from other lands, but a continent that joins them.

6 He that defers his charity until he is dead is, if a man weighs it rightly, rather liberal of another man's than his own.

7 The desire for power caused the angels to fall; the desire for knowledge in excess caused man to fall, but in charity there is no excess, neither can angel nor man come in danger by it.

8 There was never law, or sect, or opinion did not so much magnify goodness, as the Christian religion doth.

9 Riches are a good handmaid, but the worst mistress.

10 Man must know that in this theatre of man's life it is reserved only for God and angels to be lookers on.

11 A man that is young in years may be old in hours.

12 Men must pursue things which are just in present, and leave the future to divine Providence.

13 Knowledge is the rich storehouse for the glory of the Creator and the relief of man's estate.

14 A little philosophy inclineth man's mind to atheism, but depth in philosophy bringeth men's minds about to religion.

15 All good moral philosophy is but an handmaid to religion.

16 Read not to contradict and confute, nor to believe and take for granted, nor to find talk and discourse, but to weigh and consider.

17 By aspiring to a similitude of God in goodness, or love, neither man nor angel ever transgressed, or shall transgress.

18 It is better to have no opinion of God at all than such an opinion as is unworthy of him.

19 Be so true to thyself, as thou be not false to others.

20 No pleasure is comparable to the slandering upon the vantage-ground of truth.

21 What is truth? said jesting Pilate and would not stay for an answer.

22 Revenge is a kind of wild justice, which the more man's nature runs to, the more ought law to weed it out.

23 Virtue is like a rich stone—best plain set.

24 Virtue is like precious odours—most fragrant when they are incensed or crushed.

25 Men fear death as children fear to go in the dark; and as that natural fear in children is increased with tales, so is the other.

26 A wise man will make more opportunities than he finds.

17.6
Augustine Baker (1575-1641)
Benedictine writer on ascetical theology and history

1 Lord, of thy goodness, give me thyself.

17.7
Robert Barclay (1648-1690)
Scottish Quaker Apologist

1 In a true church of Christ gathered together by God, not only into the belief of the principles of Truth but also into the power, life and Spirit of Christ, the Spirit of God is the orderer, ruler and governor, as in each particular, so in the general.

2 According to the Scriptures the Spirit is the first and principal Leader.

3 I have found the evil weakening in me and the good raised up.

17.8
Isaac Barrow (1630-1677)
Anglican divine, clerical scholar and mathematician

1 There is no argument from natural effects discernible by us, which proves God's existence... the which doth not together persuade God to be very kind and benign; careful to impart to us all befitting good, suitable to our natural capacity and condition; and unwilling that any considerable harm, any extreme want or pain should befall us.

17.9
Elizabeth Bathurst (?1655-1685)
Quaker writer

1 As male and female are made one in Jesus Christ, so women receive an office in the Truth as well as men, and they have a stewardship and must give an account of their stewardship as well as the men.

17.10
Richard Baxter (1615-1691)
Nonconformist pastor and writer

1 Keep company with the more cheerful sort of the Godly; there is no mirth like the mirth of believers.

2 It is an evident truth, that most of the mischiefs that now infest or seize upon mankind through the earth, consist in, or are caused by the disorders and ill-governedness of families.

3 Humility is not a mere ornament of a Christian, but an essential part of the new creature. It is a contradiction to be a true Christian and not humble. All that will be Christians must be Christ's disciples and come to him to learn, and their lesson is to be 'meek and lowly'.

4 Prayer must carry on our work as much as preaching; he preacheth not heartily to his people, that will not pray for them.

5 Skill [is] necessary, to make plain the truth, to convince the hearers, to let in the irresistible light into their consciences, and to keep it there and drive all home; to screw the truth into their minds and work Christ into their affections... This should surely be done with a great deal of holy skill.

6 He that means as he speaks will surely do as he speaks.

7 To be the people of God without regeneration, is as impossible as to be the children of men without generation.

8 My knowledge of that life is small,
The eye of faith is dim;
But 'tis enough that Christ knows all,
And I shall be with him.

9 I preached as never sure to preach again,
And as a dying man to dying men.

10 I have pain (there is no arguing against sense) but I have peace, I have peace.

11 Christ leads me through no darker rooms
Than he went through before;
He that into God's kingdom comes
must enter by this door.

12 'Rest!' How sweet the sound! it is a melody in my ears.

17.11
Lewis Bayly (1565-1631)

Bishop and author of the popular The Practice of Piety

1 The conscionable keeping of the Sabbath, is the Mother of all Religion.

17.12
Robert Bellarmine (1542-1621)

Counter-Reformation Roman Catholic Apologist and theologian

1 Bernard [of Clairvaux] speaks of a living faith, joined with charity. Such a faith hungers and thirsts for righteousness and feels remorse for sins—not from fear of punishment but from love of righteousness. Therefore it is just as if Bernard had said: 'Whoever turns away from sin with his whole heart and desires to make amends to the Lord by works of penance—such a one is reconciled to the Lord through living faith and fervent charity, even before he undertakes the works'.

17.13
Pierre de Bérulle (1575-1629)

Cardinal, theologian and reformer

1 Jesus is the sun of our souls, whence they receive all grace, light, and influence. And the earth of our hearts should be in continual movement towards him in order to receive in all its parts and powers the favourable aspects and benign influences of this great luminary.

17.14
Jakob Boehme (1575-1624)

German Lutheran theosophical writer

1 We are all strings in the concert of his joy; the spirit from his mouth strikes the note and the tune of our strings.

17.15
Jacques Bénigne Bossuet (1627-1704)

French philosopher and bishop

1 If the Sermon on the Mount is the precis of all Christian doctrine, the eight beatitudes are the precis of the whole of the Sermon on the Mount.

2 Thirty years of Our Lord's life are hidden in these words of the gospel 'He was subject unto them'.

3 You can never love your neighbour without loving God.

4 The essence of a heretic, that is of someone who has a particular opinion, is that he clings to his own ideas.

17.16
Anne Bradstreet (1612-1672)
English poet who emigrated to the USA

1 If ever two were one, then surely we.
If ever man were lov'd by wife, then thee;
If ever wife was happy in a man,
Compare me with ye women if you can.
I prize thy love more than whole mines of gold,
Or all the riches that the East doth hold.
My love is such that rivers cannot quench,
Nor aught but love from thee, give recompense.
Thy love is such I can no way repay,
The heavens reward thee manifold, I pray.
Then while we live, in love let's so persever
That, as we live no more, we may live ever.

2 It is a pleasant thing to behold the light, but sore eyes are not able to look upon it. The pure in heart shall see God, but the defiled in conscience shall rather choose to be buried under rocks and mountains than to behold the presence of the Lamb.

3 I sought him whom my Soul did Love,
With tears I sought him earnestly;
He bow'd his ear down from Above,
In vain I did not seek or cry.

17.17
Jean de Brébeuf (1593-1649)
French Jesuit missionary, murdered in Canada

1 [From Jesuits on the Canadian mission to the Jesuits in France] However careworn and weary you may be, we can offer you nothing but a poor mat, or at best a skin rug for bed; added to that, you will arrive at a time of year when fleas will keep you awake almost all night. And this petty martyrdom, to say nothing of mosquitoes, sandflies, and suchlike gentry, lasts usually not less than three or four months of the summer.

17.18
William Bridge (1600-1670)
English nonconformist preacher

1 Ah Lord, my prayers are dead, my affections dead and my heart is dead; but you are a living God and I bear myself upon you.

17.19
Thomas Brooks (1608-1680)
A minister of the Congregational Way

1 To be in a state of true grace is to be miserable no more; it is to be happy for ever. A soul in this state is a soul near and dear to God. It is a soul housed in God.

17.20
Thomas Browne (1605-1682)
English doctor and author of Religio Medici

1 The man without a navel still lives in me.

2 At my devotion I love to use the civility of my knee, my hat and hand.

3 Meekness takes injuries like pills, not chewing, but swallowing them down.

4 I fear God, yet I am not afraid of him.

5 Affliction smarts most in the most happy state.

6 To believe only possibilities is not faith, but mere Philosophy.

7 Let him have the key to thy heart who hath the lock to his own.

8 But how shall we expect charity towards others, when we are uncharitable to ourselves? Charity begins at home, is the voice of the world, yet is every man his greatest enemy, and, as it were, his own executioner.

9 For this I think charity, to love God for himself and our neighbour for God.

10 By compassion we make others' misery our own, and so, by relieving them, we relieve ourselves also.

11 It is a brave act of valour to despise death, but where life is more terrifying than death it is then the truest valour to dare to stay alive.

12 The created world is but a small parenthesis in eternity.

13 There is another man within me that is angry with me.

14 There is surely a piece of divinity in us, something that was before the elements, and owes no homage unto the sun.

15 Music strikes in me a deep fit of devotion, and a profound contemplation of the First Composer. There is something in it of Divinity more than the ear discovers.

16 There is no road or ready way to virtue.

17 The long habit of living indisposeth us to dying.

18 Could the Devil work my belief to imagine I could never die. I would not outlive that very thought.

17.21
Jean de la Bruyère (c.1645-1696)
French writer

1 To laugh at men of sense is the privilege of fools.

2 The slave has but one master; the ambitious man has as many as can help in making his fortune.

3 All men's misfortunes spring from their hatred of being alone.

4 Two quite opposite qualities equally bias our minds—habit and novelty.

5 Genuine piety is the spring of peace of mind.

6 Modesty is to merit what shade is to figures in a picture; it gives it strength and makes it stand out.

7 This great misfortune—to be incapable of solitude.

17.22
John Bunyan (1628-1688)
English Non-Conformist minister and author of The Pilgrim's Progress

1 A man there was, though some did count him mad, The more he cast away the more he had.

2 In prayer it is better to have a heart without words, than words without a heart.

3 I have formerly lived by hearsay and faith, but now I go where I shall live by sight and shall be with Him in whose company I delight myself.

4 Prayer is a shield to the soul, a sacrifice to God, and a scourge to Satan.

5 The best prayers have often more groans than words.

6 I have sometimes seen more in a line of the Bible than I could well tell how to stand under, yet at another time the whole Bible hath been to me as dry as a stick.

7 Temptations, when we first meet them, are as the lion that roared upon Samson; but if we overcome them, the next time we see them we shall find a nest of honey within them.

8 He that bestows his goods upon the poor,
Shall have as much again,
and ten times more.

9 When the day that he [Valiant-for-Truth] must go hence was come, many accompanied him to the riverside, in to which as he went he said, 'Death, where is thy sting?' And as he went down deeper, he said, 'Grave, where is thy victory?' So he passed over, and all the trumpets sounded for him on the other side.

10 He that is down need fear no fall,
He that is low no pride.

11 If we have not quiet in our minds, outward comfort will do no more for us than a golden slipper on a gouty foot.

12 Better, though difficult, the right way to go
Than wrong, tho' easy, where the end is woe.

13 One leak will sink a ship, and one sin will destroy a sinner.

14 Let every tub stand upon its own bottom.

17.23
Edward Burrough (1632-1663)
English Quaker who died in prison

1 We are not for names, nor men, nor titles of Government, nor are we for this party nor against the other... but we are for justice and mercy and truth and peace and true freedom, that these may be exalted in our nation, and that goodness, righteousness, meekness, temperance, peace and unity with God, and with one another, that these things may abound.

17.24
Robert Burton (1577-1640)
English clergyman

1 One religion is as true as another.

2 Every man hath a good and a bad angel attending on him in particular, all his life long.

3 Those whom God forsakes, the devil by his permission lays hold on. Sometimes he persecutes them with that worm of conscience, as he did Judas, Saul and others. The poets call it Nemesis.

4 No rule is so general, which admits not some exception.

17.25
Samuel Butler (1612-1680)
English satirist

1 Life is the art of drawing sufficient conclusions from insufficient premises.

2 There is no bore like a clever bore.

3 There are more fools than knaves in the world, else the knaves would not have enough to live upon.

4 To do great work a man must be very idle as well as very industrious.

5 Logic is like the sword—those who appeal to it shall perish by it.

6 Silence is not always tact, and it is tact that is golden—not silence.

7 Discords make the sweetest airs.

8 What makes all doctrines plain and clear?
About two hundred pounds a year.
And that which was proved true before,
Prove false again? Two hundred more.

9 Our pains are real things, but all our pleasures, but fantastical.

17.26
Joseph of Calasanza (1556-1648)
Spanish priest, founder in Rome of an order educating poor children

1 All who undertake to teach must be endowed with deep love, the greatest patience, and, most of all, profound humility. They must perform their work with earnest zeal. Then through their humble prayers, the Lord will find them worthy to become fellow workers with him in the cause of truth.

17.27
Camillus de Lellis (1559-1614)
Italian priest and founder of the Ministers of the Sick

1 The approach of death is indeed the best news I could hear. A man must once pay the forfeit of death, and I do not value this life at a farthing if only our Lord will give me a tiny corner in paradise; nor do I worry about the future of the order, for I trust God to raise up men to assist and defend it.

2 The true apostolic life consists in giving oneself no rest or repose.

3 Now, is not God able to send, perhaps tomorrow, sacks of money to my door?

17.28
Jean Pierre Camus (1582-1652)
French bishop

1 The pilgrim who spends all his time counting his steps will make little progress.

2 Love virtue rather than fear sin.

3 Charity is the pure gold which makes us rich in eternal wealth.

4 Anger is quieted by a gentle word just as fire is quenched by water.

5 The crosses that we shape for ourselves are always lighter than the ones laid upon us.

6 There are no galley slaves in the royal vessel of divine love—every man works his oar voluntarily.

7 To desire to love God is to love to desire him, and hence to love him, for love is the root of all desire.

8 We must fear God through love, not love him through fear.

9 It takes more oil than vinegar to make a good salad.

10 God looks at the intention of the heart rather than the gifts He is offered.

11 If we judge ourselves, we will not be judged by God.

12 We must be able to find pleasure in ourselves when alone, and in our neighbour when in his company.

13 Too often do we call the truths which offend us by the name of slander.

14 Long illnesses are good schools of mercy for those who tend the sick, and of loving patience for those who suffer.

15 Mere silence is not wisdom, for wisdom consists in knowing when and how to speak and when and where to keep silent.

16 He who believes himself to be far advanced in the spiritual life has not even made a good beginning.

17 One ounce of patient suffering is worth far more than a pound of action.

17.29
Miguel de Cervantes (1547-1616)
Spanish novelist, author of Don Quixote

1 Tell me what company you keep, and I'll tell you what you are.

2 Among the attributes of God, although they are all equal, mercy shines with even more brilliance than justice.

3 Where truth is, there is God.

4 Who errs and mends, to God himself commends.

5 We are all as God made us, and oftentimes a great deal worse.

6 There's no sauce in the world like hunger.

7 The proof of the pudding is the eating.

8 A good name is better than great riches.

9 When we quit this world and are placed in the earth, the prince walks along a path as narrow as the journeyman.

10 There is a remedy for everything but death, which will be sure to lay us out flat some time or other.

11 Being a man I may come to be Pope.

12 He preaches well that lives well.

13 First then, fear God: for His fear is wisdom and being wise, thou canst not err.

14 Fear is sharp-sighted, and can see things underground, and much more in the skies.

17.30
Jeanne Françoise de Chantal (1572-1641)
French founder of the Order of the Visitation

1 Hell is full of the talented, but heaven of the energetic.

2 I have often noticed how gladly he [St Francis de Sales] left the Holy Spirit to do his work freely in souls, and he himself followed the attraction of that divine Spirit, and guided them as they were led by God, leaving them to follow the divine inspirations, rather than his own instructions.

3 The martyrs of love suffer infinitely more in remaining in this life so as to serve God, than if they died a thousand times over in testimony to their faith, their love, and their fidelity.

17.31
Charles I (1600-1649)
King of Great Britain and Ireland

1 Let my condition be never so low, I resolve by the grace of God never to yield up this church to the government of Papists, Presbyterians, or Independents.

2 How can we expect God's blessing if we relinquish his church?

3 God may at length show my subjects that I chose rather to suffer for them than with them.

4 They that have so often prayed against me shall never pray with me in this agony.

17.32
William Chillingworth (1602-1644)
English theologian

1 The Bible and the Bible only is the religion of Protestants.

17.33
Peter Claver (1580-1654)
Spanish Jesuit, devoted his life to the welfare of enslaved Africans in South America

1 Every time I do not behave like a donkey, it is the worse for me. How does a donkey behave? If it is slandered, it keeps silent; if it is not fed, it keeps silent; if it is forgotten, it keeps silent; it never complains, however much it is beaten or ill-used, because it has a donkey's patience. That is how the servant of God must behave. I stand before you, Lord, like a donkey.

17.34
Claude de la Colombière (d.1682)
French spiritual writer

1 If I am to complain, let me complain to Jesus fastened on his cross... You know my sufferings are far less than I deserve. And since all my afflictions proceed from you, to you I come; give me strength and hearten me to suffer in silence; as once you did yourself.

17.35
John Cosin (1595-1672)
Bishop of Durham

1 Anoint and cheer our soiled face
With the abundance of thy grace:
Keep far our foes, give peace at home;
Where thou art guide no ill can come.

2 Almighty God and heavenly Father,
we thank you for the children
which you have given us:
give us also grace to train them
in your faith, fear and love;
that as they advance in years
they may grow in grace,
and may hereafter be found in the number
of your elect children.

17.36
Richard Crashaw (1613-1649)
English lyrical and religious poet

1 Poor World (said I) what wilt thou do
To entertain this starry Stranger?
Is this the best thou canst bestow,
A cold, and not too cleanly manger?
Contend, ye powers of heaven and earth,
To fit a bed for this huge birth.

2 Great little one! whose all-embracing birth
Lifts Earth to Heaven,
stoops Heaven to Earth.

3 Why should his unstain'd breast make good
My blushes with his own heart-blood?
O, my Saviour, make me see
How dearly thou hast paid for me,
That lost again my life may prove
As then in death, so now in love.

4 Two went to pray? O rather say
One went to brag, the other to pray.

17.37

Oliver Cromwell (1599-1658)

English revolutionary soldier and statesman

1 Not only strike while the iron is hot, but make it hot by striking.

2 If we will have peace without a worm in it, lay we the foundations of justice and good will.

3 What are all histories but God manifesting himself.

4 Trust God and keep your powder dry.

5 [Letter to the general Assembly of the Church of Scotland, 3 August 1650] I beseech you, in the bowels of Christ, think it possible you may be mistaken.

6 Mr Lely, I desire you would use all your skill to paint my picture truly like me, and not flatter me at all but remark all these roughnesses, pimples, warts, and everything as you see me, otherwise I will never pay a farthing for it.

7 Mercies should not be temptations; yet we too often make them so.

8 It is not my design to drink or to sleep, but my design is to make what haste I can to be gone.

17.38

Samuel Crossman (c.1624-1683)

English churchman, nonconformist, later Anglican

1 Here might I stay and sing,
No story so divine;
Never was love, dear King,
Never was grief like thine!
This is my Friend,
In whose sweet praise
I all my days
Would gladly spend.

17.39

Richard Cumberland (1631-1718)

English bishop and founder of English Utilitarianism

1 It is better to wear out than to rust out.

17.40

René Descartes (1595-1650)

French philosopher

1 The chief cause of human errors is to be found in the prejudices picked up in childhood.

2 It is not enough to have a good mind. The main thing is to use it well.

3 I think, therefore I am.

17.41

William Dewsbury (1621-1688)

English Quaker

1 In the prison house I sung praises to my God, and esteemed the bolts and locks put upon me as jewels.

17.42

John Donne (1573-1631)

English Anglican poet and preacher

1 When the church baptizes a child, that action concerns me, for that child is thereby connected to that which is my head too, and ingrafted into that body whereof I am a member.

2 This is charity, to do all, all that we can.

3 Teach me how to repent for that's as good
As if thou hadst seal'd my pardon, with thy blood.

4 God clothed himself in vile man's flesh so he might be weak enough to suffer woe.

5 The rich have no more of the Kingdom of Heaven than they have purchased by their alms.

6 If every gnat that flies were an archangel, all that could but tell me is that there is a God, and the poorest worm that creeps tells me that.

7 How many times go we to comedies, to masques, to places of great and noble resort, nay even to church only to see the company.

8 I neglect God and his angels for the noise of a fly, for the rattling of a coach, for the whining of a door.

9 Christ beats his drum, but he does not press men; Christ is served with volunteers.

10 True joy is that earnest wish we have of heaven, it is a treasure of the soul, and therefore should be laid in a safe place, and nothing in this world is safe to place it in.

11 Man is not only a contributory creature, but a total creature; he does not only make one, but he is all; he is not a piece of the world, but the world itself, and next to the glory of God, the reason why there is a world.

12 In best understandings, sin began:
Angels sinned first, then Devils, then Man.

13 Let man's soul be a Sphere, and then, in this,
The intelligence that moves, devotion is.

14 There is in every miracle a silent chiding of the world, and a tacit reprehension of them who require, or who need miracles.

15 Churches are best for prayer
that have least light:
To see God only, I go out of sight.

16 Though truth and falsehood be
Near twins, yet truth a little elder is.

17 Into that gate they shall enter, and in that house they shall dwell, where there shall be no Cloud nor Sun, no darkness nor dazzling, but one equal light, no noise nor silence, but one equal music, no fears nor hopes, but one equal possession, no foes nor friends, but one equal communion and identity, no ends nor beginnings, but one equal eternity.

18 Death be not proud, though some
have called thee
Mighty and dreadful, for, thou art not so,
For those, whom thou think'st,
thou dost overthrow,
Die not, poor death, nor yet canst
thou kill me.

19 Any man's death diminishes me because I am involved in mankind, and therefore never send to hear for whom the bell tolls: it tolls for thee.

20 What is so intricate, so entangling as death? Whoever got out of a winding sheet?

21 One short sleep past, we wake eternally,
And Death shall be no more:
Death, thou shalt die!

22 The sun must not set upon anger, much less will I let the sun set upon the anger of God towards me.

23 Here in this world He bids us come, there in the next He shall bid us welcome.

17.43
John Dryden (1631-1701)
English poet and dramatist

1 When beauty fires the blood, how love exalts the mind.

2 Alms are but the vehicles of prayer.

3 No force the free-born spirit can constrain, but charity and great example gain.

4 Conscience is the royalty and prerogative of every private man.

5 Fear of death has gone farther with me in two minutes than my conscience would have gone in two months.

6 Possess your soul with patience.

7 Beware the fury of a patient man.

8 Truth is the foundation of all knowledge and the cement of all societies.

9 Refined himself to Soul, to curb the Sense;
And made almost a Sin of Abstinence.

10 [Of the Bible:]
Then for the style, majestic and divine,
It speaks no less than God in every line.

11 Creator Spirit, by whose aid
The world's foundations first were laid,
Come visit every pious mind;
Come pour thy joys on human kind;
From sin and sorrow set us free,
And make thy temples worthy thee.

12 Never ending, still beginning,
Fighting still, and still destroying,
If all the world be worth the winning,
Think, oh think, it worth enjoying.

13 Forgiveness to the injured doth belong
But they ne'er pardon who have done
the wrong.

14 Pity melts the Mind to Love.

15 He that once sins, like him that slides on ice,
Goes swiftly down the slippery way of vice:
Though conscience checks him,
yet those rubs gone o'er,
He slides on smoothly and looks back
no more.

16 How strangely high endeavours
may be blessed,
Where piety and valour jointly go.

17 Accurst ambition,
How dearly I have bought you.

18 Virtue is its own reward.

19 Even victors are by victories undone.

20 An honest man may take a fool's advice.

17.44
Mary Dyer (d.1660)
Quaker hanged in Massachusetts for her faith

1 I have been in paradise these several days.

17.45
Jean Eudes (1601-1680)
French missioner

1 You can advance farther in grace in one hour during this time of affliction than in many days during a time of consolation.

2 I no longer wish to find happiness in myself or in created and perishable things, but in Jesus my saviour. He is my All, and I desire to belong wholly to Him. It is the most extreme folly and delusion to look elsewhere for any true happiness. Let us, then, vehemently and courageously renounce all other things and seek only Him.

3 I see an infinite number of crucified persons in the world, but few who are crucified by the love of Jesus. Some are crucified by their self-love and inordinate love of the world, but happy are they who are crucified for the love of Jesus; happy are they who live and die on the cross with Jesus.

4 The Christian has a union with Jesus Christ more noble, more intimate and more perfect than the members of a human body have with their head.

5 O my well-beloved Jesus... hide me utterly with thee in God. Bury my mind, my heart, my will and my being, so that I may no longer have any thoughts, desires, or affections, any sentiments and dispositions other than thine own.

6 If you contemplate God with the eyes of faith, you will see him just as he is, and, in a certain manner, face to face.

17.46
Katherine Evans (d.1692)
English Quaker, imprisoned in Malta by the Inquisition for preaching

1 And in the greatest of our afflictions we could not say in our hearts 'Father, would thou hadst not brought us here!' but cried mightily to our God for power to carry us through whatsoever should be inflicted upon us, that the Truth of our God might not suffer through our weakness.

17.47
Margaret Fell (later Fox) (1614-1702)
English Quaker, imprisoned for refusing to take an oath of loyalty to the king

1 He is not a God far off, but one who may be witnessed and possessed.

17.48
Nicholas Ferrar (1592-1637)
English founder of the Little Gidding community

1 It was God that gave me to you and if he take me from you be not only content but most joyful that I am delivered from this vale of misery and wretchedness.

2 This God that hath kept me ever since I was born, ever since I came out of your womb, my most dear mother, will preserve me to the end, I know, and give me grace that I shall live in his faith and die in his fear and favour, and rest in his peace, and rise in his power and reign in his glory.

17.49
Fidelis of Sigmaringen (1577-1622)
Prussian-born Franciscan, murdered by Swiss Protestants

1 It is because of faith that we exchange the present for the future.

17.50
John Flavel (?1639-1691)
English Presbyterian minister

1 The scriptures teach us the best way of living, the noblest way of suffering, and the most comfortable way of dying.

2 Man's extremity is God's opportunity.

17.51
George Fox (1624-1691)
English preacher and founder of the Society of Friends

1 The Lord opened unto me that being bred at Oxford or Cambridge was not enough to fit and qualify men to be ministers of Christ.

2 I saw also that there was an ocean of darkness and death, but an infinite ocean of light and love which flowed over the ocean of darkness. In that also I saw the infinite love of God; and I had great openings.

3 There is one, even Christ Jesus, that can speak to thy condition.

4 We must not have Christ Jesus, the Lord of Life, put any more in the stable amongst the horses and asses, but he must now have the best chamber.

5 Christ has been too long locked up in the mass or in the Book; let him be your prophet, priest and king. Obey him.

6 Justice Bennett of Derby was the first that called us Quakers, because I bid them tremble at the word of the Lord. That was in the year 1650.

7 He [Oliver Cromwell] said: 'I see there is a people risen, that I cannot win either with gifts, honours, offices or places; but all other sects and people I can.'

8 Be still and cool in thy mind and spirit.

9 O Lord, baptise our hearts into a sense of the conditions and need of all men.

10 Be patterns, be examples in all countries, places, islands, nations, wherever you come, that your carriage and life may preach among all sorts of people, and to them; then you will come to walk cheerfully over the world, answering that of God in everyone.

17.52
Thomas Fuller (1608-1661)
English writer

1 Birth is the beginning of death.

2 Human blood is all of one colour.

3 We can live without our friends but not without our neighbours.

4 He that converses not, knows nothing.

5 Fear can keep a man out of danger, but courage can support him in it.

6 If we are bound to forgive an enemy, we are not bound to trust him.

7 Praise makes good men better and bad men worse.

8 Great hopes make great men.

9 Sleep is, in fine, so like death I dare not trust it without my prayers.

10 Weak things united become strong.

11 If afflictions refine some, they consume others.

12 Anger is one of the sinews of the soul: he that wants it hath a maimed mind.

13 He does not believe who does not love according to his beliefs.

14 Some are atheists only in fair weather.

15 A broad hat does not always cover a venerable head.

16 Miracles are the swaddling clothes of infant churches.

17 A quiet conscience sleeps in thunder.

18 A guilty conscience never thinketh itself safe.

19 Riches have made more covetous men than covetousness hath made rich men.

20 Great wealth and content seldom live together.

21 Riches are gotten with pain, kept with care and lost with grief.

22 He is not poor that hath not much, but he that craves much.

23 The way to be safe is never to be secure.

24 He that cannot pay, let him pray.

25 None can pray well but he that lives well.

26 A good prayer, though often used, is still fresh and fair in the eyes and ears of heaven.

27 Prayer should be the key of the day and the lock of the night.

28 Nature teaches us to love our friends, but religion our enemies.

29 Amendment is repentance.

30 Zeal is fit only for wise men, but is found mostly in fools.

31 Zeal without knowledge is fire without light.

32 He that will not live a saint cannot die a martyr.

33 Face to face the truth comes out.

17.53
Paul Gerhardt (1607-1676)
German Lutheran pastor and hymn-writer

1 O sacred head, sore wounded
With grief and shame bowed down
Now scornfully surrounded
With thorns, thy only crown.

2 Still let thy love point out my way;
How wondrous things thy love
has wrought!
Still lead me, lest I go astray;
Direct my word, inspire my thought;
And if I fall, soon may I hear
Thy voice, and know that love is near.

17.54
Thomas Goodwin (1600-1680)
English Puritan minister

1 When I was threatening to become cold in my ministry, and when I felt Sabbath morning coming, and my heart not filled with amazement at the grace of God, or when I was making ready to dispense the Lord's Supper, do you know what I used to do? I used to take a turn up and down among the sins of my past life, and I always came down with a broken and a contrite heart, ready to preach, as it was preached in the beginning, the forgiveness of sins.

17.55
John Goter (1650-1704)
English Roman Catholic controversialist

1 Since the care of Jesus was, by the eternal wisdom, left to a humble tradesman, have not all here of that degree a great instruction that sanctity and perfect is not to be thought the property of ecclesiasticks and Religious, but that their condition also is capable of it, and that in the New Law, it is expected of them.

17.56
Anthony Grassi (1592-1671)
Italian priest, noted spiritual guide

1 Abstinence is the mother of health. A few ounces of privation is an excellent recipe for any ailment.

17.57
Hugo Grotius (1583-1645)
Dutch jurist and statesman

1 Liberty is the power that we have over ourselves.

17.58
William Gurnall (1616-1679)
English Puritan clergyman

1 The sincere Christian is progressive—never at his journey's end till he gets to heaven. This keeps him always in motion, advancing in his desires and endeavours forward.

17.59
Joseph Hall (1574-1656)
English bishop and writer

1 He that hath but a form is a hypocrite but he that hath not a form is an atheist.

2 Moderation is the silken string running through the pearl chain of all virtues.

3 Superstition is godless religion.

4 Satan rocks the cradle when we sleep at our devotions.

5 Let no man think that because those blessed souls are out of sight, far distant in another world, and we are here toiling in a vale of tears, we have therefore lost all mutual regard to each other. No; there is still, and ever will be, a secret but unfailing correspondence between heaven and earth.

17.60
George Herbert (1593-1633)
Church of England clergyman and poet

1 Sundays the pillars are,
On which heaven's palace arched lies.

2 Bells call others, but themselves enter not into church.

3 When once thy foot enters the church,
be bare.
God is more there than thou.

4 Kneeling ne'er spoil'd silk stocking;
quit thy state;
All equal are within the church's gate.

5 A piece of the churchyard fits everybody.

6 Some make a conscience of spitting in the church, yet rob the altar.

7 Honour and profit lie not all in one sack.

8 Giving much to the poor
Doth enrich a man's store;
It takes much from the account
To which his sin doth amount.

9 All worldly joys go less
To the one joy of doing kindnesses.

10 Love is that liquor sweet and most divine,
Which my God feels as blood;
but I as wine.

11 Love your neighbour, yet pull not down your hedge.

12 Gossips are frogs, they drink and talk.

13 I am no link of thy great chain,
But all my company is a weed.
Lord, place me in thy consort
give one strain
To my poor reed.

14 Poverty is no sin.

15 He that hath a head of wax must not walk in the sun.

16 Heresy may be easier kept out than shook off.

17 The devil divides the world between atheism and superstition.

18 O let thy sacred will
All thy delight in me fulfil!
Let me not think an action mine own way,
But as thy love shall sway,
Refining up the rudder to thy skill.

19 Though God take the sun out of heaven, yet we must have patience.

20 Prayer, the church's banquet, angel's age
God's breath in man returning to his birth,
The soul in paraphrase, heart in pilgrimage,
The Christian plummet sounding heaven
and earth.

21 Who goes to bed and does not pray
Maketh two nights to every day.

22 He that contemplates hath a day without night.

23 He that will learn to pray, let him go to sea.

24 Religion, credit and the eyes are not to be touched.

25 Religion went to Rome, subduing those,
Who, that they might subdue,
made all their foes.

26 Love bade me welcome;
yet my soul drew back.
Guilty of dust and sin.

27 Come, my Way, my Truth, my Life!
Such a Way as gives us breath,
Such a Truth as ends all strife,
Such a Life as killeth Death.

28 He that trust in a lie shall perish in truth.

29 Virtue never grows old.

30 Good words are worth much, and cost little.

31 God's mill grinds slow, but sure.

32 Up, and away,
Thy Saviour's gone before.
Why dost thou stay,
Dull soul?

33 He that will enter Paradise must have a good key.

34 Teach me, my God and King
In all things thee to see,
And what I do in anything,
To do it as for thee.

17.61
Robert Herrick (1591-1674)
Church of England clergyman and poet

1 If any thing delight me for to print
My book, 'tis this; that thou, my God,
art in't.

2 Who after his transgression doth repent,
Is half, or altogether, innocent.

3 Attempt the end, and never stand to doubt;
Nothing's so hard, but search will find
it out.

4 In prayer the lips ne'er act the winning part,
Without the sweet concurrence of the heart.

5 God ne'er afflicts us more than our desert,
Though he may seem to overact His part;
Sometimes he strikes us more than flesh
can bear,
But yet still less than Grace can suffer here.

6 The tears of saints more sweet by far
Than all the songs of sinners are.

7 Seldom comes glory till a man be dead.

8 Give unto all, lest he whom thou deny'st
May chance to be no other man but Christ.

9 God bought man here with his heart's
blood expense,
And man sold God here for base thirty pence.

10 Noah the first was (as Tradition says)
That did ordain the fast of forty days.

11 Here a little child I stand,
Heaving up my either hand;
Cold as paddocks though they be,
Here I lift them up to thee,
For a benison to fall
On our meat, and on us all.

12 To work a wonder, God would have
her shown,
At once, a bud, and yet a rose full-blown.

13 Gather ye rosebuds while ye may,
Old Time is still a-flying.

17.62

William Howard (1613-1680)

English Roman Catholic, condemned and executed on false charges

1 [To his wife] God of his infinite mercy send us a happy meeting in heaven!

17.63

Francis Howgill (1618-1669)

English Quaker

1 The Kingdom of Heaven did gather us and catch us all, as in a net, and his heavenly power at one time drew many hundreds to land.

17.64

Isaac Jogues (1607-1646)

French Jesuit missionary murdered in Canada

1 What I suffered is known only to One for whose love and in whose cause it is pleasing and glorious to suffer.

17.65

Joseph of Copertino (1603-1663)

Italian Franciscan

1 Alas, my God, I know that thou hast made all things well and that by Thy grace I shall not sin in these temptations, but I would wish not to experience them

2 Obedience is a little dog that leads the blind.

17.66

Juana Inés de la Cruz (1651-1695)

Mexican nun, poet and scholar

1 Pride finds it less intolerable to hear a reproof, than envy to see a miracle.

2 All things proceed from God, who is at once the centre and the circumference from which all existing lines proceed and at which all end up.

17.67

Edward Lake (1641-1704)

English Anglican archdeacon

1 Lord, as your mercies do surround us, so grant that our return of duty may abound; and let this day manifest our gratitude by doing something well-pleasing unto you.

17.68

François, Duc de La Rochefoucauld (1613-1680)

French writer of maxims

1 Men too involved in details usually become unable to deal with great matters.

2 Men, not books, are the proper subject for study.

3 Nature has concealed at the bottom of our minds talents and abilities of which we are not aware.

4 Well bred thinking means kindly and sensitive thoughts.

5 The surest rule is to listen much, speak little, and say nothing that you may be sorry for.

6 If we had no faults ourselves, we should not take so much delight in noticing those of others.

7 A true friend is the most precious of all possessions and the one we take least thought about acquiring.

8 Flattery is a false coinage, which our vanity puts into circulation.

9 A man who cannot find tranquillity within himself will search for it in vain elsewhere.

10 Usually we praise only to be praised.

11 Only great men have great defects.

12 Plenty of people wish to become devout, but no one wishes to be humble.

13 We pardon as long as we love.

14 There are some people who would never have fallen in love if they had never heard love talked about.

15 The glory of great men should always be measured by the means they have used to acquire it.

16 Perfect valour consists in doing without witnesses that which would be capable of doing before everyone.

17 If we resist our passions, it is more because of their weakness than our strength.

18 We promise according to our hopes and perform according to our fears.

19 We often forgive those who bore us, but we cannot forgive those whom we bore.

20 Our repentance is not so much regret for the evil we have done as a fear of what may happen to us because of it.

21 We acknowledge our faults in order to repair by our sincerity the damage they have done us in the eyes of others.

22 Almost all our faults are more pardonable than the methods we think up to hide them.

23 Some wicked people would be less dangerous had they no redeeming qualities.

24 In jealousy there is more self-love than love.

25 Hypocrisy is the homage which vice pays to virtue.

26 Extreme avarice misapprehends itself almost always; there is no passion which more often misses its aim, nor upon which the present has so much influence to the prejudice of the future.

27 We all have enough strength to bear the misfortunes of others.

17.69
William Laud (1573-1645)
Archbishop of Canterbury, executed on Tower Hill

1 [Last words from scaffold] Lord, I am coming as fast as I can.

17.70
Brother Lawrence (1611-1691)
French Carmelite lay brother and mystic

1 Those who have the gale of the Holy Spirit go forward even in sleep.

2 All things are possible to him who believes, yet more to him who hopes, more still to him who loves, and most of all to him who practises and perseveres in these three virtues.

3 A little lifting of the heart suffices; a little remembrance of God, one act of inward worship are prayers which, however short, are nevertheless acceptable to God.

4 You need not cry very loud: he is nearer to us than we think.

5 Hold yourself in prayer before God, like a dumb or paralytic beggar at a rich man's gate: let it be your business to keep your mind in the presence of God.

6 The time of business does not differ from the time of prayer; and in the noise and clutter of my kitchen, while several persons are at the same time calling for different things, I possess God in as great tranquillity as if I were upon my knees at the Blessed Sacrament.

7 Make a virtue of necessity.

8 Lord, make me according to thy heart.

17.71
Lawrence of Brindisi (1559-1619)
Italian Franciscan theologian and missioner

1 There is a spiritual life that we share with the angels of Heaven and with the divine spirits, for like them we have been formed in the image and likeness of God.

17.72
John Locke (1632-1704)
English philosopher

1 The discipline of desire is the background of character.

2 To prejudge other people's notions before we have looked into them is not to show their darkness but to put out our own eyes.

3 Faith is the assent to any proposition not made out by the deduction of reason but upon the credit of the proposer.

4 The visible marks of extraordinary wisdom and power appear so plainly in all the works of creation that a rational creature who will but seriously reflect on them cannot miss the discovery of the deity.

5 One unerring mark of the love of truth is not entertaining any proposition with greater assurance than the proofs it is built upon will warrant.

6 To love truth for truth's sake is the principal part of human perfection in this world, and the seed-plot of all other virtues.

7 Wherever law ends, tyranny begins.

17.73
Marie de l'Incarnation (1599-1672)
Founder of the Carmelites of the Reform in France

1 The closer one lives to God, the more clearly one sees one's way in temporal things.

17.74
Louise de Marillac (1591-1660)
French co-founder of the Daughters of Charity

1 [To the Sisters of Charity in Warsaw]
As regards your own six selves, no secrets whatever; as regards the world outside, everything kept secret that passes within the family circle of six.

17.75
Andrew Marvell (1621-1678)
English metaphysical poet

1 But at my back I always hear
Time's wingèd chariot hurrying near.
And yonder all before us lie
Deserts of vast eternity.

2 The grave's a fine and private place,
But none I think do there embrace.

17.76
John Milton (1608-1674)
English poet

1 These are thy glorious works,
Parent of good.

2 Unbelief is blind.

3 Opinion in good men is but knowledge in the making.

4 Apt words have power to suage
The tumours of a troubled mind,
And are as balm to festered wounds.

5 The mind is its own place, and in itself
Can make a heaven of hell, a hell of heaven.

6 Take heed lest passion sway
Thy judgement to do aught
which else free will
Would not admit.

7 Boast not of what thou would'st have done,
but do
What then thou would'st.

8 They also serve who only stand and wait.

9 To reign is worth ambition, though in hell:
Better to reign in hell, than serve in heaven.

10 Revenge, at first though sweet—
Bitter ere long, back on itself recoils.

11 Men of most renowned virtue have sometimes by transgressing most truly kept the law.

12 O conscience, into what abyss of fears
And horrors hast thou driven me.

13 And I will place within them as a guide
My umpire Conscience,
whom if they will hear,
Light after light well used they shall attain,
And to the end persisting, safe arrive.

14 For neither man nor angel can discern
Hypocrisy, the only evil that walks
Invisible, except to God alone.

15 High on a throne of royal state, which far
Outshone the wealth of Ormus
and of Ind,
Or where the gorgeous East
with richest hand
Showers on her kings barbaric
pearl and gold,
Satan exalted sat, by merit raised
To that bad eminence.

16 Adam, the goodliest man of men since born
His sons; the fairest of her daughters Eve.

17 The infernal serpent; he it was, whose guile
Stirred up with envy and revenge, deceiv'd
The mother of mankind.

18 Of man's first disobedience, and the fruit
Of that forbidden tree, whose mortal taste
Brought death into our world,
and all our woe.

19 That thou art happy, owe to God;
That thou continuest such, owe to thyself,
That is, to thy obedience.

20 Good, the more
Communicated, more abundant grows.

21 God attributes to place
No sanctity, if none be thither brought
By men who there frequent,
or therein dwell.

22 Millions of spiritual creatures walk the earth unseen, both when we sleep and when we awake.

23 The helmed Cherubim
The sworded Seraphim
Are seen in glittering ranks with wings display'd.

24 Speak ye who best can tell,
ye Sons of Light,
Angels, for ye behold him, and with songs
And choral symphonies,
day without night,
Circle his throne rejoicing.

25 Only this I know,
That one celestial Father gives to all.

26 Solitude sometimes is best society,
And short retirement urges sweet return.

27 Though all the winds of doctrine were let loose to play upon the earth, so Truth be in the field, we do ingloriously, by licensing and prohibition, to misdoubt her strength.

28 He who receives
Light from above, from the Fountain
of Light,
No other doctrine needs, though
granted true.

29 Wisdom's best nurse is contemplation.

30 What if Earth
Be but the shadow of Heaven, and things
therein
Each to other like, more than on Earth
is thought?

31 And to the faithful, death the gate of life.

32 O unexpected stroke, worse than of death!
Must I thus leave thee, Paradise? thus leave
Thee, native soil?

17.77
James Nayler (?1617-1660)
English Quaker and writer of many tracts

1 The lower God doth bring me, and the nearer to himself, the more doth this Love and Tenderness spring and spread towards the poor, simple and despised ones, who are poor in spirit, meek and lowly Suffering Lambs, and with those I choose to suffer, and do suffer, wherever they are found.

17.78
Jean-Jacques Olier (1608-1657)
French mystical writer

1 The Christian, in fact, possesses two lives—the life of Adam and that of our Lord; the life of the flesh and that of the Spirit. These two lives are opposed to each other; it is needful for one to be wholly annihilated in order that the other become absolutely perfect.

2 There is nothing more wonderful than this life of Jesus in Mary, the holy life that he pours continuously into her, the divine life with which he animates her, loving and praising and adoring God his Father in her, giving a worthy supplement to her heart wherein he abounds with pleasure.

17.79
John Owen (1616-1683)
English Puritan theologian

1 If grace doth not change human nature, I do not know what grace doth.

2 The work of conversion itself, and in especial the act of believing, or faith itself, is expressly said to be of God, to be wrought in us by him, to be given unto us from him. The scripture says [that God gives us] faith, repentance, and conversion.

3 God works immediately by his Spirit in and on the wills of his saints.

4 Gifts... excite and stir up grace unto its proper exercise and operation. How often is faith, love, and delight in God, excited and drawn forth unto especial exercise in believers by the use of their own gifts!

5 To know God, so as thereby to be made like unto him, is the chief end of man.

6 No man preaches his own sermon well to others if he doth not first preach it to his own heart.

7 No part of Christian religion was ever so vilely contaminated and abused by profane wretches, as this pure, holy, plain action and institution of our Saviour: witness the Popish horrid monster of transubstantiation, and their idolatrous mass.

8 Custom of sinning takes away the sense of it; the course of the world takes away the shame of it; and love to it makes men greedy in the pursuit of it.

17.80
Blaise Pascal (1623-1662)
French mathematician, physicist, theologian and man of letters

1 Atheism shows strength of mind, but only to a certain degree.

2 It is your own assent to yourself, and the constant voice of your own reason, and not of others, that should make you believe.

3 The heart has its reasons, which reason knows not, as we feel in a thousand instances.

4 We know the truth, not only by the reason, but also by the heart.

5 Religion is so great a thing that it is right that those who will not take the trouble to seek it, if it be obscure, should be deprived of it.

6 Miracles enable us to judge of doctrine, and doctrine enables us to judge of miracles.

7 Console thyself, thou wouldst not seek Me, if thou hadst not found me.

8 Our soul is cast into a body, where it finds number, time, dimension. Thereupon it reasons, and calls this nature necessity and can believe nothing else.

9 Let us weigh the gain and the loss, in wagering that God is. Consider these alternatives: if you win, you win all, if you lose you lose nothing. Do not hesitate, then, to wager that he is.

10 Apart from Christ we know neither what our life nor our death is; we do not know what God is nor what we ourselves are.

11 Men never do evil so completely and cheerfully as when they do it from religious conviction.

12 Our nature consists in motion, complete inaction is death.

13 Jesus was in a garden, not of delight as the first Adam, in which he destroyed himself and the whole human race, but in one of agony, in which he saved himself and the whole human race.

14 Jesus will be in agony even to the end of the world. We must not sleep during that time.

15 Man's grandeur stems from his knowledge of his own misery. A tree does not know itself to be miserable.

16 He who hates not in himself his self-love and that instinct which leads him to make himself a God, is indeed blind.

17 There is no arena in which vanity displays itself under such a variety of forms as in conversation.

18 Nature has some perfections to show that she is the image of God, and some defects to show that she is only His image.

19 The last act is bloody, however fine the rest of the play. They throw earth over your head and it is finished for ever.

20 The [Catholic] church has three sorts of enemies: the Jews, who have never been of her body; the heretics who have withdrawn from it; the evil Christians who tear her from within.

21 Grace is indeed needed to turn a man into a saint, and he who doubts it does not know what a saint or a man is.

22 'God of Abraham, God of Isaac, God of Jacob', not of the philosophers and scholars. Certitude, certitude, feeling, joy, peace. God of Jesus Christ.

23 Reason's last step is the recognition that there are an infinite number of things which are beyond it. It is merely feeble if it does not go as far as to realise that.

24 It is not only impossible but useless to know God without Christ.

25 Knowing God without knowing our own wretchedness makes for pride. Knowing our wretchedness without knowing God makes for despair. Knowing Jesus Christ strikes the balance because he shows us both God and our own wretchedness.

17.81
Vincent de Paul (1580-1660)
French Roman Catholic priest and philanthropist

1 We should spend as much time in thanking God for his benefits as we do in asking him for them.

2 The reason why God is so great a Lover of humility is because He is the great Lover of truth. Now humility is nothing but truth, while pride is nothing but lying.

3 In this world, things that are naturally to endure for a long time, are the slowest in reaching maturity.

4 Be careful to preserve your health. It is a trick of the devil, which he employs to deceive good souls, to incite them to do more than they are able, in order that they may no longer be able to do anything.

5 If in order to succeed in an enterprise, I were obliged to choose between fifty deer commanded by a lion, and fifty lions commanded by a deer, I should consider myself more certain of success with the first group than with the second.

17.82
Isaac Penington (1616-1679)
English Puritan and Quaker

1 Be content to be a child, and let the Father proportion out daily to thee what light, what power, what exercises, what straits, what fears, what troubles he sees fit for thee.

2 Our life is love, and peace, and tenderness; and bearing one with another, and forgiving one another, and not laying accusations one against another.

17.83
Mary Penington (c.1625-1682)
English Quaker

1 By taking up the cross, I received strength against many things which I had thought impossible to deny; but many tears did I shed, and bitterness of soul did I experience, before I came thither.

17.84
Samuel Pepys (1633-1703)
English diarist

1 Music is the thing of the world that I love most.

2 I pray God to keep me from being proud.

3 Myself in constant good health, and in a most handsome and thriving condition, Blessed be Almighty God for it.

4 To Mr Rawlinson's church. A very fine store of women there is in this church, more than I know anywhere else.

5 I go to church; and this day the parson hath got one to read with a surplice on; I suppose himself will take it up hereafter for a cunning fellow he is as any of his coat.

6 And so by coaches to church—where a pretty good sermon—and a declaration of penitence of a man that had undergone the Church censure for his wicked life.

7 Strange to see how a good dinner and feasting reconciles everybody.

17.85
Alban Roe (1583-1642)
English Roman Catholic martyr

1 When you see our heads fixed up over the bridge, think that they are there to preach to you the very same faith for which we are about to die.

17.86
Samuel Rutherford (?1600-1661)
Scottish minister and theologian

1 Jesus Christ came into my prison cell last night, and every stone flashed like a ruby.

2 Whenever I find myself in the cellar of affliction, I always look about for the wine.

3 I urge upon you communion with Christ, a growing communion.

4 Grace grows better in the winter.

5 Believe God's word and power more than you believe your own feelings and experiences.

6 I would be undone if I did not have access to his chamber when I can show him all my business.

7 Be not proud of race, face, place, or grace.

8 I know no wholesome fountain but one. I know not a thing worth the buying but heaven; and my own mind is, if comparison were made betwixt Christ and heaven, I would sell heaven with my blessing and buy Christ.

17.87
François de Sales (1567-1622)
French Roman Catholic bishop and spiritual writer

1 Great works do not always lie in our way, but every moment we may do little ones excellently, that is, with great love.

2 If workmen spent as much time in church as religious, if religious were exposed to the same pastoral calls as a bishop, such devotion would be ridiculous and cause intolerable disorder.

3 Faith fills a man with love for the beauty of its truth, with faith in the truth of its beauty.

4 Since, O my soul, thou art capable of God, woe to thee if thou contentest thyself with anything less than God.

5 Blessed are they who do not their own will on earth, for God will do it in heaven above.

6 Nothing is so strong as gentleness, nothing so gentle as real strength.

7 Let us belong to God even in the thick of the disturbance stirred up round about us by the diversity of human affairs. True virtue is not always nourished in external calm any more than good fish are always found in stagnant waters.

8 God requires a faithful fulfilment of the merest trifle given us to do, rather than the most ardent aspiration to things to which we are not called.

9 The business of finding fault is very easy, and that of doing better very difficult.

10 He who is fretted by his own failings will not correct them; all profitable correction comes from a calm, peaceful mind.

11 I can show them that a vigorous and constant soul can live in the world without receiving *any* worldly taint, can find springs of sweet piety in the midst of the briny waters of the world.

12 The kindling power of our words must not come from outward show but from within, not from oratory but straight from the heart.

13 Try as hard as you like, but in the end only the language of the heart can ever reach another heart while mere words, as they slip from your tongue, don't get past your listener's ear.

14 Half an hour's listening is essential except when you are very busy. Then a full hour is needed.

15 There was never an angry man that thought his anger unjust.

16 To reflect on all our ordinary actions by a continual self-examination would be to tangle ourselves in a labyrinth from which we could never be extricated.

17.88
Henry Scougal (1650-1678)
Scottish theologian

1 [Title of a book by Scougal and John Wesley's definition of a Christian] The life of God in the soul of man.

2 True religion is an union of God with the soul, a real participation of the divine nature, the very image of God drawn upon the soul, or in the Apostle's phrase, it is Christ formed in us.

17.89
William Shakespeare (1564-1616)
English playwright and poet

1 The web of our life is of a mingled yarn, good and ill together. Our virtues would be proud if our faults whipped them not, and our crimes would despair if they were not cherished by our virtues.

2 Some say that ever 'gainst that season comes
Wherein our Saviour's birth is celebrated,
The bird of dawning singeth all night long;
And then, they say, no spirit can walk abroad;
The nights are wholesome; then no planets strike,
No fairy takes, nor witch hath power to charm,
So hallowed and so gracious is the time.

3 And what's in prayer but this twofold force,
To be forestalled ere we come to fall,
Or pardoned being down?

4 Try what repentance can. What can it not?
Yet what can it when one cannot repent?
O wretched state, O bosom black as death,
O limed soul that, struggling to be free,
Art more engaged! Help, angels, make assay.
Bow, stubborn knees; and heart with strings of steel
Be soft as sinews of the new-born babe.

5 My words fly up, my thoughts remain below;
Words without thoughts never to heaven go.

6 What a piece of work is man! how noble in reason! how infinite in faculty! in form, in moving, how express and admirable! in action how like an angel! in apprehension how like a god! the beauty of the world! the paragon of animals!

7 Cromwell, I charge thee, fling away ambition;
By that sin fell the angels. How can man then,
The image of his maker, hope to win by it?

8 I know myself now, and I feel within me
A peace above all earthly dignities,
A still and quiet conscience.

17.90
Angelus Silesius (Johann Scheffler) (1624-1677)
Mystical poet and controversialist from Silesia

1 The Godhead is my sap:
what greens and blooms of me,
That is Holy Ghost, who moves my energy.

2 I am as great as God, he is as small as I;
He can't be over me, beneath him I can't be.

3 A rose is but a rose, it blooms because it blooms;
It thinks not on itself, nor asks if it is seen.

4 The soul in whom God dwells—
it is (O blest delight!)
A wandering, flowing tent
of glory's endless light.

5 Be pure, still, learn to yield, and climb
to darkest heights:
Then you will come o'er all to contemplate
your God.

6 Take, drink as much as you want and can,
to you 'tis free—
The whole Divinity is your own hostelry!

7 Abandon all, and then you will dwell
close to God.
But then, abandon God—few men
can grasp this step!

17.91
Philipp Jakob Spener (1635-1705)
Alsace-born German Lutheran pastor, founder of Pietism

1 We must accustom the people to believe that mere knowledge is by no means sufficient for true Christianity—which is much more a matter of behaviour.

2 The beloved John in his old age (according to Jerome in his commentary on Galatians 3:6) was in the habit of saying little else to his disciples other than 'Little children, love one another'. Eventually they became so fed up with always hearing the same thing that they asked him why he constantly repeated it. He replied, 'Because it is the Lord's command and if it comes to pass, that suffices.'

3 Not the last among the reasons for the defect in the church are all the mistakes which occur in the calling of ministers.

17.92
Peter Sterry (1613-1672)
English Puritan divine

1 Divine love is the most universal and importunate beggar. It cometh to the door of every spirit. It knocketh. It presseth in.

17.93
Marmaduke Stevenson (d.1659)
English Quaker, imprisoned in Boston (North America) for his testimony

1 In the beginning of the year 1655, I was at the plough in the east parts of Yorkshire in Old England, near the place where my outward being was; and, as I walked after the plough, I was filled with the love and presence of the living God, which did ravish my heart when I felt it, for it did increase and abound in me like a living stream, so did the life and love of God run through me like precious ointment giving a pleasant smell, which made me to stand still. And, as I stood still... the word of the Lord came to me... 'I have ordained thee a prophet unto the nations'.

17.94
Jeremy Taylor (1613-1667)
Anglican Bishop of Down and Connor, and spiritual writer

1 It is impossible for that man to despair who remembers that his helper is omnipotent.

2 A man may be damned for despairing to be saved. Despair is the proper passion of damnation.

3 Our nature is very bad in itself, but very good to them that use it well.

4 Right intention is to the actions of a man what the soul is to the body, or the root to the tree.

5 No sin is small. No grain of sand is small in the mechanism of a watch.

6 If we refuse mercy here, we shall have justice in eternity.

7 God hath given to man a short time here upon earth, and yet upon this short time eternity depends.

8 In matters of conscience that is the best sense which every wise man takes in before he hath sullied his understanding with the designs of sophisters and interested persons.

9 Love is the greatest thing that God can give us for Himself is love: and it is the greatest thing we can give to God.

10 Virginity is a life of angels, the enamel of the soul.

11 The marital love is a thing pure as light, sacred as a temple, lasting as the world.

12 A husband's power over his wife is paternal and friendly, not magisterial and despotic.

13 He that loves not his wife and children feeds a lioness at home and broods a nest of sorrows.

14 The more we love, the better we are, and the greater our friendships are, the dearer we are to God.

15 Solitude is a good school, but the world is the best theatre.

16 The sublimity of wisdom is to do those things living which are to be desired when dying.

17 Every new star gilds the firmament and increases its first glories: and those, who are instruments of the conversion of others, shall not only introduce new beauties, but when themselves shine like the stars in glory, they shall have some reflections from the light of others, to whose fixing in the orb of heaven themselves have been instrumental.

18 A religion without mystery must be a religion without God.

17.95
Thomas Taylor (1576-1633)
English Puritan theologian

1 In your reading, let not your end be to seek and find out curiosities and subtleties, but to find and meet with Christ.

17.96
John Tillotson (1630-1694)
Archbishop of Canterbury

1 He who provides for this life, but takes no care for eternity, is wise for a moment, but a fool forever.

2 This life is the time of our preparation for our future state. Our souls will continue for ever what we make them in this world.

3 If God were not a necessary Being of Himself, He might seem to be made for the use and benefit of men.

4 God will not so much disparage eternal life and happiness, as to bestow it upon those who have conceived so low an opinion of it, as not to think it worth labouring for.

17.97
Thomas Traherne (?1636-1674)
English Anglican poet and writer

1 As nothing is easier than to think, so nothing is more difficult than to think well. The easiness of thinking we received from God, the difficulty of thinking well proceeded from ourselves.

2 Whether it be the soul itself, or God in the soul, that shines by love, or both, it is difficult to tell: but certainly the love of the soul is the sweetest thing in the world.

3 An empty book is like an infant's soul in which anything may be written. It is capable of all things, but containeth nothing.

4 Adam in Paradise had not more sweet and curious apprehensions of the world than I when I was a child.

5 For God hath made you able to create worlds in your own mind which are more precious to Him than those which He created.

6 Let the remembrance of all the glory wherein I was created make me more serious and humble, more deep and penitent, more pure and holy before Thee.

7 You never know yourself until you know more than your body. The image of God is not sealed in the features of your face, but in the lineaments of your soul.

8 A little grit in the eye destroyeth the sight of the very heavens; and a little malice or envy, a world of joy.

9 But with much trouble I was corrupted and made to learn the dirty devices of the world which I am now unlearning and becoming as it were a little child again, so that I may enter into the Kingdom of God.

10 You never enjoy the world aright till the sea itself floweth in your veins, till you are clothed with the heavens and crowned with the stars.

11 They in heaven prize blessings when they have them. They on earth do not prize them when they have them. They in hell prize them but do not have them.

12 A Christian is an oak flourishing in winter.

13 The cross of Christ is the Jacob's ladder by which we ascend into the highest heaven.

14 That cross is a tree set on fire with invisible flame that illumineth all the world. The flame is love.

15 By love alone is God enjoyed by love alone delighted in, by love alone approached and admired. His nature requires love. The law of nature commands thee to love him: the law of his nature, and the law of thine.

17.98
Rebecca Travers (?1609-1688)
English Quaker

1 The women's meetings are accompanied with the power and presence of the Lord as ever—our service great, and our supply faileth not.

17.99
Sebastian Valfré (1629-1710)
Italian spiritual director and preacher

1 An unpitied pain wins greater merit before God. Never say to God: 'Enough'; simply say, 'I am ready!'

2 When it is all over, you will not regret having suffered; rather you will regret having suffered so little and suffered that little so badly.

17.100
Henry Vaughan (c.1621-1695)
Welsh poet

1 I saw Eternity the other night,
Like a great ring of pure and endless light,
All calm, as it was bright;
And round beneath it,
Time in hours, days, years,
Driv'n by the spheres
Like a vast shadow moved;
in which the world
And all her twain were hurled.

2 My soul, there is a country
Far beyond the stars,
Where stands a winged sentry
All skilful in the wars:
There, above noise and danger,
Sweet Peace sits crown'd with smiles
And One born in a manger
Commands the beauteous files.

3 There is in God—some say—
A deep, but dazzling darkness.

17.101
Izaak Walton (1593-1683)
English writer

1 I love such mirth as does not make friends ashamed to look upon one another next morning.

2 You will find angling to be like the virtue of humility, which has a calmness of spirit and a world of other blessings attending upon it.

3 Blessings we enjoy daily, and for the most of them, because they be so common, men forget to pay their praises. But let not us, because it is a sacrifice so pleasing to him who still protects us, and gives us flowers, and showers, and meat and content.

4 Look to your health; and if you have it, praise God and value it next to a good conscience; for health is the second blessing that we mortals are capable of—a blessing that money cannot buy; therefore value it, and be thankful for it.

5 I have heard a grave divine say, that God has two dwellings, one in heaven, and the other in the meek and thankful heart.

6 He that loses his conscience has nothing left that is worth keeping.

7 Of this blest man, let his just praise be given:
Heaven was in him, before he was in heaven.

17.102
Mary Ward (1585-1645)

English founder of the Institute of the Blessed Virgin Mary

1 I would to God that all men understood this verity, that women, if they will, may be perfect, and if they would not make us believe we can do nothing and that we are 'but women', we might do great matters.

17.103
Rowland Watkyns (c.1610-1664)

Welsh clergyman

1 Bad company is a disease;
Who lies with dogs, shall rise with fleas.

17.104
Benjamin Whichcote (1609-1683)

English preacher, philosopher and Provost of King's College, Cambridge

1 He that never changed any of his opinions, never corrected any of his mistakes: and he, who was never wise enough, to find out any mistakes in himself, will not be charitable enough, to excuse what he reckons mistakes in others.

PART 4

Eighteenth Century

All the actions, all the movements of the saints, make up the gospel of the Holy Spirit. Their holy souls are the paper, their sufferings and their actions are the ink.

Jean Pierre de Caussade
(1675-1751)

18.1
Joseph Addison (1672-1719)
English essayist and poet

1 A woman seldom asks advice before she has bought her wedding clothes.

2 A religious hope does not only bear up the mind under her sufferings, but makes her rejoice in them.

3 Tradition is an important help to history, but its statements should be carefully scrutinised before we rely on them.

4 Irresolution on the schemes of life which offer themselves to our choice, and inconstancy in pursuing them, are the greatest causes of all our unhappiness.

5 I have often thought, said Sir Roger, it happens very well that Christmas should fall out in the middle of winter.

6 Sir Roger will suffer no one to sleep in [church] besides himself... if he sees anybody else nodding, either wakes them himself, or sends his servants to them.

7 The spacious firmament on high
With all the blue ethereal sky,
And spangled heavens, a shining frame,
Their great original proclaim:
The unwearied sun, from day to day,
Does his Creator's power display,
And publishes to every land
The work of an almighty hand.

8 A state of temperance, sobriety and justice without devotion is a cold, lifeless, insipid condition of virtue, and is rather to be styled philosophy than religion.

9 The best may err.

10 Music, the greatest good that mortals know
And all of heaven we have below.

11 Music religious hearts inspires;
It wakes the soul, and lifts it high,
And wings it with sublime desires,
And fits it to bespeak the Deity.

12 Sunday clears away the rust of the whole week.

13 If there's a power above us,
(And that there is all nature cries aloud
Through all her works) he must delight
in virtue.

14 If our zeal were true and genuine we should be much more angry with a sinner than a heretic.

15 Our real blessings often appear to us in the shape of pains, losses and disappointments; but let us have patience, and we soon shall see them in their proper figures.

16 Nothing lies on our hands with such uneasiness as time. Wretched and thoughtless creatures! In the only place where covetousness were a virtue we turn prodigals.

17 It is ridiculous for any man to criticise the works of another if he has not distinguished himself by his own performance.

18 The utmost we can hope for in this life is contentment.

19 A friendship that makes the least noise is very often the most useful; for which reason I prefer a prudent friend to a zealous one.

20 Health and cheerfulness mutually beget each other.

21 A man's first care should be to avoid the reproaches of his own heart.

22 Justice discards party, friendship, kindred, and is always, therefore represented as blind.

23 To forbear replying to an unjust reproach, and overlook it with a generous or, if possible, with an entire neglect of it, is one of the most heroic acts of a great mind.

24 Heaven is not to be looked upon only as the reward, but as the natural effect of a religious life.

25 Eternity! Thou pleasing, dreadful thought!
Through what variety of untried being,
Through what new scenes and changes
must we pass!
The wide, the unbounded prospect lies
before me,
But shadows, clouds, and darkness
rest upon it.

26 See in what peace a Christian can die.

18.2
Queen Anne (1665-1714)
Queen of Great Britain and Ireland

1 Almighty and eternal God, the Disposer of all the affairs of the world, there is not one circumstance so great as not to be subject to thy power, nor so small but it comes within thy care.

18.3
Johannes Albrecht Bengel (1687-1752)
Lutheran New Testament scholar

1 Apply yourself wholly to the scriptures, and apply the scriptures wholly to yourself.

2 [Of Mary] Not as the mother of grace, but as the daughter of grace.

18.4
John Berridge (1716-1793)
English clergyman

1 Preach nothing down but the devil, and nothing up but Jesus Christ.

2 [Epitaph, written by himself] Here lie the earthly remains of John Berridge, late vicar of Everton, and an itinerant servant of Jesus Christ, who loved his Master and his work, and after running on his errands many years was called to wait on him above. Reader, art thou born again? No salvation without new birth! I was born in sin, February 1716. Remained ignorant of my fallen state till 1730. Lived proudly on faith and works for salvation till 1754. Was admitted to Everton Vicarage, 1755. Fled to Jesus alone for refuge, 1756.

18.5
Peter Böhler (c.1712-1775)
Moravian pastor

1 Preach faith until you have it.

18.6
David Brainerd (1718-1747)
US evangelist to the North American Indians

1 My heaven is to please God and glorify him, and to give all to him, and to be wholly devoted to his glory; that is the heaven I long for.

2 I was a little better than speechless all day. O my God, I am speedily coming to thee! Hasten the day, O Lord, if it be thy blessed will. Oh, come, Lord Jesus, come quickly.

18.7
Edmund Burke (1729-1797)
Irish Protestant politician and orator who fought for Catholic emancipation

1 Nobody makes a greater mistake than he who does nothing because he could only do a little.

2 The only thing necessary for the triumph of evil is for good men to do nothing.

3 By gnawing through a dyke, even a rat may drown a nation.

4 Nothing is so fatal to religion as indifference.

5 Superstition is the religion of feeble minds.

6 Next to love, sympathy is the divinest passion of the human heart.

7 Our patience will achieve more than our force.

8 There is a limit at which forbearance ceases to be a virtue.

9 No sound ought to be heard in the church but the healing voice of Christian charity.

10 Example is the school of mankind, and they will learn at no other.

11 Too many have dispensed with generosity to practise charity.

12 All government—indeed, every human benefit and enjoyment, every virtue and every prudent act—is founded on compromise and barter.

13 Government is a contrivance of human wisdom to provide for human wants.

14 Magnanimity in politics is not seldom the truest wisdom; and a great empire and little minds go ill together.

15 Bad laws are the worst sort of tyranny.

16 There is but one law for all, namely, that law which governs all law, the law of our Creator, the law of humanity, justice, equity—the law of nature, and of nations.

17 [Morality] is not what a lawyer tells me I *may* do; but what humanity, reason, and justice tell me I ought to do.

18 It is hard to say whether the doctors of law or divinity have made the great advances in the lucrative business of mystery.

19 Power gradually extirpates from the mind every humane and gentle virtue.

20 Well is it known that ambition can creep as well as soar.

21 To reach the height of our ambition is like trying to reach the rainbow; as we advance it recedes.

22 Good order is the foundation of all good things.

23 Custom reconciles us to everything.

24 A state without the means of some change is without the means of its conservation.

25 We must all obey the great law of change. It is the most powerful law of nature.

26 No passion so effectually robs the mind of all its powers of acting and reasoning as fear.

27 They defined their errors as if they were defending their inheritance.

28 You can never plan the future by the past.

29 The arrogance of age must submit to be taught by youth.

30 To complain of the age we live in, to murmur at the present possessors of power, to lament the past, to conceive extravagant hopes of the future, are the common dispositions of the greatest part of mankind.

31 Flattery corrupts both the receiver and the giver.

32 Man is by his constitution a religious animal.

33 All protestantism, even the most cold and passive, is a sort of dissent. But [this] is a refinement of the principle of resistance: it is the dissidence of dissent, and the protestantism of the Protestant religion.

34 Religious persecution may shield itself under the guise of a mistaken and over-zealous piety.

35 The writers against religion, whilst they oppose every other system, are wisely careful never to set up any of their own.

36 The true way to mourn the dead is to take care of the living who belong to them.

18.8
Alban Butler (1710-1773)
English Roman Catholic priest and hagiographer

1 The method of forming men to virtue by example is, of all others, the shortest, the most easy, and the best adapted to all circumstances and dispositions.

2 Though we cannot imitate all the actions of the saints, we can learn from them to practise humility, patience, and other virtues in a manner suiting our circumstances and state of life; and we can pray that we may receive a share in the benedictions and glory of the saints.

18.9
Joseph Butler (1692-1752)
English bishop

1 [To John Wesley] Sir, the pretending to extraordinary revelations and gifts of the Holy Ghost is a horrid thing, a very horrid thing.

2 That which is the foundation of all our hopes and all our fears; all our hopes and fears which are of any consideration; I mean a future life.

18.10
John Byrom (1692-1763)
English hymn-writer

1 The parson leaves the *Christian* in the lurch
Whene'er he brings his politics into church.

2 The truth of the Gospel, which is essentially and initially a corporate possession, is personally appropriated by prayer in the heart of the believer.

3 My spirit longs for thee
Within my troubled breast,
Though I unworthy be
Of so divine a guest.

18.11
Jean Pierre de Caussade (1675-1751)
French Jesuit, ascetic writer and preacher

1 Each day you must say to yourself, 'Today I am going to begin.'

2 All that is good in you comes from God, all that is bad, spoilt and corrupt comes from yourself.

3 God is sufficiently wise, and good and powerful and merciful to turn even the most, apparently, disastrous events to the advantage and profit of those who humbly adore and accept his will in all that he permits.

4 God makes of *all* things mysteries and sacraments of love, why should not every moment of our lives be a sort of communion with the divine love?

5 While he strips of everything the souls who give themselves absolutely to him, God gives them something which takes the place of all; of light, wisdom, life and force: this gift is his love.

6 The Holy Spirit... writes his own gospel and he writes it in the hearts of the faithful.

7 There is but one thing to do to purify our hearts, to detach ourselves from creatures, and abandon ourselves entirely to God.

8 What God arranges for us to experience at each moment is the best and holiest thing that could happen to us.

9 The soul must be kept peaceful during prayer and end prayer in peace.

10 There is no one in the world who cannot arrive without difficulty at the most eminent perfection by fulfilling with love obscure and common duties.

11 There is nothing so small or apparently indifferent which God does not ordain or permit even to the fall of a leaf.

12 Watch over your heart that you may not give way, in the very least to bitterness, spite, complaints or voluntary rebellion.

13 One often has more delight finding refreshment anew than one ever had grief in its loss.

14 Interior disturbance renders the soul incapable of listening to and following the voice of the divine Spirit, of receiving the sweet and delightful impressions of His grace, and of applying itself to devotional exercises and to exterior duties.

15 Your foolish fears about the future come from the devil. Think only of the present, abandon the future to Providence. It is the good use of the present that assures the future.

16 God instructs the heart not by ideas, but by pains and contradictions.

17 All the actions, all the movements of the saints, make up the gospel of the Holy Spirit. Their holy souls are the paper, their sufferings and their actions are the ink.

18 All created things are living in the Hand of God. The senses see only the action of the creatures; but faith sees in everything the action of God.

18.12
Richard Cecil (1748-1810)
Anglican preacher

1 All the minister's efforts will be vanity or worse than vanity if he have not unction. Unction must come from heaven and spread a savour and feeling and relish over his ministry.

2 The leading defect in Christian ministers is want of a devotional habit.

3 We are too fond of our own will. We want to be doing what we fancy mighty things but the great point is to do small things, when called to them, in a right spirit.

4 The right way of interpreting scripture is to take it as we find it, without any attempt to force it into any particular system.

5 To love to preach is one thing—to love those to whom we preach, quite another.

18.13
Richard Challoner (1691-1781)
English Roman Catholic devotional writer

1 Consider... that the Holy Ghost came down upon the Apostles, in the shape of tongues, to signify that he came to make them fit preachers of his word; and to endow them with the gift of tongues, accompanied with heavenly wisdom, and understanding, of the mysteries of God, and all the gospel truths; to the end that they might be enabled to teach and publish, throughout the whole world, the faith and law of Christ.

18.14
William Cowper (1731-1800)
English poet

1 You must know that I should not love you half so well, if I did not believe you would be my friend to eternity. There is not room enough for friendship to unfold itself in such a nook of life as this.

2 Man may dismiss compassion from his heart, but God will never.

3 God made the country and man made the town.

4 Absence of occupation is not rest,
A mind quite vacant is a mind distress'd.

5 Remorse, the fatal egg by pleasure laid.

6 Grief is itself a medicine.

7 All truth is precious, if not all divine.

8 Knowledge is proud that he has learned
so much;
Wisdom is humble that he knows no more.

9 Nature is but a name for an effect whose cause is God.

10 All zeal for a reform, that gives offence
To peace and charity, is mere pretence.

11 Fanaticism is the false fire of an overheated mind.

12 Behind the frowning Providence
He hides a smiling face.

13 If we address [God] as children, it is because he tells us he is our father. If we unbosom ourselves to him as a friend, it is because he calls us friends.

14 And Satan trembles when he sees,
The weakest saint upon his knees.

15 But though life's valley be a vale of tears,
A brighter scene beyond that vale appears.

16 Oh! for a closer walk with God,
A calm and heavenly frame;
A light to shine upon the road
That leads me to the Lamb!

18.15
Daniel Defoe (1660-?1731)
English novelist and pamphleteer

1 And of all plagues with which mankind
are curst,
Ecclesiastic tyranny's the worst.

2 What is more frequent, than to see religion make men cynical, and sour in their tempers, morose and surly in their conversation.

3 All that can be called happy in the life of man, can be summed up in the state of marriage; that is the centre to which all the lesser delights of life tend, as a point in the circle.

4 In a Word, as my Life was a Life of Sorrow one way, so it was a Life of Mercy another and I wanted nothing to make it a Life of Comfort but to be able to make any sense of God's goodness to me and care over me in this condition to be my only consolation.

5 To pray and pay, too, is the devil.

6 Every devil has not a cloven hoof.

18.16
Philip Doddridge (1702-1751)
Congregational minister and hymn-writer

1 The present moment flies,
And bears our life away;
O make thy servants truly wise,
That they may live today.

2 He comes, the prisoners to release
In Satan's bondage held;
The gates of brass before him burst,
The iron fetters yield.

3 Watch! 'Tis your Lord's command,
And, while we speak, he's near;
Mark the first signal of his hand,
And ready all appear.

4 Through each perplexing path of life
Our wandering footsteps guide;
Give us each day our daily bread,
And raiment fit provide.

O spread thy covering wings around,
Till all our wanderings cease,
And at our Father's loved abode
Our souls arrive in peace.

18.17
Jonathan Edwards (1703-1757)
North American Christian philosopher and preacher

1 A true love of God must begin with a delight in his holiness, and not with a delight in any other attribute; for no other attribute is truly lovely without this.

2 Grace is but glory begun, and glory is but grace perfected.

3 If there be ground for you to trust in your own righteousness, then all that Christ did to purchase salvation, and all that God did to prepare the way for it, is in vain.

4 You have offended [God] infinitely more than ever a stubborn rebel did his prince—and yet it is nothing but his hand that holds you from falling into the fire every moment.

5 I am bold to assert that there never was any considerable change wrought in the mind or conversation of any person, by anything of a religious nature that ever he read, heard or saw, who had not his affections moved... In a word, there never was anything considerable brought to pass in the heart or life of any man living, by the things of religion, that had not his heart deeply affected by those things.

6 The end of God's creating the world was to prepare a kingdom for his Son.

7 None are true saints except those who have the true character of compassion and concern to relieve the poor, indigent, and afflicted.

8 We must view humility as one of the most essential things that characterize true Christianity.

9 Without the capacity of rational argument, all our proof of God ceases.

10 The bodies of those that made such a noise and tumult when alive, when dead, lie as quietly among the graves of their neighbours as any others.

18.18
Thomas Ellwood (1638-1713)
English Quaker, friend of John Milton

1 I found there were many plants growing in me which were not of the heavenly Father's planting, and that all these, of whatever sort or kind they were or how specious soever they might appear, must be plucked up.

18.19
François Fénelon (1651-1715)
Archbishop of Cambrai

1 We are told by all spiritual writers that one important point to bear in mind, as we seek to attain humility, is not to be surprised by our own faults and failures.

2 False humility is to believe that one is unworthy of God's goodness and does not dare to seek it humbly.

3 True humility lies in seeing one's own unworthiness, giving up oneself to God, not doubting for a moment that he can perform the greatest results for us and in us.

4 Humility is not a grace that can be acquired in a few months: it is the work of a lifetime.

5 Be content with doing with calmness the little which depends on yourself and let all else be to you as if it were not.

6 Faithfulness in carrying out present duties is the best preparation for the future.

7 There is nothing that is more dangerous to your own salvation, more unworthy of God and more harmful to your own happiness than that you should be content to remain as you are.

8 Knowledge is not the most important thing in the world. Love is essential.

9 To want all that God wants, always to want it, for all occasions and without reservations, that is the kingdom of God which is all within.

10 True affection is ingeniously inventive.

11 It is, however, only by fidelity in little things that a true and constant love of God can be distinguished from a passing fervour of spirit.

12 Chains of gold are no less chains than chains of iron.

13 When you meditate, imagine that Jesus Christ in person is about to talk to you about the most important thing in the world. Give him your complete attention.

14 To pray... is to desire; but it is to desire what God would have us desire. He who desires not from the bottom of his heart, offers a deceitful prayer.

15 As soon as we are with God in faith and in love, we are in prayer.

16 Listen less to your own thoughts and more to God's thoughts.

17 If you are to be self-controlled in your speech you must be self-controlled in your thinking.

18 It is when God appears to have abandoned us that we must abandon ourselves most wholly to God.

19 Let gratitude for the past inspire us with trust for the future.

18.20
Frederick the Great (1712-1786)
King of Prussia

1 All religions must be tolerated. Every man must get to heaven in his own way.

18.21
John Furz
Methodist preacher

1 As soon as I began to preach, a man came straight forward, and presented a gun at my face; swearing that he would blow my brains out, if I spake another word. However, I continued speaking, and he continued swearing, sometimes putting the muzzle of the gun to my mouth, sometimes against my ear. While we were singing the last hymn, he got behind me, fired the gun, and burned off part of my hair.

18.22
Olympe de Gourges (1745-1793)
French revolutionary republican, executed for her work on behalf of women

1 Women, rouse yourselves! The tocsin of reason resounds through the whole universe: recognize your rights. The powerful empire of

nature is no longer surrounded by prejudices, fanaticism, superstition and lies. The flame of truth has banished the clouds of stupidity and encroachment. Enslaved man doubled his efforts and still had need of yours to cast off his chains. Now that he is free he has become unjust towards his companion.

18.23
William Grimshaw (1708-1763)
English clergyman

1 If God drew up his Bible to heaven and sent me down another, it would not be newer to me.

18.24
Jean Nicholas Grou (1731-1803)
French Jesuit

1 The chief pang of most trials is not so much the actual suffering itself as our own spirit of resistance to it.

2 Among the actions which count as prayer, I include visits of courtesy and kindness, also necessary recreation of body and mind, so long as these be innocent and kept within the bounds of Christian conduct.

3 Fidelity in trifles, and an earnest seeking to please God in little matters, is a test of real devotion and love.

4 The crucified state is necessary for us, is good, is best and safest and will bring us more sooner to the height of perfection.

5 We must not forget that one of the greatest secrets of the spiritual life is that the Holy Spirit leads us in it not only by light and sweetness, by consolations, tendernesses, and facility of prayer, but also by obscurities and blindness, by insensibility, troubles, anguish of soul, sorrow and desolation, and often the rebellion of all our evil passions and tempers.

18.25
Madame Jeanne Guyon (1648-1717)
French Quietist author

1 If everyone who worked for the conversion of others was to introduce them immediately to prayer and to the interior life and made it their main aim to win over their hearts, innumerable, permanent conversions would definitely take place.

2 The more we appropriate God into our lives the more progress we make on the road of Christian godliness and holiness.

3 Prayer is the application of the heart to God, and the internal exercise of love.

4 Prayer is the guide to perfection, and delivers us from every vice, and gives us every virtue; for the one way to become perfect is to walk in the presence of God.

5 Do not turn to prayer hoping to enjoy spiritual delights; rather come to prayer totally content to receive nothing or to receive great blessing from God's hand, whichever should be your heavenly Father's will for you at that time.

6 Outward silence is indispensable for the cultivation and improvement of inner silence.

7 God gives the cross, and the cross gives us God.

8 It is impossible to love God without loving the cross; and a heart that delights in the cross, finds the most bitter things sweet.

9 Give no place to despondency. This is a dangerous temptation of the adversary. Melancholy contracts and withers the heart.

10 Be patient in all the sufferings God is pleased to send you. If your love of God is wholehearted you will seek him as much at Calvary as at Mount Tabor and you will definitely find that God's love towards you is even greater.

11 My life is consecrated to God, to suffer for him, as well as to enjoy him.

18.26
Joseph Hart (1712-1768)
English Independent minister and hymn-writer

1 How good is the God we adore,
our faithful unchangeable friend!
His love is as great as his power,
and knows neither measure nor end!

2 Convince us of our sin,
Then lead to Jesu's blood;
And to our wondering view reveal
The secret love of God.

18.27
Matthew Henry (1662-1714)
English Non-conformist Bible commentator

1 O Lord, lift up the light of your countenance upon us; let your peace rule in our hearts, and may it be our strength and our song in the house of our pilgrimage.

2 It was a common saying among the Puritans 'Brown bread and the Gospel is good fare'.

3 Shallows where a lamb could wade and depths where an elephant could drown.

4 When I cannot enjoy the faith of assurance, I live by the faith of adherence.

5 Peace is such a precious jewel that I would give anything for it but truth.

6 Grace is the free, undeserved goodness and favour of God to mankind.

7 Nothing can make a man truly great but being truly good and partaking of God's holiness.

8 The saints are God's jewels, highly esteemed by and dear to him; they are a royal diadem in his hand.

9 I take God the Father to be my God;
I take God the Son to be my Saviour;
I take the Holy Ghost to be my Sanctifier;
I take the Word of God to be my rule;
I take the people of God to be my people;
And I do hereby dedicate and yield
my whole self to the Lord:
And I do this deliberately, freely, and
for ever. Amen.

10 You have been used to take notice of the sayings of dying men. This is mine: that a life spent in the service of God, and communion with him, is the most comfortable and pleasant life that anyone can live in this world.

18.28
Lucy Herbert (1669-1744)
English Anglican lay woman

1 I am heartily sorry and beg pardon for my sins, especially for my little respect, and for wandering in my thoughts when in your presence, and for my continual infidelitys to your graces; for all which I beg pardon, by the merits of the blood you shed for them.

18.29
James Hervey (1714-1758)
English clergyman and poet

1 How thankful I am for death! It is the passage to the Lord and giver of eternal life. O welcome, welcome death! Thou mayest well be reckoned among the treasures of the Christian! To live is Christ, but to die is gain! Lord, now lettest thou thy servant depart in peace, according to thy most holy and comfortable Word; for mine eyes have seen thy precious salvation.

18.30
Selina, Countess of Huntingdon (1707-1791)
Founder of the body of Calvinist Methodists known as 'the Countess of Huntingdon's Connexion'

1 O, that my poor cold heart could catch a spark from others, and be as a flame of fire in the Redeemer's service! Some few instances of success, which God, in the riches of his mercy, has lately favoured me with, have greatly comforted me during my season of affliction; and I have felt the presence of God in my soul in a very remarkable manner.

18.31
Benjamin Jenks (1647-1724)
English clergyman and writer

1 O Lord, renew our spirits and draw our hearts unto yourself, that our work may not be as a burden but a delight.

2 O our God, let your grace be sufficient for us.

18.32
Samuel Johnson (1709-1786)
English writer and lexicographer

1 Christianity is the highest perfection of humanity.

2 To be of no church is dangerous. Religion... will glide by degrees out of the mind.

3 I have always considered a clergyman as the father of a larger family than he is able to maintain.

4 A woman's preaching is like a dog's walking on his hinder legs. It is not done well, but you are surprised to find it done at all.

5 When speculation has done its worst, two and two still make four.

6 The only method by which religious truth can be established is by martyrdom.

7 Integrity without knowledge is weak and useless, and knowledge without integrity is dangerous and dreadful.

8 Sir, don't tell me of deception; a lie, Sir, is a lie, whether it be a lie to the eye or a lie to the ear.

9 People need to be reminded more often than they need to be instructed.

10 Patriotism is the last refuge of a scoundrel.

11 Prejudice, not being founded on reason, cannot be removed by argument.

12 Abstinence is as easy to me, as temperance would be difficult.

13 He who has money to spare has it always in his power to benefit others: and of such power a good man must always be desirous.

14 A decent provision for the poor is the true test of civilisation.

15 It is better to live rich than to die rich.

16 Great works are performed not by strength but by perseverance.

17 Wickedness is always easier than virtue, for it takes the short cut to everything.

18 We live together in a world that is bursting with sin and sorrow.

19 Where there is yet shame, there may in time be virtue.

20 Adversity is the state in which a man most easily becomes acquainted with himself, being especially free from admirers then.

21 Men hate more steadily than they love.

22 We are seldom tiresome to ourselves.

23 He who makes a beast of himself gets rid of the pain of being a man.

24 The supreme end of education is expert discernment in all things—the power to tell the good from the bad, the genuine from the counterfeit, and to prefer the good and the genuine to the bad and the counterfeit.

25 Example is always more efficacious than precept.

26 Nothing has more retarded the advancement of learning than the disposition of vulgar minds to ridicule and vilify what they cannot comprehend.

27 Hope is itself a species of happiness, and perhaps, the chief happiness which the world affords.

28 Whatever enlarges hope will also exalt courage.

29 Nothing is more hopeless than a scheme of merriment.

30 Prudence is an attitude that keeps life safe, but does not often make it happy.

31 If a man does not make new acquaintances as he advances through life, he will soon find himself left alone. A man, Sir, should keep his friendship in constant repair.

32 For courteous some substitute the word humble, the difference may not be considered as great, for pride is a quality that obscures courtesy.

33 Kindness is in our power, but fondness is not.

34 Getting money is not all a man's business: to cultivate kindness is a valuable part of the business of life.

35 Life cannot subsist in society but by reciprocal concessions.

36 A fly may sting a stately horse and make him wince, but one is but an insect, and the other is a horse still.

37 It matters not how a man dies, but how he lives.

18.33
Thomas Ken (1637-1711)
English bishop and hymn-writer

1 Praise God from whom all blessings flow,
Praise him, all creatures here below,
Praise him above, angelic host,
Praise Father, Son and Holy Ghost.

2 [Above a hospital door]

O God, make the door of this house
wide enough
to receive all who need human love
and fellowship,
and a heavenly Father's care;
and narrow enough to shut out all envy,
pride and hate.

3 Teach me to live, that I may dread
The grave as little as my bed;
Teach me to die, that so I may
Rise glorious at the awful day.

4 Let those who thoughtfully consider the brevity of life remember the length of eternity.

5 To God the Father, who first loved us
and made us accepted in the Beloved:
To God the Son, who loved us, and washed us
from our sins in his own blood;
To God the Holy Ghost, who sheds the
love of God
abroad in our hearts,
Be all love and all glory,
From time and for eternity.

18.34
Benedict Joseph Labre (1748-1783)
French pilgrim and mendicant saint

1 To love God you need three hearts in one—a heart of fire for him, a heart of flesh for your neighbour, and a heart of bronze for yourself.

18.35
William Law (1686-1761)
English clergyman and religious writer

1 How paltry must be the devotions of those who are always in a hurry.

2 Solemn prayers, rapturous devotions, are but repeated hypocrisies unless the heart and mind be conformable to them.

3 Hence also has arisen another species of idolatry, even among Christians of all denominations; who, though receiving and professing the religion of the Gospel, yet worship God not in spirit and truth, but either in the deadness of an outer form, or in a pharisaical, carnal trust in their own opinions and doctrines.

4 If a man does not believe that all the world is God's family, where nothing happens by chance but is all guided and directed by the care and providence of a being that is all love and goodness to all of his creatures; if a man does not believe this from his heart, he cannot truly be said to believe in God.

5 There is nothing that makes us love a man so much as praying for him.

6 He who has learned to pray has learned the greatest secret of a holy and happy life.

7 Love is infallible; it has no errors, for all errors are the want of love.

8 The two things which, of all others, most want to be under a strict rule, and which are the greatest blessings to ourselves and others, when they are rightly used, are our time and our money.

9 You can have no greater sign of a confirmed pride than when you think you are humble enough.

10 More men live regardless of the great duties of piety through too great a concern for worldly goods than through direct injustice.

11 Hell is nothing else but nature departed or excluded from the beams of divine light.

12 Whatever is foolish, ridiculous, vain or earthly, or sensual, in the life of a Christian is something that ought not to be there. It is a spot and a defilement that must be washed away with tears and repentance.

18.36
Leonard of Port Maurice (1676-1751)
Italian Franciscan

1 We put ourselves to all sorts of inconveniences to satisfy our guilty passions but when it is a question of overcoming them we will not lift a finger. It is just this penny's worth of suffering that nobody wants to spend.

18.37
Alphonsus Liguori (1696-1787)
Italian moral theologian and founder of the Redemptorists

1 There are certain souls who desire to arrive at perfection all at once, and this desire keeps them in constant disquiet. It is necessary first to cling to the feet of Jesus, then to kiss his sacred hands, and at last you may find your way into his divine heart.

2 When those who are ever ready to criticize do not usurp authority which they do not possess, as a rule they are very useful to the community because they cause everyone to be on the lookout.

3 If you embrace all things in life as coming from the hands of God, and even embrace death to fulfil his holy will, assuredly you will die a saint.

4 A soul can do nothing that is more pleasing to God than to communicate in a state of grace.

5 We must neither judge nor suspect evil of our neighbour, without good grounds.

6 In building, we need not act as the people of the world do. They first procure the money and then begin to build, but we must do just the opposite. We will begin to build and then expect to receive what is necessary from Divine Providence. The Lord God will not be outdone in generosity.

7 He who trusts in himself is lost. He who trusts in God can do all things.

18.38
Gerard Majella (1726-1755)
Italian Redemptorist lay brother

1 O my God, how can you reproach me? Is it not you who have taught me those follies? Have you not given me the first example of folly by imprisoning yourself for me?

18.39
Louis-Marie Grignion de Montfort (1673-1716)
Popular French missionary

1 Do as the storekeeper does with his merchandise; make a profit on every article. Suffer not the loss of the tiniest fragment of the true cross. It may only be the sting of a fly or a point of a pin that annoys you; it may be the little eccentricities of a neighbour, some unintentional slight, the insignificant loss of a penny, some little restlessness of soul, a slight physical weakness, a light pain in your limbs. Make a profit on every article as the grocer does, and you will soon be wealthy in God.

2 To suffer much, yet badly, is to suffer like reprobates. To suffer much, even bravely, but for a wicked cause, is to suffer as a martyr of the devil. To suffer much or little for the sake of God is to suffer like saints.

18.40
John Morison (1750-1798)
British hymn-writer

1 Come, let us to the Lord our God
With contrite hearts return;
Our God is gracious, nor will leave
the desolate to mourn.

18.41
John Nelson (c.1707-1774)
Early English Methodist field preacher

1 But when I was in the middle of my discourse, one at the outside of the congregation threw a stone, which cut me on the head: however, that made the people give greater attention, especially when they saw the blood running down my face; so that all was quiet till I had done, and was singing a hymn.

18.42
John Newton (1725-1807)
Evangelical hymn- and letter-writer

1 Some books are copper, some are silver, and some few are gold; but the Bible alone is like a book all made up of bank notes.

2 How sweet the Name of Jesus sounds
In a believer's ear!
It soothes his sorrows, heals his wounds,
And drives away his fear!

3 Preaching should break a hard heart, and heal a broken heart.

4 When I get to heaven, I shall see three wonders there. The first wonder will be to see many there whom I did not expect to see; the second wonder will be to miss many people who I did expect to see; the third and greatest of all will be to find myself there.

5 May the grace of Christ our Saviour,
And the Father's boundless love,
With the Holy Spirit's favour,
Rest upon us from above.

6 It is indeed natural for us to wish and to plan, and it is merciful in the Lord to disappoint and to cross our wishes. For we cannot be safe, much less happy, but in proportion as we are weaned from our own wills and made simply desirous of being directed by his guidance.

18.43
Paul of the Cross (1694-1775)
Founder of the Passionists

1 I am a Lombard and I detest dissimulation. What I have in my heart I have also on my tongue.

2 Feed upon the will of God and drink the chalice of Jesus with your eyes shut, so that you may not see what is inside.

3 Alas! I have nothing to bequeath to you but my bad example.

4 Conceal yourselves in Jesus crucified, and hope for nothing except that all men be thoroughly converted to his will.

18.44
William Penn (1644-1718)
English Quaker and founder of Pennsylvania as a colony of religious liberty

1 To be like Christ is to be a Christian.

2 Though our saviour's Passion is over, his compassion is not.

3 This is the comfort of Friends, that though they may be said to Die, yet their Friendship and Society are, in the best sense, ever present because *immortal*.

4 To be furious in religion is to be unreligiously religious.

5 O God, help us not to despise or oppose what we do not understand.

6 Truth often suffers most by the heat of its defenders than from the arguments of its opposers.

7 Patience and diligence, like faith remove mountains.

8 An able yet humble man is a jewel worth a kingdom.

9 Be humble and gentle in your conversation; and of few words, I charge you; but always pertinent when you speak.

10 Right is right, even if everyone is against it; and wrong is wrong, even if everyone is for it.

11 Liberty of conscience is the first step towards having a religion.

12 Justice is the insurance we have on our lives, and obedience is the premium we pay for it.

13 Zeal dropped in charity is good; without it, good for nothing; for it devours all it comes near.

14 The humble, meek, merciful, just, pious and devout souls are everywhere of one religion and when death has taken off the mask they will know one another, though the divers liveries they wear here makes them strangers.

15 In his prayers he says 'Thy will be done' but means his own, at least acts so.

16 No pain, no palm; no thorn, no throne.

17 Death is but crossing the world, as friends do the sea; they live in one another still.

18.45
William Romaine (1714-1795)
A leader of the English Evangelical Revival

1 Let me see thee face to face, and enjoy thee, thou dearest Jesus, whom my soul longeth after. It is good to live upon thee by faith, but to live with thee is best of all.

18.46
Jean Baptiste de la Salle (1651-1719)
French founder of the Institute of the Brothers of Christian Schools

1 It is chiefly by asking questions and in provoking explanations that the master must open the mind of the pupil, make him work, and use his thinking powers, form his judgement, and make him find out for himself the answer.

2 There is a holy anger, excited by zeal, which moves us to reprove with warmth those whom our mildness failed to correct.

3 Vigilance and prayer are the safeguards of chastity.

4 The more you abandon to God the care of all temporal things, the more he will take care to provide for all your wants.

18.47
Robert South (1634-1716)
English divine

1 Covetousness is both the beginning and end of the devil's alphabet—the first vice in corrupt nature that moves, and the last which dies.

2 God expects from men that their Easter devotions would in some measure come up to their Easter clothes.

18.48
Anne Steele (1716-1778)
English hymn-writer

1 Let the sweet hope that thou art mine
my path of life attend;
Thy presence thro' my journey shine,
and crown my journey's end.

18.49
Jonathan Swift (1667-1745)
English poet and satirist

1 We have just enough religion to make us hate, but not enough to make us love one another.

2 Religion seems to have grown an infant with age, and requires miracles to nurse it, as it had in its infancy.

3 Complaint is the largest tribute heaven receives, and the sincerest part of our devotion.

4 Now hear an allusion: a mitre, you know, is divided above, but united below. If this you consider, our emblem is right; the bishops divide, but the clergy unite.

5 I never saw, heard, nor read, that the clergy were beloved in any nation where Christianity was the religion of the country. Nothing can render them popular but some degree of persecution.

6 And you will do well if you can prevail upon some intimate and judicious friend to be your constant hearer, and allow him with the utmost freedom to give you notice of whatever he shall find amiss, either in your voice or gesture; for want of which early warning many clergymen continue defective, and sometimes ridiculous, to the end of their lives.

7 That the universe was formed by a fortuitous concourse of atoms, I will no more believe than that the accidental jumbling of the alphabet would fall into a most ingenious treatise of philosophy.

8 Never be ashamed to own you have been in the wrong, 'tis but saying you are wiser today than you were yesterday.

9 Whatever you say against women, they are better creatures than men, for men were made of clay, but woman was made of man.

10 The best doctors in the world are Doctor Diet, Doctor Quiet and Doctor Merryman.

11 Good manners is the art of making those people easy with whom we converse. Whoever makes the fewest people uneasy is the best bred in the company.

12 Few are qualified to shine in company; but it is in most men's power to be agreeable.

13 I never wonder to see men wicked, but I often wonder to see them not ashamed.

14 Ambition often puts men upon doing the meanest offices: so climbing is performed in the same posture as creeping.

15 It is useless for us to reason a man out of a thing he has never been reasoned into.

16 There are few wild beasts more to be dreaded than a talking man having nothing to say.

17 Satire is a kind of glass, wherein beholders do generally discover everybody's face but their own.

18 Laws are like cobwebs, which may catch small flies, but let wasps and hornets break through.

19 No wise man ever wished to be younger.

20 A wise man is never less alone than when he is alone.

21 It is impossible that anything so natural, so necessary, and so universal as death should ever have been designed by Providence as an evil to mankind.

18.50
Nahum Tate (1672-1715) and Nicholas Brady (1659-1726)

Irish clergymen and hymn-writers

1 Through all the changing scenes of life,
In trouble and in joy,
The praises of my God shall still
My heart and tongue employ.

18.51
Gerhard Tersteegen (1697-1769)

German Protestant devotional writer

1 A comprehended God is no God at all.

2 I am my Father's child, not his counsellor.

3 The true inner life is no strange or new thing; it is the ancient and true worship of God, the Christian life in its beauty and in its own peculiar form. Wherever there is a man who fears God and lives the good life, in any country under the sun, God is there, loving him, and so I love him too.

4 God is a tranquil Being, and abides in a tranquil eternity. So must thy spirit become a tranquil and clear little pool, wherein the serene light of God can be mirrored.

18.52
Tikhon of Zadonsk (1724-1783)

Russian bishop and writer

1 If an earthly king—our tsar—wrote you a letter, would you not read it with joy? Certainly, with great rejoicing and careful attention. The King of heaven has sent a letter to you, an earthly and mortal man: yet you almost despise such a gift, so priceless a treasure. Whenever you read the Gospel, Christ himself is speaking to you. And while you read, you are praying and talking with him.

18.53
Augustus Montague Toplady (1740-1778)
English Calvinist clergyman and hymn-writer

1 Rock of Ages, cleft for me,
Let me hide myself in thee!
Let the water and the blood
From thy riv'n side which flow'd,
Be of sin the double cure,
Cleanse me from its guilt and power.

2 The sky is clear; there is no cloud; come, Lord Jesus, come quickly.

18.54
Paisius Velichkovsky (1722-1794)
Russian monk

1 Monks should give over all their will to their superior and should submit to him in everything as to the Lord himself. Receive from his lips as from the lips of God the word that is for the profit of your souls.

18.55
Isaac Watts (1674-1748)
Independent minister, educationalist and hymn-writer

1 Jesus shall reign where'er the sun
Does his successive journeys run:
His kingdom stretch from shore to shore
Till moons shall wax and wane no more.

2 When I survey the wondrous cross
On which the prince of glory died,
My richest gain I count but loss,
And pour contempt on all my pride.

3 There is a land of pure delight,
Where saints immortal reign;
Infinite day excludes the night,
And pleasures banish pain.

...

Could we but climb where Moses stood,
And view the landscape o'er;
Not Jordan's stream, nor death's cold flood,
Should fright us from the shore.

4 Satan finds some mischief still
For idle hands to do.

5 Bless me, O Lord, and let my food strengthen me to serve thee.

18.56
Charles Wesley (1707-1788)
English clergyman and hymn-writer

1 O thou who camest from above
The pure celestial fire to impart,
Kindle a flame of sacred love
On the mean altar of my heart.

2 'Tis Love, 'tis Love! Thou dieds't for me,
I hear thy whisper in my heart.
The morning breaks, the shadows flee,
Pure Universal Love thou art:
To me, to all, thy bowels move—
Thy nature, and thy name, is Love.

3 Love divine, all loves excelling,
Joy of heaven, to earth come down,
Fix in us thy humble dwelling,
All thy faithful mercies crown.
Jesus, thou art all compassion,
Pure, unbounded love thou art;
Visit us with thy salvation,
Enter every trembling heart.

4 Any unmortified desire which a man allows in will effectually drive and keep Christ out of the heart.

5 Make and keep me pure within.

6 Forth in thy name, O Lord, I go,
My daily labour to pursue;
Thee, only thee, resolved to know,
In all I think, or speak, or do.

7 Help us to help each other, Lord,
Each other's cross to bear,
Let each his friendly aid afford,
And feel his brother's care.

8 I shall be satisfied with thy likeness—satisfied, satisfied.

18.57
John Wesley (1703-1791)
Leader of the evangelical awakening, and founder of Methodism

1 I went to America to convert the Indians—but oh! who shall convert me?

2 Do all the good you can
By all the means you can
In all the ways you can
In all the places you can
To all the people you can
As long as ever you can.

3 O Lord, let us not live to be useless, for Christ's sake.

4 What is Christian perfection? Loving God with all our heart, mind, soul and strength.

5 Be ashamed of nothing but sin: not of fetching wood, or drawing water, if time permit; not of cleaning your own shoes or your neighbour's.

6 Some people have just enough religion to make them feel uncomfortable.

7 You may be as orthodox as the devil, and as wicked.

8 I have so much to do that I must spend several hours in prayer before I am able to do it.

9 Give me one hundred preachers who fear nothing but sin and desire nothing but God, and I care not a straw whether they be clergymen or laymen, such alone will shake the gates of hell and set up the Kingdom of God upon earth.

10 Once in seven years I burn all my sermons for it is a shame if I cannot write better sermons now than I did seven years ago.

11 The church has nothing to do but to save souls; therefore spend and be spent in this work. It is not your business to speak so many times, but to save souls as you can; to bring as many sinners as you possibly can to repentance.

12 I look upon all the world as my parish.

13 Let it be observed that cleanliness is no part of religion, that neither this nor any text of Scripture condemns neatness of apparel. Certainly this is a duty, not a sin. Cleanliness is indeed next to godliness.

14 I felt my heart strangely warmed. I feel I did trust in Christ, Christ alone, for salvation; an assurance was given me that he had taken away my sins, even mine, and saved me from the bore of sin and death.

15 Make all you can, save all you can, give all you can.

16 If Thy heart be as my heart, give me Thy hand.

17 The best of all is this—God is with us.

18 Author of life divine,
Who hast a table spread,
Furnished with mystic wine
And everlasting bread,
Preserve the life thyself hast given,
And feed and train us up for heaven.

18.58
Susanna Wesley (1669-1742)
Mother of John and Charles Wesley

1 There are two things to do about the Gospel—believe it and behave it.

2 Whatever weakens your reason, impairs the tenderness of your conscience, obscures your sense of God, or takes away the relish of spiritual things; in short, whatever increases the strength and authority of your body over your mind—that thing is sin to you.

18.59
George Whitefield (1714-1770)
Travelling evangelist in Britain and North America

1 He prayed me into a good frame of mind, and if he had stopped there, it would have been very well; but he prayed me out of it again by keeping on.

2 To preach more than half an hour, a man should be an angel and have angels for hearers.

3 Lord, help me to begin to begin.

4 I was delivered from the burden that had so heavily suppressed me. The spirit of mourning was taken from me, and I knew what it was to truly rejoice in God my saviour.

5 I am never better than when I am on the full stretch for God.

6 A judicious friend, into whose bosom we may pour out our souls, and tell our corruptions as well as our comforts, is a very great privilege.

7 I am to be examined. I hope to have got it pretty perfect. I have spared no pains to get it. Therefore I trust that God will support me!

8 Take care of your life; and the Lord will take care of your death.

9 I am tired in the Lord's work, but not tired of it.

10 The reformation which is brought about by a coercive power will be only outward and superficial; but that which is done by the face of God's Word will be inward and lasting.

18.60
Thomas Wilson (1663-1755)
English bishop

1 O Lord, forgive what I have been, sanctify what I am, and order what I shall be.

2 O give me light to see, a heart to close with and power to do thy will, O God.

3 Faith is the root of works. A root that produces nothing is dead.

4 The devil never tempts us with more success than when he tempts us with a sight of our own good actions.

5 A fault which humbles a man is of more use to him that a good action which puffs him up.

6 He that fancies he is perfect, may lose that pride which he attained by grace.

7 It costs more to revenge injuries than to bear them.

18.61
John Woolman (1720-1772)
North American Quaker preacher and writer

1 While I silently ponder on that change wrought in me, I find no language equal to it, nor any means to convey to another a clear idea of it. I looked on the works of God in this visible creation, and an awfulness covered me; my heart was tender and often contrite, and universal love to my fellow-creatures increased in me. This will be understood by such as have trodden the same path.

2 The office of a minister of Christ is weighty; and they, who go forth as watchmen, have need to be steadily on their guard against the snares of prosperity and an outside friendship.

3 Selfish men may possess the earth; it is the meek only who inherit it from the heavenly Father, free from all defilements and perplexities of unrighteousness.

18.62
Nicolaus von Zinzendorf (1700-1760)
German religious reformer

1 I have one passion, and it is He, only He.

PART 5

Nineteenth Century

For the attainment of divine knowledge, we are directed to combine a dependence on God's Spirit with our own researches. Let us, then, not presume to separate what God has thus united.

Charles Simeon
(1759-1836)

19.1
Lord John E.E.D. Acton (1834-1902)
English historian and politician

1 There is no worse heresy than that the office sanctifies the holder of it. That is the point at which the negation of Catholicism and the negation of Liberalism meet and keep high festival, and the end learns to justify the means.

2 Christianity introduced no new forms of government, but a new spirit, which totally transformed the old ones.

3 The man who prefers his country before any other duty shows the same spirit as the man who surrenders every right to the state. They both deny that right is superior to authority.

4 No authority has power to impose error, and if it resists the truth, the truth must be upheld until it is admitted.

5 Power tends to corrupt, and absolute power corrupts absolutely.

6 Grief drives men into the habits of serious reflection, sharpens the understanding and softens the heart.

7 I cannot conceive that [God] could make such a species as the human merely to live and die on this earth. If I did not believe in a future state, I should believe in no God.

19.2
John Adams (1735-1826)
Second President of the USA

1 The Hebrews have done more to civilize men than any other nation. If I were an atheist, and believed in blind eternal fate, I should still believe that fate had ordained the Jews to be the most essential instrument for civilizing the nations.

2 The preservation of the means of knowledge among the lowest ranks is of more importance to the public than all the property of all the rich men in the country.

3 Liberty cannot be preserved without a general knowledge among the people.

4 As the happiness of the people is the sole end of government, so the consent of the people is the only foundation of it.

5 All great changes are irksome to the human mind, especially those which are attended with great dangers and uncertain effects.

19.3
Louisa May Alcott (1832-1888)
North American writer of fiction

1 I planned my article... and then proceeded to write... It was about old maids. 'Happy Women' was the title, and I put in my list all the busy, useful, independent spinsters I know, for liberty is a better husband than love to many of us.

2 I can imagine an easier life, but with love, health, and work I can be happy, for these three help one to do, to be, and to endure all things.

19.4
Cecil Frances Alexander (1818-1895)
Irish hymn-writer

1 There is a green hill far away,
Without a city wall,
Where the dear Lord was crucified,
Who died to save us all.

2 His are a thousand sparkling rills,
That from a thousand fountains burst,
And fill with music all the hills;
And yet he saith, 'I thirst'.

3 And our eyes at last shall see him,
Through his own redeeming love,
For that child so dear and gentle
Is our Lord in heaven above;
And he leads his children on
To the place where he is gone.

4 Jesus calls us; o'er the tumult
Of our life's tempestuous sea
Day by day his sweet voice soundeth,
Saying, 'Christian, follow me'.

19.5
Mary Amadine of China (1872-1900)
Belgian-born nun, murdered in China during a massacre of Christians

1 I pray to God to fortify the martyrs, but I do not ask him to preserve them.

19.6
Thomas Arnold (1795-1842)
Classical scholar and Headmaster of Rugby

1 I know of no one fact in the history of mankind which is proved by better evidence of every sort, to the understanding of a fair enquirer, than the great sign which God has given us that Christ died and rose from the dead.

2 What we must look for here is, first, religious and moral principles; secondly, gentlemanly conduct; thirdly, intellectual ability.

19.7
Jane Austen (1775-1817)
English novelist

1 Incline us, oh God!, to think humbly of ourselves, to be severe only in the examination of our own conduct, to consider our fellow-creatures with kindness, and to judge of all they say and do with that charity which we would desire from them ourselves.

2 You ought certainly to forgive them as a Christian, but never to admit them in your sight, or allow their names to be admitted in your hearing.

3 It will, I believe, be everywhere found, that as the clergy are, or are not what they ought to be, so are the rest of the nation.

19.8
Mother Emily Ayckbowm (1836-1900)
Founder of the Anglican community of the Sisters of the Church

1 Their [the Sisters'] calling is not without its crosses and trials, but let us not doubt, it has also its compensations. Almighty God knows how to reward any sacrifices made for him; and in this case the recompense will probably be in proportion to the distance, difficulty and isolation of the position so cheerfully accepted.

2 In all that vast continent [Australia], there is not a single English Church Sister, while every town is over-run with Roman Catholic nuns.

19.9
Henry Williams Baker (1821-1877)
English hymn-writer

1 Lord, thy word abideth,
And our footsteps guideth;
Who its truth believeth
Light and joy receiveth.

19.10
Madeleine Sophie Barat (1779-1865)
French nun, founder of the Society of the Sacred Heart

1 If the world knew our happiness, it would, out of sheer envy, invade our retreats, and the times of the Fathers of the Desert would return when the solitudes were more populous than the cities.

2 Our Lord who saved the world through the cross will only work for the good of souls through the cross.

3 If God hears my prayers there will be no last words of mine to repeat, for I shall say nothing at all.

19.11
Thomas John Barnardo (1845-1905)
Irish doctor and founder of orphanages

1 God has not failed us once!

2 The living church ought to be dependent on its living members.

3 Character is better than ancestry, and personal conduct is of more importance than the highest parentage.

19.12
Henry Ward Beecher (1813-1887)
North American preacher and journalist

1 Compassion will cure more sins than condemnation.

2 'I can forgive, but I cannot forget' is only another way of saying 'I cannot forgive'.

3 Every man should keep a fair-sized cemetery in which to bury the faults of his friends.

4 Repentance may begin instantly, but reformation often requires a sphere of years.

5 Repentance is another name for aspiration.

6 Never forget what a man says to you when he is angry.

7 Flattery is praise insincerely given for an interested purpose.

8 Conceit is the most incurable disease that is known to the human soul.

9 A noble man compares and estimates himself by an idea which is higher than himself; and a mean man, by one lower than himself. The one produces aspiration; the other ambition, which is the way in which a vulgar man aspires.

10 The difference between perseverance and obstinacy is, that one often comes from a strong will, and the other from a strong won't.

11 Pride slays thanksgiving, but an humble mind is the soil out of which thanks naturally grows. A proud man is seldom a grateful man, for he never thinks he gets as much as he deserves.

12 The head learns new things, but the heart forevermore practises old experiences.

13 We never know the love of the parent until we become parents ourselves.

14 Half the spiritual difficulties that men and women suffer arise from a morbid state of health.

15 There are many persons who look on Sunday as a sponge to wipe out the sins of the week.

16 If a man cannot be a Christian where he is, he cannot be a Christian anywhere.

17 The soul without imagination is what an observatory would be without a telescope.

18 I should as soon attempt to raise flowers if there were no atmosphere, or produce fruits if there were neither light nor heat, as to regenerate men if I did not believe there was a Holy Ghost.

19 Theology is but our ideas of truth classified and arranged.

20 [St John's Gospel] is God's love letter to the world.

21 Heaven will be the endless portion of every man who has heaven in his soul.

22 The elect are whosoever will, and the nonelect, whosoever won't.

19.13
Andrew Beltrami (1870-1897)
Italian novice of Don Bosco's Salesian Order

1 I see that my chief obstacle to holiness is pride. I *will* overcome it!

19.14
Benildus (1805-1862)
French schoolteacher, member of the Christian Brothers

1 I imagine that the angels themselves, if they came down as schoolmasters, would find it hard to control their anger. Only with the help of the Blessed Virgin do I keep from murdering some of them.

19.15
Edward White Benson (1829-1896)
Archbishop of Canterbury

1 How desperately difficult it is to be honest with oneself. It is much easier to be honest with other people.

19.16
Robert Hugh Benson (1871-1914)
English Roman Catholic Apologist

1 Those who have the faith of children have also the troubles of children.

2 Faith is a gift which can be given or withdrawn; it is something infused into us, not produced by us.

3 There is but one thing in the world really worth pursuing—the knowledge of God.

4 It is in silence that God is known, and through mysteries that he declares himself.

5 Every advance in spiritual life has its corresponding dangers; every step that we rise nearer God increases the depths of the gulf into which we may fall.

6 There are few catastrophes so great and irremediable as those that follow an excess of zeal.

7 It has been said that Gothic architecture represents the soul aspiring to God, and the Renaissance or Romanesque architecture represents God tabernacling with men.

8 Every man may err, but not the whole gathered together; for the whole hath a promise.

9 Conscience illuminated by the presence of Jesus Christ in the heart must be the guide of every man.

10 Conversion has to materialise in small actions as well as in great.

11 Emotions should be servants, not masters—or at least not tyrants.

12 The heart is as divine a gift as the mind; and to neglect it in the search for God is to seek ruin.

13 The essence of a perfect friendship is that each friend reveals himself utterly to the other, flings aside his reserves, and shows himself for what he truly is.

14 The union of the family lies in love; and love is the only reconciliation of authority and liberty.

15 Individuals cannot cohere closely unless they sacrifice something of their individuality.

16 Democracy doesn't give the average man any real power at all. It swamps him among his fellows—that is to say, it kills his individuality; and his individuality is the one thing he has which is worth anything.

17 Mere physical courage—the absence of fear—simply is not worth calling bravery. It's the bravery of the tiger, not the moral bravery of the man.

18 There is no limit to the power of a good woman.

19 Cast away authority, and authority shall forsake you!

20 At death, if at any time, we see ourselves as we are, and display our true characters.

21 We can change, slowly and steadily, if we set our will to it.

22 God only asks you to do your best.

19.17
Mary Magdalen Bentivoglio (1834-1905)
Italian Poor Clare, founder of Poor Clare monasteries in the USA

1 In the convent we are without shoes and stockings; we shall see if we can stand it. It is certain that on the one hand we do not want to pamper anyone, but on the other hand we do not want to kill anyone either.

19.18
Bernadette of Lourdes (1844-1879)
French peasant girl who had visions of the Virgin

1 She [Blessed Virgin Mary] is so beautiful that to see her again one would be willing to die.

19.19
Julie Billiart (1751-1816)
French religious sister, founder of the Institute of Notre Dame

1 We have bread, salt, butter and potatoes, and we are the happiest women in Ghent.

2 How the Good God loves those who appreciate the value of his gifts.

3 Never will I suffer amongst us those souls without courage, those womanish hearts that can endure nothing. There must be nothing little amongst us. A religious must not be taken up with a headache, with those thousand aches and pains to which we are subject.

19.20
William Blake (1757-1827)
English poet, painter, engraver and mystic

1 When the stars threw down their spears,
And water'd heaven with their tears,
Did he smile his work to see?
Did he who made the Lamb make thee?

Tyger! Tyger! burning bright
in the forests of the night,
What immortal hand or eye,
Dare frame thy fearful symmetry?

2 If morality was Christianity, Socrates was the Saviour.

3 The pride of the peacock is the glory of God.
The lust of the goat is the bounty of God.
The wrath of the lion is the wisdom of God.
The nakedness of woman is the work of God.

4 The glory of Christianity is to conquer by forgiveness.

5 Gratitude is heaven itself.

6 In seed time learn, in harvest teach, in winter enjoy.

7 Joys impregnate, sorrows bring forth.

8 Every criminal was once an infant love.

9 He who would do good to another must do it in minute particulars.

10 Opposition is true friendship.

11 One law for the lion and ox is oppression.

19.21
Horatius Bonar (1808-1889)
Scottish minister, Moderator of the Free Church of Scotland

1 Faith takes up the cross, love binds it to the soul, patience bears it to the end.

2 Be what thou seemest! Live thy creed!

3 Fill thou my life, O Lord my God,
In every part with praise,
That my whole being may proclaim
Thy being and thy ways.

4 Here, O my Lord, I see thee face to face,
Here would I touch and handle things unseen,
Here grasp with firmer hand the eternal grace,
And all my weariness upon thee lean.

5 Speak but the word,
and sadness quits my soul;
Touch but my hand with thine,
and I am whole.

6 The kingdom that I seek
Is thine: so let the way
That leads to it be thine,
Else I must surely stray.

19.22
Catherine Booth (1829-1890)
English evangelist and founder of the Salvation Army

1 Don't let controversy hurt your soul. Live near to God by prayer. Just fall down at his feet and open your very soul before him, and throw yourself right into his arms.

2 If she have the necessary gifts, and feels herself called by the Spirit to preach, there is not a single word in the whole book of God to restrain her, but many, very many, to urge and encourage her.

3 What can we do to wake the church up? Too often those who have its destinies in the palm of their hands are chiefly chosen from those who are mere encyclopedias of the past rather than from those who are distinguished by their possession of Divine Power. For leadership of the church something more is required.

19.23
William Booth (1829-1912)
English evangelist and founder of the Salvation Army

1 Music is for the soul what wind is for the ship, blowing her onwards in the direction in which she is steered.

2 [On hearing his wife had cancer] I was stunned. I felt as if the whole world were coming to a standstill. Opposite me on the wall was a picture of Christ on the cross. I thought I could understand it as never before. She talked like a heroine, like an angel to me. I could only kneel with her and try to pray.

3 The greatness of a man's power is the measure of his surrender.

4 God has every bit of me.

5 I have found my destiny. I must take the gospel to the people of the East End.

6 Go for souls, and go for the worst.

7 Every cab-horse in London is given food, shelter and work. People ought to be looked after just as well as cab-horses are cared for.

8 A population sodden with drink, steeped in vice, eaten up by every social and physical malady, these are the denizens of Darkest England amidst whom my life has been spent.

9 While women weep, as they do now, I'll fight; while men go to prison, in and out, in and out, as they do now, I'll fight while there is a drunkard left, while there is a poor lost girl upon the streets, where there remains one dark soul without the light of God—I'll fight! I'll fight to the very end!

19.24
John Bosco (1815-1888)
Italian founder of the Salesian Order

1 It's a form of trade, you see. I ask God for souls, and pay him by giving up everything else.

2 Guard your eyes, since they are the windows through which sin enters into the soul. Never look curiously on those things which are contrary to modesty, even slightly.

3 I demand justice for so many poor children who, alarmed by the repeated investigations and by the appearance of police officers in their usually peaceful home, weep and tremble for their future. It grieves me to see them in such a state, held up to public reprobation, even by the press. For them, therefore, I demand justice and honourable amends, so that they may not suffer the loss of their daily bread.

4 The principal trap which the Devil sets for young people is idleness. This is the fatal source of all evil.

5 Meekness was the method that Jesus used with the apostles. He put up with their ignorance and roughness and even their infidelity. He treated sinners with a kindness and affection that caused some to be shocked, others to be scandalized, and still others to gain hope in God's mercy. Thus, he bade us to be gentle and humble of heart.

19.25
Billy Bray (1794-1868)
Cornish tin-miner and evangelist

1 Lord, if any have to die this day, let it be me, for I am ready.

19.26
Ignatii Brianchaninov (1807-1867)
Russian bishop

1 Make your one aim in life the doing of the will of Jesus in every circumstance, however important or trifling it may seem.

2 Jesus Christ in an incomprehensible way veiled the infinite divine nature with finite human nature, and from the finite human nature he displayed the actions of the infinite God.

3 We are ground between the millstones of temptation as grain that is ground into flour.

4 It is of the nature of inner prayer to reveal the hidden passions concealed in the human heart and to tame them.

19.27
William Bright (1824-1901)
Church historian and hymn-writer

1 And now, O Father, mindful of the love
That bought us once for all on Calvary's tree,
And having with us him that pleads above,
We here present, we here spread forth to thee
That only offering perfect in thine eyes,
The one true, pure, immortal sacrifice.

19.28
Charlotte Brontë (1816-1855)
English novelist

1 Sincerity is never ludicrous; it is always respectable.

19.29
Phillips Brooks (1835-1893)
Preacher and Bishop of Massachusetts

1 The great Easter truth is not that we are to live newly after death, but that we are to be new here and now by the power of the resurrection.

2 The Bible is like a telescope. If a man looks *through* his telescope, then he sees worlds beyond; but if he looks *at* his telescope, then he does not see anything but that. The Bible is a thing to be looked through, to see that which is beyond; but most people only look at it; and so they see only the dead letter.

3 Preaching is truth through personality.

4 There is no such way to attain to a greater measure of grace as for a man to live up to the little grace he has.

5 A prayer in its simplest definition is merely a wish turned Godward.

6 To know any man is not merely to be sure of his existence, but to have some conception of what his existence signifies, and what it is for.

7 No man in this world attains to freedom from any slavery except by entrance into some higher servitude. There is no such thing as an entirely free man conceivable.

8 Greatness after all, in spite of its name, appears to be not so much a certain size as a certain quality in human lives. It may be present in lives whose range is very small.

9 The true way to be humble is not to stoop until you are smaller than yourself, but to stand at your real height against some higher nature that will show you what the real smallness of your greatness is.

19.30
Elizabeth Barrett Browning (1806-1861)
English poet

1 God's gifts put man's best dreams to shame.

2 Free men freely work; whoever fears God fears to sit at ease.

3 Earth's fanatics make too frequently heaven's saints.

4 Leave results to God.

5 I felt so young, so strong, so sure of God.

19.31
Christian Burke (b.1859)
British woman hymn-writer

1 Lord of life and King of glory,
Who didst deign a child to be,
Cradled on a mother's bosom,
Throned upon a mother's knee;
For the children thou hast given
We must answer unto thee.

19.32
Josephine Butler (1828-1906)
English social reformer

1 Prayer cannot be truly called commission, if the only voice heard be the voice of the pleader.

2 You are women and a woman is always a beautiful thing. You have been dragged deep in the mud but still you are women. God calls to you, as he did to Zion long ago, 'Awake, awake! Thou that sittest in the dust, put on thy beautiful garments.' You can be the friend and companion of him who came to seek and to save that which was lost. Fractures well healed make us more strong. Take of the very stones over which you have stumbled and fallen, and use them to pave your road to heaven.

3 Women are called to be a great power in the future.

4 What dignity can there be in the attitude of women in general, and toward men in particular, when marriage is held (and often necessarily so, being the sole means of maintenance) to be the one end of a woman's life...?

19.33
Joseph Cafasso (1811-1860)
Italian priest and spiritual guide

1 Jesus Christ, in his infinite Wisdom, used the words and idioms that were in use among those whom he addressed. You should do likewise.

2 A few acts of confidence and love are worth more than a thousand 'who knows? who knows?' Heaven is filled with converted sinners of all kinds and there is room for more.

3 We were born to love, we live to love, and we will die to love still more.

4 I would be the happiest of men if I could become a saint soon and a big one.

19.34
William Carey (1761-1834)
English Baptist missionary to India and Bible translator

1 I can plod. I can persevere in any definite pursuit. To this I owe everything.

2 Expect great things from God
Attempt great things for God.

19.35
Thomas Carlyle (1795-1881)
Scottish historian

1 The universe is but one vast symbol of God.

2 If Jesus Christ were to come today people would not even crucify him. They would ask him to dinner, and hear what he has to say, and make fun of it.

3 He who has no vision of eternity will never get a true hold of time.

4 The great law of culture: let each become all that he was created capable of being.

5 Blessed is he who has found his work; let him ask no other blessedness.

6 Our main business is not to see what lies dimly at a distance, but to do what lies clearly at hand.

7 Experience is the best of schoolmasters, only the school fees are heavy.

8 Conviction, were it never so excellent, is worthless till it convert itself into conduct.

9 The merit of originality is not novelty, it is sincerity. The believing man is the original man he believes for himself, not for another.

10 The sincere alone can recognize sincerity.

11 Every noble work is at first impossible.

12 One life, a little gleam of time between two eternities.

13 The tragedy of life is not so much what men suffer, but rather what they miss.

14 For every one hundred men who can stand adversity there is only one who can withstand prosperity.

15 The fine arts once divorcing themselves from truth are quite certain to fall mad, if they do not die.

16 The man who cannot laugh is not only fit for treasons, strategems, and spoils; but his whole life is already a treason and a strategem.

17 True humour springs not more from the head than from the heart; it is not contempt, its essence is love.

18 The greatest of faults, I should say, is to be conscious of none.

19 Violence does even justice unjustly.

20 Prayer is and remains always a native and deep impulse of the soul of man.

21 Silence is deep as Eternity, speech is shallow as Time.

22 Wonder is the basis of worship.

23 So this is death—well...

19.36
Lydia Maria Child (1802-1880)
American abolitionist and writer

1 [Love] is the divine vitality that everywhere produces and restores life. To each and every one of us, it gives the power of working miracles if we will.

2 If a man doubts his way, Satan is always ready to help him to a new set of opinions.

19.37
Anthony Mary Claret (1807-1870)
Spanish missionary, founder and archbishop

1 I will imagine that my soul and body are like the two hands of a compass, and that my soul, like the stationary hand, is fixed in Jesus, who is my centre, and that my body, like the moving hand, is describing a circle of assignments and obligations.

2 I have always known that the Lord was my fuel; but on this trip all the rest knew it too. They could see that I hardly ate or drank anything except a potato and a glass of water all day. I never ate meat, fish, or eggs, or drank wine. I was always happy and they never saw me tired, despite the fact that some days I preached as many as twelve sermons.

3 Our Lord has created persons for all states in life, and in all of them we see people who have achieved sanctity by fulfilling their obligations well.

4 The first ideas I can remember date back to when I was five years old. When I went to bed, instead of sleeping—I have never been much of a sleeper—I used to think about eternity. I would think 'forever, forever, forever'. I would try to imagine enormous distances and pile still more distances on these and realize that they would never come to an end.

19.38
Matthias Claudius (1740-1815)
German poet

1 Good deeds that are done silently and for a good motive are the dead that live even in the grave; they are flowers that withstand the storm, they are stars that know no setting.

19.39
Elizabeth Clephane (1830-1869)
Member of the Free Church of Scotland and known for her good works in Melrose

1 Beneath the cross of Jesus
I fain would take my stand—
The shadow of a mighty rock,
Within a weary land;
A home within the wilderness,
A rest upon the way,
From the burning of the noonday heat,
And the burden of the day.

19.40
Constance Coleman
Anglican campaigner for women's rights

1 Would the fuller ministry of women hasten revival? Yes, because we are standing for the ultimate spiritual equality, not merely of women alongside men, but of all human souls in the sight of God.

19.41
Samuel Taylor Coleridge (1772-1834)
English poet and literary critic

1 I have found in the Bible words for my inmost thoughts, songs for my joy, utterance for my hidden griefs and pleadings for my shame and feebleness.

2 He who begins by loving Christianity better than truth will proceed by loving his own sect or church better than Christianity and end in loving himself better than all.

3 In wonder all philosophy began: in wonder it ends. But if the first wonder is the offspring of ignorance the last is the parent of adoration.

4 Prayer is the effort to live in the spirit of the whole.

5 False doctrine does not necessarily make a man a heretic, but an evil heart can make any doctrine heretical.

6 I have seen gross intolerance shown in support of tolerance.

7 If liberty is to be saved, it will not be by the doubters, the men of science, or the materialists; it will be by religious conviction, by the faith of individuals, who believe that God wills man to be free but also pure.

8 To most men, experience is like the stern lights of a ship, which illumine only the track it has passed.

9 Advice is like snow; the softer it falls, the longer it dwells upon, and the deeper it sinks into the mind.

10 Common sense in an uncommon degree is what the world calls wisdom.

19.42
Charles Caleb Colton (1780-1832)
English poet

1 He that will believe only what he can fully comprehend must have a very long head or a very short creed.

2 The greatest friend of Truth is Time, her greatest enemy is Prejudice, and her constant companion is Humility.

3 Men will wrangle for religion; write for it; fight for it; anything but—live for it.

4 The three great apostles of practical atheism that make converts without persecuting, and retain them without preaching, are health, wealth, and power.

5 True contentment depends not on what we have; a tub was large enough for Diogenes, but a world was too little for Alexander.

6 There is this difference between happiness and wisdom: he that thinks himself the happiest man, really is so; but he that thinks himself the wisest is generally the greatest fool.

7 Did universal charity prevail, earth would be heaven—and hell a fable.

8 True friendship is like sound health, the value of it is seldom known until it is lost.

9 Of all the marvellous works of the Deity, perhaps there is nothing that angels behold with such supreme astonishment as a proud man.

10 This world cannot explain its own difficulties without the existence of another.

11 Men are born with two eyes, but with one tongue, in order that they should see twice as much as they say.

12 When you have nothing to say, say nothing.

19.43
Cornelia Connelly (1809-1879)
Founder of the Society of the Holy Child Jesus

1 Take the cross he sends, as it is, and not as you imagine it to be.

19.44
Migel Febres Cordero-Munzo (1854-1910)
Ecuadorean Christian Brother, teacher, scholar and writer

1 The heart is rich when it is content, and it is always content when its desires are fixed on God. *Nothing* can bring greater happiness than doing God's will for the love of God.

19.45
Emily Dickinson (1830-1886)
North American poet

1 There is always one thing to be grateful for—that one is one's self and not somebody else.

19.46
Antoinette Doolittle
North American Shaker elder

1 Every cycle has its prophets—as guiding stars; and they are the burning candles of the Lord to light the spiritual temple on earth, for the time being. When they have done their work, they will pass away; but the candlesticks will remain, and other lights will be placed in them.

19.47
Fyodor Dostoevsky (1821-1881)
Russian novelist

1 Remember especially that you cannot be a judge of anyone. For no one can judge a criminal, until he recognizes that he himself is just such a criminal as the man standing before him, and that perhaps he is more to blame than anyone else for the crime which the man on trial has committed.

2 Love all God's creation, the whole of it and every grain of sand in it. Love every leaf, every ray of God's light. Love the animals, love the plants, love everything. If you love everything, you will perceive the divine mystery in things. Once you have perceived it, you will begin to comprehend it better every day, and you will come at last to love the world with an all-embracing love.

19.48
Henry Drummond (1851-1897)
Scottish evangelist and writer

1 Most of the stones for the buildings of the City of God, and all the best of them, are made by mothers.

2 The mind of Christ is to be learned in the family. Strength of character may be acquired at work, but beauty of character is learned at home.

3 Sin is a power in our life: let us fairly understand that it can only be met by another power.

4 No form of vice, not worldliness, not greed of gold, not drunkenness itself, does more to un-Christianise society than evil temper.

5 Life is not a holiday, but an education. And the one eternal lesson for us all is how better we can love.

6 The greatest thing a man can do for his heavenly Father is to be kind to some of his other children.

7 Love itself can never be defined... love
is something more than all its elements—
a palpitating, quivering, sensitive, living thing.

19.49
Mary Baker Eddy (1821-1910)
Founder of the Christian Scientists

1 Christianity is the summons of divine Love for man to be Christlike—to emulate the words and the works of our great Master.

2 Jesus of Nazareth was the most scientific man that ever trod the globe. He plunged beneath the material surface of things and found the spiritual causes.

3 The prayer that reforms the sinner and heals the sick is an absolute faith that all things are possible to God—a spiritual understanding of him, an unselfed love.

4 Sickness, sin and death, being inharmonious, do not originate in God nor belong to his Government.

5 If Christianity is not scientific, and Science is not God, then there is no invariable law, and truth becomes an accident.

19.50
Elizabeth of the Trinity (1880-1906)
French Carmelite nun

1 In heaven, it seems to me, my mission will be to draw souls into interior recollection, by helping them to go out from themselves in order to adhere to God by a very simple, wholly loving movement; and to maintain them in that great inner silence which allows God to imprint himself upon them and to transform them into himself.

2 The Blessed Trinity, then, is our dwelling-place, our home, our Father's house, which we should never leave.

3 I have found my heaven on earth, because heaven is God, and God is in my soul.

4 Pray hard for me, beloved sister; for me too it is no longer a veil which hides him from me, but a very thick wall. It is very hard, isn't it, after feeling him so close, but I am ready to remain in this state as long as it pleases my Beloved to leave me there, for faith tells me that he is there all the same, and what is the use of sweetness and consolations? They are not he.

5 It is he alone that we seek... so let us go to him through pure faith.

6 O my God, Trinity whom I adore, let me entirely forget myself that I may abide in you, still and peaceful as if my soul were already in eternity; let nothing disturb my peace nor separate me from you, O my unchanging God, but that each moment may take me further into the depths of your mystery.

19.51
Charlotte Elliott (1789-1871)
English hymn-writer

1 The Bible is my church. It is always open, and there is my High Priest ever waiting to receive me. There I have my confessional, my thanksgiving, my psalm of praise... and a congregation of whom the world is not worthy—prophets and apostles, and martyrs and confessors—in short, all I can want, there I find.

2 Just as I am, though tossed about
With many a conflict, many a doubt,
Fightings within, and fears without,
O Lamb of God, I come.

3 'Christian! Seek not yet repose',
Hear thy guardian angel say;
Thou art in the midst of foes;
'Watch and pray.'

19.52
Peter Julian Eymard (1811-1868)
French priest and religious founder

1 The Lord pursued me for a long time. He put me, as it were, into prison in order to force me to contemplate him and speak to him. He deprived me of everything that I might go and prostrate myself at his feet but invariably I again attached myself to nothingness in order to shun the abyss of love that Jesus had in store for me.

19.53
Frederick William Faber (1814-1863)
English convert to Roman Catholicism and co-founder of the London Oratory

1 Religious talk is a very feast to self-deceit.

2 We can only reach the delicate truth of mysticism through the commonplace sincerities of asceticism.

3 Love's secret is always to be doing things for God, and not to mind because they are such very little ones.

4 If we put an absurdly high ideal before us, it ceases to be an ideal at all, because we have no idea of acting upon it.

5 Exactness in little duties is a wonderful source of cheerfulness.

6 Nobody is kind to only one person at once, but to many persons in one.

7 Kindness has converted more sinners than zeal, eloquence, or learning.

8 There is a grace of kind listening, as well as a grace of kind speaking.

9 Kind words are the music of the world. They have a power which seems to be beyond natural causes, as though they were some angel's song which had lost its way and come to earth.

10 Controversy, for the most part, disfigures the question it seeks to elucidate.

11 We strain hardest for things which are almost but not quite within our reach.

12 We must wait for God, long, meekly, in the wind and wet, in the thunder and lightning, in the cold and the dark. Wait, and he will come. He never comes to those who do not wait.

19.54
Charles G. Finney (1792-1875)
North American revivalist leader and theologian

1 No words can express the wonderful love that was shed abroad in my heart. I wept aloud with joy and love; and I do not know but I should say, I literally bellowed out the unutterable gushings of my heart.

2 Some men will spin out a long prayer telling God who and what he is, or they pray out a whole system of divinity. Some people preach, others exhort the people, till everybody wishes they would stop and God wishes so, too, most undoubtedly.

3 Sin is the most expensive thing in the universe, pardoned or unforgiven—pardoned, its cost falls on the atoning sacrifice, unforgiven, it must forever lie upon the impenitent soul.

4 A state of mind that sees God in everything is evidence of growth in grace and a thankful heart.

5 A revival may be expected whenever Christians are found willing to make the sacrifices necessary to carry it on. They must be willing to sacrifice their feelings, their business, their time, to help forward the work.

6 Obedience to moral law cannot be partial, in the sense that a moral agent can partly obey and partly disobey at the same time... The only sense in which obedience to moral law can be partial is that obedience may be intermittent.

19.55
Caroline Fox (1819-1871)
English Quaker

1 Let truth be done in silence 'till it is forced to speak', and then should it only whisper, all those whom it may concern will hear.

2 The Roman Catholic priests are always better or worse than the Protestant clergy—either intensely devoted to God and their neighbour, or sly, covetous and sensual.

19.56
Elizabeth Fry (1780-1845)
English Quaker and prison reformer

1 Since my heart was touched at seventeen years old, I believe I never have awakened from sleep, in sickness or in health, by day or by night, without my first waking thought being, 'how best I might serve my Lord'.

2 After we had spent a pleasant evening, my heart began to feel itself silenced before God and without looking at others, I felt myself under the shadow of the wing of God... After the meeting my heart felt really light and as I walked home by starlight, I looked through nature up to nature's God.

3 I wish the state of enthusiasm I am now in may last, for today I *felt* there is a God. I have been devotional and my mind has been led away from the follies that it is mostly wrapped up in.

4 O Lord, may I be directed what to do and what to leave undone.

19.57

Gemma Galgani (1878-1903)

Italian woman who received the stigmata

1 I shrink every time I look at the cross because I feel I could die thinking of the pain of it, yet, in spite of this deep repugnance of mine, my heart welcomes all the sufferings it entails and in these I find all my delight.

2 Yesterday, on approaching the Most Blessed Sacrament, I felt myself burning and I had to withdraw. I am astounded that so many who receive Jesus are not reduced to ashes.

3 It is a great sorrow for a soul that wishes to live far from the pomps and vanities to return to the world, to put up with idle and insipid conversations instead of talking to God alone, to open one's eyes to see nothing but the earth instead of visions of heaven. A hard sacrifice indeed.

4 Mother dear, lend me your heart. I look for it each day to pour my troubles into.

19.58

William Ewart Gladstone (1809-1898)

British Prime Minister

1 We are part of the community of Europe, and we must do our duty as such.

2 The disease of an evil conscience is beyond the practice of all the physicians of all the countries in the world.

3 Justice delayed is justice denied.

4 There is one proposition which the experience of life burns into my soul; it is this, that a man should beware of letting his religion spoil his morality. In a thousand ways, some great, some small, but all subtle, we are daily tempted to that great sin.

5 Talk about the questions of the day; there is but one question, and that is the gospel. It can and will correct everything needing correction.

19.59

Macarius Glukharev (1792-1847)

Russian monk

1 God in his love separates us from one another temporarily, in order once more to unite us all in Christ for eternity... There is only one God, and in that one God you are both united. Only you cannot see each other for the time being. But this means that your future meeting will be all the more joyful, and then no one will take your joy from you. Yet even now you live together: all that has happened is that she has gone into another room and closed the door.

19.60

Vincent van Gogh (1853-1900)

Dutch Post-Impressionist painter

1 It is good to love many things, for therein lies strength. Whosoever loves much can accomplish much, and what is done with love is well done.

19.61

Charles Gordon (1833-1885)

English soldier and philanthropist

1 If you tell the truth, you have infinite power supporting you; but if not, you have infinite power against you.

19.62

Maria Goretti (1890-1902)

Italian young girl murdered by a would-be lover

1 [Last words when at 11 she was fatally stabbed while resisting the advances of a 19-year-old youth] May God forgive him! I want him in heaven.

19.63

Dora Greenwell (1821-1882)

Poet and devotional writer

1 My spirit bare before thee stands;
I bring no gift, I ask no sign,
I come to thee with empty hands,
The surer to be filled from thine.

19.64
Sarah Lynes Grubb (1773-1842)
English Quaker preacher

1 When I grew to about thirteen years of age, I began to discover something in me, or in my mind, like the heavenly anointing for the ministry; for the Lord had revealed his word as a hammer and had broken the rock in pieces in my living experience; and I was contrited under a sense of power and love.

19.65
Edward Everett Hale (1822-1909)
North American Unitarian clergyman

1 I am only one but still I am one. I cannot do everything but still I can do something; and because I cannot do everything let me not refuse to do the something that I can do.

19.66
Augustus William Hare (1792-1834)
English religious writer

1 Thus have we first the sun in the sky, secondly, the light, which issues from the sun, and thirdly, the heat, which accompanies the light—three separate and distinguishable things; yet distinct as they are, what can be more united than the sun and its rays, or than the light and heat which those rays shed abroad.

19.67
Maria Hare (1798-1870)
British religious writer

1 O Lord, this is our desire, to walk along the path of life that you have appointed us, in steadfastness of faith, in lowliness of heart, in gentleness of love.

19.68
Edwin Hatch (1835-1889)
English Anglican clergyman and scholar

1 Breathe on me, Breath of God,
Fill me with life anew,
That I may love what thou dost love,
And do what thou wouldst do.

19.69
Frances Ridley Havergal (1836-1879)
English linguist, musician and hymn-writer

1 Like a river glorious is God's perfect peace,
Over all victorious in its bright increase;
Perfect, yet it floweth fuller every day,
Perfect, yet it groweth deeper all the way.
Stayed upon Jehovah, hearts are fully blest;
Finding, as he promised, perfect peace and rest.

2 I believe my King suggests a thought, and whispers me a musical line or two, and then I look up and thank him delightedly and go on with it. That is how my hymns come.

3 Take my love; my Lord, I pour
At thy feet its treasure store;
Take myself, and I will be
Ever, only, all for thee.

19.70
Reginald Heber (1783-1826)
Hymn-writer and Bishop of Calcutta

1 Holy, holy, holy! Lord God Almighty!
Early in the morning our song shall rise to thee:
Holy, holy, holy! merciful and mighty!
God in three Persons, Blessed Trinity!

19.71
Herman of Alaska (d.1837)
Russian missionary

1 I have no fine speeches to make, but from the bottom of my heart I pray you to wipe the tears from the eyes of the defenceless orphans, relieve the suffering of the oppressed, and show them what it means to be merciful.

19.72
Gerard Manley Hopkins (1844-1889)
English poet

1 Glory be to God for dappled things.

2 The world is charged with the grandeur of God.
It will flame out, like shining from shook foil;
It gathers to a greatness, like the ooze of oil
Crushed. Why do men then now not reck
his rod?

3 I say more: the just man justices;
Keeps grace: that keeps all his goings graces;
Acts in God's eye what in God's eye he is—
Christ. For Christ plays in ten thousand places,
Lovely in limbs, and lovely in eyes not his
To the Father through the features of men's faces.

4 There is a point with me in matters of any size when I must absolutely have encouragement as much as crops rain: afterwards I am independent.

5 I am so happy, I am so happy.

19.73
William Walsham How (1823-1897)
English bishop and hymn-writer

1 O blest communion, fellowship divine!
We feebly struggle, they in glory shine;
Yet all are one in thee, for all are thine.

19.74
Julia Ward Howe (1819-1910)
North American campaigner for women's suffrage and the abolition of slavery

1 Mine eyes have seen the glory of
the coming of the Lord;
He is trampling out the vintage
where the grapes of wrath are stored;
He hath loosed the fateful lightning
of his terrible swift sword:
His truth is marching on.

19.75
Bernhard Severin Ingemann (1789-1862)
Danish poet and novelist

1 Through the night of doubt and sorrow
Onward goes the pilgrim band,
Singing songs of expectation,
Marching to the Promised Land.

19.76
Innocent of Alaska (1797-1879)
Russian missionary

1 God doesn't deprive of his heavenly Kingdom sinners who don't repent. They themselves simply can't bear its light—any more than you can bear the light of the sun.

19.77
Anne Javouhey (1798-1851)
French religious founder and educator

1 I wish that men were as resolute as women.

19.78
Thomas Jefferson (1743-1826)
President of the USA; chief writer of the Declaration of Independence

1 Grief drives men into the habits of serious reflection, sharpens the understanding and softens the heart.

2 I tremble for my country when I reflect that God is just.

3 When angry, count ten before you speak; when very angry, count a hundred.

4 Had the doctrines of Jesus been preached always as pure as they came from his lips, the whole civilized world would now have been Christian.

19.79
John of Kronstadt (1829-1908)
Russian priest

1 The Lord has become everything to you, and you must become everything to the Lord.

19.80
Benjamin Jowett (1817-1893)
Anglican priest and classical scholar

1 My dear child, you must believe in God in spite of what the clergy tell you.

19.81
Adoniram Judson (1788-1850)
North American missionary in Burma

1 Endeavour seven times a day to withdraw from business and company and lift up thy soul to God in private retirement.

19.82
John Keble (1792-1866)
Oxford Tractarian and poetry professor

1 Time's waters will not ebb nor stay.

2 Blest are the pure in heart,
For they shall see our God
The secret of the Lord is theirs,
Their soul is Christ's abode.

3 God hath sworn to lift on high
Who sinks himself by true humility.

4 New truths, in the proper sense of the word, we neither can nor wish to arrive at. But the monuments of antiquity may disclose to our devout perusal much that will be to this age new, because it has been mislaid or forgotten; and we may attain to a light and clearness, which we now dream not of, in our comprehension of the faith and discipline of Christ.

5 Help us, this and every day,
To live more nearly as we pray.

6 The trivial round, the common task,
Would furnish all we ought to ask:
Room to deny ourselves, a road
To bring us daily nearer God.

19.83
Søren Kierkegaard (1813-1855)
Danish philosopher and theologian

1 The remarkable thing about the way in which people talk about God, or about their relation to God, is that it seems to escape them completely that God hears what they are saying.

2 Faith means just that blessed unrest, deep and strong, which so urges the believer onward that he cannot settle at ease in the world and anyone who was quite at ease would cease to be a believer.

3 It is so hard to believe because it is so hard to obey.

4 When you read God's word, you must constantly be saying to yourself, 'It is talking to me, and about me'.

5 Silences are the only scrap of Christianity we have left.

6 Prayer does not change God, but it changes him who prays.

7 A possibility is a hint from God.

8 Never cease loving a person, and never give up hope for him, for even the Prodigal Son who had fallen most low, could still be saved. The bitterest enemy and also he who was your friend could again be your friend; love that has grown cold can kindle again.

9 The only true forgiveness is that which is offered and extended even before the offender has apologized and sought it.

10 Marriage is not harmed by seducers but by cowardly husbands.

11 The tyrant dies and his rule ends, the martyr dies and his rule begins.

19.84
Francis Kilvert (1840-1879)
Anglican clergyman and diarist

1 It was very sweet and lovely, the bright silent sunny morning, and the lark rising and singing alone in the blue sky, and then suddenly the morning air all alive with music of sweet bells ringing for the joy of the resurrection. 'The Lord is risen' smiled the sun, 'The Lord is risen' sang the lark. And the church bells in their joyous pealing answered from tower to tower, 'He is risen indeed'.

19.85
Edward King (1829-1910)
Bishop of Lincoln and theologian

1 I will thank [God] for the pleasures given me through my senses, for the glory of the thunder, for the mystery of music, the singing of the birds and the laughter of children... Truly, O Lord, the earth is full of thy riches!

2 I do value so highly a natural growth in holiness, a humble grateful acceptance of the circumstances that God has provided for us, and I dread the unnatural, cramped,

ecclesiastical holiness, which is so much more quickly produced, but is so human and poor.

3 Do pray for better bishops. These people might be angels and archangels straight off, if we were only decent.

4 I think I have begun to see my way to the alphabet of morality, but I have hardly begun Christianity, and I was fifty-four last Saturday.

5 Perhaps a better and a braver man would have rejoiced at fighting so good a cause; but my little experience has taught me that suffering is a very disturbing thing, and requires more grace than most of us possess.

19.86
Charles Kingsley (1819-1875)

English clergyman, novelist and social reformer

1 I do not want merely to possess a faith; I want a faith that possesses me.

2 Have thy tools ready; God will find thee work.

3 To be discontented with the divine discontent, and to be ashamed with the noble shame, is the very germ and first upgrowth of all virtue.

4 Pain is no evil, unless it conquer us.

5 There are two freedoms—the false, where a man is free to do what he likes; the true, where a man is free to do what he ought.

6 Thank God every morning when you get up that you have something to do which must be done whether you like it or not. Being forced to work, and forced to do your best, will breed in you temperance, self-control, diligence, strength of will, content, and a hundred other virtues which the idle never know.

7 We act as though comfort and luxury were the chief requirements of life, when all that we need to make us really happy is something to be enthusiastic about.

19.87
Jarena Lee (b.1783)

US-born, first female preacher in the African Methodist Church

1 That moment, though hundreds were present, I did leap to my feet, and declare that God, for Christ's sake, had pardoned the sins of my soul... That day was the first when my heart had believed, and my tongue had made confession unto salvation.

2 In the course of our conversation, he inquired if the Lord had justified my soul. I answered, yes. He then asked me if he had sanctified me. I answered, no; and that I did not know what that was. He then undertook to instruct me further in the knowledge of the Lord respecting this blessing.

3 Between four and five years after my sanctification, on a certain time, an impressive silence fell upon me, and I stood as if some one was about to speak to me, yet I had no such thought in my heart. But to my utter surprise there seemed to sound a voice which I thought I distinctly heard, and most certainly understood, which said to me, 'Go, preach the Gospel!'

4 If a man may preach, because the Saviour died for him, why not the woman? seeing he died for her also. Is he not a whole Saviour, instead of a half one? as those who hold it wrong for a woman to preach, would seem to make it appear.

5 O how careful ought we to be, lest through our bylaws of church government and discipline we bring into disrepute even the word of life. For unseemly as it may appear, nowadays, for a woman to preach, it should be remembered that nothing is impossible, heterodox or improper for a woman to preach, seeing the Saviour died for the woman as well as the man.

19.88
Robert E. Lee (1807-1870)
US Confederate army general

1 In all my perplexities and distresses the Bible has never failed to give me light and strength.

2 A true man of honour feels humbled himself when he cannot help humbling others.

3 Duty is the sublimest word in our language. Do your duty in all things. You cannot do more. You should never wish to do less.

4 It is well that war is so terrible, or we should get too fond of it.

19.89
Francis Libermann (1804-1852)
French convert from Judaism, missionary and founder

1 Do things simply, without too much analysis. If you really want to please God and intend to be in full agreement with his will, you can't go wrong.

19.90
Joseph Barber Lightfoot (1828-1889)
English biblical scholar

1 Thanksgiving is the end of all human conduct, whether observed in words or works.

2 Thus in the wilderness of Sinai, as on the Mount of the Transfiguration, the three dispensations met in one. Here Moses had received the tables of the law amid fire and tempest and thick darkness. Here again Elijah, the typical prophet, listened to the voice of God, and sped forth refreshed on his mission of righteousness. And here lastly, in the fullness of time, St Paul, the greatest preacher of Him of whom both the law and the prophets spoke, was strengthened and sanctified for his great work, and transformed... into the large-hearted Apostle of the Gentiles.

19.91
Abraham Lincoln (1809-1865)
President of the USA

1 My great concern is not whether God is on our side; my great concern is to be on God's side.

2 Human action can be modified to some extent, but human nature cannot be changed.

3 The Lord prefers common-looking people. That is the reason he makes so many of them.

4 Let us have faith that right makes might; and in that faith let us to the end dare to do our duty as we understand it.

5 You can fool some of the people all the time and all the people some of the time; but you can't fool all the people all of the time.

6 The ballot is stronger than the bullet.

7 We cannot be free men if this is, by our national choice, to be a land of slavery. Those who deny freedom to others, deserve it not for themselves.

8 The world has never had a good definition of the word liberty.

9 Public opinion in this country is everything.

10 Nothing is settled until it is settled right.

11 There is just one way to bring up a child in the way he should go and that is to travel that way yourself.

12 No man is poor who has had a godly mother.

13 Tact is the ability to describe others as they see themselves.

14 I am now the most miserable man living... To remain as I am is impossible.

15 To sin by silence when they should protest makes cowards out of men.

16 Better to remain silent and be thought a fool than to speak and remove all doubt.

17 Man was made for immortality.

19.92
David Livingstone (1813-1873)
Scottish medical missionary and explorer in Africa

1 I will go anywhere provided it is forward.

2 God had an only Son, and he was a missionary and a physician.

3 I never made a sacrifice. We ought not to talk of 'sacrifice' when we remember the great sacrifice which he made who left his Father's throne on high to give himself up for us.

4 Would you like me to tell you what supported me through all the years of exile among a people whose language I could not understand, and whose attitude toward me was always uncertain and often hostile? It was this, 'Lo, I am with you alway, even unto the end of the world.' On these words I staked everything, and they never failed.

19.93
Mary Livingstone (1821-1862)
Missionary in Africa

1 Accept me, Lord, as I am, and make me such as thou wouldst have me to be.

19.94
Hermann Lotze (1817-1881)
German logician and metaphysician

1 Perfect Personality is in God only, to all finite minds there is allotted but a pale copy thereof; the finiteness of the finite is not a producing condition of this Personality but a limit and a hindrance of its development.

19.95
Lucy Christine (1844-1908)
Pseudonym of French Roman Catholic author of a spiritual journal

1 I saw my soul under the image of a very limpid stretch of water and above that water God appeared like an incomparable Star, whose light was more brilliant than that of the sun and gentler than that of the moon. Not only did the light irradiate all the surface of the water, but the water itself was so transparent that the rays of this light penetrated into its very depths.

19.96
Henry Francis Lyte (1793-1847)
English clergyman

1 Abide with me, fast falls the eventide;
The darkness deepens; Lord, with me abide;
When other helpers fail, and comforts flee,
Help of the helpless, O abide with me.

2 Praise my soul, the King of heaven,
To his feet thy tribute bring;
Ransomed, healed, restored, forgiven,
Evermore his praises sing;
Alleluia! Alleluia!
Praise the everlasting King.

19.97
Macarius of Optino (1788-1860)
Russian monk

1 Do not expect to find in your heart any remarkable gift of prayer. Consider yourself unworthy of it. Then you will find peace. Use the empty, cold dryness of your prayer as food for your humility.

2 Do not attempt to assess the quality of your prayer. God alone can judge its value.

3 The moral qualities of the individual beggar have nothing to do with it; it is Christ's concern, not yours. Who are you to judge your brother? Christ is using his hand and mouth to test your compassion of himself. Will you fail him?

4 Refrain from reprimanding them [your children] while you are in this condition [of rage]. It will be better for you, and more impressive for them if you talk things over calmly, a little later.

5 You ask for some way of completely eradicating irritability. The inclination to irritability is given us to use against sin, and we were never meant to use it against our fellow men. When we do, we act contrary to our true nature.

6 Your chief accusations against her are touchiness, conceit, an absurdly exaggerated opinion of self. But surely, if these were not your own most prominent defects—which they quite obviously are—you would not be so greatly irritated by perceiving them in her. Beware of your own failings!

7 Your letter telling me of your little daughter's death has just arrived. I have already told you how wrong it was to pray that you should not have children. But it is quite as wrong to suppose that this could in any way lead to her death. No, you are certainly not responsible for it! The Lord has taken her to him not because of anything you did, but because he wanted her in heaven, by his side. Seek strength and consolation in the faith that she is even nearer to him now than she was in life, and that she is now entirely in his care.

8 Have great care of your children. We live in a time when much freedom is given to the expression of thought, but little care is taken that thoughts should be founded on truth. Teach them to love truth.

19.98
Robert Murray M'Cheyne (1813-1843)
Scottish minister

1 It is not great talents God blesses so much as great likeness to Jesus. A holy minister is an aweful weapon in the hand of God.

2 If I could hear Christ praying for me in the next room, I would not fear a million enemies. Yet distance makes no difference. He *is* praying for me.

3 God gave me a message to deliver and a horse to ride. Alas, I have killed the horse and now I cannot deliver the message.

19.99
George MacDonald (1824-1905)
Scottish novelist, poet and pastor

1 God's fingers can touch nothing but to mould it into loveliness.

2 I find the doing of the will of God leaves me no time for disputing about his plans.

3 Nothing is so deadening to the divine as an habitual dealing with the outsides of holy things.

4 We die daily. Happy those who daily come to life as well.

5 There is endless room for rebellion against ourselves.

6 The love of our neighbour is the only door out of the dungeon of the self.

7 Age is not all decay; it is the ripening, the swelling, of the fresh life within, that withers and bursts the husk.

8 When we are out of sympathy with the young, then I think our work in this world is over.

9 It is the heart that is not yet sure of its God that is afraid to laugh in his presence.

10 To try too hard to make people good is one way to make them worse; the only way to make them good is to be good.

11 No indulgence of passion destroys the spiritual nature so much as respectable selfishness.

12 No man ever sank under the burden of the day. It is when tomorrow's burden is added to the burden of today that the weight is more than a man can bear. Never load yourself so. If you find yourself so loaded, at least remember this: it is your doing, not God's. He begs you to leave the future to him, and mind the present.

13 Love makes everything lovely; hate concentrates itself on the one thing hated.

14 Work is not always required of a man. There is such a thing as sacred idleness, the cultivation of which is now fearfully neglected.

15 Afflictions are but the shadow of God's wings.

19.100
George Matheson (1842-1906)
Scottish minister

1 O Love, that wilt not let me go,
I rest my weary soul on thee:
I give thee back the life I owe,
That in thine ocean depths its flow
May richer, fuller be.

19.101
Frederick Denison Maurice (1805-1872)
English theologian and writer

1 The Lord's Prayer may be committed to memory quickly, but it is slowly learnt by heart.

2 We have been dosing our people with religion when what they need is not that but the living God.

3 'He descended into hell.' Mighty words!... I accept them as news that there is no corner of God's universe over which his love has not brooded, none over which the Son of God and the Son of Man has not asserted his dominion.

4 Christmas day declares that he dwelt among us... This is the festival which makes us know, indeed, that we are members of one body; it binds together the life of Christ on earth with his life in heaven; it assures us that Christmas day belongs not to time but to eternity.

5 The cry of the poor must either be heard by us, or it will ascend up against us into the ears of the Lord of Sabaoth.

6 Men must worship something; if they do not worship an unseen Being who loves and cares for them, they will worship the works of their own hands; they will secretly bow down to the things that they see, and hear, and taste, and smell; these will be their lords and masters, these will be their cruel tyrants.

7 [Christ] will not command stones to be made bread; he will take the bread and say, 'Thou also shalt live by every word which proceedeth out of the mouth of God. Eat, this is my body.'

8 When we say again, 'We believe that on the third day he rose again from the dead', we do not and cannot mean... that a certain man, by a strange and solitary departure from the law under which human creatures are formed, was permitted to break forth from the grave and revisit the world to which he had before belonged. We must mean that because he alone of all men had fulfilled the law of humanity, in him alone of all men that law fulfilled itself; that he rose out of death, as St Peter said, because it was not possible for him to be holden of it; that he arose, because he himself, and not death, is man's Lord and King.

9 [Christ's death was] not more emphatically an assertion of his relation with those who were heirs of mortality, than his resurrection was an assertion of their relation with him as the inheritor of an eternal life, of his Father's glory.

19.102
James Montgomery (1771-1854)
Newspaper proprietor and hymn-writer

1 Prayer is the Christian's vital breath,
The Christian's native air,
His watchword at the gates of death:
He enters heaven with prayer.

2 Can I Gethsemane forget?
Or there thy conflict see,
Thine agony and bloody sweat,
And not remember thee?

3 Be known to us in breaking bread,
But do not then depart;
Saviour, abide with us, and spread
Thy table in our heart.

19.103
Dwight L. Moody (1837-1899)
North American evangelist

1 The Bible without the Holy Spirit is a sun-dial by moonlight.

2 The Spirit of God first imparts love; he next inspires hope, and then gives liberty and that is about the last thing we have in many of our churches.

3 The way to be saved is not to delay, but to come and take.

4 When we preach on hell, we might at least do it with tears in our eyes.

5 God sends no one away empty except those who are full of themselves.

6 Lying covers a multitude of sins—temporarily.

7 True will-power and courage are not on the battlefield, but in everyday conquests over our inertia, laziness, boredom.

8 I'd rather get ten men to do the job than to do the job of ten men.

9 Character is what you are in the dark.

10 Earth is receding; heaven is approaching. This is my crowning day!

19.104
Hannah More (1745-1833)
English educationalist and religious writer

1 The soul on earth is an immortal guest,
compelled to starve at an unreal feast;
a pilgrim panting for the rest to come
an exile, anxious for his native home.

2 How goodness heightens beauty!

3 Activity may lead to evil; but inactivity cannot be led to good.

19.105
Lucretia Mott (1793-1880)
North American preacher, campaigner against slavery

1 It is time that Christians were judged more by their likeness to Christ than their notions of Christ.

2 Should Jesus again appear and preach as he did round about Judea and Jerusalem and Galilee, these high professors would be among the first to set him at naught, if not to resort to the extremes which were resorted to in his day.

3 Let us not hesitate to regard the utterance of truth in our age, as of equal value with that which is recorded in the scriptures.

19.106
George Müller (1805-1898)
Prussian-born member of the Open Brethren, founder of a Bristol orphanage

1 The only way to learn strong faith is to endure great trials. I have learned my faith by standing firm amid severe testings.

2 The vigour of our spiritual life will be in exact proportion to the place held by the Bible in our life and thoughts.

3 Our heavenly Father never takes anything from his children unless he means to give them something better.

4 My soul is still more enlarged respecting orphans. This word, 'a Father of the fatherless', contains enough encouragement to cast thousands of orphans upon the loving heart of God.

5 Lord, save me from being a wicked old man.

19.107
Andrew Murray (1828-1917)
Preacher in Scotland and South Africa

1 I want you to remember what a difference there is between perfection and perfectionism. The former is a Bible truth: the latter may or may not be a human perversion of that truth. I fear much that many, in their horror of perfectionism, reject perfection too.

2 Salvation consists wholly in being saved from ourselves, or that which we are by nature.

3 There is no one so far lost that Jesus cannot find him and cannot save him.

4 Faith expects from God what is beyond all expectation.

5 The one true way of dying to self is the way of patience, meekness, humility, and resignation to God.

6 Self is the root, the branches, the tree, of all the evil of our fallen state.

19.108
John Mason Neale (1818-1866)

English spiritual writer, founder, author and translator of many hymns

1 You cannot be a true Martha abroad unless you are a true Mary at home.

2 [To the Sisters of the Society of St Margaret] When I look round on all of you, there is nothing that I can despair of effecting. When I think of what God has brought you through, when I remember what, in one place or another, he has given you grace to attempt, ay, and to succeed in, I would not, God be my witness, change my office as regards you for any other work that could be offered me.

3 We must not come to our dear Lord at all, unless we can call him Friend; and we may not call him Friend unless we also call the poor our friends.

19.109
John Henry Newman (1801-1890)

Anglican leader of the Oxford Movement who later became a Roman Catholic cardinal

1 Heart speaks to heart.

2 Growth is the only evidence of life.

3 We must make up our minds to be ignorant of much, if we would know anything.

4 Quarry the granite rock with razors, or moor the vessel with a thread of silk; then may you hope with such keen and delicate instruments as human knowledge and human reason to contend against those giants, the passion and pride of man.

5 In a higher world it is otherwise but here below to live is to change, and to be perfect is to have changed often.

6 The sin of what is called an educated age, such as our own... is to account slightly of [the angels] or not at all... the danger, that is, of resting in things seen and forgetting unseen things and our ignorance about them.

7 A world of saints and angels, a glorious world, the palace of God, the mountain of the Lord of Hosts, the heavenly Jerusalem, the throne of God and Christ, all these wonders, everlasting, all-precious, mysterious and incomprehensible, lie hid in what we see.

8 I say that Christ, the sinless Son of God, might be living now in the world as our next-door neighbour and perhaps we not find it out.

9 True religion is a hidden life in the heart; and though it cannot exist without deeds, yet these are for the most part secret deeds, secret charities, secret prayers, secret self-denials, secret struggles, secret victories.

10 At present we are in a world of shadows. What we see is not substantial. Suddenly it will be rent in twain and vanish away, and our Maker will appear. And then, I say, that first appearance will be nothing less than a personal intercourse between the Creator and every creature. He will look on us while we look on him.

11 Indeed, it is not in human nature to deceive others for any long time, without in a measure deceiving ourselves too.

12 Ten thousand difficulties do not make one doubt.

13 It is as absurd to argue men, as to torture them, into believing.

14 Any obedience is better than none—any profession which is disjoined from obedience, is a mere pretence and deceit.

15 In this world no one rules by mere love; if you are but amiable, you are no hero; to be powerful, you must be strong, and to have dominion you must have a genius for organising.

16 The church is not in time or place, but in the region of spirits—it is in the Holy Ghost; and as the soul of man is not in every part of his body, yet in no part, not here nor there, yet everywhere, not in any one part, head or heart, hands or feet, so as not to be in every other; so also the heavenly Jerusalem, the mother of our new birth, is in all lands at once, fully and entirely, as a spirit in the East and in the West, in the North and in the South—that is, wherever her outward instruments are to be found.

17 Half the controversies in the world are verbal ones and could they be brought to a plain issue, they would be brought to a prompt termination.

18 No one is a martyr for a conclusion, no one is a martyr for an opinion; it is faith that makes martyrs.

19 To take up the cross of Christ is no great action done once for all; it consists in the continual practice of small duties which are distasteful to us.

20 Love of heaven is the only way to heaven.

21 O Lord, support us all the day long of this troublous life, until the shadows lengthen, and the evening comes, and the busy world is hushed, and the fever of life is over, and our work is done. Then in thy mercy grant us a safe lodging, and a holy rest, and peace at the last forever.

19.110
Florence Nightingale (1820-1910)
English nurse

1 Life is a hard fight, a struggle, a wrestling with the Principle of Evil, hand to hand, foot to foot. Every inch of the way must be disputed. The night is given us to take breath, to pray, to drink deep at the fountain of power. The day, to use the strength which has been given us, to go forth to work with it till the evening.

2 The silent power of a consistent life.

3 The coffin of every hope is the cradle of a good experience.

4 To understand God's thoughts we must study statistics, for these are the measure of his purpose.

5 In my thirty-first year I see nothing desirable but death.

6 When I was young, I could not understand what people meant by 'their thoughts wandering in prayer.' I asked for what I really wished, and really wished for what I asked. And my thoughts wandered no more than those of a mother would wander, who was supplicating her Sovereign for her son's reprieve from execution.

7 When we speak with God, our power of addressing him, of holding communion with him, and listening to his still small voice, depends upon our will being one and the same with his.

8 The very vastness of the work raises one's thoughts to God, as the only one by whom it can be done. That is the solid comfort—*he knows*.

9 [Last words when presented with the Order of Merit on her deathbed] Too kind—too kind!

19.111
Caroline Maria Noel (1817-1877)
English hymn-writer

1 At the name of Jesus
Every knee shall bow,
Every tongue confess him
King of glory now;
'Tis the Father's pleasure
We should call him Lord,
Who from the beginning
Was the mighty Word.

19.112
Phoebe Palmer (1807-1874)
North American Methodist

1 No longer think of holiness as a doctrine peculiar to a *sect*, but rather as a doctrine peculiar to the *Bible*, as the only fitness for admission to the society of the bloodwashed in heaven.

2 Holiness is a state of soul in which all the powers of the body and mind are consciously given up to God.

19.113
Ray Palmer (1808-1887)
North American Congregationalist pastor and hymn-writer

1 Jesus, these eyes have never seen
That radiant form of thine;
The veil of sense hangs dark between
Thy blessed face and mine.

Yet, though I have not seen, and still
Must rest in faith alone,
I love thee, dearest Lord, and will,
Unseen but not unknown.

19.114
Coventry Patmore (1823-1896)
English poet

1 The saint does everything that any other decent person does, only somewhat better and with a totally different motive.

2 That which you confess today, you will perceive tomorrow.

3 Great is his faith who does believe his eyes.

4 In love and divinity what is most worth saying cannot be said.

5 The power of the soul for good is in proportion to the strength of its passions. Sanctity is not the negation of passion but its order. Hence great saints have often been great sinners.

6 I love you, dear, but the Lord is my Life and my Light.

19.115
John Coleridge Patteson (1827-1871)
Bishop of Melanesia and founder of the Melanesian Mission

1 There will be seasons of loneliness and sadness, and it seems to me as it always was so in the case of all the people we read of in the Bible. Our Lord distinctly told his disciples to expect it to be so, and even experienced this sorrow of heart himself... so I don't learn that I ought exactly to wish it to be otherwise.

2 Every missionary ought to be a carpenter, mason, something of a butcher and a good deal of a cook.

3 The pride of race which prompts a white man to regard coloured people as inferior to himself is strongly ingrained in most men's minds, and must be wholly eradicated before they will ever win hearts and thus the souls of the heathen.

19.116
Peasant of Ars
Unnamed subject of an anecdote told by the Curé d'Ars

1 I don't say anything to God. I just sit and look at him and let him look at me.

19.117
Philaret of Moscow (1782-1867)
Russian theologian and Metropolitan of Moscow

1 The only pure and all-sufficient source of the doctrines of faith is the revealed word of God, contained now in the holy Scriptures.

2 Every one has not only a right, but it is his bounden duty to read the holy Scriptures in a language which he understands, and edify himself thereby.

3 O Lord, I do not know what to ask of you. You alone know what are my true needs. You love me more than I myself know how to love. Help me to see my real needs which are hidden from me. I dare not ask either a cross or a consolation. I can only wait on you. My heart is open to you. Visit and help me, for your great mercy's sake. Strike me and heal me, cast me down and raise me up. I worship in silence your holy will and your inscrutable ways. I offer myself as a sacrifice to you. I have no other desire than to fulfil your will. Teach me how to pray. Pray you yourself in me.

19.118
Pius IX (1792-1878)
Pope who summoned the First Vatican Council

1 The Roman pontiff can and ought to reconcile himself, and come to terms with progress, liberalism, and modern civilization.

19.119
Gabriel Possenti (1836-1862)
Italian monk

1 I will attempt day by day to break my will into little pieces. I want to do God's holy will, not my own.

19.120
Edward Bouverie Pusey (1800-1882)
English Tractarian leader

1 If we would serve Him in His sacrament we must serve Him also wherever He has declared Himself to be and especially in His poor.

2 He then cannot be said to have any care about continual prayer, who passes any day, between morning and evening, without it; who lets his thoughts run on through the day on his daily business, without checking them to offer at least some brief prayer to God.

3 Nothing is too little to be ordered by our Father; nothing too little in which to see his hand; nothing, which touches our souls, too little to accept from him; nothing too little to be done to him.

4 All things must speak of God, refer to God, or they are atheistic.

5 Think less about yourself, analyse your own feelings less, look to words and actions, and for the rest commit yourself to your Lord.

6 Now just watch yourself for the little occasions in which you think yourself cleverer than another. Perhaps you won't call it clever, but something more solid; a true perception of things. Set yourself against any supposed superiority to anyone.

7 One grain of love is better than a hundredweight of intellect.

8 Not one thing which you have ever done for God has been lost; not one is lost, or ever will be lost. While we each do the little we can do, we may leave the rest to him.

9 I am much more afraid for the rich in the Day of Judgement than for our 'degraded' or 'neglected populations' of which people are so fond of speaking.

10 Those [the heathen philosophers] who loved God, or dimly searched after him, have doubtless been accepted by him for his sake whom they knew not, their Redeemer.

11 The question, 'Whence is evil?' cannot be answered. We see that there is evil. Whence it came into the world of the Good God, we cannot tell. We who cannot understand the very least things, how should we understand the greatest?

12 God will not force your will. He has not created you like a rock or a stone. He knows what a bliss it is freely to love him.

13 Remember that since God has said, 'Speak not evil one of another, brethren', it is a sin to do it, unless it is a sin not to do it.

14 Pray while the hand is on the handle of the door, and then do as well as you can.

15 Every glimpse of God is his gift, to lead us to long more for that most blessed, ever-longing, ever-satisfied knowledge of him, which will be the bliss of eternity.

19.121
Sarah Betts Rhodes (1829-1904)
English teacher

1 God, who made the earth,
The air, the sky, the sea,
Who gave the light its birth,
Careth for me.

19.122
Albrecht Ritschl (1822-1889)
German theologian

1 For in order to know the world as a totality, and in order himself to become a totality in or over it by the help of God, man needs the idea of the oneness of God, and of the consummation of the world in an end which is for man both knowable and realizable. But this condition is fulfilled in Christianity alone.

2 One cannot arrive at and maintain individual conviction of faith in isolation from the already existing community of faith.

19.123
Christina Rossetti (1830-1894)
English poet

1 Were there no God, we would be in this glorious world with grateful hearts, and no one to thank.

2 Lord, purge our eyes to see
Within the seed a tree,
Within the glowing egg a bird,
Within the shroud a butterfly,
Till, taught by such, we see
Beyond all creatures, thee.

3 Open wide the windows of our spirits and fill us full of light; open wide the door of our hearts, that we may receive and entertain Thee with all our powers of adoration.

4 I take my heart in my hand—
I shall not die, but live—
Before thy face I stand;
I, for thou callest such:
All that I have I bring,
All that I am I give;
Smile thou and I shall sing,
But shall not question much.

5 Obedience is the key of knowledge.

6 A fall is not a signal to lie wallowing, but to rise.

7 O God, though our sins be seven, though our sins be seventy times seven, though our sins be more than the hairs of our head, yet give us grace in loving penitence to cast ourselves down into the depths of thy compassion.

8 If I long to improve my brother, the first step toward doing so is to improve myself.

9 When I am dead, my dearest,
Sing no sad songs for me.

10 Silence more musical than any song.

11 For there is no friend like a sister
In calm or stormy weather;
To cheer one on the tedious way,
To fetch one if one goes astray,
To lift one if one totters down,
To strengthen whilst one stands.

12 I love everybody. If ever I had an enemy I should hope to meet and welcome that enemy in heaven.

13 All these things that I have said
Awed me, and made me afraid.
What was I that I should see
So much hidden mystery?
And I straightway knelt and prayed.

14 Poetry is with me, not mechanism but an impulse and a reality, and... I know my aims in writing to be pure and directed to that which is true and right.

15 The heavenliest kind of Christian exhibits more bow than cloud, walking the world in a continual thanksgiving.

19.124
Michael Rua (1837-1910)
Italian priest and missionary

1 As regards certain customs of these savages, do not try to belittle them, but rather, after the example of the Church in ancient times amidst pagan peoples, try to sanctify such customs, provided they are not harmful to soul or body.

19.125
John Charles Ryle (1816-1900)
English evangelical, Anglican Bishop of Liverpool

1 [Jesus says] Roll every burden on me. Cast your whole weight on me. Never let go your hold on me for a moment. Be, as it were, rooted and planted in me. Do this and I will never fail you. I will ever abide in you.

2 I have had a deep conviction for many years that practical holiness, and entire self-consecration to God are not sufficiently attended to by modern Christians in this country. Politics, or controversy, or party-spirit, or worldliness, have eaten out the heart of piety in many of us.

3 Sound Protestant and Evangelical doctrine is useless if it is not accompanied by a holy life. It is worse than useless; it does positive harm.

4 There is an utter opposition between the friendship of the world and the friendship of Christ.

5 There is no devil so dangerous as evangelical formalism.

6 You will never attain simplicity in preaching without plenty of trouble.

7 Beware of new and strange doctrines about hell and the eternity of punishment.

8 Sin forsaken is one of the best evidences of sin forgiven.

9 Nothing I am sure has such a tendency to quench the fire of religion as the possession of money.

10 Truly we have learned a great lesson when we have learned that 'saying prayers' is not praying!

11 Depend on prayer; prayer is powerful.

12 Your religion, if it is real, and given by the Holy Ghost, must be in your *heart*. It must occupy the citadel. It must hold the reins. It must sway the affections. It must lead the will. It must direct the tastes. It must influence the choices and decisions. It must fill the deepest, lowest, inmost seat in your soul.

13 Before Christ comes it is useless to expect to see a perfect church.

19.126
Auguste Sabatier (1839-1901)
French Protestant theologian

1 Man cannot know himself without knowing himself to be limited. But he cannot feel these fatal limitations without going beyond them in thought and by desire, so that he is never satisfied with what he possesses, and cannot be happy except with that he cannot attain.

2 [Religion is] the rent in the rock through which the living and life-giving waters flow.

2 All the peoples of antiquity believed that their legislation came from heaven. In like manner all the Churches have believed, and many of them still believe, that their dogmas, in their official form, have been directly given to them by God himself. The history of evolution, political and religious, has dissipated these illusions.

19.127
Ira David Sankey (1840-1908)
Preacher and hymn-writer

1 In that sweet by and by we shall meet on that beautiful shore.

19.128
Friedrich Schleiermacher (1768-1834)
German theologian

1 Those proud islanders [the British] whom many unduly honour, know no watchword but *gain* and *enjoyment*. Their zeal for knowledge is only a sham fight, their worldly wisdom a false jewel, skilfully and deceptively composed, and their sacred freedom itself too often and too easily serves self-interest.

2 I maintain that in all better souls piety springs necessarily by itself; that a province of its own in the mind belongs to it, in which it has unlimited sway; that it is worthy to animate most profoundly the noblest and best and to be fully accepted and known by them.

3 Religion is not knowledge and science, either of the world or of God. Without being knowledge, it recognizes knowledge and science. In itself it is an affection, a revelation of the Infinite in the finite, God being seen in it and it in God.

4 The sum total of religion is to feel that, in its highest unity, all that moves us in feeling is one; to feel that anything singular and particular is only possible by means of this unity; to feel, that is to say, that our being and living is a being and living in and through God.

5 The true nature of religion is... immediate consciousness of the Deity as he is found in ourselves and in the world.

6 In the midst of finitude to be at one with the Infinite and in every moment to be eternal is the immortality of religion.

19.129
Seraphim of Sarov (1759-1833)
Russian monk

1 When I am with you no longer, come to my grave, and the more often the better. Whatever is on your heart, all your sorrow, prostrate on the ground tell it all to me, speaking as to one alive. And I will hear you and take away all your bitterness. For to you I am alive, and I shall be so always.

2 Man must be lenient with his soul in her weakness and imperfections and suffer her failings as he suffers those of others, but he must not become idle, and must encourage himself to better things.

3 Sow everywhere the good seed given to you. Sow in good ground, sow in sand, sow among the stones, sow on the road, sow among the weeds. Perhaps some of these seeds will open up and grow and bring forth fruit, even if not at once.

4 Prayer, fasting, vigils and all other Christian exercises, however good in themselves are not the goal of our Christian life, although they are the necessary means to its attainment. The true goal of the Christian life consists in the acquisition of the Holy Spirit.

5 God the Word, our Lord, the God-man Jesus Christ, likens our life to a market place. Our life on earth he calls trading. He says to all: Trade till I come, redeeming the time because the days are evil.

19.130
Bruno Serunkuma of Uganda (d.1886)
Ugandan martyr

1 A fountain fed from many springs will never dry up. When we are gone, others will rise in our place.

19.131
Elizabeth Seton (1774-1821)
US-born religious founder and educator

1 The heart preparing for Communion should be as a crystal vial filled with clear water in which the least mote of uncleanness will be seen.

19.132
Anthony Ashley Cooper, Earl of Shaftesbury (1801-1885)
Politician and social reformer

1 What is morally wrong can never be politically right.

2 I would rather be Head of the Ragged Schools than have the command of armies.

3 The first principle God's honour, the second man's happiness, the means prayer and unremitting diligence.

4 If I followed my own inclination I would sit in my armchair and take it easy for the rest of my life. But I dare not do it. I must work as long as life lasts.

5 My hands are too full, Jews, chimney-sweeps, factory children, church extension, etc., etc. I shall succeed I fear, partially in all, and completely in none. Yet we must persevere; there is hope.

6 Time was when I could not sleep for ambition. I thought of nothing but fame and immortality. I could not bear the idea of dying and being forgotten.

7 It is a wonderful accomplishment, and a most bountiful answer to one's prayers, to have obtained a wife in the highest matters and the smallest details after my imagination and my heart.

8 I wish, I ardently wish, that some other had been found to undertake the cause; nothing but the apprehension of its being lost induced me to acquiesce in Mr Bull's request. I entertain such strong opinions on the matter that I did not dare as a Christian, to let my diffidence or love of ease, prevail over the demands of morality and religion.

9 I think a man's religion, if it is worth anything, should enter into every sphere of life and rule his conduct in every relation.

19.133
Charles Simeon (1759-1836)
English evangelical clergyman

1 [In the liturgy] The influences of the Holy Spirit, from whom all holy desires, all good counsels, and all just works do proceed, are stated; and the inspiration of the Holy Spirit is sought; but all is conveyed in a way of humble devotion, without reflection on others, or even a word that can lead to controversy of any kind.

2 I do not sit down to the perusal of scripture in order to impose a sense on the inspired writers, but to receive one, as they give it me. I pretend not to teach them, I wish like a child to be taught by them.

3 Don't let Satan make you overwork and then put you out of action for a long period.

4 For the attainment of divine knowledge, we are directed to combine a dependence on God's Spirit with our own researches. Let us, then, not presume to separate what God has thus united.

19.134
Sydney Smith (1771-1845)
English clergyman and wit

1 In the midst of your highest success, in the most perfect gratification of your vanity, in the most ample increase of your wealth, fall down at the feet of Jesus, and say, 'Master, what shall I do to inherit eternal life?'

19.135
Vladimir Solovyov (1853-1900)
Russian philosopher and theologian

1 When Orthodox and Catholics, who abide in the unity of the Body of Christ, become aware of that mystical unity and are moved to confirm it by the moral bond of love and communion, the Protestant principle of freedom will find its true application and occupy a high position in the completion of the Church, for that completion is free theocracy.

2 The body of Christ, which first appeared as a small embryo in the form of the not very numerous community of the early Christians, gradually grows and develops so as to embrace, at the end of time, all humanity and the whole of nature in one universal organism of God-manhood; because the rest of nature, in the words of the Apostle, is awaiting, with hope, the manifestation of the sons of God...

19.136
Charles Haddon Spurgeon (1834-1892)
English Baptist preacher

1 By perseverance the snail reached the ark.

2 It needs more skill than I can tell
To play the second fiddle well.

3 Some are dead; you must rouse them. Some are troubled; you must comfort them. Others are burdened; you must point them to the burden-bearer. Still more are puzzled; you must enlighten them. Still others are careless and indifferent; you must warn and woo them.

4 A fellow of Billingsgate cannot understand a fellow of Brasenose. Now as the costermonger cannot learn the language of the college, let the college learn the language of the costermonger.

5 There are more flies caught with honey than with vinegar.

6 Wisdom is the right use of knowledge. To know is not to be wise... There is no fool so great as the knowing fool. But to know how to use knowledge is to have wisdom.

7 Quietude, which some men cannot abide, because it reveals their inward poverty, is as a palace of cedar to the wise, for along its hallowed courts the King in his beauty deigns to walk.

8 Every generation needs re-generation.

9 The worst thing that can happen to a man who gambles is to win.

10 Those who are quick to promise are generally slow to perform.

11 Anxiety does not empty tomorrow of its sorrows, but only empties today of its strength.

12 Whether we like it or not, asking is the rule of the Kingdom.

13 Some temptations come to the industrious, but all temptations attack the idle.

14 There are some sciences that may be learned by the head, but the science of Christ crucified can only be learned by the heart.

15 Feel for others—in your pocket.

16 Some ministers would make good martyrs. They are so dry, they would burn well.

17 Sometimes God send his love-letters in black-edged envelopes.

18 Train your child in the way in which you know you should have gone yourself.

19 When your heart is full of Christ, you want to sing.

20 As sure as ever God puts his children in the furnace he will be in the furnace with them.

19.137
Elizabeth Cady Stanton (1815-1902)

North American social reformer and women's suffrage leader

1 While their clergymen told them on the one hand, that they owed all the blessings and freedom they enjoyed to the Bible, on the other, they said it clearly marked out their circumscribed sphere of action: that the demands for political and civil rights were irreligious, dangerous to the stability of the home, the state and the church.

2 Come, come, my conservative friend, wipe the dew off your spectacles, and see that the world is moving.

3 A few of the more democratic denominations accord women some privileges, but invidious discriminations of sex are found in all religious organizations, and the most bitter outspoken enemies of woman are found among clergymen and bishops of the Protestant religion.

19.138
Caroline E. Stephen (1834-1909)

English Quaker and religious writer

1 A Friends' meeting, however silent, is at the very lowest a witness that worship is something other and deeper than words, and that it is to the unseen and eternal things that we desire to give the first place in our lives.

2 If it be our lot to stand apart from those close natural ties by which life is for most people shaped and filled, let us not be in haste to fill the gap.

3 Our wisdom therefore must lie in learning not to shrink from anything that may be in store for us, but so to grasp the master key of life as to be able to turn everything to good and fruitful account.

4 That which seems to others a cutting short of activity, may be to ourselves the laying down of arms no longer needed; our eyes may see the haven, where our friends can only see the storm.

19.139
Harriet Beecher Stowe (1811-1896)
North American writer

1 So shall it be at last, in that bright morning
when the soul waketh and life's shadows flee;
O, in that hour, fairer than daylight dawning,
Shall rise the glorious thought—I am with
thee.

2 The bitterest tears shed over graves are for words left unsaid and deeds left undone.

19.140
James Hudson Taylor (1832-1905)
English medical missionary and founder of the China Inland Mission

1 There are three indispensable requirements for a missionary: 1. Patience. 2. Patience. 3. Patience.

2 There are three stages in the work of God: Impossible; Difficult; Done.

3 I used to ask God to help me. Then I asked if I might help him. I ended up by asking him to do his work through me.

4 When God wants to do his great works he trains somebody to be quiet enough and little enough, then he uses that person.

5 Depend on it! God's work done in God's way will never lack God's supply.

6 There is a living God. He has spoken in the Bible. He means what he says and will do all he has promised.

7 I am so weak that I can hardly write,
I cannot read my Bible, I cannot even pray.
I can only lie still in God's arms like a little child, and trust.

19.141
Frederick Temple (1821-1902)
Archbishop of Canterbury

1 It is quite impossible to evolve the Moral Law out of anything but itself.

2 The principle of the Moral Law, its universality, its supremacy, cannot come out of any development of human nature any more than the necessity of mathematical truth can so come. It stands not on experience, and is its own evidence.

19.142
Alfred Tennyson (1809-1892)
English poet

1 There lives more faith in honest doubt,
Believe me, than in half the creeds.

2 Christ's character was more wonderful than the greatest miracle.

3 Knowledge comes, but wisdom lingers.

4 I am a part of all that I have met.

5 Her eyes are homes of silent prayer.

6 No life that breathes with human breath
Has ever truly longed for death.

7 My strength is as the strength of ten,
Because my heart is pure.

8 The happiness of a man in this life does not consist in the absence but in the mastery of his passions.

19.143
Theophan the Recluse (1815-1900)
Russian monk and spiritual writer

1 The principal thing is to stand before God with the mind in the heart, and to go on standing before him unceasingly day and night until the end of life.

2 Prayer is the test of everything; prayer is also the source of everything; prayer is the driving force of everything; prayer is also the director of everything. If prayer is right, everything is right. For prayer will not allow anything to go wrong.

3 The infusion of the Holy Spirit does not lie within our power. It comes as the Spirit himself wishes. And when it comes, this infusion will so greatly animate the powers of our spirit that the song to God breaks out of itself.

4 The practice of the Jesus prayer is simple. Stand before the Lord with the attention in the heart, and call to him: 'Lord Jesus Christ, Son of God, have mercy on me!' The essential part of this is not in the words, but in faith, contrition, and self-surrender to the Lord. With these feelings one can stand before the Lord even without any words, and it will still be prayer.

5 When remembrance of God lives in the heart and there maintains the fear of him, then all goes well; but when this remembrance grows weak or is kept only in the head, then all goes astray.

19.144
Thérèse of Lisieux (1873-1897)
French Carmelite nun

1 Suffering is the very best gift He has to give us. He gives it only to His chosen friends.

2 Jesus alone IS; the rest IS NOT.

3 My God, I choose the whole lot. No point in becoming a Saint by halves. I'm not afraid of suffering for your sake; the only thing I'm afraid of is clinging to my own will. Take it, I want the whole lot, everything whatsoever that is your will for me.

4 The loveliest masterpiece of the heart of God is the heart of a mother.

5 I will try to find a lift by which I may be raised to God, for I am too small to climb the steep stairway to perfection.

19.145
Francis Thompson (1859-1907)
English poet

1 O world invisible, we view thee,
O world intangible, we touch thee,
O world unknowable, we know thee,
Inapprehensible, we clutch thee.

2 Short arm needs man to reach to Heaven, so ready is Heaven to stoop to him.

3 To most, even good people, God is a belief. To the saints he is an embrace.

4 Power is the reward of sadness. It was after the Christ had wept over Jerusalem that he uttered some of his most august words; it was when his soul had been sorrowful even unto death that his enemies fell prostrate before his voice. Who suffers, conquers. The bruised is the breaker.

5 An atheist is a man who believes himself an accident.

19.146
Leo Tolstoy (1828-1910)
Russian novelist

1 Everyone thinks of changing humanity and no one ever thinks of changing himself.

2 There never has been, and cannot be, a good life without self-control.

3 The vocation of every man and woman is to serve other people.

4 A good portion of the evils that afflict mankind is due to the erroneous belief that life can be made secure by violence.

5 In order to obtain and hold power a man must love it. Thus the effort to get it is not likely to be coupled with goodness, but with the opposite qualities of pride, craft, and cruelty.

19.147
Henri de Tourville (1842-1903)
French priest and spiritual writer

1 Remember that God loves your soul, not in some aloof, impersonal way, but passionately, with the adoring, cherishing love of a parent for a child.

2 God eliminates illness through the growth of knowledge and of human wisdom.

3 Perfection never exists apart from imperfection, just as good health cannot exist without our feeling effort, fatigue, hunger or thirst, heat or cold; yet none of those prevent the enjoyment of good health.

4 When you think you are going to die say to yourself, 'So much the better! I am about to behold the Adorable!'

5 Every Saint is a pattern; but no Saint is a pattern of everything.

6 It is a splendid habit to laugh inwardly at yourself. It is the best way of regaining your good humour and of finding God without further anxiety.

7 Life is a glorious road which leads to incomparable splendour, to the very life of God, to the goal of all things, to the full fruition of all that our hearts hold within them—as if in a broken but carefully riveted vessel of which the pieces though broken, yet hold firmly together.

8 Everything which in creation bears the mark of an active energy, intelligence and love has its infinite prototype in the Father, the Son and the Holy Spirit.

9 [The God-Man] has reserved for himself the right to act directly and independently. Who could doubt that he does so, and with a generosity which should put our rigorism to shame if we were aware of the laws and the wonders of his uncovenanted grace.

10 In the new world of today... man is no longer enclosed in his own mind nor is he any more in passive contact with nature. He acts upon nature powerfully, intelligently, scientifically, triumphantly, extraordinarily, and invincibly. It is for mysticism now to praise this splendid humanity, which is in active contact with every natural force, this combination of intellect and nature, in order to fill man's life and to give him divine enjoyment of all his faculties.

11 As a rule when we are told not to be a half-hearted Christian, the meaning is that one should increase one's burden. I mean here just the opposite. I mean that we should enjoy in all its fullness the supreme gladness which Christian truth gives us.

12 We believe, but we do not know how to enjoy what we believe!

13 Many people only arrive at God by the front door, with all their luggage... Go straight from your soul to God without all this help, when you have not got it, and you will be admitted at the side door.

14 Death is the flowering of life, the consummation of union with God.

19.148
Richard Chevenix Trench (1807-1886)
Anglican Archbishop of Dublin

1 None but God can satisfy the longings of an immortal soul; that as the heart was made for Him, so He only can fill it.

2 Humility comes from the constant sense of our own creatureliness.

3 Prayer is not overcoming God's reluctance; it is laying hold of his highest willingness.

19.149
Sojourner Truth (b.1790s)
North American preacher and social activist

1 I have done a great deal of work; as much as a man, but I did not get so much pay... I suppose I am about the only colored woman that goes about to speak for the rights of colored women. I want to keep the thing stirring, now that the ice is cracked.

2 That [man] says women can't have as much rights as men, because Christ wasn't a woman! Where did your Christ come from?... From God and from a woman! Man had nothing to do with him... If the first woman God ever made was strong enough to turn the world upside down all alone, these women together ought to be able to turn it back, and get it right side up again! And now they are asking to do it, the men better let them.

3 We'll have our rights. See if we don't. And you can't stop us from them, see if you can.

19.150
George Tyrrell (1861-1909)
Irish 'modernist' theologian

1 I drifted into the church for a thousand paltry motives and reasons; some good, some bad; some true, some false or fallacious—much as an ignorant and drunken navigator gets his vessel into the right port by a mere fluke. I am more satisfied to think, as I fondly perhaps do, that my lots were in other hands—at least I still hope so.

2 In a word, I would study Aquinas as I would study Dante, in order that knowing the mind of another age we might know the mind of our own more intelligently.

3 It is extremely hard for a Christian to look straight at his religion without regarding science out of the corner of his eye, or to face science without a similar side-glance at religion.

4 By a Modernist I mean a churchman, of any sort, who believes in the possibility of a synthesis between the essential truth of his religion and the essential truth of modernity.

5 The value of the gospel is not that it gives us an ideal life, but that that life was actually lived.

6 Authority, then, is not an external influence streaming down from heaven like a sunbeam through a cleft in the clouds and with a finger of light singling out God's arbitrarily chosen delegates from the multitude, over and apart from which they are to stand as his vice-regents. Authority is something inherent in, and inalienable from, that multitude itself; it is the moral coerciveness of the Divine Spirit of Truth and Righteousness inherent in the whole, dominant over its several parts and members; it is the imperativeness of the collective conscience.

7 The too literal acceptance of the metaphor which calls the Church a kingdom has led insensibly to the debasing of the heavenly reality to the level of its earthly symbol.

8 The labyrinth of my difficulties may possibly suggest the right path to some quieter spectator of my struggles.

19.151
Charles John Vaughan (1816-1897)
Dean of Llandaff

1 If I wished to humble anyone, I should question him about his prayers. I know nothing to compare with this topic for its sorrowful self-confessions.

19.152
Theophanes Vénard (1829-1861)
French missionary priest and martyr

1 Suffering is the money with which one buys heaven.

2 Happiness is to be found only in the home where God is loved and honoured, where each one loves, and helps, and cares for the others.

19.153
Innocent Veniaminov (1797-1879)
Russian missionary and the first Orthodox bishop to work on the American continent

1 When the Holy Spirit enters the heart of man, he shows him all his inner poverty and weakness, the corruption of his soul and heart, and his remoteness from God.

2 The Holy Spirit teaches prayer. No one, until he receives the Spirit, can pray in a manner truly pleasing to God.

19.154
Joseph de Veuster ('Father Damien') (1840-1889)
Leper missionary

1 I thank God that now when I preach I shall be able to say instead of 'dear brethren', 'my fellow lepers'.

19.155
Jean-Baptiste Marie Vianney (Curé d'Ars) (1786-1859)
French priest

1 It is always springtime in the heart that loves God.

2 The greatest of all evils is not to be tempted, because there are then grounds for believing that the Devil looks upon us as his property.

3 The Devil only tempts those souls that wish to abandon sin and those that are in a state of grace. The others belong to him: he has no need to tempt them.

4 Repentance—it is always to start over again.

5 Where there is true purity in the home, purity of moral reigns supreme.

19.156
Queen Victoria (1819-1901)
Queen of the United Kingdom of Great Britain and Ireland

1 Here is the secret of England's greatness.

2 I wish he would come in my lifetime so that I could take my crown and lay it at his feet.

19.157
Maria Droste zu Vischering (1863-1899)
German nun, promoter of devotion to the Sacred Heart

1 I began to understand that the love of the Sacred Heart without a spirit of sacrifice is but empty illusion.

19.158
The Way of a Pilgrim
Anonymous Roman Orthodox spiritual writing

1 When I began to pray with all my heart, everything around me seemed delightful and marvellous. The trees, the grass, the birds, the earth, the air, the light seemed to be telling me that they existed for man's sake, that they witnessed to the love of God for man, that everything proved the love of God for man, that all things prayed to God and sang his praise. Thus it was that I came to understand what the *Philokalia* calls 'the knowledge of the speech of all creatures'.

2 They brought me presents, treated me with reverence and pampered me. I endured all this for a week. Then, fearing that I might succumb to the temptation of vainglory, I left the place in secrecy at night.

3 Ceaseless interior prayer is a continual yearning of the human spirit towards God. To succeed in this consoling exercise we must pray more often to God to teach us to pray without ceasing. Pray more, and pray more fervently. It is prayer itself which will reveal to you how it can be achieved unceasingly; but it will take some time.

19.159
Bruce Foss Westcott (1825-1901)
Bishop of Durham and scholar of the Greek New Testament

1 Temptation commonly comes through that for which we are naturally fitted.

2 We make a great mistake if we connect with our conception of heaven the thought of rest from work. Rest from toil, from weariness, from exhaustion—yes; rest from work, from productiveness, from service—no.

3 The end of prayer is the perfection of the whole Christian body.

4 When Christ serves, he serves perfectly.

5 Taking all the evidence together, it is not too much to say that there is no single historic incident better or more variously supported than the resurrection of Christ.

19.160
Anna White (late 19c.)
North American Shaker

1 Shakers regard all life and activity animated by Christian love as worship. They invoke the Divine Father-Mother in silent prayer together before each meal, partake of their food in a worshipful spirit and go about their duties in a cheerful, happy, helpful temper, feeling the 'Labour is worship and prayer'.

2 No form of worship, however sacred, is regarded as established, only so far as it expresses the gift and leading of the Spirit; no form but may be changed or dispensed with. The life of the spirit, not the form of expression, is regarded as essential.

19.161
John Greenleaf Whittier (1807-1892)
North American poet

1 If we are not full grown men and Christians, the fault is not in Quakerism, but in ourselves.

2 Drop thy still dews of quietness,
Till all our strivings cease;
Take from our souls the strain and stress,
And let our ordered lives confess
The beauty of thy peace.

3 God gives quietness at last.

19.162
William Wilberforce (1759-1833)
English philanthropist

1 Let true Christians with suitable earnestness strive to recommend their faith in everything, and to silence the idle gibes of ignorant objectors. Let them vindicate boldly the cause of Christ in an age when so many who bear the name of Christians are ashamed of him.

2 Being aware of the absolute importance and arduous nature of the service in which he is engaged, the true Christian sets about his task with vigour and diligence. He is prepared to meet difficulties and is not discouraged when they occur.

3 A man who acts from the principles I profess reflects that he is to give an account of his political conduct at the judgement seat of Christ.

4 This perpetual hurry of business and company ruins me in soul if not in body.

5 Our motto must continue to be *perseverance*. And ultimately I trust the Almighty will crown our efforts with success.

19.163
Frances Willard (d.1898)
North American Methodist and social activist

1 While alone on my knees one sabbath... as I lifted my heart to God crying, 'What wouldst thou have me to do?' there was borne in my mind, as I believe from loftier regions, this declaration, 'You are to speak for woman's ballot as a weapon for protection for her home.'

19.164
Love Maria Willis (1824-1908)
North American writer and editor

1 Father, hear the prayer we offer;
Not for ease that prayer shall be,
But for strength that we may ever
Live our lives courageously.

19.165
Christopher Wordsworth (1807-1885)
English Anglican bishop

1 Lord, be thy word my rule,
In it may I rejoice;
Thy glory be my aim,
Thy holy will my choice.

Thy promises my hope;
Thy providence my guard;
Thine arm my strong support
Thyself my great reward.

19.166
William Wordsworth (1770-1850)
English poet

1 Small service is true service while it lasts.

2 The best portion of a good man's life,
His little, nameless, unremembered acts
Of kindness and of love.

3 Even such a shell the universe itself
Is to the ear of Faith; and there are times,
I doubt not, when to you it doth impart
Authentic tidings of invisible things;
Of ebb and flow, and ever-during power;
And central peace, subsisting at the heart
Of endless agitation.

PART 6

Twentieth Century to 1950

To believe in God is one thing, to know God another. Both in heaven and on earth the Lord is made known only by the Holy Spirit, and not through ordinary learning.

Staretz Silouan
(1866-1938)

20.1
Karl Adam
German-born Roman Catholic theologian

1 We must bring unto subjection the European in us, cramped as he is by the influence of his peculiar history, in order to set free the original, genuine, true, living man from the smothering undergrowth which encompasses him.

20.2
Henry Brooks Adams (1838-1918)
North American historian

1 Man knows mighty little, and may some day learn enough of his own ignorance to fall down and pray.

2 All experience is an arch to build upon.

3 They know enough who know how to learn.

4 A teacher affects eternity; he can never tell where his influence stops.

20.3
Roland Allen (1868-1947)
British Anglican missionary

1 The coming of the Holy Spirit at Pentecost was the coming of a missionary Spirit... Those who received the Holy Spirit became witnesses.

20.4
Florence Allshorn (1887-1950)
English missionary, educator and writer

1 The dissipation of egoism is always a tearing, tormenting process, but without it there is no hope of grasping something beyond. You cannot have both.

2 The Christian religion is fundamentally authoritative; a strict demand calling for obedience, not a suggestion, one among many you could take up and tinker with, or take up and lay down.

3 The Holy Spirit is not something that stands by itself, something that we can pray for and have as a thing in itself, it is born from Love and is of Love, all its treasures are of Love, and if we are to believe our Gospels it is received by Love and Love only.

4 Love is our adventure now, and not primarily righteousness.

5 True repentance brings an urge to be different, because of the sense of the incessant movement of what I am, forming, forming, forming what I shall be in the years to come.

6 An ideal is never yours until it comes out of your finger tips.

7 I begin to think that guts come next to love; anyway, love without them is a flimsy, sentimental thing.

20.5
Ethel Ambrose (1874-1934)
Australian-born doctor who served in India

1 The medical missionary tries to win souls by healing bodies. People who would not sit and listen to the Gospel in an ordinary way, will willingly listen to the Story of Salvation, even if only to pass the time while waiting for a surgical dressing or a bottle of medicine, and at a time when hearts are softened through suffering the Gospel brings its message of comfort.

20.6
Eberhard Arnold (1883-1935)
German Protestant, founder with his wife Emmy of the Bruderhof, a Christian communal movement in the eastern USA

1 In the ultimate depths, everything good and true that men have ever known, thought, or lived comes from the one source of light. Our vocation is to make the way free for it.

2 If your heart is not clear and undivided—'single', as Jesus put it—then it will be weak, flabby, and indolent, incapable of accepting God's will, of making important decisions, and of taking strong action. That is why Jesus attached the greatest significance to singleness of heart, simplicity, unity, solidarity, and decisiveness.

3 Unless we prove our readiness to die for God's kingdom in the trivialities of daily life, we shall not be able to muster up courage in the critical hour of history.

4 A person must be converted twice; once from the natural to the spiritual, and then again from the spiritual to the natural.

5 If we in our human life take our surrender to God seriously; if God enters us as the strength of light, of the tree, as the elemental energy which alone makes new life possible—then we shall be able to live the new life.

6 As an educator, you must learn wonder... Only those who look with the eyes of children can lose themselves in the object of their wonder.

7 An open word spoken directly to another person deepens friendship and is not resented.

20.7
Sabine Baring-Gould (1834-1924)
English clergyman and hymn-writer

1 Through the night of doubt and sorrow
Onward goes the pilgrim band,
Singing songs of expectation,
Marching to the Promised Land.

...

One the object of our journey,
One the faith which never tires,
One the earnest looking forward,
One the hope our God inspires.

...

Soon shall come the great awaking,
Soon the rending of the tomb;
Then the scattering of all shadows,
And the end of toil and gloom.

2 Now the day is over,
Night is drawing nigh,
Shadows of the evening
Steal across the sky.

3 Crowns and thrones may perish,
Kingdoms rise and wane,
But the Church of Jesus
Constant will remain;
Gates of hell can never
'Gainst that Church prevail;
We have Christ's own promise,
And that cannot fail.

4 To that brightest of all meetings
Bring us, Jesus Christ, at last;
By thy Cross, through death and judgment
holding fast.

20.8
Hilaire Belloc (1870-1953)
Roman Catholic historical writer and critic

1 ['Padre Eterno' speaks:] Here and there are some not doing as the rest, or attending to their business, but throwing themselves into all manner of attitudes, making the most extraordinary sounds, and clothing themselves in the quaintest of garments. What is the meaning of that?... Oh! they are worshipping *me*! Well, that is the most sensible thing I have heard of them yet, and I altogether commend them. *Continuez, continuez!*

20.9
Richard Meux Benson (1824-1915)
Founder of the Anglican Society of St John the Evangelist

1 If we use God's talents, we shall find that they become multiplied in the use. We thought we had two; we find we have five.

2 We live in the gaslight of our earthly reason instead of the sunlight of our Father's glory!

3 We can only come to know sin as Christ is revealed within us. He gives the knowledge of God by his Holy Spirit, and thus he gives the knowledge of sin.

4 We are not to look for manifestations of divine power to make natural faith easier.

20.10
Nicolas Berdyaev (1874-1948)
Russian philosopher

1 Every time in history man has tried to turn crucified truth into coercive truth he has betrayed the fundamental principle of Christianity.

2 The mystery of the world abides in freedom: God desired freedom and freedom gave rise to tragedy in the world.

3 Fear is never a good counsellor and victory over fear is the first spiritual duty of man.

4 Civilization has a fatal way of engendering smugness and complacency, of destroying originality and individuality, and severing man from the primary sources of life.

5 The transfiguration of the world is the attainment of beauty. The Kingdom of God is beauty. Art gives us merely symbols of beauty. Real beauty is given only in the religious transfiguration of the creature. Beauty is God's idea of the creature, of man and of the world.

6 The whole life of this world must be made to pass through death and crucifixion, else it cannot attain resurrection and eternity. If death is accepted as a part of the mystery of life, it is not final and has not the last word.

7 Act as though you could hear the Divine call to participate through free and creative activity in the Divine work.

8 It is an illusion that revolution breaks with the old. It is only that the old makes its appearance with a new mask on. The old slavery changes its dress, the old inequality is transformed into a new inequality.

9 Freedom which is the result of necessity cannot be real freedom; it is only an element in the dialectic of necessity.

20.11
Georges Bernanos (1888-1948)
French writer

1 Angers, daughters of despair, creep and twist like worms. Prayer is, all things considered, the only form of revolt that stays standing up.

20.12
Edwyn Bevan (1870-1943)
British theologian, historian and philosopher

1 It is only... in the sense of giving rational comfort to people who already believe in God that the standard arguments can be regarded as demonstrating the existence of God. What actually causes anyone to believe in God is direct perception of the Divine.

20.13
Léon Marie Bloy (1846-1917)
French author and social critic

1 I am simply a poor man who seeks his God, sobbing and calling Him along all roads.

2 What must some day be so terrible an indictment of the rich is the Desire of the poor. Here is a millionaire who, beyond his needs, clings to or spends in a minute what for fifty or sixty years has been the object of the desperate prayers of a poor man.

20.14
Christoph Friedrich Blumhardt (1842-1919)
German Protestant missioner and theologian

1 It is a pity that Christianity has exploited Christ in a selfish way, which is probably the reason for the shadow that is cast over all Christendom... We remain hampered by a petty, selfish attitude in which everyone has his own dear Saviour and eats his own sweet pudding, so to speak, to his heart's content. But we never cast off the old nature; we never really learn how to live in a way worthy of God.

2 If we want to fight for the kingdom of God, then it might be more important and more necessary to do away with the nine-tenths of all Christian religion that has become false... Then the Saviour himself could live and rule, instead of the systems that, while pretending to be from God, really derive from man.

3 I call it an illusion for Christians to seek peace, as though the gospel wanted to make life comfortable for them. The contrary is true. 'I have not come to bring peace on earth, but a sword.' As long as the fight is going on, we have peace only in the fight. Our peace is not a well-being; it is a participation in Christ, in God in the flesh against all other things in the flesh.

20.15 Dietrich Bonhoeffer (1905-1945)

German Lutheran theologian, executed for his resistance to National Socialism

1 Action springs not from thought, but from a readiness for responsibility.

2 Death is the supreme festival on the road to freedom.

3 A God who let us prove his existence would be an idol.

4 Cheap grace is grace without discipleship, grace without the cross, grace without Jesus Christ, living and incarnate.

5 Costly grace is the treasure hidden in the field; for the sake of it a man will gladly go and sell all that he has. It is costly because it costs a man his life, and it is grace because it gives a man the only true life.

6 The 'heart' in the biblical sense is not the inward life, but the whole man in relation to God.

7 No actions are bad in themselves; even murder can be justified.

8 Would it not be a blasphemous frivolity to think that the devil could be exorcised with the cry 'No more war' and with a new organisation?

9 We are silent at the beginning of the day because God should have the first word, and we are silent before going to sleep because the last word also belongs to God.

10 When Jesus blessed sinners, they were real sinners, but Jesus did not make everyone a sinner first. He called them away from the sin, not into their sin.

11 It is infinitely easier to suffer in obedience to a human command than to accept suffering as free, responsible men.

12 The commandment of absolute truthfulness is really only another name for the fullness of discipleship.

13 When Christ calls a man he bids him come and die.

14 The essence of chastity is not the suppression of lust, but the total orientation of one's life towards a goal. Without such a goal, chastity is bound to become ridiculous. Chastity is the sine qua non of lucidity and concentration.

15 A Christian is someone who shares the sufferings of God in the world.

16 We must learn to regard people less in the light of what they do or omit to do, and more in the light of what they suffer.

17 Our brother has been given to us to help us. He hears the confession of our sins in Christ's stead and he forgives our sins in Christ's name.

18 Happy are they who know that discipleship simply means the life which springs from grace, and that grace simply means discipleship.

19 If Jesus Christ is not true God, how could he *help* us? If he is not true man, how could he help *us*?

20 It is part of the nature of fanaticism that it loses sight of the totality of evil and rushes like a bull at the red cloth instead of at the man who holds it.

21 In ordinary life we hardly realise that we receive a great deal more than we give, and that it is only with gratitude that life becomes rich. It is very easy to overestimate the importance of our own achievements in comparison with what we owe others.

22 It may be that the day of judgement will dawn tomorrow; in that case, we shall gladly stop working for a better future. But not before.

23 God would have us know that we must live as men who manage our lives without him... Before God and with God we live without God. God lets himself be pushed out of the world onto the cross.

24 Give me such love for God and men, as will blot out all hatred and bitterness.

25 In Jesus the service of God and the service of the least of the brethren were one.

26 One can acquire 'simplicity', but 'simpleness' is innate. Education and culture may bring 'simplicity'—indeed, it ought to be one of their essential aims—but simpleness is a gift.

27 The figure of the Crucified invalidates all thought which takes success for its standard.

28 Here and there people flee from public altercation into the sanctuary of private virtuousness. But anyone who does this must shut his mouth and his eyes to the injustice around him... What he leaves undone will rob him of his peace of mind.

29 The Church knows nothing of the sacredness of war. The Church which prays the 'Our father' asks God only for peace.

30 When a madman is tearing through the streets in a car, I can, as a pastor who happens to be on the scene, do more than merely console or bury those who have been run over. I must jump in front of the car and stop it.

20.16
Robert Bridges (1844-1930)
English poet

1 Friendship is in loving rather than in being loved.

2 Boundless is thy love for me,
Boundless then my trust shall be.

3 From this dilemma of pagan thought,
this poison of faith,
Man-soul made glad escape
in the worship of Christ;
for his humanity is God's personality,
and communion with him
is the life of the soul.

20.17
Sergius Bulgakov (1871-1944)
Russian theologian

1 Man must become not only a good and faithful worker in the world; he must not only 'dress and keep it' (Genesis 2.15), as he was commanded in paradise, but he must also become its artist; he must render it beautiful. Because he has been created by God, he is called to create.

2 This intercession by prayer is a participation in the destiny of the world.

3 All the harmonies of creation find their resonance in man, the centre of the universe.

20.18
Frances Xavier Cabrini (1850-1917)
Italian founder of the Missionary Sisters of the Sacred Heart

1 I have started houses with no more than the price of a loaf of bread and prayers, for with him who comforts me, I can do anything.

2 I travel, work, suffer my weak health, meet with a thousand difficulties, but all these are nothing, for this world is so small. To me, space is an imperceptible object, as I am accustomed to dwell in eternity.

20.19
Alexander Carmichael (1832-1912)
Scottish collector of prayers and compiler of the Carmina Gadelica

1 The people say that the sun dances on this day in joy for a risen Saviour.

20.20
Oswald Chambers (d.1917)
English spiritual writer

1 If you make a god of your best moments, you will find that God will fade out of your life and never come back until you do the duty that lies nearest, and have learned not to make a fetish of your rare moments.

2 The one mark of the saint is the moral originality which springs from abandonment to Jesus Christ.

3 Never make a principle out of your experience; let God be as original with other people as he is with you.

4 Simplicity is the secret of seeing things clearly. A saint does not think clearly for a long while, but a saint ought to *see* clearly without any difficulty.

5 Walking on the water is easy to impulsive pluck, but walking on dry land as a disciple of Jesus Christ is a different thing.

20.21
John Chapman (1865-1933)
English Benedictine monk

1 I think spiritual pride is not dangerous to anyone who tries seriously to serve God; the greater danger is usually *despondency* (though this arises from a kind of pride: wounded pride), because one is not better.

2 The longer one prays, the better it goes.

3 Prayer, in the sense of union with God, is the most crucifying thing there is.

4 Live for God and one's neighbour, and don't let's look into our heart.

5 As to being 'worthy' of receiving [holy communion], no Angel is, nor was our blessed Lady. Our preparation consists in saying: 'I am *not* worthy.'

6 Do not worry at being worried; but accept worry peacefully. Difficult, but not impossible.

7 Pray as you can, and do not try to pray as you can't.

8 If God sees best for me to die, what in the world should one wish to live for?

20.22
G.K. Chesterton (1874-1936)
English Roman Catholic essayist

1 The world will never starve for wonder; only for want of wonder.

2 Art is limitation; the essence of every picture is the frame.

3 You can never have a revolution in order to establish a democracy. You must have a democracy in order to have a revolution.

4 It is the test of a good religion whether you can make a joke of it.

5 Tradition may be defined as an extension of the franchise. Tradition means giving votes to the most obscure of all classes, our ancestors. It is the democracy of the dead.

6 It is arguable that we ought to put the State in order before there can really be such a thing as a State school.

7 The rich are the scum of the earth in every country.

8 The word 'orthodoxy' not only no longer means being right; it practically means being wrong.

9 Happiness is a mystery like religion, and should never be rationalized.

10 Charity is the power of defending that which we know to be indefensible. Hope is the power of being cheerful in circumstances which we know to be desperate.

11 A third-class carriage is a community, while a first-class carriage is a place of wild hermits.

12 Angels can fly because they take themselves lightly.

13 The point of having an open mind, like having an open mouth, is to close it on something solid.

14 Christianity has died many times and risen again; for it had a God who knew the way out of the grave.

15 Civilisation in the best sense merely means the full authority of the human spirit over all externals.

16 True contentment is a real, even an active, virtue—not only affirmative but creative. It is the power of getting out of any situation all there is in it.

17 Adventure is the champagne of life.

18 A stiff apology is a second insult.

19 [Of Thomas Aquinas and Francis of Assisi] Perhaps it would be too paradoxical to say that these two saints saved us from spirituality: a dreadful doom.

20 They have given us into the hand of
new unhappy lords,
Lords without anger or honour,
who dare not carry their swords.
They fight by shuffling papers;
they have bright dead alien eyes;
They look at our labours and laughter
as a tired man looks at flies.
But we are the people of England;
and we have not spoken yet.
Smile at us, pay us, pass us.
But do not quite forget.

20.23
George Congreve (1835-1918)
Member of Anglican Society of St John the Evangelist

1 I find growing old something quite new and a surprise... I feel it is a sort of undressing of the soul for the next and better stage of our journey. I am so sure of the purpose of God for us, an increasing purpose from good to better, that I determine not to notice even in my thoughts (if I can help it) the inconveniences and absurdities, mortifications that come with the years. We are not at home in them, only pushing on through them on the way home.

20.24
Frances Crosby (1820-1915)
Blind North American hymn-writer

1 My very soul was flooded with celestial light... for the first time I realized that I had been trying to hold the world in one hand and the Lord in the other.

20.25
James Denney (1856-1917)
Scottish theologian

1 No man can at one and the same time prove that he is clever and that Christ is wonderful.

2 To put the matter at its simplest, Jesus Christ came to make bad men good.

3 The kingdom of God is not for the well-meaning but for the desperate.

4 To be a Christian or not to be, is not a matter of being a somewhat better man, or a man perhaps not quite so good. It is a matter of life or death.

20.26
Alexander Elchaninov (1881-1934)
Russian Orthodox parish priest in France

1 The world is crooked and God straightens it. That is why Christ suffered (and still suffers), as well as all the martyrs, confessors and saints—and we who love Christ cannot but suffer as well.

2 Holiness and knowledge are given by the spirit of *sobornost* [catholicity]. Ignorance and sin are the characteristics of isolated individuals. Only in the unity of the Church do we find these defects overcome. Man finds his true self in the Church alone: not in the helplessness of spiritual isolation but in the strength of his communion with his brothers and with his Saviour.

3 You cannot cure the soul of others or 'help people' without having changed yourself. You cannot put in order the spiritual economy of others so long as there is chaos in your own soul. You cannot bring peace to others if you do not have it yourself.

20.27
Paul Florensky (1882-1943)

Russian Orthodox theologian and mathematician, imprisoned in Soviet camps

1 Certainly the Holy Spirit is indeed at work in the Church. But knowledge of the Spirit has always been a pledge or reward—at special moments and with exceptional people; and this is how it will be until 'all is fulfilled'.

20.28
Peter Taylor Forsyth (1848-1921)

Congregationalist pastor and theologian

1 It also pleased God by the revelation of his holiness and grace... to bring home to me my sin... I was turned from a Christian to a believer, from a lover of love to an object of grace.

2 When we are not so much questioning the fact [of Christ's self-emptying] as discussing the manner of it—not the *what* but the *how*—it is a matter of theological science not of religious faith. And the science of it can wait, but the religion of it cannot.

3 We pray because we are made for prayer, and God draws us out by breathing himself in.

4 It is not a world out of joint that makes our problem, but the shipwrecked soul in it. It is Hamlet, not his world, that is wrong.

5 The worst sin is prayerlessness.

6 It is possible to be so active in the service of Christ as to forget to love him.

7 The word of God is in the Bible as the soul is in the body.

8 You must live with people to know their problems, and live with God in order to solve them.

9 The Incarnation would be equally a miracle however Jesus entered the world.

20.29
Charles de Foucauld (1858-1916)

French explorer and 'Hermit of the Sahara'

1 [Letter to his cousin] What must come first in all prayers, however varied they may be, and what gives them real value is the love with which they are made.

2 Cry the gospel with your whole life.

3 Is it not true that someone in love feels that he has made perfect use of all the time he spends in the presence of his beloved? Apart from then, is not that time used best which is employed in doing the will of furthering the welfare of his beloved in some other place?

4 Above all, we must not be discouraged by difficulties, but must remind ourselves that the more difficult a work is, the slower and more unrewarding it is, the more necessary it is to set to work with great dispatch and make great efforts.

5 I must believe no work beneath me, since Jesus was a carpenter for thirty years, and Joseph all his life.

6 Now that life is almost at an end for us, the light into which we shall enter at our death begins to shine and to show us what are realities and what are not.

7 Difficulties are not a passing condition that we must allow to blow over like a storm so that we can set to work when calm returns. They are the normal condition.

8 Live as though today you may die a martyr's death.

9 The more we lack anything in this world, the more we find the best the world can give us: the cross.

10 The deeper into agony we fall, the more necessary it is for us to throw ourselves into the embrace of our Beloved, pressing ourselves against him in uninterrupted prayer.

11 Father, I put myself into your hands; Father, I abandon myself to you, I entrust myself to you. Father, do with me as it pleases you. Whatever you do with me, I will thank you for it. Giving thanks for anything, I am ready for anything, I accept anything, give thanks for anything.

12 There will always be unhappiness in our lives, and it is right that there should be: unhappiness for the sake of the love we bear... But right as these sufferings are, they should not last long in our souls. They should be transitory. What should endure and be our normal state—the state to which we should constantly return—is joy in the glory of God, joy at seeing that Jesus is suffering no longer, and will suffer no more, but is in bliss forever at the right hand of God.

13 Wherever the sacred Host is to be found, there is the living God, there is your Saviour, as really as when he was living and talking in Galilee and Judea, as really as he now is in heaven.

20.30
Temple Gairdner (1873-1928)
English Anglican missionary to the Middle East

1 *'Behold I make all things new.'* It seemed the one text in the Bible for me that day; for I was walking in a world indescribably beautified, indescribably lovely.

2 That nothing may be between me and her, be thou between us, every moment. That we may be constantly together, draw us into separate loneliness with thyself. And when we meet breast to breast, my God, let it be on thine own. Amen. Amen.

3 I won't waste more time hating myself. The self that I hate and that [Christ] hates I leave on the Cross or in the tomb. And that which rises with him is a new self.

4 From the very outset every penny shall be consecrated to God. I think there is an *art* of simplicity. It will need no end of thinking out, and it is worth learning.

5 If the efforts to evangelize Islam had not resulted in a single conversion, they would have been worth while; for they represent Christianity as a religion that is not afraid, a religion with a message of love and goodwill evinced in deeds of love and goodwill.

20.31
Eric Gill (1882-1940)
Sculptor, letterist and wood-engraver

1 Every artist may not be a special kind of person. But every person is a special kind of artist.

2 The frightful, the truly frightful horror, of the corruption of the ancient [i.e. Roman Catholic] Church was as nothing to the essential dirtiness, dirtiness in its very being and nature, of the industrial-capitalist world.

3 When I was 'under instruction' they told me all sorts of things that seemed pretty rum, but I was past that sort of worrying.

4 I cannot forget the dream in which I was walking in heaven... with Mary [his wife] and the children. We came upon our Lord... And I said to him: 'This is Betty... and this is Petra... and this is Joanna... and this is Gordian'... And then I said: 'And this is Mary.' And he said: 'Oh, Mary and I are old friends.'

5 Holy, Holy, Holy, and that means hale and hearty and whole and healthy with a mind set heavenwards.

6 The Mass and the Eucharist are not only the centre of Christian worship, they are also the centre of Christian merry-making.

7 I became a catholic because I fell *in love* with the truth. And love is an experience. I saw. I heard. I felt. I tasted. I touched. And that is what lovers do.

8 [Jesus is] Very God, yes. And dear Jesus also. He speaks to us and we speak to him. We kiss the hem of his garment. We also thank him for our bread and butter. He ordained that our bodily motions should be pleasant and gratifying and that the pleasure of marriage should be beyond the dreams of avarice. He ordained the thunderstorms and the lion's voracity; he also blessed the daisies and the poor.

20.32
Charlotte Perkins Gilman (1860-1935)
North American sociologist

1 Eternity is not something that begins after you are dead. It is going on all the time. We are in it now.

20.33
Isabella Gilmore (1842-1923)
Reformer of the Anglican Deaconess Order

1 [The clergy] will find that they will be the gainers in the end, by their deaconesses being kept fresh and bright.

2 I see the crowded churches, with hundreds and thousands of seemingly devout women worshippers, I wonder if they know the need; surely if Christ is real to them, if they believe in any way the message that it is for all, they must be longing to carry it; once the desire is there, once the word comes 'Lord here I am, send me', difficulties will vanish.

3 I went to early service alone, and to the 11 o'clock with the children. The preacher was a stranger; he gave out his text, 'Go work for me today in my vineyard'. To me it was a trumpet call; I never heard any of the sermon. I could hardly keep from off my knees until it was finished; it was just as if God's voice had called me, and the intense rest and joy were beyond all words.

20.34
Bishop Charles Gore (1853-1932)
Bishop of Oxford and theologian

1 We must never separate what God does for us from what God does in us.

2 God does not want us to do extraordinary things; He wants us to do the ordinary things extraordinarily well.

3 [To a pious clergyman] Can you lend me a Bible? I remembered my pipe but have forgotten my Bible.

4 [To a woman puzzled about an aspect of ritual] An octave is something idolatrous and wicked and smells of incense and witchcraft.

5 If there *is* to be a resurrection, we must hold on to our toasting forks.

6 I am increasingly convinced that the *Church Times* is now edited by the Devil in person.

7 But for the miracles, I should consider Nero the ideal man.

20.35
Nikolaus Gross (1898-1945)
German miner executed for opposition to National Socialism

1 [To his family] I have long since realized that your fate does not depend on me. If it is God's will that I should no longer be with you, then indeed he has some other aid that will work without me. God abandons no one who is faithful to him, and he will not abandon you if you rely on him.

20.36
Louis Guanella (1842-1915)
Italian religious founder

1 I worry until midnight and from then on I let God worry.

20.37
Augustin Guillerand
French Carthusian monk

1 If you would cross friendship's threshold, do not forget that the primary and essential condition is renunciation: that is to say, perfect disinterestedness in the search for your friend's good, his interests, his happiness, all that is to his advantage.

20.38
Adolph von Harnack (1851-1930)
German church historian and theologian

1 We cannot hesitate to believe that the great mission of Christianity was in reality accomplished by means of informal missionaries.

2 The amount of this debt [that the Christian faith has to Judaism] is so large that one might almost venture to claim the Christian mission as a continuation of the Jewish propaganda.

3 Either the gospel is in all respects identical with its earliest form (in which case it came with its time and has departed with it); or else it contains something which, under differing historical forms, is of permanent validity. The latter is the true view.

4 If we were right in saying that the gospel is the knowledge and recognition of God as the Father, the certainty of redemption, humility and joy in God, energy and brotherly love; if it is essential to this religion that the founder must not be forgotten over his message, nor the message over the founder, history shows us that the gospel has, in point of fact, remained in force, struggling again and again to the surface.

20.39
Hannsgeorg von Heinschel-Heinegg (d.1944)
A leader of the Austrian resistance, executed in Vienna

1 What is worthy of our love? You alone, O God. What is worth our searching, never again to leave it? You alone, O God. What is worth our never leaving it? You, my Lord, you alone. And in you we find everything again, and everything renewed—a new heaven and a new earth, all good human beings, and every glory in thousandfold sweetness. Here we are reflected light. There we will be light itself.

20.40
Herbert Hensley Henson (1863-1947)
Bishop of Durham

1 I do not think that 'Spiritual = ecclesiastical', but the latter presupposes the former, and has no validity if the presupposition fails.

2 The Church retains these ancient Creeds, not because they are wholly satisfying, but because they express with great dignity, and the large prestige of their antiquity and Catholick authority, truths which it holds to be vital. When we can gain a more satisfactory formulation of what we believe, we may replace the Creeds.

3 [To someone who thought that 'publicans' in the Gospels meant pub landlords] Many public-house keepers have been my personal friends, and I have often admired the courage and ability with which they have carried on a profession, which is honourable and, indeed, indispensable, but marked by some special and formidable difficulties.

4 We must be good members of our branch of Christ's Church, seeking ever to remove its evident defects, and to develop whatever is good in it.

5 I am more and more convinced that there is little virtue of edification in discourses, however eloquent and well-justified, which dilate on general failures and faults. They leave the heart untouched, and the conscience unstirred.

6 To confess my whole mind, I am not greatly attracted by the enthusiastic laudations of the literary excellence of the English Bible [Authorized Version], which are now freely offered by men who have no use for its deeper claims on their attention.

7 Indeed that is the worst trial of the preacher's life, that he is ever set up on a pedestal, where he himself is seen in a false perspective, and may easily come to see himself as others see him. Still he *does* want encouragement sometimes, poor thing: and an honest, loving friend, who blames as well as praises, can give it.

8 What possesses our brother of Chelmsford to take up his parable against the frequent use of familiar hymns in our hymn-book? Familiarity, so far from being a disadvantage, invests forms of praise and prayer with a kind of inevitableness, which adds greatly to their spiritual value. Is the 'Te Deum' to be laid aside because it is so often used? Does the Lord's Prayer suffer from its habitual use?

20.41
Henry Scott Holland (1847-1918)
English theologian and preacher

1 Co-operation! That is the key-ideal. God invites men to help in the evolution of the purpose. That is man's call—the summons to be a fellow-worker with God in that eternal counsel which shall bring man to his final consummation, as God designed him.

2 Indeed, it is a Father to whom we are listening, crying for a lost son whom he never will allow himself to disown, because, indeed, he is his own. 'When Israel was a child I loved him.'... That is the most poignant word, surely, ever put into God's mouth by man.

3 Only by being his children can we see our failure to correspond with all his desire... By crying 'Depart from me' we are called to his closer following, and to his more effective service.

4 Personalities must be social in order to be personalities. God is personal because God is three in one.

5 The individuality of a man draws its sap out of the community. The stronger the emphasis on the one, the more vivid grows the other.

20.42
Dorothy Hosie (b.1885)
Writer and lecturer on Chinese subjects

1 If Jesus is, in truth, then, Very Man as well as Very God, He is bone of woman's bone, flesh of her flesh: it was a woman's heart blood which first nourished His frame, and which filled His veins. Could he, who fathomed the depths of pain and climbed the heights of Joy, forget the human race, and leave Woman out of His philosophy of life, whether temporal or eternal?

2 [Jesus] sat down gratefully to Martha's good meal; he also took joy in Mary's acceptance of his wisdom. His Courtesy to Woman includes the liberty of the whole of the personality, the use of all the gifts with which God has endowed her. The Parable of the Talents is for her equally with man.

20.43
Friedrich von Hügel (1858-1925)
English Roman Catholic philosopher

1 The most fundamental need, duty, honour and happiness of mankind is not petition, nor even contrition, nor again even thanksgiving—these three kinds of prayer which, indeed, must never disappear out of our spiritual lives—but adoration.

2 Christianity has taught us to care. Caring is the greatest thing, caring matters most.

3 Behind every saint stands another saint.

4 I have always loved to think of devoted suffering as the highest, purest, perhaps the only quite pure form of action.

5 [On religion which ignores the adoration of God] A triangle with one side left out.

6 The primary and full Bride of Christ never is, nor can be, the individual man at prayer, but only this complete organism of all faithful people throughout time and space.

7 How poor and thin a thing is all purely personal religion. Religion to be deep and rich must be historical.

8 Be silent about great things; let them grow inside you. Never discuss them: discussion is so limiting and distracting. It makes things grow smaller. You think you swallow things when they ought to swallow you. Before all greatness, be silent—in art, in music, in religion: silence.

9 For a person came, and loved and loved, and did and taught, and died and rose again, and loves on by his power and his Spirit for ever within us and amongst us, so unspeakably rich and yet so simple, so sublime and yet so homely, so divinely above us precisely in being so divinely near.

10 But with him, and alone with him and those who still learn and live from and by him, there is the union of the clearest, keenest sense of all the mysterious depth and breadth and length and height of human sadness, suffering, and sin, *and*, in spite of this and through this and at the end of this, a note of conquest and of triumphant joy.

11 Nothing ousts the sense of God's presence so thoroughly as the soul's dialogues with itself—when these are grumblings, grievances, etc.

20.44
Rufus Jones (1863-1948)
North American Quaker and philosopher

1 I wasn't christened in a church, but I was sprinkled from morning to night with the dew of grace.

2 There is a native, elemental homing instinct in our souls which turns us to God as naturally as the flower turns to the sun.

3 Silence itself, of course, has no magic. It may be just sheer emptiness, absence of words or noise or music. It may be an occasion for slumber, or it may be a dead form. But it may also be an intensified pause, a vitalised hush, a creative quiet, an actual moment of mutual and reciprocal correspondence with God.

4 Beauty has no function, no utility. Its value is intrinsic, not extrinsic. It is its own excuse for being. It greases no wheels, it bakes no puddings. It is a gift of sheer grace, a gratuitous largesse. It must imply behind things a Spirit that enjoys beauty for its own sake and that floods the world everywhere with it.

20.45
John Henry Jowett (1841-1923)
English Congregational preacher and devotional writer

1 We get no deeper into Christ than we allow him to get into us.

2 The real measure of our wealth is how much we'd be worth if we lost all our money.

3 I am not sure which of the two occupies the lower sphere, he who hungers for money or he who thirsts for applause.

4 God does not comfort us to make us comfortable, but to make us comforters.

5 True intercession is a sacrifice, a bleeding sacrifice.

20.46
Thomas Kelly (1893-1941)
North American Quaker

1 Men and women everywhere... have a deep, deep demand within them for an absolutely vital religion, for an absolute ground and validation of life.

2 The meek and mild mediocrity of most of us stands in sharp contrast to that volcanic, upheaving, shaggy power of the prophets, whose descendants we were meant to be.

3 Our immersion in the world's suffering is like tickling our toes in the ocean of sorrow and need, in comparison with that Calvary-life which plunges into the whole flood.

4 We must hasten *unto God*; and we must hasten *into the world*.

5 Woo him. Pursue him. Yet, he, the Hound of Heaven, has been pursuing us through the years, baying ever on our track. It was we who needed to give assent to his presence, not he who had to be attracted and come to us. And when he enters in and sups with us and we with him, what unspeakable joy! At last we are Home.

20.47
Ewald von Kleist-Schmenzin (1889-1945)

Pomeranian opponent of National Socialism, imprisoned and executed

1 It is allowable to mourn the loss of earthly things, the ruin of something for which one has worked all one's life long. But we need not and must not despair. It is a loss for only a short moment, as short as the duration of life, and our happiness is not in the least affected by it. Happiness lies in the hands of God alone. It lies beyond life, and the gate that brings us to it is death.

20.48
Abraham Kuyper (1837-1920)

Dutch Calvinist theologian and politician

1 A Christianity which does not prove its worth in practice degenerates into dry scholasticism and idle talk.

2 Justification is at once an accomplished fact, but sanctification is gradual.

3 Inspiration is the name of that all-comprehensive operation of the Holy Spirit whereby he has bestowed on the church a complete and infallible Scripture.

4 The saint is a saint because he received the Holy Spirit, who took up his abode with him and inwardly married himself to the soul.

20.49
Mary Artemisia Lathbury (1841-1913)

North American artist, writer and editor

1 Break thou the bread of life,
O Lord, to me,
As thou didst break the loaves
Beside the sea.
Beyond the sacred page
I seek thee, Lord;
My spirit longs for thee,
O. living Word!

20.50
Elisabeth Leseur (1866-1914)

French housewife

1 Above all, to live is to fight, to suffer, and to love!

20.51
Nettie Fowler McCormick (1835-1923)

North American philanthropist and missions supporter

1 We plan—and God steps in with another plan for us and he is all-wise and the most loving friend we have always helping us.

20.52
Frederick B. MacNutt (1873-1949)

Anglican clergyman, writer and collector of prayers

1 Lord Jesus Christ, the Way by which we travel: show me thyself, the Truth that we must walk in; and be in me the Life that lifts us up to God, our journey's ending.

20.53
Kim Malthe-Bruun (1923-1945)

Canadian-born seaman, executed for his opposition to the National Socialist regime

1 Immediately afterwards it dawned upon me that I have now a new understanding of the figure of Jesus. The time of waiting, that is the ordeal. I will warrant that the suffering endured in having a few nails driven through one's hands, in being crucified, is something purely mechanical that lifts the soul into an ecstasy comparable with nothing else. But the waiting in the garden—that hour drips with blood.

20.54
Columba Marmion (1858-1923)

Irish-born Abbot of Maredsous

1 Christ gives himself to us according to the measure of the desire that we have to receive Him, and the capacity of the soul is increased by the desires that it expresses: 'Open your mouth wide, and I shall fill it'.

2 Our life in heaven will be to know the Eternal Light unveiled, and to rejoice in the splendour of this Light.

3 This star [Epiphany] is the symbol of the inward illumination that enlightens souls in order to call them to God.

20.55
Alice Meynell (1847-1922)
English Catholic poet and social activist

1 'You never attained to Him?' 'If to attain
Be to abide, then that may be.'
'Endless the way, followed with how much pain!'
'The way was He.'

20.56
Helmut James, Count von Moltke (1907-1945)
Silesian-born, executed for opposition to National Socialism

1 First I must tell you that quite evidently the last twenty-four hours of one's life are no different from any others. I had always imagined that it would come as a shock to say to oneself: 'Now the sun is setting for the last time for you, now the hour hand will make only two more revolutions before twelve, now you are going to bed for the last time.' Nothing of the sort. Perhaps I am a little cracked. For I cannot deny that I am in really high spirits. I only pray to God in heaven to sustain me in this mood.

20.57
Helen Barrett Montgomery (1861-1934)
North American Baptist minister and translator of the Bible

1 Few missionaries have found the expected in the work awaiting them in the field. We went to teach women and children of Christ, their Saviour and deliverer, and to teach them to read the story for themselves... We have found sickness and poverty to relieve, widows to protect, advice to be given in every possible difficulty or emergency, teachers and Bible women to be trained, houses to be built, horses and cattle to be bought, gardens to be planted, and accounts to be kept and rendered. We have found use for every faculty, natural and acquired, that we possessed, and have coveted all we lacked.

20.58
Lottie Moon (1840-1912)
North American missionary to China

1 I hope no missionary will ever be as lonely as I have been.

2 If I had a thousand lives, I would give them all for the women of China.

20.59
Handley C.G. Moule (1841-1920)
English Anglican theologian and bishop

1 I seek no more to alter things, or mend,
Before the coming of so great a friend;
All were at best unseemly; and 'twere ill
Beyond all else to keep thee waiting still.

2 Come, not to find, but make this troubled heart
A dwelling worthy of thee as thou art;
To chase the gloom, the terror, and the sin;
Come, all thyself, yea come, Lord Jesus, in!

20.60
Rudolph Otto (1869-1937)
German Protestant theologian

1 The nature of the numinous can only be suggested by means of the special way in which it is reflected in the mind in terms of feeling... We are dealing with something for which there is only one appropriate expression, *mysterium tremendum*.

20.61
Francis Paget (1851-1911)
Bishop of Oxford

1 The joy of the Lord, the joy that is strength, the joy that no man taketh from us, the joy wherewith we joy before God, the abundant joy of faith and hope and love and praise—

this it is that gathers like a radiant, fostering, cheerful air around the soul that yields itself to the grace of God, to do his holy, loving will.

20.62
Charles Péguy (1873-1914)
French Roman Catholic writer

1 What is most contrary to salvation is not sin, but habit.

2 The weakest of sinners can either frustrate or crown a hope of God.

3 Everything begins in mysticism and ends in politics.

4 Love is rarer than genius itself. And friendship is rarer than love.

5 The triumph of demagogies is passing. But the ruins are eternal. Order, and order alone, definitively makes liberty. Disorder makes servitude. Only demagogues have an interest in trying to make us believe the contrary.

6 Tyranny is always better organized than freedom.

7 He who does not bellow the truth, when he knows the truth, makes himself the accomplice of liars and forgers.

8 Nobody comes so close to the heart of Christianity as the sinner. Nobody except perhaps the saint.

9 Unless he has genius, a rich man cannot imagine what poverty is like.

10 Suffering passes: having suffered never passes.

11 When you love someone, you love him as he is.

12 We do not run after the new; we do not run after the unknown; we do not run after the extraordinary; we seek what is right and fitting, and much that is right and fitting was said before us much better than we know how to say it ourselves.

13 Night, you are for a man more nourishing than bread and wine.

20.63
Maud D. Petre (1863-1942)
Roman Catholic laywoman

1 To love is, as it were, to lay heart and soul open to our friend; it is to strip ourselves, not only of all artificial armour, but even of the covering that nature herself provides for the feelings and the heart. And this is the love that Christ has for all men: the best and the worst have power to wound because he gives it to them by the mere fact of his love.

2 Prayer is practical when it affects our outer conduct, but still more when it affects our inward activity.

3 To confess our sins is to accuse ourselves of them; quite a different thing from merely telling them.

4 The doubt which precedes belief is not necessarily painful; the doubt which follows is like the freezing of a warm limb, the blinding of a sound eye.

20.64
Christoph Probst (1919-1943)
German executed under National Socialist regime

1 I thank you for having given me life. When I really think it through, it has all been a single road to God. Do not grieve that I must now skip the last part of it. Soon I shall be closer to you than before. In the meantime I'll prepare a glorious reception for you all.

2 I never knew that dying is so easy.

20.65
Pandita Ramabai (1858-1920)
Indian social activist

1 No caste, no sex, no work, and no man was to be depended upon to get salvation, this everlasting life, but God gave it freely to any one and every one who believed on his Son whom he sent to be the 'propitiation for our sins'.

2 Who could have described [the blind man's] joy in seeing the daylight, when there had not been a particle of hope of his ever seeing it? Even the inspired evangelist has not attempted to do it. I can give only a faint idea of what I felt when my mental eyes were opened, and when I who was 'sitting in darkness saw Great Light'.

20.66
Walter Rauschenbusch (1861-1918)
Pacifist, 'Father of the Social Gospel' in the USA

1 We have a social gospel. We need a systematic theology large enough to match it and vital enough to back it.

2 It is not a matter of getting individuals into heaven, but of transforming the life on earth into the harmony of heaven.

20.67
Franz Reinisch (1903-1942)
Austrian priest, beheaded for opposition to National Socialism

1 May you then join me in a glorious and joyful *Magnificat* and *Te Deum* when you hear that my mission has ended in this world, only really to begin in the other.

20.68
Placid Riccardi (1844-1915)
Monk

1 The heart of God invites everyone to put it to the proof. The more he gives, the more he desires to give. He loves to see the trust which makes us persist in knocking unceasingly.

20.69
Theodore Roosevelt (1858-1919)
President of the USA

1 Power undirected by high purpose spells calamity; and high purpose by itself is utterly useless if the power to put it into effect is lacking.

2 The things that will destroy America are peace at any price, prosperity at any cost, safety first instead of duty first, the love of soft living, and the get-rich-quick theory of life.

3 Every reform movement has a lunatic fringe

4 Do what you can, with what you have, where you are.

5 It is better to be faithful than famous.

6 A thorough knowledge of the Bible is worth more than a college education.

7 Wisdom is nine-tenths a matter of being wise in time.

8 Some men can live up to their loftiest ideals without ever going higher than a basement.

9 Death is always, under all circumstances, a tragedy, for if it is not then it means that life has become one.

20.70
Paul Schneider (1897-1939)
Prussian pastor and martyr

1 Once again the chestnut tree is preaching a sermon to me. Its bare black branches reach out to me so promisingly the small brown buds for next spring. I can see them close to the window and also in the top branches.... Should we be so thankless and of so little faith that we deliberately overlook among the falling withered leaves of the church the buds that here too cling tenaciously to trunk and branches?

2 New sorrows should bring us new experiences of our God and a new glory. Christ says: 'I am with you all your days.'

20.71
Hugh Richard Laurie (Dick) Sheppard (1880-1937)
Anglican clergyman and founder of the Peace Pledge Union

1 Love is the only weapon we need.

2 There is only one influence that converts, and that is the example of a life which is shot through and through with the glory and strength of the spirit of Christ.

3 A parson should light fires in a dark room, and go on lighting them all his life.

4 I would rather smell incense than varnish in the house of God.

5 I resent with all my soul that the orthodox have so complicated the perfectly straight-forward teaching of Christ that common people neither hear him gladly, nor with understanding.

20.72
Staretz Silouan (1866-1938)
Russian Orthodox monk

1 The man who has the Holy Spirit within him, in however slight a degree, sorrows day and night for all mankind.

2 God is love, and in the saints the Holy Spirit is love. Dwelling in the Holy Spirit, the saints behold hell and embrace it too in their love.

3 The Lord bestows such grace on his chosen that they embrace the whole earth, the whole world, with their love, and their souls burn with longing that all should be saved and behold the glory of the Lord. Blessed is the soul that loves her brother, for 'our brother is our life'.

4 When I think of my father, I say to myself, 'That is the sort of *staretz* [spiritual guide] I would like to have.' He never got angry, he was always even-tempered and humble. Just think— he waited half a year for the right moment to correct me without upsetting me!

5 The Lord is meek and humble, and loves his creature. Where the Spirit of the Lord is, there is love for enemies and prayer for the whole world.

6 The Lord himself taught me the way to humble myself. 'Keep thy mind in hell, and despair not,' he said. Thus is the enemy vanquished.

7 To believe in God is one thing, to know God another. Both in heaven and on earth the Lord is made known only by the Holy Spirit, and not through ordinary learning.

8 My soul weeps for the whole world.

9 Adam lost the earthly paradise and sought it weeping. But the Lord through his love on the cross gave Adam another paradise, fairer than the old—a paradise in heaven where shines the light of the Holy Trinity.

10 This is true freedom—to be in God. And I did not know this before. Until I was seven and twenty I simply believed that God was, but I did not know him; but when my soul knew him by the Holy Spirit I was consumed with longing for him, and now day and night I seek him with a burning heart.

11 The soul of a humble man is like the sea: throw a stone into the sea—for a moment it will ruffle the surface a little, and then sink to the bottom.

12 Who is there who can realize what paradise is? He who bears within him the Holy Spirit can realize it in part, since paradise is the kingdom of the holy Spirit, and the Holy Spirit both in heaven and on earth is one and the same.

20.73
Mary Slessor (1848-1915)
Scottish missionary to West Africa

1 Half the world's sorrows comes from the unwisdom of parents.

2 Christ sent me to preach the gospel and he will look after results.

20.74
Amanda Berry Smith (1837-1915)
North American evangelist

1 These words rang through me like a bell: 'God in you, God in you.'... O what glory filled my soul! The great vacuum in my soul began to fill up; it was like a pleasant draught of cool water, and I felt it. I wanted to shout Glory to Jesus! but Satan said, 'Now, if you make a noise they will put you out.'

20.75
Hannah Whitall Smith (1832-1911)

Founder member of the Women's Christian Movement and of the suffrage movement in the USA

1 In the very nature of things emotions are more or less variable, while convictions, where they are really convictions, and are not purely notions or ideas, are permanent... I learned therefore not to seek emotions, but to seek only for convictions.

2 We were made to be human beings here, and when people try to be anything else, they generally get into some sort of scrapes.

3 I believe sympathy is one of the most helpful helps one can bestow upon one's fellow creatures; and it seems a great pity that so many people feel it is their duty to criticize rather than sympathize.

4 Faith is nothing at all tangible. It is simply believing God; and, like sight, it is nothing apart from its object. You might as well shut your eyes and look inside to see whether you have sight, as to look inside to discover if you have faith.

20.76
Nathan Söderblom (1866-1931)

Lutheran Archbishop of Upsala

1 Saints are persons who make it easier for others to believe in God.

20.77
Ludwig Steil (1900-1945)

German pastor who was arrested and died in Dachau

1 Greet my congregation for me.... Where will God's way lead us now? But HE himself stands always at the end of the road.

20.78
Edith Stein (1891-1942)

German Carmelite nun who died at Auschwitz

1 I am satisfied with everything. The only way of winning a knowledge of the Cross is by feeling the whole weight of the Cross. I have been convinced of this from the first moment.

20.79
Mary Stewart (d.1943)

North American superintendent of education for Californian Indians

1 Keep us, O Lord, from pettiness; let us be large in thought, in word, in deed.

20.80
Barbara Stoddart (1865-1915)

Scottish member of the Salvation Army

1 Blessed Lamb of Calvary,
Let thy Spirit fall on me;
Let the cleansing, healing flow
Wash and keep me white as snow,
That henceforth my life may be
Bright and beautiful for thee.

20.81
Janet Erskine Stuart (1857-1914)

English member of the Religious of the Sacred Heart

1 Take yourself as you are, and do not try to live by one part alone and starve the other.

2 Oh! the thrilling breathlessness of seeing the flash of four shining hoofs over one's head, as one extricates oneself from a muddy ditch.

3 I believe that the more one idealizes, the nearer one comes to the truth; the only thing is to stop at nothing, to 'bear all things, believe all things, hope all things, and endure all things' with a persuasion of faith that they will all work out for the very best. They are incomprehensible at first, but the thing is to trust them and to let the magic work.

4 God wants to take you sailing out into the glory of his thoughts and love, and through sheer fright you cling to the rope and the steps of the bathing machine... I say 'Let go', and so does God.

5 God knows and loves. We cannot understand. If we could understand, all the best beauty of our life would wither away. It is glorious in its faith and hope and adherence to what we don't understand. May our Lord give you light on this, and love for the adventurous journey of faith and hope with him in the dark.

6 To be a joy-bearer and a joy-giver says everything, for in our life, if one is joyful, it means that one is faithfully living for God, and that *nothing else counts*; and if one gives joy to others one is doing God's work; with joy without and joy within, all is well... I can conceive no higher way.

7 Oh, how he loves me! Oh, *how He longs for me*!

20.82
C.T. Studd (1862-1931)
English cricketer, missionary to India and Africa

1 Some want to live within the sound
Of Church or Chapel bell;
I want to run a rescue shop
Within a yard of hell.

2 When I came to see that Jesus Christ had died for me, it didn't seem hard to give up all for him. It seemed just common, ordinary honesty.

20.83
Geoffrey A. Studdert-Kennedy (1883-1929)
English army chaplain in World War I

1 God is love, and a three times divorced cinema actor is the perfect lover, and heaven gets mixed up with hell.

2 War is kinder than a Godless peace.

3 Nobody worries about Christ as long as he can be kept shut up in churches. He is quite safe inside. But there is always trouble if you try and let him out.

4 If Christ be not risen, the dreadful consequence is not that death ends life, but that we are still in our sins.

20.84
Sadhu Sundar Singh (1889-1929)
Indian Christian and mystic who converted from Sikhism

1 I am not worthy to follow in the steps of my Lord, but, like him, I want no home, no possessions. Like him I will belong to the road, sharing the suffering of my people, eating with those who will give me shelter, and telling all men of the love of God.

2 Those who determine not to put self to death will never see the will of God fulfilled in their lives. Those who ought to become the light of the world must necessarily burn and become less and less.

3 The true Christian is like sandalwood, which imparts its fragrance to the axe which cuts it, without doing any harm in return.

4 The capital of heaven is the heart in which Jesus is enthroned as King.

20.85
Alfred Edward Taylor (1869-1945)
British Anglican philosopher

1 If we are to be genuinely in earnest with a high ethical rule of living, it would seem to be indispensable that we should be convinced that there is something really at stake in moral effort, and that the something which may be won or lost is no less than the supreme good which makes life worth living.

2 It is possible to do better than to abstain from complaints or to cultivate pride; it is possible... to make acceptance of the worst fortune has to bestow a means to the development of a sweetness, patience, and serene joyousness which are to be learned nowhere but in the school of sharp suffering... But this attitude is possible only on one condition: the affliction must be regarded as 'God's messenger'.

20.86
Marguerite Teilhard de Chardin (d.1936)
French theologian and scientist

1 I have done nothing for thee... Yet, O Lord, this sense of deprivation could well be a part of thy divine plan. It could well be that in thine eyes our self-complacency is the most despicable of sins and that we shall come before thy presence in our nakedness that thou, and thou alone, mayest clothe us.

20.87
William Temple (1881-1944)
Archbishop of Canterbury, theologian and preacher

1 The ascension of Christ is his liberation from all restrictions of time and space. It does not represent his removal from the earth, but his constant presence everywhere on earth.

2 The atheist who is moved by love is moved by the spirit of God; an atheist who lives by love is saved by his faith in the God whose existence (under that name) he denies.

3 I believe in the Church, only holy Catholic and Apostolic Church; and nowhere does it exist.

4 Only one petition in the Lord's Prayer has any condition attached to it: it is the petition for forgiveness.

5 It is a mistake to suppose that God is only, or even chiefly, concerned with religion.

6 Love of God is the root, love of our neighbour the fruit of the Tree of Life. Neither can exist without the other, but the one is cause and the other effect.

7 Every revelation of God is a demand, and the way to knowledge of God is by obedience.

8 We affirm, then, that unless all existence is a medium of Revelation, no particular revelation is possible.

9 The principle of sacrifice is that we choose to do or to suffer what apart from our love we should not choose to do or to suffer.

20.88
Ernst Troeltsch (1865-1923)
German theologian and philosopher

1 It is the lower classes which do the really creative work, forming communities on a genuine religious basis. They alone unite imagination and simplicity of feeling with a non-reflective habit of mind, a primitive energy, and an urgent sense of need.

20.89
Eugene Trubetskoy (1863-1920)
Russian Orthodox religious philosopher

1 The royal doors are opening! The great Liturgy is about to begin.

20.90
Kanzo Uchimura (1861-1930)
Japanese teacher and preacher, founder of the mukyokai

1 Christian monotheism laid its axe at the root of all my superstitions. All the vows I had made, and the manifold forms of worship with which I had been attempting to appease my angry gods could now be dispensed with by owning this one God and my reason and my conscience responded 'Yes'!

20.91
Evelyn Underhill (1875-1941)
English mystical writer

1 This is adoration: not a difficult religious exercise, but an attitude of the soul.

2 We spend most of our lives conjugating three verbs: to want, to have and to do. But none of these verbs has any ultimate significance until it is transcended by and included in the fundamental verb—to be.

3 The adoration to which you are avowed is not an affair of red hassocks and authorized hymn books; but a burning and consuming fire.

4 Love makes the whole difference between an execution and martyrdom.

5 Mysticism is the name of that organic process which involves the perfect consummation of the love of God.

6 In religion our exclusions are nearly always wrong, and our inclusions, however inconsistent, nearly always right.

7 A saint is a human creature devoured and transformed by love: a love that has dissolved and burnt out those instinctive passions, acquisitive and combative, proud and greedy, which commonly rule the lives of men.

8 The spiritual man or woman can afford to take desperate chances, and live dangerously in the interests of their ideals; being delivered from the many unreal fears and anxieties which commonly torment us, and knowing the unimportance of possessions and of so-called success.

9 It is so much better just to be able to say, 'Send me' without having to add 'where I shall have my position properly recognized, or opportunities to use my special gifts'. It is God whom we want to get recognized, not us.

20.92
Simone Weil (1909-1943)
French philosopher and mystic

1 If we go down into ourselves we find that we possess exactly what we desire.

2 Belief in the existence of other human beings as such is love.

3 We must try to love without imagining. To love the appearance in its nakedness without interpretation. What we love then is God.

4 Imagination and fiction make up more than three-quarters of our real life. Rare indeed are the true contacts with good and evil.

5 God only comes to those who ask him to come; and he cannot refuse to come to those who implore him long, often, and ardently.

6 What hope is there for innocence if it is not recognized?

20.93
Charles Williams (1889-1945)
English poet and theologian

1 It is as difficult to be quite orthodox as to be quite healthy. Yet the need for orthodoxy, like the need for health, is imperative.

2 Nothing is certain: everything is safe.

3 The strong hands of God twisted the crown of thorn into a crown of glory: and in such hands we are safe.

4 It has not pleased God to build either the congregation of Israel or the fellowship of the church on prophets. They are the warning, the correction, the voice in the wilderness.

20.94
Thomas Woodrow Wilson (1856-1924)
President of the USA

1 When you have read the Bible you will know that it is the word of God, because you will have found it the key to your own heart, your own happiness, your own duty.

2 The object of love is to serve, not to win.

3 I fancy that it is just as hard to do your duty when men are sneering at you as when they are shooting at you.

20.95
Kiye Sato Yamamuro (1874-1917)
Woman who began the Salvation Army in Japan

1 It seems too adventurous, perhaps, but God is able. I have no one save the Holy Ghost to rely upon. My weak health and lack of ability seem to deny me success, but when I am weak, God is strong. Depending on him alone, I go forward to establish the Sanatorium.

20.96
Peter, Count Yorck von Wartenburg
(1904-1944)
Executed for opposition to National Socialism

1 That God has guided events as they have turned out, belongs to the inscrutableness of his will which I humbly accept. I believed myself to be impelled by a sense of the guilt that is weighing all of us down, and to be pure in heart. That is why I confidently hope to find in God a merciful judge.

PART 7

Twentieth Century after 1950

No generation can claim to have plumbed to the depths the unfathomable riches of Christ. The Holy Spirit has promised to lead us step by step into the fullness of truth.

Leon Joseph Suenens

20.97
Eric S. Abbott
English Anglican clergyman

1 Because God is the Ceaseless Worker, we can afford to stop, and to rest, and to commit to him the arrears in our work, as well as the work done. *We* do not 'bear up the pillars of the world'. God does that.

2 Of what did Jesus die? It is true that he died of a broken body. It would be even truer so say, both medically and spiritually, that he died of a broken *heart*.

3 It is sometimes better to stand still and wait. It is sometimes better to make a withdrawal that later on we may advance more surely.

4 There is something which only you can bring into the Kingdom.

20.98
Miriam Adeney
North American author and missionary

1 Why do we say no? In order to say yes to what really matters.

20.99
Ahn Byung-Mu
Pioneer of Korean minjung *theology*

1 Jesus proclaims the coming of God's Kingdom. He stands with the *minjung* [common people], and promises them the future of God. The God whom Jesus presented is not like Yahweh of the Old Testament who manifests a tension between love and justice. God's will is to side with the *minjung* completely and unconditionally.

20.100
Arthur Macdonald Allchin
British Anglican priest and writer

1 We can become ourselves only by transcending ourselves.

2 God's glory is at work in all things. Everything that exists, exists because it is held, sustained, enlivened by God's wisdom and God's power. The Word of God who is God, God expressing himself towards his creation, wills at all times to work the mystery of his embodiment.

3 All things were altered by Christ's passion, past and future, East and West. Time and space are no longer barriers which separate us from one another, but ways of communion, paths by which we may come to meet one another in the life which flows from the side of Christ. Injury itself, evil and wrong, all that can cause men and women to hate and destroy one another, that too is overcome, for with life there comes forgiveness, the life-giving power of reconciliation and peace.

4 They were all books which were useful for life in the Spirit. Their authors were fathers and teachers who had become friends, to whom one spoke in church and at other times; it was of little importance whether they had lived six hundred, twelve hundred or fifty years ago.

20.101
Rubem Alves
Brazilian philosopher

1 We speak words in order not to hear the Word which comes out of silence.

2 We have forgotten that to be radical means simply to go to the root of things.

3 The inevitable by-product of our healthy economy is the destruction of nature. The ecological problem is not an accident. Our economy has to deliver death.

4 Children's play ends with the universal resurrection of the dead. Adults' play ends with universal burial. Whereas the resurrection is the paradigm of the world of children, the world of adults creates the cross.

5 Play reveals that beyond the dissolution of reality we find, not chaos, but rather new possibilities. The impossible becomes possible.

6 History does not tell us of a single case in which the powerful have given up power willingly.

7 Gross national product and economic growth are not enough. Bread must be more than bread. Production must bring joy and psychic satisfaction. It must be a sacrament.

8 Hope is hearing the melody of the future. Faith is to dance it.

9 Psychoanalysis was born when it was realized that words are full of silence.

10 Cooking is a liturgical ritual.

11 Whenever action is reaction, it is bound to be reactionary.

12 For creation to take place, suffering and hope cannot be separated... Suffering without hope produces resentment and despair. Hope without suffering creates illusions, naïveté, and drunkenness.

13 We must live by the love of what we will never see.

14 Imagination is the mother of creativity.

15 Understanding is a miracle which grows out of an unspoken secret: the common paths trodden by individuals who nevertheless have never met and will never meet.

20.102
D.S. Amalorpavadass
Indian Roman Catholic theologian

1 The best way to conclude my experience of the Biblical Word is through silence! Where there is fullness and wholeness there is stillness and silence! Where there is silence there is peace.

20.103
Christine Amjad-Ali
Theologian from Pakistan

1 In my view, we cannot hope to manifest the *substance* of what it means to say that we—as women—are created in God's image if we hold on to the *forms* which symbolize the belief that we are created as secondary beings, for the glory of man, and not in the image of God.

20.104
Elizabeth Amoah
African theologian

1 The presence of the silent majority of women in the hierarchical structures of many churches in Africa is a shameful contradiction of the Christian faith.

20.105
Marian Anderson
African-American singer

1 Good habits can be fine things... A child who learns to repeat after his mother, 'Now I lay me down to sleep', may get a little thrill out of just saying it, at the beginning. After a time he realizes that he can do nothing about keeping his own soul when he is asleep.

20.106
George Appleton
Anglican archbishop in Jerusalem and religious writer

1 It takes faith to believe that God actually wants us to take part in His ongoing Spiritual warfare and to participate in the accomplishment of His purpose.

2 Increase my capacity for love and decrease my impulses to throw stones, actual or mental.

20.107
Luz Beatriz Arellano
Roman Catholic sister from Nicaragua

1 Our first experience of God was that of allowing ourselves to feel the impact of the situation of suffering and oppression that our people were undergoing. From that moment on, we began to discover God present in the suffering, oppressed, and outcast countenance of our poorest brothers and sisters.

2 Out of their participation in the suffering of our people, while also battling through their own struggle, women discover a new image of Jesus—a Jesus who is brother and sister, in solidarity on the journey toward liberation, the people's journey, and their own journey; a

Jesus who is a *compañero* (fellow revolutionary) in building the new society.

3 'Mother' does not mean being the woman who gives birth to and cares for a child; to be a mother is to feel in your own flesh the suffering of all the children, all the men, and all the young people who die, as though they had come from your own womb.

20.108
Johann Christoph Arnold
German-born leader in Bruderhof movement

1 Never force religious instruction on your child. It is far more important for him to feel the impact of your faith... If your faith is really living in you, you will not need to depend on pious words: your children will sense it in your daily life and in your contact with them.

2 God's Spirit does not let itself be tied down to a lesson or a text.

20.109
J. Heinrich Arnold
Elder of the Bruderhof, a Christian communal movement in the eastern USA

1 Becoming like children means becoming completely dependent on God and on one another.

2 What a great gift it would be if we could see a little of the great vision of Jesus—if we could see beyond our small lives!

3 What a mighty thing it is to live for God's kingdom! Live for it; look for it—it is so powerful it will completely overwhelm you.

4 It is clear that a family without love is godless, but a family ruled by the clouded emotions of blood-ties will have no love to God and Christ.

20.110
Naim Stifan Ateek
Palestinian canon of St George's Cathedral, Jerusalem

1 Justice belongs to God, not to governments and politicians.

2 To speak the truth is to transcend both self and national interests and to give allegiance to God.

3 Truth, even crucified and buried, still has a way of rising faith out of the grave, reasserting itself and challenging people to repentance and change.

4 For example, when Christians recite the *Benedictus*, with its opening lines 'Blessed be the Lord God of Israel...', what does it mean for them today? Which Israel are they thinking of? What redemption?

5 To understand God, therefore, the Palestinian Christian, like every other Christian, begins with Christ and goes backward to the Old Testament and forward to the New Testament and beyond them.

20.111
W.H. Auden
Anglo-American poet and essayist

1 No man can do properly what he is called upon to do in this life unless he can learn to forget his ego and act as an instrument of God.

2 [In 'Epitaph for an Unknown Soldier']

> To save your world you asked this man to die:
> Would this man, could he see you now,
> ask why?

3 To ask the hard question is simple.

4 Only those in the last stage of disease could believe that children are true judges of character.

5 It is nonsense to speak of 'higher' and 'lower' pleasures. To a hungry man it is, rightly, more important that he eats than that he philosophise.

6 Released by Love from isolating wrong,
Let us with Love unite our various song,
Each with his gift according to his kind
Bringing this child his body and his mind.

7 As a rule it was the pleasure-haters who became unjust.

20.112
Gustav Aulén
Swedish theologian

1 The Atonement is, above all, a movement of God to man, not in the first place a movement of man to God.

2 For my own part, I am persuaded that no form of Christian teaching has any future before it except such as can keep steadily in view the reality of the evil in the world, and go to meet the evil with a battle-song of triumph.

20.113
Gladys Aylward
Missionary to China

1 If God has called you to China or any other place and you are sure in your own heart, let nothing deter you... remember it is God who has called you and it is the same as when he called Moses or Samuel.

2 I wasn't God's first choice for what I've done in China.

3 I have two planks for a bed, two stools, two cups and a basin. On my broken wall is a small card which says, 'God hath chosen the weak things—I can do all things through Christ who strengthens me.' It is true I have passed through fire.

20.114
Peter Baelz
English Anglican theologian

1 God's activity in the world, whether in creation or redemption, remains in an important sense mysterious.

2 Telling God what I want is like throwing the world into the pool of Divinity and seeing what happens to it.

20.115
Donald M. Baillie
Scottish theologian

1 It is only when God speaks and awakens human faith that the natural object becomes sacramental. But this can happen to material things only because this is a sacramental universe, because God created all things visible and invisible.

2 God is what we really desire in every simple, spontaneous, disinterested choice of the ideal in our daily lives. God is what we really love whenever we truly love our fellows. God is what we dimly know, even in apprehending our duty in the common-place details of practice. But the more we live ourselves into the ideal, in a daily life of duty and love, the clearer becomes our conscious knowledge of God, in which alone we can rest, and which alone, in its turn, can empower us to realize the ideal. And this is more than morality: this is religion.

3 Nothing in God is impersonal. His Word is personal. His Spirit is personal. Personality in God must indeed be a very different thing from personality in us. But that is because we are far from being perfectly personal. God is the only perfectly personal Being.

20.116
John Baillie
Scottish theologian

1 A true Christian is a man who never for a moment forgets what God has done for him in Christ, and whose whole comportment and whole activity have their root in the sentiment of gratitude.

2 We may suspect, then, that the real reason why Christians are less distinguishable from the world than they used to be is not that there is more of the quality of holiness in the world, but that there is less of it in the Church.

3 He lays upon us no other burden than that of putting our whole trust in him—no difficult self-immolation, no exaggerated austerities, no excesses of ascetic practice. He want us to be kind and just and true in all the little dealings of our daily life, but even that he does not expect of us in our own strength.

4 No single hour beyond the present is promised to me for setting life upon a firm foundation, and finding a steadfast anchor for my immortal soul, and making my peace with God and my neighbour.

5 Near to losing heart? Are you overborne with labour? Or worn out with worry? Or consumed with hopeless longings? Then won't you take your Lord's advice? Don't try to keep the whole thing pent up within your own heart. Share it with God. Tell him all about it, yes, down to the last and absurdest annoying detail.

6 During the long black-out evenings of our war-time winters I found myself re-reading a great many of the books that were written about the First World War. In one of these books the question is asked as to what kind of man it was who really won the war for us, and the answer proposed is this: 'He was a plain man awake all night in a ditch.' Is not that the kind of man who by the grace of God will always win the battle of life—a plain man on the watch?

20.117
John Austin Baker
British theologian and Anglican bishop

1 Sorrow is at most only half of reality. In a thousand, often surprising ways our humanness is matched to its environment, and enabled to find it good; indeed, the ways in which mankind finds or makes its pleasures are far more varied than its pains.

2 Love begins as love for one or for a few. But once we have caught it, once it has taken possession of us, and has set up its own values in the heart of the self, there are no limits to those it can touch, to the relationships which it can transform.

3 To be alive to the reality of God is to be aware of his glorious foolishness, and of the infinite sufferings which make him the Father and friend of all the fools of love.

4 On what grounds do you call millions of light-years of inter-galactic space a 'waste'?

5 'Ought', then, not only expresses an internal attitude possible only to a free agent, but by its very logic rests on the freest of free acts, one springing purely from the inner resources of the self.

6 Love does not send others to suffer in its place. Love comes itself... The Cross is not a picture of God. This was God himself.

7 It is all grace. It is not even that there is a door which Christ has unbolted, and we, standing outside it, have to stretch out our hand, lift the latch, and walk through. We are already inside.

8 If I can now forgive, it is only because I have been forgiven, I and all other men and women who have ever lived.

20.118
Tissa Balasuriya
Sri Lankan theologian

1 We have to take a fresh look at the central core of the Christian message. This requires a direct return to the sources of revelation—the Scriptures—especially to the person of Jesus Christ as we see him in the gospels. We must purify our minds of the restrictive Christendom-centred theologies that have blurred the universality of Jesus Christ. We must ask ourselves how we are to understand the gospels in our times.

2 Our growth to a planetary dimension is an invitation to spiritual deepening, a purification from selfishness to a more universal communion in real life, to our own humanization.

3 Religionism is the result of a lack of respect for the followers of another religious faith. But, then, it is also a lack of respect for God.

4 [A religion must] above all not try to make God its own monopoly.

5 Christ is... the principle of a universal human solidarity.

6 Christian mission to Europe and north America is a matter of urgent necessity because it is these countries that do the most harm to humanity and nature as a whole; exercise more power for good or evil; call themselves Christian and hence are more damaging to the witness of the gospel; and are more dehumanized, more alienated from the values of the kingdom, and more difficult to convert.

7 The faith of Christian believers is like that of pilgrims on a journey. They have to face many obstacles both within themselves and from society.

8 Hope is the unshakeable certainty in the realization of the promises of God in Jesus Christ, based on Jesus' life, death and resurrection.

9 Love cannot be practised without justice. Love cannot be built on injustice, for injustice is lovelessness. Love is not an alternative to justice... Justice is the beginning of love.

10 Prudence will decide on the issues that are worth fighting for, as well as the means to be used in the struggle. Prudence tells us when it is necessary to bypass an issue or pursue it to the extent of polarization.

11 The virtue of moderation can be understood as a balancing of patience and impatience, action and reflection, haste and caution, compromise and polarization. It will also teach us to respect others and challenge them to social justice.

12 The churches and their institutions will live only in dying to self for others—for this is the law of the gospel. It is the poor, the weak, the marginalized, and defenceless nature that may point the churches to the way of the cross—the unique path to the resurrection.

20.119
Hans Urs von Balthasar
Swiss theologian

1 When we abandon our neighbour to God he continues to be supported by our love and the pain of being unable to help him accomplishes more than any self-confident action.

2 Christian love is not the world's last word about itself—it is God's final word about himself, and so about the world.

3 The contemplative act is the permanently basic act of all external action: it is active and effective, fruitful and missionary beyond all external undertakings of the Church.

4 Any one who's not prepared to listen to God in the first place has nothing to say to the world.

20.120
William Barclay
Scottish theologian, religious writer and broadcaster

1 Christian humility is based on the sight of self, the vision of Christ, and the realisation of God.

2 The essential fact of Christianity is that God thought all men worth the sacrifice of his Son.

3 The fact of Jesus' coming is the final and unanswerable proof that God cares.

4 One of the highest of human duties is the duty of encouragement. There is a regulation of the Royal Navy which says: 'No officer shall speak discouragingly to another officer in the discharge of his duties.'

5 The man who is poor in spirit is the man who has realised that things mean nothing, and that God means everything.

6 Pride is the ground in which all the other sins grow, and the parent from which all the other sins come.

7 Self-admiration is the death of the soul. To admire ourselves as we are is to have no wish to change. And with those who don't want to change, the soul is dead.

8 Truth which is merely told is quick to be forgotten; truth which is discovered lasts a lifetime.

20.121
Michael Barnes
English Jesuit and interfaith theologian

1 We cannot study God.

2 Faith aims to unite the sacred and the profane in everyday life, not keep them rigidly separate.

3 All spirituality is about the right ordering of desire—that quality without which no one can begin but which all too easily can lead the unwary into falsehood, not truth.

4 If God is 'always greater' then there can be no limit to what is to be known about God.

20.122
Karl Barth
Swiss Protestant theologian

1 Rightly understood, there are no Christians: there is only the eternal opportunity of becoming Christians—an opportunity at once accessible and inaccessible to all men.

2 Faith is awe in the presence of the divine incognito.

3 Whether the angels play only Bach praising God I am not quite sure. I am sure however that *en famille* they play Mozart.

4 Jesus does not give recipes that show the way to God as other teachers of religion do. He is himself the way.

5 In God alone is there faithfulness and faith in the trust that we may hold to him, to his promise, and to his guidance. To hold to God is to rely on the fact that God is there for me, and to live in this certainty.

6 [Summary of his theology]
'Jesus loves me, this I know,
for the Bible tells me so.'

7 Men have never been good, they are not good, they never will be good.

8 We are justified, from the point of view of exegesis, in regarding the democratic conception of the state as an expansion of the thought of the New Testament.

9 The Devil may also make use of morality.

10 Faith is never identical with piety.

11 If a man believes and knows God, he can no longer ask, 'What is the meaning of my life?' But by believing he actually lives the meaning of his life.

12 As I look back on my course, I seem to myself as one who, ascending the dark staircase of a church tower and trying to steady himself, reached for the banister, but got hold of the bell-rope instead. To his horror, he had then to listen to what the great bell had sounded over him and not over him alone.

13 God is not an abstract category by which even the Christian understanding of the word has to be measured, but he who is called God [in the Bible] is the one God, the single God, the sole God.

14 When once the day comes when I have to appear before my Lord, then I will not come with my deeds, with the volumes of my *Dogmatics* on my back. All the angels there would have to laugh. But then I shall also not say, 'I have always meant well; I had good faith'. No, then I will only say one thing: 'Lord, be merciful to me, a poor sinner!'

20.123
James Keir Baxter
New Zealand poet

1 Lord, Holy Spirit,
You blow like the wind in a thousand
paddocks,
Inside and outside the fences,
You blow where you wish to blow.

20.124
George Kennedy Allen Bell
Bishop of Chichester

1 Theologians are the servants of the Church.

2 I believe... that we ought to make a real effort to see that the ordinary members of our congregation understand what they believe, and can give an answer for the faith that is in them.

3 It ought not to be, that in denial of brotherly love the Church of Jesus Christ should, through the domination of force, be made a kingdom of this world.

4 I wrote and I spoke as a lover of my country; as a convinced and public opponent of Hitler and the Nazis from the beginning... as one who abhors cruelty and barbarism such as Hitler and his followers practised for so long; and as a profound believer in the ideals of liberty and justice in defence of which Great Britain went to war.

5 The Church in any country fails to be the Church if it forgets that its members in one nation have a fellowship with its members in every nation.

6 We do not know what are the limits of human achievement, of our own personal history, or of the history of the race. We do not know what possibilities are in store for us or what time is before us. We do know, however, that there is a limit, for we must all die. If we do not know Christ, death is the only limit we know. But with Christ death is transcended. He who has died for us, and is alive for us, confronts us with a totally new reality, a new limit, a new boundary to our existence. With him and in him the new world has begun!

20.125
Gerrit C. Berkouwer
Dutch Reformed theologian

1 Theology is relative to the word of God... It means that theology is occupied in continuous attentive and obedient listening to the word of God.

2 Theology is not a complex system constructed for their own entertainment by scholars in the quiet retreat of ivory towers. It must have significance for the unquiet times; but it can achieve its proper relevance only in obedient attentiveness, not to the times first of all, but to the word.

20.126
Daniel Berrigan
North American Jesuit and peace activist

1 The ironies of God are strange indeed. And one of the most striking of them all is the fact that those countries which are meeting with the harshest kind of cultural and political upheaval are at present giving the Church her best leads on renewal.

2 One final thing, however, does remain for those whose vision is not enslaved to this world. It is the only thing, after all has been said, that is worth preserving or dwelling on. It is the sublime example of a Lord who binds up and saves, who has poured himself out, taking the form of a servant. It is the example of One who cannot be finally exiled from this world, since he claims nothing from it except the privilege of being the last and the least of all.

20.127
Thomas Berry
North American Jesuit theologian

1 Our children need to learn not only how to read books composed by human genius but also how to read the Great Book of the World. Reading this Great Book is natural to children.

2 Gardening is an active participation in the deepest mysteries of the universe.

3 By gardening our children learn that they constitute with all growing things a single community of life.

4 Awakening to the cosmic/earth/human process whereby all things have a genetic relationship with each other is the most significant intellectual achievement of humankind since the higher civilization came into being some 2,500 years ago. Nothing can be itself without being in communion with everything else, not can anything truly be the other without first acquiring a capacity for interior presence to itself.

20.128
John Betjeman
English poet

1 He is not the common man, but the average man, which is far worse.

2 We accept the collapse of the fabrics of our old churches, the thieving of lead and objects from them, the commandeering and butchering of our scenery by the services, the despoiling of landscaped parks and the abandonment to a fate worse than the workhouse of our country houses, because we are convinced we must save money.

3 Too bored to think, too proud to pray, too timid to leave what we are used to doing, we have shut ourselves behind our standard roses; we love ourselves only and our neighbours no longer. As for the Incarnation, that is a fairy story for children, if we think it healthy for children to be told fairy stories.

20.129
Ana María Bidegain
Colombian Catholic church historian

1 It was the Latin American woman of the people who bore, firmly and stubbornly, subtly and tactfully, the burden of humiliation and subjugation placed on her shoulders by the colonial structure. And therefore the gospel was handed down by successive generations of women—not so much from mother to child, but from female generation to female generation, just as in the Afro-American cults today.

2 Among the popular masses, the mother has always been the best catechist.

3 Mary's yes is a free, responsible yes by which she accepts being the vessel of the new creation to be embodied by her son Jesus. It is not the yes of self-denial, almost of irresponsibility, as it has been traditionally presented to us. Mary knows to whom she is committing herself.

20.130
Steve Biko
South African political activist

1 [Black Theology] wants to describe Christ a[s] a fighting god, not a passive god who allows a lie to rest unchallenged.

20.131
María Clara Bingemer
Brazilian Catholic theologian

1 A faith in a God that is identified only with masculine traits is incompatible with Christian revelation and with the God of love.

2 The *chesed* of God, God's profound mercy, God's faithfulness to the people in spite of their infidelity and sin, comes from God's motherly heart, *rachamim*; God will always be compassionate and infinitely tender.

3 Why can't the same God who is known and adored by the chosen people as a strong liberator, a dread warrior, and a powerful lord also be known as a loving and tender mother?

20.132
Stuart Blanch
English Anglican, former Archbishop of York

1 Whatever value I attach to other religions, from my point of view they are ancillary—not an alternative to revelation in Christ.

20.133
Joost de Blank
Anglican Archbishop of Capetown

1 Christ in this country [South Africa] would quite likely have been arrested under the Suppression of Communism Act.

2 I suffer from an incurable disease—colour blindness.

20.134
Kathleen Bliss
Anglican theological writer and broadcaster

1 Often a woman's zeal has been damped down and discouraged by the Church, her gift of mind and spirit refused, her devotion and labour frittered away on trifles.

2 If we are open to the possibilities of language we will be sensitive to the use of it by others and recognize that others may be speaking of profoundly religious matters without using traditional language.

3 This may well be a form of conversion experience in the modern world: that from searching the heavens to find God and attempting to be very spiritually minded one slowly or suddenly becomes aware that what one needed but could not express was discernible by clues or flashes of insight or unexpected awareness as one's life was opened up to receive whatever would come largely unsought through events, sights, sounds, encounters, delights and afflictions.

4 It is nonsense to say that women have never had any power in the Churches: they have had immense power in the form of influence, which is irresponsible power. Nobody can call to account the wife or mother who gets her way with husband or son and is known to be the real director of his opinion and vote.

20.135
Anthony Bloom
Russian-born Orthodox monk, bishop, spiritual teacher

1 It is not the constant thought of their sins, but the vision of the holiness of God that makes the saints aware of their own sinfulness.

2 A miracle is not the breaking of the laws of the fallen world, it is the re-establishment of the laws of the kingdom.

3 Christian action should be defined as an action of God mediated through a person.

4 Our vocation is to live in the Spirit—not to be more and more remarkable animals.

5 We should always approach God knowing that we do not know him. We must approach the unsearchable, mysterious God who reveals himself as he chooses; whenever we come to him, we are before a God we do not yet know.

6 Prayer is an adventure which brings not a thrill but new responsibilities.

7 As long as the soul is not still there can be no vision, but when stillness has brought us into the presence of God, then another sort of silence, much more absolute, intervenes.

8 It is easy to live superficially and never to take the risk of diving into the depths and facing the terrors of the deep. The result is... we are unable to reach out to God—because God is deep.

20.136
Edith L. Blumhofer
American Methodist historian

1 Today evangelical and pentecostal congregations continue to depend on the prodigious efforts of women, women whose presence is absence according to the overwhelmingly masculine language of sermons, prayers, and songs.

20.137
Alan Boesak
South African theologian and political leader

1 To preach about the loneliness of persons in our secular world is all right; to preach about the terrible estrangement that is the result of apartheid is wrong, because it is 'politics'. As if the one is less real than the other!

2 I argue for preaching that speaks to the *whole* person and to *all* of life.

3 The names of some evangelical ideals are today treated with suspicion, because of years of facile misuse. Reconciliation and forgiveness—essential in the lives of Christians and Christian congregations—are examples of it. There are many black Christians who frown when someone talks of reconciliation—not so much because reconciliation is regarded as unnecessary but because 'reconciliation', 'forgiveness', 'love' are words that have been glibly used by 'Christian' authorities to frustrate opposition and progress.

4 The child was not seen as the model of purity and innocence. Rather, the child stood more or less on a par with those who counted for nothing, those peripheral to the real world, the good life; they were the 'little people' who could claim no status at all. If Jesus promises the kingdom to these children... he makes it known the kingdom of God is destined for the nobodies, the despised, the unimportant ones!

5 When they introduced slavery and enforced it with the most vicious forms of dehumanization and violence, it was the Bible read through Reformed eyes and arguments from the Reformed tradition that gave them justification for such acts of violence and human tragedy. The God of the Reformed tradition was the God of slavery, fear, persecution, and death. Yet, for those black Christians this was the God to whom they had to turn for comfort, for justice, for peace.

20.138
Clodovis Boff
Servite priest and theologian from Brazil

1 Christian consciousness—that vital element of theology—can be maintained as such only if it is steeped in the *memoria Jesu* [the memory of Jesus], if it is activated by his 'dangerous memory'.

20.139
Leonardo Boff
Brazilian liberation theologian

1 The missionary is either a contemplative and mystic, or is no authentic missionary at all.

2 To reduce the gospel to a single valid expression is to condemn ourselves to mediocrity: it means we are attempting to compress mystery to the point where it can be forced into the dimensions of our head.

3 Jesus will continue to be condemned to death so long as we do not establish the human and historical conditions that will allow justice to flower and right to flourish. And without justice and right, the kingdom of God will not be established.

4 A cross is not just a piece of wood. It is everything that makes life difficult.

5 No trace is left in human or divine memory of those who inflicted the cross on others. Only those are remembered who carried a cross for the sake of others.

6 God really does lie hidden and unknown beneath every person in need.

7 There is a whole army of irretrievable people, who are considered dead weight in history. And yet they count in God's eyes. Salvation exists precisely for them.

20.140
Betsie ten Boom
Sister of Corrie ten Boom

1 The centre of God's will is our only safety.

20.141
Corrie ten Boom
Writer, speaker and survivor of a concentration camp

1 A religion that is small enough for our understanding would not be big enough for our needs.

2 If God has called you, do not spend time looking over your shoulder to see who is following you.

3 God raises the level of the impossible.

4 Is prayer your steering wheel or your spare tyre?

5 We are not a post-war generation; but a pre-peace generation. Jesus is coming.

6 The first step on the way to victory is to recognise the enemy.

7 If God sends us on stony paths, he provides strong shoes.

8 Worry does not empty tomorrow of its sorrow; it empties today of its strength.

9 It is not on our forgiveness any more than on our goodness that the world's healing

hinges, but on his. When he tells us to love our enemies, he gives, along with the command, the love itself.

10 Forgiveness is the key that unlocks the door of resentment and the handcuffs of hate. It is a power that breaks the chains of bitterness and the shackles of selfishness.

11 He who cannot forgive others, breaks the bridge over which he himself must pass.

20.142
Evangeline Booth
Worldwide General of the Salvation Army

1 There is no depth of misery, of despair, or iniquity that is concealed from the steady eyes of the women of the Salvation Army.

2 The forces of prejudice, of selfishness, of ignorance, which have arrested the progress and curtailed the influence of womankind for centuries, are receding from the foreground of the future, and with astonished vision we look upon the limitless fields of progress.

3 Across all oceans, however tempestuous, over all frontiers, however mountainous, into all countries, however remote and inhospitable, the women's movement is spreading, the exhilaration and invigoration of its spirit is in the very air we breathe, bracing the nerves, stimulating the will, and reinforcing the faculties.

4 For what we call the women's movement is not social merely, not political merely, not economic merely. It is the direct fulfilment of the gospel of the Redeemer.

20.143
Florence Booth
Prominent member of the Salvation Army

1 In God's sight, the fact that we are women does not make us unfit or incapable of performing the highest service in his kingdom.

2 God's love and power and faithfulness are the same, whether he deals with women or with men.

3 What mighty channels for the outpouring of God's love upon the world would be represented here to-day if each woman before me were prepared to obey the heavenly vision!

20.144
Stanley Booth-Clibborn
English Anglican bishop

1 Love and justice march together...
You cannot have one without the other.

2 It is no good talking sentimentally about love towards the new and hungry nations of the earth unless we are prepared to recognise the *justice* of their demands.

20.145
Ladislaus Boros
Jesuit writer on spirituality, born in Budapest

1 Perhaps our most urgent task is to testify that heaven exists.

2 Tenderness is never a sign of weakness or inferiority. On the contrary, it is a readiness for love and affection which protects all that is most precious in the world and which acts with great sensitivity and restraint.

3 Optimism, a 'taste for happiness', is a basic and essential aspect of being a Christian.

4 There is an inescapable logic in the Christmas message: we experience joy, quite simply, in self-surrender, in giving up our lives. Joy calls for renunciation.

5 This is perhaps the most shattering aspect of Christ: that he was *hidden*. His intention was to remain nameless.

6 The most beautiful words, those that give the most genuine help, are often born in a silence filled with suffering. Silence is the glowing furnace of the word, the forge of true speech and sensitivity.

7 Christ's existence was ruled by a great silence. His soul was listening. It was given over to the needs of others.

8 Those who have known what it is to be freed from great mental distress and brought out again into light and joy by God, lose all desire to pass judgement and bear grudges.

20.146
Anne Borrowdale
English Anglican writer

1 Television is not all bad news... It may show us violence as entertainment, but it also helps us to know more about the world we live in, and encourages generosity.

2 The idea that people sin, and that therefore their behaviour at times needs to be restricted, is fair enough; but the emphasis on control through fear, shame, and punitiveness does not create a society at ease with itself.

3 Honouring fathers and mothers may mean recognizing them as frail human beings who are not the gods or devils our childish memories make them. We may come to understand why our parents behaved as they did—even if we are critical of it.

4 Despite the fears that permissiveness has taken over, the message many parents still need to hear is 'lighten up'.

20.147
Henri Boulard
Egyptian Jesuit

1 Never say that you have no time. On the whole it is those who are busiest who can make time for yet more, and those who have more leisure-time who refuse to do something when one asks. What we lack is not time, but heart.

2 Today is the reality which is born at this moment as it were from nothing, fresh as the dew at the first moment of creation.

3 Contemplation is a state of mind which does not need either a monastery or a desert to be practised in. We can develop the contemplative gaze which penetrates to the heart of reality in order to reach its soul in the midst of our ordinary everyday life. Contemplation is the capacity to live out the present fully.

4 I don't need someone to repair my past; I need someone to transform me—to transform is to recreate.

5 We emerge from repentance like a baby coming out of the bath.

6 Painful though the effects of war are to experience, it is also certain that they bring out the truth about men and women.

20.148
Louis Bouyer
French Roman Catholic theologian

1 The holy makes its first appearance as something to be feared.

2 Prayer, Christian prayer, is the supreme weapon in the struggle in which we are called to take part.

3 We attain to true liberty, not by rejecting all authority, but by obedience, even to death. At the same time, no authority should have any other aim than to develop in us the liberty of the children of God.

4 Life and liturgy are one.

20.149
John Bowker
English Anglican theologian

1 Religion will never disappear into the sea of its own errors... It will always pick itself up and dust itself down, precisely because of what goes on in the love of God and of one's neighbour as oneself.

2 Religions are corrigible pictures about something that makes its demands upon us, that calls out for explanation.

20.150
Veronica Brady

Australian writer and commentator on contemporary society

1 A society which excludes and oppresses a group of its own people and refuses to recognise their right to their own culture and way of life cannot call itself tolerant or peaceful.

2 We need our artists to remind us not only of who we are but also of what the world is.

3 Over the frontier, in the wilderness, it can seem as if the world is falling to pieces... and yet the call keeps coming, a call, I think, which is not so much to power as to community with all those others who are wounded, whose worlds or lives also seem to be falling apart, yet who are actually—we must believe—giving birth to something new.

20.151
Peter G. van Breemen

Dutch Jesuit

1 The experience of guilt has always been one of the most excruciating problems in the history of mankind.

2 Prayer cannot be measured in terms of 'usefulness'. It can only be understood as a complete surrender without wanting 'to get something out of it'.

3 For how can we ever manage to love unselfishly, to serve humbly and patiently in spite of frustration if we do not live on God's forgiveness?

4 There is no mass production with God.

5 To pray is to sit
Open-handed before God.

20.152
George Wallace Briggs

English Anglican clergyman and hymn-writer

1 Come, risen Lord, and deign to be our guest;
Nay, let us be thy guests, the feast is thine;
Thyself at thine own board make manifest,
In thine own sacrament of bread and wine.

2 Unfathomed love divine,
Reign thou within my heart;
From thee nor depth nor height,
Nor life nor death can part;
My life is hid in God with thee,
Now and through all eternity.

20.153
Jill Briscoe

English-born Bible teacher and writer

1 There are a lot of things that only happen once. Remembering that simple fact will help us live through them.

2 Change interrupts my nesting habits, intrudes into my comfort zone. Say the word change, and I freeze. I have learned to live to the full—wherever I am—by pretending I'll be there for ever. Otherwise I'd never get involved in a new project, or invest myself in someone's life, or bother to contribute to a group.

3 A man of quality is never threatened by a woman of equality.

4 If only God would lean out of heaven and tell me [my children] are going to make it, I could relax. But God doesn't do that. He tells us to be the parents he has called us to be in his strength and promises to do his part. Driven to prayer (after discovering that manipulation didn't work), I began to realize I was only truly positive and confident when I'd been flat on my face before the Lord.

20.154
Rita Nakashima Brock
Japanese-American feminist theologian

1 I have a growing sense that the models for relationships in community that the church has offered us—models of self-sacrifice, servanthood, and harmonious/homogeneous unity—are neither healthy nor viable. I suspect that these models are in many ways models of exploitative and abusive relationships.

2 I refuse to surrender the church to those who want me out of it. The church belongs to no one group but to all God's people baptized into Jesus Christ. Ultimately, it is the church of all its members, not just its leaders and theologians; it belongs to God.

3 My commitment to the transformation of the church makes me as essential to its life as those who want to preserve the church as it has been in the past.

20.155
Raymond Brown
Baptist

1 I'm not too enamoured of church unity discussions if in the end they mean uniformity.

20.156
F.F. Bruce
Scottish classicist, biblical scholar and author

1 We must first make up our minds about Christ before coming to conclusions about the miracles attributed to him.

2 The doctrine of the final perseverance of the saints has as its corollary the salutary teaching that the saints are the people who persevere to the end.

3 Sanctification is glory begun. Glory is sanctification completed.

20.157
Walter Brueggemann
German biblical scholar

1 What God does first and best and most is to trust his people with their moment in history. He trusts them to do what must be done for the sake of his whole humanity.

2 Every totalitarian regime is frightened of the artist. It is the vocation of the prophet to keep alive the ministry of imagination, to keep on conjuring and purposing alternative futures to the single one the king wants to urge as the only thinkable one.

3 Jesus of Nazareth is the fulfilment and quintessence of the prophetic tradition.

4 The Jordan looms as a decisive boundary in the Bible. It is not simply between east and west but it is laden with symbolic power. It is the boundary between the precariousness of the wilderness and the confidence of at-homeness. The crossing of the Jordan is the most momentous experience that could happen to Israel. The Jordan crossing represents the moment of the most radical transformation of any historical person or group, the moment of empowerment or enlandment, the decisive event of being turfed and at home for the first time.

5 The preaching moment is the moment for the gift of God's life in the midst of our tired alienation.

20.158
Emil Brunner
Swiss Reformed theologian

1 God wills to do something quite definite and particular through us, here and now, something which no other person could do at any other time.

2 What oxygen is to the lungs, such is hope for the meaning of life.

3 God does not desire 'something' from us—he desires us, ourselves; not our works, but our personality, our will, our heart.

4 Indeed, without being guilty of exaggeration, we may well maintain that the crisis in marriage presents the Christian ethic with the most serious and the most difficult problem with which a Christian ethic has to deal.

5 The Church exists by mission, as fire exists by burning.

6 The first and most important thing we know about God is that we know nothing about him except what he himself makes known.

20.159
Christopher Bryant
English priest, Anglican religious

1 In the spiritual journey we travel through the night towards the day. We walk not in the bright sunshine of total certainty but through the darkness of ignorance, error, muddle and uncertainty. We make progress in the journey as we grow in faith.

2 Anger is the child of pride.

3 The Godward journey is a journey on which every individual is launched, all unknowingly, at birth.

4 The splash of wealth can distance the rich from the needs of the poor and make them forget their humanity.

5 There is a deep wisdom inaccessible to the wise and prudent but disclosed to babes.

20.160
Frank Buchman
American evangelist, founder of the Moral Re-Armament movement

1 Suppose everybody cared enough, everybody shared enough, wouldn't everybody have enough? There is enough in the world for everyone's need, but not enough for everyone's greed.

20.161
Walbert Bühlmann
Swiss-born Capuchin missiologist

1 The church is a cause of suffering to many within its pale, as well as to many on the outside.

2 The church is missing its chance to arrive in the world of tomorrow.

3 No one can know any religion in its inmost depth without having affirmed it, said 'yes' to it, from within, with ultimate existential passion.

4 A new day of interchurch and interreligious ecumenism is dawning. We are on our way to a catholicity of salvation history. We are drawing nearer to the breadth of God.

5 All criticism of the church... all church reform, all hope for the church, must begin with you and me.

20.162
Rudolph Bultmann
German New Testament scholar

1 It is impossible to use electric light and the wireless and to avail ourselves of modern medical and surgical discoveries and at the same time to believe in the New Testament world of spirits and miracles.

2 The real purpose of myth is not to present an objective picture of the world as it is, but to express man's understanding of himself in the world in which he lives.

3 To demythologize is to deny that the message of Scripture and of the church is bound to an ancient world-view which is obsolete.

20.163
John Burnaby
English theological writer

1 God's promise to the pure of heart is of that knowledge of himself through love which is eternal life; and the heart will be pure when it is filled with the love of God 'in all things and above all things'. To be filled with such love is to have obtained the promises which exceed all that we can desire.

20.164
Ruth Burrows
English Carmelite nun

1 Faith is not a thing of the mind, it is not an intellectual certainty or a felt conviction of the heart, it is a sustained decision to take God with utter seriousness as the God of our life; it is to live out the hours in a practical, concrete affirmation that he is Father and he is 'in heaven'.

2 Sin is not a thing; it is not a moral stain or blemish, it is a damage to a relationship, a rejection of love. It is a gap, a chasm, and those who have chosen to be far off must be brought close.

20.165
Manas Buthelezi
South African theologian and Lutheran pastor

1 The black man must be enabled through the interpretation and application of the Gospel to realise that blackness, like whiteness, is a good natural face cream from God and not some cosmological curse.

20.166
Christopher Butler
English Benedictine monk and bishop

1 The gospel is not simply a noble humanism; it is also a message of divine redemption.

2 *Aggiornamento* means 'bringing up to date', something which any human institution may need from time to time.

20.167
Herbert Butterfield
English historian

1 There are times when we can never meet the future with sufficient elasticity of mind, especially if we are locked in the contemporary systems of thought. We can do worse than remember a principle which both gives us a firm Rock and leaves us the maximum elasticity for our minds: the principle: Hold to Christ, and for the rest be totally uncommitted.

20.168
Lavinia Byrne
British Roman Catholic religious sister, broadcaster and writer

1 When we talk about questions of authority or leadership in our churches, we must do so in a way which empowers our own leadership, our own holiness, our own sense of discernment, and the gift of obedience, which means listening.

2 [Discerning] is not about arguing one's corner. It is about trying to listen to one another in order to listen to the voice of God.

20.169
Mildred Cable and Francesca French
Explorers and missionaries to Chinese Turkestan

1 Every Gobi trade route carries all these people and many more, and the missionary's problem is how to convey a message which fits every one of them. Only one book can do this, because it is the Word of God which is for every man of every nation, but it must be taken to him in his own language or it is of no use to him. This means that some one must learn the language so well that he can translate the Bible into it.

20.170
George Caird
Free Church biblical scholar

1 When God pronounces his last word in the drama of this world's redemption, he will vindicate the way of the Cross, and he will vindicate nothing else.

2 The only glory which Jesus ever sought for himself or offered to his disciples was to be caught up into God's redemptive purpose.

20.171
Helder Camara
Brazilian Roman Catholic archbishop and theologian

1 When you let the Lord launch you, you have to be ready for anything, even for the unimaginable, even for being a bishop!

2 The Mass is so high, so broad, so deep, that it covers the whole day.

3 Those who do not believe have one thing in common with those who believe—namely, that the Lord believes in them.

4 All the denominations have fallen prey to the capitalist machine. With what remnant of moral authority can we demand structural change if our own institutes are linked to the old structures?

5 What horror has the world come to when it uses profit as the prime incentive in human progress, and competition as the supreme law of economics?

6 Beware of invoking the fear of Communism as an excuse for avoiding a change in the structures which confine millions of the sons of God in a sub-human condition.

7 There is no single definition of holiness: there are dozens, hundreds. But there is one I am particularly fond of; being holy means getting up immediately every time you fall, with humility and joy. It doesn't mean never falling into sin. It means being able to say, 'Yes, Lord, I have fallen a thousand times. But thanks to you I have got up again a thousand and one times.' That's all. I like thinking about that.

8 I hurry wherever I am beckoned, in search of what can bring men together in the name of the essential.

20.172
Ernesto Cardenal
Nicaraguan priest, poet and political activist

1 Towards God all creatures strain. And all things speak to us of God, because all things long for him, the starry sky and all insects, the huge galaxies and the chipmunk playing all day long...

2 All human eyes have longing in them.

3 And my body was made for the love of God. Every cell in my body is a hymn to my creator and a declaration of love.

4 We are mirrors of God, created to reflect him. Even when the water is not calm, it reflects the sky.

5 God's image was blurred by sin (devils are faces which have lost God's image), but with Christ it was reprinted on man.

6 Prayer is complaining and sighing and gasping and the quickened heartbeat.

7 We do not know that at the centre of our being we find not ourselves but another, that our identity is in another, that turning inwards and finding ourselves is to fall into the arms of another.

8 Bitterness and distress are in the depths of all things. This is the groaning of the creatures, of which St Paul speaks. But in us creation rests from its anguish, when our hearts rest in God.

9 The world is not like a picture painted by an artist centuries ago which now hangs untouchable in a museum. It is more like a work of art in constant process of creation, still in the studio.

10 This is the dogma of love, the dogma of the Holy Trinity. The mystery that God is not alone, that God is union, communion and communism.

11 The atheists are right, in a certain sense, to deny God. For by God they mean an anthropomorphic God, a God who does not exist, a fairytale God. But when they feel the existence of something vague and incomprehensible and mysterious and they themselves do not know what it is or what it is called, then they are also darkly affirming the existence of God, a being they can neither understand or imagine, that no man can look upon and live.

12 'To create something new you always have to make it ugly,' Picasso said. And God is infinite newness.

13 God also has a sense of humour, an infinite one.

14 You are terrified of being alone... And all the while your best friend is knocking outside, his head wet with dew.

15 We want God's voice to be clear but it is not... We want it to be clear as day, but it is deep as night. It is deep and clear, but with a dark clarity like an x-ray. It reaches our bones.

20.173
George Carey
English Archbishop of Canterbury

1 There can be no future for the Church unless we have collaborative styles of ministry.

2 The Church is not in the business of maintaining buildings: we're in the job for promoting the values of Christ and the gospel.

20.174
Amy Carmichael
Irish-born missionary in India

1 Prayer is the core of our day. Take prayer out and the day would collapse.

2 Souls are more or less securely fastened to bodies... and as you can't get the souls out and deal with them separately, you have to take them both together.

3 You can give without loving, but you cannot love without giving.

4 Learn the blessedness of the unoffended in the face of the unexplainable.

5 Not by travelling, Lord,
men come to you,
but by the way of love.

6 From silken self, O Captain, free
Thy soldier, who would follow thee:
From love of softening things,
From easy choices, weakenings,
From all that dims thy Calvary,
O Lamb of God, deliver me.

7 It may be he has only sent me here as a stopgap. Part of a soldier's duty is to fill gaps, you know. One must as willingly be nothing, as something.

8 Sorrow is one of the things that are lent, not given. A thing that is lent may be taken away; a thing that is given is not taken away. Joy is given; sorrow is lent.

20.175
Merlin R. Carothers
North American army chaplain

1 Without Christ as Saviour, without the cross, there would be no plan of salvation, no possible way to be forgiven of sin. In fact, there would be no gospel.

2 Satan can't do a thing to us unless he first gets God's permission.

3 Jesus didn't promise to change the circumstances around us, but he did promise great peace and pure joy to those who would learn to believe that God actually controls *all things*.

4 Dying to self is a progressive journey and I have come to believe that it is travelled only through praise.

5 The very act of praise releases the power of God into a set of circumstances and enables God to change them if this is his design.

20.176
Carlo Carretto
Little Brother of Jesus, and spiritual writer

1 I am not afraid that God will destroy the world, but I am afraid that he may abandon it to wander blindly in the sophisticated wasteland of contemporary civilisation.

2 Why go miles and miles to see the dubious stigmata on someone or other's hands, yet move not a step to contemplate the sore-covered hands of the poor?

3 The joy that comes from not having harmed one's brother far surpasses the joy given by some object that has been obtained at the cost of a mountain of corpses.

4 There is something much greater than human action—prayer.

5 To stand poor beside the brother I love means being his equal in terms of cultural values, intelligence and human dignity far more than in terms of money.

6 Prayer takes place in the heart, not in the head.

7 Jesus was killed by a group of those 'respectable pharisees' because they were not waiting for salvation; they thought they were saved already.

8 The desert does not mean the absence of men, it means the presence of God.

9 The violence of Jesus is deep love, not the sword or the prison, which is how we always want to resolve the problems which seem insoluble to us.

10 It is love which gives things their value. It makes sense of the difficulty of spending hours and hours on one's knees praying while so many men need looking after in the world.

11 We are the wire, God is the current. Our only power is to let the current pass through us.

12 The degree of our faith
is the degree of our prayer.
The strength of our hope
is the strength of our prayer.
The warmth of our charity
is the warmth of our prayer.

13 Living in our selfishness means stopping at human limits and preventing our transformation into Divine Love.

14 Don't try to reach God with your understanding; that is impossible. Reach him in love; that is possible.

15 When I have learned to do the Father's will, I shall have fully realised my vocation on earth.

20.177
Sydney Carter
Musician, songwriter

1 I danced in the morning
when the world was begun,
And I danced in the moon
and the stars and the sun,
I came down from heaven
and I danced on the earth,
At Bethlehem I had my birth.
Dance, then, wherever you may be;
I am the Lord of the dance, said he,
And I'll lead you all, wherever you may be,
And I'll lead you all in the dance, said he.

20.178
Carthusians (anonymous)
Monks

1 Mysteries are not dark shadows, before which we must shut our eyes and be silent. On the contrary, they are dazzling splendours, with which we ought to sate our gaze.

2 Discipline puts back in its place that something in us which should serve but wants to rule.

3 Why weep? I do not know. Perhaps it is because of the utter gratuitousness of life, of being, which we experience in such moments, like the occasions when we know what it is to be loved, truly, deeply, for ourselves.

4 In heaven, the mystery of God, precisely as mystery, will be our eternal blessedness.

5 Let us live like people who see the invisible, who are animated by the Spirit of God.

20.179
Pablo Casals
Spanish cellist, conductor and composer

1 Beauty is all about us, but how many people are blind to it! People take little pleasure in the natural and quiet and simple things of life.

2 When will we teach our children in school what they are? We should say to each of them: Do you know what you are? You are a marvel... And when you grow up, can you then harm another who is, like you, a marvel?

3 There is of course no substitute for work. I myself practised constantly, as I have all my life. I have been told I play the cello with the ease of a bird flying. I do not know with how much effort a bird learns to fly, but I do know what effort has gone into my cello.

20.180
Sheila Cassidy
English doctor, imprisoned in Chile

1 We only deliberately waste time with those we love—it is the purest sign that we love someone if we choose to spend time idly in their presence when we could be doing something more constructive.

2 The tension between the call to the desert and to the market place arises not from the greater presence of God in one or the other, but from our varying psychological needs to apprehend him in different ways.

3 When one is in very great pain and fear it is extremely difficult to pray coherently, and I could only raise my mind in anguish to God and ask for strength to hold on.

4 To shelter or give medical aid to a man on the run, from a police force which will torture and perhaps kill him, is an act of Christian love demanded by Christ in the Gospel and is no more a political act than giving first aid and a cup of tea to a Member of Parliament who has a car smash outside your door.

5 Do we not owe it to those we serve to accept our limitations and cherish our minds and bodies so that we will be available to serve them a little longer? I have learned to be very wary of the famous prayer of St Ignatius, 'to give and not to count the cost'.

20.181
Charles Causley
Australian poet

1 I am the truth, but you will not believe me,
I am the city where you will not stay,
I am your wife, your child,
but you will leave me,
I am that God to whom you will not pray.

20.182
Tereza Cavalcanti
Brazilian university teacher

1 In fact, there is no rupture, but continuity between what was revealed to the people of God in the past and the breath of the Spirit that accompanies the reading of the Bible within faith communities today.

2 The cry of the women prophets of the Bible is in line with the cries of Israel in Egypt, and it will lead to the cry of Jesus, who, throughout his life and until the time of his death, took up the cry of the suffering and the oppressed of the world.

20.183
Elsie Chamberlain
Congregational minister and first woman chaplain to the British Women's Royal Air Force

1 I believe that we get an answer to our prayers when we are willing to obey what is implicit in that answer. I believe that we get a vision of God when we are willing to accept what that vision does to us.

20.184
J. Russell Chandran
Theologian

1 The liberation of the poor is a journey full of grief, marked by both the passion of Christ and by the signs of resurrection. The liberation of the poor is a vast history that embraces all of human history and gives it true meaning.

20.185
T.C. Chao
Protestant theologian from China

1 There has been no time... when God has not been breaking into our human world; nor is there a place where men have been that he has not entered and ruled.

20.186
Guillermo Chavez
Ecuadorean writer

1 We believe in God, creator of the earth,
creator of life and freedom,
hope of the poor.

We believe in Jesus Christ,
friend in suffering,
companion in the resurrection,
way of peace.

We believe in the Spirit,
that holy force impelling the poor
to build a church of the beatitudes.

20.187
Thomas Obadiah Chisholm
North American teacher, journalist, hymn-writer

1 Great is thy faithfulness, O God my Father,
There is no shadow of turning with thee:
Thou changest not, thy compassions
they fail not.
As thou hast been, thou for ever wilt be.

20.188
Joan Chittister
North American Benedictine nun

1 Religious congregations are not faced with a vocation crisis... Religious life is faced with a crisis of significance and a crisis of spirituality. Religious life is at the brink of renewal and faced with two choices: personal comfort or prophetic presence, individual commitments or charismatic congregations. Neither choice is an easy one but one does not preclude the other.

2 The church is waiting, the world is waiting, the young people of the world are waiting to see if there is such a thing as a religious life so immersed in the contemplative moment that it does significant things in significant ways at this significant moment in history.

3 Prayer is not work and work is not prayer.

20.189
Agatha Christie
English author

1 [Quoting a classroom teacher of her youth] 'To be a Christian you must face and accept the life that Christ faced and lived; you must enjoy things as he enjoyed things; be as happy as he was at the marriage at Cana, know the peace and happiness that it means to be in harmony with God and with God's will. But you must also know, as he did, what it means to be alone in the garden of Gethsemane, to feel that all your friends have forsaken you, that those you love and trust have turned away from you, and that God himself has forsaken you. Hold on then to the belief that that is not the end. If you love, you will suffer, and if you do not know love, you do not know the meaning of a Christian life.'

20.190
Chung Hyun Kyung
Korean theologian

1 Where there is no mutual relationship, there is no human experience of God.

2 Only in community can humanity reflect God and fulfil the image of God in which we were created for mutual relationship.

3 In their suffering, Asian women meet God, who in turn discloses that they were created in the divine image, full and equal participants in the community with men.

20.191
David Clark
English Methodist minister and community activist

1 We are supposed to be a pilgrim people unencumbered and on the move yet we are chained to plant and property; we proclaim the hollowness of riches yet still have great wealth. The Church preaches about servanthood and humility yet is classically hierarchical; it offers wholeness to man yet ministers to only a fraction of his personality and needs; it speaks about love and reconciliation yet is as divided and divisive as any other institution.

2 There is no way to the rediscovery of the meaning of spirituality until holy communion is born out of holy community.

3 The church has turned its back on politics because it does not wish to acknowledge that its activities are just as political as those of any other institution.

20.192
Edith Margaret Clarkson
Canadian poet, teacher and hymn-writer

1 Saviour, I seek your face,
I here confess you;
Within your holy place
I kneel to bless you.
I gaze upon your board—
Love's mystic token;
For me, your blood outpoured,
Your body broken;
I fall, amazed, before you;
I worship, I adore you.

20.193
Paul Claudel
French poet, essayist and dramatist

1 The Cross is God at work. It is not only his rack, it is his active self, his extracting and unifying role.

20.194
Sarah Coakley
British theologian

1 Only... by facing—and giving new expression to—the paradoxes of 'losing one's life in order to save it', can feminists hope to construct a vision of the Christic 'self' that transcends the gender stereotypes we are seeking to up-end.

20.195
Donald Coggan
Former Archbishop of Canterbury

1 Wherever ugliness is kept at bay, there the Spirit of God, who is the God of Beauty, is doing His creative and re-creative labour.

2 Just as good literature and good art raise and ennoble character, so bad literature and bad art degrade it.

3 The purpose of the Church in the world is to be the worshipping and witnessing spear-head of all that is in accordance with the will of God as it has been revealed in Jesus Christ.

4 Wherever the bounds of beauty, truth and goodness are advanced, there the Kingdom comes.

5 The expertise of the pulpit can only be learned slowly and, it may well be, with a strange mixture of pain and joy.

6 God loves us *in* our sin, and *through* our sin, and goes on loving us, looking for a response.

7 The highest education is that which brings the student face to face, not simply with something great but with someone great, namely Christ.

8 If Jesus isn't the Lord of your life someone else will be.

20.196
Tito Colliander
Orthodox writer from Finland

1 Prayer is the science of scientists and the art of artists… The working material of the praying person is living humanity. By his prayer he shapes it, gives it pregnancy and beauty: first himself and thereby many others.

2 When you pray, you must yourself be silent. You do not pray to have your own earthbound desires fulfilled, but you pray: Thy will be done. It is not fitting to wish to use God as an errand boy. You yourself must be silent; let the prayer speak.

20.197
Charles Colson
North American politician, founder of the Prison Fellowship

1 Conversion may occur in an instant, but the process of coming from sinfulness into a new life can be a long and arduous journey.

2 It is absurd for Christians constantly to seek new demonstrations of God's power, to expect a miraculous answer to every need, from curing ingrown toenails to finding parking spaces; this only leads to faith in miracles rather than the Maker.

20.198
Kate Compston
English United Reformed Church minister and writer

1 Christ, crucified and risen,
is set free—
from one time
for all times
from one community
for all communities
from one sex
for both sexes
from one culture
for all cultures
from one world
for all worlds
from life as one individual
for life within every
trusting heart.

20.199
James Cone
Black American theologian

1 The significance of Black Theology lies in the conviction that the content of the Christian gospel is liberation, so that any talk about God that fails to take seriously the righteousness of God as revealed in the liberation of the weak and downtrodden is not Christian language.

2 White pictures of Jesus in Christian churches and homes are nothing but an ideological distortion of the biblical portrait.

3 It is not easy to speak with restraint and civility in a context in which your history and culture have been marginalized and thus not considered with the same respect and recognition as other histories and cultures.

4 After much reflection, I have come to the conclusion that most of the North American Whites who talk about liberation theology do nothing more than talk.

20.200
Yves Congar
French Dominican theologian

1 God's ways are always truth and justice and mercy.

2 There is nothing more urgent than doing all we can to know and to make known the *true* God, the God whose last name is pronounced Jesus Christ.

20.201
Frederick Copleston
English Catholic philosopher

1 The notion of certainty need not be linked with the notion of a static and fossilized system.

20.202
Jim Cotter
English Anglican priest and liturgical writer

1 I don't think it far-fetched to draw a comparison between making love and making

Eucharist. Perhaps the one reflects the other, the one a personal focus, the other a corporate focus, for the generating of love in the world. After all, at the heart of each are the statements, of person to person, and of God to the community of persons, 'You matter to me', and 'I am willing to die for you', i.e. grace and sacrifice.

2 Spirituality is nothing less than the whole of life orientated towards God, shaped by God, graced by God. That *includes* the sexuality of each individual and the sexuality of all, in our personal and corporate desire to come together and to create.

3 The roots of Godwardness are in matter, flesh and blood, material stuff, earth; they are not to be rejected, however painful our experience of them might be.

4 Everything you need to know about God but were always afraid to ask is conveyed in and through flesh-body. Incarnation is a fleshly and sexual doctrine. Flesh-body receives the highest affirmation through the divine presence becoming clear to us, being revealed to us, not *in* but *as* flesh. Flesh is a *means* of human loving, not an obstacle to it.

5 Do not be afraid of being close,
of loving each other,
of taking risks,
of weakness,
of being vulnerable.
Let love cast out fear.
Let steady warmth melt anxiety.

6 Let your love be exclusive, but not exclusive:
special, but not excluding.
You do not matter to each other more
than anything else
or more than anyone else in the world.
But you matter to each other in a unique way
that no one can replace,
And that matters to each of you very much
indeed.

7 Let there be space.
Remember that the ones you love
in your heart
are but guests in your soul.

20.203
William Countryman
North American Episcopal theologian

1 In reality, humility means nothing other than complete honesty about yourself.

2 Since God loves you anyway, there is no point in making yourself out to be better than you are—and none in making yourself out to be worse.

3 The person you are now, the person you have been, the person you will yet be—*this* person God has chosen as beloved.

4 Jesus could have written books, but he chose not to. He could have had his disciples memorise a fixed message word for word, but we have no convincing evidence that he ever did. Instead, he worked by exposing people to the good news, letting it do its work on them, and then sending them out to expose others.

5 Whenever the church wants to think of itself as immaculate, infallible, unerringly right or good, completely trustworthy, it falls into a kind of idolatry.

6 Hearing the good news is a beginning. The rest of our life forms our response.

20.204
Harvey Cox
North American theologian

1 The early church's belief in the Ascension can be read as its refusal to allow its Lord to be localized or spatially restricted. The Ascension in its simplest terms means that Jesus is mobile. He is not a baal, but the Lord of all history.

2 Entirely too much has been said in most churches about the stewardship of money and too little about the stewardship of power. The modern equivalent of repentance is the responsible use of power.

3 Sermons remain one of the last forms of public discourse where it is culturally forbidden to talk back.

4 Not to decide is to decide.

5 The real ecumenical crisis today is not between Catholic and Protestants but between traditional and experimental forms of Church life.

6 God has created a world, and we have messed it up.

7 One could view the whole life of Jesus from first to last as a single continuing exploit in breaking down the walls that separate the people.

8 There is no place for a priestly hierarchy in the church.

9 The starting point for any theology of the church today must be a theology of social change.

10 The Kingdom of God does not come in the same way everywhere. Mankind is not monochromatic.

11 Perhaps one day we will outgrow our ridiculous obsession with sex, of which our fixation with chastity and virginity is just the other side of the coin.

20.205
Kenneth Cragg
British scholar of comparative religion

1 The Church... is the trustee community of the gospel which interprets the nature of God as responsible love, for ever grounds that interpretation in the person and the wounds of Jesus as the Christ, and presents him as, for all mankind, the where and how of grace, of forgiveness, and peace.

20.206
Janet Crawford
New Zealand theologian

1 The Decade of Evangelism poses new questions for women in the church—questions about faith, about commitment. As women we may have questions of our own—questions about the nature of evangelism, the purpose of mission. In the past, Christian women have had to struggle for freedom to be active in mission and ministry. As a result the church's witness has been impoverished, its mission weakened. If today the Gospel is to be proclaimed in its wholeness to women and to men, then women and men must work as partners in mission and evangelism.

20.207
Don Cupitt
English Anglican priest and theologian

1 God both represents to us what we are to become and shows us the way to become it.

2 We need a spirituality to direct our freedom and make it fruitful, so that human lives can gain something of the nothing-wasted integrity and completeness of a work of art.

20.208
Jean Daniélou
French cardinal and theologian

1 Some day, indeed, the visible sun will be extinguished, and the true light will shine alone. Then we shall no longer need images and figures; then our eyes shall see, in the heaven of an eternal day, the sun that knows no setting, a perpetual Orient, the ever-renewed arising of the Sun of righteousness.

20.209
M.C. D'Arcy
British Jesuit writer

1 Knowledge is the soul's delight, its positive and personal bliss, but without the balancing desire to live in and by the life of another, this desire would be nothing but an enlightened selfishness. The two serve each other's ends, and bring it about that perfect love is mutual giving and taking, possessing and being possessed.

20.210
Robert Davidson
Scottish Old Testament scholar

1 There are those today who wish to live unquestioningly within the security of

inherited structures of belief and practice; for such people the Old Testament must be a very disturbing or a closed book, since it lives in the tension of faith and doubt.

2 It is in the struggle to maintain certainties in the midst of uncertainty, in the painful groping for new light in the midst of a darkness that seems total, that the Old Testament bears its clearest witness to the courage to doubt.

3 If we go to the Old Testament to find definitions of God or comprehensive credal statements, we shall look in vain.

4 At least if you are 'battling with God' you still believe that there is someone there with whom it is important and worthwhile to do battle—in truth.

5 It is hard to live with broken symbols, hard indeed to accept that the breaking of such hallowed symbols may be a necessary element in continuing faith.

20.211
Charles Davis
Roman Catholic theologian

1 The commitment of Christians to working with others in secular society for human values is a key part of their mission today. They must... meet God's grace as it is operative among their fellow citizens.

20.212
Michaela Davis
Australian-born poet

1 Love needs to be made
like good bread, newly each day,
to keep its freshness.

20.213
Dorothy Day
North American Roman Catholic writer and radical social reformer

1 I was lonely, dead lonely. And I was to find out then, as I found out so many things, over and over again, that women especially are social beings, who are not content with just husband and family, but must have a community, a group, and exchange with others.

2 No one has a right to sit down and feel hopeless. There's too much work to do.

3 God is our Creator. God made us in his image and likeness. Therefore we are creators... The joy of creativeness should be ours.

4 God gave us a garden to till and cultivate. We became co-creators by our responsible acts, whether in bringing forth children, or producing food, furniture or clothing.

5 It is not love in the abstract that counts. Men have loved brotherhood, the workers, the poor—but they have not loved 'personally'. It is the hardest thing in the world to love... It is never the brothers next to us, but the brothers in the abstract that are easy to love.

6 Paper work, cleaning the house, cooking the meals, dealing with innumerable visitors who come all through the day, answering the phone, keeping patience and acting intelligently—which is to find some meaning in all these encounters—these things too are the work of peace, and often seem like a very little way.

20.214
Hassan Barnaba Dehqani-Tafti
Iranian Anglican Bishop

1 [Of his murdered son, Bahram]
O God, Bahram's blood has multiplied the fruit of the Spring in the soil of our souls
So when his murderers stand before thee on the day of judgement
Remember the fruit of the Spirit by which they have enriched our lives,
And forgive.

20.215
Consuelo Del Prado
Peruvian Catholic sister

1 Spirituality is a way of living; it is also a way of following Jesus.

2 The richness of the message we [women] bring to the community depends much on the profundity of our dialogue with the Lord. This dialogue will be richer if we meditate in solitude on the challenges, questions, and gifts we receive from the community.

20.216
Annie Dillard
North American author

1 There is not a guarantee in the world. Oh your needs are guaranteed, your needs are absolutely guaranteed by the most stringent of warranties, in the plainest, truest words: knock; seek; ask. But you must read the fine print. 'Not as the world giveth, give I unto you.'

2 Beauty and grace are performed whether or not we will or sense them. The least we can do is try to be there.

3 I think that the dying pray at the last not 'please,' but 'thank you,' as a guest thanks his host at the door. Falling from airplanes the people are crying thank you, thank you, all down the air; and the cold carriages draw up for them on the rocks. Divinity is not playful. The universe was not made in jest but in solemn incomprehensible earnest. By a power that is unfathomably secret, and holy, and fleet. There is nothing to be done about it, but ignore it, or see.

20.217
Charles Harold Dodd
Welsh biblical scholar and Congregational pastor

1 To accept His Kingdom and to enter in brings blessedness, because the best conceivable thing is that we should be in obedience to the will of God.

2 A miracle in the sense of the New Testament is not so much a breach of the laws of nature, but rather a remarkable or exceptional occurrence which brought an undeniable sense of the presence and power of God.

3 The entire New Testament is witness that the real presence of Christ was not withdrawn when the Resurrection 'appearances' ceased. The unique and evanescent meetings with the risen Lord triggered off a new kind of relation which proved permanent.

4 Jesus Christ, with a confidence that to the timid traditionalism of his time appeared blasphemous, asserted that he knew the Father and was prepared to let others into that knowledge. He did so, not by handing down a new tradition about God, but by making others share in his own attitude to God.

20.218
Jack Dominian
Roman Catholic British psychiatrist

1 There is a powerful instinct in society, whether we are Christians or not, to find constant daddies telling us what to do.

2 Christianity has failed abysmally to help people realise that when they feel guilty they do not have to reject themselves totally as bad.

3 You never lose the love of God. Guilt is the warning that temporarily you are out of touch.

20.219
Vincent J. Donovan
North American missionary to the Masai in Africa

1 Evangelization is a process of bringing the gospel to people where they are, not where you would like them to be.

2 Repent, believe, be baptized, witness to Christ in the Spirit until he comes again. This is the response to the Christian message. That is the Church.

3 The preaching of the gospel in the American accent must come face to face with the fact that the creed of stark and rugged individualism running through the fiber of our society, through our business and economic and spiritual world, has nothing to do with Christianity.

20.220
Petru Dumitru
Rumanian-born poet and novelist

1 All that comforts, all that relaxes the grimace of suffering, of anger, madness, is Christian; all that comes with open arms, holds out loving hands, and gentles life, gives back hope, is [Christ's] word. We have to follow God, and not speak about him. We must speak with God, and wait patiently, in silence, until he is willing to reply in silence.

20.221
John S. Dunne
North American Roman Catholic theologian

1 Only when [contemporary man] actually takes a chance on God, so to speak, can he pray and does the dark God begin to resemble Abba.

20.222
Enrique D. Dussel
Latin American theologian

1 For God to reveal himself again, for him to rise from his apparent death, it is necessary to resurrect the real corpse, which is the colonial brother or sister. That is, the one who is dead is not God... the one who is dead is the Indian, the African, the Asian. When justice is done them, God will reveal himself.

20.223
Gerhard Ebeling
German-born theologian

1 To keep your distance from the question of [faith's] power, not to let it lay claim upon you, not to make use of faith's power, means to deny faith.

2 Faith makes the world what it truly is, the creation of God.

20.224
Alan Ecclestone
Anglican priest, writer and social activist

1 To be able to pray 'let go' is so important a part of our life that it deserves the practice it requires to become part of our maturing way of living, and its connection with final letting go should not be forgotten.

2 Prayer is, however feeble and immature, a gesture of faith, the gesture we go on making in order that the Yes of mankind may be uttered and known.

20.225
Ruth B. Edwards
Scottish biblical scholar

1 Sooner or later the strange idea must go that women are properly concerned only with domesticity and with private, 'behind-the-scenes' ministry. The Church needs its Marthas: we are all grateful to those who selflessly devote themselves to the traditional 'feminine' tasks... But this is not the sum total of women's gifts. The Church needs also its Marys, its Phoebes, and its Priscillas—perhaps even its Deborahs—who in a twentieth-century context are likely to find themselves in the forefront of public ministry, pastoral, priestly and episcopal.

20.226
Bette Ekeya
Kenyan theological writer

1 One teaching that has hurt a certain percentage of African women and placed them outside the salvation community is the interpretation of Matthew 19.4-6... Those unfortunate women who were not chosen to become Christian wives were declared concubines and their children bastards. The once happily married women found themselves abandoned and homeless, for they could not return to their fathers' homesteads.

2 By emphasizing woman's subjection to man in marriage, the church has directly given men the excuse for laxity and tyranny in their dealings with their wives.

20.227
Jean-Marc Ela
Sociologist and theological writer from Cameroon

1 Our faith in the God of revelation cannot be lived and understood abstractly, in some atemporal fashion. It can only be lived through the warp and woof of the events that make up history.

2 The divine name of the exodus not only unveils the mystery of God's personhood, but is at the same time a name to be used on a journey, a name revealing God in the direction of the future, a name of promise to show forth, in the darkness of an unknown future, what it is that can be relied upon.

3 As the oppressed of all times have turned to this primordial event [the exodus], thence to draw hope, we shall never come to any self-understanding without ourselves taking up that same history and discovering there that God intervenes in the human adventure of servitude and death to free the human being.

20.228
T.S. Eliot
American-born British poet, critic and dramatist

1 The majority of people live below the level of belief or doubt. It takes application and a kind of genius to believe anything.

2 Those who talk of the Bible as a 'monument of English prose' are merely admiring it as a monument over the grave of Christianity.

3 Most of the trouble in the world is caused by people wanting to be important.

4 Destiny waits in the hand of God, not in the hands of statesmen.

5 Tradition by itself is not enough; it must be perpetually criticised and brought up to date under the supervision of what I call orthodoxy.

6 [Wit] involves, probably, a recognition, implicit in the expression of every experience, of other kinds of experience that are possible.

7 A good deal of confusion could be avoided, if we refrained from setting before the group, what can be the aim only of the individual; and before society as a whole, what can be the aim only of a group.

8 The only wisdom we can hope to acquire is the wisdom of humility.

20.229
Virgil Elizondo
Latin American theologian

1 We have become aware that the structures of society can be either the incarnation of sin or the incarnation of grace. It is our duty to become involved in them so that they may serve the people and not continue to be the vehicle for the exploitation of the people.

20.230
Charles Elliott
English Anglican clergyman and theological writer

1 God does not demand of us that we become saints, least of all plaster saints or plastic saints, before he can use us.

2 Hypocrites we are: but we are on the way to liberation even from our own hypocrisy.

3 It's tough in the desert. It's bewildering. It's destructive. It's hellish. Yet the testimony of the Old Testament, and ever more strongly, of the New, is that out of it comes new growth, new insight, new certainty that a God of love is at home among us.

4 A spirituality that refuses to acknowledge the winter of the heart, the great sorrowfulness of human experience, is not only refusing to take seriously the life that people actually lead: it is in danger of encouraging too much leaf and too little fruit.

20.231
Jacques Ellul
French theologian and sociologist

1 The desert is the place where human powers must be renounced. In the desert there can be no more trickery, no illusions as to getting out by one's own means, no possibility of placing hope in natural sources of help.

20.232
Grace Eneme
Presbyterian from Cameroon

1 Christ's family is bigger than any human family. It includes people of all races and colors, and it is bound together by his Spirit.

2 Yes, we are a people groping in darkness. We need light, but that light must come with great healing power. For decades we [women] have been taught to be subordinate 'little angels', and all the way through those social tapes play back to us.

3 Christ was the only rabbi who did not discriminate against women in his time.

20.233
Julia Esquivel
Guatemalan writer

1 I live each day to kill death;
I die each day to beget life,
and in this dying unto death,
I die a thousand times and
am reborn another thousand
through that love.

20.234
Ruth Etchells
English Anglican theological teacher

1 I wish we could dispel the notion that the church is anything other than a gathering of sinners.

20.235
Paul Evdokimov
Russian Orthodox lay theologian

1 God can do everything, except compel a man to love him.

2 Man is free, for he is in the image of divine liberty; and that is why he has the power to choose.

20.236
George Every
English theologian

1 [Addressed to Mary]

Teach us, dear Lady, even in this hour
When we are afraid of the small
Electron that no engine can control.
Planets and atoms the same law obey,
And when they swerve, explode, and die away.

20.237
Erice Fairbrother
New Zealand teacher, school chaplain, poet and writer

1 To be engaged in building communities that are inclusive of all, where the sharing of resources and decisionmaking is equitable, is to be communicating about the deepest truths of our Christian faith, and integrates our lives with our worship.

2 When the bread is broken and the wine is poured into the cup at the eucharist, we are brought face to face with our own need for evangelism, with our own need for brokenness and the call for our lives to be outpoured... We are brought into a sacramental relationship with the broken and bleeding and with the unloved in our communities—those living with AIDS, the elderly, abused children—the list could be very long. As we listen to them, it is they who also evangelise us.

20.238
Austin Farrer
English theologian

1 The best way to find the heart of God is to trust our own best affections whatever we are looking at.

2 If Christ offers up his own death in this sacrament, it is that we may die a voluntary and daily death, and merit a daily resurrection.

3 The Resurrection is not a miracle like any other. It is a unique manifestation within this world of the transition God makes for us out of this way of being into another.

4 Salvation is the receiving of Christ's body and blood, as paupers existing on the divine charity of the Son of God. We are not our own; we are bought with a price.

5 The gift of the Holy Ghost closes the last gap between the life of God and ours...
When we allow the love of God to move in us, we can no longer distinguish ours and his; he becomes us, he lives us. It is the first fruits of the spirit, the beginning of our being made divine.

6 When we contemplate the physical creation, we see an unimaginable complex, organized on many planes one above the other; atomic, molecular, cellular; vegetable, animal, social. And the marvel of it is that at every level the constituent elements run themselves, and, by their mutual interaction, run the world. God not only makes the world, he makes it run itself; or rather, he causes its innumerable constituents to make it.

7 In so far as we are in Christ, we are filled with the Holy Ghost, and the Father's good pleasure rests upon us; infinite love delights in us.

8 To be a loyal churchman is hobbyism or prejudice, unless it is the way to be a loyal Christian.

20.239
G.P. Fedotov
Russian Orthodox church historian

1 In the Kingdom of God reigns a complete inversion of our earthly values. Folly for Christ's sake expresses essentially the need to lay bare the radical contradiction between the Christian truth and both the common sense and the moral sense of the world.

20.240
Tammy Felton
North American writer

1 We cannot abandon life because of its storms. The strongest trees are not found sheltered in the safety of the forest, rather they are out in the open spaces—bent and twisted by winds of all seasons. God provides deep roots when there are wide-spreading branches.

2 Even the hurricane is quiet in the eye
Buried never so deep in its heart
the stillness is found
A nucleus that is mysteriously calm.
Engulfed in the hurry, worry, hubbub
of our day
When everyone is flying aimlessly
in all directions
Try to find a silence of your own.
Discover your personal bit of inner peace
and cherish every minute.

20.241
Gonville ffrench-Beytagh
Anglican Dean of Johannesburg

1 Jesus alone can make atonement because he is the atonement—the at-onement of God and man.

2 To do nothing is very good, but to have nothing to do is very bad.

3 You are not drawn to God primarily for your own benefit but for his.

4 Religion means binding together.

20.242
Barbara Fiand
North American religious sister

1 Great holiness demands great sacrifice.

2 Trends in communal lifestyles are worth taking seriously only to the extent to which they are backed by vision and purpose.

3 The vision is already here. The revolution has already claimed its first hero. He dwells now in our midst and calls us to conversion.

20.243
Kathleen Fischer
North American spiritual director and writer

1 Like the Samaritan woman, contemporary women thirst for living water. They stand at the well, hoping to draw life from ancient traditions. They long to discover their own inner wells, to meet God within, as source of their wisdom, power, creativity and strength.

2 What is a healthy Christian approach to anger? Anger is a message, a revelation. Looking at and understanding the conflict we experience is a key step in illuminating the situation we find ourselves in... If we are attempting to hear God's word, we must listen to anger as carefully as we listen to joy, peace, fear, and fatigue.

20.244
Geoffrey Fisher
Archbishop of Canterbury

1 [To Pope John XXIII on the occasion of the first meeting of the Archbishop of Canterbury and the Pope since the Reformation] I'm sorry we're late, we misread the timetables. But there—nobody's infallible.

20.245
George Florovsky
Russian Orthodox theologian

1 Creation by its very existence witnesses to and proclaims its creaturehood, it proclaims that it has been produced.

20.246
Gertrude von le Fort
Roman Catholic writer on women and religion

1 [To the Church]

Mother, I lay my head between your hands:
protect me from yourself.

20.247
Harry Emerson Fosdick
North American Baptist minister

1 The man of faith may face death as Columbus faced his first voyage from the shores of Spain. What lies beyond the sea he cannot tell; all his special expectation may be mistaken, but his insight into the clear meaning of present facts may persuade him beyond doubt that the sea has another shore.

2 God is not a cosmic bell-boy for whom we can press a button to get things.

3 No man need stay the way he is.

4 An atheist is a man who has no invisible means of support.

5 Democracy assumes that there are extra-ordinary possibilities in ordinary people.

6 It is cynicism and fear that freeze life; it is faith that thaws it out, releases it, sets it free.

7 Hating people is like burning down your own house to get rid of a rat.

20.248
Lona Fowler
North American poet

1 Jesus Christ was the Human of
God's Middle-Time
Between Creation and... Accomplishment.
Through him God said of Creation,
'Without mistake'.
And of Accomplishment,
'Without doubt'.

2 Jesus Christ is the Completer
of unfinished people
with unfinished work
in unfinished times.

20.249
Matthew Fox
North American priest and theologian

1 There is no Easter without a Good Friday.

2 There is one flow, one divine energy, one divine word in the sense of one creative energy flowing through all things, all time, all space. We are part of that flow and we need to listen to it rather than to assume arrogantly that our puny words are the only words of God.

3 When humans cannot welcome the cosmos and reverence it as the blessing it is, then we will fight it. Along with everything else. An ad on television in our time boasts a man in suit and tie talking tranquilly of our need to buy an Atari game for adults and children alike in which we can 'destroy entire planets'.

4 The Good News that Jesus brings is News that all are considered royal persons by God, all have rights, all have divine dignity. He is sensitive to the pain that the oppressed undergo but insists that no one can rob them of their divine and royal dignity.

5 Hospitality is about a relationship—one cannot be hospitable without guests. God not only plays the host for us and becomes the banquet for us; God also has become guest for us. This is one of the deep meanings of the incarnation, that God let go of hosting long enough to become guest as well.

6 Jesus chose the way and the lifestyle of the storyteller, the parable-maker who fashions a new creation out of the holy materials of the only creation that we all share in common: the birds, the lilies of the field, the fishes caught, the fig tree in bloom, the sheep versus the goats, the leaven in the bread, the mustard seeds of the world, and the rains that fall on just and unjust alike.

7 The wonderful working mysteries that are our bodies are filled with darkness. Our heart works just fine—in the dark. Our livers, our intestines, our brain, all the beautiful and harmonious and working parts of our blessed bodies go about their everyday business... completely in the dark. Isn't that wonderful?

8 Facing the darkness, admitting the pain, allowing the pain to be pain, is never easy. That is why courage—big-heartedness—is the most essential virtue on the spiritual journey.

9 Still another energy derived from suffering is the manner in which letting pain be pain links us with others. All social movements and organization were born of pain.

10 A visit to the desert is a letting go of all things that occupy one; therefore the desert represents a 'no-thing' or a nothingness experience. One is refreshed in this desert.

11 Pruning creates strength, richness, depth, though temporarily pruning hurts and conjures up doubt and fear. It takes a wise gardener to know when and how and how much to cut back a beautiful rose. It takes a wise parent to prune each child according to the needs of that child. So it takes a wise individual to prune himself or herself according to one's unique needs and timing.

20.250
Frances Dominica
English Anglican religious sister

1 With death there is the pain of loss, the pain of separation, and there is the promise of eternal life, and the two things can't be separated.

2 Some of our oldest sisters in community are the most courageous about abandoning old ways and accepting new.

20.251
Lawrence Freeman
English Benedictine

1 Solitude is essentially the discovery and acceptance of our uniqueness.

2 To see God is not to see anything extraordinary but to see ordinary things as they really are.

3 Silence is the quickest cure for intolerance and the best antidote for religious arrogance.

20.252
Paolo Freire
Latin American radical educationalist

1 The oppressed must realize that they are fighting not merely for freedom from hunger, but for... freedom to create and to construct, to wonder and to venture.

20.253
Joan Mary Fry
Quaker

1 I believe it is of real value to our earthly life to have the next life in mind, because if we shut it out of our thoughts we are starving part of our spiritual nature—we are like children who fail to grow up—none the finer children for that.

20.254
Aurelia T. Fule
Hungarian-American Presbyterian theologian

1 It would be hard to say what hurts women more—the church's separation from human reality or from divine reality.

2 We cherish the church as a corporate and committed body whose government is theologically informed and intended to involve the whole people of God through elected representatives. We are therefore a church that is non-clerically governed.

20.255
Monica Furlong
English feminist writer

1 We cannot treat the human embryo as cheap and worthless without passing judgement on all human life, including our own.

2 It is not surprising that boredom—in human beings so often the mask of fear—is a problem in marriage as it is in prayer.

3 It used to irritate a friend of mine that when he went to confession he never got the chance to tell the priest the good things he had done.

4 If envy was not such a tearing thing to feel it would be the most comic of sins. It is usually, if not always, based on a complete misunderstanding of another person's situation.

5 To fast is to learn to love and appreciate food, and one's own good fortune in having it.

6 Our problem is not that we take refuge from action in spiritual things, but that we take refuge from spiritual things in action.

7 The extraordinary expression, 'making love', 'to make love', might have lent sexuality, the joining of men and women in wholeness, a very special place in Christian thought, instead of which we have scorned and denied the marvellous gift.

8 I feel that the human condition is rather like being a fly crawling slowly over a huge and complicated pattern on the wallpaper and trying, from this point of disadvantage, yet also of immediate experience, to calculate the appearance of the whole.

20.256
Kathy Galloway
Scottish minister, writer and poet

1 Let us be different,
Let us not be the same,
You will be you, I will be me,
Each of us has our own name.

20.257
Alan Gaunt
English hymn-writer

1 Love's trinity, self-perfect, self-sustaining;
love which commands, enables and obeys:
you give yourself, in boundless joy, creating
one vast increasing harmony of praise.

20.258
Ivone Gebara
Roman Catholic sister from Brazil

1 Previously, there was never any mention of sexual difference with regard to those who wrote theology, since it was obvious that the task was something proper to men.

2 It is as though a strong wind had begun to blow, opening eyes and loosening tongues, shifting stances, enabling arms to reach out to new embraces and hands to take up other tools, impelling feet to take other steps, raising the voice so its song and its lament might be heard. Woman begins to take her place as agent of history.

20.259
Giulio Girardi
Latin American theologian

1 I believe you won't find anywhere absolute criteria that will give you the certainty of not being wrong, and this risk of being wrong has to be taken because you can't be a person without taking the risk of being wrong.

20.260
Aruna Gnanadason
Indian feminist theologian

1 Asian feminists are growing in consciousness of the need to affirm the community dimension of Asian society... Women find their dignity, their selfhood, and reclaim their right to define what their womanhood is, what their femininity means—all *in community*.

20.261
Bonganjalo Goba
South African Congregational minister and writer

1 God is calling every black person to sacrifice his or her individual longing and luxury to long for a dynamic community of love where every black person finds meaningful existence breaking through oppression, injustice and disinheritance.

20.262
Betty Govinden
Representative of the Anglican Church of the Province of Southern Africa

1 There must be responsible openness, a willingness to probe questions systematically and consistently, to wrestle with them, under the guidance of the Holy Spirit, in order to discern new understandings. It saddens me when the virtues of 'the stature of waiting' are cited in a formulaic way as a solution to controversy and deadlock, particularly when the waiting has not been active, interactive, and creative.

20.263
Aelred Graham
English Benedictine monk

1 It is the unitive knowledge of God which... is what salvation is all about. The test of its genuineness, needless to say, is not in any feelings or emotions or private visions, but in how realistically we recognise the people we meet with day by day, not as individuals separated off from us, but as one with ourselves.

2 Love without insight is blind, frustrating to the lover and the beloved alike. Wisdom without compassion operates only in the realm of theory.

20.264
Billy Graham
North American evangelist

1 The Christian life is not a way 'out', but a way 'through' life.

2 I just want to lobby for God.

3 Christians are the only people in the world who have anything to be happy about.

4 Just because you go to church it doesn't mean to say that you are a born again Christian.

5 Anxiety is the natural result when our hopes are centred in anything short of God and his will for us.

6 We take excellent care of our bodies, which we have for only a lifetime; yet we let our souls shrivel, which we will have for eternity.

7 Being a Christian is more than just an instantaneous conversion—it is a daily process whereby you grow to be more and more like Christ.

8 It is unnatural for Christianity to be popular.

9 To deny self is to become a nonconformist. The Bible tells us not to be conformed to this world either physically or intellectually or spiritually.

10 Most of us follow our conscience as we follow a wheelbarrow. We push it in front of us in the direction we want to go.

11 Envy takes the joy, happiness, and contentment out of living.

12 God has given us two hands—one for receiving and the other for giving.

13 A real Christian is a person who can give his pet parrot to the town gossip.

14 Be to the world a sign that while we as Christians do not have all the answers, we do care and know about the questions.

15 If a person gets his attitude toward money straight, it will help straighten out almost every other area in his life.

16 The Devil is sincere, but he is sincerely wrong.

17 If I had my time again, I would be stronger on social injustices and less involved in parties and politics.

18 The kingdom of God needs you.

20.265
Ruth Bell Graham
North American writer

1 I think it's important to teach our children—as the Bible says—line upon line, precept upon precept, here a little, there a little. If you try to teach a child too rapidly, much will be lost. But the time for teaching and training is preteen. When they reach the teenage years, it's time to shut up and start listening.

20.266
Jacquelyn Grant
North American theologian

1 If theology, like the church, has no word for Black women, its conception of liberation is inauthentic.

20.267
Caroline C. Graveson
Quaker educationalist

1 There is a daily round for beauty as well as for goodness.

20.268
Frederick Pratt Green
English Methodist minister, poet, playwright

1 Of all my prayer, may this be chief:
Till faith is fully grown,
Lord, disbelieve my unbelief,
And claim me as your own.

20.269
Michael Green
Anglican clergyman and evangelist

1 What died in Adam and Eve when they ate the apple was that intimate, unspoiled relationship they'd had with God.

2 Death, that final curb on freedom, has itself suffered a death blow through the resurrection of Jesus.

3 Each of us will have our own different ways of expressing love and care for the family. But unless that is a high priority, we may find that we may gain the whole world and lose our own children.

4 Don't be so arrogant as to suppose that the truth is no bigger than your understanding of it.

5 The Devil has got to be resisted, not merely deprecated.

6 If it takes temptation and sin to show God in his true colours and Satan in his, something has been saved from the wreck.

7 Jesus is alive and doing things!

20.270
Graham Greene
English Roman Catholic novelist

1 The church condemns violence, but it condemns indifference more harshly. Violence can be the expression of love, indifference never.

20.271
Mary Grey
British feminist theologian

1 Those who criticize women for rocking the boat, for not keeping the peace, for disturbing order, fail to grasp the sheer power of women's love and loyalty for Church and faith in the transforming leaven of community. What is unseen is the pure generosity of service, the capacity to suffer for the realization of an ideal.

2 If we carry on investing our spiritual energies in words which have become overloaded with the baggage of centuries from which we are attempting to break free, it has to be asked if God's word can still speak to us today with power.

3 In the birthing experience we are given a 'letting go' of self—in pain and struggle—for the creation of new being. We are given the sense of our physical bodies falling or even being torn apart. We have lost our 'centred self'. Nobody can reach us in this struggle, neither husband, lover, nor parent. We are in the dark, alone, in that primeval womb of chaos from which all life emerged. And yet, in that very darkness we can meet God as creative centre.

4 The more we love and are interconnected, the more we suffer separation.

20.272
Bede Griffiths
English Benedictine monk who lived in an ashram in India

1 In Jesus we see the point in the evolution of the universe when the divine consciousness took possession of a human soul and body and the plan of God in creation from the beginning was revealed.

20.273
Gustavo Gutiérrez
Peruvian liberation theologian

1 Men are called to meet the Lord insofar as they constitute a community, a people. It is a question not so much of a vocation to salvation as a convocation.

2 Knowledge is not the conformity of the mind to the given, but an immersion in the process of transformation and construction of a new world.

3 For me theology is the consciousness that a community or a Christian generation has about its faith at a given moment. Theologies are called upon to succeed one another: they are successive understandings of faith.

4 Mystical language expresses the gratuitousness of God's love; prophetic language expresses the demands this love makes.

5 Emphasis on the practice of justice and on solidarity with the poor must never become an obsession and prevent our seeing that this commitment reveals its value and ultimate meaning only within the vast and mysterious horizon of God's gratuitous love.

6 Jesus did not compose this psalm [22], he inherited it. It had its origin in the suffering of a believer, perhaps someone who in some way represented his people. The important thing is that Jesus made it his own and, while nailed to the cross, offered to the Father the suffering and abandonment of all humankind. This radical communion with the suffering of human beings brought him down to the deepest level of history at the very moment when his life was ending.

7 Jesus' cry on the cross renders more audible and more penetrating the cries of all the Jobs, individual and collective, of human history. To adopt a comparison that Bonhoeffer uses in another context, the cry of Jesus is the *cantus firmus*, the leading voice to which all the voices of those who suffer unjustly are joined.

8 Only if we know how to be silent and involve ourselves in the suffering of the poor will we be able to speak out of their hope. Only if we take seriously the suffering of the innocent and live the mystery of the cross amid that suffering, but in the light of Easter, can we prevent our theology from being 'windy arguments'.

9 Theology does not produce pastoral activity—rather it reflects upon it... This is a theology which does not stop with reflecting on the world, but rather tries to be part of the process through which the world is transformed.

20.274
John Habgood
English Anglican, former Archbishop of York

1 My conversion was embarrassingly quick.

2 It *offends* me if people think they know too much about God... because the language about God only makes sense if it refers to that which is actually *beyond* human experience.

3 The growth of Christian experience over the centuries can be interpreted as some sort of conversation of faith where people have learned to trust that the world has a meaning, and so have found one.

4 In man's very freedom there is the possibility that it might be used in ways that are destructive.

5 I see the whole point of pain of creation as being precisely to create that which can respond freely to a reality which otherwise could so easily dominate it.

6 A constant feature of liberalism is the wish to take seriously the intellectual climate in which faith has to be lived.

20.275
Catharina J.M. Halkes
Dutch feminist theologian

1 Spirituality does not begin in an empty place; it does not just hang in mid-air or drift aimlessly. It arises in a given context, is based on certain values, and can be an inspiration for individual people but equally for groups and movements striving for a particular goal or moved by a particular ideal.

2 We can only grow as people by living in relationships, by in-depth communication, and by orientating ourselves towards justice and charity. Through this attitude we learn to live in 'correct proportions'.

3 The Church is not a goal in itself; it is an instrument of salvation for people, for everyone. We therefore defraud the world if we only speak of God's presence when God's word is proclaimed or the sacraments are celebrated... If we can imagine the world as God's body, we not only include all people, but also all structures in which people gather together; we include the whole of created reality.

20.276
Dag Hammarskjöld
Swedish statesman

1 For what has been—thanks!
For what shall be—yes!

2 If even dying is to be made a social function, then, please, grant me the favour of sneaking out on tip-toe without disturbing the party.

3 Your cravings as a human animal do not become a prayer just because it is God you ask to attend to them.

4 The longest journey is the journey inward.

5 Never, for the sake of peace and quiet, deny your own experience or convictions.

6 We are not permitted to choose the frame of our destiny. But what we put into it is ours.

7 We cannot afford to forget any experience, even the most painful.

8 Goodness is something so simple:
Always live for others, never to seek one's own advantage.

9 Is life so wretched? Isn't it rather your hands which are too small, your vision which is muddied? You are the one who must grow up.

10 To let oneself be bound by a duty from the moment you see it approaching is part of the integrity that alone justifies responsibility.

11 Your life is without a foundation if, in any matter, you choose on your own behalf.

12 You have not done enough, you have never done enough, so long as it is still possible that you have something to contribute.

13 Pray that your loneliness may spur you into finding something to live for, great enough to die for.

14 In our era the road to holiness necessarily passes through the world of action.

15 In the last analysis, it is our conception of death which decides our answers to all the questions that life puts to us.

16 Do you create or do you destroy?

20.277
Charles Handy
British economist and management consultant

1 Sin, in a way, is God's gift to man.

2 The two classes of people who are my particular friends in the gospels are the crooks and the crocks... Our weakness and our sinfulness are our greatest claims on the mercy of God.

3 The Church is rather like a compost heap... the whole point of a compost heap is that after due process of maturing, it should be spread around.

20.278
F.C. Happold
English schoolmaster and writer

1 The spiritual exercise of the radiation of love is perhaps the most important prayer of transformation which anyone can make.

20.279
Michael Hare Duke
Scottish Episcopal bishop, peace activist and hymn-writer

1 I believe that the first thing about the cross is that it is a declaration of the way God is: not an attitude of 'Down on your knees you rotten little sinner'... but a statement that God is vulnerable.

2 Love releases us for taking
one more risk than we might dare;
glory breaks through dark and danger,
shows the Lord transfigured there.
God who planted our affections,
help your gifts to grow more free,
fan in us the fires of loving,
daring, dancing Trinity.

20.280
Georgia Harkness
North American Methodist theologian and social activist

1 The assumption that what we take on faith we take with closed minds, as if we had blinders on to shut out whatever light might creep in from other sources, lies at the root of the quarrel between religion and science.

2 One can believe in God with a very complete set of arguments, yet not have any faith that makes a difference in living.

3 The basic atheism is unwillingness to commit our lives to God's keeping.

20.281
Richard Harries
English Anglican Bishop of Oxford

1 It's fundamental to my belief in God that he or she discloses him- or herself to all people in all cultures at all times, because all human beings are capable of having an apprehension of God.

2 The church has been pushed to the edges and is now largely associated with people's pastimes and leisure activities. People go to church in the same way they might play bowls or skittles or go to the pub.

3 The Church is walking a tightrope. The clergy are walking a tightrope. And as we near the end of this century, I sometimes wonder how we will keep our balance.

20.282
Beverly Wildung Harrison
North American social ethicist

1 Anger denied subverts community. Anger expressed directly is a mode of taking the other seriously, of caring.

2 If we lack self-respect we... become the sorts of people who can neither see nor hear each other.

3 I believe that our world is on the verge of self-destruction and death because the society as a whole has so deeply neglected that which is most human and most valuable and the most basic of all the works of love—the work of human communication, of caring and nurturance, of tending the personal bonds of community.

20.283
Adrian Hastings
British theologian

1 Without prayer and its grounding in faith... the human city and its politics remain irredeemable. Selfishness and the corruption of sectional interests are too strong. But without politics prayer becomes a selfish ego-trip, an escape from that burden of secular reality for which every one of us is inherently responsible. A way to God which is not a way back hour by hour to our neighbour on the streets of Sarajevo is the way to a God who does not deserve either to be worshipped or to exist.

2 For better or worse, the world sets the Church's agenda, and in so far as the Church ignores that fact, it must become irrelevant and marginal.

20.284
Stanley Hauerwas
North American theologian

1 For the Christian people there are no people beyond the power of God's word. Christians know no 'barbarians', but only strangers whom we hope to make our friends.

2 The church is finally known by the character of the people who constitute it.

3 Our greatest illusion and deception, therefore, is that we are a peaceable people, nonviolent to the core. We are nonviolent as long as no one challenges our turf.

20.285
Rosemary Haughton
North American theologian and writer on spirituality

1 Each of us has a theological work to do. We may think we haven't but we can't help it, because every time we make a decision, or refuse to make one, we are showing whether we are with Jesus or against him. We are saying something about what we think Christianity is.

2 The incarnation is a happening both unique and ordinary. It is so complete and absolute of its kind that it has no parallels, no precedents, no successors, but the flesh-taking of God as Jesus is a unique example of the kind of ordinary event I want to call 'breakthrough'.

3 I think it's natural historically that Christianity developed the idea of a separate priesthood, but it's not scriptural.

20.286
Mary Hayter
British Anglican minister

1 Any attribution of sexuality to God is a reversion to paganism.

20.287
Margaret Heathfield
Quaker, professional counsellor

1 Over and over again our spiritual tradition tells us that our will is the part of us which

God is interested in, which is needed to fulfil the Kingdom. It is the hardest part of ourselves to commit trustfully, but it is the part of us which is most of use. If we fail to follow our promptings we shall miss God, and God will miss us.

2 There is also a potential clash between our spiritual liberty and our need for coherence. How many variations can we hold together before we cease to feel any coherence ourselves, or before we appear incoherent to others outside?

3 We [Quakers] often say we have no priest, but that is not so. The fact is that we are all priests, or potential priests. In the same way, we may think we have no leaders, but that is not so either. We are all leaders, or potential leaders. Just as we are all required to be prepared to minister through the spoken word, we are all required to be prepared to receive a leading, or a prompting which may call us and others in directions we had not dreamt of.

20.288
John Heath-Stubbs
Anglican poet and critic

1 Look, I am one of the morning stars,
shouting for joy—
And not the least honoured among
those shining brothers,
O my planetary children—now that my
dark daughter,
The prodigal Earth, is made an honest
woman of;
Out of her gapped womb, her black
and grimy tomb,
Breaks forth the Crowned, victory in
his pierced hands—
Benedicite, benedicite, benedicite omnia opera.

20.289
Margaret Hebblethwaite
Journalist, theologian and writer on spirituality

1 We will not find God in our homes unless we stop and pray there.

2 If God is love, then let our love speak to us of God. If God is good, then let what is good speak to us of God. If God is joy, then let what fills us with joy speak to us of God. If God is peace, then let what brings us peace speak to us of God. If God is life, then let what is full of life speak to us of God.

3 If God can be found in all things, then there is nothing at all that can happen to us that we need fear.

20.290
John Heenan
Roman Catholic prelate

1 I knew that prudence was the most highly prized virtue in episcopal candidates and I did not count it among my attributes.

20.291
Monika Hellwig
North American theologian and ecumenist

1 Unfortunately, in our society we keep death hidden. Few people have or seek the opportunity to witness the death of others... We do not have a Christian understanding of death in which the spectator is not idle at all but represents the active support and encouragement of the community. To witness death, however... demands that one have come to terms rather radically with one's own approaching death as a dimension of life in the present.

20.292
Carter Heyward
North American feminist theologian

1 Vulnerability... is the willingness and ability to be seen as well as to see, to be touched as well as to touch. Vulnerability is the giving up of control, the turning of oneself over to the common life, not to be absorbed, stepped on, or negated, but rather to experience ourselves as co-creators of the world we want and believe in.

20.293
John Hick
British theologian

1 Jesus' specially intimate awareness of God, his consequent spiritual authority and his efficacy as Lord and as giver of new life, required in his disciples an adequate language in which to speak about their master. He had to be thought of in a way commensurate with the total discipleship which he evoked.

2 The outgrowing of biblical fundamentalism was a slow and painful process which has unhappily left the church scarred and divided, and we are still living amidst the tension between a liberal and a continuing and today resurgent fundamentalist Christianity. The church has not yet found a way to unite the indispensable intellectual and moral insights of the one with the emotional fervour and commitment of the other.

3 It is not the religions themselves that are true, and save anyone, but God. God saves men and women within the Christian way, the Muslim way, the Jewish way, the Buddhist way.

20.294
Teresa M. Hinga
Lecturer at Kenyatta University, Kenya

1 It could be said, then, that these two images of Christ, that of Christ the conqueror who seemed to legitimize the subjugation of whole races, and Christ the liberator, glimpses of whom could sometimes be seen in some of the charity work that missionaries were doing for Africans, found expression in missionary praxis. The Christ of the missionary enterprise was, therefore, an ambivalent one.

2 For Christ to become meaningful in the context of [African] women's search for emancipation, he would need to be a concrete and personal figure who engenders hope in the oppressed by taking their (women's) side, to give them confidence and courage to persevere...

20.295
H.A. Hodges
English theologian

1 However one may analyse in detail the work of Christ for us and in us, one must always at last sum it up and draw it together in the simple formula: 'He in us and we in him'.

2 Christ is the true Temple, the Bethel, over which the heavens stand open and the angels of God ascend and descend; and we who are his members are also the loving stones of the temple which is his Body.

3 As all the prayers of the Church cluster around that supreme prayer [of the eucharist], it follows that all the faithful, whenever they pray as Christians... are in their degree performing a priestly act.

4 Our salvation has nothing in common with paying a ransom except this, that we are delivered from slavery at a great personal cost to the deliverer.

20.296
Leonard Hodgson
English Anglican theologian

1 How many clergy, as Trinity Sunday draws near, groan within themselves at the thought that it will be their duty to try to expound this dry and abstract doctrine to congregations for whom they anticipate that it will have but little interest?

2 Our first task... must be to consider how to teach trinitarian religion, how to initiate our congregations into the trinitarian way of life.

3 The formula for the Christian life is seeking, finding and doing the Father's will in the Father's world with the companionship of the Son by the guidance and strength of the Spirit. That is the meaning of our membership of the Church.

20.297
Violet Holdsworth
English Quaker

1 'Cream must always rise to the surface.' True. But other substances rise to the surface besides cream... 'Is my message cream or scum?' may be an unusual and is certainly a very homely query. Still, it is one that every speaker... should honestly face.

20.298
Jean Fox Holland
North American writer

1 How many am I?
With all my children's children
Love makes me plural.

2 One who knows sorrow
For a long or little while
Learns a new language.

3 Journeying is more
Than reaching destinations.
Journeying is more.

20.299
Michael Hollings
English Roman Catholic priest and writer

1 Making a space in life for God and prayer radically changes the whole of that life, if it is lived out seriously.

2 God is the great listener. Out of his silent being, he is with us silently, he speaks to us silently, he asks us to learn the response which comes from the deep part of our being. He asks us to learn from him how to listen.

3 The Christian is not there always to 'jolly people along', but rather to weep sometimes, be silent sometimes and rejoice sometimes.

20.300
Richard Holloway
Scottish Episcopalian bishop and writer

1 I'm glad now that I discovered God before I discovered the Bible.

2 The Bible is its own best critic. It points us to the bible within the Bible, the god beyond God. The key to it all... is the warning against idolatry.

3 Establishment, ministry, ecclesial structures, theological methods are all temporary instruments that inevitably reach their use-by date. If we cling to them beyond that they become idols.

4 We either treat Scripture ahistorically, denying everything we know about its origin and development, or we treat it heuristically, recognizing that God's mystery comes through it, but has to be searched for and interpreted and can no longer be read off like an automatic computer print-out.

5 There are no more tragic figures in life and in literature than the cold and lonely figures who are so afraid of the fires in their own hearts that they would put them out rather than run the danger of being burned by them.

20.301
Theressa Hoover
North American theologian

1 To be a woman, black, and active in religious institutions in the American scene is to labor under triple jeopardy.

20.302
Julie Hopkins
British Baptist minister and theologian

1 Women who claim to be church whilst simultaneously rejecting the exclusively male language and androcentric world-view of Christian liturgy, doctrine and morality are women engaged on a pilgrimage into the heart of faith beyond structures and images.

2 Each woman is a temple of the Holy Spirit and is a full member of the Body of Christ (in other words she can have a messianic function).

20.303
Frank Houghton
English missionary bishop in China

1 This is the road of my desire—
Learning to love as God loves me,
Ready to pass through flood or fire
With Christ's unwearying constancy.

20.304
Leslie Houlden
English Anglican biblical scholar

1 ['Everything bends.'] There is nothing in life, or in belief, which is rigid, unchanging, not subject to movement and development, not (we may even say) more beautiful for giving itself readily—and being seen to do so—to such readiness to 'bend'.

20.305
Caryll Houselander
English Roman Catholic spiritual writer

1 Our Lord said to his Apostles: 'It is expedient for you that I go away.' It is the same for us. We know him only by continually learning him anew; we get away from false gods only by continually seeking him; we hold him only by losing him.

2 There should be, even in the busiest day, a few moments when we can close our eyes and let God possess us.

3 And we,
syllables of the word,
are uttering Him
who utters the secret of God.

20.306
Trevor Huddleston
English Anglican missionary, anti-apartheid campaigner

1 The cliché 'charity begins at home' has done more damage than any other in the English language.

2 We must recognise that the motives and forces behind racism are the Anti-Christ, denying that man is made in the divine image.

3 The young want to be challenged by something sacrificial. They are rejecting phoney values and standards. The only hope is to create a community that doesn't live by false values.

4 If we are truly Catholic, then universality, the proclamation that this is God's world, God's universe—is surely a prior concern to that which would make institutionalized Christianity our chief objective. It is inter-faith ecumenism... that should be the aim for us all at this moment in history.

5 Living perpetually with a flood of information pouring over us from radio and television and the press [makes it] almost physically impossible to stand back and hear what is being said, still less to stand back and understand it.

20.307
Joyce Huggett
English author

1 Saying goodbye to a loved one is not the same as forgetting them or ceasing to think of them. It is simply the way of owning the loss, integrating it, accepting its restrictions and limitations and saying yes to life without the one who has died.

20.308
Gerard W. Hughes
British Jesuit writer

1 In our journey towards God we proceed like those small birds whose flight is in loops. They always seem to be about to drop, but the drop in their flight seems to urge them forwards.

2 The Church must encourage the critical element in its members. If it fails to do so, then the individual will not be able to integrate religious belief with everyday experience or, put in other words, God will be excluded from most of the individual's life until religion comes to be considered a private but harmless eccentricity of a minority.

3 The source of most pain is in the conflict between the reality we would like to encounter and the reality in which we find ourselves, in our inability to shape reality to our own requirements. Yet the obdurate quality of reality, its refusal to be shaped by our demands, is a blessing, because it forces us out of the prison of our own conditioning, our own narrowness, and frees us from the grooves of our habitual thinking.

4 All ideologies and 'isms', all visions and dreams, all plans and policies are dangerous and destructive if they are not conceived in hearts which are sensitive to beauty and can appreciate things for their own sake. That is why a religion which cannot see beyond rules and regulations, doctrinal and moral formulae, can have such a negative effect upon its followers.

20.309
Basil Hume

English Roman Catholic Cardinal Archbishop of Westminster

1 If you accept that Jesus is the revelation and manifestation of the Father, then you are a follower of Christ and so a Christian.

2 Whenever the poor are afflicted or neglected, or whenever human freedom and dignity is not respected, then the Church has a duty to sound a prophet's note, and it must be prepared to be unpopular on matters which concern politicians as well.

20.310
Mary Hunt

North American Roman Catholic feminist theologian

1 Because in friendships people express their worst capacities as well as their best, we all learn something about limitations. We see how capable we are of evil, of hurting and being hurt, of forgiving and being forgiven.

2 Friendship is an honest mirror, but it must be allowed to reflect or its power is lost.

20.311
William Ralph Inge

English theologian and Dean of St Paul's Cathedral

1 Christianity is a revolutionary idealism which estranges revolutionaries by its idealism and conservatives by its drastic revaluation of earthly goods.

2 I am afraid the clergyman's God is too often head of the clerical profession.

3 The clergy should regard themselves as physicians of the soul.

4 The Gospel is essentially a message of spiritual redemption, not of social reform.

5 Prayer gives a man the opportunity of getting to know a gentleman he hardly ever meets. I do not mean his maker, but himself.

6 I know as much about the afterlife as you do—nothing. I must wait and see.

7 A cat can be trusted to purr when she is pleased, which is more than can be said about human beings.

8 The gospel was not good advice but good news.

9 I have never understood why it should be considered derogatory to the Creator to suppose that he has a sense of humour.

10 Christianity promises to make men free; it never promises to make them independent.

11 Whoever marries the spirit of this age will find himself a widower in the next.

12 Worry is interest paid on trouble before it falls due.

13 The aim of education is the knowledge not of fact but of values.

14 When our first parents were driven out of Paradise, Adam is believed to have remarked to Eve: 'My dear, we live in an age of transition.'

15 Religion is a way of walking, not a way of talking.

16 The enemies of Freedom do not argue; they shout and they shoot.

17 Revivals are shallow things, since they aim at reproducing what never existed or what has perished with the age that gave it birth.

18 The world is a much worse place than I ever thought it.

19 Religion is caught, not taught.

20.312
Ada María Isasi-Díaz
Cuban-born liberation theologian

1 To name oneself is one of the most powerful human acts... In our [Hispanic women's] search for a name of our own, we have turned to our music, an intrinsic part of the soul of our culture. In our songs, love songs as well as protest songs, we are simply called *mujer*. And so, those of us who make a preferential option for *mujeres* are *mujeristas*.

2 *Mujerista* theology helps us to discover and affirm the presence of God in the midst of our communities and the revelation of God in our daily lives.

3 Our preferred future breaks into our present oppression in many different ways. We must recognize those eschatological glimpses and rejoice in them and struggle to make those glimpses become our whole horizon.

20.313
Martin Israel
Lecturer in pathology; priest and spiritual director

1 In this strange life we grow through adversity rather than through success. The greatest lessons we have to learn are those concerned with loss, not gain.

2 Wholeness does not consist in removing a present source of travail; it demands a complete transformation of the person's attitude to life, which in turn is an outward sign of a transfigured personality.

3 Only one who has borne the wounds of suffering and has emerged battered but regenerated can offer much practical help to the person seeking liberation.

4 We can do nothing if we hate ourselves, or feel that all our actions are doomed to failure because of our own worthlessness. We have to take ourselves, good and bad alike, on trust before we can do anything.

5 Holidays, relaxation, and the simple pleasures of life are as important for the mystic as they are for other people.

6 Meditation is no panacea.

7 The spiritual quest is a continuous act of faith, a faith that spiritual experience is the most real thing in human life and that all other categories of experience are subordinate to the fact of God.

20.314
Jesse Jackson
US civil-rights leader, politician, minister of religion

1 Don't let them break your spirit, we have picked too much cotton for that.

2 You know the politicians will always ask the question 'Is it expedient?', then the question 'Is it right?', but the prophets ask the question 'Is it right?'. The Church must keep asking the question 'Is it right?'.

20.315
Mahalia Jackson
American gospel singer

1 God can make you anything you want to be, but you have to put everything in his hands.

20.316
Eric James
English Anglican priest and activist

1 Travel suddenly opens the windows of the soul to the reality of God in other people.

2 If the humble Hindu on the Ganges can't be saved unless he become C. of E. or Baptist or R.C., then God is not the God I want to believe in.

3 Protest for the Christian is fundamentally positive, not negative. It is always fundamentally affirmation at cost, at risk, grounded in the present and central truths of the Christian faith.

4 The motive of protest for the Christian is always provided in him whose nature and whose name is love.

5 There is never an act of faith without risk.

6 Christian political action is the wielding of power in subordination to love, subordinate not in a general sort of way but in minute particulars.

20.317
Grace Jantzen
Canadian-born feminist theologian and ethicist

1 If one is going to do philosophy of religion, one ought to know something about religion, not learnt without the life of prayer, and without giving and receiving love of God and neighbour.

20.318
Karl Jaspers
German-born Swiss philosopher

1 I *am* only through communication with the other.

20.319
David Jenkins
English Anglican bishop and theologian

1 The world does not cohere. It shows manifestations of heavenly goodness and hellish badness—for which I have a word, and that is sin.

2 I often think that the glorious future will come when the Church of England is finally broken down and some of us will be able to break out. You never know, do you, how God is going to make or re-make things? But it will not happen easily, or without pain.

20.320
Elizabeth Jennings
English poet

1 Now deep in my bed
I turn and the world turns on the other side.

20.321
John XXIII
Pope who summoned the Second Vatican Council

1 [Letter to a boy who wanted to know whether to be a pope or a policeman] Anybody can be pope; the proof of this is that I have become one.

2 My bags are packed and I am ready to go.

3 [Said two days before his death] I am able to follow my own death step by step. Now I move softly towards the end.

4 The Ten Commandments, completed by the evangelical precepts of justice and charity, constitute the framework of individual and collective survival.

5 The habit of thinking ill of everything and everyone is tiresome to ourselves and to all around us.

6 It is not true that some human beings are by nature superior and others inferior. All men are equal in their natural dignity.

7 One must never confuse error and the person who errs.

8 It is easier for a father to have children than for children to have a real father.

9 Italians come to ruin most generally in one of three ways—women, gambling, and farming. My family chose the slowest one.

10 Perfume all your actions with the life-giving breath of prayer.

11 Even though human beings differ from one another by virtue of their ethnic peculiarities, they all possess certain common elements and are inclined by nature to meet each other in the world of spiritual values.

12 The accumulation of vast wealth while so many are languishing in misery is a grave transgression of God's law, with the consequence that the greedy, avaricious man is never at ease in his mind: he is in fact a most unhappy creature.

13 I offer my life as a sacrifice for the successful outcome of the Ecumenical Council and for peace among men.

14 Do not walk through time without leaving worthy evidence of your passage.

15 For a Christian who believes in Jesus and his Gospel, war is an iniquity and a contradiction.

16 It is becoming humanly impossible to regard war, in this atomic age, as a suitable means of re-establishing justice when some right has been violated.

20.322 John Paul II

Pope

1 Our divisions prevent our neighbours from hearing the Gospel as they should.

2 Every effort to make society sensitive to the importance of the family is a great service to humanity.

3 There is no law which lays it down that you must smile! But you can make a gift of your smile; you can be the heaven of kindness in your family.

4 Only love lasts forever. Alone, it constructs the shape of eternity in the earthly and short-lived dimensions of the history of man on the earth.

5 Man lives a really human life thanks to culture.

6 Only a world that is truly human can be a world that is peaceful and strong.

7 A constant danger with priests, even zealous priests, is that they become so immersed in the work of the Lord that they neglect the Lord of the work.

8 Sin is always a squandering of our humanity, a squandering of our most precious values.

9 Violence is always an offence, an insult to man, both to the one who perpetrates it and to the one who suffers it.

10 When Christ said 'I was in prison and you visited me,' he did not draw a distinction between the guilty and the innocent.

20.323 Malcolm Johnson

English Anglican priest, Vicar of St Botolph's, Aldgate

1 [St Botolph's] steeple points to 'The Other', not despising the world of money, markets and marriages but giving them meaning and direction.

20.324 William Johnston

Jesuit writer

1 To build one's activity on love and non-violence demands the greatest inner purification; one must constantly rid one's heart of inordinate desires, fears, and anxieties, but above all, one must cleanse oneself of anger.

2 If we are to be faithful to Jesus of Nazareth, if we are to be faithful to the gospel in the modern world, if we are to be faithful to the Holy Spirit acting in the Council and in the masses of people, in short if we are to be faithful to our vocation as Christians, we must join hands with people of other faiths.

3 Christian contemplation is the experience of being loved and of loving at the most profound level of psychic life and of spirit.

20.325 Alan Jones

North American Episcopalian clergyman and author

1 The desert... is a place of revelation and revolution. In the desert we wait, we weep, we learn to live.

2 Tears are agents of resurrection and transformation... They are a gift, and their fruit is always joy.

3 The believer is one who finds something of genuine substance under the sometimes exotic and exaggerated language of religion.

4 Both religion and therapy are in danger of idolatrous devotion to the God of the normal.

20.326
David Jones
English/Welsh poet

1 If we do not like our churches to reflect the sort of life we have, let us have a different sort of life, and the churches will change inevitably.

20.327
Roxanne Jordaan
Congregational minister, South Africa

1 Being black is synonymous with being oppressed and being exploited.

2 God used Moses to deliver the people of Israel, but it was Moses' mother who defied Pharaoh's orders. Consequently she saved a child and eventually she saved the house of Israel. And isn't it also wonderful that God so designed the body of the woman that it would bear Christ the Liberator?

20.328
Toyohiko Kagawa
Japanese social reformer and evangelist

1 I read somewhere that this young man, Jesus Christ, went about doing good. But I just go about.

2 Your greatest lack is that you do not know how to pray.

3 Theology is but an appendix to love, and an unreliable appendix!

4 [Speaking about helping the slum-dwellers of Kobe] If Christ were here, he would help them, and so must I.

5 O God, make me like Jesus Christ.

6 It is not necessary for me to go far afield in search of miracles. I am a miracle myself. My physical birth and my soul's existence are miracles. First and foremost, the fact that I was even born is a miracle.

7 Those who draw water from the wellspring of meditation know that God dwells close to their hearts.

8 All this famine of love, how it saddens my soul. There is not a drop of love anywhere.

20.329
Marianne Katoppo
Author of the first Asian women's theology

1 It is interesting to see how Jesus dealt with prostitutes. Perhaps it is not admissible to say that Mary Magdalene, commonly accepted as the first person Jesus revealed himself to after his resurrection, was a prostitute. The woman at the well in Samaria (John 4) definitely was, though, yet Jesus treated her as a person, not as an object: a safety-valve for male passion, or part of a sewage system.

20.330
Jacob Kattackal
Indian theological writer

1 Christianity teaches that Salvation is not merely a posthumous experience, but starts here in this life on earth; the life of grace is incipient already in our earthly sojourn; it sprouts here though it blossoms and fructifies in heaven. The relation between the 'this-worldly life of grace' and 'the next-world life of heaven' is that of the seed and the tree.

20.331
Helen Keller
North American author

1 When one door of happiness closes, another opens; but often we look so long at the closed door that we do not see the one which has been opened for us.

2 I am too happy in this world to think much about the future, except to remember that I have cherished friends awaiting me there in God's beautiful Somewhere.

20.332
Morton Kelsey
North American theologian and spiritual writer

1 With only sense experience and reason to go on, and with no rational place for an evil first cause, enlightened people simply dropped the devil from consideration. With direct psychic experience no longer admissible as evidence of his reality, the devil was as good as dead.

20.333
Bruce Kent
British Roman Catholic campaigner for nuclear disarmament, and peace activist

1 Above all I have been blessed with a sense of purpose which still hasn't failed.

2 One day it is going to dawn on the human race that war is as barbaric a means of resolving conflict as cannibalism is [as] a means of coping with diet deficiencies.

20.334
Alec King
Australian scholar

1 The artist's vision... is, when deeply undertaken, always a little shocking at first, for it means moving out of ourselves to a peremptory strangeness of life outside; but this shocking adventure into the unknown is the way to the experience of being taken over and fulfilled—to the sense of belonging to life which is finally so immeasurably richer in satisfaction than the illusion that life belongs to us.

20.335
Martin Luther King Jr
North American Baptist pastor and black civil-rights leader

1 The richer we have become materially, the poorer we have become morally and spiritually. We have learned to fly the air like birds and swim the sea like fish, but we have not yet learned the simple art of living together like brothers.

2 The church must be reminded that it is not the master or the servant of the state, but rather the conscience of the state.

3 I have lived with the conviction that unearned suffering is redemptive. There are some who still find the cross a stumbling block, others consider it foolishness. But I am more convinced than ever that it is the power of God to social and individual salvation.

4 A man who won't die for something is not fit to live.

5 It is still one of the tragedies of human history that the 'children of darkness' are frequently more determined and zealous than the 'children of light'.

6 Shattered dreams are the hallmark of our mortal life.

7 Forgiveness is not an occasional act, it is a permanent attitude.

8 Freedom is never voluntarily given by the oppressor; it must be demanded by the oppressed.

9 He who passively accepts evil is as much involved in it as he who helps to perpetuate it.

10 Courage faces fear and thereby masters it. Cowardice represses fear and is thereby mastered by it.

11 Injustice anywhere is a threat to justice everywhere.

12 Like anybody else, I would like to live a long life. Longevity has its place. But I'm not concerned about that now. I just want to do God's will.

13 I have a dream that my four little children will one day live in a nation where they will not be judged by the colour of their skin but by the content of their character.

14 We must learn that to expect God to do everything while we do nothing is not faith, but superstition.

15 I have decided to stick with love.
Hate is too great a burden to bear.

16 The good neighbour looks beyond the external accidents and discerns those inner qualities that make all men human and, therefore, brothers.

17 I want to be the white man's brother, not his brother-in-law.

18 Returning violence for violence multiplies violence, adding deeper darkness to a night already devoid of stars.

19 The modern choice is between non-violence and non-existence.

20 I've been to the mountain top. And I've looked over, and I've seen the promised land... I'm not fearing any man. Mine eyes have seen the glory of the coming of the Lord.

20.336
Ursula King
Theologian

1 The greatest religious problem today is how to be both a mystic and a militant; in other words, how to combine the search for an expansion of inner awareness with effective social action, and how to feel one's true identity in both.

2 Asia is the continent that challenges us most with its religious pluralism and its ancient spiritual traditions.

20.337
Bill Kirkpatrick
Canadian-born Anglican priest

1 When God's dead, I am dead. God inhabited me, created me. I'm in God and God's in me. You can't escape God. Sitting on the loo you're still with God. Having sex with somebody you're still with God.

2 I have been alongside 1,250 people living with HIV/AIDS during the past ten years. And I've been alongside about 350 when they've died, and buried about half of them. And it's been a wonderful experience in a way, a wonderful experience. Humbling. Taught me a lot about spirituality.

3 If you don't get close to people you can't love them.

20.338
Kazoh Kitamori
Japanese theologian

1 Our pain defeats us, and we fear it... because we regard it as an inevitable disaster falling upon us from *outside* us. As long as we try to escape it, we cannot resolve it.

2 We can conquer [pain] only when we seek it within ourselves and long for it. We can strengthen ourselves when we earnestly seek and desire pain to be part of our nature.

20.339
Kosuke Koyama
Japanese missionary and theologian

1 God walks 'slowly' because he is love. If he is not love he would have gone much faster. Love has its speed. It is an inner speed. It is a spiritual speed. It is a different kind of speed from the technological speed to which we are accustomed... It goes on in the depth of our life, whether we notice or not, whether we are currently hit by storm or not, at three miles an hour. It is the speed we walk and therefore it is the speed the love of God walks.

20.340
Una Kroll
English doctor and Anglican deacon

1 The cross preceded the resurrection; but the Resurrection has not abolished the cross. Suffering, sin, betrayal, cruelty of every kind, continued to exist after the crucifixion and they continue still. This is the failure of the cross. God made failure an instrument of victory.

2 [Shouted to the Church of England's General Synod from the gallery when they voted against the ordination of women, 1978] We asked you for bread and you gave us a stone.

3 Nothing else can withstand evil except the power of love.

4 The non-institutional Church throws up its own priests.

20.341
Bernadette Kunambi
Tanzanian laywoman and MP

1 While Christianity and a Western type of education gave the African woman the feeling of independence and the ability to stand on her own, to make decisions both in the family and in society, it robbed her of the traditional protection of the extended family system and of society, which in the past was the corner-stone of stability in married life... This is the dilemma for the African woman today: she is gaining what she wants, but she is losing what she needs.

20.342
Hans Küng
Swiss Roman Catholic theologian

1 When a pope's theoretically infallible, doctrinal opinions are treated as infallible; authoritarian abuse of power begins.

2 A Church which abandons the truth abandons itself.

3 It is without any doubt, then, significant that today there is a fundamental agreement between Catholic and Protestant theology, precisely in the theology of justification—the point at which Reformation theology took its departure. Despite all the difficulties, have we not, after these 400 years, come decidedly closer to one another also on the theological level?

4 The pope exists for the church, and not the church for the papacy. His primacy is not the primacy of sovereignty, but the primacy of service.

20.343
Kwok Pui-lan
Chinese biblical scholar

1 In the so-called 'non-Christian' world, we tell our sisters and brothers the biblical story that gives us inspiration for hope and liberation. But it must be told as an open invitation: what have you got to share?

2 The lifting up of every voice, the celebration of diversity, the affirmation of plurality, help us to see glimpses of the amazing grace of God in all cultures and all peoples.

3 Many of the metaphors of Christianity come out of the familial context and sexual relationships between persons, such as the Father and the Son, the Church as the Bride of Christ, and Adam and Eve as the first couple. The experiences of women, whose sexuality has been controlled and who suffer violence to their bodies, challenge these 'beloved' images.

20.344
Frank Lake
English psychiatrist and missionary

1 Preaching without listening may fail to create the communion of saints.

2 It is an astonishing fact that the events of the crucifixion of Jesus Christ portray every variety of human suffering and evil.

3 When a Christian minister becomes primarily a moralist he is creating insuperable difficulties in the way of pastoral dialogue. He remains a religious man, but he has ceased to be a Christian.

20.345
Geoffrey W.H. Lampe
English theologian and priest

1 Sight, or objective proof, is not the proper ground of faith.

2 I believe that Christ's Resurrection was not different in kind from what we may hope for through him; that our rising will be a sharing in that Resurrection.

20.346
William Q. Lash (Will Quinlan)
English Anglican Franciscan and Bishop of Bombay

1 The final retreat from the world must be earned in the world by the attainment of the right attitude to the things of the world which can only be learned there and nowhere else... Not only in his will, but in the season appointed by his will, is our peace. My hour will come, when it is his hour.

20.347
Mary Jo Leddy
North American journalist

1 The desire to live freely, to live meaningfully, robs death of its power. For some in El Salvador, a chosen death is preferable to mute submission to the murderous machinery of terror. It is a choice that promises liberation not only for oneself, but also for others.

20.348
Archie C.C. Lee
Chinese Old Testament scholar

1 Being the servant or spokesman of God the prophetic church should be brave enough to risk herself to remind the government that it has the power and responsibility to maintain the well-being and prosperity for the people.

20.349
Lee Shiu Keung
Chinese historian and theologian

1 The Chinese Church has come of age... The Church should not hesitate to experiment and be willing to take the risk of indigenization and thereby help its members to be truly Christians and truly members of their own culture. But our vision does not stop with an indigenous church. We are looking forward to a world culture and a world church, in which the Chinese tradition has an important role to play.

20.350
Madeleine L'Engle
North American author

1 How many of us call the devil by name today? If we see God's love manifested to us in the Incarnation, the life and death and resurrection of Jesus, then we need to also recognize the malignant force that would try to destroy God's love in a particular way too.

2 We live under illusion that if we can acquire complete control, we can understand God, or we can write the great American novel. But the only way we can brush against the hem of the Lord, or hope to be part of the creative process, is to have the courage, the faith, to abandon control.

3 I want to be open to God, not to what man says about God. I want to be open to revelation, to new life, to new birth, to new light.

4 This is the irrational season
When love blooms bright and wild.
Had Mary been filled with reason
There'd have been no room for the child.

5 The artist is a servant who is willing to be a birthgiver. In a very real sense the artist (male or female) should be like Mary who, when the angel told her that she was to bear the Messiah, was obedient to the command. Obedience is an unpopular word nowadays, but the artist must be obedient to the word, whether it be a symphony, a painting, or a story for a small child. I believe that each work of art, whether it is a work of great genius, or something very small, comes to the artist and says, 'Here I am. Enflesh me. Give birth to me.'

6 Half the world is starving; the other half is on a diet. We are not privileged because we deserve to be. Privilege accepted should mean responsibility accepted.

20.351
Graham Leonard

English Roman Catholic priest, former Anglican Bishop of London.

1 As far as I am concerned, the priesthood is not about performing priestly functions. It is about *being* a priest, like being a father.

2 I don't believe it was an accident that God became incarnate in a patriarchal society. I don't think it's a trivial argument to say that Our Lord only chose twelve male apostles.

3 The ordination of women involves a rejection of the way in which God chose to redeem us, a way which reflected the way he made us. I do not believe it was an accident that God chose to redeem us by being incarnate as a male.

20.352
C.S. Lewis

Irish-born writer, academic and Christian Apologist

1 Chastity is the most unpopular of our Christian virtues.

2 [On the death of his mother] It was sea and islands now. Atlantis had sunk.

3 Passionate grief does not link us with the dead, but cuts us off from them.

4 Forgiveness needs to be accepted, as well as given, before it is complete.

5 Joy is the serious business of heaven.

6 The long, dull, monotonous years of middle-aged prosperity or middle-aged adversity are excellent campaigning weather for the Devil.

7 The old Puritans took away the maypoles and the mince pies, but they did not bring in the millennium, they only brought in the Restoration.

8 Anxiety is not only a pain which we must ask God to assuage but also a weakness we must ask him to pardon—for he's told us to take no care for the morrow.

9 You never know how much you really believe anything until its truth or falsehood becomes a matter of life or death to you.

10 Christianity, if false, is of no importance, and if true, of infinite importance. The one thing it cannot be is moderately important.

11 Every story of conversion is a story of blessed defeat.

12 Relying on God has to begin all over again every day as if nothing had yet been done.

13 Everyone says forgiveness is a lovely idea, until they have something to forgive.

14 God cannot give us happiness and peace apart from himself, because it is not there. There is no such thing.

15 God whispers in our pleasures but shouts in our pain.

16 When pain is to be borne, a little courage helps more than much knowledge, a little human sympathy more than much courage, and the least tincture of the love of God more than all.

17 Joy is never in our power, and pleasure is. I doubt whether anyone who has tasted joy would ever, if both were in his power, exchange it for all the pleasure in the world.

18 We are born helpless. As soon as we are fully conscious we discover loneliness. We need others physically, emotionally, intellectually; we need them if we are to know anything, even ourselves.

19 The divine art of miracle is not an art of suspending the pattern to which events conform, but of feeding events into that pattern.

20 Gratitude looks to the past and love to the present; fear, avarice, lust and ambition look ahead.

21 If people knew how much ill-feeling Unselfishness occasions, it would not be so often recommended from the pulpit.

22 She's the sort of woman who lives for others—you can always tell the others by their hunted expression.

23 At present we are on the outside of the world, the wrong side of the door. We discern the freshness and purity of morning, but they do not make us fresh and pure. We cannot mingle with the splendours we see. But all the leaves of the New Testament are rustling with the rumour that it will not always be so. Someday, God willing, we shall get *in*.

20.353
Saunders Lewis
Welsh dramatist and poet

1 O thief who took paradise from the nails
of a gibbet,
Foremost of the *nobilitas* of heaven,
Before the hour of death pray that it may
be given to us
To perceive him and to taste him.

20.354
Pauline Reeder Liddle
North American writer

1 Dear God,
My props are out from under me today,
maybe they were the wrong kind of props.
Fear is creeping through the cracks
like little insects of prey.
My aloneness gathers round my shoulders.
I long for the feel of loving arms instead.

...

With power, and love, and a sound mind
help me to be free from fear.
I can move forward with joy
even through the dark moments that come.

Thank you, God.

20.355
David Martyn Lloyd-Jones
Welsh preacher and writer

1 Putting all the ecclesiastical corpses into one graveyard will not bring about a resurrection.

2 People who think that once they are converted all will be happy, have forgotten Satan.

3 The Gospel is open to all; the most respectable sinner has no more claim on it than the worst.

4 Everything must be decided by Scripture.

5 There is a sense in which every man when he begins to pray to God should put his hand upon his mouth.

6 The more we live and try to practise the Sermon on the Mount, the more shall we experience blessing.

7 The Church is failing in her mission if her dual conception of sin and joy are defective and inadequate.

8 Faith always shows itself in the whole personality.

9 Whatever may happen to you, God is your Father, and He is interested in you, and that is His attitude towards you.

10 The glory of the gospel is that when the Church is absolutely different from the world, she invariably attracts it.

11 If we really know Christ as our Saviour our hearts are broken and cannot be hard, and we cannot refuse forgiveness.

12 The way to understand the Scriptures and all theology is to become holy. It is to be under the authority of the Spirit.

20.356
Frank Pakenham, Lord Longford
British Roman Catholic peer and social critic

1 If you can't believe in God, Humanism is the next best thing.

20.357
David Lonsdale
English Jesuit writer

1 Poverty..., for Jesus, was not so much a matter of arbitrary choice (still less of enforced destitution) as a consequence and a sign of who he was and of his wholehearted fidelity to his mission.

2 [Ignatius'] view is that all of our lives and all that they contain are a gift from God, as is the whole universe in which we live.

3 The whole mystery of Christ, summed up in the folly of the cross and resurrection of Jesus, also offers us the gift of God's wisdom, a way of seeing what for us in our own circumstances is the path of true Christian discipleship.

4 God is endlessly imaginative, and the function of discernment is to enter creatively into God's vision for the world and to collaborate with the Spirit in making that vision a reality.

20.358
Kathleen Lonsdale
Irish Quaker and pacifist

1 When you have to make a vital decision about behaviour, you cannot sit on the fence. To decide to do nothing is still a decision, and it means that you remain on the station platform or the air strip when the train or plane has left.

20.359
Vladimir Lossky
Russian-born theologian

1 Baptismal grace, the presence of the Holy Spirit—inalienable and personal to each one of us—is the foundation of all Christian life.

20.360
Harold Loukes
British Quaker

1 An act of love that fails is just as much a part of the divine love as an act of love that succeeds. For love is measured by its fullness and not by its reception.

20.361
Janani Luwum
Anglican Archbishop of Uganda, assassinated for his outspokenness

1 I do not know for how long I shall be occupying this chair. I live as though there will be no tomorrow. I face daily being picked up by the soldiers. While the opportunity is there, I preach the gospel with all my might.

20.362
Mongameli Mabona
South African Roman Catholic lecturer

1 Why are forms of Christian worship so stilted and so restrained? Are we in worship communicating with an aristocratic or a capitalistic God who wants the little people to be very well behaved or even muted when they approach his majesty? Let there be less cringing and scraping in liturgy... Why should we have to cringe and scrape even in our father's house?

20.363
Rose Macaulay
English novelist and essayist

1 'And when all the years have passed, there will gape the uncomfortable and unpredictable dark void of death, and into this I shall at last fall headlong, down and down and down, and the prospect of that fall, that uprooting, that rending apart of body and spirit, that taking off into so blank an unknown, drowns me in mortal fear and mortal grief.'

20.364
Sallie McFague
North American theologian

1 A parable is... an assault on the conventions, including the social, economic, and mythic structures that people build for their own comfort and security. A parable is a story meant to invert and subvert these structures and to suggest that the way of the kingdom is not the way of the world.

20.365
Alister McGrath
Anglican evangelical theologian

1 Theology may help the community of faith to judge, reformulate, contextualize and better articulate its vision—but it cannot create that vision in the first place.

2 Anglicanism is a glorious accident of history.

3 There is an urgent need in Anglicanism, as within all mainline churches, to foster the development of local theologies, sensitive and responsive to local situations, rather than encourage the false belief that western assumptions and values have universal validity.

20.366
Donald Mackinnon
Scottish Episcopal theologian

1 At the heart of human history, then, stands for the Christian the agony, the struggle of Christ; this mysterious and awful patience of his which yet seems big with inexhaustible energy of mercy and compassion. It is deed: not idea.

2 Revelation is not in a charade but in an agony, with flesh racked with pain, and human consciousness lost in a sense of the meaninglessness of the world.

3 [Resurrection] is the raising of the whole life and death of Christ to a place where men can see it, as the merciful act of God's love.

20.367
George MacLeod
Scottish Presbyterian minister and founder of the Iona Community

1 Jesus was crucified not in a cathedral between two candles, but on a cross between two thieves.

2 The living Church, though never neat, keeps God's world from complete disaster.

3 We must each of us be humbled by this fresh wind of the Spirit that has come to lift us up from the nadir our civilisation has reached.

4 Some of us worked long enough in a shipbuilding district to know that welding is impossible except the materials to be joined are at white heat. When you try to weld them, they only fall apart.

5 We have become too spiritual in a 'holy holy' sense, whereas we should be Biblically holy—that means facing up to the totality of life, in the power of the Cross.

6 Where people are praying for peace the cause of peace is being strengthened by their very act of prayer, for they are themselves becoming immersed in the spirit of peace.

7 If Christianity cannot be based on atheism one must nevertheless acknowledge that the challenge of atheism is a constant safeguard against idolatry.

20.368
John Macmurray
Scottish moral philosopher

1 The capacity to love objectively is the capacity which makes us persons. It is the ultimate source of our capacity to behave in terms of the object. It is the core of rationality.

2 The capacity for reason belongs to our emotional nature, just as much as to the intellect.

3 If we are to be full of life and fully alive, it is the increase in our capacity to be aware of the world through our senses which has first to be achieved.

4 Complete individual integrity is the condition of personal relationship... Moral relations are dependent on the absolute value of the human being, as a free human spirit, not as a man or a woman.

5 Dependence and freedom are incompatible.

6 Science grows out of our rationality in relation to material things. Art grows out of our relation to living things. Religion grows out of our relation to persons.

7 Human life cannot be mature until it is conscious of its own maturity, that is to say until it has become fully conscious of its real nature, and begins to live in that consciousness... Until we know ourselves we cannot be ourselves.

8 Spirit is not other than body but more than body.

20.369
John Macquarrie
Scottish-born theologian

1 Religion is refusing to die.

2 Theology makes sense only in the context of worship and action.

3 It is because God has first of all made us in his own image that we find implanted in us the desire to worship him and to grow in likeness to him. It is God's Spirit working in us that first brings us to worship the mystery of Holy Being and to seek God's peace.

4 Christian action in the world will not be sustained or carried out in an intelligent and effective manner unless it is supported by doctrinal convictions that have achieved some degree of clarity.

5 I think that for a long time it's been realised that talk of incarnation—God sending his Son and so on—is a pictorial kind of language, not conceptual language, and, if one wishes to use the expression, it is a mythological language.

20.370
Laurenti Magesa
Tanzanian Roman Catholic priest and theologian

1 Africa is crying for a Christian spirituality which has form, which is incarnated; which acts and so offers tangible results in terms, that is, of bringing about peace, justice and reconciliation among men just as Jesus came to do.

20.371
John Main
English Benedictine monk

1 The Kingdom of God is simply God's power enthroned in our hearts. Faith in the Kingdom of God is what makes us light of heart and what Christian joy is all about.

2 The first step in personhood is to allow ourselves to be loved. To know ourselves loved is to have the depths of our own capacity to love opened up.

3 The all-important aim in Christian meditation is to allow God's mysterious and silent presence within us to become more and more not only a reality, but the reality in our lives; to let it become that reality which gives meaning and shape and purpose to everything we do; to everything we are.

20.372
Sara Maitland
English writer and theologian

1 The medieval idea that all creation suffered with Christ in the crucifixion—the sun darkened, the earth trembled, even the robin stained its breast trying to share that agony, his friends stayed as close as they could and afterwards took his body and tended to it—is more in tune with modern thinking, the suffering servant, rendered wordless and howling in desolation, rather than the warrior king stoical but noble, forgiving his enemies, making arrangements for his family and encouraging his companions.

2 So, as it turns out, we do not have a little tame domestic God, thank God, but we do have a huge, wild, dangerous God—dangerous of course only if we think that God ought to be manageable and safe; a God of almost manic creativity, ingenuity and enthusiasm; a Big-Enough God, who is also a supremely generous and patient God; a God of beauty and chance and solidarity.

3 Still in the enormous silence of the desert we sing like birds.

20.373
Mary John Mananzan
Benedictine social worker and educationalist in the Philippines

1 To be a Christian today in a land where injustice and oppression abide is a challenge. To be a religious woman in such a situation is doubly so. It calls for a radical rethinking of the meaning of being a Christian and of the imperative of religious commitment.

2 To confront in others time and time again one's own prejudice, one's own blind spots, one's own doubts, is to relive time and time again one's own metanoia without the sense of relief at the thought that the decision and choice lies within one's power.

3 Perhaps the greatest anguish is the yawning gap between one's insight and one's generosity.

20.374
Monikka Mannau
Bangladeshi Christian

1 Such was the justice and mercy of the owner [of the vineyard] that the needs of the men and their families meant more to him than the concept of payment for work done. At the end of the day, all were paid the same.

20.375
Gabriel Marcel
French philosopher

1 I have always felt that admiration was of the same order as creation.

20.376
Maribel of Wantage
English Anglican religious sister and sculptor

1 Dog-tiredness is such a lovely prayer, really, if only we would recognize it as such... Our Lord can pray just as well through a dog-tired body as though a well-rested one, better perhaps.

20.377
Jacques Maritain
French philosopher

1 The Christian is not shut up in a tragedy from which there is no issue. The solution, in the spiritual order, the saints have taught him is a love stronger than hell. In the temporal order, also, I hold, there is a solution; it can only be found by going ahead, by accepting the risks of our creative freedom...

20.378
Raissa Maritain
French writer

1 God is, at first, Truth and then Love. But he is only that love which is but one with the sovereign and eternally living truth. In himself, God is love as he is truth.

2 Art proceeds from a spontaneous instinct like love does; and it must be cultivated like friendship.

20.379
Catherine Marshall
North American religious writer

1 When the dream in our heart is one that God has planted there, a strange happiness flows into us. At that moment all of the spiritual resources of the universe are released to help us. Our praying is then at one with the will of God and becomes a channel for the Creator's always joyous, triumphant purposes for us and our world.

2 Acceptance says, True, this is my situation at the moment. I'll look unblinkingly at the reality of it. But I'll also open my hands to accept willingly whatever a loving Father sends.

3 Only joyous love redeems.

4 Obedience is all over the Gospels.
The pliability of an obedient heart must be complete from the set of our wills right on through our actions.

5 Real power in prayer flows only when man's spirit touches God's spirit.

6 God insists that we ask, not because *He* needs to know our situation, but because *we* need the spiritual discipline of asking.

7 The purpose of all prayer is to find God's will and to make that will our prayer.

8 In the middle of the night I was awakened. The room was in total darkness. Instantly sensing something alive, electric in the room, I sat bolt upright in bed. Past all credible belief, suddenly, unaccountably, Christ was there, in Person, standing by the right side of my bed.

9 Our spiritual bodies will have every faculty of our earthly tabernacles, only with heightened sensitivity and wonderful new freedom.

10 There's nothing pretty about death. Those who sentimentalize it, lie.

11 The Holy Spirit will not come to us in his fullness until we see and assent to his priority—his passion for ministry.

12 The adventure of living has not really begun until we begin to stand on our faith legs and claim... the resources of our God.

20.380
Mary Clare of Fairacres
English Anglican nun

1 There is something in the female, in her need for love and to give love, that comes out in the silent, compassionate awareness of prayer.

20.381
John Masefield
English poet and novelist

1 Death opens unknown doors. It is most grand to die.

2 To most of us the future seems unsure; but then it always has been; and we who have seen great changes must have great hopes.

3 The Englishman is naturally wasteful, especially of public money. It is a question of a blunted sense of life, a dullness towards a bright design, an apathy. Let us blame the climate for it: we pass, but the climate stays.

20.382
John Mbiti
Kenyan-born Swiss Reformed pastor and African theologian

1 The uniqueness of Christianity is in Jesus Christ. He is the stumbling block of all ideologies and religious systems... He is 'the man for others' and yet beyond them. It is he, therefore, and only he, who deserves to be the goal and standard for individuals and mankind... I consider traditional religions, Islam and the other religious systems to be preparatory and even essential ground in the search for the Ultimate. But only Christianity has the terrible responsibility of pointing the way to that ultimate Identity, Foundation and Source of security.

20.383
Anthony de Mello
Indian Jesuit

1 There is only one cause of unhappiness: the false beliefs you have in your head, beliefs so widespread, so commonly held, that it never occurs to you to question them.

2 If you wish to be fully alive you must develop a sense of perspective. Life is infinitely greater than this trifle your heart is attached to and which you have given the power to so upset you.

3 Love springs from awareness. It is only inasmuch as you see someone as he or she really is here and now and not as they are in your memory or your desire or in your imagination or projection that you can truly love them, otherwise it is not the person that you love but the idea that you have formed of this person, or this person as the object of your desire not as he or she is in themselves.

4 Happy events make life delightful but they do not lead to self-discovery and growth and freedom. That privilege is reserved to the things and persons and situations that cause us pain.

5 Every painful event contains in itself a seed of growth and liberation.

6 Love can only exist in freedom. The true lover seeks the good of his beloved which requires especially the liberation of the beloved from the lover.

7 Put your books and formulas aside; dare to abandon your teacher whoever your teacher may be and see things for yourself. Dare to look at everything around you without fear and without formula and it won't be long before you see.

20.384
Rigoberta Menchú
Guatemalan Indian writer

1 We began to study with the Bible as our main text. Many relationships in the Bible are like those we have with our ancestors, our ancestors whose lives were very much like our own.

2 When I first became a catechist, I thought that there was a God up there and that he had a kingdom for the poor. But we realized that it is not God's will that we should live in suffering, that God did not give us that destiny, but that men on earth have imposed this suffering, poverty, misery, and discrimination on us.

20.385
Thomas Merton
North American Cistercian monk and writer

1 Churches in cities are most wonderful solitudes.

2 There is no wilderness so terrible, so beautiful, so arid, so fruitful, as the wilderness of compassion. It is the only desert that shall truly flourish like a lily.

3 The desert was also the country of madness... the sterile paradise of emptiness and rage.

4 O God, my God, the night has values that the day never dreamed of.

5 The ox and the ass understood more of the first Christmas than the high priests in Jerusalem. And it is the same today.

6 Agnosticism leads inevitably to moral indifference. It denies us all power to esteem or to understand moral values, because it severs our spiritual contact with God who alone is the source of all morality.

7 Christianity is more than a doctrine. It is Christ Himself, living in those whom He has united to Himself in One Mystical Body.

8 We become contemplatives when God discovers Himself in us.

9 If you want to help other people you have got to make up your mind to write things that some men will condemn.

10 Despair is the absolute extreme of self-love. It is reached when a man deliberately turns his back on all help from anyone else in order to taste the rotten luxury of knowing himself to be lost.

11 Underlying all life is the ground of doubt, as I understand the subject; difficulty and doubt are incommensurate.

12 Duty does not have to be dull. Love can make it beautiful and fill it with life.

13 Ultimately, faith is the only key to the universe. The final meaning of human existence, and the answers to the questions on which all our happiness depends cannot be found in any other way.

14 A happiness that is sought for ourselves alone can never be found: for a happiness that is diminished by being shared is not big enough to make us happy.

15 If there were no humility in the world, everybody would long ago have committed suicide.

16 Love seeks only one thing: the good of the one loved. It leaves all the other secondary effects to take care of themselves. Love, therefore, is its own reward.

17 Our minds are like crows. They pick up everything that glitters, no matter how uncomfortable our nests get with all that metal in them.

18 It is very important to live your faith by confessing it, and one of the best ways to confess it is to preach it.

19 There is no solitude except interior solitude.

20 In God there can be no selfishness, because the three selves of God are three subsistent relations of selflessness, overflowing and superabounding in joy in the perfection of their gift of their one life to one another.

21 This is the secret of the Psalms. Our identity is hidden in them. In them we find ourselves and God. In these fragments he has revealed not only himself to us but ourselves in him.

20.386
John Baptist Metz
German Roman Catholic theologian

1 The Catholic Church no longer simply *has* a third world church, it now *is* a third world church—with Western and European origins.

20.387
José Miguez-Bonino
Argentinian Protestant liberation theologian

1 Jesus never speaks of wealth *in itself* or poverty *in itself* but of rich and poor as they are, historically.

20.388
Jürgen Moltmann
German Lutheran pastor and theologian

1 Hope disposes the believer toward change. Hope is oriented toward what is coming tomorrow. In hope we count on the possibilities of the future and we do not remain imprisoned in the institutions of the past.

2 From first to last, and not merely in the epilogue, Christianity is eschatology, is hope, forward looking and forward moving, and therefore also revolutionizing and transforming the present.

3 The eschatological is not one element *of* Christianity, but it is the medium of Christian faith as such, the key in which everything in it is set, the glow that suffuses everything here in the dawn of an expected new day... The eschatological outlook is characteristic of all Christian proclamation, of every Christian existence and of the whole church.

4 What happens in Jesus' passion is the giving up of the Son through the Father. In giving up his own Son, God cuts himself off from himself and sacrifices his own self. The giving up of the Son reveals a pain in God which can only be understood in trinitarian terms, or not at all.

5 Friendship is an unpretentious relationship, for 'friend' is not an official term, nor a title of honour, nor a function. It is a personal designation. Friendship unites affection with respect. There is no need to bow down before a friend. We can look him in the eye. We neither look up to him nor down on him.

6 One can rely on a friend. As a friend one is a person for other people to rely on. A friend remains a friend, even in disaster, even in guilt.

7 Prayer and the hearing of prayer are the marks of man's friendship with God and God's friendship with man.

8 I have an idea that laughter is able to mediate between the infinite magnitude of our tasks and the limitation of our strength.

20.389
Elisabeth Moltmann-Wendel
German Lutheran journalist and author

1 The search for female conceptions of God is the search for total conceptions of life which point beyond our patriarchal limitations and constrictions.

2 Anyone who lives by the power of the God who loves unconditionally is accepted with all his or her existence, from top to toe, inside and out, negative and positive.

20.390
Hugh Montefiore
English Anglican bishop

1 Christianity is about acceptance, and if God accepts me as I am, then I had better do the same.

2 The Holy Spirit of God does not and cannot alter our limitations: he can only fulfil our potentialities.

3 The truth is a reality which we can hardly bear.

4 Just as a birth does not take place without nine months of intensive preparation, so spiritual rebirth can only take place when we are ready for it and our time has come. It is as dangerous to try to force it as it is to induce a premature birth.

20.391
Cyris H.S. Moon
Korean Old Testament scholar

1 The *minjung* are the oppressed who have their rights infringed upon by rulers. They are 'uprooted people' who have no national identity or legal protection and who are considered to be slaves. In Korea, the pattern of slavery, like that experienced by the Hebrews in Egypt, was not questioned and was considered reasonable by those who benefited from the social system.

20.392
Gareth Moore
British Dominican

1 The believer exhibits trust in God when he trusts, yet there is nobody he trusts in. You have the kind of confidence that comes from looking to somebody trustworthy to save you from a situation of peril; you trust in God when you are imperilled yet look to nobody (not even yourself) for your salvation.

20.393
Sebastian Moore
English Benedictine monk

1 A sense of human worthlessness makes God unbelievable; a sense of human greatness is the threshold of belief.

20.394
Gabriel Moran
Roman Catholic theologian

1 The Eucharist is the Church at her best.

2 Every act formed by charity is revelation of God. Every word of truth and love, every hand extended in kindness, echoes the inner life of the Trinity.

20.395
Janet Morley
English feminist theologian, liturgist and poet

1 Vulnerable God,
you challenge the powers that rule this world
through the needy, the compassionate,
and those who are filled with longing.
Make us hunger and thirst to see right prevail,
and single-minded in seeking peace;
that we may see your face
and be satisfied in you,
through Jesus Christ, Amen.

2 O God for whom we long
as a woman in labour
longs for her delivery:
give us courage to wait,
strength to push,
and discernment to know the right time;
that we may bring into the world
your joyful peace,
through Jesus Christ, Amen.

3 'Inclusive language' does not have to mean replacing 'Almighty Father' with an (equally problematic) 'Almighty Mother'. I have found that to discover how and why the feminine has been omitted from our way of addressing God is to discover also what else has been left out. To release ourselves from the habit of always using certain predictable (and perhaps scarcely noticed) formulae for the beginning of a prayer, may free the imagination to explore the unimaginable ways in which God reaches us.

20.396
Colin Morris
British Methodist preacher, writer and broadcaster

1 Your theology is what you are when the talking stops and the action starts.

2 The Church is not dead... it is Hope that has died.

3 Only the renewal of hope can liberate Christians from morbid preoccupation with their own fate and make them available for the service of their fellows.

4 Jesus had flair.

5 Ironic though it may seem, I doubt that the world will ever take Christians seriously again until they are prepared to become fools for Christ's sake.

6 Christians by definition are a possible danger to any state.

7 When you are compelled to weave barbed wire around yourself as a protection against your fellow-citizens, your security is a form of imprisonment—you can only shut others out at the price of shutting yourself in.

8 When you have such a chronic distrust of your fellow-citizens of a different colour that you dare not place yourself at their mercy; when you have so little confidence in the justice of your past dealings with them that you live in terror that one day you may be on the receiving end of the treatment you have handed out to them for centuries—then you are prisoners of despair.

20.397
Charles F.D. Moule
English Baptist theologian

1 Remember John the Baptist. It's all very well to be popular as a free-lance evangelist, but this is no way to earn one's living.

2 Idolatry is an attempt to use God for man's purposes, rather than to give oneself to God's service.

3 The birth and rapid rise of the Christian Church therefore remain an unsolved enigma for any historian who refuses to take seriously the only explanation offered by the Church itself.

20.398
Malcolm Muggeridge
English journalist

1 The fallacy of the liberal mind is to see good in everything. This has been of great assistance to the devil.

2 The only ultimate disaster that can befall us is to feel ourselves at home on this earth.

3 What is called Western civilisation is in an advanced stage of decomposition.

4 I don't think that television has corrupted me. But I do think that man has invented it to flee from reality.

5 I consider that the way of life in urbanised, rich countries, as it exists today, and as it is likely to go on developing, is probably the most degraded and unillumined ever to come to pass on earth.

6 The more we receive in silent prayer, the more we can give in active life.

20.399
Robert Murray
Roman Catholic Jesuit priest

1 All theology starts with the human mind reaching out to evoke some echo or reflection of the ineffable by means of poetic imagery, knowing that the ineffable cannot be pinned down.

20.400
Christopher Mwoheka
Roman Catholic Bishop of Rulenge, north-west Tanzania

1 Material things are not accidental. They are necessary for our condition here on earth. We cannot do without them.

20.401
Lewis Namier
British historian, born in Poland of Russian Jewish origin, baptized in 1947

1 Nineteen centuries ago our people divided: one branch, the Hebrew Nazarenes, carried into the world our national faith coupled with their new tidings, the other, as a closed community preserved the old tradition. Yet both were part of one nation, and both are part of our national history.

20.402
Stanislaw Napiorkowski
Polish Franciscan theologian

1 Christian theology is not a closed theology but a theology in motion.

20.403
Michael Nazir-Ali
Anglican bishop

1 The sharing of the gospel of a suffering God leads people to make sense of their own and the world's suffering. It leads to a high view of the significance of human life, not only created by God but redeemed by him. It leads to a confidence in human destiny, which is eternal fellowship with the loving and suffering God who has made this possible again at such great cost to himself.

2 The preaching of the gospel brings about a crisis in human affairs which leads to conversion.

20.404
Watchman Nee (Nee To-Sheng)
Chinese evangelist

1 God... has only one answer to every human need—his Son, Jesus Christ.

2 The Blood [of Jesus] deals with what we have done, whereas the Cross deals with what we are.

3 Our old history ends with the Cross; our new history begins with the resurrection.

4 The greatest negative in the universe is the Cross, for with it God wiped out everything that was not of himself. The greatest positive in the universe is the resurrection, for through it God brought into being all he will have in the new sphere. Therefore resurrection is God's new starting point.

5 Man's thought is always of the punishment that will come to him if he sins, but God's thought is always of the glory man will miss if he sins.

6 God's purpose in redemption is glory, glory, glory.

7 Think! We who are mere nonentities can have the same Spirit resting on us as rested upon Moses the friend of God, upon David the beloved king, and upon Elijah the mighty prophet.

8 God does not blame me for being an individual, but for my individualism.

20.405
Stephen Neill
English bishop

1 Man is always a unity. He *is* body, and he *is* mind and soul; and he *can be* spirit.

2 Life is filled with meaning as soon as Jesus Christ enters into it.

3 The purpose of revelation is restoration, the renewal in us of that likeness to God which man lost by sin.

4 There is power here [in Jesus], but there is no violence. There is authority, but it is the authority of one who has taken upon himself the form of a servant.

5 Christian holiness, whether for the Church or for the individual, can never be a static thing, something gained once for all. It has to be maintained amid conflicts and perils that are renewed day by day. It is a moving thing; it can only exist as a function of pilgrimage.

20.406
James Nelson
North American theologian

1 I see in Jesus a compelling picture of male sexual wholeness, of creative masculinity, and of the redemption of manhood from both oppressiveness and superficiality.

20.407
Lesslie Newbigin
British United Reformed Church theologian

1 The Christian is one who has forever given up the hope of being able to think of himself as a good man.

2 Qualifications for leadership in younger churches have been defined too largely in terms of Western cultural and educational attainments, and it is the missions of the older churches which have set these standards. This is in the sharpest possible contrast to the Pauline method.

3 Properly speaking, the Church is just the people of God, just humanity remade in Christ. It should therefore have as much variety as the human race itself.

4 [The Church] exists wherever God in His sovereign freedom calls it into being by calling His own into the fellowship of His Son. And it exists solely by His mercy.

5 I think the great difficulty about the *invisible* church is that one always chooses the members oneself. The invisible church is a kind of extension of the ego. The very essence of the church is that it is a visible body, and it is *one* body.

6 The life of faith is a continually renewed victory over doubt, a continually renewed grasp of meaning in the midst of meaninglessness.

20.408
H. Richard Niebuhr
North American theologian

1 The humility of Christ is not the moderation of keeping one's exact place in the scale of being, but rather that of absolute dependence on God and absolute trust in him, with the consequent ability to move mountains. The secret of the meekness and the gentleness of Christ lies in his relation to God.

2 In his moral sonship to God Jesus Christ is not a median figure, half God, half man; he is a single person wholly directed as man toward God and wholly directed in his unity with the father toward men. He is mediatorial not median.

20.409
Reinhold Niebuhr
North American theologian

1 There is an ethical paradox in patriotism which defies every but the most astute and sophisticated analysis. The paradox is that patriotism transmutes individual unselfishness into national egoism.

2 It is the evil in man that makes democracy necessary, and man's belief in justice that makes democracy possible.

3 A democratic society must use every stratagem of education and every resource of religion to generate appreciation of the virtues and good intentions of minority groups which diverge from the type of the majority, and to prompt humility and charity in the life of the majority.

4 All men who live with any degree of serenity live by some assurance of grace.

5 God, give us grace to accept with serenity the things that cannot be changed, courage to change the things that should be changed, and the wisdom to distinguish the one from the other.

6 The ethic of Jesus is the perfect fruit of prophetic religion.

7 The problem of politics and economics is the problem of justice. The question of politics is how to coerce the anarchy of conflicting human interests into some kind of order, offering human beings the greatest possible opportunity for mutual support.

8 Nothing true or beautiful or good makes complete sense in any immediate context of history; therefore we must be saved by faith.

20.410
Martin Niemoller
German Lutheran pastor

1 First they came for the Jews. I was silent. I was not a Jew. Then they came for the Communists. I was silent. I was not a Communist. Then they came for the trade

unionists. I was silent. I was not a trade unionist. Then they came for me. There was no one left to speak for me.

2 There is no faith without repentance, and there is no church without repentance.

3 Easter is not a part of the old accustomed divine order, of the ordered world in which we live, but it is an absolutely new, unexpected act of the living God, which interrupts and runs counter to the uniform rise and fall of the world's rhythm. Here we have the beginning of something new.

20.411
Dennis Nineham
British theologian

1 People of different periods and cultures differ very widely; in some cases so widely that accounts of the nature and relations of God, men and the world put forward in one culture may be unacceptable, as they stand, in a different culture, even though they may have expressed profound truth in their time and expressed it in a form entirely appropriate to the original situation.

20.412
Simeon Nkoane
South African religious and bishop

1 It's important to think big. It's wonderful if it comes off.

20.413
Albert Nolan
South African theologian

1 To come to Jesus or to follow him is to accompany him into the kingdom. Becoming a disciple is an alternative way of speaking about entering into the kingdom.

2 The remarkable thing about Jesus was that, although he came from the middle class and had no appreciable disadvantages himself, he mixed socially with the lowest of the low and identified himself with them. He became an outcast *by choice*.

3 Nothing could be more unauthoritative than the parables of Jesus. Their whole purpose is to enable the listener to discover something for himself. They are not illustrations of revealed doctrines; they are works of art which reveal or uncover the truth about life.

4 Joy was in fact the most characteristic result of all Jesus' activity amongst the poor and the oppressed.

20.414
Edward Norman
English historian

1 In their death agonies the Western churches are distributing the causes of their own sickness—the politicisation of religion—to their healthy offspring in the developing world.

20.415
Henri Nouwen
Dutch Dominican and writer on spirituality

1 Much violence is based on the illusion that life is a property to be defended and not a gift to be shared.

2 The movement from loneliness to solitude... is not a movement of a growing withdrawal from, but rather a movement towards, a deeper engagement in the burning issues of our time.

3 The basis of the Christian community is not the family tie, or social or economic equality, or shared oppression or complaint, or mutual attraction... but the divine call. The Christian community is not the result of human efforts.

4 No human being can understand us fully, no human being can give us unconditional love, no human being can offer constant affection, no human being can enter into the core of our being and heal our deepest brokenness.

5 Probably no word better summarizes the suffering of our times better than the word 'homeless'. It reveals one of our deepest and most painful conditions, the condition of not having a sense of belonging, of not having a place where we can feel safe, cared for, protected, and loved.

6 Poverty of mind as a spiritual attitude is a growing willingness to recognise the incomprehensibility of the mystery of life. The more mature we become the more we will be able to give up our inclination to grasp, catch, and comprehend the fullness of life and the more we will be ready to let life enter into us.

20.416
Sabelo Ntwasa
South African black theologian

1 The Church... cannot be seen simply as the company of believers who have had spiritual experiences. It is the company of those whose lives are perceived to have the quality of Christ-in-his-struggle-against-human-bondage. It is thus the company of liberators, or it is not the Church.

20.417
Charles Nyamiti
Roman Catholic dogmatic theologian from Tanzania

1 The uniformization of cultures would be a great evil for humanity.

20.418
Julius Nyerere
President of Tanzania

1 Unless we participate actively in the rebellion against those social structures and economic organizations which condemn men to poverty, humiliation and degradation, then the Church will become irrelevant to man and the Christian religion will degenerate into a set of superstitions accepted by the fearful.

2 The Church cannot uplift a man; it can only help him to provide the conditions and the opportunity for him to co-operate with his fellows to uplift himself.

3 Exploiting the poor does not become a right thing to do because communists call it a wrong thing.

20.419
Flannery O'Connor
North American novelist

1 I wouldn't spend much time worrying about dryness. It's hard to steer a path between indifference and presumption and [there's] a kind of constant spiritual temperature-taking that don't do any good or tell you anything either.

2 There is a question whether faith can or is supposed to be emotionally satisfying. I must say that the thought of everyone lolling about in an emotionally satisfying faith is repugnant to me.

3 I'm glad you've figured out free will or whatever. It's great to be able to figure it out but dangerous to put too much faith in your figuring.

4 Ignorance is excusable when it is borne like a cross, but when it is wielded like an ax, and with moral indignation, then it becomes something else indeed.

5 Making grace believable to the contemporary reader is the almost insurmountable problem of the novelist who writes from the standpoint of Christian orthodoxy.

6 What people don't realize is how much religion costs. They think faith is a big electric blanket, when of course it is the cross.

20.420
William Oddie
English Roman Catholic writer

1 Women priests could be a step towards a new religion.

20.421
Mercy Amba Oduyoye
African theologian from Ghana

1 Feminism is anything but the imperialist ploy some would like us to take it for. There may be a lot of red herrings to come, but feminism is certainly not one of them. It is a fact of experience, not a thesis.

2 We do have one *earth*, granted, but it is also true to say that we live in *different* worlds.

3 To strive for unity in diversity is a task we cannot evade—and there are no shortcuts.

4 People of the Church who are ordinarily in daily converse with one another are the carriers of religion. How they live and what they live by is what constitutes Christianity for the observer.

5 African women's strength lies in the belief that the spirit-world is on the side of those who protect life and combat all that carries death in its wake.

6 I have arrived at a point where I no longer wish to be patient with sexism, racism, and injustices against the dignity that rightly belongs to beings made in the image of God. Those labels are losing their force, but the realities they point to, the burden and the evil we are naming, continue. Those who live under them feel their iron weight.

7 The irruption of women in Church and society is an integral part of the voice of the earth's voiceless that is beginning to penetrate the atmosphere and stir up the peace of the principalities and powers that hold the structures of our so-called one world in their hands.

20.422
Paul Oestreicher
German-born theologian and social activist

1 I cannot explain the mystery of how someone who is a human being just like I am can also be worshipped. And yet the more real the mystery has become for me, it isn't that Jesus has become more like God, but that all my brothers and sisters have.

2 A humiliated and defenceless church must go out into a hostile world to re-discover the God-man in the least of his brethren.

3 On the whole, the Church isn't worse than the world around it. It can't pretend to be better and, when it does, other people recognise the hypocrisy of it.

4 There are various paths to Christian obedience. The essential point, however, is that this obedience can only be measured by its commitment to the world.

20.423
J.H. Oldham
Scottish-born ecumenist

1 Man is more than scientist and technician, explorer and transformer. The concern of Christianity is with man as a being who exists, who acts and suffers, who has the responsibility of choice, who is exposed to fate, who sees at the end of the road death waiting for him, who needs a faith by which he can live, who can be free from anxiety only when he knows where he may place his trust.

2 The real is what limits me—the thing I cannot alter or do away with.

3 The belief that man is essentially man *with* man, that life is essentially dialogue, is not one among a thousand other interesting ideas. In the assertion man's humanity is at stake.

4 Christians often talk far too easily and glibly about God.

5 I have no wish to question the legitimacy of committing our journeys to God in prayer... But what we must on no account do is to put God on the same level as a tourist agency. If what you have set your heart on is a corner seat, you will get more efficient service from Mr Thomas Cook.

6 Faith is an active creative force.

7 To learn that God is not part of his own creation and cannot therefore be objectified is one of the lessons which atheism may help to teach us... The habit of objectifying God and regarding his action as on the same plane as human action, and consequently as an alternative to it, has too often led Christians to leave to God things that they were meant to do themselves.

8 There is inexhaustible meaning in the statement that God has chosen the foolish things of the world to put to shame them that are wise, and the weak things to confound those that are strong, but there is all the difference in the world between believing that and supposing that God takes delight in immaturity, incompetence, wishy-washiness and muddle.

9 If dialogue and communication belong to the ultimate nature of reality, the heart of religion is prayer.

10 To many people today the mention of Jesus Christ is a source, not so much of illumination, as of perplexity.

11 A living faith is not something you have to carry, but something that carries you.

12 The Church is most true to its own nature when it seeks nothing for itself, renounces power, humbly bears witness to the truth but makes no claim to be the *possessor* of truth, and is continually dying in order that it may live.

20.424
Timothy Olufosoye
Theologian

1 In thy journeys to and fro
God direct thee;
In thy happiness and pleasure
God bless thee;
In care, anxiety or trouble
God sustain thee;
In peril and in danger
God protect thee.

20.425
Akin J. Omoyajowo
Nigerian black theologian

1 In their zeal to save the souls of Africans from eternal damnation, the early missionaries mixed Christian principles with Western culture, not to say beliefs... The god that was introduced to Africa was a completely foreign god, and this robbed Christianity of its universality.

2 Unless the widening gap between the rich and poor is arrested, and if possible reversed, the very peace and stability of any society will be seriously jeopardized.

3 As we separate everyday life from religion, we are breaking up the unity and wholeness of life.

4 The rather discriminatory attitude to women of the Western-related Churches, ostensibly in obedience to Pauline injunctions, is in matters of religion quite alien to Africa.

20.426
Huub Oosterhuis
Dutch Jesuit

1 Make us receptive and open
and may we receive your kingdom
like children taking bread from the hands of their father.
Let us live in your peace, at home with you,
all the days of our life.

20.427
Helen Oppenheimer
Anglican theologian and writer

1 Death has suddenly become so discussable as to be almost fashionable.

2 Our capacity to communicate makes us what we are.

20.428
James I. Packer
British theologian

1 One of the many divine qualities of the Bible is this, that it does not yield its secrets to the irreverent and the censorious.

2 Happiness is never found until we have the grace to stop looking for it.

3 In revelation, God is the agent as well as the object. It is not just that men speak about God, or for God; God speaks for himself, and talks to us in person.

4 God the Father is the giver of Holy Scripture; God the Son is the theme of Holy Scripture; and God the Spirit is the author, authenticator, and interpreter, of Holy Scripture.

5 I question the adequacy of conceptualizing the subject-matter of systematic theology as simply revealed truths about God, and I challenge the assumption that has usually accompanied this form of statement, that the material, like other scientific data, is best studied in cool and clinical detachment.

20.429
Raimundo Panikkar
Indian Roman Catholic theologian

1 We believe we may speak not only of the unknown God of the Greeks but also of the *hidden Christ of Hinduism*—hidden and unknown and yet present and at work because he is not far from any one of us.

2 In the trinity a true encounter of religions takes place, which results, not in a vague fusion or mutual dilution, but in an authentic enhancement of all the religious and even cultural elements that are contained in each.

3 No man can live without symbols. The symbol is the true appearance of reality; it is the form in which, in each case, reality discloses itself to our consciousness, or rather, it is that particular consciousness of reality. It is in the symbol that the real appears to us.

20.430
Wolfhart Pannenberg
German Lutheran theologian

1 Faith as the fulfilment of life is really the same thing as trust. And trust is one of the fundamental aspects of life for every human existence... Only trust allows the soul room to breathe.

2 The kingdom of God and of his Christ is greater than the Church.

20.431
Sun Ai Lee Park
Poet and theologian from Korea

1 If we really want the church to be the community of Jesus Christ, a community that lives in love as one body seeking the Reign of God with others, then the practice of classism, sexism and racism in the church cannot be permitted.

2 All the broken hearts
shall rejoice;
all those
who are heavy laden,
whose eyes are tired
and do not see,
shall be lifted up
to meet with
the motherly healer.

20.432
Alan Paton
South African writer and educator

1 No Christian should ever think or say that he is not fit to be God's instrument, for that in fact is what it means to be a Christian. We may be humble about many things, but we may never decline to be used.

2 The ground is holy, being even as it came from the Creator. Keep it, guard it, care for it, for it keeps men, guards men, cares for men. Destroy it and man is destroyed.

20.433
Paul VI
Pope

1 It must be borne in mind that the purpose of interpretation—hermeneutics—is to understand and elicit the meaning conveyed by the text, taking into account the words used, not to invent some new sense on the basis of arbitrary conjecture.

20.434
M. Scott Peck
US psychiatrist and author

1 In and through community lies the salvation of the world.

2 Good theology makes good psychology.

20.435
Max Picard
German philosopher

1 Silence is not simply what happens when we stop talking... When language ceases, silence begins. But it does not begin *because* language ceases. The absence of language simply makes the presence of silence more apparent.

2 Silence contains everything within itself. It is not waiting for anything; it is always wholly present and it completely fills out the space in which it appears.

3 Silence is the only phenomenon today that is 'useless'. It does not fit into the world of profit and utility; it simply *is*. It seems to have no other purpose; it cannot be exploited.

20.436
Aloysius Pieris
Sri Lankan Jesuit theologian

1 It is sad that whereas yesterday's feudalism turned some monasteries into oases of plenty amid deserts of poverty, pushing them into the hands of today's revolutionaries who *force* monks to practice *voluntary* poverty for the benefit of the masses (as has happened in Tibet and Mongolia), today's capitalism has entrenched some ashrams, zendos, and prayer centers in the grip of wealth-accumulating patrons who frequent them for spells of tranquility and return unconverted and unrepentant, awaiting another revolution to disrupt that unholy alliance with mammon.

2 The term 'Third World' is a theological neologism for God's own people. It stands for the starving sons and daughters of Jacob—of all places and all times—who go in search of bread to a rich country, only to become its slaves.

20.437
Norman Pittenger
US-born process theologian

1 A sermon is a proclamation of the generous love of God in Christ, or it is not a Christian sermon.

2 The honest effort to do one's duty, the living of human life in love and charity with others, the pursuit of truth and goodness, and all else that conforms our lives to the pattern of their intended perfection, can only be explained in the last resort by grasping the truth that deep down within us is this working of the Spirit of God.

3 Christianity is not a simple, fixed entity; it is itself a living and developing process. To be committed to the Christian faith is to be caught up into a community of life which does not continue in one stay but which goes on towards the future, incorporating in itself all sorts of novelty, changing whilst it remains ever the same in that its deepest engagement is with the movement of love, of relationship in love, of deepest concern, as these have been expressed in the life of Jesus and his saints.

4 To love is to be willing to put the beloved in the first place and oneself in the second place.

5 To say that God is Love is to say that God is the living, active, dynamic, ceaselessly desiring reality who will not let go until he has won the free response of his creation—and won this response, not by the employment of methods other than love, but by the indefatigable quality of his loving.

20.438
Ruth Pitter
English poet

1 If You are Love, You won't mind if I scold.
We laugh when creatures nag. It can be funny.
We like their impudence. I know an old
Blackbird I wouldn't sell for any money,
Who curses as to heaps because it's cold.
It's all our fault. We laugh till we are weak.

20.439
Nyameko Pityana
South African student leader

1 Black Theology seeks to commit black people to the risks of affirming the dignity of black personhood.

20.440
John Polkinghorne
British scientist and theologian

1 In the end, whatever shift may be made intellectually to grapple with the problem of evil, the only satisfactory conclusion to the matter will come if it is indeed true that 'all shall be well'.

2 God does not fussily intervene to deliver us from all discomfort, but neither is he the impotent beholder of cosmic history. Patiently, subtly, with infinite respect for the creation with which he has to deal, he is at work within the flexibility of its process.

3 The old image of the divine Clockmaker presiding over a steadily ticking universe has been replaced by One responsible for a world at once more open to innovation in its process and more dangerously precarious in its possible outcome.

20.441
Maen Pongudom
Thai theologian

1 God has revealed himself through other religions and philosophical systems besides the Jewish system. God loved and loves other people besides the Jews. He has never forsaken any tribe of human beings at any moment.

20.442
Enoch Powell
English politician

1 Christianity is an intellectual religion... [It] is a faith which makes demands upon people's minds, and relates its promises to the results of mental activity.

2 Christianity is not for us unless we are able to face the fact that failure exists.

3 In a sugary, romantic, cosy religion, suitable to match the Welfare State, there would not only be equality of opportunity to be saved, but an insurance scheme thrown in, to ensure that nobody missed salvation through being born in the wrong place at the wrong time, or not happening to entertain the necessary belief, or being incapable of doing so.

20.443
John Powell
North American Jesuit

1 If you knew me yesterday, please do not think that it is the same person that you are meeting today.

2 The fully human person is an Actor, not a Reactor.

20.444
Ianthe Pratt
English Roman Catholic feminist

1 Liturgy can only really live, worship can only truly express joy, sorrow, hope, faith and love if it is firmly rooted in the actual lives and experience of the people who are worshipping.

20.445
Gerald Priestland
BBC Religious Affairs Correspondent

1 The Church of England is the perfect church for people who don't go to church.

2 Creeds are devices to keep heretics out rather than draw people in.

3 I remain suspicious of piety in the young—eleven to twenty-one is probably a decade which is better left spiritually alone.

4 I submit that Christians ought not to be scared of a moral issue just because someone has stuck a political flag on it.

20.446
Anne Primavesi
Irish theologian and writer on ecological issues

1 The bodily complementarity of males and females is something much more than a source of agreeable sensation. It can be a central manifestation of the wider human delight in existence, a focal point, symbolizing and providing expressive release for the whole of our erotic connectedness to the world.

2 I have to view ecology and theology as two complementary dimensions of my life that must both be taken into account if I am to meet the needs of the world as it exists.

3 It is the combination of both power and love which makes a community workable and sustainable. It is the combination of power and love which Christians call the Spirit, and which empowers us to shape our common future for the good of all.

20.447
Joan Puls
North American Franciscan and ecumenist

1 Often nothing requires more courage than admission of fault. The disturbance that repentance evokes in our personal and collective psyches is so jarring that we tend to exhaust every other available dynamic before we succumb. We dread the bald admission of our wrong-doing!

2 The church of Jesus Christ is above all ecumenical in its suffering.

3 The most glaring scandal of Christianity is its division over the eucharist, its unwillingness to distribute bread and wine to all who approach the table.

20.448
Michel Quoist
French writer of popular prayers

1 Tomorrow God isn't going to ask
What did you dream?
What did you think?
What did you plan?
What did you preach?
He's going to ask *What did you do?*

2 The adolescent is a child who is in the process of receiving from the hands of God, through the intermediary of his parents, personal care of and responsibility for his body, his affections, and his mind.

3 Adolescence, physical, emotional and intellectual, is a sign from God that this is a time of preparation, the time to prepare for union with another person.

4 There's no such thing as a person alone. There are only people bound to each other to the limits of humanity and time.

5 Hunger and thirst are healthy drives unless you eat and drink solely for your own pleasure and in excess of what is reasonable. We must eat to live, and not live to eat.

6 Only love enables humanity to grow, because love engenders life and it is the only form of energy that lasts forever.

7 A man will be effective to the degree that he is able to concentrate. Concentration is not a mode of doing, but above all a mode of being.

8 We must welcome the night. It's the only time that the stars shine.

9 Psychosomatic illnesses are illnesses of the soul transmitted to the body; a sick spirit and a healthy body inevitably come into conflict and finally break down.

20.449
Alan Race
British theologian

1 We have a foot in two camps. We celebrate and share what we know of God through the impact of Jesus in our world. We also wait to hear, learn and be judged by others who tell of a different experience, without defining their experience by virtue of our criterion of the Christ. We participate according to the Christian norm, yet with other norms which are also universally binding.

20.450
Philip Rack
Quaker writer

1 Please be patient, those of you who have found a rock to stand on, with those of us who haven't and with those of us *who are not even looking for one*. We live on the wave's edge, where sea, sand and sky are all mixed up together: we are tossed head over heels in the surf, catching only occasional glimpses of any fixed horizons. Some of us stay there from choice because it is exciting and it *feels like the right place to be*.

20.451
Gerhard von Rad
German biblical scholar

1 Creation not only exists, it also discharges truth… Wisdom requires a surrender, verging on the mystical, of a person to the glory of existence.

20.452
Hugo Rahner
German Roman Catholic theologian

1 Mere seriousness does not get down to the roots of things, and... a spirit of fun, of irony and of humour often digs deeper and seems to get more easily—because more playfully—down to the truth.

2 Without the divine drop of oil we call humour the great world machine would soon grind to a standstill.

3 Not everything in our society is in the hands of the devil and thundering from the pulpit is not always in place.

20.453
Karl Rahner
German Roman Catholic theologian

1 Only when human beings are taken seriously—to the utmost—is it possible to know something of God, and only when we know something of God is it possible to take human beings seriously—to the utmost.

2 The Church is not a finished, solidly built and furnished house, in which all that changes is the successive generations who live in it. The Church is a living reality which has had a history of its own and still has one.

3 The Ascension is a festival of the future of the world. The flesh is redeemed and glorified, for the Lord has risen for ever. We Christians are, therefore, the most sublime materialists.

4 Prayer can be like a slow interior bleeding, in which grief and sorrow make the heart's blood of the inner man trickle away silently into his own unfathomed depths.

5 To renounce all is to gain all; to descend is to rise; to die is to live.

20.454
Arthur Michael Ramsey
Archbishop of Canterbury

1 When an Anglican is asked 'Where was your Church before the Reformation?' his best answer is to put the counter-question, 'Where was your face before you washed it?'

2 Despite our wicked divisions, there is a unity which is a fact.

3 No resurrection. No Christianity.

4 A church which starves itself and its members in the contemplative life deserves whatever spiritual leanness it may experience.

5 I want to want to want to want you God.

6 Your prayer then will be a rhythmic movement of all your powers, moving into the divine presence in contemplation and moving into the needs of the people in intercession.

7 The point of the Daily Office is to root your prayer in the scriptures and in the Church's corporate prayer.

8 Beware of attitudes which try to make God smaller than the God who has revealed himself to us in Jesus.

9 You will never be nearer to Christ than in caring for the one man, the one woman, the one child.

10 To repent is to turn, and to have a change of mind. The turning and the change of mind are God's gift, and they are a turning and a change of mind towards God.

11 We are all of us infinitesimally small and ludicrous creatures. You have to be serious, but never be solemn, because if you are solemn about anything there is the risk of becoming solemn about yourself.

20.455
Ian T. Ramsey
British theologian and philosopher

1 For the religious man 'God' is a key word, an irreducible posit, and ultimate of explanation expressive of the kind of *commitment* he professes.

2 In a miracle the Universe declares itself personal at a point where persons are not; and the miracle story must be odd enough to make this remarkable claim. We shall never measure the logic of miracle stories by reading them off against scientific assertions; the point they make is one very different from any which can be made in scientific language.

3 Being sure in religion does not entail being certain in theology; to be aware of our Duty does not necessarily give us an infallible prescription.

4 As an attempt to chart a mystery, Christian social theory must be intrinsically tentative, ever open to reform and modification—striving at all times to be faithful alike to our vision of God as to our deepest insights into human personality.

20.456
David Randall
British Anglican priest

1 I had to learn that it was all right not doing anything except being the loving presence of God in a situation which is about sharing the pain as much as it is about offering cheap comfort. So much spirituality is cheap and meaningless, because it's about making people feel better, and the reality is that people *don't* get better from AIDS. When you're dying, you're dying.

20.457
Irina Ratushinskaya
Russian poet

1 I will live and survive and be asked
How they slammed my head against a trestle,
How I had to freeze at nights
How my hair started to turn grey...
I will smile. And I will crack some joke
And brush away the encroaching shadow
And I will render homage to the dry September
That became my second birth.
And I'll be asked: 'Doesn't it hurt you
to remember?'

20.458
Joseph Ratzinger
Cardinal and Roman Catholic theologian

1 The purely calculating mind will always find it absurd that for man's sake, God would spend himself to the full. Only the love can understand the foolishness of a love for which extravagance is a law, and only excess is sufficient.

2 It is always disagreeable to have to prophesy!

3 Christian brotherhood, unlike the purely secular brotherhood of Marxism, is above all brotherhood based on the common paternity of God.

4 Christian faith lives on the discovery that not only is there such a thing as objective meaning, but this meaning knows me and

loves me, I can entrust myself to it like the child that knows all its questions answered in the 'You' of its mother.

20.459
Charles E. Raven
English theologian and scientist

1 For mankind there are two unique sacraments which disclose the meaning and convey the experience of reality: they are the created universe and the person of Jesus Christ.

2 We must be broken into life.

20.460
Samuel Rayan
Indian theologian

1 To enable the church to be the sign of God's liberating presence, theology will have to engage in a sustained critique of the church. We need to become aware of the ambiguity of the church's role in history.

2 [The church's] eschewal of politics usually amounts to support for the status quo and the powers that be.

3 Indian theology seeks to discern, illumine, and support the people's struggle for human wholeness in freedom and dignity. Its endeavour is to make a meaningful contribution to the march of our people toward human fullness in a just society.

4 New Testament spirituality is the spirituality of broken bread (our earth) and shared wine (a life of friendship).

20.461
Ernest Raymond
English novelist and religious writer

1 Am I then home again at last? I do not know. Perhaps I shall never know. I hope and trust and do not know.

20.462
Ranjini Rebera
Theologian from Sri Lanka, now living in Australia

1 The phrase 'a group of women' appears many times in the Jesus narratives. The strongest evidence of this group was at the foot of the cross. The women stood in solidarity with each other in a situation that must have been frightening and bewildering to them... Later, when the disciples refused to believe Mary's report of her encounter with the risen Christ, a group of women went back to the empty tomb. Women believing in women.

2 Any institution that accepts patriarchy as its model and patriarchal images as its symbols and its vision will have little credibility in the process of building a just and equal society.

20.463
Bridget Rees
British feminist and preacher

1 Most of the prophets were on the edge, on the outside, over against the institution. Perhaps this is my vocation, at least for the moment.

2 It is hard to turn my back on an organization, on a community of people I love, but it is harder to go on living a lie. I want to witness in my not receiving communion to the brokenness of our community, to make this visible rather than pretend that everything is all right.

20.464
Donald Reeves
English Anglican clergyman

1 We need theologians to help us reflect on our experience of trying to create a just and caring society, for which the Church is there to offer its life. What we do *not* need is white, male, middle-class theologians writing books to each other in universities, in jargon which hardly anyone except themselves can understand.

2 The Church of England simply fails to understand the contradictions with which it lives, let alone the great questions of whether we are going to survive as a human race.

3 Some people think liturgy's like saying Beanz Meanz Heinz over and over again beautifully. I don't see that at all.

20.465
Douglas Rhymes
English priest and author

1 The meeting of Christ in us with the Christ in others will mean that we shall be willing to expose ourselves in openness to others without fear, seeing each person we meet as having a significance because both of us are accepted and loved by God.

2 To have a prayerful approach to people is to have eyes to see, a mind intent upon seeing, a heart hopeful of seeing the image of God in each person I meet, to see them in themselves and in God.

20.466
Cliff Richard
English pop singer

1 What's important is that God is so much part and parcel of life that spontaneous mental chat becomes second nature.

2 What other people think of me is becoming less and less important; what they think of Jesus because of me is critical.

3 The more we depend on God, the more dependable we find he is.

20.467
Alan Richardson
British theologian

1 All Christian doctrine arises from Christian experience.

2 Christian theology has never suggested that the 'fact' of Christ's resurrection could be known apart from faith.

3 It is Christ himself, rather than any of the things which he did, who is the supreme miracle and chief attestation of the truth of the biblical revelation.

4 The Christian missionaries did not bring Christ to India: they found him there.

5 'Religion' is one of the slipperiest words in the dictionary... Many of the wisest and most God-fearing men of past ages, and some of the leading theologians of our own day, unhesitatingly declare that religion is a bad thing.

6 Where there are no prophets, there can be no special revelation.

20.468
Nelly Ritchie
Superintendent of the Evangelical Methodist Church in Argentina

1 The statement: Jesus is the Christ! covers new dimensions. It does not have to do with an applied doctrine but with a truth to discover, with a response which, translated into words and deeds, takes on historical truthfulness and liberating force.

2 Nothing separates us from God like a piety that is sure of itself. Nothing draws us closer to God than acknowledgement of the grace of pardon, the offer of a new chance for abundant grace.

20.469
John A.T. Robinson
English theologian

1 Jesus never claims to be God, personally, yet he always claims to bring God, completely.

2 All I can do is to try to be honest—honest to God and about God—and to follow the argument wherever it leads.

3 All true awareness of God is an experience at one and the same time of ultimacy *and* intimacy.

4 The life of God, the ultimate Word of Love in which all things cohere, is bodied forth completely, unconditionally and without reserve in the life of a man—the man for others and the man for God. He is perfect man and perfect God—not as a mixture of oil and water, of natural and supernatural—but as the embodiment through obedience of 'the beyond in our midst', of the transcendence of love.

5 We do not know anything about his [Jesus'] sex-life.

20.470
Aracely de Rocchietti
Methodist pastor in Uruguay

1 It is the hope generated by belief in justice as an historical constant which reveals to us both God's love for all creation and the human capacity to proclaim.

20.471
Raquel Rodríguez
Lutheran pastor from Puerto Rico

1 [On John 4: Jesus and the Samaritan woman] This passage and others like it open our eyes to the reality that social, ethnic, religious, ethical, and sexist prejudices cannot be allowed to keep us from announcing the message of life, which has also been announced to us as women and which social constraints have tried to diminish or take away from us.

2 Love and service will come to be substituted for the old relationship with God, which was based on sacrifice, humiliation, and religious ritual. The relationship and the encounter with the God of life are to be found in this Spirit of life, in the struggle to achieve that life for ourselves and for others.

3 The time is coming, in fact it is already here when we are asked for proof of our gratitude to God.

20.472
Roger of Taizé
Co-founder and Prior of the Taizé community

1 There are three gestures, in particular, which are capable of being signs of God at work, paths of communion and ways of discovering new dimensions of ecumenism: Avoid separating the generations; Go to meet those who cannot believe; Stand alongside the exploited.

2 The man of prayer finds his happiness in continually creating, searching, being with Christ.

3 Generosity and detachment are not enough. Communion with the poverty-stricken in the world also means participating in the world's struggle against its poverty. The Christian's place is in the thick of this struggle, at the front lines, in the rich countries as well as in the poor.

4 The love which we bear for others remains the mark of the authenticity of our contemplation.

20.473
Oscar Romero
Roman Catholic Archbishop of El Salvador, murdered while preaching

1 I speak a word of encouragement,
For the Lord's light will always brighten
these ways.
New shepherds will come,
But always the same gospel.

2 We can't enrich the common good of our country by driving out those we don't care for.

3 Christianity is not a collection of truths to be believed, of laws to be obeyed, of prohibitions. That makes it very distasteful. Christianity is a person, one who loved us so much, one who calls for our love. Christianity is Christ.

4 We cannot segregate God's word from the historical reality in which it is proclaimed. It would not then be God's word. It would be history, it would be a pious book, a Bible that

is just a book in our library. It becomes God's Word because it vivifies, enlightens, contrasts, repudiates, praises what is going on today in this society.

5 We have never preached violence, except the violence of love, which left Christ nailed to a cross, the violence that we must each do to ourselves to overcome our selfishness and such cruel inequalities among us.

6 A religion of Sunday Mass but of unjust weeks does not please the Lord. A religion of much praying but with hypocrisy in the heart is not Christian. A church that sets itself up only to be well off, to have a lot of money and comfort, but that forgets to protest injustices, would not be the true church of our Redeemer.

7 God is the judge of all social systems.

8 I cannot change except to seek to follow the gospel more closely. And I can quite simply call to everyone: let us be converted so that Christ may look upon our faith and have mercy on us.

9 I want to repeat to you what I said once before: the shepherd does not want security while they give no security to his flock.

10 God's reign is already present on our earth in mystery. When the Lord comes, it will be brought to perfection.

11 That is the hope that inspires Christians. We know that every effort to better society, especially when injustice and sins are so ingrained, is an effort God blesses, that God wants, that God demands of us.

20.474
Eleanor Roosevelt
US diplomat

1 No one can make you feel inferior without your consent.

2 I could not at any age be content to take my place in a corner by the fireside and simply look on. One must never, for whatever reason, turn one's back on life.

3 Understanding is a two-way street.

20.475
Agnes Maud Royden
English preacher, campaigner for women's suffrage

1 The Church should no longer be satisfied to represent only the Conservative Party at prayer.

2 I believe that the average man and woman are not quite normal about sex; I think most of us are rather unnaturally over-sexed, and over-preoccupied with sex, and that this greatly complicates the question of birth control.

3 Not even a beginning has been made in breaking down the peculiarly loathsome superstitions which bar the sanctuary to women... It remains a fact that it crystallizes a prejudice indescribably insulting to womanhood, and one which, when a young woman first hears it, fills her with a very deep (and honourable) sense of resentment.

20.476
Rosemary Radford Ruether
North American feminist theologian

1 The church as historical institution tends to sacralize the established social order—its political as well as its familial hierarchies... By contrast, the concept of the church as spirit-filled community tends to break down these social hierarchies.

2 The church as spirit-filled community thus believes itself called into an exodus from the established social order and its religious agents of sacralization. It is engaged in witnessing to an alternative social order demanded by obedience to God.

3 The church cannot be defined only as historical institution or only as spirit-filled community. Rather, the church exists as a dialectical interaction between the two elements... Seldom does the interplay between the two take place with optimal creativity.

4 The feminism we envision is one that is able constantly to build an integral vision of a new humanizing culture beyond patriarchy without becoming closed or sectarian toward any living cultural option or human community.

5 The full personhood of women is one of the touchstones for testing our faithfulness to the vision of redemption in Christ. By this norm much of mainstream tradition must be judged as deficient.

20.477
Robert Runcie
Archbishop of Canterbury

1 I think I am the only person who was actually converted at his own confirmation service.

2 I can't believe, when I see the promise of Christ expressed in a particular person, that that's all coming to an end. But as for the geography and climate of an after-life—well, I'm agnostic about that.

3 War springs from the love and loyalty being offered to God being applied to some God-substitute, one of the most dangerous being nationalism.

4 When a man realises that he is a beloved child of the Creator of all, then he is ready to see his neighbours in the world as brothers and sisters.

5 What does being redeemed in Christ mean if you are a Jew about to be gassed?

6 I can't believe in a God who only saves people who live in certain latitudes. If I had happened to be born in Delhi I'd probably be a Hindu; or in Iran a Muslim.

20.478
Letty M. Russell
North American theologian

1 The Bible is especially dangerous if we call it 'the Word of God' and think that divine inspiration means that everything we read is right. But divine inspiration means that God's Spirit has the power to make the story speak to us from faith to faith. The Bible is accepted as the Word of God when communities of faith understand God to be speaking to them in and through its message.

20.479
Stanley J. Samartha
Indian writer on interfaith issues

1 Mere scholarship does not yield Truth or reach God... Without disciplining the body, focusing the mind, purifying the emotions, and controlling the will no one can *hear* the sound of Truth or *see* the vision of God.

20.480
W.E. Sangster
English Methodist preacher

1 Jesus chose the Apostles to be with him that they might observe the life he lived and then live it themselves.

2 Some people are so strong in faith, and so sure of God, that they can praise him in pain, and pass through the valley of the shadow with songs on their lips. But they are rare souls. For most people it is a time for mute obedience.

3 The fullness of the Christian life cannot be known except in fellowship—fellowship with God and fellowship with one another. Moreover, the purposes of God in this world require a social organism by which to express themselves.

4 Tell God that you have, alas! no inclination to pray, and that you have dragged yourself to your knees. Still you will be welcome!

5 Our best self points out the hard and costly way; our lower self derides it and urges us to 'play for safety'. Our best self challenges us to be the highest we have power to be; our lower self tells us that we must always take care of 'number one'. So the struggle goes on. So our essential character is shaped. The light of eternity will reveal what we have become.

6 Every day the choice between good and evil is presented to us in simple ways.

7 Even the most sudden conversion does not leap like the genie of the lamp out of nothing, but has at its heart some dazzling conscious insight of the true relation of the soul and God.

20.481
Siegfried Sassoon
English poet and novelist

1 Heart's miracle of inward light,
What powers unknown have sown your seed
And your perfection freed?...
O flower within me wondrous white,
I know you only as my need
And my unsealed sight.

2 Let There Be Life, said God.
And what He wrought
Went past in myriad marching lines,
and brought
This hour, this quiet room,
and my small thought
Holding invisible vastness in its hands.

20.482
Cicely Saunders
Pioneer of the English hospice movement

1 Life is learning to love and most of us have merely begun when we die. This is the main reason why many of us long for and expect another life.

20.483
Harry Sawyerr
Protestant theologian from Sierra Leone

1 To represent Jesus Christ as the first-born among many brethren who with him together form the Church is in true keeping with African notions.

2 If the African lives with his dead, he would naturally feel himself in the wrong place if there was no opportunity for him to realize the hoped-for comradeship with his ancestors, just because he had become a Christian.

20.484
Dorothy L. Sayers
English detective-story writer, Christian Apologist

1 God was executed by people painfully like us, in a society very similar to our own... by a corrupt church, a timid politician, and a fickle proletariat led by professional agitators.

2 At the name of Jesus, every voice goes plummy, every gesture becomes pontifical, and a fearful creeping paralysis slows down the pace of the dialogue.

3 The great thing, I am sure, is not to be nervous about God—and to try and shut out the Lord Immanuel from any sphere of truth. Art is not He—we must not substitute art for God; yet this also is He, for it is one of His images and therefore reveals His nature.

4 The one and only thing that seems to have roused the 'meek and mild' Son of God to a display of outright physical violence was precisely the assumption that 'business is business'.

5 The Churches are shocked when 'unfortunates' are reduced to selling their bodies; they are less shocked when journalists are reduced to selling their souls.

6 We, as a nation, are not very ready to harbour resentment, and sometimes this means that we forget without forgiving—that is, without ever really understanding either our enemy or ourselves.

7 Not Herod, not Caiaphas, not Pilate, not Judas ever contrived to fasten upon Jesus Christ the reproach of insipidity; that final indignity was left for pious hands to inflict. To make of his story something that could neither startle, nor shock, nor terrify, nor excite, nor inspire a living soul is to crucify the Son of God afresh.

8 Work is the natural exercise and function of man—the creature who is made in the image of his Creator.

9 Nobody but a god can pass unscathed through the searching ordeal of incarnation.

10 The artist does not see life as a problem to be solved, but as a medium for creation.

11 [The artist] is not necessarily an artist in handling his personal life, but (since life is the material of his work) he has at least got thus far, that he is using life to make something new.

12 As for the common man, the artist is nearer to him than the man of any other calling, since his vocation is precisely to express the highest common factor of humanity—that image of the Creator which distinguishes man from the beast.

20.485
Edith Schaeffer
North American writer and speaker

1 The family should be a place where each new human being can have an early atmosphere conducive to the development of constructive creativity. Parents, aunts and uncles, grandparents, and sisters and brothers can squash, stamp out, ridicule, and demolish the first attempts at creativity, and continue this demolition long enough to cripple spontaneous outbursts of creation.

20.486
Francis Schaeffer
North American theologian

1 Man, made in the image of God, has a purpose—to be in relationship to God, who is there. Man forgets his purpose and thus he forgets who he is and what life means.

2 God has established Government but he has not made it autonomous. Thus if the office bearer commands that which is contrary to God's Law his authority is abrogated. At this point it is the Christian's duty to disobey.

3 Made in God's image, man was made to be great, he was made to be beautiful and he was made to be creative in life and art. But his rebellion has led him into making himself into nothing but a machine.

20.487
Edward Schillebeeckx
Dutch Dominican theologian

1 There are people who damage or destroy everything they touch, but there are others who manage to leave everything with which they come in contact, whether it be with their hands or with their reason, with their mind or with their heart, somehow changed for the better... So it is in an incomparable way with... Jesus.

2 Each sacrament is the personal saving act of the risen Christ himself, but realised in the visible form of an official act of the Church.

3 If liberation is the real hallmark of the power of good, then for anyone who consistently continues to regard the world from the standpoint of the victims and thus from solidarity with these victims, this solidarity, if it inspires all action, is a power which is literally stronger than death, a power which disarms evil and makes it yield.

4 The history of human beings and the life of human beings who hold on to one another or let one another go is the place where the cause of salvation or damnation is decided.

20.488
Basilea Schlink
Mother and co-founder of the Lutheran Community at Darmstadt

1 Today the approaching kingdoms of darkness and light are clearer than ever before. They are taking shape here on earth.

2 The ecumenical assignment is really a sacred commission—because it allows us to take part in the suffering of Jesus, who suffers today on account of his torn body. It is a task which should move us to the depths of our very being and should impel us, through love of Jesus, to do all that we can to heal those wounds whatever it costs.

3 If the glory of God is to break out in your service, you must be ready to go out into the night.

20.489
Alexander Schmemann
Russian Orthodox theologian

1 There must be someone in this world—which rejected God and in this rejection, in this blasphemy, became a chaos of darkness—there must be someone to stand in its centre, and to discern, to see it again as full of divine riches, as the cup full of life and joy, as beauty and wisdom, and to thank God for it. This 'someone' is Christ.

2 Each year Lent and Easter are, once again, the rediscovery and the recovery of what we were made through our own baptismal death and resurrection.

20.490
Sandra Schneiders
North American religious sister

1 Unless we can find a way to understand scripture which denies neither its normative status in the community of faith nor the very real problems raised by its sometimes morally unacceptable treatment of women, the foundations of the Christian faith itself are fatally undermined.

2 How does one relate to a male savior who represents a male God who is invoked to legitimate the claim that maleness is normative for humanity?

3 'Can this be the Christ?' [John 4.29]. Women today are asking this same question of the institutional church. Can you recognize in us, in our persons and in our experience, the image of Christ, and will you choose to act accordingly?

20.491
L. Alonso Schoekel
Spanish Jesuit and biblical scholar

1 People ask us for bread and we offer them a handful of theories about each verse of John 6. They ask questions about God and we offer them three theories about the literary form of one psalm. They thirst for justice and we offer them discussions about the root of the word *sedaga* ('justice' in Hebrew). I am examining my conscience out loud, and the reply I hear is: the one must be done without neglecting the other.

20.492
Albert Schweitzer
Missionary

1 We cannot possibly let ourselves get frozen into regarding everyone we do not know as an absolute stranger.

2 Only through Love can we attain communion with God.

3 The most important quality in a person connected with religion is absolute devotion to the truth.

4 As soon as man does not take his existence for granted, but beholds it as something unfathomably mysterious, thought begins.

5 One thing stirs me when I look back at my youthful days, the fact that so many people gave me something or were something to me without knowing it.

6 A man is ethical only when life, as such, is sacred to him, that of plants and animals as that of his fellow men, and when he devotes himself helpfully to all life that is in need of help.

7 The ethic of relation of man to man is not something apart by itself: it is only a particular relation which results from the universal one.

20.493
Lesbia Scott
Hymn-writer

1 I sing a song of the saints of God,
Patient and brave and true,
Who toiled and fought and lived and died
For the Lord they loved and knew.
And one was a doctor, and one was a queen,
And one was a shepherdess on the green;
They were all of them saints of God; and I mean,
God helping, to be one too.

20.494
Richenda Scott
English Quaker historian

1 Men and women still feel, in a way they cannot explain, that in the sacrifice of the cross

something has happened to them, has been done for them. It is nothing so simple as averting the wrath of a just and outraged God through the sacrifice offered in appeasement on behalf of sinful man. As we grope for understanding, do we find that the conquest of sin at the unconscious as well as the conscious depths did achieve something for the human race, did break a bond that held human nature in its grip, so that the way is opened for a fresh approach to God and to the whole universe in which our existence is set?

20.495
Ida Scudder

North American missionary doctor to India

1 Do not always look for gratitude, for sometimes when you are most deserving, you will get the least.

20.496
Vida Scudder

North American literary scholar, religious writer and social activist

1 Man is most truly himself, as the Eastern Church well knows, not when he toils but when he adores. And we are learning more and more that all the innocent joy in life may be a form of adoration.

2 When the time came to retire on a Carnegie pension... I wanted to refuse that money, and I could have done so and not starved. But I took it. I decided that my legal claim on it involved moral responsibility for its use. So I spend it year by year, on radical social causes mostly religious in character and inspired if not endorsed by the Church; thereby seeking to hack off the branch I sit on.

3 One may sometimes attend church for a year, and hear excellent discourses on international peace, on industrial justice, on civil liberties, sex relations, social ethics in every phase; but rarely or never a word to help one's poor little soul in its effort to enter into commerce with the Eternal.

20.497
Juan Luis Segundo

Uruguayan Jesuit liberation theologian

1 I believe that this is the greatest danger: to think that faith is a kind of possession of the church that is best preserved when the formulas are repeated in a strictly orthodox way and when the Christian stays far away from dialogue with others who do not keep the faith in the same orthodox way.

2 For me the greatest danger for faith continues to be the divorce between faith and life with its commitments.

20.498
Peter Selby

English theologian

1 It is human to want things to be different.

2 The Church is the first fruit of God's longing. Its life together, therefore, does not depend on excluding people and groups, but on a witness to the constantly inclusive activity of a God whose concern extends to a sparrow that falls on the ground.

3 The Church is not a tribe like other tribes.

4 The fear that often comes to the surface in the Church by talk of women as priests and of homosexual relationships is above all else the fear of desire.

5 The struggle against what is in shorthand called racism deserves to be seen as source and ground of the struggles which humankind has to make.

20.499
Jane Shaw

North American-born Anglican church historian

1 The average Anglican is now black and female. What would it mean for us to make central to the life and mission of the Anglican Church the theological reflections of such women...? In what ways would this require us to 'deconstruct' our ideas not only about gender and theology but also concerning race, ethnicity and mission?

2 One of the most remarkable things about Christianity is that it can not only bear the contradictions and complexities of multiple understandings of what it means to be fully human, but that it embraces such multiplicity.

20.500
Fulton John Sheen
North American Roman Catholic archbishop

1 Perfection is being not doing; it is not to effect an act but to achieve a character.

2 God does not love us because we are valuable. We are valuable because God loves us.

3 You are not tempted because you are evil; you are tempted because you are human.

4 Character is not in the mind. It is in the will.

5 Sex has become one of the most discussed subjects of modern times. The Victorians pretended it did not exist; the moderns pretend that nothing else exists.

20.501
Philip Sheldrake
English pastoral theologian and writer

1 King Alfred, on the run from the Danish invaders of Saxon Wessex, found hospitality at a simple hearth where he was berated for allowing the cakes to burn. He was thus reminded that ordinary people see the real story of life in the ordinary daily round.

2 The pages of Christian history are strewn with marginalized people and traditions as well as forgotten or disparaged ideas. Allowing for an inner weakness in some of them, it seems nonetheless fair to say that many have been left behind or actively repressed in the name of progress, institutional development or orthodoxy.

3 True desire is non-possessive. It is an openness to the future, to possibility, to the other—whether a human other or God.

4 [For Celtic Christians] the natural landscape was both a concrete reality where people lived and, at the same time, a doorway into another, spiritual, world.

5 The sense of living in a 'between place' enabled Celtic Christians to make connections between the physical and the intangible, the seen and the unseen, this world and a permanently present 'other' world.

6 Holiness is a process, a continual movement towards God.

7 Passion, for all its dangers, needs uncaging if we are to move towards completeness as human beings and if our walking with Christ in faith is to pass beyond the cerebral and the emotionally anaemic.

8 The salvation that is effected by the Cross of Jesus is not merely a healing for individuals but it is also the ultimate destruction of the deadness at the heart of human history.

20.502
David Sheppard
Anglican Bishop of Liverpool

1 As part of its listening, the Church is called to commit itself to action on behalf of the poor.

2 The call to justice jars on many ears.

3 The Church is called to reflect God's character in the world... Reflecting this character of God will mean that the Church must risk losing its innocence by becoming involved in the corporate life of cities. It must sometimes take sides, even if that leads to great unpopularity rather than growth in the number of worshippers.

4 The character of Christian love is that we should reject snappy catch answers and slogans, and refuse to withdraw when the subject becomes difficult.

5 When powers and institutions are reconciled to God, they become more modest, and take on their proper place in His purposes.

20.503
Ronald J. Sider
North American theologian

1 Western Christians have failed... to declare God's perspective on the plight of our billion hungry neighbours.

2 God longs for the salvation of the rich as much as for the salvation of the poor... Salvation for the rich will include liberation from their injustice.

3 God requires radically transformed economic relationships among his people.

4 The present division between the haves and have-nots in the body of Christ is a major hindrance to world evangelism.

20.504
Ulrich Simon
German-born theologian

1 The possibility of freedom in slavery is a spiritual act, in which everything that is done is first received.

2 The lasting significance of Auschwitz for humanity lies in its disclosure of the human condition as something incomprehensible and insoluble in merely human terms. The conflict occurred on a dimension which cannot be understood according to any theories or myths.

20.505
Cardinal Sin
Roman Catholic cardinal of the Philippines

1 [On getting his hat] Now there is an eighth Cardinal Sin.

20.506
Edith Sitwell
English poet

1 Still falls the Rain—
Dark as the world of man, black as our loss—
Blind as the nineteen hundred and forty nails
Upon the Cross.

20.507
Herbert Slade
English Anglican monk

1 All life is growth. This is especially true of the spiritual life. It continually grows. To stand still, to look back is death.

2 Easy forms of theological harmonisation are like committee schemes of reunion: always premature and almost always wrong.

3 One of the most perplexing situations of the present time is the uncertainty among the clergy about the essentials of their calling and as a result the confused methods of training they are being given.

20.508
Nicola Slee
British feminist theologian and liturgical writer

1 Christians are those who remember the story of Jesus within the community of the church, in and for their own time and in their own lives.

2 There is not and never has been *one* 'story of Jesus', but many stories. From New Testament times onwards, the stories told about Jesus have been at least as remarkable for their diversity as their commonality, and the attempt to recapture a 'core' of *either* unassailable historical fact *or* doctrinal consensus is almost certainly doomed.

3 There is no feminist 'solution' to the question of Christian identity which will miraculously dissolve the centuries of male bias and oppression enshrined in the tradition or which will recover the lost lives and witness of countless unremembered women.

4 Women whose lives have been shaped by feminism can no longer continue to read ancient scriptural texts and patriarchal traditions in old, established ways.

20.509
Mary F. Smith
Quaker and later Scottish Episcopalian

1 Prayer is an exercise of the spirit, as thought is of the mind.

2 To pray about any day's work does not mean to ask for success in it. It means, first to realize my own inability to do even a familiar job, as it truly should be done, unless I am in touch with eternity, unless I do it 'unto God', unless I have the Father with me.

20.510
Patti Smith
North American pop singer

1 Who was Jesus out to get? The thieves and the whores. He was looking to get the lowest of the low; he was looking to help the lepers to pray for themselves. They didn't need to go to these fancy scribes and Pharisees, and, like, bring a lamb or a gold shekel and say, 'Will you say a prayer for me?' He was saying, 'If you want to talk to God, you can talk for free: mention my name—you're in.'

20.511
Ivor Smith-Cameron
Indian-born Anglican priest

1 The Christian community has, through much of its missionary endeavour, failed to take seriously the spiritual journeys of others. In doing so it has lost out on its own fullness.

2 Christian unity itself is only part of a deeper unity of people of all faiths, and that is only part of a deeper unity of all mankind.

3 I don't think that Jesus primarily called us to Himself. What He did was to call us together *with* Him in doing His Father's will. Jesus is the key to our greater understanding of the nature of God, though God is greater... than simply being limited to the person of Christ.

4 Whenever I hear about Christ as Saviour it appears that He saves us from sin—and I don't wish to deny that—but in my experience he does more than that: He releases us from *fear*, and I think fear is the great killer.

20.512
George M. Soares-Prabhu
Indian New Testament scholar

1 Western exegesis [scriptural interpretation], part of the immense ideological production of an affluent and intensely acquisitive society built on principles diametrically opposed to those of Jesus, has... tried systematically to spiritualize the gospel understanding of the poor.

2 The poor of the Bible are all those who are in any way, and not just economically, deprived of the means or the dignity they need to lead a fully human existence; or who are in a situation of powerlessness which exposes them to such deprivation. The poor of the Bible are thus the 'wretched of the earth', the marginalized, the exploited, all those who are actually or potentially oppressed.

3 Real poverty, as distinct from metaphorical or 'spiritual poverty', is never valued in the Bible for itself. As a state of economic or social deprivation brought about by exploitation, it is an evil... So Yahweh promises to vindicate the poor so that they will be poor no more. And Jesus, who blesses not poverty but the poor, announces the dawning of the eschatological age which will bring all poverty to an end.

4 The Kingdom comes indeed as a gift but it comes also as a responsibility inviting urgent and active response from those to whom it is given. Salvation comes from God, but it is actualized in and through the struggles of the poor.

20.513
Jon Sobrino
El Salvadorean liberation theologian

1 The cross does not offer us any explanatory model that would make us understand what salvation is and how it itself might be salvation. Instead it invites us to participate in a process within which we can actually experience history as salvation.

2 It would be illusory, useless, and even blasphemous to claim to bear witness to God without engaging in practical activity to repair creation.

3 In the pain, misfortune, oppression,
and death of the people,
God is silent.
God is silent on the cross,
in the crucified.
And this silence is God's word, God's cry.
In solidarity,
God speaks the language of love.

20.514
Dorothee Soelle
German theologian

1 To need consolation and to console are human, just as human as Christ was.

2 In the face of suffering you are either with the victim or the executioner—there is no other option.

3 To watch with Jesus, not to fall asleep during the time of his fear of death, which lasts till the end of the world and has in view all the fearful, is an ancient Christian demand that is contrary to every natural response to affection.

4 To attain the image of Christ means to live in revolt against the great Pharaoh, is to remain with the oppressed and the disadvantaged. It means to make their lot one's own.

5 A society is conceivable in which no person is left totally alone, with no one to think of him and stay with him. Watching and praying are possible.

6 One can say that in every prayer an angel waits for us, since every prayer changes the one who prays, strengthens him, in that it pulls him together and brings him to the utmost attention, which in suffering is forced from us and which in loving we ourselves give.

7 The more strongly we affirm reality, the more we are immersed in it, the more deeply we are touched by these processes of dying which surround us and press in upon us.

8 Death is what takes place within us when we look upon others not as gift, blessing or stimulus but as threat, danger, competition. It is the death that comes to all who try to live by bread alone. This is the death that the Bible fears and gives us good reason to fear. It is not the final departure we think of when we speak of death; it is that purposeless, empty existence devoid of genuine human relationships and filled with anxiety, silence and loneliness.

20.515
Solentiname Christians
Christian community on the island of Solentiname, Nicaragua

1 [Community study of Matthew 26.6-13]

Oscar: If they'd sold [the perfume] it would have gone to only a small number of the poor, and the poor of the world are countless. On the other hand, when she offered it to Jesus, she was giving it, in his person, to all the poor. That made it clear that it was Jesus we believe in. And believing in Jesus makes us concerned about other people, and we'll even get to create a society where there will be no poor.

Thomas Pena: There's lots of ways of being poor: a poor person can be somebody with an arm missing. A poor person is somebody born stupid, or an orphan child, without parents. There'll always be people like that in need, but of course if we're Christians they won't be poor, in poverty; if they are among us, that is, we won't let them perish.

Laureano: We can offer our lives as Jesus did. Then it'll be also for us, that perfume that the woman poured on Jesus.

20.516
Alexander Solzhenitsyn
Russian writer

1 The disappearance of nations would have impoverished us no less than if all men had become alike, with one personality and one face. Nations are the wealth of mankind, its collective personalities; the very least of them

wears its own special colours and bears within itself a special facet of divine intention.

2 Violence can only be concealed by the lie, and the lie can be maintained only by violence... Once the lie has been dispersed, the nakedness of violence will be revealed in all its repulsiveness, and then violence, become decrepit, will come crashing down.

3 Not everything has a name. Some things lead us into a realm beyond words. Art thaws even the frozen, darkened soul, opening it to lofty spiritual experience. Through Art we are sometimes sent—indistinctly, briefly—revelations not to be achieved by rational thought.

20.517
Choan-Seng Song
Theologian from Taiwan

1 Most of us [who write theology] do not listen as we write.

2 Perhaps a poet can tell us how we should go about theology. Look out the window of your workroom and imbibe the colours with which God has adorned nature! Then there will be more colour in your theology. Listen to dogs bark, birds sing and insects hum outside your workroom. Then your theology will become audible as well as legible.

3 Can sun and moon and stars praise God? Of course they can. Theologians must regain the ability to hear them sing and praise God. Then their theological mind will expand.

4 What Jesus showed us is how to do theology with people daily involved in the joys and sorrows of this life.

5 If popular theology has to be invented by a handful of Christian thinkers, then it is no longer theology of the people.

6 The people, the masses, the undertrodden, are *theo*-logical beings. They are human beings with whom God dwells.

7 The last supper was not a political event. It was a meal of redemption prepared by the compassionate God... The broken body of Jesus is different from ours. It is broken to release the redemptive power of God. Its blood is shed to give rise to a community of wholeness. It is the reign of God that breaks out of that broken body of Jesus.

8 God seems especially patient in Asia. Space is vast. History is long. Culture is rich. Persons are numerous. The heart nourished by such culture embraces deep emotions. The soul formed in such history is very patient. And the mind grown out of such vast space has plenty of room.

9 Is it that the passion shown in the birth of a child gives us a glimpse into the passion of God giving birth to creation?

10 Theology of compassion is the theology of love with no strings attached. It does not predetermine how and where God should do God's saving work. It does not assume that God left Asia in the hands of pagan powers and did not come to it until missionaries from the West reached it.

11 There is always a danger in religion, any religion, to idolize—idolizing everything from power, pomp, doctrine, and creed to some minute detail of how a believer is to be initiated into the mystery of faith.

12 Power is essentially exhibitionistic.

13 The power of God's reign is not exhibitionistic. It is self-effacing, self-concealing. That power, like the leaven buried inside the mass of dough, is a fermentative power in the depth of humanity, in the womb of God's creation. It is the power of compassion. It is the power of the cross.

14 We are more likely to catch glimpses of truth when we allow what we think and believe to be tested.

15 Let us be clear, then, that it is not our business to protect the truth. Rather it is our business to serve the truth, wherever and whenever it is found.

20.518
Donald Soper
British Methodist preacher

1 Capitalism is an evil thing, because it is based on what is called enlightened self-interest, and that is a baptismal name for selfishness. Poverty is a crime. The Church has been very specific on other matters. It hasn't hesitated to speak arbitrarily on most intimate affairs like sex. I don't see why it should restrict its particularity to those and not extend them to the world of the unemployed.

2 I can't see any future for a church that in God's world doesn't accept that it must be involved in that part of it which is political and economic. A Church which claims that the world is for Christ must be up to its neck in politics.

3 We must begin with people where they are, not where we like them to be. They are not where our fathers were.

20.519
Janet Martin Soskice
British theologian

1 Churches that do not ordain women need to demonstrate how their ecclesial practice is consonant with their Christology.

2 The symbols by which we structure our world have direct and substantive effect on how we act in that world.

20.520
John Spong
US Episcopalian bishop

1 The only churches that grow today are those that do not, in fact, understand the issues, and can therefore traffic in certainty.

20.521
Dumitru Staniloae
Romanian Orthodox theologian

1 The whole world ought to be regarded as the visible part of a universal and continuing sacrament, and all man's activities as a sacramental, divine communion.

20.522
Douglas V. Steere
North American Quaker and philosopher

1 If something apart from ourselves is seeking to make itself known to us, it will not succeed unless we know how to wait, to persist in waiting.

2 In learning to pray, no laboratory is needed but a room; no apparatus but ourselves. The living God is the field of force into which we enter in prayer, and the only really total failure is to stop praying and not to begin again.

3 To come near to God is to change.

4 Intercession is the most intensely social act that the human being is capable of.

20.523
David Steindl-Rast
Austrian-born Benedictine monk

1 Community is always poised between two poles: solitude and togetherness. Without togetherness community disperses; without solitude community collapses into a mass, a crowd.

2 Contemplative life as a 'vocation' means a particular form of life in which, ideally at least, every detail of daily living is oriented towards recollection.

3 Responsive listening is the form the Bible gives to our basic religious quest as human beings.

4 Suddenly everything is simple. We can drop all the big, cumbersome terms. Gratefulness says it all.

5 To recover a healthy understanding of leisure is to come a long way toward understanding contemplation.

20.524
Baroness Mary Stocks
English advocate of women's suffrage and the welfare state

1 We don't call it sin today, we call it self-expression.

20.525
Elaine Storkey
British sociologist

1 The consensus appears to be that as it is presented and practised in our churches the gospel is NOT Good News for women.

20.526
John Stott
British theologian

1 The Christian should resemble a fruit tree, not a Christmas tree! For the gaudy decorations of a Christmas tree are only tied on, whereas fruit grows on a fruit tree.

2 Christianity is unique. It is peerless.

3 Christianity is not primarily a theological system, an ethical system, a ritual system, a social system or an ecclesiastical system—it is a person: it's Jesus Christ, and to be a Christian is to know Him and to follow Him and believe in Him.

4 Ultimately, evangelism is not a technique. It is the Lord of the Church who reserves to Himself His sovereign right to add to His Church.

5 Every church should be engaged in continuous self-reformation, scrutinising its traditions in the light of Scripture and where necessary modifying them.

6 Before Christ sent the church into the world he sent the Spirit into the church. The same order must be observed today.

7 Without the Spirit, the Word is a lifeless and dead letter.

8 Christianity is in its very essence a resurrection religion. The concept of resurrection lies at its heart. If you remove it, Christianity is destroyed.

9 Verbally in Scripture, visually in sacrament, Jesus Christ is set forth as the only Saviour of sinners.

10 Grace is love that cares and stoops and rescues.

11 The Bible has the authority of God because God himself has spoken... I do not believe that there could be a more authentic or authoritative witness to the historic Jesus. We may have more to learn, but I don't believe God has any more to teach than what he has once and for all revealed in His incarnate Son.

20.527
Elizabeth Stuart
British Roman Catholic theologian

1 Liturgy is dangerous.

2 Lesbian, gay and bisexual people, along with people from different races, children and many more have been deprived of a liturgical language to make sense of their experience. Linguistic deprivation is a particularly effective way of keeping people silent and disempowered.

3 The Church as the people of God is larger than buildings, larger than institutions, larger than hierarchies and denominations, larger than any religion. Where two or three are gathered together in God's name there is the Church.

4 Friendship is *political* when it motivates people to come together to change structures and situations which damage and diminish their friends.

5 Gay and lesbian Christians know that God's spirit is not a tame dove but a wild goose, free of ecclesiastical attempts to control and confine it, that makes its home in the most unlikely places. The Spirit comes not in quiet conformity but demanding to be heard.

20.528
Evelyn Sturge
English Quaker and social activist

1 We must be confident that there is still more 'life' to be 'lived' and yet more heights to be scaled. The tragedy of middle age is that, so often, men and women cease to press 'towards the goal of their high calling'. They cease learning, cease growing; they give up and resign from life. As wisdom dawns with age, we begin to measure our experiences not by what life gives to us, not by the things withheld from us, but by their power to help us to grow in spiritual wisdom.

20.529
Leon Joseph Suenens
Belgian cardinal

1 We are not criticised for being Christians, but for not being Christian enough.

2 Christ cannot live his life today in this world without our mouth, without our eyes, without our going and coming, without our heart. When we love, it is Christ loving through us.

3 No generation can claim to have plumbed to the depths the unfathomable riches of Christ. The Holy Spirit has promised to lead us step by step into the fullness of truth.

4 The preaching of the Gospel and its acceptance imply a social revolution whereby the hungry are fed and justice becomes the right of all.

5 We find in the Spirit unity and plurality at the same time. There is plurality in that unity and unity in that plurality. There is no uniformity. It is the fullness of the Father, of the Son and of the Spirit.

6 O Lord, pray for us, because we so strongly need someone to be our go-between, to bring us from this level of coexistence to a new stage of communion.

7 Come, Holy Spirit! I do not ask of you any special gift but neither do I refuse any gift either, because we receive those manifestations not for ourselves but for the Kingdom of God, for the building up of his Church. One person will receive a certain manifestation of the Spirit, another a different one, but all will use their particular gifts to share in the upbuilding of the Church.

20.530
R.S. Sugirtharajah
Sri Lankan theologian

1 Conversion does not necessarily mean changing from one religion to another. It can mean a conversion to a new dimension of one's own faith. One can be rooted in one's tradition and yet learn more and be open to its forgotten aspects.

2 [In the Cornelius–Peter episode] what we often overlook is that Peter too was converted. It was a rude shock to him, as it was to Jonah before him, that God's grace knows no bounds and extends to outsiders who are not normally recipients of such love.

3 In the new figure of Jesus as a sage, we discover one who helps us to find a way to respond to religious pluralism and the greater problems of human suffering and injustice. Jesus as a sage is open and less imperialistic, and at the same time committed to the lifting up of the poor.

20.531
Stephen Sykes
British theologian

1 Realism and honesty compel us to admit that it is not self-evident for Anglicans to speak enthusiastically about evangelism.

2 Liberalism is a cuckoo in the Anglican nest, and the all-too-facile inclusion of it under the guise of a 'party' with a long and honoured history in Anglicanism was bound to be no more than a temporary measure.

20.532
Elsa Tamez
Methodist theologian from Mexico

1 The earth of our continent [South America], waiting for justice and fulfilment, has already been fertilized by the blood of thousands and thousands of people who have been killed throughout its history, and especially in the last twenty years.

2 To distance oneself [from the biblical text] means to be new to the text (to be a stranger, a first-time visitor to the text), to be amazed by everything, especially by those details that repeated readings have made seem so logical and natural. It is necessary to take up the Bible as a new book, a book that has never been heard or read before.

3 It is clear from this process of gaining distance and coming closer that in Latin America the Bible is not read as an intellectual or academic exercise; it is read with the goal of giving meaning to our lives today.

20.533
Richard Henry Tawney
English economic historian

1 When men have gone so far as to talk as though their idols have come to life, it is time that someone broke them.

2 Those who seek God in isolation from their fellow-men... are apt to find, not God, but a devil whose countenance bears an embarrassing resemblance to their own.

20.534
John V. Taylor
English Anglican bishop

1 The whole doctrine of justification by faith hinges, for me, on my painfully reluctant realisation that my Father is not going to be more pleased with me when I am good than when I am bad. He accepts me and delights in me as I am. It is ridiculous of him, but that is how it is between us.

2 God is ultimately interested in my being totally alive: everything that comes from him is life-giving.

3 Nothing is more needed by humanity today, and by the church in particular, than the recovery of a sense of 'beyondness' in the whole of life to revive the springs of wonder and adoration.

4 Whatever we do that creates deadness is a sin.

5 My own attempt to understand the Holy Spirit has convinced me that he is active in precisely those experiences that are very common—experiences of recognition, sudden insight, an influx of awareness when you wake up and become alive to something... Every time a human being cries 'Ah! I see it now!', that's what I mean by the Holy Spirit.

6 All true intercession is a deepening of awareness towards others rather than a request.

7 Jesus Christ is much more naturally at ease and at home in non-European cultures than most of his missionaries.

8 This is the true sequence of mission: a surpassing awareness of the reality of Christ, corporately shared, expressing itself in thankfulness and wonder, causing the world to ask questions to which an answer must be given in a form that every hearer can understand.

9 Other faiths have their mystics but only in Jesus, I believe, can we find such spontaneous and personal communion with God combined with such a passionate ethical concern for humanity. Both awareness of God and awareness of the world attain their zenith in him.

20.535
Michael Taylor
English Baptist Director of Christian Aid

1 For me, Christianity is about the Kingdom, not about the Church: it has to do with human growth and development, not church growth and development.

2 If Christ is present in human life, He is present all the time.

3 I do not think heresy is coming to the wrong conclusions. It is coming to any conclusion alone; no longer listening to all the other voices in history and the world around you, but coming to your own conclusions without being enriched by others, being jolted by others, and being called on to something where all of you are converted into something better than any of them.

20.536
Pierre Teilhard de Chardin

French theologian and scientist

1 We have only to believe. And the more threatening and irreducible reality appears, the more firmly and desperately must we believe. Then, little by little, we shall see the universal horror unbend, and then smile upon us, and then take us in its more than human arms.

2 Faith has need of the whole truth.

3 Those who die in grace go no further from us than God—and God is very near.

4 Lord, enfold me in the depths of your heart; and there, hold me, refine, purge, and set me on fire, raise me aloft, until my own self knows utter annihilation.

5 Old age comes from God, old age leads on to God, old age will not touch me only so far as He wills.

6 The most satisfactory thing in life is to have been able to give a large part of oneself to others.

7 It is finally the Utopians, not the 'realists', who make scientific sense. They at least, though their flights of fancy may cause us to smile, have a feeling for the true dimensions of the phenomenon of Man.

8 Expectation—anxious, collective and operative expectation of an end of the world, that is to say, of an issue for the world—that is perhaps the supreme Christian function and the most distinctive characteristic of our religion.

9 To act is to create and creation is for ever.

10 Something is afoot in the universe, a result is working out which can best be compared to a gestation and birth: the birth of a new spiritual reality formed by souls and the matter they draw after them. Laboriously, by way of human activity and thanks to it, the new earth is gathering, isolating and purifying itself. No, we are not like flowers in a bunch, but the leaves and flowers of a great tree, on which each appears at its time and place, according to the demands of the All.

11 We have not, in us, a body which takes its nourishment independently of the soul. Everything that the body has admitted and has begun to transform must be transfigured by the soul in its turn.

12 The masters of the spiritual life incessantly repeat that God wants only souls. To give those words their true value, we must not forget that the human soul, however independently created our philosophy represents it as being, is inseparable, in its birth and its growth, from the universe into which it is born.

13 In each soul, God loves and partly saves the whole world which that soul sums up in an incommunicable and particular way.

14 Owing to the interrelation between matter, soul and Christ, we bring part of the being which he desires back to God *in whatever we do*.

20.537
Elizabeth Templeton

Scottish philosopher and theologian

1 The Church is, of course, odd.

2 Unless our ecclesiastical strangeness is our transparency to the generous strangeness of God, we lose all but trivial sociological interest for a world as fragmented and fragile as ours.

3 The core of the Christian gospel is a promise and an invitation to belong in, to be at home in, the abolition of all exclusiveness, in sharing the outgoing life of a non-excluding God with the whole of creation.

20.538
Mother Teresa of Calcutta
Albanian-born nun and founder of the Missionaries of Charity

1 A beautiful death is for people who have lived like animals to die like angels.

2 It is by forgiving that one is forgiven.

3 Holiness consists of doing the will of God with a smile.

4 I have found the paradox that if I love until it hurts, then there is no hurt, but only more love.

5 There is a net of love by which you can catch souls.

6 A family that prays together stays together.

7 God is the friend of silence. Trees, flowers, grass grow in silence. See the stars, moon and sun, how they move in silence.

8 Now let us do something beautiful for God.

9 If you are humble, nothing will touch you, neither praise nor disgrace, because you know what you are.

20.539
Adrian Thatcher
British theologian

1 Merriment is an antidote to the deadening seriousness that has attached itself to sexual activity in much of Christian history. Unless sex is playful, it is intolerable.

20.540
Margaret Thatcher
English Prime Minister

1 When Christians... take counsel together, their purpose... should not be to ascertain what is the mind of the majority, but what is the mind of the Holy Spirit—something which may be quite different.

20.541
Helmut Thielicke
German Lutheran theologian and preacher

1 Tell me how much you know of the sufferings of your fellow men and I will tell you how much you have loved them.

2 There is no more sensitive conscience than that of a person who loves God. It registers every shadow that passes over the heart of God.

3 Man becomes a holy thing, a neighbour, only if we realise that he is the property of God and that Jesus Christ died for him.

4 Heaven is not a space overhead to which we lift our eyes; it is the background of our existence, the all-encompassing lordship of God within which we stand.

5 You ought never to believe something that you dare not think over.

20.542
Susan Brooks Thistlethwaite
North American theologian

1 Denial is the way to the continuation of the abuse of women. Consciousness of the violence against women with which we all live every day is the beginning of its end. A feminist biblical interpretation must have this consciousness at its center.

20.543
R.S. Thomas
Welsh poet

1 He stands at the grave's
entrance and rubs death from his eyes,
while thought's fountain recommences
its play, watering the waste ground
over again for the germination
of the blood's seed, where roses should blow.

20.544
Angela Tilby
English television producer and Anglican theologian

1 I am drawn to those strands in our spiritual tradition which see human beings as priests of creation, gifted with consciousness and with the power of naming, but always in a relationship of dependence on the natural world.

2 Being honest to God means being prepared to question God about the world and to suffer the blazing encounter with God's strange and un-human holiness.

3 Love remains the vocation of all who are baptised, and love is a sign of God to the whole community. Yet love hurts. Here it is that some of us make our most costly mistakes. Here it is often that our personal story looks most wobbly and incomplete. Here it is, also, that we come to know God not only as our Creator, but as our redeemer, our lover, the hound of heaven who will not let us go.

20.545
Paul Tillich
German-born American Protestant theologian and philosopher

1 In the depth of the anxiety of having to die is the anxiety of being eternally forgotten.

2 Accept the fact that you are accepted.

3 Language has created the word *loneliness* to express the pain of being alone, and the word *solitude* to express the glory of being alone.

4 The first duty of love is to listen.

5 Grace strikes us when we are in great pain and restlessness. It strikes us when we walk through the dark valley of a meaningless and empty life. It strikes us when we feel that our separation is deeper than usual.

6 The courage to be is the courage to accept oneself as accepted in spite of being unacceptable... this is the genuine meaning of the Paulinian–Lutheran doctrination of justification by faith.

7 Personality is that being which has power over itself.

8 The courage to be is rooted in the God who appears when God has disappeared in the anxiety of doubt.

9 The saint is saint, not because he is 'good' but because he is transparent for something that is more than he himself is.

20.546
Florence Tim Oi Li
Born in Hong Kong, first woman Anglican priest

1 Here was I, a simple girl wishing to devote my life to [God's] service. The wider issues of the ordination of women were far from my mind as I entered the little church. I was being obedient to God's call.

20.547
J.R.R. Tolkien
British Roman Catholic philologist and writer

1 'Trends' in the Church are... serious, especially to those accustomed to find in it a solace and a 'pax' in times of temporal trouble, and not just another arena of strife and change.

20.548
Edicio de la Torre
Priest in the Philippines

1 Blessed are those who hunger and thirst
after justice
For they shall be satisfied
But when, O Lord, and how?

20.549
Camillo Torres
Columbian priest

1 We believe in a loving God,
whose Word sustains our lives
and the work of our hands in the universe.

God is life.

We believe in God's son among us
who brought the seed of renewal.
He lived with the poor to show the meaning of love.

Jesus Christ is Lord.

We believe in the Spirit of Life
who makes us one with God,
whose strength and energy renews our own.

The Spirit is love.

20.550
Sergio Torres
Latin American theologian

1 The poor call into question the mission and identity of the church.

2 In Latin America a liberative reading of the Bible has its roots in the practice of the poor working in the organization of basic ecclesial communities. It is not just reading passages that speak about oppression or liberation. The whole Bible is seen as a project with a liberation message.

3 Personal conversion and social transformation are proposed in the Bible. The reign of God is a utopian horizon, but it also begins to be built here on earth.

20.551
Paul Tournier
Swiss doctor and counsellor

1 For the fulfilment of his purpose God needs more than priests, bishops, pastors and missionaries. He needs mechanics and chemists, gardeners and street sweepers, dressmakers and cooks, tradesmen, physicians, philosophers, judges and shorthand typists.

2 In trying to do everything for the best, we do not avoid all mistakes. So the Christian life is not a huge effort to do good, but abdication and a prayer that God will guide us through all the reefs.

3 A man's judgment of another depends more on the judging and on his passions than on the one being judged and his conduct.

4 You can never establish a personal relationship without opening up your own heart.

5 No one can develop freely in this world and find a full life without feeling understood by at least one person.

20.552
Phyllis Trible
North American theologian

1 Prophetic movements are not exempt from sin. Even as feminism announces judgment on patriarchy and calls for repentance and change, it needs ever to be aware of its own potential for idolatry. No document teaches this lesson better than scripture.

20.553
Simon Tugwell
British Dominican

1 It is time we woke up to the fact that people want more from the church than bingo and dance: they want God.

2 When the Tradition is healthy, it communicates a wholeness of personal and corporate experience, an understanding of and familiarity with Scripture, not as dead words from the past, but as a kind of living language, and a mature and developing Christian culture and wisdom.

3 God's love sets us truly free. Our love finds its fulfilment in being transformed into God's love, and only then will our works be truly fruitful.

4 There is a kind of reticence about the saints, like the reticence of the Lord himself, and it is this that makes them able to do God's work and to speak his word, without making people feel threatened or 'got at' by them, without crushing the bruised reed or extinguishing the smouldering wick.

5 There is no justification for supposing that anyone who receives the gift of tongues has received any special 'fullness of the Spirit'.

6 In the last analysis, it is not the *experience* of God that we must preach, but his reality.

20.554
Desmond Tutu
South African archbishop

1 We believe that there can be no real peace in our beloved land until there is fundamental change.

2 The wealthy consume a great deal more than can be justified by the population figures.

3 Desperate people use desperate methods.

4 The dividedness of the Churches makes it difficult for people to believe in the Gospel of Jesus Christ.

5 Women, we need you to give us back our faith in humanity.

6 [Of 29 February 1988] What we did today was not the negative thing of saying we disobeyed. It was the positive thing of saying we obeyed God.

7 We who advocate peace are becoming an irrelevance when we speak peace. The government speaks rubber bullets, live bullets, tear gas, police dogs, detention and death.

8 There are three good reasons for a cleric not to harbour political ambition: Archbishop Makarios, Ayatollah Khomeini and Bishop Musorewa.

9 Thank God I am black. White people will have a lot to answer for at the last judgement.

10 Goodness is stronger than evil;
love is stronger than hate;
light is stronger than darkness;
life is stronger than death;
victory is ours through him who loved us.

20.555
Colin Urquhart
English Anglican clergyman and author

1 The world around us will recognise us as disciples of Jesus when they see our prayers being answered.

2 The cross that Jesus tells us to carry is the one that we willingly take up ourselves—the cross of self-denial in order that we might live for the glory of the Father.

3 God is the God of promise. He keeps his word, even when that seems impossible; even when the circumstances seem to point to the opposite.

20.556
Sister Vandana
Indian member of the Order of the Sacred Heart and theological writer

1 When wine, used liberally on merry-making occasions—gave out, it was Mary's presence that saved the situation. She turned to Jesus instinctively for help with the certainty of a true *bhakta* (a lover of God). When he seemed to refuse to do anything about it, with equal certainty and the equanimity of a *sthitaprajna* (one of steadfast wisdom), she told the servants just to obey him... Thus through the miracle of water, he revealed his glory and his disciples believed in him.

2 Water! An ordinary, everyday, familiar thing, usually taken for granted and unnoticed—except when found absent and needed. This the Lord used as an instrument to 'manifest his glory'... 'and his disciples believed in him'. God often used very ordinary things and lets his glory shine out through them.

3 Mary and water have much in common. Mary, like water, was creature—ordinary, unnoticed, quiet, serviceable, lovely, and precious. As there can be no life without water, so God ordained that there would be no new life without Mary.

20.557
Robert Van de Weyer
English Anglican clergyman

1 Just as the Passover festival of the Jews pointed towards Jesus, so too does our village harvest festival.

2 Once the clergyman stops rushing, and once he and his people discover the advantages of small congregations, then worship in the countryside is second to none.

3 If country parsons sought to emulate Herbert's style of ministry, the stress which so many feel would melt away.

4 The parson of many parishes has no choice but to confine himself to being an apostle and, like the first apostles in Jerusalem, he must politely and humbly ask his people to choose from among themselves deacons who can run their affairs, in the form of churchwardens and PCC members.

5 There is in Anglican circles an unfortunate and misguided assumption that individuals should only be ordained if they first experience an inner calling, and then offer themselves for selection. This was not, of course, how Peter, James, John and the rest became apostles; Jesus invited them and, without any prior sense of vocation, they accepted.

20.558
Jean Vanier
French-Canadian founder of the L'Arche communities

1 Is it not one of the problems of religious life today that we have separated ourselves from the poor and the wounded and the suffering? We have too much time to discuss and to theorize, and we have lost the yearning for God which comes when we are faced with the sufferings of people.

2 A community—and especially a Christian one—will always be running against the tide of society, with its individualistic values of wealth and comfort and resulting rejection of people who get in the way of these.

3 When we are at peace, when we have assumed our deep wounds and weakness, when we are in touch with our own heart and capacity for tenderness, then actions flow from our true selves.

4 Even the most beautiful community can never heal the wound of loneliness that we carry. It is only when we discover that this loneliness can become a sacrament that we touch wisdom, for this sacrament is purification and presence of God.

5 To grow is to emerge gradually from a land where our vision is limited, where we are seeking and governed by egotistical pleasure, by our sympathies and antipathies, to a land of unlimited horizons and universal love, where we will be open to every person and desire their happiness.

20.559
W.H. Vanstone
English Anglican clergyman

1 Such is the likeness of God, wholly given, spent and drained in that sublime self-giving which is the ground and source and origin of the universe.

2 When we love we hand ourselves over to receive from another our own triumph and our own tragedy.

3 In artistic creation, as in human relationships, the authenticity of love is denied by the assurance of control. Love aspires for each that which, being truly an 'other', cannot be controlled.

4 He went to the garden of Gethsemane to wait upon the outcome. Waiting can be the most intense and poignant of all human

experiences—the experience which, above all others, strips us of our needs, our values and ourselves.

5 The Church is what man is and does when he recognises what is happening in the being of the universe.

20.560
Chad Varah
Founder of the Samaritans

1 I am the only man in the world who cannot commit suicide.

20.561
Michael Vasey
British theologian and liturgist

1 It may be that the healing of the masculine imagination in the Western church would, of itself, have profound effects for others.

2 In the end, death may be too powerful for people to trust a church that is afraid of reality and mess in human life.

20.562
Alida Verhoeven
Dutch-born minister of the Methodist Church of Argentina

1 Today we say, 'Enough! It's over!' Never again will we use a language, an image, or a symbol that excludes the life, experience, and reflection of millions of human beings: women, young people, peoples and nations of other races or skin colors.

20.563
Stephen Verney
English Anglican bishop

1 Prayer is not us trying to grab hold of God. Prayer is to recognise God coming to us.

2 Contemplation is to open our whole personality to God so that he can take possession of our emotions, our thinking and our will.

3 Gradually, as we grow and develop, we become aware that there is... a centre of authority within us, which lays claim upon us, and keeps us in a true relation to the rest of the universe.

20.564
Alec Vidler
English religious writer

1 It is the Church of the saints and martyrs and prophets, who have been the lights of the world in their several generations, that has the demand upon your allegiance—not the Church which has been corrupted by wealth and worldly power. But the true Church is embedded in the existing Churches—you will not find it elsewhere.

20.565
John J. Vincent
Methodist industrial missioner

1 The obedience of Jesus is not simply submission, but real striving, cooperation, activity.

2 The Bible does not theologize; it tells stories.

3 We need a radical theology based on discipleship to Jesus, a new systematic based on faithful practice. We do not need creeds, but 'rules for the road', for those who wish to be disciples to the ongoing, emerging God incarnate in the Christ today.

4 Liturgy is rehearsal of the whole story of Jesus' ministry, passion, death, resurrection; liturgy is doing something together in the light of the gospel.

20.566
Willem Adolf Visser'T Hooft
Dutch ecumenist

1 It belongs to the very life of the people of God that it must accept again and again to have its life renewed by a new confrontation with its Lord and his holy will.

2 Unity in the New Testament sense is the goal of a living Church. And that means that

the rediscovery of what the living Church is must come before we can go much further on the road to unity.

20.567
René Voillaume
French Little Brother of Jesus and spiritual writer

1 The desert bears the sign of man's complete helplessness as he can do nothing to subsist alone and by himself, and he thus discovers his weakness and the necessity of seeking help and strength in God.

2 To love as Jesus loves; that is not only the Lord's precept, it is our vocation. When all is said and done it is the one thing we have to learn, for it is perfection.

3 The language of the mystics cannot meet the language of science and reason, but nevertheless in a world that craves experimental testimonies it will always be one of the roads by which our contemporaries can find God.

20.568
Helen Waddell
Irish Presbyterian scholar

1 The desert has bred fanaticism and frenzy and fear: but it also bred heroic gentleness.

20.569
Gordon S. Wakefield
English Methodist theologian

1 We are to give our heart to God that he may make it happy, with a happiness which stretches its capacity to the full.

20.570
Jim Wallis
North American Christian activist, writer and founder of the Sojourners Community

1 It is time for a faith decision on nuclear weapons, an altar call in the face of nuclear war. It is time for Christians to get up out of their seats, walk down the aisle of history, and take their place alongside brothers and sisters from all church traditions to form a new peace church in our time.

2 Conformity can go on for generations at a time, but, as the history of the church testifies, the explosive power of the gospel will always be recovered and felt again when men and women have their eyes and lives opened to the living Christ.

3 The gospel gives us different priorities from those of the popular culture and offers us a different agenda from that of the political economy.

4 Contrary to the dominant attitude of our own society, one's economic life and standard of living is not a private matter. It is a critical issue of faith and discipleship.

5 The making of community is essentially a revolutionary act. It proposes to detach men and women from their dependence upon the dominant institutions of the world system and creates an alternative corporate reality based upon different social values.

6 The Holy Spirit is the source of community and the Spirit's work is more related to the building of community than to the edification of the isolated individual.

7 Our Christian institutions are often dependent on parts of the American establishment that oppress the poor of the earth. To come to terms with the gospel will cost the churches a great deal.

8 The church's service and mission in the world is absolutely dependent on its being *different* from the world, being *in* the world but not *of* the world.

20.571
Wandera-Chagenda
East African poet

1 In Limbo
Our weary bodies
Moan, wrestling in our dreams
With the impertinent question:
Why don't you resurrect your
Humanity?

20.572
Neville Ward
British writer on spirituality

1 Adoration is a rejoicing in what we believe God is in himself, in the more that he must be that we cannot understand; it is a reaching out to this in love and longing, wanting to know and prove as much of this as is permitted here on earth, going to that rim of experience where something tells you to turn back to life because this is as far as you can go in wonder at the devastating richness of life. The rest we may hope to know after death, but it is not for now.

2 We are meant to be continually encouraged and discouraged, and to hope in God.

3 Real intercession is not merely a petition but a piece of work, involving perfect, costly self-surrender to God for the work he wants done on other souls.

4 God cannot want from us what is not possible.

5 The fulfilment of marriage is that joy in which each lover's true being is flowering because its growth is being welcomed and unconsciously encouraged by the other in the infinite series of daily decisions which is their life together.

20.573
Kallistos (Timothy) Ware
Greek Orthodox monk and bishop

1 The Christian is saved not in isolation but as a member of the community; he is saved in and through others. We can only be saved when praying for the salvation of all and with the aid of the prayers of all.

20.574
Max Warren
General Secretary of the Church Missionary Society

1 Our first task in approaching another people, another culture, another religion, is to take off our shoes, for the place we are approaching is holy. Else we may find ourselves treading on men's dreams. More serious still, we may forget that God was here before our arrival.

20.575
Robert Allen Warrior
North American journalist

1 The exodus, with its picture of a God who takes the side of the oppressed and powerless, has been a beacon of hope for many in despair.

2 So long as people believe in the Yahweh of deliverance, the world will not be safe from Yahweh the conqueror. But perhaps, if they are true to their struggle, people will be able to achieve what Yahweh's chosen people in the past have not: a society of people delivered from oppression who are not so afraid of becoming victims again that they become oppressors themselves.

20.576
David Watson
English Anglican evangelist

1 The real and important world is the world inside us, not the world outside.

2 If we are willing to learn the meaning of real discipleship and actually to become disciples, the Church in the West would be transformed, and the resultant impact on society would be staggering.

3 There is nothing negative or killjoy about holiness.

4 Faith essentially means taking someone at their word.

5 What other society has as its symbol a horrifying instrument of torture and death—especially when the marks of that society are meant to be love and peace.

6 We have broken God's commandments again and again, and in the court of God's presence we are manifestly guilty. I believe it is

only because Jesus actually took our sin and God's righteous judgment upon Himself that we are saved.

7 I have seen the manifestation of demonic power in the lives of individuals which would make it very hard for me to deny the existence of evil as an intelligent force.

20.577
Evelyn Waugh
English novelist

1 The haunted, trapped, murdered priest is our contemporary and Campion's voice sounds to us across the centuries as though he were walking at our elbow.

20.578
Leslie Weatherhead
British Methodist minister

1 Perhaps we have done everything in the world to find health and radiance, happiness and peace, except to listen to, and heed the soul, crying always that same plaintive cry, the cry of the stream for the ocean, the cry of the prisoner for freedom, the cry of the watcher for morning, the cry of the wanderer for home, the cry of the starving for food, the cry of the soul for God.

2 Nothing can ever destroy truth.

3 But whatever you have ever read or heard, concerning which there has been that inner flash, that sudden certainty, then in God's name heed it, for it is the truth.

4 A miracle is a law-abiding event by which God accomplishes His redemptive purposes through the release of energies which belong to a plane of being higher than any with which we are normally familiar.

5 It is one thing to be told that the Bible has authority because it is divinely inspired, and another thing to feel one's heart leap out and grasp its truth.

20.579
Pauline Webb
English Methodist, ecumenist, preacher and broadcaster

1 Christianity brings liberation through the Gospel in faith and action. But the Christian Church has not been a sufficiently liberating institution for women, in the sense of not opening up to them the full range of possibilities.

20.580
Wang Weifan
South-East Asian writer

1 My Lord is the source of love;
I the river's course.
Let God's love flow through me.
I will not obstruct it.
Irrigation ditches can water
but a portion of the field;
the great Yangtze River can water
a thousand acres.
Expand my heart, O Lord,
that I may love yet more people.
The waters of love can cover vast tracts,
nothing will be lost to me.

20.581
Angela West
British feminist theologian and peace activist

1 The garment of the faith we profess must fit us also for our death.

2 It is our theory (mode of seeing) that to a large extent determines how we experience.

3 [1980s feminism] was particularly insistent on the value of women's experience for doing theology. Yet... I have become acutely aware of the dangers of the tendency to falsely universalise our own experience.

20.582
Morris West
Roman Catholic novelist

1 Every man must be allowed to judge himself; but he must not be allowed to bury the evidence.

20.583
Ikoli Harcourt Whyte
Nigerian writer

1 Come to the world!
Yes, God the Creator, come!
Things are not as you created them
in the beginning.
Come, God, for it is your help
we need in the world.

20.584
E.R. Wickham
British industrial missioner and bishop

1 The Church thinks and plans within the context of the Church instead of setting her mission and her obedience within the given context of society and the world at large. And her 'zeal without knowledge' is responsible for grossly inadequate expressions of mission... Missionary planning in the Church must measure up to the realities of the situation.

2 Too often the Gospel is preached wide outside the context of man's life in this world, thrown to him from outside like a lifebuoy (or even a brick) inscribed with a soteriological text that is meaningless to the secular mind and indifferent to the social context in which men are rooted.

3 In no area of life is it more crucial for us to learn how to communicate Christian truth than in the field of politics and industry.

4 The Church must be more concerned with 'principalities and powers' if she would more faithfully save 'flesh and blood'. This is the hardest lesson for the Church to learn.

5 A church whose structure is mapped out in a wholly territorial and geographical shape cannot impinge effectively on the functional structures and social projections of a highly industrialized society.

20.585
Maurice Wiles
British Anglican theologian

1 The appeal to mystery can be an evasion of proper critical questioning. But that is not its true implication... For while mystery warns us against the speciously attractive answers that would dissolve it, it also encourages us to continue with the looking, for we can never tell whether we have reached the limits of human understanding. Indeed it is to such a continued search for understanding that faith commits us.

2 All belief about God is problematic. For in our beliefs about God we are reaching out to speak of a realm beyond the level of our ordinary experiencing.

3 Language about the Holy Spirit is language designed to describe the occasions in which the divine purpose finds effective realization in human life.

4 It is a very proper and healthy thing to be sceptical of philosophers or others who try to tell us that it is impossible to do something which people appear to have done for a long time and to be continuing to do.

20.586
David Wilkerson
North American evangelist and pastor

1 What is it about tears that should be so terrifying... I knew from my work in the church how important a role tears play in making a man whole. I think I could almost put it down as a rule that the touch of God is marked by tears.

2 Christ's love is a love without angles: a love that asks nothing in return... this is the quality that redeems.

3 The Holy Spirit is in charge here.

4 It took me years to discover the premier lesson that God has a timing all His own and that I must not be impatient when His timing doesn't coincide with mine.

5 My parish is the gutter.

6 Every word and deed of a parent is a fibre woven into the character of a child, which ultimately determines how that child fits into the fabric of society.

20.587
Jan Willebrands
Roman Catholic cardinal

1 Theological discussion is a necessary help to discover and to manifest the unity in faith which we already enjoy and to restore that unity where it has been lost.

2 Unity is vital only if it is a vital unity.

20.588
Phoebe Willetts
British peace activist and poet

1 God has feasted the empty-bellied,
and the rich have discovered their void.
God has made good the word
given at the dawn of time.

20.589
Basil Willey
English literary scholar

1 The learned and ingenious attempts by theologians of all times to explain exactly how the divine and human natures were united in Christ seem to me a standing example of the misuse of reason in regions beyond its competence.

20.590
Delores S. Williams
Black womanist theologian from the USA

1 Womanist theology should teach Christians new insights about moral life based on ethics supporting justice for women, survival, and a productive quality of life for poor women, children, and men. This means that the womanist theologian must give authoritative status to black folk wisdom... and to black women's moral wisdom... when she responds to the question, 'How ought the Christian to live in the world?'

20.591
Harry Williams
English theologian

1 Often we shall have to change the direction of our thinking and our wishing and our striving. That is what repentance really means—taking our bearings afresh and trying a new road.

2 Most people's wilderness is inside them, not outside. Thinking of it as outside is a trick we play on ourselves—a trick to hide from what we really are, not comfortingly wicked, but incapable, for the time being, of establishing communion.

3 The background of resurrection is always impossibility. And with impossibility staring us in the face, the prelude to resurrection is invariably doubt, confusion, strife, and the cynical smile which is our defence against them. Resurrection is always the defiance of the absurd.

4 No society can be run on the basis that its members are saints. Any state has to take into account that it has to govern sinners, which means there are going to be tensions between one group and another—but it's better to work that out than have bloody revolution.

5 The wonder and curiosity which welcomes what is new and regards it not as threatening but enriching life—that wonder and curiosity is God.

20.592
Rowan Williams
Welsh Anglican bishop, theologian and social activist

1 A sermon is not a lecture, not a vehicle for instruction and nothing else, certainly not a vehicle for bright ideas and speculations. Good sermons happen when the twofold listening, to tradition and to the present, really becomes a listening to and for God, so that something emerges almost begging to be put into words.

2 The dark night is God's attack on religion. If you genuinely desire union with the

unspeakable love of God, then you must be prepared to have your 'religious' world shattered.

3 Any culture which is terrified—as ours is—of silence and aloneness is one in which the sense of human reality, human truth, is being eroded.

4 The gospel will not ever tell us we are innocent, but it will tell us we are loved; and in asking us to receive and consent to that love, it asks us to identify with, and make our own, love's comprehensive vision of all we are and have been. That is the transformation of desire as it affects our attitude to our own selves—to accept what we have been, so that all of it can be transformed.

5 Peace is the first casualty of untruthfulness.

20.593
John Wimber

Charismatic leader of the 'signs and wonders' movement

1 There is no difference between the *words* and *works* of Jesus. The *works* have exactly the same message as the *words*. The message and words concentrate on the announcement of the Kingdom of God. The miracles and works show us what the Kingdom is like.

20.594
Walter Wink

North American theologian

1 Our culture resolutely refuses to believe in the real existence of evil, preferring to regard it as a kind of systems breakdown that can be fixed with enough tinkering.

2 Satan is... God's holy sifter.

3 Satan has been called a snake. Better he had been called a chameleon. For Satan is never quite the same from moment to moment.

4 There are some churches, like some marriages, where no one seems to be happy unless the members are at each other's throats.

20.595
Miriam Therese Winter

North American Medical Mission Sister and liturgist

1 The ability to find joy in the world of sorrow and hope at the edge of despair is woman's witness to courage and her gift of new life to all.

2 If you want to test the validity of anyone's claim to inclusivity, try referring to God as she.

3 With courage and with love, we must expand our religious images, open up our metaphors, and make sure that our God-language is representative of all.

20.596
Women's Department, Burma Council of Churches

1 Jesus' own mother offered us a song which tells us what God means by Development. This song offers no false promises, nor hope to the proud or the rich, but firmly states that God our Saviour, by taking the side of the poor, makes all people equal and creates justice. This is how those who fear God will receive God's mercy.

20.597
Derek Worlock

Roman Catholic Archbishop of Liverpool

1 When you spell things out, you're accused of politics. If you don't spell them out, you're accused of being an interesting social philosopher.

20.598
Brian Wren

English hymn-writer

1 If our naming of God is distorted, our knowledge of God will be also.

2 To speak of God as the Mother of Creation seems to me a beautiful image, entirely consistent with Christian faith in God who surpasses and contains all created things, yet expressing in a new way God's profound care for creation and involvement with it.

3 Masculinity is a problem for Christian theology and ought to be felt as such.

4 Patriarchal Christianity is in danger of worshipping an idol, and we are not protected from idolatry by the fact that much of our God-language is biblical.

20.599
Olive Wyon
British Anglican laywoman and devotional writer

1 We must begin where we are. For many people the heavy responsibilities of home and family and earning a living absorb all their time and strength. Yet such a home—where love is—may be a light shining in a dark place, a silent witness to the reality and the love of God.

2 To ears which have been trained to wait upon God in silence, and in the quietness of meditation and prayer, a very small incident, or a word, may prove to be a turning-point in our lives, and a new opening for his love to enter our world, to create and to redeem.

3 One of the first things for which we have to pray is a true insight into our condition.

4 Silence is precious: but we have to pay the price it demands. Silence does not reveal its treasures until we are willing to wait in darkness and emptiness.

5 The Christian ideal... is not that of a number of 'integrated' individuals, concerned about their own spiritual progress, but of growth into Christ, as members of the Body of Christ, in which we all live by the same Life, which flows through the Body, and animates us all.

20.600
John Howard Yoder
North American theologian

1 Jesus was, in his divinely mandated (i.e., promised, anointed, messianic) prophethood, priesthood, and kingship, the bearer of a new possibility of human, social, and therefore political relationships.

20.601
Frances Young
British theologian

1 For that is spirituality—thinking, feeling, and acting in love, and singing praises to our Divine Lover. When we sing love-songs we may use the classic scores of scripture or tradition, or we may make our own improvisations. But the themes are universal.

2 We worship a mysterious, not an anthropomorphic God.

20.602
Katherine Zappone
North American-born feminist theologian

1 The most basic requirement for an authentically integrated self is knowledge of one's own inherent value.

2 Vulnerability means that we let go of protective mechanisms that close us to the possibility of being deeply influenced by the other. We allow others virtually to change our lives.

20.603
Jean Zaru
Christian Palestinian

1 Peace for my mother meant submission and relinquishment of rights. I have come to see that this results in doing violence to ourselves and others.

2 As we opt for violence or non-violence in revolution, we know that the liberty to choose is not always there.

20.604
Hubert van Zeller
English Benedictine monk

1 By letting themselves be cynical, unhappy people aggravate their melancholy. They are like a dog which tears at its wounded paw so as to hurt the pain.

2 More people are destroyed by unhappiness than by drink, drugs, disease, or even failure. There must be something about sadness which attracts or people would not accept it so readily into their lives.

3 Achievement is not the lot of all, so the Christian would be wise to cultivate the disposition of being content to do without it.

4 If we do not listen we do not come to truth. If we do not pray we do not even get as far as listening.

5 Peace comes not by establishing a calm outward setting so much as by inwardly surrendering to whatever the setting.

20.605
Nicolas Zernov
Russian-born theologian

1 The artistic perfection of an icon is not only a reflection of the celestial glory—it is a concrete example of matter restored to its original harmony and beauty, and serving as a vehicle of the Spirit. The icons are part of the transfigured cosmos.

2 To become a 'passion-bearer', to be an innocent victim, slain for Christ's sake, to refuse the use of violence even in the face of death, these were the implications of Christianity which produced the deepest impression upon the newly converted Russians.

20.606
John Zoa
Roman Catholic Archbishop of Yaounde, Cameroon

1 The problem that faces us is the problem of a race that has already been evangelised.

INDEX OF SOURCES

A

B

C

D

E

I

J

K

L

M

S

X

Y

Z

INDEX OF THEMES

A

abandonment 17.90.7, 18.11.7, 18.11.15, 18.19.18, 18.25.5, 18.46.4, 19.22.1, 19.23.3, 19.30.4, 19.120.5, 20.20.2, 20.29.11, 20.350.2, 20.379.2

action 17.37.1, 17.76.7, 18.7.1, 18.7.2, 18.59.5, 19.35.6, 19.65.1, 20.15.1, 20.28.6, 20.43.4, 20.48.1, 20.101.11, 20.135.3, 20.180.4, 20.255.6, 20.276.14, 20.316.4, 20.369.2, 20.448.1, 20.474.2, 20.513.2, 20.536.9; and contemplation 13.33.1, 13.38.1, 16.65.22, 20.336.1, 20.369.2

Adam and Eve 2.13.5, 2.13.7, 2.13.18, 7.9.3, 14.19.2, 16.33.5, 17.20.1, 17.76.16, 17.97.4, 20.72.9, 20.269.1, 20.311.14, 20.343.3

adoration 19.123.3, 20.43.1, 20.43.5, 20.91.1, 20.91.3, 20.496.1, 20.534.3, 20.572.1

Advent 12.17.2, 18.16.2, 18.16.3

adventure 20.22.17, 20.81.2, 20.91.8

adversity 6.5.1, 15.14.4, 17.5.1, 17.5.2, 18.11.16, 18.32.20

advice 16.26.1, 17.43.20, 19.41.9, 20.45.3

affection 5.22.3, 11.1.9, 13.25.2, 13.25.3, 17.2.1, 18.19.10, 18.32.33, 20.145.2, 20.238.1

affliction 17.20.5, 17.46.1, 17.50.2, 17.52.11, 17.61.5, 17.86.2, 19.99.15, 20.85.2

afterlife 15.2.2, 18.9.2, 18.14.15, 18.44.14, 19.2.7, 19.59.1, 19.127.1, 20.253.1, 20.311.6, 20.331.2, 20.379.9, 20.398.2, 20.477.2

age, old 17.39.1, 18.7.29, 18.49.19, 19.20.6, 19.99.7, 19.106.5, 20.23.1, 20.250.2, 20.335.12, 20.536.5

agnosticism 20.450.1, 20.461.1

almsgiving 17.5.6, 17.5.7, 17.20.10, 17.22.1, 17.22.8, 17.28.3, 17.42.5, 17.43.2, 17.60.8, 17.61.8, 18.7.11, 19.136.15, 20.174.3

ambition 16.24.8, 16.62.2, 17.21.2, 17.43.17, 17.76.9, 17.89.7, 18.7.20, 18.7.21, 18.49.14, 19.12.9, 19.132.6, 20.228.3

angels 1.1.7, 3.9.4, 3.12.10, 4.26.8, 5.35.2, 6.14.8, 7.17.7, 7.18.2, 7.20.7, 12.15.3, 13.23.1, 13.37.7, 14.2.1, 14.11.18, 16.52.7, 16.65.1, 17.24.2, 17.71.1, 17.76.22, 17.76.23, 17.76.24, 19.109.6, 20.22.6

anger 4.35.3, 5.10.4, 5.10.24, 5.21.1, 17.28.4, 17.42.22, 17.52.12, 17.87.15, 18.46.2, 19.12.6, 19.48.4, 19.78.3, 19.97.4, 20.11.1, 20.159.2, 20.243.2, 20.282.1, 20.324.1

animals 7.9.3, 7.14.1, 20.311.7

anxiety 4.4.16, 14.26.7, 19.136.11, 20.264.5, 20.352.8, 20.545.1

art/s 12.10.1, 12.11.1, 13.13.2, 16.60.1, 16.60.2, 17.37.6, 19.35.15, 19.123.4, 20.22.2, 20.31.1, 20.150.2, 20.157.2, 20.172.9, 20.195.2, 20.196.1, 20.334.1, 20.350.5, 20.368.6, 20.378.2, 20.399.1, 20.484.3, 20.484.10, 20.484.11, 20.484.12, 20.516.3, 20.559.3, 20.605.1

asking *see* petition

atheism 2.14.1, 17.5.3, 17.5.4, 17.52.14, 17.80.1, 18.7.35, 19.42.4, 19.145.5, 20.87.2, 20.172.11, 20.247.4, 20.280.3, 20.367.7

atonement 20.112.1, 20.120.2, 20.241.1, 20.576.6

authority 7.21.2, 9.5.4, 16.24.3, 16.24.4, 16.51.5, 19.1.4, 19.16.9, 19.150.6, 20.168.1, 20.218.1

authorship 12.21.1, 16.28.1, 20.100.4

avarice 13.24.5, 17.52.22, 17.68.26

B

baptism 2.8.1, 2.13.12, 2.20.1, 3.1.9, 4.2.5, 4.2.17, 4.15.1, 4.15.5, 4.15.7, 4.35.1, 8.1.2, 14.3.1, 16.61.1, 16.61.2, 17.42.1, 19.54.1, 20.44.1, 20.359.1, 20.489.2

beauty 5.8.24, 7.13.1, 16.38.1, 17.43.1, 19.99.1, 19.104.2, 20.10.5, 20.44.4, 20.179.1, 20.195.1, 20.216.2, 20.267.1, 20.308.4, 20.538.8

begging 16.45.21

belief 12.7.1, 17.20.6, 17.80.9, 18.35.4, 19.42.1, 19.109.13, 19.147.12, 20.12.1, 20.122.11, 20.171.3, 20.228.1, 20.325.3, 20.352.9, 20.356.1, 20.383.1, 20.393.1, 20.526.2, 20.585.2

belonging 20.154.2, 20.415.5, 20.536.1, 20.541.5

bereavement 13.15.3, 19.97.7, 20.307.1, 20.352.2

Bible *see* Scripture/s

Bible translation 16.19.1, 16.26.2, 16.67.4, 16.67.5, 20.40.6, 20.169.1, 20.228.2

birth, new 5.24.6, 16.62.3, 17.10.7, 19.136.8, 20.90.4, 20.395.2, 20.536.10

bishops 4.27.1, 4.45.1, 7.10.1, 16.35.5, 16.36.1, 16.42.1, 18.49.4, 19.85.3

Black theology 20.130.1, 20.137.5, 20.165.1, 20.199.1, 20.327.1, 20.439.1

blessing 13.11.10, 18.33.5, 18.42.5, 20.424.1

blessings 17.97.11, 17.101.3, 18.1.15

blindness *see* spiritual blindness

body 7.13.5, 20.172.3, 20.202.3, 20.202.4, 20.249.7, 20.275.3, 20.368.3; and soul 2.9.3, 3.12.9, 4.9.1, 14.13.4, 15.2.1, 17.80.8, 19.37.1, 20.174.2, 20.264.6, 20.368.8, 20.448.9, 20.536.11, 20.536.12; of Christ 5.8.18, 11.8.2, 19.135.2, 20.407.5, 20.431.1, 20.483.1, 20.599.5

busyness 13.35.1, 18.57.8, 19.162.4

C

calling/vocation 5.32.4, 6.4.6, 7.4.1, 17.42.23, 17.87.2, 17.93.1, 19.4.4, 19.12.22, 19.64.1, 19.87.3, 19.123.13, 19.123.14, 19.132.2, 19.146.3, 19.163.1, 20.33.3, 20.113.1, 20.113.2, 20.135.4, 20.141.2, 20.158.1, 20.171.1, 20.176.15, 20.180.2, 20.241.3, 20.242.3, 20.415.3, 20.480.1, 20.544.3, 20.546.1, 20.557.5, 20.563.3, 20.567.2

capitalism 20.171.5, 20.171.6, 20.518.1

care 20.43.2, 20.160.1, 20.180.4

celebration 3.1.1, 17.10.1, 20.31.6

D

E

F

G

H

I

J

K

L

licence 16.45.13

life, this 17.96.2, 19.48.5; *see also* human life; Jesus, our life; public life; spiritual life

life together 5.3.1, 20.118.2, 20.335.1

life, true 2.13.3, 4.8.5, 16.40.6, 16.44.1, 17.96.4, 19.109.2, 20.6.5, 20.50.1

light 2.5.3, 4.35.16, 7.19.1, 20.481.1; divine/uncreated 8.10.3, 11.9.2, 11.9.6; *see also* Jesus, light of the world

likeness *see* image and likeness

listening 17.87.14, 18.19.16, 19.53.8, 20.145.7, 20.299.2, 20.299.3, 20.517.1, 20.523.3, 20.545.4, 20.604.4

little things 4.26.1, 4.26.2, 4.35.10, 16.70.6, 18.2.1, 18.7.1, 18.11.10, 18.11.12, 18.19.5, 18.24.3, 19.53.3, 19.53.5, 19.109.19, 19.120.3, 19.120.8, 19.166.2, 20.20.1, 20.179.1

liturgy 20.148.4, 20.362.1, 20.464.3, 20.527.1, 20.565.4

logic *see* reason

loneliness 17.21.3, 19.115.1, 20.58.1, 20.276.13, 20.354.1, 20.545.3, 20.558.4

longing 14.7.16, 16.38.25, 18.10.3, 20.49.1, 20.92.5, 20.172.2, 20.578.1

long-suffering *see* patience/long-suffering

love 3.12.11, 4.4.6, 4.20.3, 4.27.5, 5.8.1, 5.8.16, 5.10.5, 5.22.2, 5.22.9, 6.13.2, 7.17.1, 7.17.3, 13.6.1, 13.20.2, 13.20.4, 14.4.12, 14.22.2, 16.38.8, 16.38.9, 16.39.1, 16.60.3, 16.63.1, 17.30.3, 17.52.13, 17.91.2, 17.97.2, 18.7.9., 18.35.7, 19.33.3, 19.60.1, 19.83.8, 19.120.7, 20.62.11, 20.106.2, 20.117.2, 20.202.5, 20.202.6, 20.212.1, 20.213.5, 20.263.2, 20.271.4, 20.298.1, 20.303.1, 20.322.4, 20.328.8, 20.368.1, 20.371.2, 20.383.3, 20.385.16, 20.448.6, 20.492.2, 20.538.5, 20.559.2; love is 12.7.3, 14.21.6, 18.19.8, 19.36.1, 19.48.7, 20.4.4, 20.63.1, 20.71.1, 20.92.2, 20.119.2, 20.437.4, 20.502 4; of God/Jesus Christ 5.14.8, 5.23.9, 6.2.2, 12.17.4, 13.11.9, 14.1.1, 14.4.6, 14.24.1, 16.38.7, 16.38.10, 16.38.12, 16.65.17, 16.70.1, 17.97.15, 18.17.1, 18.34.1, 19.113.1, 19.155.1, 20.39.1, 20.91.5, 20.92.3, 20.174.5; *see also* God, love of; Jesus, love of; love-of-God-and-neighbour

love-making 20.202.1, 20.255.7

love-of-God-and-neighbour 6.12.1, 7.17.7, 8.4.1, 11.9.3, 12.3.2, 13.26.1, 17.15.3, 17.20.9, 19.99.6, 20.15.24, 20.21.4, 20.40.3, 20.46.4, 20.72.3, 20.87.6, 20.115.2, 20.149.1, 20.317.1, 20.454.9, 20.465.1, 20.477.4, 20.534.9, 20.580.1

loyalty 16.65.23, 17.31.2, 20.40.4

lying 18.32.8, 19.103.6, 20.62.7

M

mankind *see* humankind

marks of the Christian 4.9.11, 4.9.12, 4.9.13, 5.34.1, 12.16.4, 17.23.1, 17.29.8, 17.72.1, 17.97.2, 18.44.1, 20.116.1

marriage 16.13.2, 16.20.2, 16.24.10, 16.40.3, 16.67.2, 17.16.1, 17.62.1, 17.94.11, 17.94.12, 18.15.3, 19.3.1, 19.32.4, 19.83.10, 19.132.7, 20.30.2, 20.32.4, 20.31.8, 20.226.1, 20.226.2, 20.255.2, 20.572.5

Martha *see* Mary and Martha

martyr/s, prayer of 2.7.1, 2.7.2, 2.7.3, 3.8.1, 4.11.1, 4.23.1, 4.31.1, 4.59.1

martyrdom 2.12.6, 3.9.3, 3.12.3, 9.3.1, 16.26.12, 16.51.11, 18.32.6, 19.5.1, 19.83.11, 19.109.18, 20.91.4; willingness for 4.2.13, 14.4.5, 5.33.5, 16.9.1, 16.11.1, 16.14.1, 16.34.2, 17.31.3

martyrs, witness of 2.6.1, 2.12.5, 2.16.2, 2.16.3, 2.20.2, 3.3.1, 3.4.1, 3.11.1, 4.1.1, 4.13.1, 4.64.1, 12.5.1, 16.42.7, 16.62.5, 19.130.1, 20.577.1

Mary (mother of Jesus) 2.12.3, 2.17.1, 5.12.1, 5.36.1, 9.7.2, 12.16.3, 13.11.5, 13.17.1, 13.20.11, 14.18.1, 15.1.1, 16.15.2, 16.45.23, 16.66.1, 17.61.12, 17.78.2, 18.3.2, 19.18.1, 19.57.4, 20.129.3, 20.236.1, 20.350.4, 20.556 1, 20.556.3, 20.596.1

Mary and Martha 4.58.1, 16.65.22, 19.108.1, 20.42.2

matter/material things 8.9.6, 20.202.3, 20.400.1, 20.605.1

maturity 17.81.3, 19.161.1, 20.368.7

media, the 20.146.1, 20.306.5, 20.398.4, 20.484.5

meditation 4.49.1, 12.12.2, 12.12.3, 14.20.1, 18.19.13, 20.313.6, 20.328.7, 20.371.3

meekness 16.32.1, 17.20.3, 18.61.3, 19.24.5, 20.174.4

memory of Jesus 20.138.1, 20.508.1, 20.508.2

men/masculinity 16.40.4, 17.29.11, 20.351.2, 20.351.3, 20.406.1, 20.490.2, 20.561.1, 20.598.3

men and women 15.1.2, 17.9.1, 19.77.1, 20.143.2, 20.153.3, 20.206.1, 20.258.1, 20.446.1

middle age 20.352.6, 20.528.1

mind 4.26.5, 4.26.10, 5.23.8, 16.51.10, 16.65.24, 17.40.2, 17.76.5, 19.16.12, 20.385.17, 20.442.1; and heart 14.7.11, 19.143.1, 19.143.5, 20.176.6, 20.209.1

ministry 4.12.2, 5.33.6, 16.33.9, 17.27.2, 17.51.1, 17.91.3, 18.12.1, 18.12.2, 18.61.2, 19.136.16, 20.71.3, 20.173.1, 20.379.11, 20.557.3, 20.557.4

minjung *see* common people

miracles 17.42.14, 17.52.16, 17.80.6, 18.49.2, 20.135.2, 20.141., 20.156.1, 20.197.2, 20.217.2, 20.328.6, 20.352.19, 20.455.2, 20.467.3, 20.578.4

mission 6.14.2, 8.5.1, 8.6.1, 8.6.2, 8.13.1, 17.17.1, 17.51.10, 18.57.1, 19.50.1, 19.124.1, 20.3.1, 20.5.1, 20.38.1, 20.38.2, 20.118.6, 20.158.5, 20.534.8, 20.570.8, 20.584.1

missionaries 7.3.1, 19.92.2, 19.115.2, 19.140.1, 20.57.1, 20.58.1, 20 82.1, 20.113.3, 20.139.1, 20.294.1, 20.425.1, 20.467.4, 20.511.1, 20.534.7

moderation 6.4.1, 17.59.2, 20.118.11

modesty 3.7.1, 17.21.6, 19.24.2

monastic/religious life 4.44.1, 6.9.2, 7.2.1, 12.12.11, 16.35.7, 18.54.1, 19.8.2, 19.17.1, 19.19.1, 19.19.3, 20.188.1, 20.188.2, 20.436.1, 20.558.1

money 7.17.2, 13.1.1, 17.25.8, 18.32.13, 18.35.8, 18.37.6, 18.57.15, 19.125.9, 20.30.4, 20.45.2, 20.204.2, 20.264.15, 20.496.2

morality/moral issues 18.7.17, 18.44.10, 19.20.2, 19.58.4, 19.132.1, 19.141.1, 19.141.2, 20.85.1, 20.115.2, 20.122.9, 20.385.6, 20.445.4, 20.492.6

motherhood 2.19.1, 4.43.1, 9.2.1, 19.48.1, 19.91.12, 19.144.4, 20.107.3, 20.129.2, 20.131.3, 20.271.3, 20.352.2, 20.517.9

Q

R

S

T

U

V

W

Y

Z

INDEX OF KEY WORDS

A

abandon: a. all 17.90.7
a. ourselves entirely to God 18.11.7
afraid that he may a. it 20.176.1
Father, I a. myself to you 20.29.6
the courage, the faith, to a. control 20.350.2
the more perfectly you a. yourself 14.4.13
the more you a. to God 18.46.4
when we a. our neighbour to God 20.119.1
abandoned: when God appears to have a. 18.19.18
abandonment: in sweet a. 13.20.7
springs from a. to Jesus Christ 20.20.2
abandons: a Church which a. the truth, a. itself 20.342.2
God a. no one 20.35.1
abasement: His a. is our glory 4.30.1
abba: dark God begin to resemble A. 20.221.1
abbot: a. aim to be loved 6.4.5
receives the name of a. 6.4.7
abdication: a. and a prayer that God 20.551.2
abide: a. in me, fast falls the eventide 19.96.1
good to a. fast in him 12.16.5
Saviour, a. with us, and spread 19.102.3
abides: a. there in bliss for ever 14.18.13
ability: may despair of his own a. 16.45.8
able: an a. yet humble man 18.44.8
abode: their soul is Christ's a. 19.82.1
above: O thou who camest from a. 18.56.1
Abraham: God counselled A. to leave 6.1.1
the stock of A.—A. who was 10.5.1
abroad: no need for us to go a. 4.4.12
absence: the desert does not mean the a. 20.176.8
absolucion: and plesaunt was his a. 14.5.1
absolute: a. power corrupts absolutely 19.1.5
abstain: a. from certain foods 15.13.4
abstains: a. from a fault 13.2.1
abstinence: a. is as easy to me 18.32.12
a. is the mother of health 17.56.1
almost a Sin of A. 17.43.9
deceived by too much a. 14.24.3
abstract: dry and a. doctrine 20.296.1
absurd: always the defiance of the a. 20.591.3
abundant: more Communicated, more a. grows 17.76.20
abuse: authoritarian a. of power begins 20.341.1
abyss: [Christ's] power in the a. 12.23.1
in order to shun the a. of love 19.52.1
accept: a. me, Lord, as I am 19.93.1
a. the fact that you are accepted 20.545.2
God, give us grace to a. 20.409.5
to a. his Kingdom 20.217.1
to a. willingly whatever a loving Father 20.379.2
acceptable: to will what is most a. 15.14.1
acceptance: a. says, True 20.379.2
Christianity is about a. 20.390.1
make a. of the worst fortune 20.85.2
accepted: accept the fact that you are a. 20.545.2
a. by him for his sake 19.120.10
forgiveness needs to be a. 20.352.4
is a. with all his or her existence 20.389.2
accepts: he who passively a. evil 20.335.9
accident: who believes himself an a. 19.145.5
accidental: material things are not a. 20.400.1
accidie: a. This spirit must be cast out 5.41.3
accomplice: the a. of liars and forgers 20.62.7
accomplishment: and of A. 'without doubt' 20.248.1
account: an a. must be given 5.22.16
be of no a. in our own eyes 16.49.4
takes much from the a. 17.60.8
accusations: your chief a. against her 19.97.6
accuse: to a. ourselves of them 20.63.3
accused: you're a. of politics 20.597.1
achieve: enable him to a. it? 12.12.2
acquaintances: not make new a. 18.32.31
acquainted: becomes a. with himself 18.32.20
act: always a. with the same fervour 13.7.1
an a. of Christian love 20.180.4
contemplative a. is the permanently basic a. 20.119.3
every a. of kindness and compassion 14.18.3
how we a. in that world 20.519.2
right to a. directly and independently 19.147.9
the last a. is bloody 17.80.19
to a. is to create 20.536.9
to wish to a. like angels 16.65.1
action: a. springs not from thought 20.15.1
basic act of all external a. 20.119.3
by this a. Christ our Master 15.1.4
Christian a. in the world 20.369.4
Christian a. should be defined 20.135.3
greater than human a.—prayer 20.176.4
human a. can be modified 19.91.2
in the context of worship and a. 20.369.2
more than any self-confident a. 20.119.1
on the same plane as human a. 20.423.7
only quite pure form of a. 20.43.4
passes through the world of a. 20.276.14
put you out of a. 19.133.3
talking stops and the a. starts 20.396.1
we take refuge from a. 20.255.6
whenever a. is reaction 20.101.11
worth far more than a pound of a. 17.28.17
actions: a sight of our own good a. 18.60.4
a. flow from our true selves 20.558.3

become: let each b. all 19.35.4
we can b. ourselves 20.100.1
what we are to b. 20.207.1

becomes: he b. us, he lives us 20.238.5

bed: approach your b., say B. 7.9.1
b. too cold is to go to b. colder 16.7.2
goes to b. and does not pray 17.60.21
made your cross my b. 13.6.2

beggar: like a dumb or paralytic b. 17.70.5
moral qualities of the individual b. 19.97.3
most universal and importunate b. 17.92.1
that I may die a b. 4.53.1

begging: ought to go b. 16.45.21

begin: b. every day of his life with new ardour 16.7.3
help me to b. to b. 18.59.3
how to b. where we are 14.7.8
'today I am going to b.' 18.11.1
we must b. where we are 20.599.1

beginning: a b. of any great matter 16.23.1
for the first time—as it were—b. 13.7.1
from the b. of time 1.1.4
God is without b. 4.7.3
God the b. and end of our love 14.24.1
hidden there from the b. 12.23.1
in my end is my b. 16.46.1
let us have reason for b. 4.2.10
never ending, still b. 17.43.12
the Son had a b. 4.7.3

behave: Gospel—believe it and b. it 18.58.1

behaviour: a vital decision about b. 20.358.1

beheld: I b. that which cannot be related 13.6.12
if you b. him with your eyes 16.26.3

behold: ardently long to b. you 11.1.9
I long for release, to b. 5.31.1
pleasant thing to b. the light 17.16.2
until we b. your face 8.10.2
what we are, that we b. 14.17.6

beholding: life of man consists in b. 2.13.3

being: bring part of the b. which he desires 20.536.14
but above all a mode of b. 20.448.7
God is a tranquil B. 18.51.4
perfection is b. not doing 20.500.1

belief: all b. about God is problematic 20.585.2
below the level of b. or doubt 20.228.1
God is a b. 19.145.3
is the threshold of b. 20.393.1
the doubt that precedes b. 20.63.4

beliefs: not love according to his b. 17.52.13
the false b. you have in your head 20.383.1

believe: b., but that we may b. 6.13.1
b. God's word and power 17.86.5
b., so that you may understand 5.8.21
b. that you have it 16.26.7
be slow to b. 4.17.8
but you will not b. me 20.181.1
genius to b. anything 20.228.1
Gospel—b. it and behave it 18.58.1
he does not b. 17.52.13
he that will b. only 19.42.1
how much you really b. anything 20.352.9
I b. in order that I may understand 11.1.7
I b. in the living God 4.1.1
I had rather b. all the fables 17.5.3
if you can't b. in God 20.356.1
it is so hard to b. because 19.83.3
O man, b. in God 15.11.1
one can b. in God with 20.280.2
that I b., and take it 16.24.7
those who do not b. 20.171.3
to b. in God is one thing 20.72.7
we b. but we do not know 19.147.12
we b. in a loving G. 20.549.1
we b. in God, creator 20.186.1
we b. in one God 4.7.4
we have only to b. 20.536.1
who does b. his eyes 19.114.3
you must b. in God in spite 19.80.1
you ought never to b. something 20.541.5

believed: the first when my heart had b. 19.87.1

believer: the b. exhibits trust in God 20.392.1
the b. is one who finds 20.325.3
what is the mark of a b.? 4.9.11

believers: describe the great joy of b. 6.14.2
the faith of Christian b. 20.118.7

believes: if a man b. and knows God 20.122.11
possible to him who b. 17.70.2
possible to one who b. 12.7.1

believing: argue men, as to torture them, into b. 19.109.13

bell: for whom the b. tolls 17.42.19
listen to what the great b. 20.122.12
the sound of Church or Chapel b. 20.82.1

bell-boy: God is not a cosmic b. 20.247.2

bellow: he who does not b. the truth 20.62.7

bells: b. call others 17.60.2

belong: I desire to b. wholly to Him 17.45.2
let us b. to God 17.87.7

belonged: gave to God what b. to him 13.15.1

belonging: not having a sense of b. 20.415.5

beloved: as long as it pleases my B. 19.50.4
far above love is the B. 14.21.1
he belongs only to the B. 5.14.8
in the presence of his b. 20.29.3
made us accepted in the B. 18.33.5
put the b. in the first place 20.437.4

below: my thoughts remain b. 17.89.5

bend: to such readiness to b. 20.304.1

beneath: believe no work b. me 20.29.5
b. him I can't be 17.90.2

Benedictus: when Christians recite the B. 20.110.2

benefit: for the use and b. of men 17.96.3
for your own b. but for his 20.241.3
in his power to b. others 18.32.13

benefits: on whom to bestow his b. 2.13.5
thanking God for his b. 17.81.1

the more shall we experience b. 20.355.6
they in heaven prize b. 17.97.11

blessings: b. we enjoy daily 17.101.3
our real b. often appear 18.1.15
praise God from whom all b. flow 18.33.1
with an abundance of b. 12.26.4

blind: content willing to wax b. 16.51.4
therefore represented as b. 18.1.22

blinded: may be b. to all other things 16.8.2

blinding: the b. of a sound eye 20.63.4

blindness: an incurable disease— colour b. 20.133.2
such b. and ignorance 16.19.1

blood: as often as the Lord's b. is shed 4.2.14
b. running down my face 18.41.1
Christian b. that is the seed 3.12.3
fertilized by the b. of thousands 20.532.1
gave his life b. 1.1.9
human b. is all of one colour 17.52.2
I desire his b., which is 2.12.8
my b. has been mingled 11.9.8
O God, Bahram's [his son's] b. 20.214.1
sharing our flesh and b. 5.12.3
the b. [of Jesus] deals with what 20.404.2
the heart's b. of the inner man 20.453.4
to the point of shedding your b. 4.26.11
when beauty fires the b. 17.43.1

blood-ties: ruled by the clouded emotions of b. 20.109.4

blooms: it b. because it b. 17.90.3
when love b. bright and wild 20.350.4

blossom: which b. early in the season 13.20.10

blot: b. out all hatred and bitterness 20.15.24

boast: b. not of what thou 17.76.7

boat: launch out thy b. 16.34.1

bodies: hard hearts and unruly b. 3.6.3
heavenly, so our b. 2.13.17
our b. are filled with darkness 20.249.7
our spiritual b. will have every faculty securely fastened to b. 20.174.2
reduced to selling their b. 20.484.5
take excellent care of our b. 20.264.6

body: a b. which takes its nourishment 20.536.11
an wanton horse and an unchaste b. 4.29.1
b. and the soul conversing together 15.2.1
b. feels while our mind thinks 13.37.2
b. is of great service to the soul 12.7.9
b. of a man I bring thee 5.37.2
every part of my b. is ready 4.64.1
gave his b. for our b. 1.1.9
he built himself a temple, a b. 4.8.1
He is b., and he is mind 20.405.1
hear the words 'the b. of Christ' 5.8.18
how can I hate this b. of mine 7.13.5
I confess that Christ's b. 16.58.1
I will imagine that my soul and b. 19.37.1
illnesses of the soul transmitted to the b. 20.448.9
it is a visible b., and it is *one* b. 20.407.6
[Jesus] gave up his one b. 12.23.3
members of the B. of Christ 20.599.5
my b. was made for the love of God 20.172.3
not degraded by receiving a b. 4.8.3
not other than b. but more than b. 20.368.8
our b. is not made of iron 13.11.7
refreshment for the b. 13.10.12
ruins me in soul, if not in b. 19.162.4
that b. and heart in which 4.12.1
the b. derives its stedfastness 5.33.4
the b. is deified along with the soul 14.13.4
the b. of Christ 19.135.2
there indeed is the whole b. 11.8.2
this lowly b. of mine 7.15.1
until you know more than your b. 17.97.7
we are members of one b. 19.101.4
what death is to the b. 13.24.4
what the soul is to the b. 2.9.3
when the b. is constrained 12.23.5

bold: when we feel us too b. 16.51.9

bolts: esteemed the b. and locks 17.41.1

bond: loose every unjust b. 4.2.18
love who is the b. 15.10.1

bones: it reaches our b. 20.172.15

Boniface: resolved to send our brother B. 8.6.1

book: an empty b. is like 17.97.1
in the mass or in the b. 17.51.5
the reading of this holy b. 16.20.1
to read the Great B. of the World 20.127.1

books: in the sacred b. shines 5.22.19
Jesus could have written b. 20.203.4
men, not b. 17.68.2
some b. are copper 18.42.1
the prophets wrote b. 4.17.7
theologians writing b. to each other in universities 20.464.1
they were all b. which were useful 20.100.4

bore: forgive those who b. us 17.68.19
no b. like a clever b. 17.25.2

boredom: it is not surprising that b. 20.255.2

born: by being b. again 5.24.6
from you was b. Christ 9.7.2
I felt myself absolutely b. again 16.45.1
that I was even b. is a miracle 20.328.6
to be b. according to Christ 14.3.1
when we are b. anew 14.17.8
you are a b. again Christian 20.264.4

bought: God b. man 17.61.9
how dearly I have b. you 17.43.17
we are b. with a price 20.238.4

bound: he was so b. [to his brethren] 11.9.3
people b. to each other 20.448.4

boundary: decisive b. in the Bible 20.157.4

boundless: b. is thy love 20.16.2

bow: exhibits more b. than cloud 19.123.15

Bradford: there goes John B. 16.8.1

brag: one went to b. 17.36.4

brake: he took the bread and b. it 16.24.7

branches: when there are wide-spreading b. 20.240.1
bravery: not worth calling b. 19.16.17
Brasenose: cannot understand a fellow of B. 19.136.4
breach: yet the b. of his commandment 16.22.1
bread: all b. is *ours* 14.11.12
appear as pure b. 2.12.5
be known to us in breaking b. 19.102.3
b. must be more than b. 20.101.7
break thou the b. of life 20.49.1
breaking one b. 2.13.2
broken b. was scattered 2.8.4
brown b. and the Gospel 18.27.2
in the b. we eat the power 4.20.7
just as the b. 2.13.17
like good b., newly each day 20.2112.1
over the broken b. 2.8.3
served with b. 2.1.2
the b. and wine in his house 13.24.5
the B. of Life himself changes 14.3.2
the spirituality of broken b. 20.460.4
to God who gives our daily b. 16.64.1
we asked you for b. 20.340.2
will not command stones to be made b. 19.101.7
breadth: drawing nearer to the b. of God 20.161.4
break: don't let them b. your spirit 20.314.1
some of us will be able to b. out 20.319.2
to b. my will into little pieces 19.119.1
breakdown: regard it as a kind of systems b. 20.594.1
breaking: b. down the walls 20.204.7
God has not been b. into 20.185.1
breast: why should his unstain'd b. 17.36.3
breath: as the b. which comes out 4.54.1
born of the b. of God 3.12.9
breathes with human b. 19.142.6
God's b. in man 17.60.20
the life-giving b. of prayer 20.321.10
breathing: draws us out by b. himself in 20.28.3
bred: being b. at Oxford or Cambridge 17.51.1
brethren: instead of 'dear b.' 19.154.1
we are seven b. 5.3.1
brevity: consider the b. of life 18.33.4
bride: let me, then, be the b. of Christ 7.4.1
bridge: breaks the b. over which 20.141.11
bright: b. and beautiful for thee 20.80.1
bring: all that I have I b. 19.123.4
b. to the Lord, O you peoples 13.16.7
sorrows b. forth 19.20.7
broken: all the b. hearts 20.431.2
a sacramental relationship with the b. 20.237.2
hard to live with b. symbols 20.210.5
he died of a b. body 20.97.2
the b. body of Jesus 20.517.7
we must be b. into life 20.459.2
brokenness: the b. of our community 20.463.2
brooks: shallow b. murmur most 16.60.6
brooms: in the midst of saucepans and b. 16.41.1
brother: a b. also wanting to make bread 4.63.1
against your b. 4.48.1
and feel his b.'s care 18.56.7
if I long to improve my b. 19.123.8
love and care for his b. 13.16.3
loves her b., for 'our b. is our life' 20.72.3
merciful Redeemer, Friend and B. 13.36.2
my life is with my b. 4.4.1
not having harmed one's b. 20.176.3
our b. has been given to us 20.15.17
when you see your b. 5.4.1
white man's b. not his b.-in-law 20.335.17
brotherhood: Christian b., unlike 20.458.3
brotherly: bonded together in b. love 6.14.9
brothers: as b. and sisters 29.477.4
equal, since they are b. 4.35.7
make all men human and, therefore, b. 20.335.16
the simple art of living together like b. 20.335.1
brought: what God has b. you through 19.108.2
bruised: the b. is the breaker 19.145.4
brutes: not made to live like b. 14.8.2
buds: the b. that here too cling 20.70.1
build: all experience is an arch to b. 20.2.2
man in turn was to b. 5.9.1
buildeth: wheresoever God b. a church 16.2.1
building: in b., we need not act 18.37.6
bullet: the ballot is stronger than the b. 19.91.6
bullets: the government speaks rubber b. 20.554.7
burden: he lays upon us no other b. 20.116.3
I was delivered from the b. 18.59.4
roll every b. on me 19.125.1
sank under the b. of the day 19.99.12
the b. of the day 19.39.1
burdens: by the weight of their b. 5.31.1
burial: glory to you for your b. 4.38.4
buried: body should be b. outside 12.25.1
burn: I b. all my sermons 18.57.10
I cannot b. 16.58.3
must b. eternally 16.70.1
so dry, they would b. well 19.136.16
burning: anyone who is not b. 13.34.1
b. down your own house 20.247.7
I felt myself b. and I had to withdraw 19.57.2
I seek him with a b. heart 20.72.10
mission, as fire exists by b. 20.158.5
burns: she so b. with desire for him 13.9.2
bury: b. my mind, my heart 17.45.5
b. the faults of his friends 19.12.3
bush: the b. seen by Moses 16.66.1
busiest: even in the b. day 20.305.2
those who are b. 20.147.1
business: also a man of b. 5.22.4
the assumption that 'b. is b.' 20.484.4
the b. of maintaining buildings 20.173.2
the time of b. does not differ 17.70.6

busy: peace if we did not b. ourselves 15.14.16
buys: money with which one b. heaven 19.152.1

C

cab-horse: every c. in London 19.23.7
Calais: you shall find 'C.' lying in my heart 16.47.1
call: hear the divine c. to participate 20.10.7
I c. upon my God 9.6.2
I was being obedient to God's c. 20.546.1
it was a trumpet c. 20.33.3
tension between the c. to the desert 20.180.2
the c. to justice jars 20.502.2
the divine c. 20.415.3
what he did was to c. us together 20.511.3
when you c. upon him 12.26.4
called: if God has c. you 20.141.2
it is God who has c. you 20.113.1
things to which we are not c. 17.87.8
you were c. and really are 9.7.2
calling: c. is not without its crosses 19.8.1
constant c. on the name of God 6.3.1
calls: c. it into being by calling His 20.407.4
God c. to you 19.32.2
when Christ c. a man 20.15.13
calm: a nucleus that is mysteriously c. 20.240.2
not always nourished in external c. 17.87.7
set to work when c. returns 20.29.7
Calvary: Blessed Lamb of C. 20.80.1
that C.-life which plunges 20.46.3
you will seek him as much at C. 18.25.10
came: first they c. for the Jews 20.410.1
Jesus c. into the world to save 16.3.1
Campion: C.'s voice sounds to us 20.577.1
can: pray as you c. 20.21.7
canal: c. For a c. spreads abroad 12.7.16
candle: this day light such a c. 16.42.7
candles: not in a cathedral between two c. 20.367.1
our lighted c. are a sign 7.19.1
they are the burning c. 19.46.1
cannibalism: as c. is [as] a means of coping 20.333.2
capable: thou art c. of God 17.87.4
capacity: our c. to communicate 20.427.2
capital: the c. of heaven is the heart 20.84.4
capitalism: C. is an evil thing 20.518.1
today's c. has entrenched 20.436.1
capitalist: fallen prey to the c. machine 20.171.4
capitalistic: an aristocratic or a c. God 20.362.1
captive: heart may be c. to no earthly thing 16.38.3
car: jump in front of the c. and stop it 20.15.30
cardinal: now there is an eighth C. Sin 20.505.1
care: a man's first c. 18.1.21
c. must be taken of the sick 6.4.4
Christianity has taught us to c. 20.43.2
let us silence every c. 13.10.6
providence is the c. God takes 8.9.3
take c. of me 4.23.1
take c. of your life 18.59.8
will he not himself c. for you 4.17.4
careful: be very c. how we speak 16.35.8
careless: the c. soul will be punished 4.66.1
carelessness: our c. and our weakness 4.4.4
cares: free of the c. of this passing 7.7.2
careth: who gave the light its birth, c. for me 19.121.1
caring: c. is the greatest thing, c. matters 20.43.2
nearer to Christ than in c. 20.454.9
carried: because we are being c. high 12.6.1
carriers: the c. of religion 20.421.4
carry: for power to c. us through 17.46.1
not something you have to c. 20.423.11
cast: c. away authority 19.16.19
c. yourself into the arms of God 16.52.8
the more he c. away 17.22.1
cat: a c. can be trusted to purr 20.311.7
catastrophes: few c. so great and irremediable 19.16.6
catch: by which you can c. souls 20.538.5
catechist: the mother has always been the best c. 20.129.2
when I first became a c. 20.384.2
category: God is not an abstract c. 20.122.13
cathedral: not in a c. between two candles 20.367.1
catholic: agreement between C. and Protestant theology 20.342.3
I became a c. 20.31.7
if we are truly c. 20.306.4
over-run with Roman C. nuns 19.8.2
see you a C. Christian 4.43.1
the C. Church no longer 20.386.1
the Roman C. priests 19.55.2
Catholicism: the negation of C. 19.1.1
Catholics: when Orthodox and C. 19.135.1
caught: being c. up in God 16.38.15
cause: an effect whose c. is God 18.14.9
in whose c. it is pleasing and glorious 17.64.1
ceasing: pray without c. 6.2.5
cedar: a palace of c. to the wise 19.136.7
celebration: all our life is a c. 3.1.1
cell: build yourself a c. in your heart 14.4.3
c., and your c. will teach 4.44.1
dear c., what happy hours 6.9.2
cellar: find myself in the c. of affliction 17.86.2
cello: I play the c. 20.179.3
celtic: enabled C. Christians to make 20.501.5
cement: the c. of all societies 17.43.8
cemetery: keep a fair-sized c. 19.12.3
censure: Church c. for his wicked life 17.84.6
centre: at once the c. and the circumference 17.66.2
at the c. of our being 20.172.7
centuries: overloaded with the spiritual baggage of c. 20.271.2

the making of c. 20.570.5
the trustee c. of the gospel 20.205.1
very useful to the c. 18.37.2
we receive from the c. 20.215.2
companion: c. in the resurrection 20.186.1
companionship: this demands c. 13.37.11
company: bad c. is a disease 17.103.1
in our neighbour when in his c. 17.28.12
it is thus the c. of liberators 20.416.1
only to see the c. 17.42.7
tell me what c. you keep 17.29.1
compass: like the two hands of a c. 19.37.1
compassion: by c. we make others' misery 17.20.10
c. will cure more sins 19.12.1
deserve my tenderness and c. 9.3.1
first outburst is always c. 14.11.13
God is full of c. 16.65.27
God's c. 4.6.1
I hope that in his c. 7.15.1
it is the power of c. 20.517.13
man may dismiss c. 18.14.2
passion is over, his c. is not 18.44.2
the depths of thy c. 19.123.7
the true character of c. 18.17.7
the wilderness of c. 20.385.2
theology of c. 20.517.10
wisdom without c. 20.263.2
with your boundless c. 14.10.1
you will seek to do c. 13.31.8
compassionate: God will always be c. 20.131.2
compel: no part of religion to c. religion 3.12.2
compensations: it has also its c. 19.8.1
competition: c. as the supreme law 20.171.5
complacency: engendering smugness and c. 20.10.4
complain: if anyone should c. to you of another 16.38.2
if I am to c., let me c. 17.34.1
no one would c. about his cross 16.59.1
complaint: c. is the largest tribute 18.49.3
with a c. against me 4.21.1
complementarity: bodily c. of males and females 20.446.1
complete: c. organism of all faithful people 20.43.6
completeness: to move towards c. as human beings 20.501.7
completer: Jesus Christ is the C. 20.248.2
composer: contemplation of the First C. 17.20.15
compost: the Church is rather like a c. heap 20.277.3
comprehend: what he can fully c. 19.42.1
comprehended: a c. God 18.51.1
compromise: is founded on c. and barter 18.7.12
compunction: I would far rather feel c. 15.14.19
conceal: c. yourselves in Jesus crucified 18.43.4
concealed: a talent that is c. 16.26.10
concealing: I am c. myself from you 13.29.5
conceit: c. is the most incurable disease 19.12.8
pluck me down in my own c. 16.24.1
conceived: nothing greater can be c. 11.1.2
concentrate: he is able to c. 20.448.7
concert: strings in the c. of his joy 17.14.1
concessions: by reciprocal c. 18.32.35
conclusions: drawing sufficient c. 17.25.1
concupiscence: fasting can overcome c. 13.22.1
condemn: if you c. another 7.13.12
write things that some men will c. 20.385.9
condemnation: cure more sins than c. 19.12.1
condition: a true insight into our c. 20.599.3
can speak to thy c. 17.51.3
handsome and thriving c. 17.84.3
let my c. be never so low 17.31.1
they are necessary for our c. 20.400.1
they are the normal c. 20.29.7
conditioning: the prison of our own c. 20.307.3
conduct: judged and his c. 20.551.3
personal c. is of more importance 19.11.3
rule his c. in every relation 19.132.9
till it convert itself into c. 19.35.8
when it affects our outer c. 20.63.2
conference: keep clear of every c. of bishops 4.27.1
confess: as Lord we c. you 5.29.1
every tongue c. him 19.111.1
that which you c. today 19.114.2
to c. our sins 20.63.3
confessing: live your faith by c. it 20.385.18
confession: c. must be our own 13.5.2
ingenuous kind of c. 5.22.20
when he went to c. 20.255.3
confessioun: ful swetely herde he c. 14.4.1
confidence: a few acts of c. 19.33.2
our c. in Christ 16.72.2
place all our c. 13.25.4
the path of prayer with c. 4.26.7
confirmation: at c. he gives 5.17.1
converted at his own c. service 20.477.1
conflict: looking at and understanding the c. 20.243.2
the crown without the c. 4.35.5
to engage in spiritual c. 6.14.6
conformed: tells us not to be c. 20.264.9
conformity: c. can go on for generations 20.570.2
entire c. and resignation 16.52.9
knowledge is not the c. 20.273.2
the spirit comes not in quiet c. 20.527.5
conforms: c. our lives to the pattern 20.437.2
confrontation: life renewed by a new c. 20.566.1
congregation: at the outside of the c. threw a stone 18.41.1
congregations: advantages of small c. 20.557.2
conquer: c. by forgiveness 19.20.4
in the end truth will c. 14.31.1
pain is no evil, unless it c. 19.86.4
conquered: as through a c. man 2.13.7
you have c. death 4.22.1

D

damnation: despair is the proper passion of d. 17.94.2
the cause of salvation or d. is decided 20.487.4

damned: you d. spirits! 13.16.5

dance: blessed, eternal and indissoluble d. 7.20.7
if elephants can be trained to d. 16.26.4

danced: I d. in the morning 20.177.1

dancing: with d. and hymns in city and country 4.24.2

danger: a possible d. to any state 20.396.6
glory breaks through dark and d. 20.279.2
the greatest d. for faith 20.497.2

dangerous: liturgy is d. 20.527.1
we do have a huge, wild, d. God 20.372.2
wicked people would be less d. 17.68.23

dangerously: live d. in the interests 20.91.8

dangers: attended with great d. 19.2.5
has its corresponding d. 19.16.5

Dante: would study Aquinas as I would study D. 19.150.2

dappled: Glory be to God for d. things 19.72.1

dare: d. to look at everything around you 20.383.7

dark: a d. night through which the soul passes 16.38.20
as children fear to go in the d. 17.5.25
d. as the world of man 20.506.1
hope with him in the d. 20.81.5
light fires in a d. room 20.71.3
our heart works just fine—in the d. 20.249.7

darkest: the denizens of D. England 19.23.8

darkness: a deep, but dazzling d. 17.100.3
a people groping in d. 20.232.2
abandoned to outer d. 4.66.1
adding deeper d. to a night 20.335.18
an ocean of d. and death 17.51.2
cast them into outer d. 4.18.1
d. in our entire body 5.10.10
d. that is supremely bright 14.13.1
facing the d., admitting the pain 20.249.8
in that very d. we can meet God 20.271.3
kingdoms of d. and light 20.488.1
reconcile yourself to wait in this d. 14.7.4
the 'children of d.' are frequently 20.335.5
this d. which is between you 14.7.3
transformation of d. and chaos 2.14.10
willing to wait in d. and emptiness 20.599.4

darting: frequently d. them up to Heaven 16.52.11

darts: the longing d. of love 14.7.16

date: 'bringing up to d.' 20.166.2

daughter: but as the d. of grace 18.3.2
I am his d. 13.29.7
in a d. of man 2.3.1
your little d.'s death 19.97.7

dawn: all our sunsets into d. 3.1.5
rise at d. for prayer 5.32.6

day: contemplates hath a d. without night 17.60.22
he who gives you the d. 4.28.3
human life is but a single d. 4.27.5
if you spend the d. fruitfully 15.14.2
it covers the whole d. 20.171.2
let this d., O Lord 17.3.5
prayer is the core of our d. 20.174.1
the entire course of the d. 5.23.13
the Lord's D. is called this 7.10.4
the night has values that the d. 20.385.4
through the night towards the d. 20.159.1

daylight: fairer than d. dawning 19.139.1
Truth walks by d. 14.21.3

days: desires to see good d.?' 6.4.6
I believe my d. are few 16.30.2

dazzling: they are d. splendours 20.178.1

deaconesses: d. being kept fresh and bright 20.33.1

deacons: choose from among themselves d. 20.558.4

dead: devout husband, you are d. 13.15.3
much sorrow for the d. 16.62.3
not link us with the d., but cuts us off 20.352.3
seldom comes glory till a man be d. 17.61.7
some are d.; you must rouse them 19.136.3
the d. I give thee 5.37.2
when God's d., I am d. 20.337.1
when I am d. and opened 16.47.1
when I am d. my dearest 19.123.9

deadness: whatever we do that creates d. 20.535.4

dearly: love thee more d. 13.36.2

death: a beautiful d. is for people 20.538.1
a good d. does honour 14.22.1
a matter of life or d. 20.25.4
act of valour to despise d. 17.20.11
and D. shall be no more 17.42.21
antidote against d. 2.13.2
any man's d. diminishes me 17.42.19
as then in d., so now in love 17.36.3
at d., if at any time 19.16.20
becomes a matter of life or d. to you 20.352.9
before the hour of d. 20.353.1
birth is the beginning of d. 17.52.1
bringing in d. 2.13.19
combat all that carries d. 20.421.5
dark d. is destroyed 3.6.1
D. be not proud 17.42.18
d. has suddenly become so discussable 20.427.1
d. is always, under all 20.69.9
D. is but crossing the world 18.44.17
d. is no more 4.42.1
d. is the flowering of life 19.147.14
d. is the only limit we know 20.124.6
d. is the supreme festival 20.15.2
d. is what takes place within us 20.514.8
d. may be too powerful 20.561.2
d. opens unknown doors 20.381.1
d., that final curb on freedom 20.269.2
d. the gate of life 17.76.31
'd. where is thy sting?' 17.22.9
die a voluntary and daily d. 20.238.2
do not be afraid of d. 2.19.1
embrace d. to fulfil his holy will 18.37.3
eternal d. is more bitter 16.34.2
fear of d. has gone farther 17.43.5

drawn: you are not d. to God 20.241.3
draws: God d., but he d. 4.35.14
dread: why are you in such d.? 15.9.2
dreadful: some have called thee Mighty and d. 17.42.18
dream: I cannot forget the d. 20.31.4
I have a d. that my four little children 20.335.13
when the d. in our heart 20.379.1
dreams: put man's best d. to shame 19.30.1
shattered d. are the hallmark 20.335.6
wrestling in our d. 20.571.1
dressed: now you are foppishly d. 4.32.1
drink: a population sodden with d. 19.23.8
d. the chalice of Jesus 18.43.2
d. with heartfelt reverence 3.10.1
take, d. as much as you want 17.90.6
driven: and horrors hast thou d. me 17.76.12
driving: by d. out those we don't care for 20.473.2
dross: d. is consumed by the fire 16.25.1
drown: even a rat may d. a nation 18.7.3
drum: Christ beats his d. 17.42.9
dry: my spirit has become d. 16.38.22
they are so d., they would burn well 19.136.16
dryness: empty, cold d. of your prayer 19.97.1
time worrying about d. 20.419.1
dungeon: only door out of the d. of the self 19.99.6
dust: I who am but d. and ashes! 7.16.1
duties: exactness in little d. 19.53.5
in carrying out present d. 18.19.6
in the fulfilment of your d. 16.49.1
one of the highest of human d. 20.120.4
the continual practice of small d. 19.109.19
duty: do the d. that lies nearest 20.20.1
d. does not have to be dull 20.385.12
d. is the sublimest word 19.88.3
first spiritual d. of man 20.10.3
just as hard to do your d. 20.94.3
our return of d. may abound 17.67.1
to let oneself be bound by a d. 20.276.10
dwarfs: we are like d. on the shoulders of giants 12.6.1
dwell: God does not d. 13.24.1
you will d. close to God 17.90.7
dwelling: d. in the Holy Spirit 20.72.2
fix in us thy humble d. 18.56.3
he has made the d. 12.17.6
Spirit of God d. within us 6.15.1
dwellings: God has two d. 17.101.5
dwells: Christ d. in us 4.30.3
God d. close to their hearts 20.328.7
soul in whom God d. 17.90.4
dying: as a d. man to d. men 17.10.9
continually d. in order that it may live 20.423.12
even if d. is to be made 20.276.2
habit of living indisposeth us to d. 17.20.17
I never knew that d. is so easy 20.64.2
the d. pray at the last 20.216.3
the most comfortable way of d. 17.50.1
the one true way of d. to self 19.107.5
the sayings of d. men 18.27.10
to be desired when d. 17.94.16
touched by these processes of d. 20.514.7
when you're d. you're d. 20.456.1
dyke: by gnawing through a d. 18.7.3
dynamic: God is the living, active, d., ceaselessly 20.437.5

E

eagerly: e. and entirely 16.13.19
they seek most e. to hear 16.70.2
early: e. in the morning our song 19.70.1
earn: no way to e. one's living 20.397.1
earned: food that I have not e. 4.50.1
ears: unexpected news make both e. tingle 4.9.3
earth: a lump of muddy e. 16.72.3
a short time here upon e. 17.94.7
e. is receding; heaven is approaching 19.103.10
e. would be heaven 19.42.7
God is on e. 7.20.2
how he fills heaven and e. 6.10.4
lifts E. to Heaven, stoops Heaven to E. 17.36.2
placed in the e. 17.29.9
so may it be done on e. 13.15.4
the e. is full of thy riches! 19.85.1
the e. of our continent [South America] 20.532.1
the new e. is gathering, isolating 20.536.10
the present life of humans on e. 8.4.2
the prodigal e. 20.288.1
things of e. should be put 5.10.15
throw e. over your head 17.80.19
to feel ourselves at home on this e. 20.398.2
we do have one e. 20.421.2
when the Saviour was on e. 2.18.1
wherever you are on e. 4.4.16
earthly: every e. possession is just 6.14.5
here lie the e. remains 18.4.2
stripped of e. possessions 11.8.1
ease: cannot settle at e. in the world 19.83.2
fears to sit at e. 19.30.2
easier: I can imagine an e. life 19.3.2
make it e. for others to believe 20.76.1
east: to the people of the E. End 19.23.5
Easter: each year Lent and E. 20.489.2
E. is not a part 20.410.3
night before E. in vigil 7.10.3
the E. joy, the threshold 9.6.1
the great E. truth 19.29.1
their E. devotions 18.47.2
there is no E. without a Good Friday 20.249.1
easy: sit in my armchair, and take it e. 19.132.4
than wrong, tho' e. 17.22.12
eat: e. as a hungry man eats 3.10.1
'e., this is my body' 19.101.7
we must e. to live, and not live to e. 20.448.5

lest your e. question 5.15.1
sown in him by the e. 5.21.1
the bitterest e. 19.83.8
the e. will fill them with bad ones 16.51.10
to recognize the e. 20.141.6

energetic: but heaven of the e. 17.30.1

energies: the release of e. 20.578.4

energy: as the elemental e. 20.6.5
bears the mark of an active e. 19.147.8
one flow, one divine e. 20.249.2
only form of e. that lasts forever 20.448.6

enflame: God will sometimes e. 14.7.13

engagement: a deeper e. 20.415.2

engine: that no e. can control 20.236.1

England: but we are the people of E. 20.22.20
here is the secret of E.'s greatness 19.156.1
not ordained that E. shall perish 16.24.5
the Church of E. is the perfect church 20.445.1

English: not a single E. Church Sister 19.8.2

Englishman: the E. is naturally wasteful 20.381.3

engraven: e. the glory of his power 16.13.9

enjoy: how to e. what we believe 19.147.12
in winter e. 19.20.6
should e. in all its fullness 19.147.11

enjoyed: by love alone is God e. 17.97.15

enjoyment: know no watchword but *gain* and *e.* 19.128.1

enlighten: e. the darkness of my heart 13.16.11

enlightened: arise and be e.! 12.3.3
being e., we are adopted 3.1.9

enlightens: e. the mind with its light 14.4.10
illumination that e. souls 20.54.3

enough: everybody cared e., everybody shared e. 20.160.1
Father, and it is e. for us' 13.36.1
never say to God: 'E.' 17.99.1
you have not done e. 20.276.12

enquiry: we come in e. and by e. 12.1.3

enslave: you will e. yourself 5.23.4

entangling: so intricate, so e. as death? 17.42.20

enter: e. into the glory of the heavenly 16.13.15

enthusiasm: I wish the state of e. 19.56.3

enthusiastic: something to be e. about 19.86.7

entirely: eagerly and e. 16.13.19

envy: e. and hatred try to pierce 5.8.8
e. takes the joy, happiness 20.264.11
if e. was not such a tearing thing 20.255.4
than e. to see a miracle 17.66.1
the joy of someone you e. 7.20.4
too many Christians e. the sinners 16.45.22

episcopal: highly prized virtue in e. candidates 20.290.1

epistle: this e. [Romans] is in truth 16.45.2

equal: all e. are within the church's gate 17.60.4
all men are e., since 4.35.7
means being his e. 20.176.5
men are e. in their natural dignity 20.321.6
one e. communion and identity 17.42.24
process of building a just and e. society 20.462.2

equality: standing for the ultimate spiritual e. 19.40.1

equally: who can love all men e. 7.17.1

erases: only the hand that e. 14.11.19

erotic: our e. connectedness to the world 20.446.1

err: being wise, thou canst not e. 17.29.13
every man may e. 19.16.8
the best may e. 18.1.9
to e. in daring to embody 4.30.2
to e. is human 5.8.5

errand: use God as an e. boy 20.196.2

error: dispelled the darkness of e. 5.11.1
it has no e., for all e. 18.35.7
no authority has power to impose e. 19.1.4
one must never confuse e. 20.321.7
to persist in e. is devilish 5.8.5

errors: chief cause of human e. 17.40.1
imitation of the common e. of our life 16.60.5
see my own e. and not judge 4.20.8
they defined their e. 18.7.27

errs: confuse error and the person who e. 20.321.7

escape: as long as we try to e. it 20.338.1
e. from his mighty hand 1.1.8

eschatological: the e. is not one element *of* Christianity 20.388.3

eschatology: Christianity is e. 20.388.2

establishment: dependent on parts of the American e. 20.570.7

eternal: but e. life is more sweet 16.34.2
disparage e. life and happiness 17.96.4
essence of everything that is e. 15.11.1
e. death is more bitter 16.34.2
its reward is e. 13.11.6
the promise of e. life 4.8.5
unspeakable glory of e. life 5.32.3

eternity: a teacher affects e. 20.2.4
but a small parenthesis in e. 17.20.12
e. is not something 20.32.1
E.! Thou pleasing 18.1.25
he acquired e. 12.23.3
he who has no vision of e. 19.35.3
in God, time and e. are one 14.26.1
I am accustomed to dwell in e. 20.18.2
I saw E. the other night 17.100.1
I used to think about e. 19.37.4
it constructs the shape of e. 20.322.4
remember the length of e. 18.33.4
silence is deep as E. 19.35.21
takes no care for e. 17.96.1
unless I am in touch with e. 20.509.2
upon this short time e. depends 17.94.7
we shall have justice in e. 17.94.6

ethic: the e. of Jesus 20.409.6
the e. of relation of man to man 20.492.7
with which a Christian e. has to deal 20.158.4

ethical: a man is e. only when 20.492.6
in earnest with a high e. rule 20.85.1

F

failures: dilate on general f. and faults 20.40.5
faith: a continuous act of f., a f. 20.313.7
a living f. is not something 20.423.11
boldly for the f. 11.8.1
by exalting the merit of f. 16.35.6
Christians should possess: knowledge, f. 5.34.1
could be known apart from f. 20.467.2
emotionally satisfying f. is repugnant to me 20.419.2
eyes: those of flesh and those of f. 4.35.1
f. aims to unite 20.121.2
f. alone justifies us 16.45.3
f. always shows itself 20.355.8
f. as the fulfilment of life 20.430.1
f. essentially means 20.576.4
f. expects from God 19.107.4
f. fills a man with love 17.87.3
f. has need of the whole truth 20.536.2
f. has no merit 6.14.11
f., however, is something that 16.45.4
f. is a big electric blanket 20.419.6
f. is a gift 19.16.2
f. is a kind of possession of the church 20.497.1
f. is an active creative force 20.423.6
f. is awe in the presence 20.122.2
f. is never identical with piety 20.122.10
f. is not a thing of the mind 20.164.1
f. is nothing at all tangible 20.75.4
f. is the assent to any proposition 17.72.3
f. is the only key to the universe 20.385.13
f. is the root of works 18.60.3
f. is to believe 5.8.7
f. is to dance it 20.101.8
f. keeps watch for that day 3.12.12
f. makes the world 20.223.2
f. means just that blessed unrest 19.83.2
f. ought in silence to fulfil 4.30.2
f. sees in everything the action of God 18.11.18
f. takes up the cross 19.21.1
f. tells us of things 16.38.23
f. that thaws it out 20.247.6
f. was my guide 2.1.2
for those whose f. is weak 15.13.4
from f. thus flow forth love 16.45.12
give an answer for the f. 20.124.2
in the concord of your f. 2.12.2
in which f. has to be lived 20.274.6
increase us in f. 2.16.1
is not f., but superstition 20.335.14
it is because of f. 17.49.1
it is f. that makes martyrs 19.109.18
it is through f. 1.1.4
let us go to him through pure f. 19.50.5
live your f. by confessing it 20.385.18
must rest in f. alone 19.113.1
my f. began to grow 5.32.6
necessary element in continuing f. 20.210.5
never an act of f. without risk 20.316.5
not the proper ground of f. 20.345.1
not to make use of f.'s power 20.223.1
possess a f.; I want a f. that possesses 19.86.1
preach f. until you have it 18.5.1
show how great our f. is 7.21.1
so the F. was planted 16.14.1
the divorce between f. and life 20.497.2
the garment of f. we profess 20.581.1
the life of f. is 20.407.6
the only way to learn strong f. 19.106.1
the seat of f. is not in the brain 16.31.1
there lives more f. 19.142.1
they are successive understandings of f. 20.273.3
till f. is fully grown 20.268.1
to feel the impact of your f. 20.108.1
to make natural f. easier 20.9.1
unfaltering f. can savour it 13.37.19
we begin to stand on our f. 20.379.12
we must be saved by f. 20.409.8
what is required of you is f. 15.14.9
what we take on f. 20.280.1
when God speaks and awakens human f. 20.115.1
when they hear of this freedom of f. 16.45.13
yet not have any f. 20.280.2
faithful: and to the f., death 17.76.31
better to be f. than famous 20.69.5
if we are to be f. to Jesus 20.324.2
the f. person lives 3.1.3
the lips of all the f. 5.33.8
faithfulness: f. in carrying out 18.19.6
God's f. to the people 20.131.2
great is thy f. 20.187.1
faiths: a deeper unity of people of all f. 20.511.2
join hands with people of other f. 20.324.2
fall: a f. is not a signal to lie wallowing 19.123.6
being afraid to f. headlong 5.8.4
each time you f. and in this way 7.12.5
every time you f. 20.171.7
f. down at the feet of Jesus 19.134.1
is down need fear no f. 17.22.10
make them f. down 14.24.3
power caused the angels to f. 17.5.7
to rise by other's f. 16.62.2
fallen: all the evil of our f. state 19.107.6
falling: not by violence, but by oft f. 16.42.4
false: as thou be not f. to others 17.5.19
but you show yourself f. 6.10.1
Christian religion that has become f. 20.14.2
he is a f. prophet 2.8.7
falsehood: f. by night 14.21.3
though truth and f. be 17.42.16
fame: for what is f. in itself 16.51.7
I thought of nothing but f. 19.132.6
familiarity: f. so far from being 20.40.8
families: the disorders and ill-governedness of f. 17.10.2
family: a f. that prays together 20.538.6
a f. without love is godless 20.109.4
all the world is God's f. 18.35.4
Christ's f. is bigger than any human f. 20.232.1
clergyman as the father of a larger f. 18.32.3
love and care for the f. 20.269.3

protection of the extended f. system 20.341.1
the f. should be a place 20.485.1
the union of the f. lies in love 19.16.14
to be learned in the f. 19.48.2
to the importance of the f. 20.322.2

famine: all this f. of love 20.328.8

famous: better to be faithful than f. 20.69.5

fanaticism: f. is the false fire 18.14.11
part of the nature of f. 20.15.20
the desert has bred f. 20.568.1

fanatics: Earth's f. 19.30.3

fancies: he that f. he is perfect 18.60.6

fantasies: unsubstantial f. slide easily 12.23.6

farewell: f. in the Lord 6.11.1
f. my dear child 16.51.15

farther: nearer to church, the f. from God 17.3.3

fashionable: as to be almost f. 20.427.1

fast: a true f. means refraining from evil 4.2.18
did ordain the f. of forty days 17.61.10
he must f. and be clean 14.5.3
I am coming as f. as I can 17.69.1
they f. for two or three days 2.3.2
to f. is to learn to love 20.255.5

fasting: do not limit the benefit of f. 4.2.18
easy to talk of f. 5.22.5
f. can overcome concupiscence 13.22.1
what we gain from f. 5.10.4

fasts: the immoderate long f. 5.22.18

fate: share this f. with you 2.7.1
your f. does not depend on me 20.35.1

father: 'a F. of the fatherless' 19.106.4
and a heavenly F.'s care 18.33.2
as you pray to the eternal F. 16.48.2
asserted that he knew the F. 20.217.4
clergyman as the f. of a larger family 18.32.3
concrete affirmation that he is F. 20.164.1
do for his heavenly F. 19.48.6
do not refuse me, F.! 16.57.1
doing the F.'s will in the F.'s world 20.296.3
equality with the F.'s glory 5.24.4
giving up of the Son through the F. 20.388.4
God is your F. 2.356.9
have God for his f. 3.2.1
he tells us he is our f. 18.14.13
hear the voice of the F. 14.17.7
I am my F.'s child 18.51.2
I take God the F. to be my God 18.27.9
if the F. begot the Son 4.7.1
it is a F. to whom we are listening 20.41.2
it is easier for a f. 20.321.8
let the F. proportion out daily to thee 17.82.1
my f. was the only one 3.11.1
one celestial F. gives to all 17.76.25
one God the F. 2.13.9
our heavenly F. never takes anything 19.106.3
pass out of this world to the F. 13.10.6
show us the F. 13.36.1
the F. does not exist 3.1.7
the F. of all has no name 2.14.6
the F. of all things 3.1.8
the F.'s boundless love 18.42.5
the F. to my soul 5.42.1
through the Son to the F. 2.13.11
to be ordered by our F. 19.120.3
when I think of my f. 20.72.4
with God the F. 10.5.1

fatherly: having tasted his f. love 16.13.18

fathers: they are not where our f. were 20.518.3

fault: a f. which humbles a man 18.60.5
abstains from a f. 13.2.1
more courage than admission of f. 20.447.1
person who likes finding f. 7.17.4
the business of finding f. 17.87.9

faults: almost all our f. 17.68.22
bury the f. of his friends 19.12.3
do not think of the f. of others 16.65.21
if we had no f. ourselves 17.68.6
not to be surprised by our own f. 18.19.1
the greatest of f. 19.35.18
we acknowledge our f. 17.68.21

fear: a man who is in the grip of f. 16.45.6
and the f. of God. 4.54.1
f. can keep a man out of danger 17.52.5
f. God: for his f. is wisdom 17.29.13
f. God through love 17.28.8
f. is never a good counsellor 20.10.3
f. is sharp-sighted 17.29.14
f. is the great killer 20.511.4
f. the Lord 2.11.3
help me to be free from f. 20.454
I f. God, yet 17.20.4
in very great pain and f. 20.180.3
let love cast out f. 20.202.5
of acting and reasoning as f. 18.7.26
that we need f. 20.289.3
this f. of Almighty God 16.20.1

feared: appearance as something to be f. 20.148.1
one thing to be f. 4.35.26

fearful: if you have a f. thought 9.1.1

fears: all our hopes and all our f. 18.9.2
fightings within, and f. without 19.51.2
perform according to our f. 17.68.18
whoever f. God f. to sit 19.30.2

feast: the f. is thine 20.152.1
the name of the f. explains 3.12.11
to share in God's own f. 12.9.1

feasted: God has f. the empty-bellied 20.588.1

feeble: begin from one's f. state 4.26.1
the religion of f. minds 18.7.5

feebleness: bold, remember our own f. 16.51.9

feed: f. upon the will of God 18.43.2
it forgets to f. on you 16.38.22
you f. the hungry in your sweetness 14.4.1

feeds: Christ always f. with his own blood 4.35.20

f. is not an occasional act 20.335.7
f. is the key 20.141.10
f. needs to be accepted 20.352.4
f. to the injured 17.43.13
if we do not live on God's f.? 20.151.3
it is poured out for the f. of sins 4.2.14
reconciliation and f.—essential 20.137.3
the f. we display to those 5.10.17
the only true f. 19.83.9
the petition for f. 20.87.4
we cannot refuse f. 2.356.11

forgiving: f. one another 17.82.2
it is by f. that one is forgiven 20.538.2
we forget without f. 20.484.6

forgot: it's folly to become f. 12.21.1

forgotten: of dying and being f. 19.132.6
the anxiety of being eternally f. 20.545.1

forks: we must hold onto our toasting-f. 20.34.5

form: f. the mind of the young 4.35.23
he that hath but a f. 17.59.1
identical with its earliest f. 20.38.3
no f. of worship, however sacred 19.160.2
the deadness of an outer f. 18.35.3

formalism: no devil so dangerous as evangelical f. 19.125.5

formed: f. in the image and likeness of God 17.71.1
f. me and reformed me 11.1.5

forming: what I am, f., f., f. what I shall be 20.4.5

formula: the f. for the Christian life 20.296.3
without fear and without f. 20.383.7

fornication: 'do not commit f.' 4.62.1

forsake: therefore f. everything for God 14.27.3

forsaken: he has never f. any tribe 20.442.1
sin f. is one of the best 19.125.8
thou hast never f. 16.5.1

forsakes: those whom God f. 17.24.3

forth: f. in thy name, O Lord, I go 18.56.6

fortify: to f. the martyrs 19.5.1

fortune: in every down-turn of f. 6.5.1
one's own good f. in having it 20.255.5
the worst f. has to bestow 20.85.2

fortune-telling: reject all divination, f. 8.7.1

forward: I will go anywhere provided it is f. 19.92.1
is hope, f. looking and f. moving 20.388.2

found: cannot be f. by anything 14.7.6
even when he cannot be f. 12.7.8
if God can be f. in all things 20.289.3
if God could not be f. 6.16.1
if thou hadst not f. me 17.80.7

foundation: laying f. stones 13.19.1
setting life upon a firm f. 20.116.4
the church's f. is unshakeable 4.2.15
truth is the f. of all knowledge 17.43.8
your life is without a f. 20.276.11

foundations: first lay deep f. of humility 5.8.28
lay we the f. of justice 17.37.2

founder: the f. must not be forgotten 20.38.4

fountain: a f. fed from many springs 19.130.1
for he is the f. 14.24.1
the unique f. of truth 16.13.12

fragrance: imparts its f. to the axe 20.84.3
nor the f. of love in the soul 7.20.1

fragrant: most f. when they are incensed 17.5.24

frailties: never listen to accounts of the f. 16.38.2

frame: essence of every picture is the f. 20.22.2
not permitted to choose the f. of our destiny 20.276.6

France: I am from F. 12.21.1
it is different in F. 12.23.6

franchise: an extension of the f. 20.22.5

Francis: F. whittled a little cup 13.10.10
in beautiful things F. saw Beauty 13.10.7
St F. ordered a plot 13.39.2

free: a Christian is a perfectly f. lord of all 16.45.7
a man is f. to do what he likes 19.86.5
accept suffering as f., responsible 20.15.10
adoring, imploring, O set me f. 16.46.2
be both a servant, and f. 5.23.6
Christianity promises to make men f. 20.311.10
crucified and risen, is set f. 20.198.1
f. men freely work 19.30.2
f. us from the tyranny 7.20.7
God's love sets us truly f. 20.553.3
in order to set f. the original 20.1.1
man is f., for he is in the image 20.235.12
no such thing as an entirely f. man 19.29.7
possible only to a f. agent 20.117.5
to f. the human being 20.227.3
we cannot be f. men if 19.91.7
works of mercy set a man f. 5.8.17
you've figured out f. will 20.419.3

freed: the Lord has f. me 5.27.1

freedom: attains to f. from any slavery 19.29.7
better organized than f. 20.62.6
dependence and f. are incompatible 20.368.5
f. from hunger, but for... f. to create 20.252.2
f. into subjection to God 5.13.2
f. is never voluntarily given 20.335.8
f. which is the result of necessity 20.10.9
God desired f. and f. gave rise 20.10.2
in man's very f. 20.274.4
love can only exist in f. 20.383.6
out of a sheer f. 13.13.3
sensitivity and wonderful new f. 20.379.9
the enemies of f. do not argue 20.311.16
the possibility of f. in slavery 20.504.1
the Protestant principle of f. 19.135.1
this is true f. 20.72.10
those who deny f. to others 19.91.7
to direct our f. and make it fruitful 20.207.2
when they hear of this f. of faith 16.45.13

freedoms: there are two f. 19.86.5

freely: God gave it f. 20.65.1
that which can respond f. 20.274.5
what a bliss it is f. to love him 19.120.12

G

gale: the g. of the Holy Spirit 17.70.1
gambles: man who g. is to win 19.136.9
game: as though it were just a g. 7.16.2
gap: Holy Ghost closes the last g. 20.238.5
it is a g., a chasm 20.164.2
not be in haste to fill the g. 19.138.2
unless the widening g. 20.425.2
gaps: part of a soldier's duty is to fill g. 20.174.7
garden: God gave us a g. 20.213.4
Jesus was in a g. 17.80.13
gardener: it takes a wise g. to know 20.249.11
gardening: by g. our children learn 20.127.3
g. is an active participation 20.127.2
garment: distribute my g. as follows 4.4.13
possession is just a kind of g. 6.14.5
you are the g. that covers 14.4.1
garments: our fathers… wore old g. 4.32.1
gaslight: we live in the g. 20.9.1
gate: entering through the narrow g. 6.18.1
faithful, death the g. of life 17.76.31
strive to enter by the narrow g. 4.61.1
the g. of heaven to man below 13.37.15
gather: g. ye rosebuds while ye may 17.61.13
gathered: God g. us out of all lands 4.4.11
let thy Church be g. 2.8.4
they are g. into me 14.26.9
was g. together 2.8.4
where two or three are g. together 20.527.3
gave: God that g. me to you 17.48.1
so many people g. me something 20.492.5
gay: Lesbian, g. and bisexual people 20.527.2
gaze: let us fix our g. 1.1.6
ought to sate our g. 20.178.1
so that he can turn his g. 4.3.1
when our g. has wandered 5.10.6
gazelles: like the man who chases after g. 6.2.4
gender: transcends the g. stereotypes 20.194.1
general: no rule is so g. 17.24.4
generation: every g. needs re-generation 19.136.8
the children of men without g. 17.10.7
we are not a post-war g. 20.141.5
generations: avoid separating the g. 20.472.1
generosity: and encourages g. 20.146.1
dispensed with g. 18.7.11
one's insight and one's g. 20 374.3
to show his great g. 4.35.8
genius: love is rarer than g. itself 20.62.4
unless he has g., a rich man 20.62.9
gentle: anger is quieted by a g. word 17.28.4
nothing so g. as real strength 17.87.6
gentleman: getting to know a g. 20.311.5
gentlemanly: g. conduct 19.6.2
gentleness: it also bred heroic g. 20.568.1
nothing is so strong as g. 17.87.6
the infinite g. of my God! 13.29.7
Germany: certain peoples in G. 8.6.1
gestation: compared to a g. and birth 20.536.10
gesture: a g. of faith, the g. we go on 20.224.2
gestures: there are three g. 20.472.1
we ought to use g. 15.1.4
Gethsemane: alone in the garden of G. 20.189.1
can I G. forget? 19.102.2
He went to the garden of G. 29.559.4
ghost: if I did not believe there was a Holy G. 19.12.18
giants: like dwarfs on the shoulders of g. 12.6.1
gift: a g. from God 20.357.2
a g. to be shared 20.415.1
endow them with the g. of tongues 18.13.1
faith is a g. 19.16.1
God's g. to man 20.277.1
neither do I refuse any g. 20.529.7
no g. is more precious 16.26.1
properly the g. of another 6.10.2
suffering is the very best g. 19.144.1
this g. is his love 18.11.5
gifts: all g. have been given 5.10.5
appreciate the value of his g. 19.19.2
g. … excite and stir up 17.79.4
God's g. put man's best dreams 19.30.1
if she have the necessary g. 19.22.2
rather than the g. he is offered 17.28.10
share all the g. they have 14.11.11
that my natural g. might not 10.3.2
the best of all your g. 5.42.1
whatever g. God bestowed upon us 13.20.11
gird: I g. myself today 8.3.1
girl: what shall I do with this g.? 2.17.1
give: g. all you can 18.57.15
g. and you will receive 5.8.17
g. me, good Lord, a humble 16.51.2
g. what you command 5.8.11
g. yourself entirely to God 13.20.1
of thy goodness, g. me thyself 17.6.1
rather than to g. oneself to God's service 20.397.2
the more we can g. in active life 20.398.6
to g. up all for him 20.82.2
to have been able to g. 20.536.6
we are to g. our heart 20.569.1
when you g., see that you g. 14.21.7
you can g. without loving 20.174.3
given: God will truly be g. to you 14.27.3
I have g. myself to God 12.16.5
to be accepted as well as g. 20.352.4
gives: no one g. himself freely 16.13.18
the more he g. 20.68.1
the soul g. up all for love 14.18.11
giving: more beautiful for g. itself readily 20.304.1
one for receiving and the other for g. 20.264.12
that which multiplies in g. 14.21.7
glad: a g. spirit attains to perfection 16.52.10
gladden: thereby g. someone's mind 5.23.1

G. on the same level as a tourist agency 20.423.5
G. really does lie hidden 20.139.6
G. should be greatly loved by women 12.16.3
G. speaks for himself 20.428.3
G., the author of all marvels 7.5.1
G. the beginning and end of our love 14.24.1
G. the Father of our Lord 2.16.1
G. wants to come down to us 16.45.19
G. who knows everything 8.9.4
G. who made the eath, the air 19.121.1
G. will fade out of your life 20.20.1
G. wills to do something 20.158.1
G. would not be true to himself 4.8.8
G.'s house is the Catholic Church 12.17.4
G.'s love and power and faithfulness 20.143.2
G.'s own people 20.436.2
G.'s promise to the pure of heart 20.163.1
He alone is G. who 12.7.8
he always claims to bring G. 20.469.1
heaven is G., and G. is in my soul 19.50.3
He is not a G. far off 17.47.1
honoured and valued by G. 13.18.2
how to be with G. 5.23.5
human beings with whom G dwells 20.517.6
human sins afflict with grief even G. 3.9.2
I am as great as G. 17.90.1
I am that G. to whom 20.181.1
I fear G., yet 17.20.4
I need nothing but G. 17.1.1
I should believe in no G. 19.2.7
I want to be open to G. 20.350.3
I want to want to want to want you G. 20.454.5
I was created to see G. 11.1.6
if G. could not be found 6.16.1
if G. in his love for the human race 7.13.3
if G. is 'always greater' 20.121.4
if G. is love, then let our love speak 20.289.2
if G. were not a necessary Being 17.96.3
if you contemplate G. 17.45.6
if you do not become G. for me 14.11.3
important thing we know about G. 20.158.6
is the one G., the single G., the sole G. 20.122.13
it is G. contemplating G. 14.17.1
leads him to make himself a G. 17.80.16
life of G. in the soul of man 17.88.1
make G. its own monopoly 20.118.4
make G. smaller than the G. 20.454.8
make known the *true* G., the G. 20.200.2
my G. and my all! 13.16.14
my G. who is and who abides 4.13.1
nearer to church, the farther from G. 17.3.3
no one can know G. unless 2.13.14
nothing can be said properly of G. 9.5.2
not that, but the living G. 19.101.2
not the *experience* of G. 20.553.6
one G. and one Christ 1.1.5
one G. the Father 2.13.9
one vast symbol of G. 19.35.1
possible to know something of G 20.453.1
power for good is derived from G. 3.2.7
seed of G. grows into G. 14.11.17
so like G. as stillness 14.11.10
something beautiful for G. 20.538.8
soul is in G. and G. in the soul 14.4.11
the cross gives us G. 18.25.7
the cross is G. at work 20.193.1
the g. beyond G. 20.300.2
the G. of the Reformed tradition was the G. of slavery 20.137.5
the infinite gentleness of my G.! 13.29.7
the living G. is the field of force 20.522.2
the more we appropriate G. 18.25.2
the soul seeks G. in his majesty 13.9.2
there is a living G. 19.140.6
there is in G.—some say 17.100.3
there is no human experience of G. 20.190.1
they that deny a G. 17.5.4
they want G. 20.553.1
think or say can G. be exalted 13.6.9
this fire is G. 13.10.5
thus there was born true G. 5.24.3
to be alive to the reality of G. 20.117.3
to keep the thought of G. 5.10.22
to know G. 17.79.5
to listen to the voice of G. 20.168.2
to love G. for himself 14.7.1
to say that G. is love 20.437.5
to show G. in his true colours 20.269.6
to speak of G. as the Mother of Creation 20.598.2
to the most true G. 2.14.1
too easily and glibly about G. 20.423.4
try referring to G. as she 20.595.2
we all wish to be G. with G. 13.20.6
we cannot study G. 20.121.1
were there no G. 19.123.1
whatever G. does 14.11.13
what G. is and where G. is 14.25.1
what is impossible to G.? 4.2.9
where truth is, there is G. 17.29.3
why can't the same G. 20.131.3
you can't escape G. 20.337.1

God-and-Man: then was seen G. 14.4.2

Godhead: the G. is my sap 17.90.1
united also to your G. 11.9.8

godliness: cleanliness is indeed next to g. 18.57.13
the road of Christian g. 18.25.2

godly: we wish to be g. in church 13.20.9

God-man: life of the G. 13.6.4
rediscover the G. in the least 20.422.2

Godward: the G. journey 20.159.3

Godwardness: the roots of G. 20.202.3

gold: chains of g. are no less chains 18.19.12
he who loses g. 4.17.11
like g. in the furnace 16.25.1

golden: Jerusalem the g. 12.8.1

good: all kinds of g. things 3.12.8
all our power for g. 3.2.7
all that is g. in you 18.11.2

and the g. raised up 17.7.3
being truly g. and partaking 18.27.7
blessed is he who does g. 13.18.1
but of what is g. in them 16.65.21
choosing between g. and evil 3.9.5
do all the g. you can 18.57.2
given us by God for a g. purpose 4.9.6
God is everything that is g. 14.18.7
God made nothing that was not g. 5.13.1
g., and since the highest g. is above 13.10.14
g., the more communicated 17.76.20
hallmark of the power of g. 20.487.3
he knows those who do g. 5.18.1
he who would do g. to another 19.20.9
how g. is the God we adore 18.26.1
knowest best what is for my g. 16.6.1
made g. before we can do g. 16.42.5
men have never been g., they are not g. 20.122.7
more store by our g. will 15.6.1
music, the greatest g. 18.1.10
not a huge effort to do g. 20.551.2
power is never g. 9.1.3
saint, not because he is 'g.' 20.545.9
supreme g. which makes life worth 20.85.1
the choice between g. and evil 20.480.6
the g. of the one loved 20.385.16
the only way to make them g. is to be g. 19.99.10
the power of the soul for g. 19.114.5
the true contacts with g. 20.92.4
to see g. in everything 20.398.1
to think of himself as a g. man 20.407.1

goodbye: saying g. to a loved one 20.307.1

goodness: beauty as well as for g. 20.267.1
Christ is g. itself 4.28.6
did not so much magnify g. 17.5.8
g. is something so simple 20.276.8
g. is stronger than evil 20.554.10
how g. heightens beauty 19.104.2
make any sense of God's g. 18.15.4
the thought of the divine g. 16.30.1

goods: who seek for g. before 12.7.6

gospel: application of the g. 20.165.1
be a proclaimer of the g. 5.23.12
'brown bread and the G. 18.27.2
but always the same g. 20.473.1
Christ sent me to preach the g. 20.73.2
content of the Christian g. is liberation 20.199.1
cry the G. with your whole life 20.29.2
difficult for people to believe in the G. 20.554.4
doing something together in the light of the g. 20.565.4
fulfilment of the g. of the Redeemer 20.142.4
g. is in all respects identical 20.38.3
hearing the G. as they should 20.322.1
hidden in these words of the g. 17.15.2
Holy Spirit... writes his own g. 18.11.6
I must take the g. 19.23.5
I preach the g. with all my might 20.361.1
listen to the G. in an ordinary way 20.5.1
one question, and that is the g. 19.58.5
process of bringing the g. 20.219.1
seek to follow the g. more closely 20.473.8
the core of the Christian g. 20.537.3
the explosive power of the g. 20.570.2
the glory of the g. 2.356.10
the g. gives us different priorities 20.570.3
the g. in the American accent 20.219.3
the g. is essentially a message 20.311.4
the g. is NOT Good News for women 20.525.1
the g. is not simply 20.166.1
the g. is open to all 20.355.3
the g. is the knowledge 20.38.4
the g. things he had done 20.255.3
the g. was not good advice 20.311.8
the g. will not ever tell us 20.592.4
the preaching of the G. 20.529.4
the trustee community of the g. 20.205.1
the truth of the G. 18.10.2
the value of the gospel 19.150.5
there would be no g. 20.175.1
to reduce the g. 20.139.2
too often the G. is preached 20.584.2
two things to do about the G. 18.58.1
we have a social g. 20.66.1
whenever you read the G. 18.52.1

gospels: my particular friends in the g. 20.277.2
to understand the g. in our times 20.118.1

gossip: do not listen gleefully to g. 7.17.4
give his pet parrot to the town g. 20.264.13

gossips: g. are frogs 17.60.12

gothic: g. architecture represents the soul aspiring 19.16.7

govern: g. your will 16.60.8

government: all g. 18.7.12
God has established g. 20.486.2
g. is a contrivance of human wisdom 18.7.13
no new forms of g. 19.1.2
remind the g. that it has the power 20.348.1
the g. speaks rubber bullets 20.554.7
the sole end of g. 19.2.4
whose g. is theologically informed 20.254.2

governments: God, not to g. and politicians 20.110.1

grace: a gift of sheer g. 20.44.4
advance farther in g. 17.45.1
attain to a greater measure of g. 19.29.4
beauty and g. are performed 20.216.2
but for the g. of God 16.8.1
cheap g. is g. without discipleship 20.15.4
consult g., not doctrine 13.10.4
costly g. is the treasure hidden 20.15.5
divine g. that did not fail them 16.62.5
g., but as the daughter of g. 18.3.2
G. can suffer here 17.61.5
g. comes after tribulation 16.59.2
G. does not want to be praised 13.18.3
G. grows better in the winter 17.86.4
g. is but glory begun 18.17.2
g. is indeed needed 17.80.21
g. is love that cares 20.526.10
g. is the free, undeserved 18.27.6
g. sometimes precedes the sacrament 5.43.1
g. strikes us when 20.545.5

guided: that God has g. events 20.96.1
guideth: and our footsteps g. 19.9.1
guilt: g. is the warning 20.218.3
impelled by a sense of the g. 20.96.1
the experience of g. has always been 20.151.1
guilty: distinction between the g. and the innocent 20.322.10
g. conscience never thinketh 17.52.18
g. of dust and sin 17.60.26
we are manifestly g. 20.576.6
when they feel g. 20.218.2
gulf: depths of the g. into which we may fall 19.16.5
gun: presented a g. at my face 18.21.1
guts: g. come next to love 20.4.7
gutter: my parish is the g. 20.586.5

H

habit: h. and novelty 17.21.4
not sin, but h. 20.62.1
habits: good h. can be fine things 20.105.1
hairshirt: as for my h., keep it 4.4.13
Hamlet: it is H., not his world 20.28.4
hand: a willing heart and a ready h. 16.20.4
give me thy h. 18.57.16
I take my heart in my h. 19.123.4
living in the H. of God 18.11.18
only the h. that erases 14.11.19
pray while the h. is on the handle 19.120.14
the work of an almighty h. 18.1.7
this was the h. that wrote it 16.20.5
thou dost open thy h. 16.24.2
we h. ourselves over 20.559.2
your h. upholds the universe 4.16.1
your right h. is extended 8.10.1
handiwork: revealed in his h. 13.7.2
handmaid: but an h. to religion 17.5.15
riches are a good h. 17.5.9
hands: but I'll also open my h. 20.379.2
coming from the h. of God 18.37.3
God has given us two h. 20.264.12
I put myself into your h. 20.29.11
into your h., O Father 13.14.1
my hands are too full 19.132.5
put everything in his h. 20.315.1
the strong h. of God 20.93.3
the works of their own h. 19.101.6
happen: nothing at all that can h. to us 20.289.3
things that only h. once 20.153.1
happened: something has h. to them 20.494.1
happiest: I would be the h. of men 19.33.4
we are the h. women in Ghent 19.19.1
happiness: a h. that is sought for ourselves 20.385.14
a strange h. flows into us 20.379.1
as the h. of the people 19.2.4
difference between h. and wisdom 19.42.6
God cannot give us h. and peace 20.352.14
h. is a mystery like religion 20.22.9
h. is never found until 20.428.2
h. is nothing but the enjoyment 13.10.14
h. is the natural life of man 13.37.6
h. is to be found only 19.152.2
h. lies in the hands of God alone 20.47.1
hope is itself a species of h. 18.32.27
if the world knew our h. 19.10.1
in providing for true h. 16.22.2
lives as to make h. impossible 5.8.13
nothing can bring greater h. 19.44.1
optimism, 'a taste for h.' 20.145.3
the chiefest point of h. 16.26.9
the h. of a man in this life 19.142.8
the joys of everlasting h. 8.4.8
the second, man's happiness 19.132.3
unspeakable good and everlasting h. 16.51.11
when one door of h. closes 20.331.1
happy: a nature should be perfectly h. 13.13.4
all that can be called h. 18.15.3
and work I can be h. 19.3.2
anything to be h. about 20.263.3
Dear cell, what h. hours 6.9.2
does not often make it h. 18.32.30
h. events make life delightful 20.383.4
h. the man whose words 13.7.3
I am so h., I am so h. 19.72.5
I am too h. in this world 20.331.2
in the most h. state 17.20.5
Man still wishes to be h. 5.8.13
that he may make it h. 20.569.1
that thou art h., owe to God 17.76.19
to have once been h. 6.5.1
harbour: back to the h. of God's will 4.28.7
the church offers the safest h. 4.2.15
you are the calm of the h. 4.57.1
harm: do the most h. to humanity and nature 20.118.6
since they h. themselves 16.71.1
useless; it does positive h. 19.125.3
harmonization: easy forms of theological h. 20.507.2
harp: nothing his own but his h. 12.19.1
harvest: abundant h. of true faith 8.6.2
our village h. festival 20.557.1
hassocks: not an affair of red h. 20.91.3
hasten: h. the day, O Lord 18.6.2
we must h. *unto God* 20.46.4
hat: a broad h. 17.52.15
hate: can do nothing if we h. ourselves 20.313.4
h. concentrates itself 19.99.13
h. is too great a burden to bear 20.335.15
just enough religion to make us h. 18.49.1
men h. more steadily 18.32.21
hated: h. for our name 2.4.1
hates: he who h. not in himself 17.80.16
hating: h. people is like burning down 20.247.7
waste more time h. myself 20.30.3
hatred: rebuke h. rather by 5.23.10

humility: as we seek to attain h. 18.19.1
Christian h. is based on 20.120.1
example of h., look at the cross 13.37.9
false h. is to believe 18.19.2
first lay deep foundations of h. 5.8.28
God is so great a Lover of h. 17.81.2
her constant companion is H. 19.42.2
h. comes from the constant 19.148.2
h. is not a grace 18.19.4
h. is not a mere ornament 17.10.3
h. means nothing other than 20.203.1
h. restrains the heart. 7.1.6
I would rather have a defeat with h. 4.17.13
if there were no h. in the world 20.385.15
let us learn h. from Christ 8.8.1
like the virtue of h. 17.101.2
not worth the least act of h. 16.38.13
quickest path to h. 14.7.7
so do we need h. 4.54.1
that leads to h. 4.60.1
the h. of Christ 20.408.1
the resurrection of h. 7.13.8
the spirit of chastity, h., patience 4.20.8
the wisdom of h. 20.228.8
true h. lies in seeing 18.19.3
we must view h. 18.17.8
wherever such mock h. 14.7.9
who sinks himself by true h. 19.82.2
without h. is like someone 6.14.13

humour: God also has a sense of h. 20.172.13
he has a sense of h. 20.311.9
regaining your good h. 19.147.6
the divine drop of oil we call h. 20.452.2
true h. springs 19.35.17

hunger: h. and thirst are healthy drives 20.448.5
h. and thirst, O Christ 10.6.1
I would rather die of h. 14.12.1
men are dying of h. 13.12.2
no sauce in the world like h. 17.29.6
starve for h. 10.2.1
to h. for her is to feed 13.20.4

hungers: Christ h. now 6.7.1
he who h. for money 20.45.3

hungry: makes us h. and yearning 14.17.2
our billion h. neighbours 20.503.1

hunted: tell the others by their h. expression 20.352.22

hurricane: even the h. is quiet 20.240.2

hurry: perpetual h. of business and company 19.162.4
those who are always in a h. 18.35.1

hurt: love until it hurts, then there is no h. 20.538.4

hurts: yet love h. 20.544.3

husband: a h.'s power over his wife 17.94.12
for liberty is a better h. than love 19.3.1

husbands: but by cowardly h. 19.83.10

hymn: every cell in my body is a h. 20.172.3

hymns: frequent use of familiar h. 20.40.8
over, with h. of victory 8.9.2
that is how my h. come 19.69.2

hypocrisies: are but repeated h. 18.35.2

hypocrisy: h. is the homage 17.68.25
nor angel can discern H. 17.76.14
other people recognise the h. 20.422.3

hypocrite: hath but a form is a h. 17.59.1

hypocrites: h. we are: but we 20.230.2

I

I: I am nothing, I have nothing 14.14.1
I am what I am. 12.9.2
to live as myself and yet not I 13.24.2

ice: like him that slides on i. 17.43.15
now that the i. is cracked 19.149.1

icon: the act of painting an i. 9.7.1
the artistic perfection of an i. 20.605.1

idea: by an i. which is higher 19.12.9
it is deed: not i. 20.366.1

ideal: absurdly high i. before us 19.53.4
an i. is never yours 20.4.6
the Christian i. 20.599.5

idealism: Christianity is a revolutionary i. 20.311.1

idealizes: the more one i. 20.81.3

ideals: live up to their loftiest i. 20.69.8
our i. are far higher 4.9.8

ideas: he clings to his own i. 17.15.4
instructs the heart not by i. 18.11.16

identity: our i. is in another 20.172.7
to the question of Christian i. 20.508.3

ideological: i. distortion of the biblical portrait 20.196.2

idealogies: all i. and 'isms' 20.308.4

idioms: used the words and i. 19.33.1

idle: all temptations attack the i. 19.136.13
for i. hands to do 18.55.4
he must not become i. 19.129.2
never be entirely i. 15.14.3
very i. as well as very industrious 17.25.4
virtues which the i. never know 19.86.6

idleness: Devil sets for young people is i. 19.24.4
put aside i. 12.7.7
such a thing as sacred i. 19.99.14

idol: in danger of worshipping an i. 20.598.4
prove his existence would be an i. 20.15.3

idolatry: another species of i. 18.35.3
atheism is a constant safeguard against i. 20.367.7
i. is an attempt to use God 20.397.2
it falls into a kind of i. 20.203.5
the warning against i. 20.300.2

idolize: to i.—idolizing everything from power 20.517.11

idols: beyond that they become i. 20.300.3
talk as though their i. 20.533.1

ignorance: i. and lack of learning 7.13.15
i. is excusable when it is borne 20.419.4
orthodoxy synonymous with i. 16.26.8
the first wonder is the offspring of i. 19.41.3

insight: gap between one's i. 20.373.3

J

even more brilliance than j. 17.29.2
generated by belief in j. 20.470.1
I demand j. 19.24.3
in the spectacle of his j. 5.10.8
is the problem of j. 20.409.7
j. becomes the right of all 20.529.4
j. belongs to God 20.110.1
j. delayed is j. denied 19.58.3
j. discards party, friendship 18.1.22
j. is the insurance 18.44.12
love and j. march together 20.144.1
love cannot be practised without j. 20.118.9
love the j. of Jesus Christ 13.31.8
makes all people equal and creates j. 20.596.1
man's belief in j. 20.409.2
recognize the j. of their demands 20.144.2
revenge is a kind of wild j. 17.5.22
so little confidence in the j. 20.396.8
such was the j. and mercy 20.374.1
that will allow j. to flower 20.139.3
the call to j. jars 20.502.2
they thirst for j. 20.491.1
violence does even j. unjustly 19.35.19
waiting for j. and fulfilment 20.532.1
we shall have j. in eternity 17.94.6
when j. is done them 20.222.1
when we speak about j. 4.2.1

justification: a question of our j. 16.13.13
doctrination of j. by faith 20.545.6
doctrine of j. by faith 20.534.1
j. is at once 20.48.2
precisely in the theology of j. 20.342.3

justified: Almighty God has j. 1.1.4
inquired if the Lord had j. my soul 19.87.2
we are j. 20.122.8

justifies: faith alone j. us 16.45.3

K

keep: K. yourself, my son, from everything 13.28.2
make and k. me pure within 18.56.5

keepeth: that God k. it 14.18.4

kept: God k. for us what was yours 13.15.1
God that hath k. me 17.48.2

key: grasp the master k. of life 19.138.3
is there then no k. to fit 16.18.1
must have a good k. 17.60.33
the k. of the day 17.52.27
the k. to thy heart 17.20.7
the k. to your own heart 20.94.1

keys: Peter was first given the k. 7.12.6

kill: to k. a man is not to defend a doctrine 16.16.1
we do not want to k. anyone either 19.17.1

killed: I have k. the horse 19.98.3

kin: if he be not of k. to God 17.5.4

kind: be k. to some of his other children 19.48.6
k. words are the music of the world 19.53.9
nobody is k. to only one person 19.53.6
too k.—too k.! 19.110.9

kindle: we also must k. the fire 5.41.3

kindness: every act of k. 14.18.3
k. has converted more sinners 19.53.7
k. is in our power 18.32.33
the heaven of k. in your family 20.322.3
to cultivate k. 18.32.34

kindnesses: one joy of doing k. 17.60.9

king: and K. of glory 19.31.1
I am like a k. with my legs stretched out 4.17.3
I were an unkind k. 14.19.6
if an earthly k. 18.52.1
no K. but him whom I have seen 3.4.1
praise my soul, the K. of heaven 19.96.2
the K. in his beauty deigns to walk 19.136.7
the K. of kings is here 16.42.3
the K.'s Highway 17.3.2
the warrior k. stoical but noble 20.372.1
win the friendship of the K. 11.9.7

kingdom: as ruler of his k. 12.17.4
asking is the rule of the K. 19.136.12
calls the Church a k. 19.150.7
Christianity is about the K. 20.535.1
doesn't deprive of his heavenly K. 19.76.1
entering into the k. 20.413.1
in the K. of God reigns 20.239.1
k. of God is destined 20.137.4
k. of God or the k. of heaven 5.10.2
lovers of his heavenly k. 15.14.7
may we receive your k. 20.426.1
only you can bring into the k. 20.97.4
prepare a k. for his Son 18.17.6
rich have no more of the K. 17.42.5
that I may enter into the K. of God 17.97.9
the glory of the heavenly k. 16.13.15
the k. comes indeed as a gift 20.512.3
the k. of God and of his Christ 20.430.2
the k. of God does not come 20.204.10
the k. of God is not for 20.25.3
the k. of God is simply 20.371.1
the k. of God needs you 20.264.18
the k. of God which is all within 18.19.9
the k. of heaven can be reached 6.16.1
the k. of heaven did gather us 17.63.1
the miracles and works show us what the k. 20.593.1
the way of the k. is not the way 20.364.1
there the k. comes 20.195.4
to accept his k. 20.217.1
to attain the k. of heaven 4.4.12
to live for God's k. 20.109.3
without justice and right, the k. of God 20.139.3

kingdoms: k. of darkness and light 20.488.1

kings: not only are we [Christians] the freest of k. 16.45.10
the King of k. is here 16.42.3

kiss: I cannot give you a k., so 8.5.4
we embrace each other with a k. 2.14.4

kitchen: in the noise and clutter of my k. 17.70.6
penitent is like a k. utensil 4.26.4
when you are in the k. 16.65.14

knaves: more fools than k. 17.25.3

kneeling: k. ne'er spoiled silk stocking 17.60.4

knees: bend our k., using outward actions 15.1.4
the weakest saint upon his k. 18.14.14

knew: if you k. me yesterday 20.443.1

knives: a pair of k., as a token 15.9.1

knock: he would never come and k. 4.2.12

knocketh: it k. It presseth in 17.92.1

knocking: persist in k. unceasingly 20.68.1
your best friend is k. outside 20.172.14

know: because you k. what you are 20.538.9
celebrate and share what we k. 20.449.1
for all who k. themselves 4.4.9
I do not k. Perhaps I shall never k. 20.461.1
I k. how much I do not k. 10.3.1
if we would k. anything 19.109.3
if you k. yourself well 14.29.1
light, that we may k. you 4.56.1
never k. yourself until you k. 17.97.7
no one can k. God 2.13.14
one thing, to k. God another 20.72.7
persons who best k. God 13 6 5
they k. enough who k. how to learn 20.2.3
think they k. too much about God 20.274.2
to k. any man 19.29.6
to k. God 17.79.5
to k. thee as true God 11.11.1
to see and to k. truly 5.14.7
to seek wisely, to k. surely 13.37.12
we do not k. him 20.135.5
we k. about God 15.10.3
we k. nothing about him 20.158.6
what we could not bear to k. 8.9.4
wish to k. how such things 13.10.4

knower: the k. and the known are one 14.11.6

knowingly: take care not k. to do 13.28.1

knowledge: a humble k. of yourself 15.14.17
but k. in the making 17.76.3
by k. and by love 12.17.5
Christians should possess: k. 5.34.1
desire for k. in excess 17.5.7
do not despise those whose k. 5.23.2
ever-longing, ever-satisfied k. 19.120.15
for the attainment of divine k. 19.133.4
general k. among the people 19.2.3
he gives the k. of God 20.9.3
if by k. only, and reason 17.3.2
if k. can cause most people 7.13.15
k. comes, but wisdom lingers 19.142.3
k. is not the conformity 20.273.2
k. is not the most important 18.19.8
k. is proud 18.14.8
k. is the rich storehouse 17.5.13
k. is the soul's delight 20.209.1
k. not of fact but of values 20.311.13
k. that never had a beginning 5.5.1
k. without integrity 18.32.7
light of the k. of himself 5.11.1
obedience is the key of k. 19.123.5
our k. of God 20.598.1
not the source of your own k.? 14.4.9
preservation of the means of k. 19.2.2
that k. of himself through love 20.163.1
the k. of a simple [i.e. real] thing 14.30.1
the k. of God 19.16.3
the k. of God and of ourselves 16.13.4
through the growth of k. 19.147.2
value k. of God above all 7.17.3
we cannot have k. of God 14.7.11
who has no k. of himself 16.26.11
wisdom is the right use of k. 19.136.6
zeal without k. 17.52.31

known: it is in silence that God is k. 19.16.4
just as its fruit makes k. 7.20.5
knower and the k. are one 14.11.6
nothing can be k. naturally 14.30.2
seeking to make itself k. to us 20.522.1
what he himself makes k. 20.158.6
what is to be k. about God 20.121.4

knows: God who k. everything 8.9.4
he who k. himself, k. everyone 4.4.6
man k. mighty little 20.2.1B

Knox: I fear John K.'s prayers 16.46.3

Korea: in K., the pattern of slavery 20.391.1

L

labour: always in l. and 4.28.8
day, to those who l. with love 4.27.5
exercising yourself in the field of l. 6.14.10
give us Thy grace to l. for 16.51.1
'l. is worship and prayer' 19.160.1
my daily l. to pursue 18.56.6
when we are engaged in manual l. 14.13.2
without truth your l. is in vain 12.24.4

labours: all the l. Jesus undertook 12.7.10
he l. in vain 4.44.2
the end of my l. is come 13.37.14

labyrinth: tangle ourselves in a l. 17.87.16
the l. of my difficulties 19.150.8

lack: heart that is little from l. of love 14.23.1
see what you l. 14.7.7
the more we l. anything 20.29.9
your greatest l. 20.328.2

ladder: a l. by which he could climb 13.10.7
cross of Christ is the Jacob's l. 17.97.13

lady: I saw our Blessed L. 14.18.1

laid: lighter than the ones l. upon us 17.28.5

laity: paintings are the Bible of the l. 12.11.1

lamb: gave us a l. for a lion 13.20.11
led forth like a l. 2.15.2
road that leads me to the L.! 18.14.16
shallows where a l. could wade 18.27.3

lamp: eye and l. of the body 5.10.10

land: go to the l. whose love 7.6.1
in the l. of the living 11.4.1

Israel entered the promised l. 4.17.2
I've seen the promised l. 20.335.20
so men forget their own l. 5.33.2
to leave their country and their l. 6.1.1
when you reach that l. 4.17.2

landscape: [for Celtic Christians] the natural l. 20.501.4

language: an adequate l. in which to speak 20.293.1
deprived of a liturgical l. 20.527.2
I find no l. equal to it 18.61.1
inclusive l. does not have to mean 20.395.3
l. about the Holy Spirit is l. 20.585.3
l. of the heart 17.87.13
learns a new l. 20.298.2
learn the l. of the costermonger 19.136.4
masculine l. of sermons 20.136.1
never again will we use a l. 20.562.1
one must learn the l. 20.169.1
open to the possibilities of l. 20.134.2
our God-l. is biblical 20.598.4
our God-l. is representative of all 20.595.3
pictorial kind of l., not conceptual l. 20.369.5
read the Holy Scriptures in a l. 19.117.2
the absence of l. 20.435.1
the l. about God only makes 20.274.2
the l. of the mystics 20.567.3

large: let us be l. in thought 20.79.1

last: so shall it be at l. 19.139.1

late: too l. I came 5.8.24

Latimer: L.! L.! L.! Be careful what you say 16.42.3

laugh: the man who cannot l. 19.35.16
that is afraid to l. in his presence 19.99.9
to l. at men of sense 17.21.1
to l. inwardly at yourself 19.147.6
we l. when creatures nag 20.438.1

laughter: l. almost ever cometh 16.60.4
l. is able to mediate 20.388.8

launch: when you let the Lord l. you 20.171.1

law: atoms the same l. obey 20.236.1
but one l. for all 18.7.16
custom is a kind of l. 7.10.2
had fulfilled the l. of humanity 19.101.8
impossible to evolve the Moral L. 19.141.1
justifies us and fulfils the l. 16.45.3
most powerful l. of nature 18.7.25
'not under the l. but under grace' 6.18.1
of L. there can be no less acknowledged 16.33.2
one l. for the lion 19.20.11
put away all thinking about the L. 16.13.13
rigid letter of the l. 11.6.1
the old l. gives strength to the new 5.33.1
the principle of the Moral L. 19.141.2
wherever l. ends, tyranny begins 17.72.7

laws: bad l. are the worst 18.7.15
l. are like cobwebs 18.49.18
re-establishment of the l. 20.135.2

lay: will be sure to l. us out flat 17.29.10

laymen: whether they be clergymen or l. 18.57.9

laziness: take from me the spirit of l. 4.20.8

lead: I'll l. you all in the dance 20.177.1
trials, through which thou didst l. me 16.5.1

leaders: we are all l., or potential l. 20.287.3

leadership: empowers our own l. 20.168.1
for l. of the church 19.22.3
qualifications for l. in younger churches 20.407.2

leaf: even to the fall of a l. 18.11.11

league: we have made a l. 16.14.1

leak: one l. will sink a ship 17.22.13

lean: and make his body l. 14.5.3

learn: in seed time l. 19.20.6
l. everything you possibly can 12.17.1
l. quickly, for I know not 8.4.3
may be l. by the head 19.136.14
they will l. at no other 18.7.10
we also wait to hear, l. 20.449.1
who know how to l. 20.2.3

learned: by the l. seeking 11.1.4
l. to do the Father's will 20.176.15
we have l. a great lesson 19.125.10

learning: by identifying the new l. 16.26.8
extensive search after l. 15.14.17
more retarded the advancement of l. 18.32.26
not through ordinary l. 20.72.7
with all our l. grovel 5.8.15

leave: we may l. the rest to him 19.120.8

lecture: the morning hour when you l. 13.19.1

led: let us be l. by their light 5.14.1
think they are l. by the spirit 13.20.3

leisure: a healthy understanding of l. 20.523.5
people's pastimes and l. activities 20.281.2

lent: a thing that is l. 20.174.8
each year L. and Easter 20.489.2

lepers: 'my fellow l.' 19.154.1
the sight of l. nauseated me 13.16.2

lesbian: gay and l. Christians 20.527.5

less: burn and become l. and l. 20.84.2

let: I say, 'L. go', and so does God 20.81.4
or l. on another go 20.487.4
to be able to pray 'l. go' 20.224.1

letter: a lifeless and dead l. 20.526.7
God's love l. to the world 19.12.20
when you receive a l. from a friend 7.10.8

letting: a l. go of all things that occupy 20.249.10
we are given a 'l. go' of self 20.271.3

liberal: the tension between a l. and 20.293.2
the fallacy of the l. mind 20.398.1

liberalism: a constant feature of l. 20.274.6
l. is a cuckoo 20.531.2
the negation of l. 19.1.1

liberation: a project with a l. message 20.550.2
choice that promises l. 20.347.1
Christianity brings l. 20.579.1
God as revealed in the l. 20.199.1

help to the person seeking l. 20.313.3
his l. from all restrictions 20.87.1
if l. is the real hallmark 20.487.3
its conception of l. is inauthentic 20.266.1
the l. of the poor 20.184.1
we are on the way to l. 20.230.2
whites who talk about l. theology 20.199.4

liberator: Christ the l. 20.294.1

liberators: it is thus the company of l. 20.416.1

liberty: clash between our spiritual l. 20.287.2
good definition of the word l. 19.91.8
if l. is to be saved 19.41.7
l. cannot be preserved 19.2.3
l. is a better husband than love 19.3.1
l. is the power that we have 17.57.1
l. of conscience 18.44.11
order alone, definitively makes l. 20.62.5
then gives l. 19.103.2
we attain to true l. 20.148.3

lie: a l., Sir, is a l. 18.32.8
harder to go on living a l. 20.463.2
he that trust in a l. 17.60.28
the l. can be maintained only by violence 20.516.2

life: a matter of l. or death 20.25.4
absolute ground and validation of l. 20.46.1
adventure is the champagne of l. 20.22.17
all the changing scenes of l. 18.50.1
as my L. was a L. of Sorrow 18.15.4
be in me the L. 20.52.1
becomes a matter of l. or death to you 20.352.9
but eternal l. is more sweet 16.34.2
cry the gospel with your whole l. 20.29.2
cynicism and fear that freeze l. 20.247.6
death as a dimension of l. in the present 20.291.1
death is the flowering of l. 19.147.14
enter into every sphere of l. 19.132.9
especially true of the spiritual l. 20.507.1
for having given me l. 20.64.1
for the gift of God's l. 20.157.5
growth is the only evidence of l. 19.109.2
have the next l. in mind 20.253.1
honour to a whole l. 14.22.1
human l. seems rather like this 8.4.2
I am tired of this l. 11.7.1
I die each day to beget l. 20.233.1
I have had a long l. 8.4.4
ideal l., but that l. was actually lived 19.150.6
in the joys and sorrows of this l. 20.517.4
is l. so wretched? 20.276.9
last twenty-four hours of one's l. 20.56.1
let there be l. said God 20.481.2
l. and liturgy are one 20.148.4
l. as a problem to be solved 20.484.10
l. cannot subsist in society 18.32.35
l. is a hard fight, a struggle 19.110.1
l. is a property to be defended 20.415.1
l. is filled with meaning 20.405.2
l. is not a holiday 19.48.5
l. is stronger than death 20.554.10
l. is the art of drawing 17.25.1
l. well spent is long 16.44.1
long for and expect another l. 20.482.1
means that l. has become one 20.69.9
more in remaining in this l. 17.30.3
my knowledge of that l. is small 17.10.8
my l. is hid in God with thee 20.152.2
my l. is with my brother 4.4.1
neither what our l. nor our death is 17.80.10
no wise man wants a soft l. 9.1.2
one l., a little gleam 19.35.12
our l. is grounded in faith 14.18.5
our l. is love, and peace 17.82.2
possess a blessed and eternal l. 13.11.2
reveal or uncover the truth about l. 20.413.3
sickness at the end of his l. 12.25.1
such a L. as killeth Death 17.60.27
such is hope for the meaning of l. 20.158.2
take care of your l. 18.59.8
the divorce between faith and l. 20.497.2
their gift of their one l. to one another 20.385.20
the Lord is my L. and my Light 19.114.6
the promise of eternal l. 4.8.5
the real story of l. 20.501.1
the search for total conceptions of l. 20.389.1
the sort of l. we have 20.326.1
the tragedy of l. 19.35.13
this is the tree of l. 12.17.7
to *all* of l. 20.137.2
turn one's back on l. 20.474.2
we ascend to l. 2.13.7
we cannot abandon l. because 20.240.1
we must be broken into l. 20.459.2
which leads to certain l. 2.19.1
will always win the battle of l. 20.116.6

life-giving: everything that comes from him is l. 20.534.2

lifestyles: trends in communal l. 20.242.2

lifetime: I wish he would come in my l. 19.156.2

lift: God hath sworn to l. on high 19.82.3
I will try to find a l. 19.144.5

lifted: he that is mighty l. me 5.32.1

lifting: a little l. of the heart suffices 17.70.3

light: a great chain of l. 5.14.6
a parson should l. fires 20.71.3
absorbed into the uncreated L. 13.6.12
attain to the divine l. 16.38.20
because sees the l. blazing 4.35.15
best for prayer that have least l. 17.42.15
but one equal l. 17.42.24
fill us full of l. 19.123.3
flooded with celestial l. 20.24.1
give us the spirit of l. 4.56.1
giving l. to all who want 2.13.20
here we are reflected l. 20.39.1
he who receives l. from above 17.76.28
his l. is received by those 4.2.4
kingdoms of darkness and l. 20.488.1
know the Eternal L. unveiled 20.54.2
l. has been made 14.2.2
l. was first 7.5.2

men do not see the divine l. 11.9.6
O give me l. to see 18.60.2
O L. that none can name 11.9.2
pleasant thing to behold the l. 17.16.2
simply can't bear its l. 19.76.1
remains one dark soul without the l. of God 19.23.9
the brightness of his eternal l. 7.19.1
the l. into which we shall enter 20.29.6
the l., which issues from the sun 19.66.1
the one true source of l. 20.6.1
the true l. will shine alone 20.208.1
the Way of L. 2.5.3
those who ought to become the l. 20.84.2
through whom you give us l. 13.16.1
we need l., but that l. must come 20.232.2
who gave the l. its birth, careth for me 19.121.1
zealous than the 'children of l.' 20.335.5

lighten: need to hear is 'l. up' 20.146.4

lightly: they take themselves l. 20.22.12

like: a bishop is most l. God 16.35.5
O God, make me l. Jesus Christ 20.328.5

likeness: great l. to Jesus 19.98.1
I shall be satisfied with thy l. 18.56.8
l. to Christ 19.105.1
possesses a l. to its prototype 4.41.2
renewal in us of that l. to God 20.405.3
such is the likeness of God 20.559.1
to be in his l. is granted 5.13.2
to grow in l. to him 20.369.3

limbo: in l. our weary bodies 20.571.1

limbs: l. that have become your own? 11.9.9

limit: absolutely and without l. 5.14.9
death is the only l. we know 20.124.6

limitation: art is l. 20.22.2
the l. of our strength 20.388.8

limitations: does not and cannot alter our l. 20.390.2
to accept our l. and cherish 20.180.5
we all learn something about l. 20.310.1

limited: without knowing himself to be l. 19.126.1

limits: absolutely not have l. set on it 16.65.19
stopping at human l. 20.176.13
the real is what l. me 20.423.2

line: speaks no less than God in every l. 17.43.10

lingering: with l. delight 14.20.1

links: letting pain be pain l. us 20.249.9

lion: for Judah's L. bursts his chains 11.5.1
one law for the l. 19.20.11

lioness: feeds a l. at home 17.94.13

lions: fifty l. commanded by a deer 17.81.5
"to the l. with the Christians!" 3.12.4

lips: hang upon the l. 5.33.8
in prayer the l. 17.61.4
let no word pass your l. in vain 4.2.16

liquor: love is that l. sweet 17.60.10

listen: do not l. as we write 20.517.1
first duty of love is to l. 20.545.4
if we do not l. 20.604.4
l. less to your own thoughts 18.19.16
l. much, speak little 17.68.5
l. to, and heed the soul, crying 20.578.1
l. to anger as carefully as we l. 20.243.2
l. to your heart 15.13.2
never l. to accounts of the frailties 16.38.2
not prepared to l. to God 20.119.4
trying to l. to one another 20.168.2
we need to l. to it 20.249.2

listener: God is the great l. 20.299.2

listening: as part of its l., the Church 20.502.1
faith that comes from l. 7.8.1
half an hour's l. 17.87.14
no longer l. to all the other voices 20.535.3
obedient l. to the word of God 20.125.1
preaching without l. 20.344.1
responsive l. is the form 20.523.3
there is a grace of kind l. 19.53.8
the twofold l., to tradition and to the present 20.592.1

literal: furthest from the l. is commonly the worst 16.33.4

literary: l. excellence of the English Bible 20.40.6

literature: just as good l. 20.195.2

little: attention to l. things is a great thing 4.35.10
be great in l. things 16.70.6
great L. one! 17.36.2
nothing is too l. 19.120.3
often seem like a very l. way 20.213.6
please God in l. matters 18.24.3
there must be nothing l. amongst us 19.19.3

littleness: great in his l. 4.27.3

liturgical: cooking is a l. ritual 20.101.10
deprived of a l. language 20.527.2

liturgy: life and l. are one 20.148.4
l. can only really live 20.444.1
l. is a rehearsal of the whole story 20.565.4
l. is dangerous 20.527.1
some people think l.'s like 20.464.2
the great l. is about to begin 20.89.1

live: anything but—l. for it 19.42.3
as we l. no more, we may l. ever 17.16.1
contemplation is the capacity to l. 20.147.3
desire to l. freely, to l. meaningfully 20.347.1
finding something to l. for 20.276.13
I have learnt to l. to the full 20.153.2
let us l. like people 20.178.5
l. as men who manage our lives 20.15.23
l. as though today 20.29.8
l. for God and one's neighbour 20.21.4
l. in Christ, l. in Christ 16.40.6
l. no longer for oneself 4.45.1
l. thy creed! 19.21.2
not fit to l. 20.335.4
observe the life he lived and then l. 20.480.1
teach me to l., that I may dread 18.33.3
they l. in one another still 18.44.17
to die is to l. 20.453.5
to l. as myself and yet not I 13.24.2

to l. for God's kingdom 20.109.3
to l. in the spirit of the whole 19.41.4
to l. is to change 19.109.5
to l. is to fight 20.50.1
to l. more nearly as we pray 19.82.5
to l. without speaking is better 4.33.1
we learn to l. in 'correct proportions' 20.275.2
who is it that wants to l. 6.4.6
you must l. with people 20.28.8

lived: how religiously we have l. 15.14.14
I have formerly l. 17.22.3
observe the life he l. and then live 20.480.1

lives: he preaches well that l. well 17.29.12
he that l. well 17.52.25
if I had a hundred l. 16.11.1
if I had a thousand l. 20.58.2
in the evening of our l. 16.38.9
lay down their l. 2.3.3
live our l. courageously 19.164.1
l. the meaning of his life 20.122.11
man dies, but how he l. 18.32.37
rooted in the actual l. and experience 20.444.1
she's the sort of woman who l. for others 20.352.22

living: more to comfort the l. 5.8.9
take care of the l. who belong to them 18.7.36
teach us the best way of l. 17.50.1
the adventure of l. 20.379.12
the l. church 19.11.2
the long habit of l. 17.20.17
you are a l. God 17.18.1

load: never l. yourself so 19.99.12

loaf: lump of dough, or a l. 2.13.12

loaves: as thou didst break the l. 20.49.1

lobby: I just want to l. for God 20.264.1

local: to foster the development of l. theologies 20.365.3

lock: the l. of the night 17.52.27
who hath the l. to his own 17.20.7

lodging: grant us a safe l. 19.109.21

loftier: so the l. the life 14.31.5

logic: l. is like the sword 17.25.5

Lombard: I am a L. 18.43.1

loneliness: filled with anxiety, silence and l. 20.514.8
l. can become a sacrament 20.558.4
l. to express the pain of being alone 20.545.3
movement from l. to solitude 20.415.2
pray that your l. 20.276.13
seasons of l. and sadness 19.115.1
to preach about the l. 20.137.1
we discover l. 20.352.18

lonely: cold and l. figures 20.300.5
I was l., dead l. 20.213.1
missionary will ever be as l. 20.58.1

long: all things l. for him 20.172.1
heart, for by inspiring it to l. 5.8.11
life well spent is l. 16.44.1
O God for whom we l. 20.395.2

longevity: l. has its place 20.335.12

longing: all human eyes have l. in them 20.172.2
go on l. after him 14.7.4
I was consumed with l. for him 20.72.10

longings: it pours out its l. to God 5.10.18
satisfy the l. of an immortal soul 19.148.1

longs: my spirit l. for thee 18.10.3
Oh, *how he l. for me* 20.81.7

longsuffering: l. is a sovereign virtue 14.19.1

look: does not dare l. at you 4.35.15
l. at him and let him l. at me 19.116.1
l. upon him present within us 16.65.11

lookers: for God and angels to be l. on 17.5.10

looking: by l. at what he can see 4.28.5
the grace to stop l. for it 20.428.2

lord: a powerful l. 20.131.3
hand and the L. in the other 20.24.1
if a L. so great and good 13.11.8
if J. isn't the Lord of your life 20.195.8
it is the L. of the church 20.526.4
L., of thy goodness, give me thyself 17.6.1
made useful for the L. 2.11.5
power and presence of the L. 17.98.1
the L. has become everything to you 19.79.1
the L. is a wrecker of evil 11.10.1
the L. is meek and humble 20.72.5
the L. is my Life and my Light 19.114.6
the L. was my fuel 19.37.2
the L.'s prayer may be committed 19.101.1
they neglect the L. of the work 20.322.7
thirty years of Our L.'s life 17.15.2
you alone are the L. 12.26.2

lords: do you address as l. 5.33.7
the hand of new unhappy l. 20.22.20

lordship: the all-encompassing l. of God 20.541.4

lore: Christ's l. 14.5.5

lose: if you l. you l. nothing 17.80.9
it is more serious to l. hope 7.12.7
l. myself in the heart of Jesus 17.1.1
l. our own children 20.269.3
may very well l. his head 16.51.11
to l. our way 13.20.4

losing: the paradoxes of l. one's life 20.194.1
we hold him only by l. him 20.305.1

loss: mourn the l. of earthly things 20.47.1
the pain of l. 20.250.1
the way of owning the l. 20.307.1
those concerned with l. not gain 20.313.1

lost: Adam l. the earthly paradise 20.72.9
I have l. everything 13.15.3
it has l. out on its own fullness 20.511.1
l.; not one is l., or ever will be l. 19.120.8
not l., but only sent on ahead 3.2.3
rotten luxury of knowing himself to be l. 20.385.10
seldom known until it is l. 19.42.8
the apprehension of its being l. 19.132.8
there is no one so far l. 19.107.3

lot: My God, I choose the whole l. 19.144.3

incomprehensibility of the m. of life 20.415.6
O wonderful m.! 3.1.8
so much hidden m.? 19.123.13
the appeal to m. 20.585.1
the lucrative business of m. 18.7.18
the m. of God, precisely as m. 20.178.4
the m. of his embodiment 20.100.2
the m. of yourselves 5.8.18
what is this strange m.? 2.15.1
your thoughts are a m. 5.20.1
you will perceive the divine m. 19.47.2
mystic: as important for the m. 20.313.5
how to be both a m. and a militant 20.336.1
m., or is no authentic missionary 20.139.1
mystical: m. language expresses 20.273.4
mysticism: everything begins in m. 20.62.3
m. is the name 20.91.5
the delicate truth of m. 19.53.2
mystics: the language of the m. 20.567.3
myth: the real purpose of m. 20.162.2
mythological: it is a m. language 20.369.5

N

nag: whenever his wife began to n. 16.45.25
naked: n. and to be seen n. 11.9.10
we shall not be found n. 4.18.1
when you see him n. 4.35.19
nakedness: come before thy presence in our n. 20.86.1
garment that covers every n. 14.4.1
name: good n. is better than great riches 17.29.8
hated for our n. 2.4.1
how sweet the n. of Jesus sounds 18.42.2
not everything has a n. 20.516.3
the Father of all has no n. 2.14.6
the n. of Jesus 14.24.4
to n. oneself 20.312.1
nameless: intention was to remain n. 20.145.5
names: or allow their n. to be admitted 19.7.2
we are not for n. 17.23.1
naming: if our n. of God is distorted 20.598.1
with the power of n. 20.544.1
narrow: entering through the n. gate 6.18.1
strive to enter by the n. gate 4.61.1
nation: a royal and priestly n. 8.1.2
its members in one n. 20.124.5
may be exalted in our n. 17.23.1
our n. will cease to be strong 8.5.3
so are the rest of the n. 19.7.3
national: carried into the world our n. faith 20.401.1
individual unselfishness into n. egoism 20.409.1
nationalism: one of the most dangerous being n. 20.477.3
nations: n. are the wealth of mankind 20.516.1
new and hungry n. 20.144.2
natural: by our n. senses 16.38.23
impossible that anything so n. 18.49.21
no argument from n. effects 17.8.1
once from the n. to the spiritual 20.6.4
naturally: nothing can be known n. 14.30.2
nature: a n. should be perfectly happy 13.13.4
does not desert our human n. 5.24.4
foster and seek their own n. 13.31.1
human n. cannot be changed 19.91.2
human n. has ineffable dignity 13.13.1
I looked through n. up to n.'s God 19.56.2
N. has concealed 17.68.3
N. has some perfections to show 17.80.18
N. is but a name 18.14.9
N. teaches us to love 17.52.28
N., the vicaire of the almyghty lorde 14.5.4
nothing else but n. departed 18.35.11
our n. is very bad in itself 17.94.3
perfect n. of true man 5.24.3
sharer in the divine n. 5.24.5
that which is contrary to his n. 4.2.9
that which we are by n. 19.107.2
the ardent heat of my n. 5.22.12
the destruction of n. 20.101.3
the divine n. is really 13.37.17
to change their n. 4.2.17
we never cast off the old n. 20.14.1
with finite human n. 19.26.2
natures: combined both n. 5.24.1
to give new n. to things 4.2.17
nauseated: previously n. me became a source 13.16.2
navel: the man without a n. 17.20.1
near: God is n. to all who call upon him 6.16.1
God is very n. 20.536.3
live n. to God by prayer 19.22.1
precisely in being so divinely n. 20.43.9
they draw n. to God 4.4.8
to come n. to God is to change 20.522.3
nearer: he is n. to us than we think 17.70.4
n. to church, the farther from God 17.3.3
necessary: cling only to what is n. 4.28.4
the things n. for the day 4.28.3
they are n. for our condition 20.400.1
necessity: calls this nature n. 17.80.8
make a virtue of n. 17.70.7
make a virtue of n. 12.16.1
the result of n. 20.10.9
need: all life that is in n. of help 20.492.6
conditions and n. of all men 17.51.9
enough in the world for everyone's n., but 20.160.1
he knows what we n. 4.40.1
I know you only as my n. 20.481.1
I n. nothing but God 17.1.1
one answer to every human n. 20.404.1
thy n. is yet greater than mine 16.60.7
unknown beneath every person in n. 20.139.6
we n. others physically, emotionally 20.352.18
needed:nothing is more n. by humanity today 20.534.3
needs: given over to the n. 20.145.7
know what are my true n. 19.117.3

O

P

the source of most p. 20.308.3
they can praise him in p. 20.480.2
when p. is to be borne 20.352.16
when we are in great p. 20.545.5
when we earnestly seek and desire p. 20.338.2
where p. and grief and sighing 5.16.1

painful: every p. event contains in itself 20.383.5

pains: by p. and contradictions 18.11.16
of all the p. that lead 14.18.15
our p. are real things 17.25.9

paint: p. my picture truly like me 17.37.6

paintings: p. are the Bible of the laity 12.11.1

Palestinian: the P. Christian 20.110.5

palm: no pain, no p. 18.44.16

pamper: we do not want to p. anyone 19.17.1

pangs: my birth p. are at hand 2.12.6

papers: they fight by shuffling p. 20.22.20

parable: a p. is... an assault 20.364.1
the gospel p. comes to my mind 12.17.8

parables: more unauthoritative than the p. 20.413.3

paraclete: O faithful p. 12.14.1

paradise: Adam in P. 17.97.4
Adam lost the earthly p. 20.72.9
as in an unseen p. 12.17.7
give me a tiny corner in p. 17.27.1
God set man in p. 2.21.2
had p. at will. 14.19.2
he that will enter P. 17.60.33
I have been in p. 17.44.1
of p. above 12.2.1
P. is our native country 16.31.3
parents were driven out of P. 20.311.14
Pasch opens to us the gates of p. 4.38.3
the sterile p. of emptiness and rage 20.385.3
what is p.? 14.29.3
who can realize what p. is? 20.72.12

paradox: I have found the p. 20.538.4
this is a p. 13.24.2

paragon: the p. of animals! 17.89.6

paralysis: a fearful creeping p. 20.484.2

pardon: as if thou hadst seal'd my p. 17.42.3
God may p. you, but I 16.24.9
my religion teaches me to p. 16.50.1
p. one another 15.5.1
sorry and beg p. for my sins 18.28.1
the grace of p. 20.468.2
we p. as long as we love 17.68.13

pardonable: more p. than the methods 17.68.22

pardoned: had p. the sins of my soul 19.87.1

parent: every word and deed of a p. 20.586.6
love of a p. for a child 19.147.1
never know the love of the p. 19.12.13
p. of good 17.76.1

parenthesis: but a small p. in eternity 17.20.12

parents: he tells us to be the p. 20.153.4
the message many p. 20.146.4
the unwisdom of p. 20.73.1
understand why our p. behaved 20.146.3

parish: all the world as my p. 18.57.12
my p. is the gutter 20.586.5

parrot: give his pet p. to the town gossip 20.264.13

parson: a p. should light fires 20.71.3
the p. leaves the *Christian* 18.10.1
the p. of many parishes 20.558.4
this day the p. hath got 17.84.5

parsons: if country p. sought 20.557.3

part: do not try to live by one p. 20.81.1
God actually wants us to take p. 20.106.1
in every p. of the world 16.13.9
ne'er act the winning p. 17.61.4
to fit in with any p. 11.8.2

participate: God is so much p. and parcel of life 20.466.1
invites us to p. in a process 20.513.1
p. in the accomplishment 20.106.1

participation: a p. in Christ 20.14.3
gardening is an active p. 20.127.1
real p. of the divine nature 17.88.2

particular: quite definite and p. through us 20.158.1

particulars: must do it in minute p. 19.20.9

partner: from his side to be his p. 12.20.1

partners: women and men must work as p. 20.206.1

party: under the guise of a 'party' 20.531.2

Pasch: this is the P. 4.38.3

pass: days of our life p. swiftly 8.2.2

passes: suffering p.: having suffered never p. 20.62.10

passing: all things are p. 16.65.13

passion: a glimpse into the p. of God 20.517.9
all the ways of the p. and the cross 13.6.6
altered by Christ's p. 20.100.3
I have one p. 18.62.1
imitator of the p. 2.12.6
no p. which more often misses 17.68.26
p., for all its dangers 20.501.7
sometimes we are filled with p. 15.14.20
sympathy is the divinest p. 18.7.6
take heed lest p. sway 17.76.6
the p. and pride of man 19.109.4
though our saviour's P. is over 18.44.2
with ultimate existential p. 20.161.3

passions: according to the nature of our p. 7.13.7
combat in which we kill our p. 10.4.1
if we resist our p. 17.68.17
in proportion to the strength of its p. 19.114.5
inwardly their p. still 14.26.8
on the judging and on his p. 20.551.3
protect them against all evil p. 3.6.3
ruler of his p. 13.12.5
the mastery of his p. 19.142.8
the tyranny [of the p.] 7.20.7
to any of the p. 5.23.6
to excite the p. or not 8.9.5

perspective: you must develop a sense of p. 20.383.2
persuade: goeth about to p. a multitude 16.33.1
persuaded: be p. by me 14.28.2
pertinent: always p. when you speak 18.44.9
Peter: P. too was converted 20.530.2
P. was first given the keys 7.12.6
petition: one p. in the Lord's Prayer 20.87.4
trouble, offer up p. 4.5.8
petticoat: out of the Realm in my p. 16.24.3
pettiness: keep us, O Lord, from p. 20.79.1
pharisees: group of those 'respectable p.' 20.176.7
more P. among the Christians 13.29.4
to these fancy scribes and P. 20.510.1
philosopher: an interesting social p. 20.597.1
philosophers: be sceptical of p. 20.585.4
philosophy: a little p. inclineth 17.5.14
all good moral p. 17.5.15
if one is going to do p. of religion 20.317.1
in wonder all p. began 19.41.3
not faith, but mere P. 17.20.6
the highest point of p. 4.35.27
the wisdom of p. 13.8.1
to be styled p. than religion 18.1.8
together the whole of p. 4.33.1
torn from the old garment of p. 10.3.2
physical: mere p. courage 19.16.17
physician: he was a missionary and a p. 19.92.2
there is only one p. 2.12.1
physicians: as p. of the soul 20.311.3
beyond the practice of all the p. 19.58.2
picture: paint my p. truly like me 17.37.6
piety: cling totally to this formula for p. 5.10.22
eaten out the heart of p. 19.125.2
faith is never identical with p. 20.122.10
genuine p. is the spring 17.21.5
like a p. that is sure of itself 20.468.2
mistaken and over-zealous p. 18.7.34
moves it most to p. is the best 16.37.4
p. springs necessarily by itself 19.128.2
regardless of the great duties of p. 18.35.10
suspicious of p. in the young 20.445.3
weaker sex, to p. more prone 17.2.2
piglets: like a litter of p. pressed close 13.40.1
Pilate: crucified under Pontius P. 2.14.3
what is truth? said jesting P. 17.5.21
pilgrim: a p. panting for the rest to come 19.104.1
onward goes the p. band 19.75.1
onward goes the p. band 20.7.1
the p. who spends all his time 17.28.1
we are supposed to be a p. people 20.191.1
pilgrimage: as a function of p. 20.405.5
go in perfect p. in imitation 6.1.1
in the house of our p. 18.27.1
in this place of p. 13.25.5
pilgrims: as p., for p. are we all 14.19.4
like that of Christian p. on a journey 20.118.7
p. ever sigh for and desire our homeland 6.10.3
pillars: Sundays the p. are 17.60.1
pious: he who is p. does not contend 16.72.4
indignity was left for p. hands 20.484.7
pity: p. melts the mind to love 17.43.14
place: always and in every p. 13.11.10
God attributes to p. 17.76.21
here and in every p. 12.14.1
it *feels like the right p. to be* 20.450.1
know where the p. is 4.43.2
nor is there a p. 20.185.1
smaller the p. the more extended 12.23.5
plagues: of all p. with which mankind 18.15.1
plan: building according to his p. 5.33.3
we p.—and God steps in 20.51.1
planetary: our growth to a p. dimension 20.118.2
plans: no time for disputing about his p. 19.99.2
planted: so the Faith was p. 16.14.1
planting: p. that Peter and Paul did 2.10.1
plants: many p. growing in me 18.18.1
virtue that p. the other virtues 6.14.3
play: adult's p. ends with universal burial 20.101.4
however fine the rest of the p. 17.80.19
p. reveals that beyond the dissolution 20.101.5
playing: just p. about 12.7.15
pleader: the voice of the p. 19.32.1
pleading: p. comes forth 5.10.14
pleasant: it is a p. thing to behold 17.16.2
please: my heaven is to p. God 18.6.1
that you may p. him 16.40.3
the need to p. others. 5.23.4
pleased: God is p. so long as 11.1.8
not going to be more p. 20.534.1
pleasing: most p. in thy sight 15.14.1
nothing that is more p. to God 18.37.4
pleasure: able to find p. in ourselves 17.28.12
desire for p. 7.17.2
joy is never in our power, and p. is 20.352.17
no p. is comparable 17.5.20
that you may have p. in everything 16.38.21
the fatal egg by p. laid 18.14.5
we would die of p. 14.2.1
pleasure-haters: the p. who became unjust 20.111.7
pleasures: all our p., but fantastical 17.25.9
ceaselessly ask to taste my p. 13.29.1
finds or makes its p. 20.117.1
God whispers in our p. 20.352.15
'higher' and 'lower' p. 20.111.5
the simple p. of life 20.313.5
pliability: the p. of an obedient heart 20.379.4
plod: I can p. 19.34.1
ploughed: p. by your teaching 8.6.2
ploughman: I would to God that a p. 16.26.2
plucked: must be p. up 18.18.1
plural: love makes me p. 20.298.1

condemn men to p., humiliation 20.418.1
I desire and choose p. 16.35.1
imagine what p. is like 20.62.9
in the great heart of P. 13.24.1
inner p. and weakness 19.153.1
O blessed p., who bestows 13.11.1
or p. *in itself* 20.387.1
p. and misfortune 5.32.7
p. …, for Jesus, was not so much 20.357.1
p. is a crime 20.518.1
p. is having nothing 13.24.3
p. is no sin 17.60.14
p. of mind 20.415.6
p. should be the badge of religious 16.54.2
p. was not found in heaven 12.7.12
real p., as distinct 20.512.3
receive p., want, sickness 4.40.2
reduced to such a state of p. 16.12.1
the world's struggle against its p. 20.472.3

powder: trust God and keep your p. dry 17.37.4

power: a husband's p. over his wife 17.94.12
anyone who lives by the p. of the God 20.389.2
authoritarian abuse of p. begins 20.342.1
average man any p. at all 19.16.16
being which has p. over itself 20.545.7
combination of both p. and love 20.446.3
for our p. comes not from us 3.11.1
God has all p. 14.27.1
God's p. enthroned in our hearts. 20.371.1
health, wealth, and p. 19.42.4
if there's a p. above us 18.1.13
in the bread we eat the p. 4.20.7
it is a p. that breaks 20.141.10
liberty is the p. that we have 17.57.1
manifestations of divine p. 20.9.4
no limit to the p. of a good woman 19.16.18
not to make use of faith's p. 20.223.1
of such p. a good man 18.32.13
our only p. is to let the current 20.176.11
p. gradually extirpates 18.7.19
p. is essentially exhibitionistic 20.517.12
p. is never good 9.1.3
p. is the reward of sadness 19.145.4
p. tends to corrupt 19.1.5
p. to do thy will 18.60.2
p. undirected by high purpose 20.69.1
powerful have given up p. willingly 20.101.6
praise releases the p. of God 20.175.5
real p. in prayer flows 20.379.5
seek new demonstrations of God's p. 20.197.2
sin is a p. in our life 19.48.3
subject to thy p. 18.2.1
that p. of his which controls 5.10.9
the desire for p. 17.5.7
the greatness of a man's p. 19.23.3
the p. of God's reign 20.517.13
the presence and p. of God 20.217.2
the responsible use of p. 20.204.2
the silent p. of a consistent life 19.110.2
the supreme expression of his p. 4.28.2
their possession of Divine P. 19.22.3
there is p. here [in Jesus] 20.405.4
to obtain and hold p. a man 19.146.5
wielding of p. in subordination to love 20.316.6
women have never had any p. 20.134.4
you have infinite p. supporting you 19.61.1

powerful: p. have given up power willingly 20.101.6

powerlessness: who are in a situation of p. 20.512.2

powers: all the p. of the body and mind 19.112.2
when p. and institutions 20.502.5
with 'principalities and p.' 20.584.4

practical: p. holiness, and entire self-consecration 19.125.2

practice: Fathers who put them into p. 4.17.7
new systematic based on faithful p. 20.565.3
prove its worth in p. 20.48.1

practise: does not p. what 2.8.7
to p. his job well 13.23.3

praise: either to empty p. 5.23.6
fill my mouth with your p. 4.20.6
flattery is p. insincerely given 19.12.7
increasing harmony of p. 20.257.1
I p. you God my beloved 13.6.2
it is travelled only through p. 20.75.4
let his just p. be given 17.101.7
may fill our hearts with p. 16.64.1
p. God! 14.25.1
p. God from whom all blessings flow 18.33.1
p. makes good men better 17.52.7
psalmody and p. of which he is worthy 7.1.3
the very act of p. releases 20.175.5
we p. only to be praised 17.68.10
with the light of another's p. 12.7.2
your mind rejoices, offer up p. 4.5.8

praised: not been pleased at being p. 4.35.25
p. be you, my Lord 13.16.1

praises: singing p. to our Divine Lover 20.601.1

pray: above all, p. for the gift of tears 15.13.1
anyone who prays should p. 6.15.4
cannot pay, let him p. 17.52.24
difficult to p. coherently 20.180.3
every man when he begins to p. 20.355.5
first things for which we have to p. 20.599.3
God wants us to p. 14.7.8
goes to bed and does not p. 17.60.21
he that will learn to p. 17.60.23
he who has learned to p. 18.35.6
if we do not p. 20.604.4
if you p. truly 4.26.8
in learning to p. 20.522.2
must p. with all his heart 5.44.1
no inclination to p. 20.480.4
none can p. well 17.52.25
p. as you can 20.21.7
p. at your trade, on a journey 4.35.12
p. in this fashion 13.6.4
p. inwardly 14.18.10
p. while the hand is 19.120.14
retire there to p. 14.4.3
shall never p. with me in this agony 17.31.4

these three kinds of p. 20.43.1
the soul which gives itself to p. 16.65.19
this is indeed p. 4.5.5
to struggle hard in p. 4.26.6
we are in p. 18.19.15
we are made for p. 20.28.3
without p. and its grounding in faith 20.283.1
you would spend more of it in p. 16.65.10
your p. will then be a rhythmic movement 20.454.6

prayerful: to have a p. approach 20.465.2

prayerlessness: the worst sin is p. 20.28.5

prayers: ah Lord, my p. are dead 17.18.1
arm ourselves with devout p. 13.12.3
as all the p. of the Church 20.295.3
dare not trust it without my p. 17.52.9
deceived into multiplying p. 9.3.2
Gabriel who offers up p. will receive 4.5.4
increase your p. 5.26.1
must come first in all p. 20.29.1
our p. being answered 20.555.1
question him about his p. 19.151.1
'saying p.' is not praying! 19.125.10
solemn p., rapturous devotions 18.35.2
the same kind of p. 5.10.13

praying: or know he is p. 4.4.7
our p. is then at one 20.379.1
so much as p. for him 18.35.5
the moment you start p. 4.5.3

prays: a family that p. together 20.538.6
a lively person p. one way 5.10.13
anyone who p. should pray 6.15.4
the longer one p. the better 20.21.2

preach: as soon as I began to p. 18.21.1
best ways to confess it is to p. it 20.385.18
Christ sent me to p. the gospel 20.73.2
feels herself called by the Spirit to p. 19.22.2
for a woman to p. 19.87.5
'Go, p. the Gospel!' 19.87.3
I p. as many as twelve sermons 19.37.2
I p. the gospel with all my might 20.361.1
if a man may p. 19.87.4
practise what you p.?' 5.22.10
preachers can be taught to p. 16.26.4
p. faith until you have it 18.5.1
p. nothing down but the devil 18.4.1
some people p., others exhort 19.54.2
there are a few who p. Christ 16.45.11
they are there to p. to you 17.85.1
to love to p. is one thing 18.12.5
to p. about the loneliness 20.137.1
to p. more than half an hour 18.59.2
to p. unless we p. as we walk 13.16.12
your carriage and life may p. 17.51.10

preached: I p. as never sure to preach 17.10.9
purely p. and heard 16.13.16
too often the Gospel is p. 20.584.2

preacher: a p. must apply himself 13.23.3
the p. was a stranger 20.33.3
worst trial of the p.'s life 20.40.7

preaches: he p. well that lives well 17.29.12
no man p. his own sermon 17.79.6

preachers: give me one hundred p. 18.57.9
in angels being called p. 13.23.1
surely p. can be taught to preach 16.26.4

preaching: a bishop should die p. 16.36.1
a woman's p. is like a dog's 18.32.4
carry on our work as much as p. 17.10.4
carry on your p. 8.13.1
his p. was a blazing fire 15.1.3
I argue for p. that speaks 20.137.2
if teaching and p. is your job 16.7.1
never obtain simplicity in p. 19.125.6
p. is truth through personality 19.29.3
p. of both the Old and the New 8.5.1
p. should break a hard heart 18.42.3
p. without listening 20.344.1
the church's p. shines everywhere 2.13.20
the p. moment is the moment 20.157.5
the p. of the gospel 20.403.2
when you are p. in church 5.22.1
without p., which sows 13.23.2

precept: more efficacious than p. 18.32.25

precepts: his most holy p. 13.16.7

precious: all that is most p. in the world 20.145.2

predestined: saved unless he is p. 16.35.8
some are not p. to salvation 16.4.1

prejudge: to p. other people's notions 17.72.2

prejudice: greatest enemy is p. 19.42.2
it crystallizes a p. 20.475.3
one's own prejudice 20.373.2
p., not being founded on reason 18.32.11
the forces of p. 20.142.2

prejudices: p. cannot be allowed to keep us 20.471.1
p. picked up in childhood 17.40.1

premises: conclusions from insufficient p. 17.25.1

preparation: life is the time of our p. 17.96.2
this is a time of p. 20.448.3
without nine months of intensive p. 20.390.4

pre-peace: but a p. generation 20.141.5

presence: being the loving p. of God 20.456.1
God's mysterious and silent p. within us 20.371.3
his constant p. everywhere 20.87.1
it means the p. of God 20.176.8
purification and p. of God 20.558.4
stand in his p. for evermore 11.8.5
the joy of your p. 13.29.6
the real p. of Christ 20.217.3
the sense of God's p. 20.43.11
we are always in the p. of God 16.65.18
we stand laxly in his p. 7.16.2

present: death as a dimension of life in the p. 20.291.1
think only of the p. 18.11.15
we exchange the p. for the future 17.49.1
you are wholly p. everywhere 11.1.3

presents: they brought me p. 19.158.2

preserve: p. the church as it has been 20.154.3

Q

R

S

when God calls for it as a s. 4.64.1
without a spirit of s. 19.157.1
sacrificed: he was s. in the passover lamb 2.15.3
I choose to be s. 4.2.13
sacrifices: every day bring God s. 4.35.18
in other s. the flesh 6.14.4
willing to make the s. necessary 19.54.5
sacrificial: challenged by something s. 20.306.3
sacrilegious: all those s. practices 8.7.1
sadness: I will have no s. in my house 16.52.2
joy that comes after s. 11.8.3
must be something about s. 20.604.2
not do their work in s. 6.4.2
power is the reward of s. 19.145.4
seasons of loneliness and s. 19.115.1
safe: he is quite s. inside 20.83.3
keeps life s. 18.32.30
never thinketh itself s. 17.52.18
nothing is certain: everything is s. 20.93.2
see me s. up 16.51.14
the way to be s. 17.52.23
safeguards: the s. of chastity 18.46.3
safety: centre of God's will is our only s. 20.140.1
urges us to 'play for s.' 20.480.5
sage: Jesus as a s. is open 20.530.3
sailing: God wants to take you s. 20.81.4
saint: a s. is a human creature 20.91.7
become a s. soon and a big one 19.33.4
behind every s. stands another s. 20.43.3
every S. is a pattern; but no S. 19.147.5
he that will not live a s. 17.52.32
nobody except perhaps the s. 20.62.8
no point in becoming a S. by halves 19.144.3
the one mark of the s. 20.20.2
the s. does everything that any 19.114.1
the s. is a s. because 20.48.4
the s. is s., not because 20.545.9
to turn a man into a s. 17.80.21
saints: a kind of reticence about the s. 20.553.4
all the movements of the s. 18.11.17
a share in the glory of your s. 3.8.1
become s., least of all plaster s. 20.230.1
divine things are given to the s. 14.13.1
dwelling in the Holy Spirit, the s. 20.72.2
final perseverance of the s. 20.156.2
God deliver us from sullen s. 16.65.8
great s. have often been great sinners 19.114.5
makes the s. aware 20.135.1
make too frequently heaven's s. 19.30.3
none are true s. except 18.17.7
on the wills of his s. 17.79.3
part and lot among his s. 2.16.1
s. are persons who make it easier 20.76.1
s. in each generation are joined 11.9.4
the case with all the s. 7.17.7
the s. are God's jewels 18.27.8
the s. of the past 16.13.7
the whole science of the s. 7.10.5
sake: not to love me for your own s. 14.4.6
salad: to make a good s. 17.28.9
salt: disciples the s. of the earth 5.11.2
put s. in our mouths 5.8.20
salvation: a catholicity of s. history 20.161.4
all that Christ did to purchase s. 18.17.3
baptism, they have no s. 4.15.1
dangerous to your own s. 18.19.7
experience history as s. 20.513.1
for the s. of mankind 2.3.1
is what s. is all about 20.263.1
it is an instrument of s. 20.275.3
let your s. be founded in the Lord 4.48.1
long for s. 14.28.2
look to nobody (not even yourself) for your s. 20.392.1
made confession unto s. 19.87.1
necessary for the s. of man 13.37.16
not necessary for s. 16.65.2
our s. gives joy and refreshment 4.4.4
our s. has nothing in common 20.295.4
s. comes from God 20.512.4
s. consists wholly in being saved 19.107.1
s. exists precisely for them 20.139.7
s. for none outside the church 3.2.4
s. for the rich 20.503.2
s. is found in the day of affliction 4.34.1
s. is not merely a posthumous 20.330.1
s. is the receiving 20.238.4
the cause of s. or damnation is decided 20.487.4
the s. that is effected 20.501.8
the way of s. is easy 13.29.3
the work for our s. 6.19.1
they were not waiting for s. 20.176.7
this s. of love 12.15.1
through community lies the s. 20.434.1
through matter that my s. came 8.9.6
to be depended upon to get s. 20.65.1
to social and individual s. 20.335.3
visit us with thy s. 18.56.3
what is most contrary to s. 20.62.1
while our s. is truth 4.15.7
would be no plan of s. 20.175.1
Samaritan: like the S. woman 20.243.1
same: Satan is never quite the s. 20.594.3
Samson: as the lion that roared upon S. 17.22.7
sanctification: but s. is gradual 20.48.2
inexhaustible source of s. 14.13.3
s. is glory begun 20.156.3
sanctified: asked me if he had s. me 19.87.2
sanctify: s. what I am 18.60.1
the Lord s. and bless you 16.40.3
try to s. such customs 19.124.1
sanctity: s. is not the negation of passion 19.114.5
sand: no grain of s. is small 17.94.5
sandalwood: the true Christian is like s. 20.84.3
sang: little singing birds s. of God 16.13.10

sap: draws its s. out of the community 20.41.5
the Godhead is my s. 17.90.1

Satan: a scourge to S. 17.22.4
don't let S. make you overwork 19.133.3
have forgotten S. 20.355.2
S. can't do a thing to us 20.175.1
S. exalted sat 17.76.15
S. has been called a snake 20.594.3
S. is... God's holy sifter 20.594.2
S. trembles when he sees 18.14.14.
the forces of S. 2.12.2
while Hades so debated with S. 4.46.1

satire: s. is a kind of glass 18.49.17

satisfactory: the most s. thing in life 20.536.6

satisfied: I am s. with everything 20.78.1
s. with thy likeness—s., s. 18.56.8

satisfying: emotionally s. faith is repugnant to me 20.419.2

sauce: no s. in the world like hunger 17.29.6

saucepans: in the midst of s. and brooms 16.41.1

savages: certain customs of these s. 19.124.1

save: convinced we must s. money 20.128.2
faithfully s. 'flesh and blood' 20.584.4
find him and cannot s. him 19.107.3
nothing to do but to s. souls 18.57.11
s. all you can 18.57.15
to s. your world you asked 20.111.2
who died to s. us all 19.4.1
you s. your people and bless them 12.26.2

saved: and so to be s. 2.14.8
being s. from ourselves 19.107.2
damned for despairing to be s. 17.94.2
our Lord who s. the world 19.10.2
s. unless he is predestined 16.35.8
the Christian is s. 20.573.1
the way to be s. is not to delay 19.103.3
those being s. would be few 7.13.3
what shall I do to be s.? 7.11.1

saves: God loves and partly s. 20.536.13
God s. men and women 20.293.3
he that s. you 5.8.27
only s. people who live 20.477.6
s. himself as well 13.21.1

saving: to know his s. benefits 16.48.1
who helps in the s. of others 13.21.1

Saviour: how does one relate to a male s. 20.490.2
I hear about Christ as S. 20.511.4
in joy for a risen S. 20.19.1
may the grace of Christ our S. 18.42.5
Prince and S. of the faithful. 12.15.1
qualities practised by your S. 13.7.4
really know Christ as our S. 2.356.11
saving deeds of God our S. 12.26.3
Socrates was the S. 19.20.2
the Mysteries of our S. 6.15.2
the only s. of sinners 20.526.9
there is your S. 20.29.13
the S. died for the woman as well 19.87.5
the works of our S. 2.18.1
thy S.'s gone before 17.60.32
when the S. was on earth 2.18.1
wherein our S.'s birth is celebrated 17.89.2
without Christ as S. 20.175.1

say: all we can s. about him 16.13.5
each day you must s. to yourself 18.11.1
have nothing to s., s. nothing 19.42.12
he did not s., 'You shall not 14.18.2
I don't s. anything to God 19.116.1
knowingly to do or s. 13.28.1
not attend to what we s. 4.35.2
nothing to s. to the world 20.119.4
they suspect everything we s. 16.13.3

saying: what is most worth s. cannot be said 19.114.4

scales: come to know the s. 16.59.1

scandal: if you want to avoid giving s. 4.2.7
most glaring s. of Christianity 20.447.3

scenes: through all the changing s. 18.50.1
through what new s. 18.1.25

sceptical: healthy thing to be s. 20.585.4

schemes: irresolution on the s. of life 18.1.4

scholarship: mere s. does not yield Truth 20.479

scholasticism: dry s. and idle talk 20.48.1

school: example is the s. of mankind 18.7.10
solitude is a good s. 17.94.15
such a thing as a State s. 20.22.6

schoolmasters: experience is the best of s. 19.35.7
if they came down as s. 19.14.1

science: and S. is not God 19.49.5
regarding s. out of the corner 19.150.3
s. grows out of our rationality 20.368.6
the language of s. and reason 20.567.3
the men of s. 19.41.7
the quarrel between religion and s. 20.280.1
the s. of it can wait 20.28.2

sciences: there are some s. 19.136.14

scientific: can be made in s. language 20.455.2
if Christianity is not s. 19.49.5
the most s. man 19.49.2

scold: be slow to s. 16.70.5
you won't mind if I s. 20.438.1

scorch: love can both fiercely s. 13.31.2

scorn: things that worldly men s. 13.18.2

scornful: that of not being s. 4.65.1

scoundrel: the last refuge of a s. 18.32.10

scriptural: can no longer continue to read ancient s. 20.508.
priesthood, but it's not s. 20.285.3

scripture: a complete and infallible S. 20.48.3
a selection from S. was read 4.19.1
a thousand testimonies in S. 14.27.4
a way to understand s. 20.490.1
based on his reading of S. 5.22.1
everything must be decided by S. 20.355.4
familiarity with S. 20.553.2

Holy S. is so sublime 13.6.3
in the light of S. 20.526.5
mind was not made for divine S. 9.5.3
reading of the words of S. 5.23.5
right way of interpreting s. 18.12.4
rule in the exposition of s. 16.33.4
so the S. guides those adrift 4.28.7
teaches this lesson better than s. 20.552.1
the authority of S. 9.5.5
the giver of Holy S. 20.428.4
the message of S. 20.162.3
the perusal of s. 19.133.2
the s. at his plough 16.26.2
the strength of what S. says 4.9.11
they read the S. literally 14.4.8
to understand S. fully 13.6.3
truly divine words of S. 5.30.1
we either treat S. ahistorically 20.300.4
whole of s. took on another look 16.45.1

criptures: according to the S. 17.7.2
apply yourself wholly to the s. 18.3.1
brothers to study the S. 13.16.9
contained in the holy s. 16.53.1
contained now in the holy S. 19.117.2
duty to read the holy Scriptures 19.117.2
in the S. be the fat pastures 16.20.3
know more of the s. than you do 16.67.1
root your prayer in the s. 20.454.7
s. alone, in which he has willed 16.13.8
sources of revelation—the S. 20.118.1
that which is recorded in the s. 19.105.3
the s. teach us 17.50.1
the way to understand the S. 20.355.12
well learned in the Holy S. 16.28.2
when he reads the holy S. 5.26.3

crupulous: s. people, forever tormented 14.26.7

cum: the rich are the s. of the earth 20.22.7

ea: adrift on the s. of life 4.28.7
a s. without shore and fathomless 16.30.1
God is a s. of infinite substance 8.9.1
it was s. and islands now 20.352.2
like the s.: throw a stone 20.72.11
pray, let him go to s. 17.60.23
the s. has another shore 20.247.1
till the s. itself floweth in your veins 17.97.10

eal: set his s. on each of your souls 4.15.5

earch: make haste, s. persistently 14.28.2
nothing's so hard, but s. 17.61.3

earched: dimly s. after him 19.120.10

earching: s., being with Christ 20.472.2

eason: 'gainst that s. comes 17.89.2

easoning: faith is the s. 13.37.19

easons: s. of loneliness and sadness 19.115.1

eat: her s. is the bosom of God 16.33.2

ecret: grows out of an unspoken s. 20.101.15
love's s. is always 19.53.3
pray in s. to your Father 4.5.3
s. struggles, s. victories 19.109.9
the greatest s. of a holy and happy life 18.35.6
the s. of the Lord is theirs 19.82.2
uttering him who utters the s. of God 20.305.3

secrets: it does not yield its s. 20.428.1
no s. whatever 17.74.1
our conscience know our s. 5.26.2
to the s. of the artistry 12.10.1
which the s. of the heart cannot evade 5.10.9

sect: proceed by loving his own s. or church 19.41.2

secular: working with others in s. society 20.211.1

secure: life can be made s. by violence 19.146.4
never to be s. 17.52.23

security: they give no s. to his flock 20.473.9
your s. is a form of imprisonment 20.396.7

see: heart, for they shall s. God 3.9.8
I was created to s. God 11.1.6
in all things thee to s. 17.60.34
in the desire to s. him. 4.28.5
Lord, purge our eyes to s. 19.123.2
not to s. what lies dimly 19.35.6
or s. the vision of God 20.479.1
rekindle his desire to s. more 4.28.5
saint ought to s. clearly 20.20.4
s. beyond our small lives 20.109.2
s. things for yourself 20.383.7
that I may s. only those things 16.8.2
to have eyes to s. 20.465.2
to s. and to know truly 5.14.7
to s. God is not to s. anything 20.251.2
what you do not let s. 5.8.7

seed: a s. of growth and liberation 20.383.5
Christian blood that is the s. 3.12.3
O s. cast into the ground 2.2.1
sow everywhere the good s. 19.129.3
that of the s. and the tree 20.330.1
the s. of David 2.12.8
the s. of God is in us 14.11.17
within the s. a tree 19.123.2

seed-plot: the s. of all other virtues 17.72.6

seeing: joy in s. the daylight 20.65.2

seek: desiring, we may s. 11.1.1
in vain I did not s. or cry 17.16.3
it is he alone that we s. 19.50.5
s. by reading 16.38.6
s. for goods before they s. 12.7.6
those who s. God in isolation 20.533.2
thou wouldst not s. me 17.80.7
to s. wisely 13.37.12
who s. the Lord, evening and morning 6.2.6

seeking: by continually s. him 20.305.1

seeks: a poor man who s. his God 20.13.1
s. God in some external routine 14.11.16

seen: and yet he can be s. 3.9.8
heart's eye through which God is s. 5.8.14
resting in things s. 19.109.6
the s. and the unseen 20.502.5

sides: I saw in myself two s. 13.6.1
it must sometimes take s. 20.502.3
sifter: Satan is... God's holy s. 20.594.2
sight: destroyeth the s. 17.97.8
I go out of s. 17.42.15
like s., it is nothing apart 20.75.4
s. or objective proof 20.345.1
where I shall live by s. 17.22.3
while I am present to your s.! 11.1.3
with s. of thee may he 10.6.1
sign: be to the world a s. 20.264.14
significance: each person we meet as having a s. 20.465.1
significant: does s. things in s. ways 20.188.2
signs: s. of God at work 20.472.1
silence: a certain secret and hidden s. 15.10.6
an impressive s. fell upon me 19.87.3
born in a s. filled with suffering 20.145.6
for s. is not God 14.7.6
God is s., and in s. 7.1.3
God is the friend of s. 20.538.7
hidden in the depths of s. 5.10.18
in luminous s. within the mind 4.20.2
in perfect s. 5.10.21
in s. man can most readily 14.11.2
it is better to keep s. 16.35.4
it is in s. that God is known 19.16.4
let truth be done in s. 19.55.1
mere s. is not wisdom 17.28.15
outward s. is indispensable 18.25.6
ruled by a great s. 20.145.7
s. contains everything within itself 20.435.2
s. is deep as Eternity 19.35.21
s. is not always tact 17.25.6
s. is not simply what happens 20.435.1
s. is precious 20.599.4
s. is the mystery 7.9.2
s. is the only phenomenon today 20.435.3
s. is the quickest cure 20.251.3
s. itself has no magic 20.44.3
s. more musical than any song 19.123.10
s. the idle gibes of ignorant 19.162.1
still in the enormous s. of the desert 20.372.3
terrified, as ours is, of s. 20.592.3
the prayer of s. 4.5.1
the word which comes out of s. 20.101.1
then another sort of s. 20.135.7
to sin by s. 19.91.15
try to find a silence of your own 20.240.2
where there is s. there is peace 20.102.1
words are full of s. 20.101.9
silenced: my heart began to feel itself s. 19.56.2
silences: s. are the only scrap of Christianity 19.83.5
silent: be solitary, be s. 5.6.1
better to remain s. 19.91.16
God is s. God is s. on the cross 20.513.3
I was s. I was not a Jew 20.410.1
like God when he is s. 16.35.5
only if we know how to be s. 20.273.8
out of his s. being, he is with us 20.299.2
the more we receive in s. prayer 20.398.6
we are s. at the beginning 20.15.9
when and where to keep s. 17.28.15
you must yourself be s. 20.196.2
silently: good deeds that are done s. 19.38.1
silk: by wearing s., while you neglect 4.35.19
silkworm: Die! Die as the s. does 16.65.6
similitude: aspiring to a s. of God in goodness 17.5.17
simple: natural and quiet and s. things of life 20.179.1
suddenly everything is s. 20.523.4
the knowledge of a s. [i.e. real] thing 14.30.1
to ask the hard question is s. 20.111.3
to be both wise and s. 4.35.27
simpleness: but s. is innate 20.15.26
simplicity: an *art* of s. 20.30.4
hold fast to s. of heart 2.11.4
in complete s., showing 13.6.10
never obtain s. in preaching 19.125.6
O holy s.! 14.15.1
one can acquire s. 20.15.26
s. is the secret 20.20.4
simply: do things s. 19.89.1
sin: a word, and that is s. 20.319.1
be ashamed of nothing but s. 18.57.5
bring home to me my s. 20.28.1
bursting with s. and sorrow 18.32.18
come to know s. as Christ is revealed 20.9.3
committed every imaginable s. 14.26.5
contrary to salvation is not s. 20.62.1
do not grieve about a s. that is 4.4.2
do to death s. 2.13.10
God's image was blurred by s. 20.172.5
hardhearted and persist in s. 4.4.8
her dual conception of s. and joy 20.355.7
in our s. and *through* our s. 20.195.6
love virtue rather than fear s. 17.28.2
more serious to lose hope than to s. 7.12.7
no s. is small 17.94.5
not exempt from s. 20.552.1
now there is an eighth Cardinal S. 20.505.1
one s. will destroy a sinner 17.22.13
prevent him from continuing in s. 2.13.19
sickness, s. and death, being inharmonious 19.49.4
s. forsaken is one of the best 19.125.8
s., in a way, is God's gift to man 20.277.1
s. is always a squandering 20.322.8
s. is a power in our life 19.48.3
s. is not a thing 20.164.2
s. is the most expensive thing 19.54.3
s. is to the soul, but worse 13.24.4
so love wipes away s. 16.39.1
so the holy man is still afraid of s. 7.12.3
souls that wish to abandon s. 19.155.3
that creates deadness is a s. 20.534.4
the conquest of s. 20.494.1
the idea that people s. 20.146.2
the promptings of s. 5.22.12

only trust allows the s. room to breathe 20.430.1
our s. is cast into a body 17.80.8
possess your s. with patience 17.43.6
prayer is light to the s. 6.2.5
receive my s. 2.7.2
refined himself to S. 17.43.9
ruins me in s., if not in body 19.162.4
sin is to the s., but worse 13.24.4
s. is increased by the desires 20.54.1
s. is in God and God in the s. 14.4.11
s. resembles a ship 8.11.1
souls well-beloved of my s. 1.1.9
take my s. and give it peace 4.11.1
the s. is dead 20.120.7
the s. of man is not in every part of his body 19.109.16
the s. must be kept peaceful 18.11.9
the s. seeks God in his majesty 13.9.2
the s. that is united with God 16.38.11
the s. without imagination 19.12.17
to help one's poor little s. 20.496.3
transfigures by the s. in its turn 20.536.11
true relation of the s. and God 20.480.7
we define the s. 3.12.9
what the s. is to the body 2.9.3
which exalts the s. above the world 13.6.11
yet my s. drew back 17.60.26
you destroy your own s. 7.13.12

souls: go for s., and go for the worst 19.23.6
God wants only s. 20.536.12
homing instinct in our s. 20.44.2
I ask God for s., and pay him 19.24.1
in our s., Lord, prepare 4.20.5
open windows into men's s. 16.24.6
our s. will continue for ever 17.96.2
reduced to selling their s. 20.484.5
s. are more or less securely fastened 20.174.2
s. well-beloved of my soul 11.1.9
we let our s. shrivel 20.264.6

sound: no s. ought to be heard 18.7.9

source: my Lord is the s. of love 20.580.1

sources: four rich s. of prayer 5.10.14
from the primary s. of life 20.10.4

sow: s. everywhere the good seed 19.129.3

space: let there be s. 20.202.7
light-years of inter-galactic s. 20.117.4
making a s. in life for God 20.299.1
s. is an imperceptible object 20.18.2

spake: twas God the word that s. it 16.24.7

spare: if God s. my life 16.67.1

sparrow: one s. should appear and fly swiftly 8.4.2

speak: all things must s. of God 19.120.4
asked if God's will can still s. 20.271.2
because God does not s. 16.13.8
better than to s. without living 4.33.1
knowing when and how to s. 17.28.15
listen much, s. little 17.68.5
no one left to s. for me 20.410.1
not s. about him. We must s. with 20.220.1
s. not evil one of another 19.120.13
s. ye who best can tell 17.76.24
to s. and remove all doubt 19.91.16
to s. the truth 20.110.2
when we s. with God 19.110.7
who least presume to s. of him 13.6.5

speaking: a grace of kind s. 19.53.8
someone was s. 5.32.8

speaks: God s. for himself 20.428.4
s. ill of his flock s. ill 14.21.4
s. will surely do as he s. 17.10.6

spectator: right path to some quieter s. 19.150.8

speculation: when s. has done its worst 18.32.5

speech: a s. that is wearisome 4.2.10
love's finest s. is without words 13.20.5
s. is shallow as Time 19.35.21
s. is the organ of this present world 7.9.2
to be self-controlled in your s. 18.19.17

speeches: I have no fine s. to make 19.71.1

speed: love has its s. It is an inner s. 20.339.1

spent: life well s. is long 16.44.1

sphere: let man's soul be a S. 17.42.13

spheres: driv'n by the s. 17.100.1

spices: carrying powdered s. in the open air 6.14.13

spinsters: all the busy, useful, independent s. I know 19.3.1

spirit: allow the S. of God to dwell 4.26.3
and he *can be* s. 20.405.1
animated by the S. of God 20.178.5
any special 'fullness of the S.' 20.553.5
attempt to understand the Holy S. 20.534.5
because he received the Holy S. 20.48.4
bound together by his S. 20.232.1
by reason of the S. 6.15.1
come, Holy S.! 20.529.7
come, thou Holy S., come 13.27.1
coming of the Holy S. at Pentecost 20.3.1
consists in the acquisition of the Holy S. 19.129.4
cool in thy mind and s. 17.51.8
Creator S., by whose aid 17.43.11
divine Love, that is, the Holy S. 14.14.5
don't let them break your s. 20.314.1
dwelling in the Holy S., the saints 20.72.2
filled with the Holy S. 11.9.7
flesh and s. must not be understood 16.45.5
found in this S. of life 20.471.2
freedom and the bondage of the s. 16.45.7
full authority of the human s. 20.22.15
give us by your Holy S. 16.20.4
God's S. is not a tame dove 20.527.5
God works immediately by his S. 17.79.3
government, but a new s. 19.1.2
here must the s. rise to grace 17.3.1
he sent the S. into the church 20.526.6
Holy S., S. of truth 16.54.3
if we recognize the S. of God 16.13.12
knowledge of the S. 20.27.1
language about the Holy S. 20.585.3

make up the gospel of the Holy S. 18.11.17
meditate on the oracles of the S. 7.12.8
my s. has become dry 16.38.22
no force the free-born s. 17.43.3
not received the S. of God because 6.13.1
one S. of grace 1.1.5
operation of the Holy S. 20.48.3
our vocation is to live in the S. 20.135.4
people think they are led by the s. 13.20.3
prayer is an exercise of the s. 20.509.1
send, O Christ, the S. 5.42.1
serving as a vehicle of the S. 20.605.1
share in the Holy S. 12.26.4
silence of the Holy S. 14.31.3
S. does not let itself be tied down 20.108.2
s. is not other than body 20.368.8
S. is the source of community 20.570.6
s., seeing that he is s. 7.1.2
the Bible without the Holy S. 19.203.1
the bird of the Holy S. 13.32.1
the church as s.-filled community 20.476.1
the gale of the Holy S. 17.70.1
the gift and leading of the S. 19.160.2
the Holy S. has promised 20.529.3
the Holy S. himself 2.4.2
the Holy S. is in charge here 20.586.3
the Holy S. is not something that stands 20.4.3
the Holy S. is one 3.1.8
the Holy S. is within us always 6.15.3
the Holy S. of God 20.390.2
the Holy S. will not come to us 20.379.11
the Holy S. ... writes his own gospel 18.11.6
the influences of the Holy S. 19.133.1
the infusion of the Holy S. 19.143.3
the kingdom of the Holy S. 20.72.12
the man who has the Holy S. 20.72.1
the mark of him who is born of the S.? 4.9.12
the mind of the Holy S. 20.540.1
the presence of the Holy S. 20.359.1
the radiance of the Holy S. 5.10.24
the same S. resting on us 20.404.7
the S. of God first imparts love 19.103.2
the s., in turn, gives us 16.45.3
the S. is the first and principal Leader 17.7.2
the S. of God is the orderer 17.7.1
the S. of truth, possess your heart 13.25.2
the voice of the divine S. 18.11.14
there is the S. of God 2.13.1
this fresh wind of the S. 20.367.3
this working of the S. of God 20.437.2
through the S. humankind 2.13.11
to be under the authority of the S. 20.355.12
we believe in the S. of Life 20.549.1
we find in the S. unity 20.529.5
we free our s. to win and use 4.9.10
when I had drunk the S. 3.2.2
when man's s. touches God's s. 20.379.5
when the Holy S. enters the heart 19.153.1
when the Holy S. teaches prayer 19.153.2
where the S. of the Lord is 20.72.5
which Christians call the S. 20.446.3
whoever marries the s. of this age 20.311.11
without the S., the Word 20.526.7
words come from the Holy S. 13.7.3

spirits: evil s. driven away 15.1.1
the love of all s. is measured 14.17.4
you damned s.! 13.16.5

spiritual: advancing on the s. way 7.12.4
arm ourselves against our s. enemies 7.13.9
cannot live a s. life for 5.10.16
destroys the s. nature 19.99.11
doorway into another, s., world 20.501.2
far advanced in the s. life 17.28.16
half the s. difficulties 19.12.14
impossible to engage in s. conflict 6.14.6
once from the natural to the s. 20.6.4
people who aim at a s. life 16.52.6
's. = ecclesiastical' 20.40.1
starving part of our s. nature 20.253.1
take refuge from s. things 20.255.6
there is a s. life that we share 17.71.1
the s. combat 10.4.1
the s. man or woman 20.91.8
the s. quest is a continuous 20.313.7
those who wish to live a s. life 14.26.4
to image s. things 13.10.13
whatever s. leanness it may experience 20.454.4

spirituality: all s. is about the right ordering 20.121.3
a s. that refuses 20.230.4
for that is s. 20.601.1
New Testament s. is the s. of broken 20.460.4
saved us from s. 20.22.19
so much s. is cheap and meaningless 20.456.1
s. does not begin 20.275.1
s. is a way of living 20.215.1
s. is nothing less than 20.202.2
taught me a lot about s. 20.337.2
the meaning of s. 20.191.2
we need a s. to direct 20.207.2

spiritualize: tried systematically to s. the gospel 20.512.1

spiritually: better left s. alone 20.445.3

spitting: s. in the church 17.60.6

splendour: leads to incomparable s. 19.147.7

spoil: letting his religion s. his morality 19.58.4

sponge: look on Sunday as a s. 19.12.15

spoon: behoveth him a full long s. 14.5.2

spot: it is a s. and a defilement 18.35.12

spread: maturing, it should be s. around 20.277.3

springs: a fountain fed from many s. 19.130.1

springtime: always s. in the heart that loves God 19.155.1

squandering: sin is always a s. 20.322.8

stability: dangerous to the s. of the home 19.137.1
will give s. to the soul 5.10.23

stable: put any more in the s. 17.51.4

staff: fetch me my coat and s.! 7.7.1

stages: three s. in the work of God 19.140.2

the s. of our hope 20.176.12
we all have enough s. 17.68.27
strengthen: we can s. ourselves when 20.338.2
strengthening: helping me, s. 4.13.1
stress: the s. which so many feel 20.557.3
stresses: pounded by the waves of life's various s. 8.5.2
stretch: on the full s. for God 18.59.5
strike: not only s. while the iron is hot 17.37.1
string: moderation is the silken s. 17.59.2
strings: we are all s. in the concert 17.14.1
strip: it is to s. ourselves 20.63.1
strips: s. us of our needs 20.559.4
while he s. of everything 18.11.5
strive: s., my brothers, to attain 4.49.1
strivings: till all our s. cease 19.161.2
stroke: O unexpected s. 17.76.32
strong: nothing is so s. as gentleness 17.87.6
one often comes from a s. will 19.12.10
s. may not be held back 6.4.5
to be powerful, you must be s. 19.109.15
weak things united become s. 17.52.10
stronger: God is the s. 16.65.5
structures: impinge effectively on the functional s. 20.584.5
inherited s. of belief and practice 20.210.1
the hierarchical s. of many churches 20.104.1
struggle: if they are true to their s. 20.575.2
in the s. in which we are called 20.148.2
in the s. to achieve that life 20.471.2
in the thick of this s. 20.472.3
means to be used in the s. 20.118.10
so the s. goes on 20.480.5
to s. hard in prayer 4.26.6
struggled: unless you have s. for it 4.26.11
struggles: gifts of grace increase as the s. increase 16.59.2
through the s. of the poor 20.512.4
study: I refuse to s. dead skins 13.12.2
proper subject for s. 17.68.2
s. diligently and apply yourself 16.7.1
we cannot s. God 20.121.1
stunned: I was s. 19.23.2
stupid: O s. people 14.4.9
style: then for the s., majestic 17.43.10
sub-human: in a s. condition 20.171.6
subjection: by emphasising women's s. 20.226.2
subjects: God may at length show my s. 17.31.3
submission: not simply s., but real striving 20.565.1
peace for my mother meant s. 20.603.1
submit: s. to a higher authority 4.9.2
subordinate: taught to s. 'little angels' 20.232.2
substance: all made of the same s. 4.4.9
God is a sea of infinite s. 8.9.1
succeed: if in order to s. in an enterprise 17.81.5
success: Almighty will crown our efforts with s. 19.162.5
in the midst of your highest s. 19.134.1
let us work as if s. depended 16.35.11
tempts us with more s. 18.60.4
thought which takes s. for its standard 20.15.27
suffer: all the voices of those who s. 20.273.7
cannot but s. as well 20.26.1
I choose to s., and do s. 17.77.1
if you love, you will s. 20.189.1
in the light of what they s. 20.15.16
now it is I who s. 3.3.1
rather to s. for them than with them 17.31.3
s. with Christ, and for Christ 15.14.5
to fight, to s., and to love 20.50.1
to see your love s. 14.18.15
to s. for him, as well as to enjoy 18.25.11
to s. in obedience to a human 20.15.10
to s. much, yet badly, is to s. 18.39.2
to s. pain without sin 13.31.5
we hope to s. torment 2.14.8
what we w. from others 15.14.18
would God I might s. ten times 16.69.1
suffered: by the ills they have s. 6.17.1
having s. never passes 20.62.10
s. for God's sake 15.14.21
what I s. is known only 17.64.1
suffering: above all ecumenical in its s. 20.447.2
borne the wounds of s. 20.313.3
devoted s. as the highest 20.43.4
energy derived from s. 20.249.9
I am now s. for him 3.3.1
in sorrow and s., go straight 16.38.16
in the face of s. 20.514.2
in their s., Asian women meet 20.190.3
it is just this penny's worth of s. 18.36.1
not God's will that we should live in s. 20.384.2
not so much the actual s. 18.24.1
one ounce of patient s. 17.28.17
our immersion in the world's s. 20.46.3
sense of my corporal s. 16.70.4
sharing of the gospel of a s. God 20.403.1
s. for his sake 16.52.5
s. is a very disturbing thing 19.85.5
s. is the money 19.152.1
s. is the very best gift 19.144.1
s. passes 20.62.10
s. without hope produces resentment 20.101.12
summarizes the s. of our times 20.415.5
take part in the s. of Jesus 20.488.2
the church is a cause of s. 20.161.1
the noblest way of s. 17.50.1
the purest s. hears and carries 16.38.17
the s. servant, rendered wordless 20.372.1
this radical communion with the s. 20.273.6
unearned s. is redemptive 20.335.3
when you experience s. and troubles 13.20.7
whether this means unending s. 7.15.1
which in s. is forced from us 20.514.6
sufferings: be patient in all the s. 18.25.10
my heart welcomes all the s. 19.57.1

T

frivolous t. and making fun of things 7.12.2
if you want to t. to God, you can t. 20.510.1
no need to t. a lot in prayer 4.40.1
religious t. is a very feast 19.53.1
the way in which people t. about God 19.83.1
to be, than to t. 16.35.4

talking: a t. man having nothing to say 18.49.16
'it is t. to me, and about me' 19.83.4
way of walking, not a way of t. 20.311.15
when the t. stops 20.396.1

tangible: faith is nothing at all t. 20.75.4

target: a t. and an end 5.10.1
for anyone to reach our t. 5.10.2

task: no t. is difficult if your desire 5.22.2
our most urgent t. 20.145.1
true Christian sets about his t. 19.162.2

taste: a t. of the holy blessed spirit 16.51.2
ceaselessly ask to t. my pleasures 13.29.1
to perceive him and to t. him 20.353

taught: afterward he t. 14.5.6
religion is caught, not t. 20.311.19
unless he is t. by God 2.13.14

teach: all who undertake to t. 17.26.1
if you try to t. a child 20.265.1
in harvest t. 19.20.6
t. me, my God and King 17.60.34

teacher: a t. affects eternity 20.2.4

teachers: authors were fathers and t. 20.100.4

teaches: does not contend but t. in love 16.72.4

teaching: if t. and preaching is your job 16.7.1
no form of Christian t. has any future 20.112.2
one t. that has hurt 20.226.1
perfect follower of Christ's t. 14.14.3
straightforward t. of Christ 20.71.5
strong enough to receive more advanced t. 7.3.1
t. that lacks grace 7.10.7

tears: above all, pray for the gift of t. 15.13.1
do it with t. in our eyes 19.103.4
had not given us t. 7.13.3
in this vale of t., yearning 13.10.8
life's valley be a vale of t. 18.14.15
many t. did I shed 17.83.1
so we ought to have t. 4.17.1
t. are agents of resurrection 20.325.1
the bitterest t. shed over graves 19.139.2
the fruit of those t. that I sowed 16.30.1
the t. of saints 17.61.6
the touch of God is marked by t. 20.586.1
through t. and hard work 5.41.2
to shed t. over what has happened 8.8.1
with t. I sought him earnestly 17.16.3

telescope: an observatory would be without a t. 19.12.17
the Bible is like a t. 19.29.2

television: from radio and t. and the press 20.306.5
I don't think that t. has corrupted me 20.398.4
t. is not all bad news 20.146.1

tell: God. T. him all about it 20.116.5
t. him of our needs and troubles 8.8.2
t. it all to me 19.129.1

telling: beyond all t. 13.30.1

temper: evil t. 19.48.4

temperance: a state of t. 18.1.8
as t. would be difficult 18.32.12

temple: Christ is the true T. 20.295.2
let us make a t. 13.16.8
make thy t. worthy thee 17.43.11
sacred as a t. 17.94.11
this t. has two porches 5.33.1

temples: if then you are t. 6.15.1
no reason for the t. of God 10.2.1

temporal: sees one's way in t. things 17.73.1
the care of all t. things 18.46.4

temporary: theological methods are all t. instruments 20.300.3

temptation: hindered by a small t. 7.12.4
if it takes t. and sin 20.269.6
t. commonly comes through 19.159.1
t. is like a river 4.15.2
the great usefulness of t. 14.27.4
the millstones of t. 19.26.3

temptations: in the t. of all she is tried 4.2.6
I shall not sin in these t. 17.65.1
mercies should not be t. 17.37.7
some t. come to the industrious 19.136.13
t., when we first meet them, are 17.22.7
the more you are attacked by t. 13.16.6

tempted: greatest of all evils is not to be t. 19.155.2
not t. because you are evil 20.500.3
you shall not be t. 14.18.2

tempts: Devil only t. those souls 19.155.3

ten: as much again, and t. times more 17.22.8

tenderness: t. is never a sign of weakness 20.145.2

tent: a wandering, flowing t. 17.90.4

test: ceremonies are the t. of the righteousness 16.45.14
God wishes to t. you 16.25.1
O Lord, who puts us to the t. 4.6.2
prayer is the t. of everything 19.143.2

testament: believe in the New T. world 20.162.1
for such people the Old T. 20.210.1
go the the Old T. to find 20.210.3
New T. spirituality is the spirituality of broken 20.460.4
Old T. bears its clearest witness 20.210.2
testimony of the Old T. 20.230.3
the thought of the New T. 20.122.8

testaments: both the Old and the New T. 8.5.1
Church has two t. 5.33.1

tested: what we think and believe to be t. 20.517.14

testimonies: more than a thousand t. 14.27.4

testings: standing firm amid severe t. 19.106.1

text: tied down to a lesson or a t. 20.108.2

thank: grateful hearts, and no one to t. 19.123.1
I t. you, Lord 4.17.3

troublous: all the day long of this t. life 19.109.21

true: be so t. to thyself 17.5.19
one religion is as t. as another 17.24.1

trumpet: the creature is like a mighty t. 4.28.1
the First Blast of the T. 16.40.5
to me it was a t. call 20.33.3

trumpets: t. sounded for him on the other side 17.22.9

trust: believer exhibits t. in God when he trusts 20.392.1
boundless then my t. 20.16.2
confidence in God and absolute t. in him 20.408.1
if they t. in him alone 16.65.27
like a little child, and t. 19.140.7
not bound to t. him 17.52.6
O Lord, put no t. in me 16.52.3
on t. before we can do anything 20.313.4
ostentation, and lack of t. 7.17.2
putting our whole t. in him 20.116.3
to t. his people with their moment 20.157.1
t. God and keep your powder dry 17.37.4
t. is one of the fundamental aspects 20.430.1

trusting: wisdom lies in t. no one 13.24.6

trusts: believer exhibits trust in God when he t. 20.392.1
he who t. in himself is lost 18.37.7

truth: absolute devotion to the t. 20.492.3
a Church which abandons the t. 20.342.2
all t. is precious 18.14.7
bellow the t., when he knows the t. 20.62.7
but our ideas of t. 19.12.19
down to the t. 20.452.1
face to face the t. comes out 17.52.33
faith has need of the whole t. 20.536.2
firm in standing for the t. 8.4.6
God is, at first, t. 20.378.1
God's ways are always t. 20.200.1
greatest friend of T. is Time 19.42.2
he is the great Lover of t. 17.81.2
heart leap out and grasp its t. 20.578.5
heed it, for it is the t. 20.578.3
his t. is marching on 19.74.1
human reason supplies the t. 6.14.11
I am the t. 20.181.1
I teach or wonder what is t. 9.6.2
if it resists the t., the t. must 19.1.4
if you tell the t. 19.61.1
in it we have the t. 9.5.5
in the end t. will conquer 14.31.1
into the fullness of t. 20.529.3
learn how to communicate Christian t 20.584.3
let t. be done in silence 19.55.1
likely to catch glimpses of t. 20.517.14
loving Christianity better than t. 19.41.2
method by which religious t. 18.32.6
nothing can ever destroy t. 20.578.2
not our business to protect the t. 20.517.15
on our road towards t. 3.1.2
preaching is t. through personality 19.29.3
quick to speak the t. 4.17.8
shall perish in t. 17.60.28
slandering upon the vantage-ground of t. 17.5.20
so T. be in the field 17.76.27
teach them to love t. 19.97.8
that the t. may live in us 14.10.1
the nearer one comes to the t. 20.81.3
the supreme comforter, the Spirit of t. 13.25.2
the t. is a reality which we can hardly bear 20.390.3
the t. is no bigger than your 20.269.4
the t. that we must walk in 20.52.1
the utterance of t. in our age 19.105.3
though t. and falsehood be 17.42.16
to love t. for t.'s sake 17.72.6
to speak the t. 20.110.2
T. and Love are wings 4.20.3
t., even crucified and buried 20.110.3
t. is on the persecuted side 16.42.6
t. is the foundation of all knowledge 17.43.8
t. is the highest thing 14.5.7
t. often suffers most 18.44.6
t. on the lips 12.16.4
T. walks by daylight 14.21.3
t., we shall never despise the t. 16.13.12
t. which is merely told 20.120.8
turn crucified t. into coercive t. 20.10.1
we do not come to the t. 20.604.4
we know the t. 17.80.4
what is t.? said jesting Pilate 17.5.21
where t. is, there is God 17.29.3
willed that his t. should be published 16.13.8
with a t. to discover 20.468.1
without t. your labour is in vain 12.24.4

truthfulness: the commandant of absolute t. 20.15.12

truths: call the t. which offend us 17.28.13
communicating about the deepest t. 20.237.1
new t., in the proper sense 19.82.4

tub: let every t. stand 17.22.14

tumult: Jesus calls us; o'er the t. 19.4.4
withdraw our hearts completely from the t. 5.10.20

turbulent: rid me of this t. priest? 12.13.1

turn: they have only to t. back 5.14.2
to repent is to t. 20.454.10
t. everything to good 19.138.3

turned: I was t. from a Christian 20.28.1
those who have t. away 5.14.2

turning-point: a word, may prove to be a t. 20.599.2

turns: the world t. on the other side 20.320.1
which t. us to God 20.44.2

twelve: how could t. uneducated men 4.35.22

two: if ever t. were one 17.16.1
t. went to pray? 17.36.4

twins: be near t., yet truth 17.42.16

Tyburn: a man left to enjoy your T. 16.14.1

tyranny: the worst sort of t. 18.7.15
t. is always better organized 20.62.6
wherever law ends, t. begins 17.72.7

tyrant: nothing is more abhorrent to the t. 15.12.1
the t. dies and his rule ends 19.83.11

tyrants: all the t. that the world affords 17.2.1
these will be their cruel t. 19.101.6

J

unoffended: learn the blessedness of the u. 20.174.4
unpopularity: even if that leads to great u. 20.502.3
unreligiously: loathsomely and u. to come 16.58.2
unrest: faith means just that blessed u. 19.83.2
unrighteousness: perplexities of u. 18.61.3
unseen: forgetting u. things 19.109.6
the seen and the u. 20.502.5
to the u. and eternal things 19.138.1
u. but not unknown 19.113.1
unselfishness: how much ill-feeling u. occasions 20.352.21
transmutes individual u. 20.409.1
unsought: would come largely u. 20.134.3
untaught: pour into their u. minds 8.5.1
untroubled: we go to sleep u. 5.23.14
untrue: statement that I knew to be u. 16.28.1
untruthfulness: first casualty of u. 20.592.5
unwisdom: the u. of parents 20.73.1
unworthiness: seeing one's own u. 18.19.3
unworthy: one is u. of God's goodness 18.19.2
upheaval: cultural and political u. 20.126.1
uphold: fail if thou u. me not 16.52.3
uplift: the church cannot u. a man 20.418.2
uprooted: they are 'u. people' 20.391.1
upwards: by instinct to fly u. 13.7.2
urgent: there is nothing more u. 20.200.2
use: saints, before he can u. us 20.230.1
the main thing is to u. it well 17.40.2
used: we may never decline to be u. 20.432.1
useful: I shall be more u. to you 13.12.1
usefulness: cannot be measured in terms of u. 20.151.2
useless: let us not live to be u. 18.57.3
only phenomenon today that is u. 20.435.3
worse than u.; it does positive harm 19.125.3
utopians: it is finally the U. 20.536.7

V

vacuum: the great v. in my soul 20.74.1
vainglory: succumb to the temptation of v. 19.158.2
vale: life's valley be a v. of tears 18.14.15
validity: is of permanent v. 20.38.3
valley: I still dwell in the v. of care 13.33.1
valour: it is a brave act of v. 17.20.11
perfect v. consists in doing 17.68.16
where piety and v. 17.43.16
valuable: we are v. because God loves us 20.500.2
value: it is love which gives things their v. 20.176.10
v. knowledge of God above all 7.17.3
v. of it is seldom known 19.42.8
values: community that doesn't live by false v. 20.306.3
inversion of our earthly v. 20.239.1
knowledge not of fact but of v. 20.311.13
v. that the day never dreamed of 20.385.4
vanity: no arena in which v. 17.80.17
our v. puts into circulation 17.68.8
variety: have as much v. as the human race 20.407.3
varnish: rather smell incense than v. 20.71.4
vastness: holding invisible v. in its hands 20.481.2
the very v. of the work 19.110.8
veil: no longer a v. which hides him from me 19.50.4
the v. of sense hangs dark between 19.113.1
venerate: I v. the Creator of matter 8.9.6
vengeance: virtue, and a swift v. 14.19.1
verbs: conjugating three v. 20.91.2
versified: poets that have never v. 16.60.2
vessel: carefully riveted v. 19.147.7
in the royal v. of divine love 17.28.6
vice: homage which v. pays to virtue 17.68.25
no form of v. 19.48.4
prosperity doth best discover v. 17.5.2
sodden with drink, steeped in v. 19.23.8
the slippery way of v. 17.43.15
this is the definition of v. 4.9.6
v. does not want to be scorned 13.18.3
zeal which shields us from v. 6.4.3
vices: not to dwell upon the v. of men 16.13.14
trample those same v. 5.8.22
we make a ladder of our v. 5.8.22
victim: either with the v. of the executioner 20.514.2
O saving V., opening wide 13.37.15
to be an innocent v. 20.605.2
victims: from the standpoint of the v. 20.487.3
victories: even victors are by v. undone 17.43.19
victors: even v. are by victories undone 17.43.19
victory: first step on the way to v. 20.141.6
than a v. with pride 4.17.13
view: our v. of the most sublime things 13.37.1
vigil: night before Easter in v. 7.10.3
vigilance: v. and prayer are the safeguards 18.46.3
vigils: v., meditation, and prayer 5.10.23
vigour: the v. of our spiritual life 19.106.2
vindicate: v. the way of the Cross 20.170.1
vinegar: takes more oil than v. 17.28.9
with honey than with v. 19.136.5
violence: a display of outright physical v. 20.484.4
as we opt for v. or non-v. in revolution 20.603.2
but there is no v. 20.405.4
life can be made secure by v. 19.146.4
much v. is based on the illusion 20.415.1
never preached v., except the v. of love 20.473.5
results in doing v. to ourselves 20.603.1
returning v. for v. multiplies v. 20.335.18
the Church condemns v. 20.270.1
the v. of Jesus is deep love 20.176.9
to refuse the use of v. 20.605.2
v. can only be concealed 20.516.2
v. does even justice unjustly 19.35.19
v. is always an offence 20.322.9

W

obedience is the tomb of the w. 7.13.8
our w. is the part of us 20.287.1
perform the w. of God speedily 12.15.3
ready for whatever God's w. brings 8.4.6
resignation to the divine w. 16.52.9
says 'thy w. be done' but means his own 18.44.15
the w. of God 4.2.8
then our w. is free 14.17.8
to break my w. into little pieces 19.119.1
to do his holy, loving w. 20.61.1
to find God's w. and to make that w. 20.379.7
too fond of our own w. 18.12.3
your w. is subject to changes 5.23.7
you've figured out free w. 20.419.3

willing: a w. heart and a ready hand 16.20.4
but he draws the w. 4.35.14

willingly: he does and suffers all things w. 16.45.17

willingness: laying hold of his highest w. 19.148.3

will-power: true w. and courage 19.103.7

wills: fed and strengthened their own w. 14.26.8

win: I cannot w. either with gifts 17.51.7
if you w., you w. all 17.80.9
man who gambles is to w. 19.136.9
to serve, not to w. 20.94.2
you will w. many for God 13.12.4

wind: it is as though a strong w. 20.258.2
the speed of w. 8.3.1
the stronger the w. 14.31.5
you blow like the w. 20.123.1

windows: house of our hearts, open the w. 12.17.2
I would not open w. 16.24.6
opens the w. of the soul 20.316.1
open wide the w. of our spirits 19.123.3
the w. through which sin enters 19.24.2

wine: and shared w. (a life of friendship) 20.460.4
God feels as blood; but I as w. 17.60.10
I always look about for the w. 17.86.2
in the w. we drink 4.20.7
there was an excellent w. 2.1.2
two little kegs of w. 8.5.4
when the w. is in 16.2.2
when w., used liberally 20.556.1

wing: under the shadow of the w. of God 19.56.2

wings: afflictions are but the shadow of God's w. 19.99.15
in glittering ranks with w. display'd 17.76.23
we need no w. to go in search 16.65.11
who have as it were w. 12.15.3
you take the w. of contemplation 13.33.1

winter: acknowledge the w. of the heart 20.230.4
Grace grows better in the w. 17.86.4
should fall out in the middle of w. 18.1.5

wire: compelled to weave barbed w. 20.396.7
we are the w., God is the current 20.176.11

wisdom: all the w. of the world 16.22.2
and of human w. 19.147.2
deep w. inaccessible 20.159.5
difference between happiness and w. 19.42.6
fruitless is the w. of him 16.26.11
help us to grow in spiritual w. 20.528.1
if w. delights you 11.1.10
ignorance concerning him is true w. 9.5.2
knowledge comes, but w. lingers 19.142.3
likeness of the eternal W. 13.10.13
not w., for w. consists in knowing 17.28.15
O W. of the eternal Father 16.8.2
the divine w. 9.5.4
the entire sum of our w. 16.13.4
the first key to w. 12.1.3
the only w. we can hope to acquire 20.228.8
the sublimity of w. 17.94.16
unsearchable depth of w. 5.14.5
what the world calls w. 19.41.10
when we speak about w. 4.2.1
w. cannot give way to evil 4.2.4
w. is humble 18.14.8
w. is nine-tenths 20.69.7
w. is the right use of knowledge 19.136.6
w. lies in trusting no one 13.24.6
w. requires a surrender 20.451.1
W.'s best nurse is contemplation 17.76.29
w.: She is a tree of life 3.9.9
w. that required no teaching 5.5.1
w. without compassion 20.263.2
with heavenly w. the hearts 5.11.2

wise: a w. man 18.49.20
a w. man will make 17.5.26
being w. in time 20.69.7
being w., thou canst not err 17.29.13
by the worldly w. will be called folly 6.14.7
it takes a w. parent to prune 20.249.11
no w. man wants a soft life 9.1.2
to be both w. and simple 4.35.27

wiser: w. today than you were yesterday 18.49.8
you are not w. than God 7.1.4

wish: I w., I ardently w. 19.132.8
merely a w. turned Godward 19.29.5

wished: I asked for what I really w., and really w. 19.110.6

wit: by his w. could compass upon earth 16.22.2
wine is in, the w. is out 16.2.2
[w.] involves, probably 20.228.6

witchcraft: smells of incense and w. 20.34.4

with: God is w. us 18.57.17
the Lord be w. you always 13.11.10

withdraw: w. from business and company 19.81.1

withdrawal: better to make a w. 20.97.3

within: you were w. me 5.8.24

without: God can no more do w. us 14.11.4

witness: a silent w. to the reality 20.599.1
to claim to bear w. to God 20.513.2

witnessed: one who may be w. 17.47.1
they w. to the love of God 19.158.1

witnesses: doing without w. 17.68.16

wives: in their dealings with their w. 20.226.2

woe: weak enough to suffer w. 17.42.4
where the end is w. 17.22.12

woman: a w. is always a beautiful thing 19.32.2
a w. is led by her natural love 4.35.20
a w. seldom asks advice 18.1.1
a w.'s preaching is like a dog's 18.32.4
as a w. in labour 20.395.2
because Christ wasn't a w.! 19.149.2
each w. is a temple of the Holy Spirit 20.302.2
for a w. to preach 19.87.5
God so designed the body of the w. 20.327.2
he is bone of w.'s bone 20.42.1
help the w. and the w. the 16.67.2
his courtesy to W. 20.42.2
if each w. before me was prepared 20.143.3
it was the Latin American w. 20.129.1
laudable in a married w. 15.4.1
never threatened by a w. of equality 20.153.3
no limit to the power of a good w. 19.16.18
often a w.'s zeal 20.134.1
praiseworthy forwardness in the w. who 8.4.9
the dilemma for the African w. today 20.341.1
the nakedness of w. is the work of God 19.20.3
the only coloured w. 19.149.1
to be a religious w. 20.373.1
to be a w., black and active 20.301.1
when he saw a w. of striking beauty 7.13.1
why not the w.? 19.87.4
w. begins to take her place 20.258.2
w. was made of man 18.49.9
w. who stayed behind to seek Christ 6.14.1
w.'s witness to courage 20.595.1
you are to speak for w.'s ballot 19.163.1

womanist: W. theology should teach Christians 20.590.1

womankind: curtailed the influence of w. 20.142.2

womb: had come from your own w. 20.107.3
if the w. holds back the child 4.20.1
in the little enclosure of her holy w. 13.11.5
on coming to the Virgin's w. 13.11.8

women: a certain percentage of African w. 20.226.1
accord w. some privileges 19.137.3
African w.'s strength 20.421.5
Against the Monstrous Regiment of W. 16.40.5
Asian w. meet God 20.190.3
attitude to w. of the Western-related Churches 20.425.4
bar the sanctuary to w. 20.475.3
bring out the truth about men and w. 20.147.6
churches that do not ordain w. 20.519.1
contemporary w. thirst for living water 20.243.1
continuation of the abuse of w. 20.542.1
did not discriminate against w. 20.232.3
ethics supporting justice for w. 20.590.1
experiences as w., whose sexuality 20.343.3
God should be greatly loved by w. 12.16.3
'Happy W.' was the title 19.3.1
hard to say what hurts w. more 20.254.1
has also been announced to us as w. 20.471.1
has no word for Black w. 20.266.1
issues of the ordination of w. 20.546.1
liberating institution for w. 20.579.1
men were as resolute as w. 19.77.1
ministry of w. hasten revival? 19.40.1
new questions for w. in the church 20.206.1
prodigious efforts of w., w. whose presence 20.136.1
seemingly devout w. worshippers 20.33.2
so w. receive an office in the Truth 17.9.1
the attitude of w. in general 19.32.4
the cry of the w. prophets 20.182.2
the fact that we are w. 20.143.1
the full personhood of w. 20.476.5
the gospel is NOT Good News for w. 20.525.1
the irruption of w. in Church 20.421.7
the phrase 'a group of women' 20.462.1
the silent majority of w. 20.104.1
the value of w.'s experience 20.581.3
the w.'s meetings 17.98.1
the w.'s movement is spreading 20.142.3
those who criticize w. 20.271.1
very fine store of w. 17.84.4
want to live as men and w. 13.20.6
we are the happiest w. in Ghent 19.19.1
we—as w.—are created in God's image 20.103.1
whatever you say against w. 18.49.9
what we call the w.'s movement 20.142.4
whether he deals with w. or with men 20.143.2
w. are called to be a great power 19.32.3
w. are properly concerned only 20.225.1
w. can't have as much rights as men 19.149.2
w. discover a new image of Jesus 20.107.2
w. engaged on a pilgrimage 20.302.1
w. especially are social beings 20.213.1
w. find their dignity 20.260.1
w. have never had any power 20.134.4
w., if they will, may be perfect 17.102.1
w. priests could be a step 20.420.1
w., rouse yourselves! 18.22.1
w., we need you 20.554.5
w. who have to bear nature's weakness 8.4.9
w. whose lives have been shaped 20.508.4

wonder: in the object of their w. 20.6.6
in w. all philosophy began 19.40.3
never starve for w. 20.22.1
revive the springs of w. 20.534.3
the w. and curiosity which welcomes 20.591.5
there is a new w. in heaven 7.20.2
to work a w. 17.61.12
who has lost his sense of w. 12 26.1
w. is the basis of worship 19.35.22

wonders: all these w. 19.109.7

won't: nonelect, whosoever w. 19.12.22
the other from a strong w. 19.12.10

word: a w., may prove to be a turning-point 20.599.2
accepted as the W. of God 20.478.1
because it is the W. of God 20.169.1
believing in the w. 2.5.2
cover myself with the W. of God 5.27.1
every creature is a divine w. 13.10.16
for her sake the W. 9.4.2
God's final w. about himself 20.119.2
God should have the first w. 20.15.9

God the W. restored 2.13.10
he is the W. of whom 2.14.9
he keeps his w. 20.555.3
in order not to hear the W. 20.101.1
it is the w. of God 20.94.1
let no w. pass your lips in vain 4.2.16
Lord, be thy w. my rule 19.165.1
Lord, thy w. abideth 19.9.1
my experience of the Biblical W. 20.102.1
no meaningless w. be uttered 4.2.16
out of love for us the Word of God 7.17.9
see the W. of God purely preached 16.13.16
so the W. poured out 3.1.6
stronger than all the evils in the soul is the W. 3.9.6
taking someone at their w. 20.576.4
the power of God's w. 20.284.1
the revealed w. of God 19.117.1
the W. does not withdraw 5.24.4
the W. of all things 3.1.8
the W. of God 4.8.4
the w. of God is plain in itself 16.40.1
the W. of God humanified 15.10.2
the W. was not degraded 4.8.3
tremble at the w. of the Lord 17.51.6
twas God the w. that spake it 16.24.7
was the mighty W. 19.111.1
we cannot segregate God's word 20.473.4
when you read God's w. 19.83.4
with the w. of prayer 2.14.2
w. of God is in the Bible 20.28.7
without the Spirit, the W. 20.526.7

words: for w. left unsaid 19.139.2
good w. are worth much 17.60.30
heart without w., than w. without a heart 17.22.2
however just your w. 4.35.3
in all your deeds and w. 13.10.9
indifferency of all forms of w. 14.31.3
inexpressible: w. cannot describe it 7.18.3
investing our spiritual energies in w. 20.271.2
kind w. are the music of the world 19.53.9
Love's finest speech is without w. 13.20.5
my w. fly up 17.89.5
no difference between the w. and *works* 20.593.1
no last w. of mine to repeat 19.10.3
of few w., I charge you 18.44.9
reading the w. of God 5.30.1
say five w. devoutly 9.3.2
so w. are appropriate 4.17.9
the kindling power of our w. 17.87.12
the most beautiful w. 20.145.6
used the w. and idioms 19.33.1
while mere w., as they slip 17.87.13
w. are full of silence 20.101.9

work: a piece of w., involving perfect 20.572.3
activity in the Divine w. 20.10.7
after w. a rest is welcome 12.23.4
arrears in our w., as well as the w. done 20.97.1
being forced to w. 19.86.6
believe no w. beneath me 20.29.5
do your w. in peace 4.36.2
every noble w. is at first impossible 19.35.11
fever of life is over, and our w. is done 19.109.21
free men freely w. 19.30.2
go forth to w. with it till the evening 19.110.1
he who has found his w. 19.35.5
he will fit you for the w. 16.52.8
I must w. as long as life lasts 19.132.4
it is the w. of a lifetime 18.19.4
left the Holy Spirit to do his w. 17.30.2
let us w. as if success depended 16.35.11
no substitute for w. 20.179.3
not do their w. in sadness 6.4.2
old man has left his w. 2.2.1
prayer is not w. and w. is not prayer 20.188.3
so immersed in the w. of the Lord 20.322.7
that our w. may not be as a burden 18.31.1
the very vastness of the w. 19.110.8
then I think our w. in this world is over 19.99.8
these things too are the w. of peace 20.213.6
three stages in the w. of God 19.140.2
tired in the Lord's w. 18.59.9
to do great w. 17.25.4
tools ready; God will find thee w. 19.86.2
we do not persevere in the w. 4.17.12
whatever good w. a man undertakes 5.1.1
w. awaiting in the field 20.57.1
w. is not always required of a man 19.99.14
w. is the natural exercise 20.484.8
w. not of men but of angels 12.10.1

worker: a good and faithful w. 20.17.1
because God is the Ceaseless W. 20.97.1
the wisdom of the w. 13.7.2

working: by w. hard during the day 14.2.2
w. with others in secular society 20.211.1

workmen: if w. spent as much time 17.87.2

works: faith is the root of w. 18.60.3
great w. are performed 18.32.16
great w. do not always 17.87.1
just before our w. can please God 16.42.5
no difference between the *words* and w. 20.593.1
nothing but good and holy w. 16.49.2
our w. do not ennoble us 14.11.1
relaxing in the practice of good w. 16.35.6
such are all the w. of God 14.18.9
than all other good w. together 16.38.7
the Holy Spirit w. in us 14.17.9
the marvellous w. of the Deity 19.42.9
the w. of our Saviour 2.18.1
then do we teach also good w. 16.45.16
then will our w. be truly fruitful 20.553.3
these are thy glorious w. 17.76.1
when God wants to do his great w. 19.140.4
w., being inanimate things 16.45.9
w., but God w. 5.8.23

world: a mind which misliketh this w. 16.31.2
all the ways of the w. 8.4.5
all the w. as my parish 18.57.12
Come to the w.! 20.583.1
construction of a new w. 20.273.2

wrote: this was the hand that w. it 16.20.5
wrought: that first he w. 14.5.6

Y

yarn: web of our life is of a mingled y. 17.89.1
yearning: y. of the human spirit towards God 19.158.3
yes: for what shall be—'y.!' 20.276.1
 in order that the Y. of mankind 20.224.2
 Mary's y. is a free, responsible y. 20.129.3
 say y. to what really matters 20.98.1
 saying y. to life without the one 20.307.1
yesterday: knowledge or good deed to y. 17.3.5
yoke: to the y. of Christ 5.33.6
young: a man that is y. in years 17.5.11
 Devil sets for y. people is idleness 19.24.4
 form the mind of the y. 4.35.23
 I felt so y., so strong 19.30.5
 out of sympathy with the y. 19.99.8
 still too y. for punishment 4.2.11
 suspicious of piety in the y.
 the y. want to be challenged 20.306.3
younger: ever wished to be y. 18.49.19
yourself: a humble knowledge of y. 15.14.17
 first learn to love y. 12.7.5
 if you know y. well 14.29.1
 making y. out to be worse 20.203.2
 take y. as you are 20.81.1
youth: submit to be taught by y. 18.7.29
youthful: I look back at my y. days 20.492.5

Z

zeal: an evil bitter z. 6.4.3
 if our z. were true 18.1.14
 passion and we think it is z. 15.14.20
 those that follow an excess of z. 19.16.6
 z. dropped in charity is good 18.44.13
 z. is fit only for wise men 17.52.30
 z. without knowledge 17.52.31

ACKNOWLEDGMENTS

We would like to thank all those who have given us permission to include quotations in this book, as indicated on the list below. Every effort has been made to trace and acknowledge copyright holders of all the quotations included in this anthology. We apologize for any errors or omissions that may remain, and would ask those concerned to contact the publishers, who will ensure that full acknowledgment is made in the future.

bercius: from A. Hamman (ed.), *Early Christian Prayers* translated by W. Mitchell), 1961, by permission of Longmans, Green and Co.

braham of Nathpar: from *The Syriac Fathers on Prayer and the Spiritual Life* (translated by Sebastian Brock), by permission of Cistercian Publications

gathon: from *Sayings of the Desert Fathers* (translated by Benedicta Ward), Mowbray, 1975, by permission of Cassell plc

lonius: from *Sayings of the Desert Fathers* (translated by Paul achance), 1993, by permission of Paulist Press

noub: from *Sayings of the Desert Fathers* (translated by Benedicta Ward), Mowbray, 1975, by permission of Cassell plc

phrahat: from *The Syriac Fathers on Prayer and the Spiritual Life* translated by Sebastian Brock), by permission of Cistercian ublications

pollo: from *Sayings of the Desert Fathers* (translated by Benedicta Ward), Mowbray, 1975, by permission of Cassell plc

pollos: from *The Philokalia* (translated by G.E.H. Palmer, Philip herrard and Kallistos Ware), 1979, 1983, by permission of Faber nd Faber

postolic Constitutions: from A. Hamman (ed.), *Early Christian Prayers* (translated by W. Mitchell), 1961, by permission of ongmans, Green and Co.

sterius of Amasia: from A. Hamman (ed.), *Early Christian Prayers* translated by W. Mitchell), 1961, by permission of Longmans, Green and Co.

thanasius: from *The Early Christian Fathers* (edited and translated y Henry Bettenson), 1956, by permission of Oxford University ress

V.H. Auden: from *Collected Poems*, 1966, published by Faber and aber Ltd. Reprinted by permission

abai: from *The Syriac Fathers on Prayer and the Spiritual Life* translated by Sebastian Brock), by permission of Cistercian ublications

alai: from A. Hamman (ed.), *Early Christian Prayers* (translated by V. Mitchell), 1961, by permission of Longmans, Green and Co.

obert Barclay: from *Quaker Faith and Practice*, 1994, by ermission of the Religious Society of Friends in Britain

lizabeth Bathurst: from *Quaker Faith and Practice*, 1994, by ermission of the Religious Society of Friends in Britain

ames K. Baxter: from *Collected Poems*, by permission of Oxford Jniversity Press

eatrice of Nazareth: from F. Bowie (ed.), *Beguine Spirituality* translated by O. Davies), 1989, by permission of SPCK

essarion: from *Sayings of the Desert Fathers* (translated by enedicta Ward), Mowbray, 1975, by permission of Cassell plc

onaventure: from *Works of St Bonaventure: 1: Mystical Opuscula* translated by J. de Vinck), St Anthony Guild Press, 1960

Book of Steps: from *The Syriac Fathers on Prayer and the Spiritual Life* (translated by Sebastian Brock), by permission of Cistercian Publications

Robert Bridges: from the *Yattendon Hymnal*, 1st edition 1895, by permission of Oxford University Press

Edward Burrough: from *Quaker Faith and Practice*, 1994, by permission of the Religious Society of Friends in Britain

Sydney Carter: from *Songs of Sydney Carter in the Present Tense*, Book 2, by permission of Stainer and Bell

John Cassian: from *John Cassian: Conferences* (translated by Colm Luibheid), 1982, by permission of Paulist Press

Charles Causley: from *Charles Causley: Collected Poems 1951–1975*, by permission of Macmillan Publishers and David Higham Associates

Thomas O. Chisholm: words 1923, renewal 1951, by permission of Hope Publishing

John Chrysostom: from *The Later Christian Fathers* (edited and translated by Henry Bettenson), 1970, by permission of Oxford University Press

Clare of Assisi: from *Francis and Clare* (translated by Armstrong and Brady), 1982, by permission of Paulist Press

Clement of Alexandria: from *The Early Christian Fathers* (edited and translated by Henry Bettenson), 1956, by permission of Oxford University Press

Clement of Rome: from *The Early Christian Fathers* (edited and translated by Henry Bettenson), 1956, by permission of Oxford University Press

Calvin: from François Wendel, *Calvin: The Origins and Development of His Religious Thought* (translated by P. Mairet), copyright © 1950 by Presses Universitaires de France. English translation copyright © 1963 by William Collins, Sons & Co., Ltd, and Harper & Row, Publishers, Inc. Reprinted by permission of HarperCollins Publishers, Inc.

Carpus, Papylus and Agathonike: from A. Hamman (ed.), *Early Christian Prayers* (translated by W. Mitchell), 1961, by permission of Longmans, Green and Co.

Sarah Coakley: from Daphne Hampson (ed.), *Swallowing a Fishbone?*, SPCK, 1996, by permission of the author

Colman the Irishman: from *Medieval Latin Lyrics* (translated by Helen Waddell), by permission of Penguin Books

Kate Compston: from *Encounters (Prayer Handbook)*, URC, 1988, by permission of the author

Jim Cotter: from *Pleasure, Pain and Passion*, Cairns Publications, 1988, by permission of the author

Cronius: from *Sayings of the Desert Fathers* (translated by Benedicta Ward), Mowbray, 1975, by permission of Cassell plc

Cyprian: from *The Early Christian Fathers* (edited and translated by Henry Bettenson), 1956, by permission of Oxford University Press

Cyril of Alexandria: from *The Later Christian Fathers* (edited and translated by Henry Bettenson), 1970, by permission of Oxford University Press

Cyrillona: from A. Hamman (ed.), *Early Christian Prayers* (translated by W. Mitchell), 1961, by permission of Longmans, Green and Co.

Dadisho: from *The Syriac Fathers on Prayer and the Spiritual Life* (translated by Sebastian Brock), by permission of Cistercian Publications

Desert fathers and mothers: from *The Wisdom of the Desert Fathers* (translated by Benedicta Ward), 1975, by permission of SLG Press

William Dewbury: from *Quaker Faith and Practice*, 1994, by permission of the Religious Society of Friends in Britain

Didache: from *The Early Christian Fathers* (edited and translated by Henry Bettenson), 1956, by permission of Oxford University Press

Diodochos of Photiki: from *The Philokalia* (translated by G.E.H. Palmer, Philip Sherrard and Kallistos Ware), 1979, 1983, by permission of Faber and Faber

Dionysius the Areopagite: from Andrew Louth, *Denys the Areopagite*, Geoffrey Chapman, 1989, by permission of Cassell plc

Dioscurus: from *Sayings of the Desert Fathers* (translated by Benedicta Ward), Mowbray, 1975, by permission of Cassell plc

Dominic: from *Early Dominican Writings* (translated by Simon Tugwell), 1982, by permission of Paulist Press

Dorothea of Montau: from *The Heart of Love: Prayers of German Women Mystics* (translated by Brian Pickett), 1991, by permission of St Paul Publications

Doulas: from *Sayings of the Desert Fathers* (translated by Benedicta Ward), Mowbray, 1975, by permission of Cassell plc

Michael Hare Duke: from *Hymns and Congregational Songs*, 1991, by permission of Stainer and Bell

Mary Dyer: from *Quaker Faith and Practice*, 1994, by permission of the Religious Society of Friends in Britain

Margaret Ebner: from *The Heart of Love: Prayers of German Women Mystics* (translated by Brian Pickett), 1991, by permission of St Paul Publications

Elizabeth of Schonau: from *The Heart of Love: Prayers of German Women Mystics* (translated by Brian Pickett), 1991, by permission of St Paul Publications

Ephraem the Syrian: from *The Syriac Fathers on Prayer and the Spiritual Life* (translated by Sebastian Brock), by permission of Cistercian Publications

Epiphanius: from *Sayings of the Desert Fathers* (translated by Benedicta Ward), Mowbray, 1975, by permission of Cassell plc

Epistle to Diognetus: from *The Early Christian Fathers* (edited and translated by Henry Bettenson), 1956, by permission of Oxford University Press

Epitaph: from A. Hamman (ed.), *Early Christian Prayers* (translated by W. Mitchell), 1961, by permission of Longmans, Green and Co.

Epitaph from Cairo: from A. Hamman (ed.), *Early Christian Prayers* (translated by W. Mitchell), 1961, by permission of Longmans, Green and Co.

Julia Esquivel: from *Threatened with Resurrection*, 1982, by permission of the Brethren Press

Euplus: from A. Hamman (ed.), *Early Christian Prayers* (translated by W. Mitchell), 1961, by permission of Longmans, Green and Co.

Evagrius of Pontus: from *The Syriac Fathers on Prayer and the Spiritual Life* (translated by Sebastian Brock), by permission of Cistercian Publications

Katherine Evans: from *Quaker Faith and Practice*, 1994, by permission of the Religious Society of Friends in Britain

George Every: from *Seasons of the Spirit*, 1984, by permission of SPCK

Tammy Felton: from *Images of Women in Transition* (compiled by J. Grana), St Mary's Press, 1991, by permission of the author

Lona Fowler: from *Images of Women in Transition* (compiled by J. Grana), St Mary's Press, 1991, by permission of the author

Caroline Fox: from *Quaker Faith and Practice*, 1994, by permission of the Religious Society of Friends in Britain

Margaret Fell Fox: from *Quaker Faith and Practice*, 1994, by permission of the Religious Society of Friends in Britain

Elizabeth Fry: from *Quaker Faith and Practice*, 1994, by permission of the Religious Society of Friends in Britain

Francis of Assisi: from *Francis and Clare* (translated by Armstrong and Brady), 1982, by permission of Paulist Press

Kathy Galloway: from *Love Burning Deep*, 1993, by permission of SPCK

Alan Gaunt: from *Hymn Texts of Alan Gaunt*, by permission of Stainer and Bell

Gelasios: from *Sayings of the Desert Fathers* (translated by Benedicta Ward), Mowbray, 1975, by permission of Cassell plc

Genesius of Rome: from A. Hamman (ed.), *Early Christian Prayers* (translated by W. Mitchell), 1961, by permission of Longmans, Green and Co.

Fred Pratt Green: by permission of Stainer and Bell

Sarah Lynes Grubb: from *Quaker Faith and Practice*, 1994, by permission of the Religious Society of Friends in Britain

Guigo II the Carthusian: from *Guigo II: The Ladder of Monks and Twelve Meditations* (translated by Colledge and Walsh), Mowbray, 1978, by permission of Cassell plc

Hadewijch of Brabant: from F. Bowie (ed.), *Beguine Spirituality* (translated by O. Davies), 1989, by permission of SPCK

Dag Hammarskjold: from *Markings* (translated by W.H. Auden and Lief Sjoberg), copyright © 1964 by Alfred A. Knopf, a division of Random House, Inc., and Faber and Faber Ltd. Used by permission of Alfred A. Knopf, a division of Random House, Inc.

John Heath-Stubbs: from *John Heath-Stubbs: Selected Poems*, by permission of Oxford University Press and David Higham Associates

Walter Hilton: from *Ladder of Perfection* (translated by Clifton Wolters), 1989, by permission of Penguin

Hippolytus: from A. Hamman (ed.), *Early Christian Prayers* (translated by W. Mitchell), 1961, by permission of Longmans, Green and Co.

Jean Fox Holland: from *Images of Women in Transition* (compiled by J. Grana), St Mary's Press, 1991, by permission of the author

Francis Howgill: from *Quaker Faith and Practice*, 1994, by permission of the Religious Society of Friends in Britain

Humbert of Romans: from *Early Dominican Writings* (translated by Simon Tugwell), 1982, by permission of Paulist Press

Ignatius of Antioch: from *The Early Christian Fathers* (edited and translated by Henry Bettenson), 1956, by permission of Oxford University Press

Inscription: from A. Hamman (ed.), *Early Christian Prayers* (translated by W. Mitchell), 1961, by permission of Longmans, Green and Co.

Irenaeus: from *The Early Christian Fathers* (edited and translated by Henry Bettenson), 1956, by permission of Oxford University Press

Irenaeus of Sirmium: from A. Hamman (ed.), *Early Christian Prayers* (translated by W. Mitchell), 1961, by permission of Longmans, Green and Co.

Isaac of Antioch: from A. Hamman (ed.), *Early Christian Prayers* (translated by W. Mitchell), 1961, by permission of Longmans, Green and Co.

Isaac of the Cells: from *Sayings of the Desert Fathers* (translated by Benedicta Ward), Mowbray, 1975, by permission of Cassell plc

Isaiah the Solitary: from *The Philokalia* (translated by G.E.H. Palmer, Philip Sherrard and Kallistos Ware), 1979, 1983, by permission of Faber and Faber

Isidore of Pelusia: from *Sayings of the Desert Fathers* (translated by Benedicta Ward), Mowbray, 1975, by permission of Cassell plc

Isidore the Priest: from *Sayings of the Desert Fathers* (translated by Benedicta Ward), Mowbray, 1975, by permission of Cassell plc

Elizabeth Jennings: from *Elizabeth Jennings: Collected Poems*, by permission of Carcanet Publishers and David Higham Associates

John: from *The Philokalia* (translated by G.E.H. Palmer, Philip Sherrard and Kallistos Ware), 1979, 1983, by permission of Faber and Faber

John of Apamea: from *The Syriac Fathers on Prayer and the Spiritual Life* (translated by Sebastian Brock), by permission of Cistercian Publications

John of Carpathos: from *The Philokalia* (translated by G.E.H. Palmer, Philip Sherrard and Kallistos Ware), 1979, 1983, by permission of Faber and Faber

John of Damascus: from *The Philokalia* (translated by G.E.H. Palmer, Philip Sherrard and Kallistos Ware), 1979, 1983, by permission of Faber and Faber

John the Dwarf: from *Sayings of the Desert Fathers* (translated by Benedicta Ward), Mowbray, 1975, by permission of Cassell plc

John the Elder (of Dalyatha): from *The Syriac Fathers on Prayer and the Spiritual Life* (translated by Sebastian Brock), by permission of Cistercian Publications

Jordan of Saxony: from *Early Dominican Writings* (translated by Simon Tugwell), 1982, by permission of Paulist Press

Joseph of Panephysis: from *Sayings of the Desert Fathers* (translated by Benedicta Ward), Mowbray, 1975, by permission of Cassell plc

Joseph the Visionary (Abdisho): from *The Syriac Fathers on Prayer and the Spiritual Life* (translated by Sebastian Brock), by permission of Cistercian Publications

Justin Martyr: from *The Early Christian Fathers* (edited and translated by Henry Bettenson), 1956, by permission of Oxford University Press

Robert Kilwardby: from *Early Dominican Writings* (translated by Simon Tugwell), 1982, by permission of Paulist Press

Madeleine L'Engle: from *The Irrational Season*, copyright © 1977 Crosswicks, Ltd. Reprinted by permission of HarperCollins Publishers, Inc.

Saunders Lewis: from Jones and Thomas (eds), *Beguine Spirituality*, 2nd edition 1983, by permission of the University of Wales Press

Pauline Reeder Liddle: from *Images of Women in Transition* (compiled by J. Grana), St Mary's Press, 1991, by permission of the author

Liturgical fragments: from A. Hamman (ed.), *Early Christian Prayers* (translated by W. Mitchell), 1961, 1961, by permission of Longmans, Green and Co.

Lot: from *Sayings of the Desert Fathers* (translated by Benedicta Ward), Mowbray, 1975, by permission of Cassell plc

Lucian and Marcian: from A. Hamman (ed.), *Early Christian Prayers* (translated by W. Mitchell), 1961, 1961, by permission of Longmans, Green and Co.

Macarius of Alexandria: from *Sayings of the Desert Fathers* (translated by Benedicta Ward), Mowbray, 1975, by permission of Cassell plc

Mark the Ascetic: from *The Philokalia* (translated by G.E.H. Palmer, Philip Sherrard and Kallistos Ware), 1979, 1983, by permission of Faber and Faber

Martyrius Sahdona: from *The Syriac Fathers on Prayer and the Spiritual Life* (translated by Sebastian Brock), by permission of Cistercian Publications

Hrabanus Maurus: from *Medieval Latin Lyrics* (translated by Helen Waddell), by permission of Penguin Books

Maximus the Confessor: from *The Philokalia* (translated by G.E.H. Palmer, Philip Sherrard and Kallistos Ware), 1979, 1983, by permission of Faber and Faber

Mechtilde of Hackeborn: from *The Heart of Love: Prayers of German Women Mystics* (translated by Brian Pickett), 1991, by permission of St Paul Publications

Mechtilde of Magdeburg: from F. Bowie (ed.), *Beguine Spirituality* (translated by O. Davies), 1989, by permission of SPCK

Methodius of Olympus: from A. Hamman (ed.), *Early Christian Prayers* (translated by W. Mitchell), 1961, 1961, by permission of Longmans, Green and Co.

Moses: from *Sayings of the Desert Fathers* (translated by Benedicta Ward), Mowbray, 1975, by permission of Cassell plc

Michele Najlis: from A. Hopkinson (ed.), *Lovers and Comrades*, 1989, by permission of Women's Press

James Nayler: from *Quaker Faith and Practice*, 1994, by permission of the Religious Society of Friends in Britain

Nilus: from *Sayings of the Desert Fathers* (translated by Benedicta Ward), Mowbray, 1975, by permission of Cassell plc

Or: from *Sayings of the Desert Fathers* (translated by Benedicta Ward), Mowbray, 1975, by permission of Cassell plc

Origen: from A. Hamman (ed.), *Early Christian Prayers* (translated by W. Mitchell), 1961, 1961, by permission of Longmans, Green and Co.

Origen: from *The Early Christian Fathers* (edited and translated by Henry Bettenson), 1956, by permission of Oxford University Press

Paphnoutios: from *Sayings of the Desert Fathers* (translated by Benedicta Ward), Mowbray, 1975, by permission of Cassell plc

Paul the Great: from *Sayings of the Desert Fathers* (translated by Benedicta Ward), Mowbray, 1975, by permission of Cassell plc

Paulinus of Nola: from A. Hamman (ed.), *Early Christian Prayers* (translated by W. Mitchell), 1961, 1961, by permission of Longmans, Green and Co.

Isaac Penington: from *Quaker Faith and Practice*, 1994, by permission of the Religious Society of Friends in Britain

Mary Penington: from *Quaker Faith and Practice*, 1994, by permission of the Religious Society of Friends in Britain

William Peraldus: from *Early Dominican Writings* (translated by Simon Tugwell), 1982, by permission of Paulist Press

Peter Martyr: from *Early Dominican Writings* (translated by Simon Tugwell), 1982, by permission of Paulist Press

Peter of Celle: from *Selected Works* (translated by H. Feiss), by permission of Cistercian Publications

Peter of Rheims: from *Early Dominican Writings* (translated by Simon Tugwell), 1982, by permission of Paulist Press

Philimon: from *The Philokalia* (translated by G.E.H. Palmer, Philip Sherrard and Kallistos Ware), 1979, 1983, by permission of Faber and Faber

Philoxenus of Mabbug: from *The Syriac Fathers on Prayer and the Spiritual Life* (translated by Sebastian Brock), by permission of Cistercian Publications

Poemen: from *Sayings of the Desert Fathers* (translated by Benedicta Ward), Mowbray, 1975, by permission of Cassell plc

Prudentius: from *Medieval Latin Lyrics* (translated by Helen Waddell), by permission of Penguin Books

Rabbula of Edessa: from A. Hamman (ed.), *Early Christian Prayers* (translated by W. Mitchell), 1961, by permission of Longmans, Green and Co.

Radbod of Utrecht: from *Medieval Latin Lyrics* (translated by Helen Waddell), by permission of Penguin Books

Raymond of Penafort: from *Early Dominican Writings* (translated by Simon Tugwell), 1982, by permission of Paulist Press

Richard Rolle: from *Richard Rolle: The English Writings* (translated by R.S. Allen), 1989, by permission of Paulist Press

Sarah: from *Sayings of the Desert Fathers* (translated by Benedicta Ward), Mowbray, 1975, by permission of Cassell plc

Siegfried Sassoon: 'Heart's miracle of inward light', from *Collected Poems*, by permission of George Sassoon

Schenute: from A. Hamman (ed.), *Early Christian Prayers* (translated by W. Mitchell), 1961, by permission of Longmans, Green and Co.

Lesbia Scott: by permission of Morehouse Publishing, Harrisburg, PA

Sedulius: from A. Hamman (ed.), *Early Christian Prayers* (translated by W. Mitchell), 1961, by permission of Longmans, Green and Co.

Sedulius Scotus: from *Medieval Latin Lyrics* (translated by Helen Waddell), by permission of Penguin Books

Serapion: from A. Hamman (ed.), *Early Christian Prayers* (translated by W. Mitchell), 1961, by permission of Longmans, Green and Co.

Severus of Thrace: from A. Hamman (ed.), *Early Christian Prayers* (translated by W. Mitchell), 1961, by permission of Longmans, Green and Co.

Simeon bar Sabba'e: from A. Hamman (ed.), *Early Christian Prayers* (translated by W. Mitchell), 1961, by permission of Longmans, Green and Co.

Sisoes: from *Sayings of the Desert Fathers* (translated by Benedicta Ward), Mowbray, 1975, by permission of Cassell plc

Edith Sitwell: from *Edith Sitwell: Collected Poems*, 1994, by permission of Sinclair Stevenson and David Higham Associates

Elisabeth Staeglin of Thoss: from *The Heart of Love: Prayers of German Women Mystics* (translated by Brian Pickett), 1991, by permission of St Paul Publications

Marmaduke Stevenson: from *Quaker Faith and Practice*, 1994, by permission of the Religious Society of Friends in Britain

Synesius: from A. Hamman (ed.), *Early Christian Prayers* (translated by W. Mitchell), 1961, by permission of Longmans, Green and Co.

Tertullian: from *The Early Christian Fathers* (edited and translated by Henry Bettenson), 1956, by permission of Oxford University Press

Thalassios the Libyan: from *The Philokalia* (translated by G.E.H. Palmer, Philip Sherrard and Kallistos Ware), 1979, 1983, by permission of Faber and Faber

Theodora: from *Sayings of the Desert Fathers* (translated by Benedicta Ward), Mowbray, 1975, by permission of Cassell plc

Theodore of Eleutheropolis: from *Sayings of the Desert Fathers* (translated by Benedicta Ward), Mowbray, 1975, by permission of Cassell plc

Theodore of Enaton: from *Sayings of the Desert Fathers* (translated by Benedicta Ward), Mowbray, 1975, by permission of Cassell plc

Theodore of Pherme: from *Sayings of the Desert Fathers* (translated by Benedicta Ward), Mowbray, 1975, by permission of Cassell plc

Theodoret: from *The Later Christian Fathers* (edited and translated by Henry Bettenson), 1970, by permission of Oxford University Press

Theognostus: from *The Philokalia* (translated by G.E.H. Palmer, Philip Sherrard and Kallistos Ware), 1979, 1983, permission of Faber and Faber

Theophilus of Alexandria: from *Sayings of the Desert Fathers* (translated by Benedicta Ward), Mowbray, 1975, by permission of Cassell plc

Thomas of Cantimpre: from *Early Dominican Writings* (translated by Simon Tugwell), 1982, by permission of Paulist Press

R.S. Thomas: from *R.S. Thomas: Later Poems* 1972–82, by permission of Macmillan Publishers

Jacopone da Todi: from *Jacopone da Todi: The Lauds* (translated by Serge and Elizabeth Hughes), 1982, by permission of Paulist Press

Rebecca Travers: from *Quaker Faith and Practice*, 1994, by permission of the Religious Society of Friends in Britain

Wandera-Chagenda: from Aylward Sharker (ed.), *African Christian Spirituality*, 1978, Geoffrey Chapman, by permission of Cassell plc

John Woolman: from *Quaker Faith and Practice*, 1994, by permission of the Religious Society of Friends in Britain

Zeno: from *Sayings of the Desert Fathers* (translated by Benedicta Ward), Mowbray, 1975, by permission of Cassell plc